Land Reform in Scotland

Scotland's Land
Series editor: Dr Annie Tindley

Editorial Advisory Board
Dr Calum MacLeod, University of Edinburgh
Dr Malcolm Combe, University of Aberdeen
Dr Iain Robertson, University of the Highlands and Islands
Professor Terence Dooley, Maynooth University
Professor Ewen A. Cameron, University of Edinburgh
Dr John MacAskill, University of Edinburgh

This series presents the latest scholarly work to academic and public readers on Scotland's land issues. Predominantly focusing on the history of Scotland's economic, political, and social and cultural relationships to land, landscape, country houses and landed estates, it also brings in cutting-edge approaches to explore new methodologies and perspectives around this politically contentious but stimulating issue. As an interdisciplinary series, it will necessarily contain a wide range of approaches, including history, law, economics and economic history, philosophy, environment/landscape studies, and human/cultural geography. The aim of the series is to bring together and publish the best work on land issues across a wide range of disciplines for a diverse set of audiences.

Published and forthcoming titles

The Land Agent: 1700–1920
Lowri Ann Rees, Ciarán Reilly and Annie Tindley (eds)

Scotland's Foreshore: Public Rights, Private Rights and the Crown, 1840–2017
John MacAskill

Land Reform in Scotland: History, Law and Policy
Malcolm M. Combe, Jayne Glass and Annie Tindley (eds)

edinburghuniversitypress.com/series/slf

Land Reform in Scotland

History, Law and Policy

Edited by Malcolm M. Combe, Jayne Glass
and Annie Tindley

EDINBURGH
University Press

Edinburgh University Press is one of the leading university presses in the UK. We publish academic books and journals in our selected subject areas across the humanities and social sciences, combining cutting-edge scholarship with high editorial and production values to produce academic works of lasting importance. For more information visit our website: edinburghuniversitypress.com

Edinburgh University Press Ltd
The Tun – Holyrood Road
12 (2f) Jackson's Entry
Edinburgh EH8 8PJ

Typeset in 10.5/13pt Sabon by
Servis Filmsetting Ltd, Stockport, Cheshire
and printed and bound in Great Britain

A CIP record for this book is available from the British Library

ISBN 978 1 4744 4684 6 (hardback)
ISBN 978 1 4744 4685 3 (paperback)
ISBN 978 1 4744 4686 0 (webready PDF)
ISBN 978 1 4744 4687 7 (epub)

Contents

Acknowledgements   vii
Notes on the Contributors   viii

Introduction   1
Malcolm M. Combe, Jayne Glass and Annie Tindley

Part I History

1 Land, Labour and Capital: External Influences and Internal
  Responses in Early Modern Scotland   23
  Allan I. Macinnes

2 Agricultural Enlightenment, Land Ownership and Scotland's
  Culture of Improvement, 1700–1820   39
  Brian Bonnyman

3 The Impact of Agrarian Radicalism on Land Reform in
  Scotland and Ireland, 1879–1903   56
  Brian Casey

4 'The usual agencies of civilisation': Conceptions of Land
  Ownership and Reform in the Comparative Context in the
  Long Nineteenth Century   74
  Annie Tindley

5 Still on the Agenda? The Strange Survival of the Scottish
  Land Question, 1880–1999   94
  Ewen A. Cameron

Part II Law

6 Earth and Stone: History, Law and Land through the Lens
  of Sasine   113
  Andrew R. C. Simpson

7 Legislating for Community Land Rights 154
Malcolm M. Combe

8 Towards Sustainable Community Ownership: A
Comparative Assessment of Scotland's New Compulsory
Community Right to Buy 177
John A. Lovett

9 Property Rights and Human Rights in Scottish Land Reform 213
Frankie McCarthy

10 The Evolution of Sustainable Development in Scotland: A
Case Study of Community Right to Buy Law and Policy,
2003–18 236
Andrea Ross

11 Scottish Residential Tenancies 263
Douglas Bain

12 Crofting Law 293
Eilidh I. M. MacLellan

13 Agricultural Tenancy Legislation and Public Policy
Considerations in Scotland 311
Hamish Lean

Part III Policy

14 Planning and Rights: Are there Lessons for Town Planning
We Can Borrow from Land Reform? 329
Robert G. Reid

15 Crofting Policy and Legislation: An Undemocratic and
Illegitimate Structure of Domination? 351
Iain MacKinnon

16 Does Size Really Matter? Sustainable Development
Outcomes from Different Scales of Land Ownership 368
Jayne Glass, Steven Thomson and Rob Mc Morran

17 Agricultural Models in Scotland and Norway: A Comparison 388
Annie McKee, Heidi Vinge, Hilde Bjørkhaug and Reidar
Almås

Index 410

Acknowledgements

The co-editors would like to put on record their thanks firstly to the contributors to this volume, who have added a rich and holistic set of perspectives to a constantly evolving question. Secondly, they wish to thank the Centre for Mountain Studies at Perth College UHI (University of the Highlands and Islands), the Carnegie Trust for the Universities of Scotland and the Centre for Scotland's Land Futures for funding the workshop activity that underpinned the writing of this book and for a subvention to the publisher to allow for its eventual somewhat expanded form. Thanks also to the School of Law at the University of Aberdeen, for its support of an event that allowed some of the themes in this book to be aired, and also for contributing to the subvention to the publisher.

Notes on the Contributors

Reidar Almås is Emeritus Professor of Rural Sociology at NTNU, the Norwegian University of Science and Technology, Trondheim, Norway. He is currently senior researcher at RURALIS Institute for Rural and Regional Research. His publications span the areas of agri-food restructuring, agricultural policy, agricultural history, rural and regional development.

Douglas Bain is a lecturer at the University of Aberdeen School of Law. Before returning to higher education as a mature student in 2003, he worked for fifteen years for the national campaigning charity Shelter Scotland, before which he worked for a local authority housing department. He teaches law honours courses on the Scottish Law of Leases and Charities and Voluntary Organisations in Scotland.

Hilde Bjørkhaug is a research professor at RURALIS Institute for Rural and Regional Research, Norway. Her research interests are agricultural restructuring and family farming, ethics, power relations, and financialisation in the agri-food value chain.

Brian Bonnyman is a graduate of Glasgow School of Art and the University of Edinburgh. He has taught at the universities of Dundee and Aberdeen and is currently an Honorary Fellow at the University of Dundee.

Ewen A. Cameron is the Sir William Fraser Professor of Scottish History at the University of Edinburgh. He has long-standing interests in the history of land legislation in Scotland and has published widely on the subject from the nineteenth century to the present day.

Brian Casey is a historian of late-nineteenth-century Ireland and Scotland. His research interests focus upon the land question, the dynamics of agrarian radicalism and rural history. He is the author of *Class and Community in Provincial Ireland*, published in 2018.

Malcolm M. Combe is a senior lecturer in law at the University of Strathclyde. He specialises in property law and has published on many aspects of land law and land reform, including access to land and landlord and tenant law. In June 2013, he was appointed an adviser to the Land Reform Review Group, which reported in 2014. Since January 2017, he has been a Case and Comment editor of the legal journal the *Juridical Review* and he is the general editor of the Scottish Landlord and Tenant Legislation collection of statutory materials. He is a qualified (non-practising) solicitor in Scotland and England and Wales.

Jayne Glass is a research fellow and lecturer in the Rural Policy Centre at Scotland's Rural College (SRUC) and Honorary Lecturer at the University of Edinburgh. She was previously a researcher at the Centre for Mountain Studies at Perth College UHI (University of the Highlands and Islands). Over the past decade, she has undertaken a range of theoretical and applied research and consultancy projects related to land reform and land ownership in Scotland. She is lead editor of *Lairds, Land and Sustainability: Scottish Perspectives on Upland Management* (Edinburgh University Press, 2013).

Hamish Lean is a partner in Shepherd and Wedderburn. He is accredited by the Law Society of Scotland as a Specialist in Agricultural Law, and he sits on the Law Society of Scotland's Rural Affairs Committee, the NFUS Legal and Technical Committee and is a member of the Scottish Agricultural Arbiters and Valuers Association. He is also a trustee of RSABI, Scotland's leading agricultural charity and was a member of the Scottish Government-appointed Agricultural Holdings Legislation Review Group.

John A. Lovett is the D. Van D. Daggett, Jr. Distinguished Professor of Law at Loyola University New Orleans College of Law. Educated at Haverford College, Indiana University (Bloomington) and Tulane University Law School, Professor Lovett practised law in Louisiana for seven years before joining the faculty at Loyola in 2002. He teaches and writes widely about property law in Louisiana, the United States and Scotland. He is currently Honorary Visiting Professor at the University of Edinburgh Law School.

Frankie McCarthy was appointed as a senior lecturer in private law at the University of Glasgow in August 2014 and became a professor there in

November 2019. She joined the School as a PhD researcher then became a lecturer in 2007. She is a graduate of the Universities of Edinburgh (LLB, DipLP) and Glasgow (PhD), and has been a visiting researcher at the University of Otago, New Zealand. She is also a qualified solicitor, having worked as a trainee and then solicitor at Simpson and Marwick WS (now part of Clyde & Co) prior to her doctoral studies.

Allan I. Macinnes is Emeritus Professor at the University of Strathclyde. He worked at the universities of Glasgow and Aberdeen before his appointment as professor of early modern history at Strathclyde University. He has written on the history of the Highlands, including Scottish Jacobitism and the Highland clans. His book, *Union and Empire: the Making of the United Kingdom in 1707*, was published by Cambridge University Press in 2007, which called it 'a major new interpretation of the Act of Union in a broad European and colonial context'.

Annie McKee is a social researcher in land management in the Social, Economic and Geographical Sciences Group (SEGS) at the James Hutton Institute. Her research focuses on rural governance and institutions, rural community development, and achieving sustainable development in rural areas. She received her PhD from the University of Aberdeen/ University of the Highlands and Islands in 2013 on 'the role of private landownership in facilitating sustainable rural communities in upland Scotland'. In 2016 she completed an OECD Comparative Research Fellowship, undertaking fieldwork in Central Norway, to identify lessons for Scottish land reform.

Iain MacKinnon is a researcher on the governance of land and natural resources at the Centre for Agroecology, Water and Resilience at Coventry University. His work seeks to understand and support traditional knowledge systems and land-based cultural practices of Scottish Gaels. In recent years this has led him to examine the 'domestic colonisation' of the modern Highlands and Islands and forms of resistance to that. He belongs to a crofting family on the Isle of Skye.

Eilidh I. M. MacLellan qualified as a solicitor in 2008, and since then has practised in Inverness and Skye, specialising in crofting law. In 2017 she became a crofting law consultant, launching Camus Consulting on 1 July 2017, although she remains a member of the Law Society of Scotland. She also served on the Law Society of Scotland Rural

Affairs Committee between 2008 and 2017, is a committee member of the Crofting Law Group, and a member of the Scottish Crofting Federation.

Rob Mc Morran is a researcher and lecturer at Scotland's Rural College (SRUC) and worked previously as a researcher at the Centre for Mountain Studies, part of the University of the Highlands and Islands. He has a BSc in Applied Ecology from University College Cork (Ireland), an MSc in Environmental Management from Stirling University, and a PhD in Environmental Governance. His recent research has included using interdisciplinary approaches to investigate policy mechanisms and governance processes as they relate to land ownership, rural community development and sustainable management of the uplands.

Robert G. Reid has been a town and country planner for forty years. He has studied and worked in all aspects of planning, from new towns, through Glasgow's East End to its bustling city centre. He has experience at planning directorate level with Grampian Region and then with Aberdeen City Council where he was Director of Planning. He moved to the private sector in 2004 as Director of Planning at Halliday Fraser Munro, was Convenor of the Royal Town Planning Institute in Scotland 2012 and since 2016 has been Development Director for Wildland Limited, managing development projects across eleven estates in Scotland. He teaches planning to students of various disciplines at the University of Aberdeen. He has been active within the environmental movement in Scotland, with a particular involvement in land reform, especially the Land Reform (Scotland) Act 2003.

Andrea Ross is professor of environmental law in the School of Law, University of Dundee. She was previously a lecturer in the Department of Land Economy at the University of Aberdeen. A qualified barrister and solicitor in Ontario, Canada, she has also worked as corporate counsel in the head office of investment company Midland Walwyn Inc. The co-author of a book on Scottish devolution and the editor of a collection on environmental regulation, she is best known for her extensive research into sustainable development.

Andrew R. C. Simpson is a senior lecturer at the University of Aberdeen. His research interests include Scottish and European legal history, with a particular focus on the history of legal thought, and he is the co-author of *Scottish Legal History Volume One: 1000–1707* (Edinburgh

University Press, 2017). He is also interested in property law and the law of succession.

Steven Thomson is an applied agricultural economist delivering research, consultancy and education for SRUC's Land Economy, Environment and Society research group and SRUC's Rural Policy Centre. He has a particular interest in agricultural and rural policy evaluation but is involved in a wide range of rural economy studies stemming from his comprehensive knowledge of contemporary agriculture and rural development issues. He currently coordinates the 'Adaptation to change in land based and other rural sectors' work package in the Scottish Government's ongoing strategic research programme.

Annie Tindley is a senior lecturer in modern British History at Newcastle University, specialising in rural and aristocratic elites in the nineteenth and early twentieth centuries. She is interested in the ways in which landed elites defined and translated their power – territorial, political, social, financial – across their estates, in the domestic political world of Westminster, and into the imperial context as governors and legislators. Her first book examined western Europe's largest landed estate in the later nineteenth century – the Sutherland estate – tracking its evolving priorities, powers and drivers under a framework of 'decline and fall'.

Heidi Vinge is a PhD candidate in sociology at NTNU, the Norwegian University of Science and Technology, and researcher at RURALIS Institute for Rural and Regional Research, Norway with interests in sustainable land use, political decision-making and the relationship between power and knowledge.

Introduction

Malcolm M. Combe, Jayne Glass and Annie Tindley

THIS BOOK PRESENTS A stimulating rethink of contemporary land reform in Scotland from historical, legal, and policy perspectives. It combines scholarly analysis with interdisciplinary perspectives on the journey land reform has taken in Scotland from the medieval period to the present day (2019 at the time of writing), and how it is likely to develop in the future. By examining land reform through a multidisciplinary lens, the chapters that follow capture as rounded a view as possible of an issue which has generated significant cumulative political and social acrimony in pre-modern, modern and contemporary Scottish society. As such, land reform has generated a great deal of scholarly, political and popular writing, polemic and debate, a state of play which is both a blessing and a curse for those seeking more light than heat, and particularly for those who are thinking about the future of land reform. The intention of this volume is to present to any reader interested in land reform, in Scotland or the wider world, the latest scholarly thinking on the issue. It does not aim to be the final word (that would be impossible), but it hopes to enrich, complicate and extend our collective understandings of this critical issue in Scottish history and society. It does this by exploring in-depth the critical issues relevant to each discipline and cross-referencing them to draw out shared themes, ideas and questions that enhance our understanding of the monolithic 'land question'.

By focusing on the three areas of history, law and policy, the editors are not proposing that these are the only or even the most important perspectives that could be taken. This is evidently not the case; we also recognise that experts in their relative fields of ecology, land management, geography and the social sciences have published extensively in this area, work that we and our contributors have drawn on here.[1] There is additionally a long and distinguished history of literary

---

[1] See for example the classic, F. F. Darling, *West Highland Survey: An Essay in*

responses to land questions and reform, in Gaelic, Scots and English.[2] Again, some of that material surfaces in the chapters that follow, but what we aim to do here is something a little different, through the combination of our three disciplines across an extensive chronology. This highlights an important point about the volume: that its focus is often backward rather than forward-looking. The volume begins with a section addressing the history of the land reform question (very broadly defined) in Scotland from the seventeenth to the late twentieth century, a vital task given the power of historical rhetoric and historicist thinking around the issue. There are a couple of important caveats to make here, however. Firstly, land reform was and is always of its time and place. This volume ranges across centuries and builds in, as far as possible, comparative analyses with other places, but the end focus is concerned with the specificity of land reform in and for Scotland, and the regions that make up the country. Secondly, there is no historical 'escalator' of progress which took Scottish society, step by step, up any kind of obvious or preordained path of land reform. Nothing is inevitable and – side-stepping the teleological approach – our contributors are at pains to unpack the historical, political and legal accidents and blind alleys that underpin so much of both the societal and political drivers of reform, legislative or not.

We hope that this volume effectively swerves the dangers of over-simplification which have dogged land reform debates and are in turn generated by the intensely politicised nature of the question. If tackled as an academic problem, however, there are opportunities as well as restrictions within the political nature of the land reform question in Scotland. One of the significant challenges faced by the editors and contributors to this volume was the hotly contested nature of the long-standing political controversy that is glibly summed up in the phrase 'the land question'. This points to questions with deeper roots: what role can and does academic research of any discipline play in an intensely

---

Human Ecology (Oxford: Oxford University Press, 1955); and more recent work for instance, J. H. Dickson, 'Scottish woodlands: their ancient past and precarious present', *Scottish Forestry*, 47 (1993); W. Orr, *Deer Forests, Landlords and Crofters* (Edinburgh: John Donald, 1982).

[2] See for example, G. Bruce and F. Rennie, *The Land Out There: A Scottish Land Anthology* (Aberdeen: Aberdeen University Press, 1991); K. H. Jackson, *Studies in Early Celtic Nature Poetry* (Cambridge: Cambridge University Press, 1935); D. E. Meek, 'Gaelic poets of the land agitation', *Transactions of the Gaelic Society of Inverness*, 49 (1974–6); N. Shepherd, *The Living Mountain* (Aberdeen: Aberdeen University Press, 1977).

political debate? Is there such a thing as an objective point of view on fundamental questions for our society such as the ownership, use and management of the finite resource that is land? Each of the contributors here have been considering these questions from their own disciplinary and personal perspectives, and collectively, we wish to make a contribution to a lively, important and 'unsafe' debate. As such, the volume is designed to support and inform current public debate, not become a direct part of it. The main reason for this is to prevent – as far as possible in a fast-changing field – early dating and obsolescence of the work presented here. A further reason is that this is not intended to be a 'campaigning' or polemical volume, supporting any of the myriad stances on land issues in Scotland. Instead, it is intended to present and critique the various viewpoints on, and contexts of, land reform. Land reform has long been and continues to be an 'unsafe' area for academic (and non-academic) study: it is fraught with tension and remains highly emotive. The political, economic and social stakes are high and this can be traced in some of the contributions here, both historically and in contemporary debate.

As well as the highly contested nature of the debate, there are other problems of bias and emphasis. One of these is the tendency towards the 'Highlandisation' of the land reform debate, and a reminder not to ignore either the Lowlands or urban land questions. In part this is due to historical legacy – many of the key events and reforms took place in the Highlands and Islands first, and therefore they tend to loom large. However, recent land reform has been characterised by less-expected geographies, for example, the proposed Wanlockhead community purchase, or recent provisions for urban community landownership, or, going back a little further, the Glasgow rent strikes of the First World War period. The contributors to this volume have worked to provide a much more rounded and geographically inclusive picture as a result. At the root of many of the issues outlined already are the power and problems of defining key concepts in the land reform debate. Terms such as 'community', 'private benefit' and 'public good' are used extensively in political debate and the wider literature, but conflicting or confused meanings attached to these can generate misunderstandings or even rancour, whatever disciplinary or political standpoint an observer takes. We do not propose that this volume will present the definitive word on any of these concepts but we do hope that it will help establish some common ground.

LAND REFORM – A BRIEF INTRODUCTION

As the following chapters will make clear, land reform has a relatively long pedigree in Scotland and its regions. Excluding the upheaval that followed the failed Jacobite uprisings, the first UK statutory measures that actively reworked land tenure in Scotland applied only to qualifying inhabitants in the 'crofting counties' of the Highlands and Islands in 1886; in 1911 this protection was extended to the rest of rural Scotland.[3] There is one topic of land reform not dealt with explicitly in the volume, although it is highlighted throughout: the management and ownership of the Scottish Crown Estate lands, devolved in 2017.[4] The processes and drivers of these reforms and those that came over the course of the rest of the twentieth century are traced in the first part of this volume.

In more recent terms, following the work of the Land Reform Policy Group in the late 1990s, the first key step in the contemporary land reform process was the Abolition of Feudal Tenure etc. (Scotland) Act 2000, which removed what was left of the system of feudal tenure and the influence of feudal superiors in relation to land in Scotland.[5] After devolution and the re-establishment of the Scottish Parliament in 1999, momentum for land reform increased. The first Scottish Land Fund was established in 2001, providing financial resources to communities to support land purchase, and the first Land Reform (Scotland) Act was enacted in 2003. This legislation continued a widespread and long-standing trend throughout Europe of property rights becoming progressively more restricted and qualified, introducing measures aimed at addressing greater diversity in ownership through the community (pre-emptive) right to buy (Part 2) and the crofting community (absolute) right to buy (Part 3), together with statutory non-motorised rights of responsible access over most land (and inland water) for all (Part 1).[6]

---

[3] A brief outline history of the history of crofting is provided by MacLellan in this volume. The regime introduced in 1886 stopped being Highland-centric by virtue of the Small Landholders (Scotland) Act 1911. That legislation, and various amending statutes, continue to apply outwith the crofting counties, with crofting again going its own way after Highland-centric legislation was passed in 1955.

[4] For a full treatment of the issue of the Crown Estate lands, please see J. MacAskill, *Scotland's Foreshore: Public Rights, Private Rights and the Crown 1840–2017* (Edinburgh: Edinburgh University Press, 2018).

[5] Land Reform Policy Group, 'Identifying the Problems' (Edinburgh: Scottish Office, 1998).

[6] C. Rodgers, 'Property rights, land use and the rural environment: a case for

More recently, the creation of the Land Reform Review Group (LRRG) by the Scottish Government in 2012 (which reported to Scottish Ministers in 2014), the House of Commons Scottish Affairs Committee's Inquiry into Land Reform in Scotland in 2014–15, the Community Empowerment (Scotland) Act 2015, and the Land Reform (Scotland) Act 2016 have highlighted the continued political interest in the subject and a political appetite for further progressive reform. With the Scottish Land Commission becoming fully operational in 2017 (the Commission was established by the 2016 Act), increased financial and other support exists for implementing and developing land reform legislation and policy, reinforcing a fundamental shift of the balance of power between communities and landowners.

All of the key events, drivers and outcomes of land reform in Scotland will be picked up in the chapters in much more detail, but in order to introduce and contextualise that work, we will briefly discuss here three overarching themes. First, what are the drivers for land reform up to the present day? Second, how have those drivers been translated into action and why have they taken the forms they have? Third, what have been the outcomes or implementation of reforms and their consequences over time; and are these all a means to an end or the end in themselves?

What has driven contemporary land reform in Scotland?

Since the 1980s, one of the unifying clarion calls of Scottish land reformers has been the persistence of a highly concentrated pattern of landownership. Studies carried out in the 1870s had highlighted this pattern, and – to the horror of land reform campaigners and politicians of the centre and left – despite all of the transformational adjustments made by Scottish society in the twentieth century, this particular aspect of it remained stubbornly the same.[7] The work of Bateman in the 1870s to surveys of landownership by Andy Wightman, Robin Callander and others between the 1970s and 1990s focused on this aspect of land-ownership, and from that work have spiralled (sometimes acrimonious)

---

reform', *Land Use Policy*, 26S (2009), S134–S141; A. Pillai, 'Sustainable Rural Communities? A legal perspective on the community right to buy', *Land Use Policy*, 27 (2010), pp. 898–905.

[7] It was the work of Bateman which sparked initial outrage: see, J. Bateman, *The Great Landowners of Great Britain and Ireland* (London: Harrison, 1876).

debates about land use and management, democracy and social justice.[8] As the chapters in this volume discuss, one of these drivers has been the increasing concern around climate change and environmental protection and the challenges (and opportunities) faced by Scotland, a country historically prized for the beauty of its 'natural' landscapes.[9]

Since the late 1990s, three undertakings have been charged with looking at land reform in Scotland, in the shape of two ad hoc bodies and a new specific, standing body. All three owe much to devolution of power from the UK Parliament at Westminster to the Scottish Parliament at Holyrood. Although appointed by a UK government, the Land Reform Policy Group was formed with the legislative programme for the nascent devolved legislature in mind. Thereafter, the Land Reform Review Group was appointed by the Scottish Government, and the Scottish Land Commission was introduced by legislation passed by the Scottish Parliament. The scrutiny they brought and, in the case of the Scottish Land Commission, the scrutiny that will continue, accordingly owes much to devolution, and this is before one even considers the potential impact of the quieter and Scottish-centric legislative timetabling that Holyrood has as compared to Westminster, not to mention the simple but difficult-to-quantify point that the Scottish Parliament is unicameral and land reform legislation passed by it needs to go before committees rather than through a second legislative chamber in the form of the House of Lords.

Important as all of that has been, to say modern land reform in Scotland is all about devolution would be to overlook many other factors that have contributed to the evolving debate and legal framework. The first background factor is one that has not actually featured prominently in the publicly stated justifications for twenty-first century Scottish land reform, nor has it found itself embodied expressly in legislation such that a law seeks to benefit a particular group that might have experienced a wrong in the past. This unspoken factor is history, with historical reasons for reform tending to take a back seat to other arguments. That being the case, history has axiomatically contributed to the situation that prevails today, and historic lessons can and do

---

[8] R. Callander, *A Pattern of Landownership in Scotland* (Finzean: Haughend Publications, 1987); A. Wightman, *Who Owns Scotland* (Edinburgh: Canongate, 1996); and R. Callander, *How Scotland is Owned* (Edinburgh: Canongate, 1998).

[9] For a full discussion of these issues see J. Hunter, *On the Other Side of Sorrow: Nature and People in the Scottish Highlands* (Edinburgh: Birlinn, 1994).

inform what happens in the present day, hence the coverage of historical materials in this text.

Rather than looking backwards, the stated arguments in favour of land reform tend to look forwards, perhaps by being about enterprise and community revitalisation (or at least retention). The already mentioned discussion around concentration of land ownership has also featured, in terms of the effects it can have (especially when coupled with the strong agenda-setting role that the apex property law right of ownership has traditionally afforded in Scots law). A further modern trend in the Scottish land reform debate is an increased awareness for a rights-based push for reform: whilst contemporary land reform is not characterised as being for the provision of subsistence agriculture for those who are starving nor shelter for those who are destitute, notions about housing quality and human dignity have been creeping into the Scottish debate (as discussed below), as have wider points about sustainability and the environment. All of this allows for a more nuanced analysis as to when settled property rights might be challenged.

Of course, these points raise counterpoints. Economists might only countenance intervention when there has been some kind of market failure, and simply identifying a concentration of ownership will not automatically make that case. Further, if property rights become fickle or fragile that can have an unsettling effect on the market, and anyone seeking to reform land purely on the basis of social justice needs to remember that land is but one (important) part of the overall equitable mix of society. These and other counterpoints notwithstanding, we now move to providing an overview of the important reforms that have happened in the relatively recent past.

Land reform and 'community'

The pursuit of greater economic efficiency and social equity via the redistribution of property rights is a common theme of land reform in other countries, particularly those in less developed and transitional economies.[10] In Scotland, however, land reform legislation has placed the concept of 'community' at its core, although definitions of community have shifted over the past 135 years. Liberal politicians and

[10] B. Slee, K. Blackstock, K. Brown, R. Dilley, P. Cook, J. Grieve and A. Moxey, *Monitoring and Evaluating the Effects of Land Reform on Rural Scotland – A Scoping Study and Impact Assessment.* (Edinburgh: Scottish Government Social Research, 2008).

thinkers of the late nineteenth century defined the Scottish Highlands (in a strikingly similar way to rural India) as being structured around historical 'village communities' and the Crofters Holdings (Scotland) Act 1886 set out a historical and structural definition of crofting which was built around an historicist ideal of the communal.

The powerful influence of this thinking is evident in the twenty-first century too. The 2003 Act came into force at a time of an increasingly interdisciplinary shift towards a paradigm based on community-led approaches to achieve development goals. This meant that rural development was no longer seen as a 'top-down' pursuit which focused on the subsidisation of agricultural activities. Instead, 'rural' academics discussed a shift towards integrated rural development, emphasising the importance of local community governance and the development of local resources within post-productive, non-agricultural economic activities.[11] Similar thinking evolved within literature on the commons and collaborative management since the turn of this century, with the commons representing important economic, social and environmental resources that were becoming increasingly contested arenas for political, legal and social actions by various state and community actors.[12] Defined as 'the collective and local ownership of land, resources, or ideas, held in an often communal manner, sometimes in opposition to private property', academic debate about the commons at that time invoked shared interests and investments in land, culture and nature, yet this debate was divorced from traditional models and concepts of 'ownership'.[13]

Supporters of community-led approaches tend to view community governance of natural resources as desirable because local groups are deemed to have higher levels of motivation, knowledge and experience that are inextricably bound up with their livelihoods and community.[14]

---

[11] See for example, C. Ray, 'Neo-endogenous rural development in the EU', in: P. Cloke, T. Marsden and P. Mooney (eds), *Handbook of Rural Studies* (London: Sage, 2006), pp. 278–91.

[12] A. P. Brown, 'Crofter, forestry, land reform and the ideology of community', *Social and Legal Studies*, 17:3 (2008), pp. 24–34.

[13] J. B. Holder and T. Flessus, 'Emerging Commons', *Social and Legal Studies*, 17:3 (2008), pp. 299–310; T. Xu and A. Clarke (eds), 'Legal Strategies for the Development and Protection of Communal Property', *Proceedings of the British Academy*, 216 (Oxford: Oxford University Press, 2018).

[14] J. Glass, A. Scott, M. F. Price and C. Warren, 'Sustainability in the uplands: introducing key concepts', in J. Glass, M. F. Price, C. Warren and A. Scott (eds), *Lairds, Land and Sustainability: Scottish Perspectives on Upland Management* (Edinburgh: Edinburgh University Press, 2013), pp. 3–31.

The notion that people in communities need to co-operate because they depend on each other is also at the core of arguments in favour of small-scale, common-pool resources being managed by the users themselves, rather than private individuals/entities, or public bodies. Community ownership and management of land raise important questions and contested legal and moral notions about how 'community' can be used as a means of bounding collective entitlement.[15] To that end, several commentators have argued that there is considerable added value generated in terms of motivation and collective endeavour when land or assets are actually *owned* by a community, as opposed to being managed collaboratively with the state or other local actors.[16] It is in this context that the concept of 'community' in Scotland has played (and continues to play) a key role in reimagining and reclaiming the land through its place in the collective local imagination.[17] The role of history and the politics of dispossession also provide important themes in cultural cohesion and individual and community reinterpretations of land, and these themes emerge in the chapters that follow.[18]

Another emergent theme in many land debates is that of human rights, with more recent debates moving away from an owner-centric, protection-of-property approach to a more holistic analysis that also considers relevant human rights of non-owners in appropriate circumstances. That said, protection of property rights is something that is provided for in Article 1 of the First Protocol to the European Convention on Human Rights, and its terms (not to mention the fact that the Scottish Parliament only has legislative competence to make law in a manner that does not contravene the Convention) has had some impact on land reform measures. Such impact could be (and normally would be) indirect, by shaping the laws that Holyrood has passed, but in one case there was a successful court challenge to a statutory provision that was designed to improve the rights of a narrow class of

[15] K. M. Brown, 'Reconciling moral and legal collective entitlement: implications for community-based land reform', *Land Use Policy*, 24:4 (2007), pp. 633–43.

[16] For example, see B. Quirk, 'Making assets work: the Quirk Review of community management and ownership of public assets' (London: HMSO, 2007).

[17] A. F. D. MacKenzie, 'Re-imagining the land, North Sutherland, Scotland', *Journal of Rural Studies*, 20 (2004), pp. 273–87.

[18] A. F. D. MacKenzie, 'A working land: crofting communities, place and the politics of the possible in post-Land Reform Scotland?' *Transactions of Institute of British Geographers* 31:3 (2006), pp. 383–98.

agricultural occupiers of land, which was ruled to breach a landlord's human rights.[19]

Outcomes and implementation of land reform

It is, of course, ironic that in a country where the land reform debate has, with some variation, occupied such a central position in political and economic thinking since the eighteenth century, the fundamental reality of the continued concentration of ownership of land has in fact shifted only marginally. Although there has been some diversification in the ownership of land, not least in the role of the state as a major landowner, followed by its various agencies and conservation agencies and charities, private landownership by individuals and families remains a dominant model, particularly in the principally urban public understanding of the drivers of land reform.[20] Some of the surnames of these owners are historically unfamiliar, but many are not: the Buccleuchs, the Sutherlands and the Argylls are just three examples of powerful landowning families whose names appear in the historical record from the fourteenth to the twenty-first centuries.[21] As the chapters in the history section of this volume demonstrate, many of the outcomes of changes to land use have been driven by private landowners, including early agricultural improvement and diversification. Changes to land *ownership* patterns, however, have come from the state for a wide range of reasons.

The current Scottish Government supports land reform in order to diversify the range of ownership models in Scotland: from community ownership to conservation ownership, a more balanced mixed economy is envisioned for the future. Underpinning this are a whole range of competing priorities, including environmental and climate change concerns, the increase of renewable energy sources and forestry, sustainable development, and community empowerment, several of which are outlined

---

[19] The case in question was *Salvesen* v. *Riddell* [2013] UKSC 22. Issues to do with this case are considered in this volume by McCarthy and Lean.

[20] T. Johnston, *Our Scots Noble Families* (Glasgow: Forward Publishing, 1909), for a classic example of dissatisfaction with this model.

[21] See for example, B. Bonnyman, *The Third Duke of Buccleuch and Adam Smith: Estate Management and Improvement in Enlightenment Scotland* (Edinburgh: Edinburgh University Press, 2014); A. Tindley, *The Sutherland Estate, 1850–1920* (Edinburgh: Edinburgh University Press, 2010); E. Richards, *The Leviathan of Wealth* (London: Routledge and Kegan Paul, 1973); S. Boardman, *The Campbells, 1250–1513* (Edinburgh: John Donald, 2006).

in the policy section of this volume. In this sense, land reform today is primarily a means to wider ends; although the historical thrust of much of the land reform debate has been around an end in itself: to break the private 'monopoly' of much of Scottish landownership on principle. As later chapters explore in depth, arguments around landownership as the litmus test of how equitable Scottish society has been, is and might be, have long been central to the reform debate.

STRUCTURE AND APPROACH OF THE VOLUME

This volume utilises three disciplinary perspectives to examine land reform in Scotland and makes an effort to incorporate the nature of the question in Scotland into its global context, both historically and in contemporary society. Although we have organised the chapters broadly into their disciplinary approaches, the boundaries between and within the three areas were much more porous than we perhaps expected at the start of this process. Nearly all of the chapters borrow freely from historical, legal and policy perspectives, and many others besides: economics, environmental sciences and philosophy, politics, geography and the social sciences. We hope that this enriches the picture of the evolution of land reform questions in Scotland since the seventeenth century.

The history of land reform

The volume opens with five chapters which tackle the various historical antecedents of land reform in Scotland, in both a directly legislative way for the modern period and in a more broadly contextual fashion for earlier periods. This is not designed to be a comprehensive historical survey and eagle-eyed readers will note some omissions, for instance, the history of the Forfeited Estates or a detailed chronology of the Highland Land War.[22] As outlined above, however, this is not our purpose.

A number of common themes emerge through this study. Firstly, that change has been the only real constant in the history of land ownership, use and reform. The historical picture is never static, and the interplay between competing interests and perceptions of land and how it relates to wider social and economic questions has long been with

---

[22] For detailed histories of both see J. Hunter, *The Making of the Crofting Community* (Edinburgh: John Donald, 1976); A. Smith, *Jacobite Estates of the '45* (Edinburgh: Birlinn, 2003).

us. This is a theme taken up in some detail by Allan I. Macinnes in his chapter on early modern Scotland and the emergence of capitalism and its impact on land questions. He takes a comparative perspective to examine the mobility of labour, the impact of inflation from the New World and proto-industrial diversification, as well as the impact of early Enlightenment on agricultural improvement in Highlands and Lowlands, planned villages and capital repatriation from empire. Although these significant adjustments were not always driven by legislation, and 'land reform' was not a term contemporaries would have recognised, these changes were highly innovative, disruptive and only by taking a wider global and imperial perspective, as Macinnes does in his chapter, can we situate them accurately.

The second major connecting theme that emerges from the historical perspective is that of the enduring influence and power of what we might broadly characterise as the landed classes. The aristocracy, peerage, gentry, landlords and landowners, whatever you call them, the great private landowners of Scotland have long been instrumental in thinking on land. Although regarded by contemporaries as wholly resistant to land reform because it would likely be against their fundamental economic interests, this was not always the case, and as Brian Bonnyman traces in his chapter on Agricultural Enlightenment, land ownership and improvement, landowners have been at the vanguard of change. Although the Agricultural Enlightenment has been identified as a Europe-wide and transatlantic phenomenon, arguably nowhere was its influence more profoundly felt than in eighteenth- and early-nineteenth-century Lowland Scotland. Bonnyman examines some of the distinctive elements of the Scottish Agricultural Enlightenment, its relationship to the wider improving movement, and its impact on estate management, land use and the Lowland Scottish landscape, and the developing academic field of the Lowland Clearances. Particular emphasis is placed on the effects of the improving ideology on the attitudes, beliefs and values of the Scottish landed classes, and the ways in which these changes affected leasing policy, landlord–tenant relations, and the wider transformation of Scottish agriculture.

Thirdly, and already touched on, is the importance of putting the history of Scotland's engagement with land issues into the wider European, imperial and global context. This wider context is as important as understanding Scotland's regional differences, and is discussed in two of the chapters in the History section. In the first, Brian Casey builds a detailed comparative picture between Scotland and Ireland. We move into the nineteenth century and away from the perspectives of landowners to that of small tenants in doing so. In this period, efforts were frequently made to tie the plight of the small Irish farmer and the Highland crofter, in particular, together; both, it was claimed, suffered under the hands of capricious landlordism. This sort of tenant radicalism had a long tradition in both countries but until the 1880s any action was frequently short-lived and disorganised. Yet by the 1880s, agrarian radicalism in both Scotland and Ireland became better organised and more evocative as they asserted their rights against the 'yoke of landlordism'. This context is critical to our contemporary understandings of legislative land reform, resulting as it did in the first piece of dedicated land reform legislation for (a part of) Scotland: the Crofters Holdings (Scotland) Act 1886, a measure directly influenced by the Irish Land Act 1881.

Ireland has often been used by historians as a natural comparator for historical land issues, but there are important broader contexts to consider as well, and this is attempted in Annie Tindley's chapter. Taking a macro perspective of the land question and Scotland's place in it, this chapter examines the terms of and tensions within the land question during this period, which saw the beginning and consolidation of industrialisation and massive European imperial expansion. The global land question in the nineteenth century needs to be understood in terms of these wider forces, and by tracking different reactions and responses to them, we can better judge Scotland's place in the debate and break down the view that it has been exceptional in its engagement with the land question. This chapter examines the nineteenth-century land question in countries and territories as diverse as Russia, Canada, Ireland and India, and the direct connections and linkages – both intellectual and legislative – that were made by contemporaries between and within these locations. These issues were of the first political and social importance across a wide range of locations because in most cases they were also intimately linked with questions of governance, and the legitimacy of power more broadly defined. For imperial powers such as Britain and Russia, settlements around land were part of the package of 'benefits' that imperial rule was perceived to bring subject peoples, and legislation radically in advance of what was politically possible in the domestic context was introduced in colonial territories. This chapter should provide a useful historical grounding for the contemporary comparisons made with Norway in Chapter 17.

The fourth theme considers the stubborn survival, and indeed increasing political importance of the land question during Scotland's dramatic and fast-paced shift from an agricultural and rural society to one of the most urban and industrial societies on earth. This theme is explored by

Ewen Cameron in his chapter on the strange survival of the Scottish land question in late nineteenth- and twentieth-century Scottish society and political life. Issues concerned with the ownership of, access to, and redistribution of land have remained more important in Scotland than in other parts of the United Kingdom and the politics of the land question are reflected in many areas of the cultural life of an urban industrial nation. Significant works of twentieth-century Scottish literature, in both Gaelic and English, are concerned with the histories and geographies, communities and places, grievances and aspirations, associated with land. The clearances and the Crofters War of the 1880s are prominent in this body of work. Even for those critics who perceived weakness in the Gaelic poetry of the nineteenth century, as a result of the triumph of the landlords during the clearances, the protests of the 1880s represented a political and cultural turning point. This engagement with the history of the land question continues throughout the twentieth century. This chapter examines the cultural, political and journalistic means by which the land question did not die.

The law of the land

Critical to any discussion of the history, contemporary picture, and future of land reform is of course the changing legal underpinning and understandings of the law surrounding property, the rights pertaining to it, and the process for creating and transferring property rights. The central part of this book therefore deals with these issues, and spans a long historical chronology as well as presenting detailed contemporary case studies. Andrew Simpson provides a critical bridge between the historical and legal perspectives promoted in this volume through a discussion of the development of sasine from the twelfth to the twenty-first centuries. Sasine is a legal institution which has been developed continuously in relation to claims affecting land for the last 850 years. As a result, Simpson's study of the history of sasine addresses many questions that those interested in the historical development of claims and rights in land might wish to pose and highlights the importance of the role of the legal practitioners in the development of property law and on the reform of land law.

From a legal institution over 800 years old, the four subsequent chapters engage with much a much more recent land law reform. Malcolm Combe introduces us to contemporary approaches to community land ownership, considering the framework for and the practical impact of community ownership up to the time of writing. He does this by explaining the statutory framework for community rights to buy, highlighting some of the practical and theoretical issues that arise from them, and considering examples of acquisitions which have variously taken place in accordance with statutory schemes, been driven by the prospect of those schemes as a fallback position, or occurred on ad hoc bases without any apparent reference to the modern legislation.

In Chapter 8, John Lovett drills further into the suitability of community rights to buy as a legal model for land reform; in particular, he draws on international theoretical comparators to critique recent Scottish land reform measures, particularly those that allow private property to be forcibly transferred from one private party to another under the justification of some kind of public benefit. This innovative scrutiny will highlight certain pressure points in the Scottish system that merit careful consideration, and in so doing explains how property theory can or might in the future impinge on the workings of Scotland's land reform legislation.

Frankie McCarthy then takes the legal land reform debate in a different direction, engaging with an, at times, oversimplified area in terms of land rights: that of human rights and their impact on the debate in Scotland. She argues that political and media representations of human rights and any associated impact on land reform in Scotland has been mischaracterised as a shield behind which private landowners can push back on land reform. Understood correctly, however, human rights law provides a valuable framework for ensuring *all* interests in land are given due consideration.

Staying with recent community right to buy legislation, in Chapter 10 Andrea Ross considers the evolution of sustainable development in Scotland. She explores how the law and policy relating to sustainable development in the context of the various community right to buy regimes in Scotland have matured and evolved from their introduction in 2003 to the present. Importantly, this analysis uncovers a new era in sustainable development policy in Scotland that has the potential to move well beyond the rhetoric of sustainable development to deliver transformational outcomes.

The three chapters that follow shift the focus somewhat to individual relationships, albeit towards legal relationships that can have profound impacts on land occupation and use, and, in turn, local communities. The legal relationship in question is that of landlord and tenant, the importance of that relationship having already been touched on in the analyses by Cameron and Bonnyman. These chapters look at three particularly relevant modern contexts for leasing, namely residential tenancies, crofting, and agricultural tenancies.

In Chapter 11, Douglas Bain tracks the recent, occasionally convoluted, evolution of the regimes that govern leases of dwellings to people as homes, right up to and including the introduction of the new private residential tenancy by the Private Housing (Tenancies) (Scotland) Act 2016. This statute, which will often allow a tenant to stay in a property on an open-ended basis provided rent is being paid when it falls due, represents the most recent (tenant-favouring) bounce of the landlord–tenant seesaw that has been seesawing from (at least) 1915 until the present day. As Bain notes, the law in this area is not static – a point which could be made in relation to many issues analysed in this book – but Bain offers a timely analysis of how things are poised and the innovations that the 2016 legislation has brought.

Eilidh I. M. MacLellan takes on the challenge of a critical discussion of the impact of land reform on the hugely complex and controversial area of crofting law in Chapter 12. She starts by outlining the development of crofting law from 1886, the backbone of which has always been the principles of security of tenure, controlled rents, and compensation for improvements carried out to the land. Despite demonstrable current appetite for the reform of crofting law, there have been remarkably few calls to remove the original protections. MacLellan identifies and analyses some of the challenges which face crofting in the modern era, namely, the state of crofting legislation itself, crofting law and its arguably dysfunctional relationship with the wider land reform movement, the conflicting objectives of the crofting system, and the market for crofts.

Lastly in this section, Hamish Lean considers the evolution of agricultural holdings legislation in Scotland beginning with the legislative changes of the late nineteenth century. Where crofting was restricted to the traditional crofting counties in the Highlands and Islands, agricultural holdings can operate across Scotland and (together with the less-common small landholdings) have offered an alternative form of regulated tenancy regime for rural occupiers for many years. The roots of crofting and agricultural holdings are different, however: where crofting was said to protect the people, agricultural holdings was said to protect the land. As Lean explains, ensuring the productive capacity of land was seen as a key goal of the reforms of the nineteenth century, before a shift towards security of tenure for tenants took place in the middle of the twentieth century for reasons linked to the war effort and rationing. After consolidation of relevant legislation by the Agricultural Holdings

(Scotland) Act 1991, further reforms have attempted to revitalise rural Scotland by introducing new agricultural tenancy options that might be suitable for landlords offering land to new entrant farmers, by reforming the rules for existing tenancies, and also by introducing, in some circumstances, a right to buy for secure agricultural tenants. As Lean explains, the cumulative effect of these reforms has been somewhat mixed, but one thing that is all too clear is the complexity of the system that now exists, a complexity that makes for a final analogy between agricultural tenancies and crofting law.

Taken together, these chapters provide an overview of how these significant Scots law rules operate to regulate landownership, occupation and use in a way that will be useful to present-day practitioners and professionals operating in relevant fields. They also explain where policy-oriented land law reform has taken Scots law in relation to these crucial areas of regulation that can have a real impact on the ground, and in so doing set the scene for further policy analysis. Before moving to that analysis, it is worth clarifying one regulatory area that undoubtedly can have an impact on the ground that is omitted from this legal coverage. This omission is planning law. One reason for this omission is that analysis of the blackletter of planning law is available elsewhere and there would be little point in seeking to build on that coverage here.[23] A further reason to omit detailed analysis of planning law for the moment is that legislation is currently before the Scottish Parliament, and thus this serves as another moving target. That being said, what is provided in the policy section below is a chapter by Bob Reid, who offers a view of where planning can sit within the wider Scottish land debate.

Land reform in policy and practice

The final chapters of this volume analyse contemporary land reform policy from a range of perspectives. First, Bob Reid neatly links the policy and legal sections of the book by presenting a practitioner's perspective of the lessons that can be transferred from land reform to town planning in Scotland and the rest of the UK. Reflecting on over forty years of experience in the planning profession, Reid further develops the narrative about the importance of 'rights' in land reform and explores how rights have also come to the fore within planning. He

---

[23] R. McMaster, A. Prior and J. Watchman, *Scottish Planning Law*, 3rd edn (London: Bloomsbury, 2013); N. Collar, *Planning*, 4th edn (London: Sweet & Maxwell, 2016).

reminds us that much of the work connected to the access rights in Part 1 of the Land Reform (Scotland) Act 2003 would have been carried out in planning departments and applauds the development of over 20,000 kilometres of core paths that now exist as a result. He also poses challenging questions about rights and the current housing crisis, advocating the acquisition of land by public authorities in the public interest to ensure land acquisition and development is at existing use value rather than value based on future expectation of development. This provides a timely discussion as the Scottish Land Commission simultaneously grapples with such challenges and questions.

Next, Iain MacKinnon presents the first of three chapters which use predominantly empirical approaches to draw out important themes. In his chapter on the development of crofting policy, MacKinnon considers how contending ideas about land use and governance, and the demands that accompany them, may have contributed to the current 'crofting crisis' as an extension of the ongoing land question in relation to crofting as outlined in both the history and legal sections of the volume. His analysis of the representation of crofters' views in recent crofting policy formation is based on an examination of the 2008 Committee of Inquiry on Crofting and a more recent Scottish Government response to a consultation on crofting support while it was developing the Scottish Rural Development Programme 2014–2020. This analysis allows MacKinnon to question whether the development of crofting policy and legislation in these instances was conducted in a manner that complies with national and international standards for legitimate processes of political change.

In the closing chapters of this volume, the nature of the relationships between landowners, tenants and communities is given due attention, completing the examination of this theme in the history section and helping us to understand the importance of these relationships for contemporary rural development. Jayne Glass, Steven Thomson and Rob Mc Morran explore the role of the landowner in delivering local 'sustainability outcomes' in an analysis of six Scottish parishes which have either historically undergone a process of ownership fragmentation or remained predominantly under the ownership of one large private estate. Examining the Sasines Register to chart the land ownership history of the parishes, in combination with quantitative and qualitative data collection in each place, the authors are able to illustrate the complexities involved in understanding the extent to which land ownership change affects local development. Recognising that there are no restrictions in Scotland with regard to who can own land (and how much they can own), this chapter draws some interesting conclusions that chime with discussions earlier in the volume about concentrated ownership and the challenges associated with understanding how the scale of a landholding influences local outcomes.

Finally, in a chapter which draws on international insights from agricultural models in Norway and adds to valuable international comparisons elsewhere in the volume, Annie McKee and her Norwegian co-authors Heidi Vinge, Hilde Bjørkhaug and Reidar Almås review recent legislative and policy change in Norway to reveal how the Norwegian subsidy system encourages farmers to expand unit size and invest in technology. Using a similar approach to the research described in the chapter that precedes it, the results of interviews with members of the farming community in two Norwegian parishes reveal strong links between farming and non-farming communities and a stronger 'connection with the land' than is present in Scotland. This chapter also reflects on the nature of the relationship between landowner and tenant in Norway, drawing important lessons for the Scottish context.

CONCLUSION

In summary, all of the contributions that make up this volume are designed to firstly, establish the state of academic play on particular issues relating to land reform and secondly, to constructively critique that position and point to gaps and opportunities for further research. As we noted at the beginning of this introduction, this volume does not attempt to offer anything approaching the 'final word' on such a rich and contentious issue, instead, we hope that it acts as a guide through the thickets of material around land reform, pointing out some of the clear paths and dead ends in the long history of this, one of the most unsafe contemporary issues facing Scotland today.

There are two key forward-looking themes the editors would like to suggest for the possible future direction or underpinning of land reform, however. The first is foregrounded in Chapter 5 by Ewen Cameron and continued in Chapters 7 and 8 by Malcolm Combe and John Lovett, and that is the possible – even probable – shift of focus of land reform from rural to urban Scotland. As some new definitions of communities of place and interest are developed and supported and community rights are expanded as a result of the Community Empowerment (Scotland) Act 2015 – both in geographic terms by expanding the pre-emptive right to buy to the whole of Scotland and in terms of scope by allowing neglected, abandoned or detrimental land and assets to be acquired – the potential for reform in urban Scotland is significant. The second future

– and unknowable – direction of land reform in Scotland relates to (at the time of writing) the UK's impending exit from the European Union. The reader will note the editors' and contributors' attempts to future-proof their chapters against what is currently an unknown but undoubtedly seismic forthcoming change in the legislative, environmental, economic and political climate. It is difficult to overstate the potential impact this constitutional change will have on all of Scottish society, not least the rural places under analysis in this volume and of course the land reform agenda linked to them. That necessary yet strategic manoeuvre notwithstanding, the editors hope that this volume will provide a useful starting point for future debate on land reform, in its historical, legal and policy manifestations, that will stand the test of time.

PART I

History

1

Land, Labour and Capital: External Influences and Internal Responses in Early Modern Scotland

Allan I. Macinnes

THE OWNERSHIP, MANAGEMENT AND occupancy of land in early modern Scotland were profoundly affected by dissension between the monarchy, parliament and church; by civil wars; and by Enlightenment thinking. Early modern Scotland was no less affected by inflation provoked by the continuous influx of gold and silver from mainly Spanish colonies in the New World than by the spread of the Protestant Reformation from the continent, which was facilitated and consolidated by the secularisation of the kirklands. From the mid seventeenth century, as a reaction to intensely debilitating civil war, writing commenced on political economy that postulated whether prosperity was attributable primarily to landed enterprise or to overseas trade which financed the engagement of labour in manufacturing. Political economy shaped government policy throughout Europe from the later seventeenth century. Mercantilism – in essence protectionism – played a significant role in moving Scotland to join with England in the Treaty of Union in 1707. The Union, which consolidated the presence of Scottish settlers and trading networks in North America and the Caribbean, opened up new horizons for freelance and corporate ventures to Latin America, Asia and Africa. Such ventures led to the formidable repatriation of capital that stimulated the land market, reorientated estate management and transformed the built environment. Ongoing removal and relocation of people from country to town or overseas was rationalised by the Enlightenment that condoned clearances in the Highlands and Lowlands in pursuit of agricultural improvement and industrial diversification.[1]

[1] Steve Pincus, 'Rethinking Mercantilism: Political Economy, the British Empire, and the Atlantic World in the Seventeenth and Eighteenth Centuries', *The William and Mary Quarterly* (2012), pp. 3–34; Allan I. Macinnes, 'Political Virtue and Capital Repatriation: A Jacobite Agenda for Empire' in Jean-François Dunyach and Allan I. Macinnes with Richard B. Sher (eds), 'Enlightenment and Empire', special edition, *Journal of Scottish Historical Studies*, 38 (2018), pp. 36–54.

LAND, POLITICS AND PLANTATION

Gold and silver bullion from the New World, primarily from Peru and Mexico, became a major source of inflation as too much money chased too little goods. A sustained period of price instability ensued as not just Spain, but all of Europe, attempted to absorb the vastly enhanced supplies of gold and silver for conversion into coin. Inflation also led to a major shift in economic power away from the Mediterranean towards the Atlantic that was grasped by the Dutch, the French and the English who promoted urbanisation to diversify from agriculture into manufacturing. Strong commercial and confessional links with the Dutch Republic in the later sixteenth century enabled Scots to become adept operators in the European carrying trade and also diversified into tramp-trading: that is, the conveyance of goods to and from several ports rather than directly to the ship's ultimate destination. In eastern Europe, landowners tightened their grip over agricultural production, imposed serfdom on their farmers and labourers, and left trade to Jews and enterprising immigrants. Scots grasped this trading opportunity in large numbers, especially in the Commonwealth of Poland–Lithuania. Paradoxically, as the Firth of Forth became a major supplier of coal and salt to the Dutch, coastal landlords, to consolidate their greatly increased revenues, imposed serfdom on colliers and salt-workers from 1606.[2]

Controlled redirection of labour was a pronounced feature of the secularisation of the kirklands, which comprised the wholesale transfer of the lands held by the medieval church to the Crown and the landed and mercantile elites. In effect, around 50 per cent of the landed estates in Scotland changed hands in the sixteenth century, the principal beneficiaries being not just the nobles and lairds whose acquisitions were erected into temporal lordships in 1587, but also former tenants of the church who were able to convert their redeemable leases into hereditary feus. Secularisation responded to inflation by releasing entrepreneurial energies for the development of plantations by land and sea. George Keith, 5th Earl Marischal, who controlled much of the former estates of Monymusk Priory in Aberdeenshire, established Scotland's second civic

[2] Waldemar Kowalski, 'The Placement of Urbanised Scots in the Polish Crown during the Sixteenth and Seventeenth Centuries' in Alexia Grosjean and Steve Murdoch (eds), *Scottish Communities Abroad in the Early Modern Period* (Leiden and Boston: Brill, 2005), pp. 53–101; T. C. Smout, *A History of the Scottish People 1560–1830* (London: Collins, 1970), pp. 180–3.

university at Aberdeen in 1593. Simultaneously, he planted Peterhead as a fishing village which became a model for plans by the Crown to erect towns as oases of civility in Kintyre, Lochaber and Lewis from 1597. Edward Bruce, Lord Kinloss, developed undersea coal mining at Culross where he built his Abbey House from former monastic properties in 1608. It was Scotland's first country house.[3]

The general plantation of Ulster from 1609, which followed on from private Scottish plantations in Down and Antrim, were authorised by James VI of Scotland and I of England as part of a policy of frontier pacification. Ulster became a dumping ground for members of notorious reiving families expelled from the Anglo-Scottish Borders. It also became a place of refuge for Scottish Gaels displaced through the military and legislative offensive of King James in the West Highlands and Islands. Four clans deemed notoriously disruptive were expropriated; three – the MacDonalds of Kintyre and Islay, the MacIains of Ardnamurchan and the MacLeods of Lewis – for their mercenary involved in Ireland; the other – the MacGregors in the southern Highlands – for their persistent banditry on the Lowland peripheries. With the king reluctant to meet escalating naval and military costs, expropriation became a matter of private enterprise. The MacKenzies from Wester Ross gained Lewis, the Campbells of Argyll, Calder and Glenorchy acquired the rest. The legislative offensive, marked by the Statutes of Iona of 1609 and their piecemeal reissue in 1615, aimed to expedite the assimilation of the clan elite on the western seaboard into the Scottish landed classes, a process well underway without official prompting elsewhere in the Highlands. With the *buannachan* who had made their living in Ireland as mercenaries now redundant, some were deployed to make lands more productive by shifting from small enclosed plots to large open fields. Chiefs were also required to report annually to central government on the conduct of their kinsmen and followers. On coming to Edinburgh, they usually incurred lavish expenditure on dress, entertainment and gaming. This led to debts accumulating on their estates faster than rents could be raised to pay off their creditors. Most chiefs had to mortgage or sell off lands, usually to more frugal clansmen but occasionally to acquisitive rivals such as the clan elite of the Campbells and the MacKenzies.

Changes in landownership also featured in the annexation of Orkney and Shetland to the Scottish Crown by 1612. In the later sixteenth

[3] Allan I. Macinnes, 'Making the Plantations British, 1603–38' in Steven G. Ellis and Raingard Esser (eds), *Frontiers and the Writing of History, 1500–1850* (Hannover-Laatzen: Wehrhahn Verlag, 2006), pp. 95–112.

century, the Northern Isles had been run ruthlessly by the Stewart Earls
of Orkney who oppressively exploited the native udal laws of Norse
origin. The abolition of udal law in 1611, as a prelude to annexation
and the expropriation of the Stewart Earls, was a necessary first step to
challenging the towns in Northern Germany and the Dutch Republic
that controlled the trade in herring and white fish from Orkney and
Shetland. To effect this challenge, migration was discretely encouraged
from fishing communities in the Moray Firth to the Northern Isles.
Out-migration was much about prosperity as poverty. Plantations by
land and sea both within and beyond Scotland required venture capital.
New opportunities were being opened up in the Americas. Although the
colonisation of Nova Scotia in the late 1620s failed, Scots participated
in Dutch and Swedish as well as English ventures.[4]

Feudal tenures and leases became geared towards marketing rather
than the consumption of produce. Growing commercialism was further
evident in the emergence of single-tenant farms though multiple-tenanted
townships remained the norm. While money rents from livestock had
fallen behind provender rents from crops by the 1620s, landlords led
the way in promoting the droving of cattle and sheep to urban markets.
Landlords, whose provender rents kept pace with inflation, engaged in
landscaping, creating parks, orchards and gardens. More intensive arable
farming led to a decline in periods of dearth and famine, 1621–3 and
1635–6 being noted exceptions in the early seventeenth century.[5] The
most pronounced entrepreneurial development in the countryside was
the emergence of a class of yeoman, who bridged the lesser lairds and the
substantive tenant farmers. Yeomen in the hinterland of Glasgow diversified into mining for coal and lime. Customary exactions, such as boon
work, carriages and thirling to mills were relaxed but not eradicated.
Commercial renegotiation of rents was complemented by a rise in wage
labour that was redeployed to quarrying as well as building and textile
manufacturing.[6] However, the determination of Charles I to impose

---

[4] Allan I. Macinnes, *The British Revolution 1629–1660* (Basingstoke: Palgrave
Macmillan, 2005), pp. 54–70; Aonghas MacCoinnich, *Plantation and Civility in
the North Atlantic: The Case of the Northern Hebrides 1570–1639* (Leiden: Brill,
2015), pp. 176–257.

[5] Ian Whyte, 'Poverty or Prosperity: Rural Society in Lowland Scotland in the Late
Sixteenth and Early Seventeenth Centuries', *Scottish Economic & Social History*,
18 (1998), pp. 19–31; National Records of Scotland (NRS), Messrs Tod, Murray
& Jamieson WS, GD237/boxes 105, 200–1 and Barony Court Book of Edinbellie
1625–39, GD1/223/1.

[6] Hamilton District Library, 1637 Rental of the Estates of the Marquis of

British economic uniformity led to recession in Scotland, marked by an unstable currency and eroded cost differentials for Scottish produce in overseas markets. When Charles moved from economic to religious uniformity, he instigated a revolution that started in Scotland in 1637 and spread to Ireland in 1641 and England in 1642.

LAND, CONFLICT AND REVOLUTION

The Covenanting movement, which led the revolution in Scotland, dominated the British political agenda until 1645. However, whole swathes of Scotland were debilitated by a civil war between Covenanters and Royalists supporting Charles I. The most affected areas were the Highlands and the north-east. Loss of population led to land lying waste for over a generation. In-migration was also promoted from west and south-west Scotland into Kintyre, Cowal and Mid-Argyll. The Braes of Angus were the recipients of out-migration from Badenoch and Strathspey. Royalists and subsequently lukewarm Covenanters were subject to wholesale forfeitures and sequestrations. Internal political dissension caused Scotland to fall prey to acquisitive English interests as represented by Oliver Cromwell and the New Model Army, who unilaterally executed Charles I in 1649. The Cromwellian occupation of Scotland from 1651 featured regressive taxation to pay for the New Model Army, stagnation in overseas trade and further extensive forfeiture and sequestration of Royalists and Covenanters. Wholesale changes in landownership were checked by the British restoration of Charles II in 1660. However, the English Parliament imposed Navigation Acts, which remained in force throughout the later seventeenth century. Such mercantilist legislation brought home to the Scots that bigger European powers squeezed the lesser.

Accumulating debts remained a persistent feature of estate management, leading to the raising of rents and renewed intensification of farming that had commenced before the civil wars through single-tenant farms, enclosures and the spread of fixed allotments in place of periodic parcelling of open fields as runrig. Droving actually benefited from mercantilist restrictions directed by the English government against Ireland. English markets for livestock came to be dominated by Scottish drovers as the emergence of London as Europe's foremost city encouraged farmers in the Home Counties to cut back on pasture to boost arable

Hamilton, Acc. No. 120169/133; NRS, Rentals of the Archbishopric of Glasgow, RH11/32/1–2 and Miscellaneous Church Papers, CH8/80, /89, /99.

production. Livestock travelling on the hoof from Scotland could be fed
up on the reserved pastures to cater for the expanding demand for beef
and lamb from London. Although Galloway was the Scottish district
initially to the fore in the droving trade, the Highlands were emerging into a position of dominance, particularly for cattle by the 1680s.
Commercial pastoralism promoted tenurial change including the phasing
out of tacksmen as middle managers among the clans, land reclamation
and the conversion of shielings into townships where the profits from
droving enabled grain to be imported rather than grown. Indeed, this
decade instigated the process of estate reorientation in the Highlands
that was to gain momentum from the 1730s as the removal of internal
tariffs at the Union of 1707, the expanding markets for beef and lamb
from industrial towns in the Midlands and north of England and the
increased demand for salt beef for the royal navy ensured that droving
remained a key growth point in the Scottish economy.[7]

The droving trade led to a significant expansion of landholding
through sales and mortgages mainly to frugal clan gentry. During his
stint as governor of Scotland when Duke of York, the future James VII
and II instigated a Commission for Securing the Peace of the Highlands,
which exacted bands of surety, parish by parish, from the clan elite and
other landlords between 1682 and 1684. Their willingness to accept
responsibility for the conduct of their tenants and dependants in order
to suppress thefts of livestock contrasted sharply with the reception
accorded to such bands imposed on Lowland landlords to restrain their
tenants and dependants from militant resistance to the religious and
political establishment. As Covenanting shifted from a movement of
power in the 1640s to that of protest in the later seventeenth century, its
social composition changed markedly. Nobles were conspicuous by their
absence. Lairds and merchants continued to feature, but a new status
was assumed by yeomen farmers and by women, who were coming to
prominence as tenant-framers and as skilled workers in textiles, print-
ing and shopkeeping. This later Covenanting movement reflected and
drew strength from increased commercial activity as evident from the
mushrooming of fairs and villages, competitive bidding for tenancies,
and a surge in seasonal and casual labour for wages that undercut
paternalism in the Highlands and Lowlands. Nevertheless, as evident

[7] Allan I. Macinnes, *Clanship, Commerce and the House of Stuart*, 1603–1788
(East Linton: Tuckwell Press, 1996), pp. 104–58; Allan Kennedy, *Governing
Gaeldom: The Scottish Highlands and the Restoration State, 1660–1688* (Leiden:
Brill, 2014), pp. 180–250.

from continuing migration overseas, more labour was coming on to the market than could be absorbed in Scotland either through landed enterprise or manufacturing generated by overseas trade. A committee of inquiry into trade instigated by York in 1681 was sceptical about calls to protect trade. Scotland lacked the political muscle to impose mercantilist measures. Establishing colonies in America was viewed as an alternative to political incorporation with England.[8]

When James VII and II was ousted in favour of William of Orange, the Revolution of 1688–91 was met with limited opposition in England but with steadfast resistance in Ireland and Scotland where forfeitures were again in evidence for Jacobites who supported the deposed king. But the Revolution also stimulated joint-stock companies to further manufacturing and commerce as overseas trade expanding into the Mediterranean and the Caribbean with assistance from the Bank of Scotland, licensed by William of Orange in 1695. A less successful initiative, simultaneously financed through public subscription, was the Company of Scotland trading to Africa and the Indies, which soon shifted its focus from trading to planting at Darien on the Panama Isthmus, a settlement that could potentially dominate trade to the West and the East Indies and control the overland route for Spanish gold and silver from Peru to the Gulf of Mexico. Faced with staunch opposition from the Spanish Crown and the English East India Company, William duly reneged on his commitment to the Company of Scotland. Nevertheless, shares worth £400,000 sterling were promptly subscribed in Edinburgh and Glasgow. Funding was not matched by adequate planning, however. Two expeditions to Darien foundered, the majority of the colonists succumbing to disease. The abandonment of Darien in 1700 coincided with a demographic crisis through prolonged famine in Scotland that lasted for over five years from 1695. The famine was felt acutely as dearth was no longer a regular occurrence. Even in peak years, the famine was never endemic. Towns with greater purchasing power fared better than rural areas dominated by arable farming. Districts where pastoral farming predominated were less affected. Prices for grain, as for livestock, had stabilised by 1702.[9]

[8] Neil McIntyre, 'Saints and Subverters: The Later Covenanters in Scotland, c.1648–1682', unpublished PhD thesis (University of Strathclyde, 2016), *passim*; Allan I. Macinnes, *Union and Empire: The Making of the United Kingdom in 1707* (Cambridge: Cambridge University Press, 2007), pp. 164–71.

[9] Douglas Watt, *The Price of Scotland: Darien, Union and the Wealth of Nations* (Edinburgh: Luath Press, 2007), pp. 219–42; Karen J. Cullen, *Famine in*

Darien, however, had renewed pressure for political incorporation, which was duly accomplished in 1707. The Treaty of Union was not a magnanimous act of altruism in which England rescued an impoverished Scotland. Darien had not financially crippled Scotland. No more than £153,000 sterling in venture capital was lost on the Panama Isthmus as just over 38 per cent of the shares were actually subscribed. Neither Darien nor the famine led to major changes in land ownership or estate management, which was certainly not the case when Scots got caught up in the speculative South Sea Bubble that burst in 1720. Out-migration to Ulster helped stabilise the labour market and, unlike the civil wars of the 1640s, land did not lie neglected for over a generation. Capital losses from Darien were more than compensated by returns from the carrying trade as from tramp-trading and inward and outward investment through the Dutch Republic, Sweden and Northern Germany.[10]

LAND AND THE 1707 ANGLO-SCOTTISH UNION

The Treaty of Union primarily concerned political economy, with overseas trade secondary to landed enterprise. A common market was created throughout the United Kingdom. By allowing for the free flow of capital, English investors could no longer be prevented from investing in Scottish ventures. The Scots were now guaranteed access to the American colonies of the Crown. However, all parts of the UK came under the same trading regulations and were liable to the same duties. In effect, the Scots had to adjust to English commercial regulation and meet higher duties for customs and excise.

While droving took off with unrestricted access to England, it had a negative impact in financing the absenteeism of chiefs and clan gentry. Debts accumulated from their increased consumer spending. Rents were raised. Sales and mortgages were not abated. Droving was a positive stimulus to banking. Sustained inflows of cash were invested in fishing and textiles. In an era of speculative ventures in stocks and shares, the Bank of Scotland was to the fore in promoting commercial stability through sound lending. This continued to be a feature of the dual banking

---

Scotland: The Ill Years of the 1690s (Edinburgh: Edinburgh University Press, 2010), pp. 123–56.

[10] Patrick Walsh, 'The Bubble on the Periphery: Scotland and the South Sea Bubble', *Scottish Historical Review*, 91 (2012), pp. 106–24; Kathrin Zickermann, *Across the German Sea: Early Modern Scottish Connections with the Wider Elbe-Weser Region* (Leiden and Boston: Brill, 2013), pp. 114–34.

system operative from the foundation of the Royal Bank of Scotland in 1727. Pioneering note issues, overdrafts and deposit accounts during the 1730s facilitated commercial enterprise on the basis of credit rather than secure funds, a basis which attracted inward investment from England where banking practices remained conservative. As well as advancing credit for colonial traders in tobacco, sugar and rum, increased funding was now available to boost direct exports of linen and woollens to colonial markets, developments which boosted rentals and sustained a buoyant land market. Sugar no less than tobacco became a major driver of urban and rural improvements especially after the resilience of the Scottish economy was tested by widespread famine in 1742–3.[11]

Imperial engagement had a profound impact on political management. The limited places of profit in Scotland tended to be monopolised by committed Whigs especially after political management was devolved to Archibald Campbell, earl of Islay (later 3rd duke of Argyll) in 1725. Placement in empire was different on account of the pervasive contacts of John Drummond of Quarrel. Having begun his career as an Edinburgh merchant, he moved to Amsterdam where he established himself as the leading continental financier for the British forces during the War of the Spanish Succession, 1702–13. Drummond helped shape the direction of the East India Company after he settled in London from 1724. Though he favoured Union, his strong Jacobite connections made him the ideal imperial complement to Islay. Drummond enjoyed the backing of Prime Minister Robert Walpole who had factored in Jacobites as expendable manpower to maintain the British presence in the Caribbean and secure the frontiers of American colonies such as Georgia and North Carolina. Until his death in 1740, Drummond was the chief mover in placing Scots, regardless of their political or religious affiliations, in both the military and mercantile branches of the East India Company. The governor of Madras, James MacRae, from an impoverished family in Ayr, became the first Scottish nabob in the 1720s. Drummond also aided Scottish adventurers who tramp-traded through the Indian Ocean to the South China Seas. Gaining placement in India was no guarantee of prosperity. The chances of any adventurer returning with a fortune were about one in 500.

Nevertheless, Scottish networks tainted with Jacobitism did prosper

[11] S. G. Checkland, *Scottish Banking: A History, 1695–1973* (Glasgow and London: Collins, 1975), pp. 58–71; Christopher A. Whatley, *Scottish Society 1707–1830: Beyond Jacobitism, Towards Industrialisation* (Manchester and New York: Manchester University Press, 2000), pp. 48–95.

from empire. The Duffs from the north-east, based in the shires of Aberdeen and Banff with further mercantile interests in the towns of Elgin and Inverness, repatriated funds through London from three empires – the Spanish and the Swedish as well as the British. With the network's fortunes founded on private banking, landed enterprise and overseas trade, William Duff of Dipple was ennobled in 1734 as Lord Braco (later as 1st earl of Fife). The Stirlings of Keir, landowners near Glasgow and in the shires of Stirling and Perth, focused their endeavours on the West and East Indies. Sums repatriated from tramp-trading in India to Britain by 1748 were used, in part, to improve and expand the family holdings in central Scotland, but primarily to acquire further plantations in Jamaica.[12]

After the Fifteen, prominent Jacobites had been forfeited by legal attainder rather than by the due process of law. However, their Whig opponents were determined that landed families and their commercial associates should not be utterly ruined. Forfeiture was partially obstructed by courts allowing the process of sequestration, based on bad debts, to take precedence. Estates sequestered were usually put under the charge of a kinsman of the person forfeited. But forfeiture had also enabled speculative interests, notably the York Buildings Company of London, to purchase Jacobite estates with a view to asset-stripping timber and mineral rights. Among clans where chiefs and leading gentry had been forfeited, rents continued to be paid to them in exile. Attempts by government troops to lift rents in Wester Ross in October 1721 were violently resisted.

After the Forty-Five, the British government pursued a final solution to the Jacobite problem by active terrorism directed against the clans by land and sea. Livestock was driven off and fishing boats holed to induce starvation. Banditry became a form of social protest for renegade clansmen who lifted livestock from Lowland peripheries. A more widespread practice of civil disobedience was the payment of rents from forfeited estates to chiefs and clan gentry exiled on the continent, a practice that continued until the show trial of James Stewart in Aucharn, wrongly executed in 1752 as an accessory to the murder of Colin Campbell of Glenure, the government factor in Appin.[13]

---

[12] Allan I. Macinnes, 'Union, Empire and Global Adventuring with a Jacobite Twist, 1707–53' in Allan I. Macinnes and Douglas J. Hamilton (eds), *Jacobitism, Enlightenment and Empire, 1680–1820* (London: Pickering & Chatto, 2014), pp. 123–40 and 141–57.

[13] Macinnes, *Clanship, Commerce and the House of Stuart*, pp. 203–17.

REBELLION AND LANDED ENTERPRISE

Following adverse press publicity for the atrocities in the aftermath of the Forty-Five, the British government moved away from extirpating to civilising the clans. Archibald, 3rd duke of Argyll, empowered by a war chest of £493,000 for the abolition of heritable jurisdiction, was intent on demonstrating that British patriotism trumped Scottish rebellion by expanding banking, linen manufacturing and fisheries. Landed enterprise at home, no less than commercial engagement with empire, now made improvers and adventurers British patriots.

The first significant test of this approach came when thirteen forfeited Jacobite estates were annexed to the Crown, a measure accomplished in 1752 but not implemented until 1760. Intended as models for exemplary practice, the Annexed Estates were overseen by commissioners who included in their ranks, civic leaders and noted improvers who sponsored authoritative reports on fisheries, manufactures and mineral resources. Financing was dependent on the cash surplus from the capital raised from the sale of forfeited Jacobite estates in the Lowlands, not on an annual grant from central government. Rents on the Annexed Estates, after initial survey and valuation, were frozen by the commissioners. The resultant erosion of capital impeded long-term projects. Inherited debts were continued not cleared. Bureaucracy flourished through lack of accountability and energetic management. No commissioner would appear to have personally visited any Annexed Estate. Following the end of the Seven Years War in 1763, the Estates primarily became an agency to relocate demobilised soldiers and sailors. Planning effectively ended in 1774. Offers of long leases giving greater security of tenure for improving farmers were curtailed to facilitate the movement of labour into industry and to conserve landed interests in anticipation of the full-scale restoration of the Jacobite disinherited in 1784. Although the commissioners did not transform the Highlands, they did accelerate the break-up of traditional, communal townships through the creation of single-tenant farms, planned villages and crofting communities. The consequent removal and relocation of people served as a template for clearance for restored Jacobite as well as loyalist Whig landlords.[14]

---

[14] Annette M. Smith, *Jacobite Estates of the Forty-Five* (Edinburgh: John Donald, 1982), pp. 1–53; Andrew Mackillop, *'More Fruitful Than the Soil': Army, Empire and the Scottish Highlands, 1715–1815* (East Linton: Tuckwell Press, 1999), pp. 13–76.

Rationalised by the political economy emanating from the Enlightenment, the clearance of people was propagated as integrating the Highlands into the British empire. Commercial farming of first cattle then sheep by single rather than multiple tenants removed surplus farmers and labourers or relocated them into crofting communities that too often became rural ghettos for quarrying, fishing and kelp production. The civil engineer, Thomas Telford, was employed to direct central government's programme of road, bridge and canal construction to stem what had become a tidal flow of emigration from the Highlands. Telford warned in 1802 that the removal of erstwhile clansmen to make way for sheep farming carried out to an imprudent extent would cause great hardship. It was the duty of government to curtail the excesses of profiteering landlords. This prognosis fell on deaf ears as evident from the notoriously brutal clearances in Sutherland in the next two decades. Cattle farmers, their labourers and families were removed from interior glens and straths to make way for sheep walks. Some of the evicted were relocated into coastal crofting communities to pursue a livelihood from fishing for which they were ill equipped.[15]

Although landowners in Highlands and Lowlands were increasingly on the defensive from the 1820s over their estate management, they continued to demonstrate economic and social leadership by creating planned villages – perhaps as many as 250 – that came to be dispersed throughout Scotland in the eighteenth and early nineteenth centuries. Planned villages were characterised by their geometric layouts, wide streets and hygienic standards. Their primary role was entrepreneurial: to relocate and redeploy labour not just for casual and seasonal work in agriculture but to diversify employment opportunities in textiles, fisheries, extractive industries, chemicals and distilling. Landowners advanced credit and advertised widely throughout the UK for settlers.

Around the Moray Firth and in the north-east, where planned villages proliferated from the 1720s, settlements near the coast switched from textile production to fishing, a task facilitated by parliamentary grants to encourage exports, to remove restrictions on salt for curing and, above all, to construct harbours using residual moneys from the

---

[15] Roy H. Campbell and James B. A. Dow (eds), *A Source Book of Scottish Economic and Social History* (Oxford: Basil Blackwell, 1968), pp. 44–7; Allan I. Macinnes, 'Scottish Gaeldom: the first phase of Clearance' in Thomas M. Devine and Rosalind Mitchison (eds), *People and Society in Scotland I: 1760–1830* (Edinburgh: John Donald, 1998), pp. 70–90; J. Hunter, *The Making of the Crofting Community* (Edinburgh: John Donald, 1976); E. Richards, *The Highland Clearances* (Edinburgh: Birlinn, 2008).

Annexed Estates. In 1786, the mantle of exemplary Highland development was taken over by the British Society for Fisheries. Of their four planned villages, only Pulteney in Caithness was still thriving by the 1820s, partly because of its proximity to the fishing expertise in Wick and partly because of its diversification into distilling. Continuous investment was integral to sustainability. If deficient, planned villages could and did degenerate into housing for agricultural labour or into sea towns where serfdom had been occasionally imposed upon workers to maintain fishing in the north-east and the Northern Isles.

The counterpoint to this regressive development was the depth and diversity planned villages gave to industrialisation, particularly when promoted by David Dale, the foremost textile entrepreneur in the later eighteenth century, who pioneered the switch in production from cottages for linen and wool to factories for cotton. In the west of Scotland, he founded New Lanark in partnership with Richard Arkwright, the English inventor of the water frame that had transformed productivity in cotton factories throughout Britain. The most exemplary factory village in terms of living conditions for workers was at Catrine in Ayrshire which Dale established with Claud Alexander of Ballochmyle, who had made his fortune in India. The leading importer of bird-nest yarn from India was James Menteith, with whom Dale founded the village of Blantyre in Lanarkshire. Dale's missionary zeal for industrialisation led to his promotion of villages in Newton Stewart in Galloway, Oban in Argyllshire and Spinningdale in Sutherland. Planned villages, which dispersed markets and stimulated consumerism, served as a vital bridge between agriculture and industry that offered a staged process rather than a sudden jump to urbanisation.[16]

The landscape as well as the built environment was transformed by the later eighteenth century: afforestation, enclosures, parklands, drystone dykes and single-tenant farms with steadings, barns and bothies became commonplace. The botanical distinction between leguminous and non-leguminous crops, which provided the scientific basis for crop rotation, was readily transmitted by Scottish MPs impressed by the more advanced state of English agricultural practice. National and local societies, which operated from 1723, encouraged agricultural

[16] Douglas G. Lockhart (ed.), Scottish Planned Villages (Edinburgh: Scottish Historic Society, 2012), passim; Allan I. Macinnes, 'Applied Enlightenment: its Scottish limitations in the eighteenth century' in Jean-François Dunyach and Ann Thomson (eds), The Enlightenment in Scotland: National and International Perspectives (Oxford: Voltaire Foundation, 2015), pp. 21–58.

transformation as a fashionable pursuit. The Highland and Agricultural Society was established in 1784 to bring improvements in the Highlands up to the same level as the Lowlands. Pioneer improvers, usually with external sources of income as judges, army and naval officers or as imperial adventurers, drove on agricultural change, albeit piecemeal improvements that were more haphazard than scientific.

Surveying, though used in the building of military roads in the Highlands from the 1720s, only attained commercial significance from the 1750s. Surveyors pointed out settlement potential, highlighting the neglect of cultivation, inadequate drainage, misuse of field divisions and the arbitrary location of day-labourers' holdings. Estate improvement was often not the first priority in their remit. Aesthetics and landscaping prevailed if charged to find the best site for a family seat. Technological innovation was no less transformative. The light plough designed by James Small from Berwickshire was generally introduced from the 1760s. Andrew Meikle from East Lothian devised the threshing machine in 1786. These inventions both redeployed and increased the demand for labour as later did the steam-powered reaper invented in 1827 by Patrick Bell from Angus. Mechanisation was limited by its expense, its weight and its lack of mobility. The primary driver of rural transformation came from the stimulus of the market, notably the movement of prices for grain and livestock onto higher plateaux. This was largely accomplished between the 1760s and the 1780s principally because the prior increase in agricultural productivity in England was less than population growth. Prior industrialisation in England also increased the ready market for Scottish grain and livestock. Upward price movement was the key to convincing tenant farmers to engage in agriculture not just as a scientific enterprise but as a capitalist pursuit.[17]

CONCLUSIONS

By the outset of the nineteenth century, the Union was one pillar of landed enterprise; the empire had become the other, not just through direct adventuring but also through indirect engagement by the acquisition, transfer and sale of stocks and shares in freelance and company ventures. Two Highland examples will suffice. The Malcolms of Poltalloch were minor lairds in Argyllshire until their family fortunes were transformed

---

[17] Roy H. Campbell, *Scotland Since 1707: The Rise of an Industrial Society* (Oxford: Basil Blackwell, 1971), pp. 24–37; Ian H. Adam (ed.), *Papers of Peter May, Land Surveyor, 1749–1793* (Edinburgh: Scottish History Society, 1979), pp. 1–85.

on becoming plantation owners in Jamaica from the 1750s. Profits from sugar and rum led to their vast accumulation of wealth as evident from the sixfold increase in turnover recorded in their business ledgers: from £115,174 in 1771 to £720,556 in 1826. From Jamaica they diversified as merchant adventurers and slave traders between the West Indies, Central and North America. The bulk of their wealth was repatriated, partly to build up their social position in London and Edinburgh, but principally to work and accumulate capital. They invested successfully in London's West Indian docks, in Yorkshire shipbuilding and, above all, as shipping insurers specialising in the Indian Ocean and the South China Seas. It was only the outbreak of the Napoleonic Wars in 1793 and the subsequent enforcement of an economic blockade around the British Isles that led the Malcolms to invest seriously in the Highlands. They used their colonial wealth to force up prices on the land market to such an extent that they moved from small, through medium, to large landowners in a single generation. Despite the limited featuring of the Highlands in their investment portfolio, the Malcolms had a basically sound and progressive record as improvers for their agricultural innovations, commercial developments and industrial sponsorship.[18]

The Campbells of Glenorchy were more traditional estate managers whose main source of revenue continued to rest on landed enterprise in the shires of Perth and Argyll with farming bolstered by forestry and slate quarrying. Members of the family did engage in imperial adventures from New Jersey to Brazil, from the West to the East Indies and on to China in the early eighteenth century. Under John Campbell, 1st marquess of Breadalbane, between 1791 and 1816, the family focused on interest arising from stocks and shares in imperial markets. As the economy slumped during and after the Napoleonic Wars, agricultural rents slightly declined from £48,620 to £46,700. Revenues from quarries and woods were more volatile falling from £5,000 to £3,000. In like manner, money accruing from stocks and shares fell from £7,230 to £4,000.[19] Although solid returns from rents made the Campbells of Glenorchy relatively resilient, less well placed were landowners who invested imprudently at home and abroad. A series of banking crises from 1797 to 1810 led to a major shake-out of land ownership in Argyllshire between 1802 and 1813 when long-standing landowners were themselves removed and relocated.[20]

---

[18] Argyll and Bute District Archives, Malcolm of Poltalloch Papers, DR 2/80/7–12.
[19] NRS, Breadalbane MSS, GD112/9/2.
[20] ABDA, Minute Book of the Commissioners of Supply of Argyllshire, 1808–21,

When looking at the picture of landed and economic enterprise in early modern Scotland it is clear that major structural economic reform and entrepreneurship – with all the risks and rewards that might entail – was not confined to the modern period. The drivers for these changes to landed enterprise were local, national and imperial, with regional rivalries between landed families being played out during periods of national conflict and revolution, and at the same time undercut by the global opportunities brought by the burgeoning British empire.

pp. 119–21; Allan I. Macinnes, 'Landownership and Land Use and Elite Enterprise in Scottish Gaeldom: From Clanship to Clearance in Argyllshire, 1688–1858' in Thomas M. Devine (ed.) *Scottish Elites* (Edinburgh: John Donald, 1994), pp. 1–42.

2

Agricultural Enlightenment, Land Ownership and Scotland's Culture of Improvement, 1700–1820

Brian Bonnyman

OVER THE LAST FOUR decades of the eighteenth century, Lowland Scotland's agricultural economy underwent a period of radical change, a process that not only remodelled farming practice, but transformed its society and landscape. It was a revolution which affected husbandry and land use, and radically reformed landholding itself, recasting the relationship between landlords and those who lived and worked on their estates: in terms of access to land it represented the most profound period of land reform in Scotland's history. These changes were underpinned by a distinctive culture of improvement, strongly influenced in outlook and practice by the attitudes, ideas and values of the Scottish Enlightenment. This chapter attempts to examine some of the distinctive elements of this 'Agricultural Enlightenment' in Scotland, its relationship to the wider improving movement, and its impact upon those living and working on the land.

The concept of 'Agricultural Enlightenment' is a relatively new one.[1] As an area of research it aligns with the wider recent interest in the intellectual and cultural origins of growth. In its broadest sense, it refers to the attempts to apply the methodologies and insights of the Enlightenment to agriculture: as one recent survey has summarised, it can be characterised by the production and diffusion of useful knowledge, the transfer of skills and technology, and the actions of the state and other agents in promoting agrarian improvement.[2] It rested on a belief that 'not only was agriculture susceptible of improvement', but that it 'could actually

---

[1] D. Dickson, *Old World Colony: Cork and South Munster 1630–1830* (Madison, WI: University of Wisconsin Press, 2005), p. 288; J. Mokyr, *The Enlightened Economy: An Economic History of Britain 1700–1850* (New Haven: Yale University Press, 2009), p. 171; P. Jones, *Agricultural Enlightenment: Knowledge, Technology, and Nature 1750–1840* (Oxford: Oxford University Press, 2016).

[2] Jones, *Agricultural Enlightenment*, p. 2.

be perfected with the aid of human reason and ingenuity'.[3] The concept
has particular relevance to the study of Lowland Scotland, where the
period of dramatic agrarian change coincided with the remarkable cultural flourishing that we now know as the Scottish Enlightenment.[4]
Indeed, despite the fact that the Agricultural Enlightenment has been
identified as a Europe-wide and transatlantic phenomenon, it has been
argued that in only two countries were these ideas put into practice to
such an extent that the resulting changes could merit the term agricultural revolution: Denmark and Scotland.[5] Although both revolutions
were underpinned by an enlightenment ideology and orchestrated 'from
above', the contrast between the two countries' methods and the nature
of their outcomes could not have been starker. Denmark's revolution,
pushed through on behalf of an absolutist state, reformed serfdom,
persuaded the country's feudal nobility to sell off the majority of their
lands, and created a rural society of some 40,000 small-holding peasant
proprietors.[6] In Scotland, the reforms to agriculture and landholding
served to consolidate the pre-eminent position of the existing landed
classes and transformed a rural society with almost universal access to
land to one in which only a minority retained the legal right to land use.

Although debate continues over the notion of an 'agricultural revolution' in England, in Scotland scholarship has confirmed that agrarian
change in the Lowlands was indeed revolutionary. Research has shown
that, although Scottish agriculture had been far from static during the
later seventeenth and early eighteenth centuries, the 1760s and 1770s
marked a critical watershed in terms of the rapidity, scale and extent
of agrarian change. New land management systems and farming practices facilitated by widespread enclosure, led to a complete overhaul
of Scottish farming resulting in dramatic productivity gains: over the
second half of the eighteenth century average grain yields increased by

---

[3] Jones, *Agricultural Enlightenment*, p. 6.

[4] E. J. Hobsbawm, 'Scottish Reformers of the Eighteenth Century and Capitalist
Agriculture' in E. J. Hobsbawm (ed.), *Peasants in History: Essays in Honour of Daniel
Thorner*, vol. 3 (Calcutta: Oxford University Press, 1981), pp. 3–29; H. Cheape,
'For the Betterment of Mankind: Scotland, the Enlightenment and the Agricultural
Revolution', *Folk Life-Journal of Ethnological Studies*, 40:1 (2001), pp. 7–24; N.
Davidson, 'The Scottish Path to Capitalist Agriculture 3: The Enlightenment as the
Theory and Practice of Improvement', *Journal of Agrarian Change*, 5:1 (2005),
pp. 1–72.

[5] Jones, *Agricultural Enlightenment*, pp. 6–7.

[6] Jones, *Agricultural Enlightenment*, pp. 147–54; T. C. Smout, 'Landowners in
Scotland, Ireland and Denmark in the Age of Improvement', *Scandinavian Journal
of History*, 12:1–2 (1987), pp. 92–7.

between 200 to 300 per cent, catching up with English levels by 1800.[7] In the course of a couple of generations, Scottish agriculture went from being regarded as backward and inefficient to being held up as a model of modern commercial farming and a destination for European economic tourism. Whereas early improving landlords had brought farmers from Norfolk to Scotland to spread improved practices, such was the standing of 'Scotch husbandry' by 1809 that *Farmers Magazine* could report on the demand for Scottish farmers and farm servants south of the border.[8]

Aside from its rapidity, another distinctive feature of the Scottish Agricultural Revolution was the leading role played by its landed classes. To a significant extent, particularly in its crucial early stages, this was a revolution that was instigated, funded, and implemented from above. That landlords were able to push through such a transformation was largely due to their unrivalled dominance of Scottish society. Peasant proprietorship hardly existed in Scotland and its land ownership was one of the most concentrated in Europe. It has been estimated that in 1770 the total number of landowners in Scotland numbered just over 8,000. Large estates dominated, particularly in the south and east, accounting for roughly half the total land by value. Although small proprietors, most concentrated in the south-west of the country, were the most numerous, they accounted for only a small fraction of the total land, around 5 per cent: in contrast, around 1,500 landowners (less than 0.002 per cent of the population) owned over 90 per cent of the land.[9] This concentration in land was matched by a formidable concentration of power: land remained the primary source of political, social and ecclesiastic influence, wealth, and social prestige.[10] It was a domination that was clearly expressed physically over the pre-improvement landscape, their residences and policies standing like 'islands of improved, enclosed and wooded land in an open, bare countryside'.[11]

[7] T. M. Devine, *The Transformation of Rural Scotland: Social Change and the Agrarian Economy, 1660–1815* (Edinburgh: Edinburgh University Press, 1994), p. 57.

[8] *Farmers Magazine*, 10 (1809) pp. 129, 248; T. C. Smout, 'A New Look at the Scottish Improvers', *Scottish Historical Review*, 91:1 (2012), p. 129.

[9] L. Timperley, 'The Pattern of Landholding in Eighteenth-century Scotland' in M. L. Parry and T. R. Slater (eds), *The Making of the Scottish Countryside* (London: Croom Helm, 1980), pp. 142, 150–1.

[10] R. H. Campbell, 'The Landed Classes' in T. M. Devine and R. Mitchison (eds), *People and Society in Scotland: Volume I, 1760–1830* (Edinburgh: Edinburgh University Press, 1988), pp. 91–108.

[11] I. Whyte and K. A. Whyte, *The Changing Scottish Landscape, 1500–1800* (London: Routledge, 1991), p. 53.

Below the landowners, almost all of Scotland was occupied by leaseholders or tenants-at-will, over whom landlords enjoyed considerable legal rights. Unlike England, the concept of 'custom' was hardly accounted for in Scottish legal thought, and Scotland lacked customary forms of land tenure that could form a brake on landed interests.[12] Landlord rights over their tenants had been augmented by a Court of Session Act of 1756, which clarified earlier legislation from 1555 and simplified the process of removal at the end of a tenant's lease.[13] The Act of Entail 1685 had further enhanced their position, essentially protecting their lands from bankruptcy and division. Legal decisions over the course of the eighteenth century together with the reformed Entail Act 1770 had also served to reinforce property rights.[14] Writing in 1814, Sir John Sinclair, one of the country's foremost improvers, could confidently claim, 'In no country in Europe, are the rights of proprietors so well defined, and so carefully protected, as in Scotland.'[15] When it came to altering the physical structure of their estates, two Acts passed by the Scottish Parliament in 1695 eased the process of consolidating lands intermixed with other proprietors' holdings and simplified the process of dividing up 'commonties', lands held in common by the various proprietors whose estates bordered them.[16] These were the Division of Runrig Act and the Division of Commonty Act. The Runrig Act referred to 'proprietary runrig', that is, the intermixture of lands belonging to different heritors rather than different tenants. The Act allowed proprietors to apply to sheriffs, justices of the peace or lords of regality for the division and consolidation of these lands, creating a legal framework to untangle the intermixed holdings. Unlike their English counterparts, Scottish landowners were free to enclose their estates at will with no further legislation required. As one historian has noted,

[12] R. W. Hoyle, 'Introduction: Custom, Improvement and Anti-Improvement' in R. W. Hoyle (ed.), *Custom, Improvement and the Landscape in Early Modern Britain* (Florence: Ashgate, 2011), pp. 1–2.

[13] Devine, *Transformation*, pp. 63–4.

[14] R. Mitchison, 'Patriotism and National Identity in Eighteenth-century Scotland' in T. W. Moody (ed.), *Historical Studies 11: Nationality and the Pursuit of National Independence* (Belfast: Appletree, 1978), pp. 87–8; J. E. Handley, *Scottish Farming in the Eighteenth Century* (London: Faber and Faber, 1953), pp. 202–3.

[15] Sir J. Sinclair, *General Report of the Agricultural State and Political Circumstances of Scotland, Volume 1* (Edinburgh: Constable, 1814), p. 115.

[16] Division of Runrig Act, Division of Commonty Act.

'the estate in Scotland was far more powerful than anywhere else in the British Isles'.[17]

A final consideration of the landlords' ability to improve was their financial resources. In a cash-poor country, landowners had access to the capital required to invest in the improvement of agriculture and to provide the infrastructure needed to support it. The social prestige of land ownership was such that new money from trade and empire was commonly channeled back into landed estates, adding to the funds available.[18]

While all these factors help explain the landowners' ability to instigate change, they do not, however, explain why they chose to do so. The landed classes could just as easily have hindered reform, but far from being obstructionist, they embraced improvement with an enthusiasm unmatched in contemporary Europe.[19] Most accounts of the Scottish landed classes' zeal to improve their estates have understandably tended to focus on self-interest, with the demand for higher rents and returns the overriding factor. From this perspective, traditional conceptions of landholding were quickly replaced by more commercial attitudes, with the landed estate becoming little more than a money-making enterprise. However, it can be argued that too narrow an economic explanation raises the danger of economic determinism, with improvement seen as an automatic response to rising prices. Growing demand for agricultural produce after decades of stagnation undoubtedly provided the essential economic context for the reforms to succeed. However, the attitudes, beliefs and mentalities of the landed classes were also crucial, particularly their adoption of a set of values which embraced improvement and made them receptive to change. As one historian has put it, 'in no other part of Europe were the powerful so interested in ideas and so free to act upon them.'[20] This improving ethos was important as it not only gave ideological support to the reforms but also shaped the kind of improvement that would be implemented.

Evidence of the improving mindset amongst members of the Scottish

---

[17] R. A. Houston, *Peasant Petitions: Social Relations and Economic Life on Landed Estates, 1600–1850* (Basingstoke: Palgrave Macmillan, 2014), p. 291.

[18] Devine, *Transformation*, p. 79; E. Grant and A. Mutch, 'Indian Wealth and Agricultural Improvement', *Journal of Scottish Historical Studies*, 35:1 (2015), pp. 25–44.

[19] Jones, *Agricultural Enlightenment*, p. 220.

[20] E. L. Emerson, 'The Social Composition of Enlightened Scotland: The Select Society of Edinburgh, 1754–1764', *Studies on Voltaire and the Eighteenth Century*, 114 (1973), p. 291.

landed classes can be traced back to the later seventeenth century and
the raft of improving Acts passed by the Scots Parliament in the 1690s,
legislation that has been described as amounting to 'a definite policy
of encouraging agrarian reform'.[21] The five-year subsistence crisis and
resultant famine that occurred in the same decade dramatically exposed
the comparative vulnerability of Scottish agriculture and led to a number
of publications aimed at countering its deficiencies, the first evidence of
improving literature in the country.[22] The concept of 'improvement' had
been evolving in England since the sixteenth century, broadening out
from a narrow definition that referred exclusively to increasing the rental
of an agricultural estate to one which encompassed a wide range of land
improvement activities and presented their pursuit as both a moral and
patriotic duty.[23] In this respect the early Scots improvers inherited an
already established ideology, both in terms of theory and practice. These
ideas, however, were to be shaped and adapted to Scotland's particular
circumstances, both physical (in terms of geography, topography, and
climate) and intellectual.

Closer contact with England and its more advanced agriculture
after 1707 coupled with a growing awareness of the need to improve
Scotland's struggling economy culminated in 1723 with the founding
of The Honourable the Society of Improvers of Agriculture in Scotland,
the first patriotic improving society in Europe, and the birth of what
can be seen as the improving movement in Scotland. The founding of
the Society, whose aristocratic and landed membership was drawn from
across the political spectrum, indicated that by the 1720s something
like a consensus had emerged amongst the country's landed elite that
economic improvement would not happen spontaneously but would
have to be actively encouraged from above, and that the improvement
of agriculture would be central to that goal.[24]

The Society's foundation also highlights the important patriotic element

[21] I. D. Whyte, *Agriculture and Society in Seventeenth-century Scotland*
(Edinburgh: John Donald, 1979), pp. 98–110.

[22] Whyte, *Agriculture*, pp. 252–4; Smout, 'Scottish Improvers', p. 127.

[23] P. Warde, 'The Idea of Improvement' in R. W. Hoyle (ed.), *Custom,
Improvement and the Landscape in Early Modern Britain* (Florence: Ashgate,
2011), pp. 127–48.

[24] B. Bonnyman, 'Agrarian Patriotism and the Landed Interest: The Scottish
"Society of Improvers in the Knowledge of Agriculture", 1723–1746' in
K. Stapelbroek and J. Marjanen (eds), *The Rise of Economic Societies in the
Eighteenth Century: Patriotic Reform in Europe and North America* (Basingstoke:
Palgrave Macmillan, 2012), pp. 27–32.

to improvement in Scotland. The links between agricultural improvement and patriotism would become well established in eighteenth-century Britain, underpinned by the strain of classical agrarianism that presented the agricultural way of life as 'a kind of aristocratic ideal', and a particularly appropriate role for the landed gentry and nobility.[25] But there was also a particular Scottish variant of agrarian patriotism, whose distinctiveness lay in the belief that only by achieving economic parity with England could Scotland hope to avoid economic and political dependency.[26] As the secretary of the Society of Improvers noted, regarding Scotland's 'Sister Kingdom', 'If we are far behind, we ought to follow the faster.'[27] Although exemplified by the founding of the Society of Improvers this view became even more prevalent in the aftermath of the failed Jacobite rebellion of 1745, when patriotically minded economic improvement came to play a central role in the attempts to rehabilitate 'North Britain' politically.[28] Catching up with England became seen as both a matter of national pride and an economic necessity. From around the same time, this improving ethos was given stronger impetus, justification and theoretical grounding by the particular enquiries and interests of the Scottish Enlightenment.

The first of these interests was what might be termed an agrarian-centred political economy. The development of political economy was one of the defining characteristics of the Scottish Enlightenment: given Scotland's relative poverty and its particular constitutional and political situation, it is perhaps unsurprising that the Scottish theorists were particularly concerned with economic growth, analysing why it happened and proposing the best ways to promote it.[29] A key element of this analysis was the emphasis placed on the improvement of agriculture

---

[25] K. Hudson, *Patriotism with Profit: British Agricultural Societies in the Eighteenth and Nineteenth Centuries* (London: H. Evelyn, 1972); J. A. Montmarquet, *The Idea of Agrarianism: From Hunter-Gatherer to Agrarian Radical in Western Culture* (Moscow, ID: University of Idaho, 1989), pp. 25–6, 56.

[26] C. A. Bayly, *Imperial Meridian: The British Empire and the World 1780–1830* (London: Longman, 1989), p. 85; Bonnyman, 'Agrarian Patriotism'.

[27] R. Maxwell (ed.), *Select Transactions of the Honourable the Society of Improvers in the Knowledge of Agriculture in Scotland* (Edinburgh: Sands, Brymer, Murray and Cochran, 1743), p. 1.

[28] B. Harris, *Politics and the Nation: Britain in the Mid-Eighteenth Century* (Oxford: Oxford University Press, 2002), pp. 186–7; C. A. Whatley, *Scottish Society, 1707–1830: Beyond Jacobitism, Towards Industrialisation* (Manchester: Manchester University Press, 2000), pp. 116–22.

[29] J. Robertson, *The Case for the Enlightenment: Scotland and Naples, 1680–1760* (Cambridge: Cambridge University Press, 2005), p. 375.

in the development of the wider economy. In the early part of the century, the outlook was predominantly mercantilist, concerned with increasing self-sufficiency and improving Scotland's poor balance of trade. Although actively involved in attempts to stimulate other areas of the economy, particularly the linen industry, the Society of Improvers repeatedly put forward their view that agriculture was the foundation that supported all other sectors of the economy, a position maintained by other contemporary Scottish writers on political economy.[30] However, even in the more sophisticated expression of liberal economics pioneered by David Hume and systematised by Adam Smith, agriculture continued to play a central role. Although Smith rejected the French Physiocratic notion of agriculture being the sole source of wealth, he retained the idea that the improvement of agriculture was the foundation upon which sustainable economic growth – the 'natural progress of opulence' – rested. Indeed, as long as there was unproductive land capable of cultivation and improvement, it was more beneficial for society as a whole to invest in the agricultural sector than in any other area of the economy. As Smith remarked in his correspondence, for the landed classes agricultural improvement was both a patriotic and moral duty, and failing to do so was both 'shameful' and 'foolish'.[31] Closely linked to this understanding of economic improvement was a conception of human nature which saw the drive to self-improvement and the betterment of one's condition as an inbuilt 'natural inclination'. This desire for personal betterment, given the correct conditions to flourish, would tend to result in the 'natural progress of things towards improvement', and as such, was at the heart of the Scottish Enlightenment economic theory.[32]

The Scottish philosophers' historical analysis of the natural progress of society also involved a sustained and damning critique of feudalism. The Scottish Enlightenment thinkers were the first to systematically analyse feudalism, arguing that the weakening of feudal ties was a key element in the strengthening of personal liberty and the growth

[30] Bonnyman, 'Agrarian Patriotism', pp. 45–6; G. Seki, 'Policy Debate on Economic Development in Scotland: The 1720s to the 1730s' in T. Sakamoto and H. Tanaka (eds), *The Rise of Political Economy in the Scottish Enlightenment* (London: Routledge, 2003), pp. 22–38.

[31] B. Bonnyman, *The Third Duke of Buccleuch and Adam Smith: Estate Management and Improvement in Enlightenment Scotland* (Edinburgh: Edinburgh University Press, 2014), pp. 64–9.

[32] D. Spadafora, *The Idea of Progress in Eighteenth-century Britain* (London: Yale University Press, 1990), pp. 312–13.

of commercial society.[33] Although feudalism had been on the wane in the Lowlands since the second half of the seventeenth century, it was only with the anti-feudal legislation passed after the Jacobite rebellion of 1745–6 that the process was formalised. The Tenures Abolition Act 1746, which abolished military tenure, and the Heritable Jurisdictions (Scotland) Act 1746, which removed most of the private judicial powers of feudal lords, were together regarded by the literati as an important milestone in bringing Scotland closer into line with England and more fully completing the Union.[34] Despite the reforms, feudal restrictions remained, particularly in the form of Scotland's Entail Law and the numerous servitudes that remained a common part of leaseholding.[35] Both of these areas would be targeted by the agricultural improvers as irrational relics of the feudal system, out of step with commercial society and inimical to progress. Indeed, leading Enlightenment theorists would play a key role in the debate over entail reform, culminating in the Entail Act of 1770. The reforms may not have gone as far as Lord Kames and Adam Smith would have liked, but the Act would play a vital role in facilitating the improvement of entailed estates.[36]

Another element of Enlightenment influence over Scottish improvement was the attempt to adopt a scientific approach to agriculture. Treating agriculture as 'a philosophy' or as 'any other science' that was amenable to experimental methods had been the proclaimed intention of the Scottish improvers since the 1720s. At a basic level, this meant trial and error, adopting and then adapting existing methods of husbandry for Scotland's particular environmental conditions.[37] But from the 1740s there was evidence of a more systematic approach to applying the advances in natural knowledge to agriculture, especially through the disciplines of chemistry, botany and mineralogy. In addition to the first

[33] C. Kidd, 'North Britishness and the Nature of Eighteenth-Century British Patriotisms', *The Historical Journal*, 39:2 (1996), pp. 369–74; Hobsbawm, 'Scottish Reformers', pp. 3–29; C. J. Berry, *The Idea of Commercial Society in the Scottish Enlightenment* (Edinburgh: Edinburgh University Press, 2015), pp. 50–9.

[34] C. Kidd, 'Eighteenth-Century Scotland and the Three Unions' in T. C. Smout (ed.), *Anglo-Scottish Relations from 1603–1900* (Oxford: Oxford University Press, 2005), p. 185.

[35] Whyte, *Agriculture*, pp. 46–7.

[36] N. T. Phillipson, 'Lawyers, Landowners and the Civic Leadership of Post-Union Scotland', *Juridical Review*, 21 (1976), pp. 97–120; Bonnyman, *Buccleuch*, pp. 61–71; Lord Kames, *Principles of Equity*, 3rd edn (Edinburgh: J. Bell and W. Creech, 1778), reprinted as *Old Studies in Scots Law*, vol. 4 (Edinburgh: Edinburgh University Press, 2013).

[37] Bonnyman, 'Agrarian Patriotism', pp. 48–9.

public lectures on agriculture in Britain, delivered in 1756, university lectures on natural history, mineralogy and chemistry at Edinburgh and Glasgow often included agricultural elements, and this tradition culminated in 1790 with the founding of Britain's first Chair of Agriculture, at the University of Edinburgh.[38] Scientists such as William Cullen, Joseph Black and John Walker also acted as consultants, advising landowners on the chemical properties of soil, lime and marl. Although the workings of soil chemistry and plant nutrition would not be fully revealed until Liebig's discoveries in the mid nineteenth century, Scottish scientists made a number of important early contributions to the topic.[39] The leading scientists of the Scottish Enlightenment – several of whom were improving farmers in their own right – tended to be of an extremely pragmatic nature, keen to find practical applications for their discoveries. As one scholar has noted, their approach reflected a wider concern of 'uniting through science the practical but essentially individual experience of Scottish farmers with those rational and theoretical principles thought to underlie all husbandry'.[40]

How were these ideas and values spread? An important starting point is the practical involvement and networking of the intellectuals themselves, a role enhanced by their particular standing within Scottish society. Although the majority of the thinkers were drawn from the middling classes, many were from a lesser landed or gentry background themselves. A significant number, like Lord Kames, William Cullen and James Hutton were landowners or tenant farmers and active improvers in their own right; others, such as Adam Smith, tutored and advised the nobility over the reform of their estates.[41] But of even more importance was the remarkably high status given to such intellectuals within elite Scottish society and their subsequent ability to influence and persuade the powerful. It was not just that they enjoyed the patronage and support of the nobility and political establishment: in a real sense, from the later 1750s onwards, the literati of Enlightenment Scotland were the

[38] M. D. Eddy, *The Language Of Mineralogy: John Walker, Chemistry and the Edinburgh Medical School, 1750–1800* (London: Routledge, 2016), p. 50.

[39] Jones, *Agricultural Enlightenment*, p. 163.

[40] C. W. J. Withers, 'William Cullen's Agricultural Lectures and Writings and the Development of Agricultural Science in Eighteenth-Century Scotland', *Agricultural History Review*, 37 (1989), p. 154.

[41] Bonnyman, *Buccleuch*, pp. 64–76; Ian Simpson Ross, *Lord Kames and the Scotland of his Day* (Oxford: Oxford University Press, 1972), pp. 315–32; William C. Lehmann, *Henry Home, Lord Kames, and the Scottish Enlightenment* (The Hague: Martinus Nijhoff, 1971), pp. 81–96.

establishment. Through their dominance of the law courts, the established Church, the universities, and the other administrative positions of government in Scotland, the leading literati were in a key position to shape the nature of public debate and establish the intellectual norms of polite society.[42]

A crucial convergence point for these thinkers and the landed classes were the societies and clubs that proliferated in eighteenth-century Scotland and played a central role in enlightenment culture.[43] Of particular importance in this regard was the Select Society (founded 1754), the pre-eminent Enlightenment debating society, whose membership list included almost all the major figures of the Scottish Enlightenment. Starting off as a small literary society aimed at improving the public-speaking skills of its members through polite debate, its membership expanded rapidly to include younger members of the aristocracy and landed gentry, in effect connecting 'the rising stars of Scottish intellectual life with the agrarian elite of the nation'.[44] Its remit also soon expanded, broadening out from issues of personal improvement in reasoning and eloquence to questions of national improvement and 'the most effectual methods of promoting the country'.[45] Its spin-off society, The Edinburgh Society for Encouraging Art, Science, Manufactures and Agriculture (1755), which shared the same membership, offered premiums for essays on agricultural matters and, in 1756, hosted Britain's first agricultural show.[46] Its debating topics included such practical questions as the comparable public benefits of arable and pastoral farming, the most suitable obligations for improving leases, and the proportion of produce that should be charged as rent, precisely the kind of issues that would come to the fore in the attempts of estates to instigate improvements.[47]

Perhaps even more influential at the regional level was the profusion

---

[42] Emerson, 'Select Society', pp. 291–329; S. Shapin, 'The Audience for Science in Eighteenth-Century Edinburgh', *History of Science*, 12:2 (1974), pp. 101–2.

[43] Berry, *Commercial Society*, pp. 14–17.

[44] N. T. Phillipson, 'The Scottish Enlightenment' in R. Porter and M. Teich (eds), *The Enlightenment in National Context* (Cambridge: Cambridge University Press, 1981), p. 32; F. A. Jonsson, *Enlightenment's Frontier: The Scottish Highlands and the Origins of Environmentalism* (New Haven: Yale University Press, 2013), p. 16.

[45] Emerson, 'Select Society', n. 297.

[46] H. Holmes, 'The Dissemination of Agricultural Knowledge, 1700–1850' in A. Fenton and K. Veitch (eds), *Scottish Life and Society: A Compendium of Scottish Ethnology, Volume 2, Farming and the Land* (Edinburgh: John Donald, 2011), p. 875.

[47] Jonsson, *Enlightenment's Frontier*, p. 27.

of local agricultural societies. The Society of Improvers had launched a scheme in the 1720s to set up 'small Societies of Gentlemen and Farmers', resulting in the forming of at least two local farming societies in the 1730s. By 1772, the date of the founding of the first agricultural society in England, Scotland had already produced at least eleven; by 1835 there would be over 133.[48] At the national level, the Philosophical Society (1737), the Royal Society of Edinburgh (1783), and, in particular, the Highland Society of Scotland (1784) all included agricultural improvement as part of their wider remit. Enlightenment thinkers played key roles in these societies, their involvement often overlapping with positions in such public and semi-public development agencies as the Board for the Annexed Estates, the Board of Trustees for the Encouragement of Fisheries, Arts, and Manufactures of Scotland, and the British Wool Society.[49] Although the practical impact of such improvement institutions can be debated, they undoubtedly served to foster the networks of people and knowledge which helped to disseminate the ideas and practices of improvement.[50] They also played a not-insignificant role in another key area to be considered: the publication of books on agriculture. Starting from a very low base, agricultural publishing in Scotland expanded rapidly in the second half of the century, the impact among rural communities aided by the growth of subscription libraries and agricultural journals.[51] As the most comprehensive survey of the topic has concluded, membership and subscription lists reveal 'the books were being purchased and read by key figures in the agricultural community, the people through whom agricultural changes were introduced'.[52] All in all, these societies, public bodies, educational innovations and the publishing culture amounted to a sophisticated knowledge economy, one which diffused not only practical know-how but also the wider improving ideals. And as T. C. Smout has rightly stressed, 'It is impossible

[48] R. C. Boud, 'Scottish Agricultural Improvement Societies, 1723–1835', *Review of Scottish Culture*, 1 (1984), pp. 73, 76–7; Smout, 'Scottish Improvers', pp. 144–6.

[49] Emerson, 'Select Society', pp. 305–6; Jonsson, *Enlightenment's Frontier*, p. 56.

[50] I. H. Adams, 'The Agents of Agricultural Change' in M. L. Parry and T. R. Slater (eds), *The Making of the Scottish Countryside* (Montreal: McGill-Queen's University Press, 1980), pp. 155–76; Smout, 'Scottish Improvers', p. 146.

[51] H. Holmes, 'The Circulation of Scottish Agricultural Books During the Eighteenth Century', *The Agricultural History Review* (2006), pp. 47–8; M. Towsey, '"Store Their Minds with Much Valuable Knowledge": Agricultural Improvement at the Selkirk Subscription Library, 1799–1814', *Journal for Eighteenth Century Studies*, 38:4 (2015), pp. 569–84.

[52] Holmes, 'Circulation', p. 77.

that Scotland could have advanced as quickly as it did without the agronomist information flows that the improvers facilitated.'[53]

By what means were these 'top-down' improvements put into practice? A vital component were changes in landholding arrangements that accompanied or, in some cases, preceded the changes in actual farming practice. The first of these was the move from multiple tenancies – involving communal farming arrangements, with intermixed holdings often held in 'run-rig' – towards single-tenant farms where the farm and holding were one and the same.[54] Beginning gradually in the seventeenth century and spreading out from the more advanced farming areas of the south-east, by the second half of the eighteenth century single tenancies were in the ascendant throughout the Lowlands.[55] Another major element was the move towards longer, written leases. Earlier customary leases had been in decline since the sixteenth century, and by the beginning of the seventeenth century the majority of tenants in Scotland were tenants-at-will, their leases usually renewed annually, without written record or the formal right to pass it on to their descendants. The move towards written leases can be traced from 1620s but these tended initially to be short, of three to seven years duration.[56] By the beginning of the eighteenth century these were widespread, commonly of between fifteen and nineteen years.[57] From the improvers' perspective, the long lease was seen as providing the essential security required for tenants to invest in and improve their holdings.[58] As one estate petition from 1757 put it, referring to tenancies-at-will, 'no improvement can be expected by inclosing or otherwise, while the possession of the tenant is so precarious'.[59] Looking back from 1814, Sir John Sinclair argued that, by 'inseparably' uniting the interests of the landlord and tenant towards the same goal, the long lease had played a fundamental role in the improvement of the land.[60]

---

[53] Smout, 'Scottish Improvers', p. 146.
[54] Whyte, *Agriculture*, pp. 139–41.
[55] Devine, *Transformation*, p. 27.
[56] Whyte, *Agriculture*, pp. 31, 158, 161–2.
[57] I. D. Whyte, 'Landlord–Tenant Relationships in Scotland from the Sixteenth Century to Modern Times' in J. Beech, O. Hand, M. A. Mulhern and J. Weston (eds), *Scottish Life and Society: A Compendium of Scottish Ethnology, Volume 9, The Individual and Community Life* (Edinburgh: John Donald, 2005), p. 345; Devine, *Transformation*, pp. 21–2.
[58] Devine, *Transformation*, pp. 60, 71.
[59] National Records of Scotland, Buccleuch MSS, GD224/392/14.
[60] Sinclair, *General Report*, p. 116.

The 'improving' lease was a further important development. Rare before 1750 but spreading quickly thereafter, and, by the 1790s becoming the standard form in many areas, these were long leases which contained detailed clauses stipulating land use and management practices.[61] These conditions or 'covenants' often included detailed crop rotations and manuring regimes, and specific requirements to reclaim and enclose land. While there has been some debate over the efficacy of these clauses and of the ability of estates to enforce them, the improving lease gave estates legally enforceable control over the management of land, often backed up with penalties and fines, and undoubtedly played an essential role in the diffusion of improved agricultural practices.[62]

A further crucial element of leasing strategy was the setting of rent levels. Although rack-renting could occur, the prime concern, particularly on larger, improvement-orientated estates, was to set what was termed 'an equitable' or 'moderate' rent: one which allowed the tenant a reasonable profit on the stock he employed while giving enough incentive to improve.[63] A sliding rent scale was sometimes used to make allowances for the expense of improvements over the initial period of the lease, with rents subsequently rising in the latter years.[64] In one of the clearest attempts to apply the insights of political economy to a landed estate, William Keir, Overseer of Improvements to the Duke of Buccleuch, devised and implemented a system of setting the rents of the estate's 226 sheep farms based on the average market price of their products. Rather than seeking a maximised return, the ultimate motivation behind his reforms was establish a 'moderate' rent that would both incentivise and enable the tenants to carry out the extensive improvements stipulated in their leases.[65]

How did these tenurial changes affect those living and working on the land? At the level of the tenant, the changes were, on the whole, gradual and piecemeal, with the thinning out that accompanied the move from multiple to single tenancies drawn out over an extended period beginning in the second half of the seventeenth century. By the 1760s and

[61] Devine, *Transformation*, pp. 43–4.

[62] Devine, *Transformation*, pp. 70–3.

[63] T. M. Devine, 'The Great Landlords of Lowland Scotland and Agrarian Change in the Eighteenth Century' in T. M. Devine (ed.), *Clearance and Improvement: Land, Power and People in Scotland, 1700–1900* (Edinburgh: John Donald, 2006), p. 53.

[64] Devine, *Transformation*, pp. 73–4; Bonnyman, *Buccleuch*, pp. 92, 125–6; J. E. Handley, *The Agricultural Revolution in Scotland* (Glasgow: Burns, 1963), pp. 113, 114.

[65] Bonnyman, *Buccleuch*, pp. 120–35.

the beginning of rapid improvement, single-tenant farms were already dominant, and, outside the marginal upland areas where the numbers of small tenants were further reduced, those holding a tenancy were in a comparatively secure position.[66] It was these existing tenants with their consolidated and increasingly market-orientated farms who would implement the improvements on the ground and, particularly from the early nineteenth century, begin to take over the improving initiative from the landowners. The changes at the level of the subtenant and cottar classes, who made up the substantial portion of the rural population in most areas, however, were far more dramatic and disruptive. Prior to improvement, almost everyone in the rural Lowlands had access to some land, albeit with varying degrees of tenurial security and rights of occupancy; even in the predominantly arable areas, 'there was no truly landless class in Scottish society'.[67] After the changes, only the tenants retained their stake in the land, and a new class of landless farm servants and labourers was created. This was the most fundamental social change of the Scottish agricultural revolution, with the widespread removal of cottars – who, with no written lease could be evicted at will by the tenants from whom they held land for labour services – likened to the Highland Clearances.[68] Due to a number of mitigating factors, however, it was, on the whole, a 'silent revolution'. The new agriculture and its associated trades tended to require more labour rather than less, and offered more, even year-round, employment than the marked seasonal variations of the old system. Rising wages kept ahead of inflation and the period saw a general rise in living standards. Growing urban and rural industry offered employment opportunities and many landlords, keen to retain a workforce on their estates and to encourage market centres on their estates, invested in new planned settlements, a distinctive element of Scottish improvement.[69] Nevertheless, the impact on Scottish rural society was profound and long-lasting.

One final consequence to consider is the impact of the physical reorganisation of the landscape introduced by the new farming systems. The changes in landholding prior to 1760 had taken place largely within

[66] I. D. Whyte, 'Pre-improvement Rural Communities: Lowland' in J. Beech et al., *Scottish Life and Society: The Individual and Community Life*, p. 333.

[67] Whyte and Whyte, *Changing Scottish Landscape*, p. 20.

[68] Whyte, 'Pre-improvement Communities', p. 333; Devine, *Transformation*, pp. 136–62.

[69] Devine, *Transformation*, pp. 157–62; P. Aitchison and A. Cassell, *The Lowland Clearances: Scotland's Silent Evolution* (Edinburgh: Birlinn, 2017); T. M. Devine, *The Scottish Clearances: a History of the Dispossessed* (Allen Lane: London, 2018).

the existing open-field systems, with farming still organised around the traditional infield–outfield system.[70] The move towards enclosed fields, the improvement of wasteland and the division of commonties resulted in not only a more rationally ordered and regular landscape but also a more regulated one.

Through the powers of the Commonty Act, some half a million acres of land were transferred from multiple to single ownership, the most intensive period of division lying between 1760 and 1815, but these recorded divisions underestimate the total land affected, as often the threat of the Act was enough to result in privately agreed action.[71] Although commonties were not 'commons' in the English sense, they did represent an important customary source of common grazing, building resources and fuel to those living on the adjoining estates. Their division, together with the improvement of other muir, moss and outfield, and the tighter regulation of forestry use, all served to further undermine the subsistence of the cottar class.[72]

Even more profound in terms of the creation of the improved landscape was the enclosure of land, a process that rapidly became widespread in the final quarter of the eighteenth century. Regarded by most improvers as an essential prerequisite to improvement, the rectilinear fieldscape, enclosed by hedge, ditch or dyke, not only represented a 'closing-up' of the landscape and a clearer delineation of ownership and rights of use, but psychologically marked an emphatic break with the past.[73]

One example where the restrictions of the new landscape came to the fore was in the clampdown on unauthorised hunting, trespassing, and poaching that became increasingly evident in the final quarter of the eighteenth century.[74] Hunting with dogs in particular, which could involve dozens following on foot and cause damage to enclosures, crops, and livestock, became seen as particularly inimical to the improved land use; the author of the *General View* of Dumfriesshire listed it as the first of his 'principal obstacles to improvements'.[75] Tighter controls on hunting and fishing were seen not only as ways of preserving game and protecting property rights, but also as a method of

[70] Devine, *Transformation*, p. 32.
[71] I. H. Adams, 'Division of the Commonty of Hassendean 1761–1763', *The Stair Society Miscellany*, 1 (1971), p. 176; Devine, *Transformation*, p. 51.
[72] Devine, *Transformation*, pp. 142–3.
[73] Devine, *Transformation*, p. 85.
[74] Bonnyman, *Buccleuch*, pp. 167–70.
[75] B. Johnston, *General View of the Agriculture of the County of Dumfries* (London, 1794), pp. 85–6.

discouraging perceived idleness which could undermine the more regulated and regimented work practices required by the new agriculture and its associated trades.[76]

Such restrictions were just one of a number of areas where improvement could result in encroachments upon customary rights and traditional practices. Indeed, the cumulative effects of these developments in leasing strategy and land use were that, despite the removal of feudal servitudes, improvement, at least in its initial stages, resulted in significantly more regulation and control over tenants' behaviour rather than less. This also serves to underline an important general point that, although commercialisation played a fundamental role in the improving process, it was not synonymous with improvement. 'Improvement' was a cultural as well as an economic concept, one broad enough to encompass a range of complementary values, from the personal and moral, to the patriotic and aesthetic. Deeply informed by the ideas of the Scottish Enlightenment, Scotland's distinct culture of improvement provided moral justification, theoretical rigour and ideological support to the process of agricultural change: as such, it played a pivotal role in the transformation of its rural economy, landscape and society, the effects of which are still evident today.

[76] Bonnyman, *Buccleuch*, p. 170.

3

The Impact of Agrarian Radicalism on Land Reform in Scotland and Ireland, 1879–1903

Brian Casey

IN IRELAND AND SCOTLAND, land reform became a way by which political leaders could gain access to their audiences and resulted in evocative and successful campaigns being organised within the 'Celtic fringe' of the United Kingdom. Embracing the language of an earlier generation of English agrarian radicals, Scottish Highland and Irish agrarian radicals of the late-Victorian period enumerated the dangers of unfettered exercise of property rights that they felt to have been going on since the Cromwellian upheavals in seventeenth-century Ireland and the series of Highland clearances since the eighteenth century.[1] Globally, grass roots political leaders were seen to be 'missionaries of "great traditions"', and attributable to their success was how they managed to find a poignant dilemma to carry to their audiences. If the message and the bearer were accepted they were then 'assimilated into an existing set of meanings, symbols, and practices'.[2] Like religious creeds, political creeds are usually percolated and elaborated in urban centres and then brought to the countryside as ideas trickle down from the intellectual architects and then 'lose their original features and take on the coloration of the local social environment [as] efforts to close the cognitive gap were to no avail'.[3] James C. Scott remarked that this distinctly vernacular perspective was 'more than simply a parochial version of cosmopolitan forms and values' as ideas transferred from elites to non-elites, from the city to the countryside, and from the core to the periphery as the mass

---

[1] See Malcolm Chase, *The People's Farm: English Radical Agrarianism, 1775–1840* (Oxford: Oxford University Press, 1988, 2010); Clive Dewey, 'Celtic Agrarian Legislation and the Celtic Revival: Historicist Implications of Gladstone's Irish and Scottish Land Acts 1870–1886', *Past and Present*, 64 (August 1974), pp. 30–70.

[2] James C. Scott, *Decoding Subaltern Politics: Ideology, Disguised, and Resistance in Agrarian Politics* (New York: Routledge, 2013), pp. 7–8.

[3] Scott, *Decoding Subaltern Politics*, pp. 7–8

of people did not get involved or embrace abstract ideals.[4] This essay examines aspects of agrarian radicalism in both regions between 1879 and 1891, using the foundation of the Irish National Land League and the Parnell split as the two points in which to explore the similarities and differences in terms of collection action, political engagement and historicist claims to land.

Highlanders were perceived as a warrior people that had been tamed following their losses at Culloden in 1746 and the Highland Clearances oversaw a significant transformation and destruction of an ancient way of life; yet people appeared to have remained passive, which perplexed contemporary observers. During the nineteenth century, it had become common to juxtapose the truculence of Irish violence and 'their bitter struggle against an alien landlord class with the passive stoicism of the Scottish Gaels'. This is an oversimplification as fifty-five sets of disturbances between 1780 and 1855 challenge the notion of a docile Highlands. Despite this, the majority of clearances took place with little resistance because most Highlanders were devoid of power as they did not own land and had insecure tenure; some had no rights at all as landlords had full legal control over their properties.[5]

The integration of the Scottish Highlands and Lowlands into the United Kingdom was achieved by military subjugation, a scorched earth policy and an anti-Jacobite *kulturkampf* after 1745. The resulting clearances were carried out by Anglicised clan leaders that were determined to maximise their profits with little regard for human cost. Alvin Jackson argues that the significance of this assimilation in its own terms and in comparison with Ireland was quite striking:

> in the eighteenth and nineteenth centuries, the Highlands were simultaneously defined as the ultimate locus of Scottishness and effectively (if forcefully) embraced by the union state. By way of contrast, the far west of Ireland, in particular the western islands, were being defined at the same time as the *fons et origo* both of Irish national identity and (with the birth of the Irish National Land League) of the revolution against the union.[6]

It was believed that the spread of uncivilised agrarian unrest emerged from the west of Ireland and travelled to the Scottish Highlands by the 1870s.

[4] Ibid., pp. 10–12.

[5] T. M. Devine, *Clanship to Crofters War: The Social Transformation of the Scottish Highlands* (Manchester: Manchester University Press, 1994), pp. 209–14.

[6] Alvin Jackson, *The Two Unions: Ireland, Scotland, and the Survival of the United Kingdom, 1707–2007* (Oxford: Oxford University Press, 2012), pp. 149–50.

RISING EXPECTATIONS AND AGITATION, 1850–1880

During the 1850s and 1860s, greater economic sophistication emerged in the west of Ireland which facilitated a changing relationship between town and country, and which was symptomatic of the 'revolution of rising expectations' that preceded the Land War.[7] Shopkeepers were now more visible as the country became an interconnected economic network. The rural population was now coming to terms with money more easily and railways changed people's idea of distance and place meaning that they were becoming less insular in outlook. Nevertheless, Ireland could remain a place where quite short distances could separate the consciousness of men, 'indeed ties between Connemara and Boston were probably closer than between Connemara and Donegal'.[8] The agricultural changes of the late eighteenth century, the reorganisation of husbandry in Scotland as well as the emergence of enclosure and capitalist farming, changed the previous system of rural life that consisted of the hamlet *fermtoun* in Lowland and the *baile* in the Highlands as clearances, the squaring of farms and assisted emigration schemes in both regions were carried out in the name of progress. This rationalisation of farming was used by agrarian radicals in both regions to portray a dispossessed people, with historicist assertions over the illegality of clearances, emigration and eviction becoming an evocative trope during both the Land War and Crofters War.[9] There was relative peace in the crofting areas after 1850, though crofters were seen to be living in fear and engaged in ingratiating deference in order to court favour with their landowner or his staff. They were viewed as people who were unwilling to complain because 'memories of the clearances, imprinted deep in the minds of the crofters, left them cowed and submissive; and on some estates the factors, wielding the threat of eviction to exact obedience, ruled as petty tyrants'.[10]

Serious congestion and subdivision remained despite the numerous

---

[7] J. S. Donnelly, Jr, *The Land and the People of Nineteenth-Century Cork: The Rural Economy and the Irish Land Question* (London and Boston, Routledge and Kegan Paul, 1975), pp. 250–2.

[8] K. T. Hoppen, *Elections, Politics and Society in Ireland, 1832–1887* (Oxford: Oxford University Press, 1984), p. 462.

[9] T. C. Smout, 'The landowner and the planned village in Scotland, 1730–1830' in N. T. Phillipson and Rosaline Mitchison, *Scotland in the Age of Improvement* (Edinburgh: Edinburgh University Press, 1970, 1996), pp. 73–9.

[10] I. M. M. MacPhail, 'Prelude to the Crofters' War, 1870–80' in *Transactions of the Gaelic Society of Inverness*, vol. XLIX (Inverness 1974–6), pp. 159–61.

clearances and the squaring of holdings which meant that there were still many grievances in crofting areas, even as crofter fishermen of the north and west saw a rise in living standards during the 1870s. The same period saw an increase in the number of newspapers and journals that were interested in the crofter problem. Through their pages, absentee landlords were subject to criticism for neglecting their estates as was the rationalisation of the rural economy in the name of 'improvement'.[11] Local newspapers allow for a more effective assessment of the local experience during this period than the national press. For example, in Ireland, they also reported on affairs beyond the confines of the local communities and this was important in the modernisation of west of Ireland society. Reporting on events beyond the immediate district allowed western Irish nationalism to develop a more cosmopolitan hue as speeches had inflections of Enlightenment and Chartist thought.[12] The leadership for crofters did not come from within communities initially, rather it was generally in the hands of exiled Highlanders in towns and cities.[13] During the 1860s and 1870s, Highland societies began to emerge in several large towns. Primarily a social outlet, they also provided charity to impoverished Highland brethren and developed an interest in crofters' problems.[14] In Ireland, leadership consisted generally of townsmen, shopkeepers, teachers, and priests, part of the 'challenging collectivity', which, according to Samuel Clark, consisted of 'combinations formed by and claiming to represent the interests of tenant farmers [that] became the predominant type of agrarian collective action in the post-Famine period'.[15]

Until the 1870s, protest was reactionary in Ireland and Scotland. It tended to be localised with a lack of leadership inhibiting its effectiveness and it was generally a response to immediate local concerns. However, it became more robustly organised after 1880 and was aimed at recovering land that protestors believed to be illegally appropriated.[16]

[11] Ibid., pp. 169–70, 183.

[12] Brian Casey, *Class and Community in Provincial Ireland, 1851–1914* (London: Palgrave Macmillan, 2018), p. 4.

[13] MacPhail, 'Prelude to the Crofters' War, 1870–80', p. 161; Eric Hobsbawm, *Labouring Men: Studies in Labouring History* (London: Weidenfeld and Nicolson, 1964), p. 272.

[14] MacPhail, 'Prelude to the Crofters' War, 1870–80', pp. 169–70, 183.

[15] Samuel Clark, *Social Origins of the Irish Land War* (Princeton: Princeton Legacy Library, 1979), p. 211.

[16] Iain J. M. Robertson, *Landscapes of Protest in the Scottish Highlands After 1914: The Later Highland Wars* (Farnham: Ashgate, 2013), p. 29.

The 'Great Awakening' of English agricultural labourers was led by Joseph Arch in 1874 as he began to organise them into a trade union in order to more robustly campaign for improvements in their working conditions.[17] Irish and Scottish radicals were further inspired by the coherent critiques of Irish and Highland landlordism emerging under the Irish National Land League and the Highland Land Law Reform Association during the 1880s, with meetings, lectures and pamphlets all playing an important role in highlighting the grievances felt. This became part of an effort to mobilise crofters to demand fairer access to land and challenge the increased stratification of Highland society brought about by sheep parks and sporting estates. Methods of protest were more effective after 1880, focusing their attention on recovering land that protestors claimed to be illegally appropriated.[18] In addition, a series of land reform associations emerged in the Highlands during the nineteenth century with one – the Scottish Land Reform Alliance – inspired by the Chartist Land Plan.[19] A more assertive Highland identity began to emerge. Through the use of trauma-inflected rhetoric, leaders instilled a sense of dispossession and moral entitlement for land which acknowledged the breach of unwritten codes and the evocative pathos of clearances. A similar rhetoric was used during various public meetings in the three phases of the Irish Land War between 1879 and 1909.[20]

Prior to the Land War, the conservative, anti-agrarian nature of nationalist politics in Ireland isolated it from a large proportion of the population; quests for self-determination were concentrated in the towns and cities of Leinster and Munster. While there had been periods of unrest during previous economic downturns, 'the speed at which economic adversity renewed hostilities indicates that, underlying the apparent harmony that prevailed during most of the 1860s and 1870s, there remained a basic weakness in the Irish landlord–tenant relationship'.[21] The social base of the Land League was wider than anything that preceded it. Yet, motions passed at meetings focused upon the grievances of farmers to the neglect of labourers. This nascent, loose and supposedly pragmatic alliance soon came to dominate Land League

[17] See Pamela Horn, *Joseph Arch 1826–1919: the Farm Workers' Leader* (Warwick: The Roundwood Press, 1971).

[18] Robertson, *Landscapes of Protest*, p. 29.

[19] Andy Wightman, *The Poor Had No Lawyers: Who Owns Scotland* (Edinburgh: Birlinn, 2011), p. 80.

[20] Ibid.

[21] Clark, *The Social Origins of the Irish Land War*, pp. 153–7.

ideology as stronger farmers succeeded in asserting their hegemony and became responsible for many of the periods of unrest.[22]

Violent inflections in speeches, coupled with significant increases in recorded agrarian crime, saw the Land League being proclaimed an illegal organisation on 20 October 1881. While the authorities hoped this would spell the end of agitation, the creation of the Irish National League frustrated efforts to pacify the Irish countryside and there was a revival of meetings in November and December 1882 with twenty-five recorded to have taken place, mostly in large market towns. Special Resident Magistrates were created to assist in offering a more robust response to agrarian agitation and theirs was frequently a rigid and simplistic interpretation.[23] Special Resident Magistrate Clifford Lloyd was concerned that there would be a revival by August 1883 in the west of Ireland. He further noted the more pronounced disagreements amongst nationalists as a more obvious urban–rural division began to emerge.

> There are now in [provincial] Ireland, two parties, one the farming class and other respectable people who wish to take advantage of late legislation and to enjoy its fruits, the other the village members of the late Land League who 'toil not' but are rather anxious to continue to live upon what they can extort from others and to enjoy the local influence which they possess as the recognised commanders of the 'moonlighters' of their districts.[24]

Demonstrations were an evocative representation of farmer strength, while also being an effective way of intimidating opponents of the Land League to either conform to their demands or face consequences, which was generally manifested through social ostracism within and from the local community. Once the agitation spread beyond Connaught and into Leinster and Munster towards the end of 1880, the Land League's nascent radicalism was dampened as stronger farmers became more demanding in seeking directly beneficial reforms to the neglect of the smaller farmers. The government initially ignored the Land League's meetings because they thought that they were merely Fenians seeking catharsis and would not gain any significant support. This was because previous movements, such as the Tenant League, were short-lived

---

[22] L. P. Curtis, Jr, 'On class and class conflict in the Land War' in *Irish Economic and Social History*, p. viii (1981), p. 87.

[23] Stephen Ball, 'Policing the Irish Land War: Official responses to political protest and agrarian crime in Ireland, 1879–91', PhD thesis (University of London, 2000), p. 163.

[24] National Archives of Ireland, Chief Secretary's Office, Registered Papers, CSORP/1883/20404.

and generally unsuccessful, and while tenant defence associations and farmers clubs had their activities reported on extensively in the local press during the 1870s, neither landlords nor the authorities saw them as a threat. Between the first Land League meeting in Irishtown, County Mayo, in April 1879 and the following September, twenty-two meetings were held; between September and December the same year there were 140 meetings discussing rent and land tenure. Ideas put forward were idealistic but displayed sophistication and awareness of previous land reform movements. Much to the government's annoyance, there was nothing in the speeches that initially amounted to criminality so it was difficult to effectively halt the Land League's progress.[25] The Land League had branches in twenty-three counties by December 1880 and its leaders wanted it to eventually have a branch in every county as they campaigned for fair rent, fixity of tenure and freedom of sale – the three Fs. They eventually called for peasant proprietorship as a panacea to problems in the countryside. Their hopes were evidently ambitious, especially as the success of each branch was down to the effectiveness of local leadership. Some local leaders failed to control agrarian crime which was becoming increasingly common. This limited the Land League's ability to develop a veneer of legitimacy and resulted in Michael Davitt, former Fenian and founder of the Land League who was born in Mayo but grew up in Lancashire, calling for stronger leaders.

By December 1879, Michael Davitt realised that the Scottish Highlands could potentially be an area for agitation, though there was little desire for such a campaign at the time. Angus Sutherland, a Highland-born land radical, established the Skye Vigilance Committee in 1881 and argued that that every Highlander was a born agitator because they had suffered either directly or indirectly from landlordism.[26] Davitt concluded that land nationalisation as advocated by Henry George was the best solution to the crisis as he became disgusted with the influence of larger farmers in the movement in Ireland.[27] According to Moody it was a doctrine of national ownership and taxation of lands to rid Ireland of a 'foul, pestiferous social rinderpest' landlordism and the idea of the national ownership of land became a cherished principle

---

[25] Casey, *Class and Community in Provincial Ireland*, chapters 5 and 6.

[26] Andrew G. Newby, *The Life and Times of Edward McHugh (1853–1915): Land Reformer, Trade Unionist and Labour Activist* (Lampeter: Edwin Mellen Press, 2005), pp. 74–82.

[27] Paul Bew, *Land and the National Question in Ireland, 1858–82* (Dublin: Gill and Macmillan, 1978), pp. 26–7, 53.

of Davitt's.[28] This was his reinterpretation of the cry 'the land for the people'. George's ideas were viewed with great suspicion in Ireland. They were seen to be communistic and potentially damaging to the cause of Irish nationalism and Davitt became increasingly isolated from mainstream Irish nationalism.[29] There had been conflict within the Land League, primarily between western small farmers on one hand and eastern and southern graziers and large farmers on the other, much like tensions between crofters and Highland sheep farmers. In a letter to the *Freeman's Journal* of 21 June 1882 an intellectual confidante of Davitt, Matt Harris, stated that land nationalisation was harmful and threatened to foster disunion, stating: 'where there is practical work to be done, common sense requires that men should remain steadily at that work and not be changing with every wind that blows' and also that Davitt's advocacy of land nationalisation was causing disunion.[30] Harris was concerned that 'the nationalisation of the land means the denationalisation of the country' and that farmers would become apathetic if they thought it was a solution to the land question.[31]

At a meeting in Glasgow in October 1883, Davitt argued that land nationalisation could be adopted as a social remedy to the poverty and despair being experienced in the Highlands. He encouraged Highlanders to challenge the power of landlords to claim absolute ownership of land as they sought to assert their 'privileged idleness', while decreeing that clearances, famine and emigration were part of the Malthusian political economy that was used to explain the poverty that existed in the Highlands.[32] Henry George visited the Highlands when he discussed land nationalisation and this was overseen by Edward McHugh. Despite a mixed response to the idea, it was better received in Scotland than Ireland.[33]

---

[28] T. W. Moody, *Davitt and Irish Revolution 1846–82* (Oxford: Oxford University Press, 1982), pp. 519, 521–2.

[29] Laurence Marley, *Michael Davitt: Freeland Radical and Frondeur* (Dublin: Four Courts Press, 2007), p. 167.

[30] *Freeman's Journal*, 21 June 1882.

[31] Ibid.

[32] *Speech of Michael Davitt at the meeting in favour of land nationalisation held at St. James Hall 30 October 1883* (London, 1883).

[33] Newby, *The Life and Times of Edward McHugh*, pp. 72–4.

THE LAND WARS AND RESPONSES

On 15 December 1879, *The Times* reported that there were more frequent discussions around land laws taking place in Scotland as their
reform was increasingly seen as a pressing concern and question. The
Free Church minister John MacMillan had written to the press in the
summer and autumn of 1880 highlighting the fact that at Leckmelm
in Wester Ross crofters were now becoming day labourers; the local
landowner, Pirie, was determined to commandeer croft lands for his
own farm. MacMillan accused Pirie of behaving egregiously, maintaining that the crofter was a peaceful sort, especially when juxtaposed with
the small farmer of the west of Ireland, who had encouraged the holding
of peaceful meetings throughout 1880 to highlight the problems that
crofters were facing.[34]

While Angus Sutherland had preached land restoration prior to the
Crofters Bill in 1885, the *Oban Times* warned against expecting too
much. Napier's 1884 proposal entailed longer-term economic planning while what became the Act was a response to a particular set of
circumstances, much in the same vein as the Land Law (Ireland) Act
1881. Scotland was now facing land and national questions as Davitt
began talking about the rise of popular democracy in Glasgow in 1886,
convinced of Gladstone's integrity regarding Irish Home Rule and land
reform.[35] Angus Sutherland was elected to parliament and, being a disciple of Henry George, he assured voters that securing land reform was
his main priority as the *Highland News* kept the Georgite gospel alive.

The politicisation of poverty by Fenians in the west of Ireland
and Highland campaigners gave agitation a greater coherence. In the
Highlands, 'protest was more organised and aimed at recovering land
previously expropriated (so protestors believed) under the drive to agricultural improvement or deer forest'.[36] Following the success of Irish MPs
and agrarian radicals in agitating for the creation of the Bessborough
Commission, which investigated the Landlord and Tenant (Ireland) Act
1870, and following the passing of the Land Act 1881 after a period of
sustained agitation, Highland MPs demanded something similar, which

[34] Allan W. MacColl, *Land, Faith and the Crofting Community: Christianity and
Social Criticism in the Highlands of Scotland, 1843–1893* (Edinburgh: Edinburgh
University Press, 2006), pp. 96–8.
[35] Andrew G. Newby, *Ireland, Radicalism and the Scottish Highlands, c.1870–
1912* (Edinburgh: Edinburgh University Press, 2007), pp. 138–9.
[36] Robertson, *Landscapes of Protest*, p. 29.

led to the establishment of the Napier Commission in 1883. While the Napier Commission is now a remarkable historical document in its own right, it did not attract much support for its recommendations when it first came out.[37]

The Crofters Commission was legislated for under section 17 of the Crofters Holdings (Scotland) Act 1886 and its early movements suggested that it had a policing as well as a judicial role.[38] The government hoped that it would be a calming influence on the Highlands and while it pacified the area in the long-term, the Crofters Commission's movement around the various communities fuelled agitation because of competing claims for its attention, thus becoming a cause for concern in places.[39] Its activities also attracted displeasure from one quarter or another at any point in time as every landowner believed that his cause was the most pressing.[40] They feared their property rights would be usurped and they would not be entitled to recoup arrears, especially as the Commission had the power to cancel debts if it saw fit. On the other hand, it gave crofters the false hope that their arrears could be struck off as they then drew inspiration from the Land League's controversial 'No Rent Manifesto', meaning that there were crofters determined not to pay anything until the Commission decided upon their rents.[41] The 'No Rent Manifesto' was issued by imprisoned members of the Land League that called for small farmers to withhold rents in order to obtain large rent abatements under the 1881 Land Act and to put the Act to the test in order to provide evidence of the limitations of fair rent, fixity of tenure and freedom of sale to solve the land question for farmers. It was condemned by Archbishop Croke and other priests in the *Freeman's Journal* – the mainstream nationalist organ – as they argued that it was too impracticable to implement.[42] An amending Act was passed in Scotland in 1887 whereby proceedings could be paused while a landlord sought to recover arrears.[43]

The Crofters Commission hoped the settling of rents would lead to negotiated settlements elsewhere. When this did not happen a new

---

[37] Ibid., pp. 31–2.

[38] Ewen A. Cameron, *Land for the People? The British Government and the Scottish Highlands, c.1880–1925* (East Linton: Tuckwell Press, 1996), pp. 40–1.

[39] Ibid., pp. 40–1.

[40] Ibid., pp. 43, 45.

[41] Ibid., pp. 42–5.

[42] See Walter Walsh, *Kilkenny: The Struggle for the Land, 1850–1882* (Kilkenny: Walsh Books, 2008), p. 377.

[43] Crofters Holdings (Scotland) Act 1887; Cameron, *Land for the People?*, p. 48.

cleavage emerged in the Highlands between those with judicially fixed
rents and those without. It failed to appease crofters as the more radical
element did not think that it went far enough in affecting reform. For
example, South Uist crofters believed that the Secretary for Scotland and
the Commission were using the legislation to engender a new form of
landlord tyranny because of the Secretary's power to fix the sittings
of the Commission. The Commission eventually became a component
of public policy and the Conservatives saw it as a useful way of keeping
the peace and stifling overzealous crofter demands.[44] This had strong
overtones with Constructive Unionism in Ireland, which emerged to
tame the more radical elements of Irish agrarian radicalism and became
known by the moniker 'Killing Home Rule by Kindness'. Land purchase
became the cornerstone of this policy and J. J. Lee remarked: 'moral
force unionism was based on the assumption that every native has his
price'.[45]

Alexander MacDonald acted for many proprietors in the Highlands
and was of the opinion that many crofters could pay rent but chose
not to in the hope of achieving further reductions. He also argued that
there were many magnanimous landowners that accepted the decisions
made by the commissioners.[46] Lord Stafford, son and heir of the largest
landowner in Scotland, was cultivating his image as a champion of
the crofters and he was treated with a degree of suspicion because of
this. The 8th duke of Argyll felt that Stafford betrayed his class with
his actions. However, most of the odium towards Stafford came from
crofters led by Angus Sutherland, who believed that he was using the
question, cynically, to get elected. In addition to this, because he was so
far removed from them in terms of social class, there was a belief that
he could not fully understand their plight, despite what he said.[47]

The Crofters War saw an intense revival of interest in Highland
history of the previous century. The Sutherland estate and ducal family
starred as the top villain in various narratives being constructed with
very public attacks on the family taking place. It also saw an explosion
of public and private correspondence that criticised the Sutherlands and
other landlords across the Highlands.[48] Highland estates underwent

[44] Ibid., pp. 44–6.
[45] Beckett, *The Making of Modern Ireland*, p. 406; J. J. Lee, *The Modernisation of Irish Society 1848–1918* (Dublin: Gill and Macmillan, 1971), p. 127.
[46] Cameron, *Land for the People?*, p. 50.
[47] Annie Tindley, *The Sutherland Estate, 1850–1920* (Edinburgh: Edinburgh University Press, 2010), pp. 81–2.
[48] Ibid., pp. 58–60.

various stages of retrenchment on the eve of the Crofters War, particularly between 1882 and 1886. The 3rd duke of Sutherland became increasingly absent from his estate, which became a cause of concern because of the changing political context in the Highlands during this period. Because Sutherland covered an entire crofting county, there were large-scale stresses and difficulties within landlord–tenant relations on the estate. Its management were exasperated and believed that crofters were sources of social and economic burden and this reflected a strain of thought among some landowners in both Ireland and Scotland.[49] Like their heavily indebted Irish brethren, Scottish landowners were loath to offer any major concessions to crofters. The nature of landlord–tenant relations in both countries was changing and landowners struggled to comprehend this shift in attitudes.[50]

Catholic clergy in the west of Ireland and Free Church of Scotland clergy in the Highlands came to play important roles in defusing potentially dangerous situations by acting as mediators between the civil authorities and landlords. Defiance against the law became so unprecedented during the Crofters War and the Land War that clerical involvement became imperative in order to keep unrest to a minimum, especially when there was a fear that there could be loss of life.[51] The divide between Scottish landowners and their tenants was deepened owing to landlord membership and loyalty to the Established Church.[52] There were similar cultural distinctions in Ireland, which were further distinguished by the evangelical revival of the 1820s where landlords known as the 'Bible gentry' engaged in a 'Second Reformation' in an effort to gain converts to Protestantism.[53] While this was an overwhelming failure, memory left great rancour and was used as a propaganda tool during the Land War, with the clergy forefront in delivering splenetic anti-landlord rhetoric. The clergy in both regions were expected to be vocal on behalf of their respective flocks but they were slow to do so, partially because of a fear of unnecessarily inflaming confrontation. In Ireland, the initial involvement of Fenians in the land campaign, especially in the establishment of the Ballinasloe Tenant Defence Association – the precursor to the Land

---

[49] Ibid., pp. 58–60.

[50] Ibid., p. 64.

[51] MacColl, *Land, Faith and the Crofting Community*, pp. 102–4.

[52] MacPhail, 'Prelude to the Crofters' War', pp. 159–61.

[53] See Irene Whelan, 'The bible gentry: evangelical religion, aristocracy, and the new moral order in the early nineteenth century' in Crawford Gribben and Andrew R. Holmes (eds) *Protestant Millennialism, Evangelicalism and Irish Society, 1790–2005* (Basingstoke: Palgrave Macmillan, 2006), pp. 52–82.

League – made the clergy slow to become involved; coupled with Fenian hostility, the movement had greater freedom to posit radical solutions to the land question.[54]

POLITICAL REFORM AND LAND

As Irish MPs developed more clout and discipline in Westminster, they brought attention to the condition of the Highlands in Parliament which assisted in breaking down anti-Irish prejudices in the region.[55] The issuing of notices to quit led to a rent strike on Lord MacDonald's estate in Skye during April 1882. This tactic was similar to rent strikes in Ireland and increased violence coincided with Michael Davitt's visit to Skye. He helped to coordinate crofter resistance to the military force being dispatched.[56] He believed that the crofter cause was part of a pan-Celtic struggle and the common grievances amongst farmers in Ireland, Scotland and Wales were shared partially through knowledge of what was happening on the Celtic fringe.[57] Davitt hoped that a pan-Celtic fringe could become part of a wider scheme to forge an alliance with the democratic masses of Britain and Ireland though anti-Irish sentiment remained strong in Wales.[58]

While the growth of democratic politics, assisted by Gladstonian liberalism, was now exciting previously voiceless actors in Britain and Ireland, the Irish Parliamentary Party was hesitant about running working-class candidates for election, with liberal caucuses in Britain also preferring to run bourgeois candidates instead of penniless and therefore expensive working men. Still, there were candidates that were successfully returned in Ireland as they agreed to 'sit, act and vote as one'.[59] The Irish Parliamentary Party held the balance of power at Westminster

---

[54] See Casey, *Class and Community in Provincial Ireland*, chapter 5; Gerard Moran, 'Laying the Seeds for Agrarian Agitation: The Ballinasloe Tenant Defence Association, 1876–80' in Carla King and Conor McNamara (eds), *The West of Ireland* (Dublin: Irish Academic Press, 2011), pp. 73–92.

[55] Andrew G. Newby, 'Landlordism is soon going Skye-High. Michael Davitt and Scotland, 1882–1887' in *History Scotland* (July/August 2003), p. 52.

[56] Marley, *Michael Davitt*, p. 168.

[57] David Howell, 'The land question in nineteenth-century Wales, Ireland and Scotland: A comparative study' in *Agricultural History Review*, 61:1 (June 2013), pp. 83–4, 88.

[58] Howell, 'The land question in nineteenth-century Wales, Ireland and Scotland', p. 177. Cit. in Marley, *Michael Davitt*, p. 180.

[59] See Conor Mulvagh, *The Irish Parliamentary Party at Westminster* (Manchester: Manchester University Press, 2016).

following the 1885 election and British party politics eventually pivoted towards Irish Home Rule by the 1910s. While the Conservatives were keen to suppress land agitation, they were also aware of the importance of keeping Charles Stewart Parnell onside.[60] Irish MPs represented the single greatest internal threat to the stability of the Union at this time. Conor Mulvagh has argued that 'the Irish Parliamentary Party was not merely a momentary anomaly in the House of Commons. It constituted the most powerful third party in the history of British politics until the emergence of Scottish nationalism'.[61]

Crofters were slower than their Irish counterparts to engage actively in the burgeoning democratic framework following the Secret Ballot Act of 1872 and the extension of the franchise in 1884. Nevertheless, the 1885 election also offered great promise for crofters. For example, in Sutherland the county seat was going to be contested for the first time in over fifty years. The Irish Parliamentary Party had a strong machine in place in rural Ireland through the auspices of the Irish National League but the same level of organisation was not yet evident in the Highlands. Despite this lack of organisation, Angus Sutherland became one of the six crofter candidates that ran with the support of the Highland Land Law Reform Association. All six were single-issue candidates, whose campaigns focused upon land reform and a party that came under the umbrella of the Crofters Party emerged at this election. Sutherland was the most radical of these candidates and he was also a supporter of Irish Home Rule, believing that land nationalisation was the panacea to the woes caused by an unsatisfactory resolution of the land question.[62]

Even though Irish Home Rule was the issue at play in Westminster, land still excited the Irish countryside. The return of economic distress in Ireland during 1885 eventually saw the emergence of the Plan of Campaign in October 1886 which was a form of collective bargaining on estates. The intensity of this economic depression meant that smallholders in the west of Ireland would struggle to find work locally and coupled with a decreased demand for seasonal migration in Britain, this exacerbated their problems. Parnell distanced himself from the Plan with its energy drawn from the explicit support of the agrarian wing of the Irish National League. Irish nationalist MPs were also strongly in

[60] Andrew Gailey, *Ireland and the Death of Kindness: The Experience of Constructive Unionism, 1890–1905* (Cork University Press, 1987), pp. 2–3.

[61] Mulvagh, *The Irish Parliamentary Party*, p. 2.

[62] Tindley, *The Sutherland Estate*, pp. 80–1.

favour of it, which shows how the agrarian wing still had great influence in the nationalist movement. Its promulgators maintained that it would only work effectively if every tenant on an estate signed up to it, which would then give tenants a strong negotiating hand, therefore it also pressured grudging support from reticent tenants.[63]

The Plan became part of a wider struggle for survival for both land-lords and tenants and by January 1888, the police estimated that it was operating on thirty-eight estates. Laurence Geary stated that it took place on at least 203 properties with more than 70 per cent of them being in Munster and Connaught, magnifying the extent of the problem in the west of Ireland. There was a spike in the number of evictions taking place because of the Plan, although evicted tenants received financial assistance and were assured that their evictions would only be temporary. These promises proved to be hollow as the Plan's funds ran low and Parnell's lack of support limited their ability to effectively fundraise.

Nationalist MPs stumped for the Plan of Campaign on successive Sundays during the winter of 1886–7; the spectacle of processions, parades, speeches and banners all added to a sense of rural solidar-ity amongst tenant farmers in the face of landlord oppressors.[64] These meetings succeeded in hiding the inherent class divisions amongst the non-gentry classes in the countryside as nationalists sought to present a veneer of unity. Again, they were popular manifestations of nationalist fervour and spurred the agitation on as farmers were promised a brilliant future. Tenants were further told that not only were they fighting for their survival, they were also fighting for the nationhood of Ireland and many were ruthlessly exploited by nationalists in this as they were told that they should be prepared for imprisonment to further the agitation.

The Parnellite split of 1891 bitterly divided Irish nationalism and killed off any momentum that the agrarian movement may have had. William O'Brien attempted to revive it through the United Irish League (UIL) which held its first meeting in Westport on 23 January 1898.[65] It had clearly articulated political and agrarian purposes and had three overt objectives: to revive a popular grass roots, extra-parliamentary movement in the hope of reinvigorating a decaying parliamentary nation-alism; to make the Parnellite and anti-Parnellite divisions irrelevant

---

[63] See Laurence Geary, *The Plan of Campaign, 1886–1891* (Cork University Press, 1987), pp. 1–3.

[64] Ibid., p. 34.

[65] Fergus Campbell, *Land and Revolution: Nationalist Politics in the West of Ireland, 1891–1921* (Oxford: Oxford University Press, 2005), p. 28.

through local unity; and to mount pressure to transfer ownership of land from landlords to tenant farmers through the redistribution of grazing to tillage in order to meet the needs of impoverished smallholders. Like the earlier Land League meetings, there was a strong anti-land grabbing element within the UIL. Land grabbing was the taking of the farm of an evicted neighbour. It was particularly egregious because it evoked memories of Famine clearances and was deeply frowned upon. Meetings generally took place after Mass on Sundays or on fair days as parades, bands and banners all added to the spectacle and brought their efforts to the attention of a wider audience. Police hubris returned once again as they doubted the vitality of the movement even as graziers expressed fear about potential outrages against them.[66]

The Parnellite split was a fissure through Irish nationalism. It split the movement and it struggled to recover, though the success of the United Irish League saw O'Brien organise a land conference with Captain John Shawe-Taylor, a little-known Galway landlord that culminated in the Wyndham Land Act 1903.[67] This Act offered landlords exceedingly generous terms to sell their estates, free themselves from heavy encumbrances and spelled the terminal decline of landlord presence in Ireland. Rural social relationships had been changing prior to the 1903 Act. This was particularly obvious in towns and the Act intensified such change, 'thus changing the basis for agrarian collection action in Ireland. Rather than agitating against the landlords (for land purchase), farmers began to agitate against each other (for land redistribution)'.[68] In an effort to incentivise landlords to sell, the terms of the Act were quite generous. The 12 per cent cash bonus on the final purchase price encouraged many landlords to avail of it, though it soon became obvious that it was going to be inadequate. There was also a question as to whether the land conference proposals would result in too high a price being paid to landlords.[69] Patrick Cosgrove and Terence Dooley have illustrated that the Wyndham Land Act was not the final solution to the land question and an attempt to find a solution to it was something that frustrated and stymied successive Free State governments.[70] Many smaller farmers

[66] See Paul Bew, *Conflict and Conciliation in Ireland, 1890–1910: Parnellites and the Radical Agrarians* (Oxford: Oxford University Press, 1987).

[67] Land Purchase (Ireland) Act 1903.

[68] Campbell, *Land and Revolution*, p. 289.

[69] Philip Bull, 'The significance of the nationalist response to the Irish land act of 1903' in *Irish Historical Studies*, 28:111 (May 1993), pp. 283–98.

[70] For more, see Patrick John Cosgrove, 'The Wyndham Land Act, 1903: The final solution to the Irish Land Question?', PhD thesis (Maynooth University, 2009);

realised that even after purchasing their farms, more land was needed to make them remotely viable. Therefore, the large stock-rearing ranches of many estates became the most obvious source for additional land.[71]

CONCLUSIONS

What was the impact of agrarian radicalism and resistance on late nineteenth century land reforms being demanded in the west of Ireland and the Highlands? The Land League broke down the parochialism of the previous political system as in the countryside thought they were part of a national movement that was moving towards a definitive goal: peasant proprietorship and Home Rule. For this to have happened, the people needed to be convinced that what was happening in the wider entity was of importance to them. The success of the Land League came down to its ability to identify landlords as the cause of farmer woes. National issues like Home Rule could be used to fuel agrarian discontent into something more overtly political as its leaders succeeded in using poverty to unite the lower classes into collective action. Despite the later rhetoric of the Land League, it was the farmer and not the landlord that drove his children off the land.[72]

The Irish Parliamentary Party was comprehensively successful at the 1885 election which boded well for the crofter cause as Irish MPs ensured that the Highland question was on the agenda in Westminster by 1886. Gladstone now became a firm believer in trying to bring about some reforms for the Highlands, even after the disappointing conclusions of the Napier Commission. He introduced the Crofters Bill that eventually became the Crofters Act in 1886, hoping that it would have a calming effect in the Highlands despite a belief that it was a reward for lawlessness.[73]

Animosity towards landlords became more noticeable during the late 1880s as the impact of Napier Commission became more evident and coercion was introduced. Landlords expressed surprise at the end of their passivity as they feared that there would be serious damage done to their precarious finances if the army was not brought in to assert

---

Terence Dooley, *'The Land for the People': The Land Question in Independent Ireland* (Dublin: University College Dublin Press, 2004).

[71] Patrick Cosgrove, *The Ranch War in Riverstown, Co. Sligo, 1908* (Dublin: Four Courts Press, 2012), p. 7.

[72] Lee, *The Modernisation of Irish Society*, pp. 9–11.

[73] See J. P. D. Dunbabin, *Rural Discontent in Nineteenth-Century Britain* (London: Faber and Faber, 1974), pp. 196–206; Marley, *Michael Davitt*, pp. 175–6.

control.[74] The Crofters Commission initially failed to find a middle ground as one side always felt aggrieved and this limited its effectiveness. It did learn from its mistakes as it became more technical and constructive, though its independence waned between 1895 and 1906. Nevertheless, its key initial success was achieving the trust of crofters, normally suspicious of government, doing much to quell agitation in the Highlands.[75] Highland landowners ruled with feudal might and were assisted by obsequious factors and staff in the management of their sometimes vast estates. While tenants achieved some legal rights following the assent of the Crofters Act in 1886 thanks to the efforts of Highland radicals, the increasingly centralised nature of land ownership remained unchallenged.[76]

[74] James Hunter, *The Making of the Crofting Community* (Edinburgh: Birlinn, 2015), pp. 211–13.

[75] Cameron, *Land for the People?*, pp. 58–60.

[76] Wightman, *The Poor Had No Lawyers*, pp. 43–7.

4

'The usual agencies of civilisation':[1] Conceptions of Land Ownership and Reform in the Comparative Context in the Long Nineteenth Century

Annie Tindley

INTRODUCTION

> The politics of this country will probably, for the next few years, mainly consist in an assault upon the constitutional position of the landed interest.[2]

IN 1886, THE CROFTERS HOLDINGS (Scotland) Act passed into law, granting small tenants in the crofting counties limited tenurial protections, including compensation for improvements made, freedom from eviction as long as certain conditions were met, and fair rents, set by a government agency, the Crofters Commission.[3] It was a landmark piece of legislation and has retained a powerful legal, economic and cultural hold not just in the geographies it was first applied to, but on later and continuing land reform debates in Scotland.[4] It is illustrative to consider this legislation in a wider context, however. Its closest models were the Irish Land Act 1870 and the Land Law (Ireland) Act 1881, also passed by Gladstone's Liberal government, which heralded government intervention into land and tenure management. Both of these Acts were structured in contrast to the recommendations of the Royal Commission, chaired by Lord Napier, to investigate the causes of tenant dissatisfaction in the Highlands and which had recommended very different solutions, anchored in lessons from other parts of Europe, including Russia.[5] Equally though, they took inspiration from the Bengal Tenancy Act

[1] British Library, India Office Select Papers, F130/5, fo. 85, Lord Dufferin, viceroy of India to Lord Cross, Secretary of State for India, 6 August 1886.

[2] Benjamin Disraeli, cited in J. W. Mason, 'The Duke of Argyll and the land question in nineteenth-century Britain', *Victorian Studies*, 21:2 (1978), p. 149.

[3] E. A. Cameron, *Land for the People? The British Government and the Scottish Highlands, c.1880–1925* (East Linton: Tuckwell Press, 1996), pp. 37–9.

[4] J. Hunter, *The Making of the Crofting Community* (Edinburgh: John Donald, 1976), pp. 161–4.

[5] Cameron, *Land for the People*, p. 19–39.

1885, passed by the government of India after a long and acrimonious political struggle by a viceroy who was an Ulster landowner and influential contributor to the land reform debate in Ireland, Frederick Hamilton Temple Blackwood, first marquess of Dufferin.[6] The legislative programme advanced by these Acts was in contrast to that already in place by 1874 in Prince Edward Island, which promoted government-funded and compulsory land purchase as the response to a robust tenant agitation on that island.[7] All four pieces of legislation were influenced and informed by the other, despite the striking geographical and governance disparities. Two key themes were shared: first, they were part of a wider historicist turn in thinking about land in Britain and Ireland, with a particular focus on the 'village community' among liberal thinkers; second, they were about evidencing the good governance that Britain claimed to offer its domestic population, but in particular those colonised peoples and territories over which it had imposed autocratic rule.[8] This chapter poses one central question, therefore: what was Scotland's place in the global land reform question? Further, how did it influence and how was it influenced by intellectual debate and legislative currents elsewhere; was there anything distinctive about the Scottish experience?[9]

This chapter will put Scotland's historical engagement with land

[6] Richard Davenport-Hines, 'Blackwood, Frederick Temple Hamilton-Temple-, first marquess of Dufferin and Ava (1826–1902)', *Oxford Dictionary of National Biography*, Oxford University Press, 2004, online edn, January 2008, <http://www.oxforddnb.com/view/article/31914> (accessed 26 March 2018); B. Martin, *New India, 1885* (Berkeley: University of California Press, 1969), pp. 31–4, 36; A. Gailey, *The Lost Imperialist: Lord Dufferin, Memory and Myth-making in an Age of Celebrity* (London: John Murray, 2015), pp. 212–13.

[7] This legislation was passed during Lord Dufferin's tenure as Canada's governor-general; R. Bitterman, *Rural Protest on Prince Edward Island: From British Colonisation to the Escheat Movement* (Toronto: University of Toronto Press, 2006), pp. 3–7, 272–6; J. M. Bumsted, *Land, Settlement and Politics on Eighteenth-Century Prince Edward Island* (Montreal: McGill-Queen's University Press, 1987), pp. ix–xi; I. R. Robertson (ed.), *The Prince Edward Island Land Commission of 1860* (Fredericton: Acadiensis, 1988), pp. ix–xxx.

[8] C. Dewey, 'The rehabilitation of the peasant proprietor in nineteenth century economic thought', *History of Political Economy*, 6:1 (1974); C. C. Eldridge, *England's Mission: The Imperial Idea in the Age of Gladstone and Disraeli 1868–1880* (London: Palgrave Macmillan, 1973), pp. 53–91; E. D. Steele, 'Ireland and the Empire in the 1860s. Imperial Precedents for Gladstone's First Irish Land Act', *Historical Journal*, 11:1 (1968), pp. 64–83.

[9] Questions posed by contemporaries too, e.g. J. W. Probyn (ed.), *Systems of Land Tenure in Various Countries* (London: Cobden Club, 1876 edn). An interesting comparative example in this regard is the work of C. Smith, 'Second Slavery,

issues into the comparative context, exploring contemporary debates in
the British imperial territories across the long nineteenth century. That
period is defined here as 1789 to 1918, allowing this global consideration of land reform to be grounded in the European context as well.
By beginning with the French Revolutionary period, the landed aspects
of that revolution frame at one end the radically shifting fortunes of
the landed and aristocratic classes, and by ending with the First World
War and the collapse of the Russian, Ottoman, German and Habsburg
empires, this chapter highlights the somewhat unusual survival of that
class (and the monarchy) in Britain and the British empire itself.[10] In
one sense, these macro European events demonstrate that the principles
of land reform and class decline were not unusual in a Scottish context
except in terms of scale.[11] The one exception, noted throughout, is
of course Ireland, which perhaps had more in common with eastern
Europe than Britain by 1923, due to the Anglo-Irish and Civil wars.[12]
Taking a macro perspective of the land question and Scotland's place in
it, this chapter examines the debates over land during this period, which
saw both the consolidation of industrialisation and massive European
imperial expansion.[13] The global land question in the nineteenth century
needs to be contextualised within these wider forces, and by tracking
different reactions and responses to them, we can better judge Scotland's
place in the debate and complicate the view that it has been exceptional
in its engagement. Some comparative studies have already been undertaken, particularly between Ireland and India, and between Scotland,
England and Ireland.[14] These studies highlight shared and conflicting

Second Landlordism and Modernity: A Comparison of Antebellum Mississippi and
Nineteenth-Century Ireland', *Journal of the Civil War Era*, 5:2 (2015), pp. 204, 206.

[10] See for instance, R. Gerwarth, *The Vanquished: Why the First World War
Failed to End* (London: Allen Lane, 2016); P. M. Jones, '"The Agrarian Law":
schemes for land redistribution during the French Revolution', *Past and Present*,
133 (1991), pp. 96–133.

[11] R. Gerwarth and J. Kitchen, 'Transnational approaches to the "crisis of
empires" after 1918', *Journal of Modern European History*, 13:2 (2015).

[12] T. A. Dooley, *The Decline of the Big House in Ireland: A Study of Irish Landed
Families, 1860–1960* (Dublin: Wolfhound Press, 2001).

[13] See the European comparative analysis that demonstrates this approach: E. Frie
and J. Neuheiser, 'Introduction: noble ways and democratic means', *Journal of
Modern European History*, 11:4 (2013), pp. 433–48; M. Cragoe and P. Readman,
'Introduction', in M. Cragoe and P. Readman (eds), *The Land Question in Britain,
1750–1950* (Basingstoke: Palgrave Macmillan, 2010), pp. 1–19.

[14] C. Dewey, 'Images of the village community: a study of Anglo-Indian ideology',
Modern Asian Studies, 6:3 (1972), pp. 291–9; C. Dewey, *Anglo-Indian Attitudes: the*

ideas about the nature, duties and purpose of landowning, and attacks on the principles on which it was based by campaigners such as Henry George.[15] Land issues were of the first political and social importance across a wide range of geographies because they were intimately linked with questions of governance, and the legitimacy of power more broadly defined.[16] For imperial powers, settlements around land were part of the package of 'benefits' that imperial rule was perceived to bring subject peoples, and legislation, often radically in advance of what was politically possible in Britain, was introduced in colonial territories.[17]

This chapter will examine the forces that shaped the intellectual and legislative responses to land issues in a comparative context, a context with three shared themes. First, the processes and consequences of industrialisation and urbanisation, the scale and speed of which was unusually fast in the British, and more specifically, Scottish context. Second, the impact of significant European imperial expansion across the late eighteenth and nineteenth centuries. Third, the changing nature of governance and the attempted legitimisation of power in the British, Irish and imperial contexts. These three themes underpin any comparative examination of Scottish land reform in the historical context and can best be understood as complex transnational flows, rather than binary exchanges.

The processes of industrialisation and urbanisation in Britain had significant consequences for land reform debates in Scotland and the empire. These were macro-level, complex and long-drawn-out processes

Mind of the Indian Civil Service (London: A. & C. Black, 1993); Steele, 'Ireland and the Empire', pp. 64–83; E. A. Cameron, 'Communication or Separation? Reactions to Irish land agitation and legislation in the Highlands of Scotland, c.1870–1910', *English Historical Review*, 120:487 (2005), pp. 633–66.

[15] H. George, *Progress and Poverty: An Inquiry into the Cause of Industrial Depressions and of Increase of Want with Increase of Wealth* (New York: Appleton, 1882); Steele, 'J. S. Mill and the Irish Question', pp. 419–25; E. Stokes, *The English Utilitarians and India* (Oxford: Oxford University Press, 1959); E. Sullivan, 'Liberalism and Imperialism: John Stuart Mill's defence of the British Empire', *Journal of the History of Ideas*, 44 (1983).

[16] As understood by contemporaries, see just one example on these themes and how they were related in the mid-Victorian consciousness: J. S. Mill, *England and Ireland* (London: Longmans, Green, Reader and Dyer, 1868), pp. 8–9, 11, 22–4.

[17] See, for example, the long history of land and revenues reform in British India: J. Wilson, *India Conquered: Britain's Raj and the Chaos of Empire* (London: Simon & Schuster, 2016), pp. 169, 499, 501; and for British Columbia, A. Perry, *On the Edge of Empire: Gender, Race and the Making of British Columbia, 1849–1871* (Toronto: University of Toronto Press, 2001), pp. 126–7.

whereby over the nineteenth century much of the British economy shifted from a primarily agrarian focus to a fully globalised industrial and financial system.[18] Lowland and central Scotland was in the vanguard of this process, but much of rural Scotland – aside from the mass movement of its population south and overseas – was not, and the economy there remained primarily agrarian.[19] Building on long-standing assumptions of the primitive and backward nature of the people of the Highlands and Islands in particular, the region came to be seen as falling behind the march of progress seen elsewhere in the British Isles.[20] It shared this position of ignominy with Ireland, another economy which 'failed' to industrialise (with the exception of east Ulster), and which was struck by utmost disaster in the Great Irish Famine, an agrarian catastrophe within the same polity of the world's first industrial nation.[21] Tensions around perceptions of agricultural economies as 'backward' were replicated not just in rural Scotland and Ireland, but in the empire also. Predominantly agrarian (and extractive) economies such as that of India were also placed into this category and as a consequence regarded as a necessary recipient of the benevolent application of land reform by the imperial state. This was especially the case when private landlordism was deemed to have failed to undertake this duty.[22] Increasingly, landowners were presented as rotten apples in the social cart, and as unworthy of saving from their own financial and political incompetence.[23] 'In any event it seems to me,' wrote Lord Dufferin, while viceroy of India, 'that the ruin

[18] P. J. Cain and A. G. Hopkins, *British Imperialism: Innovation and Expansion* (New York, Longman, 1993), pp. 3–52.

[19] E. Richards, *The Highland Clearances* (Edinburgh: Birlinn, 2008), pp. 415–23.

[20] See J. Loch, *An Account of the Improvements of the Marquess of Stafford* (London: Waterlow & Sons Ltd, 1820) as a key exemplar of this view; A. Mackillop, *More Fruitful than the Soil: Army, Empire and the Scottish Highlands, 1715–1815* (East Linton: Tuckwell Press, 2000); Ewen Cameron, 'Poverty, Protest and Politics: Perceptions of the Scottish Highlands in the 1880s', in D. Broun and M. Macgregor (eds), *Mìorun Mòr nan Gall, 'The Great Ill-Will of the Lowlander'? Lowland Perceptions of the Highlands* (Glasgow: Centre for Scottish and Celtic Studies, University of Glasgow, 2007).

[21] C. O'Grada, *The Great Irish Famine* (Cambridge: Cambridge University Press, 1989).

[22] For a Canadian case study see Perry, *On the Edge of Empire*, pp. 124–38; and, a comparative Irish and Indian one, see C. Boylan, 'Victorian ideologies of improvement: Sir Charles Trevelyan in India and Ireland', in T. Foley and M. O'Connor (eds), *Ireland and India: Colonies, Culture and Empire* (Dublin: Irish Academic Press, 2006), chapter 14.

[23] Although see Smith, 'Second Slavery, Second Landlordism', pp. 205, 208, 210.

of us Irish landlords is sure. I do not think the English people care a button for our interests, nor do I see . . . how they can be protected.'[24] Landowners were becoming starkly aware of their own declining power in this period, much of which was being overtaken by the state.

Fast-paced imperial expansion and consequent emigration of millions of people to 'new' worlds from European nations is the second underpinning theme.[25] As well as providing a broad geographical platform to demonstrate 'good' governance, it brought the British – and disproportionately the Scottish – into contact with indigenous landholding systems and understandings about property ownership and management.[26] As the *British Columbian* baldly stated in 1865, 'Colonisation necessarily involves the contact, and practically the collision of two races of men – one superior and one inferior, the latter being in possession of the soil, the former gradually supplanting it.'[27] Imperial expansion was crucial for thinking about land reform and a central part of what empire was thought of as being *for*, but, as the examples in the opening paragraph illustrate, would also have significant consequences for land reform in Scotland, Ireland, England and Wales.[28] The legislative and intellectual debates around Scottish land reform in the nineteenth century were

[24] British Library, F130/20, fo. 45, Dufferin to Lord Lansdowne, 17 December 1885; Gailey, *The Lost Imperialist*, pp. 279, 312, 332.

[25] Perry, *On the Edge of Empire*, pp. 133–5; C. A. Wilson, *A New Lease on Life: Landlords, Tenants and Immigrants in Ireland and Canada* (Toronto: McGill-Queen's University Press, 1994), pp. 3–4, 163.

[26] Perry, *On the Edge of Empire*, p. 132; C. Dewey, 'Celtic agrarian legislation and the Celtic revival: historicist implications of Gladstone's Irish and Scottish Land Acts', *Past and Present*, 64 (1974), pp. 30–70; S. B. Cook, *Imperial Affinities: Nineteenth-Century Analogies and Exchanges Between India and Ireland* (London and New Dehli: Sage Publications, 1992), pp. 9–37; A. G. Newby, *Ireland, Radicalism and the Scottish Highlands, c.1870–1912* (Edinburgh: Edinburgh University Press, 2007), pp. 1–8; A. Behm, 'Settler colonialism and anticolonial rebuttal in the British world, 1880–1920', *Journal of World History*, 26:4 (2015), pp. 803–4, 806; A. Nettelbeck, 'Colonial protection and the intimacies of indigenous governance', *History Australia*, 14:1 (2017), pp. 35–7, 46.

[27] Cited in Perry, *On the Edge of Empire*, p. 125; see also pp. 126–8 and C. G. Calloway, *White People, Indians and Highlanders: Tribal Peoples and Colonial Encounters on Scotland and America* (Oxford: Oxford University Press, 2010).

[28] See for example, M. Cragoe, 'A Contemptible Mimic of the Irish:' the Land Question in Victorian Wales' in M. Cragoe, and P. Readman (eds), *The Land Question in Britain, 1750–1950* (Basingstoke: Palgrave Macmillan, 2010), pp. 1–19, 97–102; P. Readman, *Land and Nation in England: Patriotism, National Identity and the Politics of Land, 1880–1914* (Woodbridge: Boydell and Brewer, 2008), pp. 110–36.

heavily influenced by empire, but also by the European context. Russia, Prussia, Belgium and France were key contexts of the Scottish debate, as writers and legislators all over Europe wrangled with the issue of small landholdings in an age of consolidated, mechanised agriculture.[29]

The third underpinning theme is around governance and the legitimisation of domestic and imperial power in a period where this was under pressure and subject to significant change. Much of the Scottish (and Irish) land reform debate in the later nineteenth century focused on the crimes and abuses of the aristocratic and landed classes and sought to redress the balance of power between that elite class, which made up a disproportionate element of the governing establishment, and the small tenant, rural and labouring people. As such, land reform was part of a broader overturning of aristocratic power, the tale of 'decline and fall' of the British and Irish aristocracy, explored by David Cannadine and F. M. L. Thompson, among others.[30] A key aspect to this was their removal from their long-standing role as a service aristocracy. Cannadine has argued that this traditional role was more durable in the imperial context, although that too faded into 'ornamentalism'.[31]

---

[29] See for instance, PP1872, C. 572, Reports from H.M. representatives respecting tenure of land in countries of Europe (parts I–V); D. Smith, *Former People: The Last Days of the Russian Aristocracy* (London: Picador, 2012), pp. 3–20; Frie and Neuheiser, 'Introduction', pp. 443–8; M. Rendle, 'Conservatism and Revolution: the All-Russian Union of Landowners, 1916–18', *Slavonic and East European Review*, 84:3 (2006), pp. 481–4; A. J. Mayer, *The Persistence of the Old Regime: Europe to the Great War* (New York: Pantheon Books, 1981); see also essays on Russian (pp. 309–46), French (pp. 287–308), Belgian (pp. 197–242), Prussian (pp. 243–86) and Indian (pp. 125–96) land systems in Probyn (ed.), *Systems of Land Tenure*.

[30] D. Cannadine, *The Decline and Fall of the British Aristocracy* (New Haven, Yale University Press, 1990), pp. 25–31 for an overview of this interpretation and F. M. L. Thompson's seminal articles, 'English Landed Society in the Twentieth Century': 'I: Property: collapse and survival', *Transactions of the Royal Historical Society (TRHS)*, 5th ser., 40 (1990); 'II: New Poor and New Rich', *TRHS*, 6th ser., 1 (1991); 'III: Self-Help and Outdoor Relief', *TRHS*, 6th ser., 2 (1992); 'IV: Prestige Without Power', *TRHS*, 6th ser., 3 (1993); D. Spring, 'The role of the aristocracy in the nineteenth century', *Victorian Studies* (1960), pp. 57–63; I. G. C. Hutchison, 'The nobility and politics in Scotland, c.1880–1939', in T. M. Devine (ed.) *Scottish Elites* (Edinburgh: John Donald, 1994), pp. 131–48; D. Cannadine, *Aspects of Aristocracy: Grandeur and Decline in Modern Britain* (New Haven: Yale University Press, 1994), pp. 165–83.

[31] D. Cannadine, *Ornamentalism: How the British Saw Their Empire* (London: Allen Lane, 2001); Z. Laidlaw, *Colonial Connections, 1815–45: Patronage, the Information Revolution and Colonial Government* (Manchester: Manchester University Press, 2005), pp. 17–21.

Nonetheless, landed power had a significant influence on imperial governance, not least the construction of the 'benefits' of empire. Across the spectrum of political beliefs, there was an underpinning agreement that land – its ownership, tenurial and legal structures – was crucial to this. There are three further aspects to be considered. First was the impact of the historicist turn from the 1870s, particularly among liberal thinkers, whose influence was felt directly via land legislation in Scotland, Ireland and India. Historicist thinking looked back and sought to 'restore' landholding systems and traditions, to right the perceived wrongs of the past.[32] In other words, historicism could be tolerated in places that were perceived as being immune to progress, such as the Scottish Highlands, India and Ireland. Second, the destruction of indigenous land rights has been highlighted by imperial historians, and increasingly in the Scottish and Irish contexts also.[33] Victorian intellectuals at once harked back to a past they wished to see restored, and at the same time were able to justify the crushing of indigenous land rights in the American colonies, Canada, Australia and New Zealand by settlers and their governments.[34] Third, we must consider the impact of agrarian radicalism and the decline of deference in rural society and how ideas about land reform were actually communicated and understood differently in different geographical contexts.[35]

Scottish land reform is not unique historically, and shared many

[32] E. D. Steele, 'J. S. Mill and the Irish Question: the principles of political economy, 1848–1865', *Historical Journal*, 13:3 (1970), pp. 419–50; G. Peatling, 'Race and Empire in nineteenth-century British intellectual life: James Fitzjames Stephen, James Anthony Froude, Ireland, and India', *Eire-Ireland*, 42 (2007); C. Dewey, 'The influence of Sir Henry Maine on agrarian policy in India', in A. Diamond (ed.), *The Victorian Achievement of Sir Henry Maine* (Cambridge: Cambridge University Press, 1991), pp. 353–74.

[33] See for instance, I. Mackinnon, 'Decommonising the Mind': historical impacts of British imperialism on indigenous tenure systems and self-understanding in the Highlands and Islands of Scotland', *International Journal of the Commons*, 12:1 (2018), and 'Colonialism and the Highlands', *Northern Scotland*, 8:1 (2017), pp. 22–48.

[34] P. Dwyer and L. Ryan, 'Reflections on genocide and settler-colonial violence', *History Australia*, 13:3 (2016), pp. 339–42, 350, in which analysis Ireland is included; Nettelbeck, 'Colonial protection', pp. 32, 34–7, 46. See also T. Summerhill, *Harvest of Dissent: Agrarianism in Nineteenth-Century New York* (Chicago: University of Illinois Press, 2005), p. 173.

[35] See for instance, Hunter, *Crofting Community*, pp. 205–10; Cameron, *Land for the People*, pp. 16–71; Cragoe and Readman, *The Land Question*, pp. 1–19. The 8th duke of Argyll was one of the most outspoken opponents in the 1880s: Argyll, 'Land Reformers', *Contemporary Review*, 48 (1885); Argyll, 'A Model Land Law:

elements with other places: ownership versus tenancy, the individual versus the communal, the state versus the landowner, understandings of historical tenure and ownership and their applications in legislation, and both opposition to and agitation for land reform.[36] Scottish land reform influenced legislative programmes and intellectual debates elsewhere and was in turn influenced by them.[37] This chapter tackles the shared and comparative aspects of Scottish land reform, underpinned by the themes explored in this introduction. So much is shared and so little exceptional: the impact of historicist thinking, the increasing tensions everywhere between private landowners and states, little-understood cultural changes such as the decline of deference, and the better-mapped economic change from agrarian to industrial economies and imperial expansion: Scotland was part of, influenced, and influenced by these global trends.[38]

THE ISSUES AT STAKE – SHARED CONTEXTS OF LAND REFORM

Some of the shared contexts of land reform stem directly from the ownership and management of land (that is, issues of property and contract), and some to understandings of historical memory and cultures of land.[39] This section will discuss three of these: first, universal complaints of land hunger and concentration of land ownership; second, the rights and responsibilities of property and how these were redefined in an increasingly democratic, industrial and globally connected age, underpinned by the drivers of economic development, progress and prosperity; third, the importance of memory and culture on understandings of the issues at

a reply to Arthur Williams MP', *Fortnightly Review*, 41 (1887); Argyll, 'New Irish Land Bill', *Nineteenth Century*, 9 (1881).

[36] See R. Bitterman and M. McCallum, 'When private rights become public wrongs: property and the state in Prince Edward Island in the 1830s', in J. McLaren, A. R. Buck and N. E. Wright (eds), *Despotic Dominion: Property Rights in British Settler Societies* (Vancouver: University of British Columbia Press, 2004), pp. 1–22; A. Ali, *The Punjab Under Imperialism, 1885–1947* (Princeton: Princeton University Press, 1988); L. P. Curtis, 'Landlord responses to the Irish Land War, 1879–1987', *Éire-Ireland*, Fall–Winter (2003), pp. 137–46; S. Gopal, *British Policy in India 1858–1905* (Cambridge: Cambridge University Press, 1965); Vaughan, *Landlords and Tenants*, pp. 9–10.

[37] M. Harper and S. Constantine (eds), *Migration and Empire* (Oxford: Oxford University Press, 2010), pp. 12–16.

[38] For the classic account see H. Newby, *The Deferential Worker: A Study of Farm Workers in East Anglia* (London: Allen Lane, 1977), pp. 414–35.

[39] See for instance, C. King (ed.), *Famine, Land and Culture in Ireland* (Dublin: University College Dublin Press, 2000).

stake over land, which had a huge impact on the construction of land reform globally.[40]

One of the aspects of Scottish land that nineteenth-century campaigners often stressed was the unusual level of concentration of ownership, and – related in their view – the consequent land hunger experienced by the small labouring tenantry.[41] As one witness said in evidence to the Royal Commission sent by Gladstone's Liberal government to investigate the agrarian agitation of the Scottish Highlands in the early 1880s: 'there are forty-two crofters in this township [Strathy]. Previous to the Sutherland Clearances there were only four . . . the immediate result of these Clearances was over crowding'. One witness described life in the congested rural areas as, 'just crowded like my fingers'.[42] This concentration of private land ownership into a small number of hands was always explained historically and in relation to the relatively poor agricultural quality of the land in Scotland, as well as the nature of specific social organisation such as clanship in the *Gàidhealtachd*.[43] By the early nineteenth century, a new class of landowner was emerging onto the scene: wealthy industrialists and financiers who purchased large estates. Putting these claims into the comparative context is illustrative, however; land hunger as a result of the concentration of landholding and certain patterns of land use, such as ranching or commercial sport was as endemic in parts of Ireland, England and Wales as in Scotland.[44] In Canada, the land of opportunity for European settlers,

[40] See for instance E. Richards, *Debating the Highland Clearances* (Edinburgh: Edinburgh University Press, 2007), pp. 3–25; Hunter, *Crofting Community*; R. E. Jones, *Petticoat Heroes: Gender, Culture and Popular Protest in the Rebecca Riots* (Cardiff: University of Wales Press, 2015).

[41] An issue which still exercises contemporaries: Hunter, *Crofting Community*, pp. 119–20; A. Tindley, *The Sutherland Estate 1850–1920: Aristocratic Decline, Estate Management and Land Reform* (Edinburgh: Edinburgh University Press, 2010), pp. 69–70.

[42] PP, XXXII–XXXVI, *Evidence given to the Commissioners of Inquiry into the Condition of the Crofters and Cottars in the Highlands and Islands*, 1884, pp. 1611, 1616.

[43] PP, XXXIII–XXXVI, *Report of the Commissioners of Inquiry into the Condition of the Crofters and Cottars in the Highlands and Islands of Scotland*, 1884; Tindley, *Sutherland Estate*, pp. 70–1; Cameron, *Land for the People*, pp. 18–23.

[44] M. Bentley, *Lord Salisbury's World. Conservative Environments in Late Victorian Britain* (Cambridge: Cambridge University Press, 2001), p. 109; J. S. Donnelly, *The Land and the People of Nineteenth-Century Cork* (London: Routledge and Kegan Paul, 1975), pp. 192–3; W. E. Vaughan, *Landlords and Tenants in Mid-Victorian Ireland* (Oxford: Oxford University Press, 1994), pp. 1–2, 4, 6, 10–11, 187–218.

land ownership was the defining model, with tenancies much more rare, and – due in part to the vast size of the dominion – where much larger landholdings were possible than in many parts of Europe.[45] The 4th duke of Sutherland, after disposing of a section of his northern estates to a Paisley dye manufacturer, went on to buy 100,000 acres of land in Alberta, translating the ownership patterns of Scotland to Canada.[46] Land hunger was of course less of an issue for settlers in the Canadian prairies, except for indigenous peoples being forced onto small reservations, constrained by violence, disease and treaty. The consequences of that land hunger are still to be worked through today.[47] Similar patterns can be seen in Australia, India and Russia, with many types of ownership underpinning it: settler, state or aristocratic. In terms of land hunger and concentration of land ownership, Scotland was not that unusual.

This was just one of the issues that made up an ecosystem of debate and disagreement over land. More broadly, conceptualisations of both the rights and the responsibilities of property were in flux across the nineteenth century.[48] Land reformers in Scotland argued that the traditional landed and aristocratic classes had been very clear as to the *rights* that ownership of property conferred, but due to a range of pressures including economic modernisation, they had abandoned their traditional *responsibilities*. So, the argument went, their rights should be curbed.[49] In Scotland, the argument that private land ownership or landowners per se should be abolished (as in France, for example), never took hold among the majority of campaigners, but rather that protections be introduced to ensure that the tenantry enjoyed a greater share of the benefits of property.[50] This approach was replicated across the world: the government of India passed a number of land reform acts which sought to curb the worst abuses of private property while avoiding an all-out

---

[45] Harper and Constantine (eds), *Migration and Empire*, pp. 11–40.

[46] Tindley, *Sutherland Estate*, pp. 131–5; Perry, *On the Edge of Empire*, p. 135.

[47] See for example the Land Rights Now UN Call for Action: <http://www.landrightsnow.org/en/home/> (last accessed 26 March 2018); A. Lester and Z. Laidlaw, 'Indigenous sites and mobilities: connected struggles in the long nineteenth century', in Z. Laidlaw and A. Lester (eds), *Indigenous Communities and Settler Colonialism: Landholding, Loss and Survival in an Interconnected World* (Basingstoke: Palgrave Macmillan, 2015), pp. 1–3, 6, 11–13, 15.

[48] Bentley, *Lord Salisbury's World*, pp. 94–124.

[49] See the classic attack in Tom Johnston, *Our Scots Noble Families* (Glasgow: Forward Publishing, 1909), especially pp. xxxi–xxxv.

[50] E. A. Cameron, 'Setting the heather on fire: the land question in Scotland', in Cragoe and Readman (eds), *The Land Question in Britain*, pp. 109–25; Tindley, *Sutherland Estate*, p. 68–75, 86.

assault on its essential principles and the traditional Indian landowning classes, which were seen as the bedrock of British and imperial society.[51] British legislators regarded their role as saving private landlordism from itself; by forcing some reforms, they were rescuing them from the very real possibility of violent and much more far-reaching reform, even revolution. What linked these processes intellectually was the belief that this insight was unique to the British perspective and their history of good governance. Victorian thinkers considered this temporally (back to Magna Carta) and geographically (the imperial world), pointing out that the only revolution Britain had undergone was a Glorious one, and that wise and moderate government, led still by the propertied classes, lay at the heart of this success.[52] Aside from the most radical of British and Irish land reformers, the view that property anchored polities was sacrosanct. What was required was a fairer distribution of the benefits of property to maintain the equilibrium.

Historical and cultural understandings and debates over their definitions and meaning played a significant role in thinking about land issues in Scotland, Britain, Ireland and the global empire.[53] Property and contract were not simply legal principles, but debatable starting points for cultural, historical, religious and social systems. In the mid to late nineteenth century, the previous romanticisation of these traditions, and the rural 'noble savage', was folded into a wider historicist turn, whereby social traditions were being reimagined, reinvented and restructured for the present, and the notion that historical wrongs had been committed and must be atoned for via reform in the present began to take hold among liberal thinkers.[54] Putting this into the global and imperial context, India stands out as the comparator most in alignment with this historicist thinking, although we see it also in parts of Canada.[55] The controversy is interesting on a number of different

[51] These abuses included rack-renting, refusal to offer tenurial security and absenteeism. See for instance C. A. Bayly, 'Ireland, India and the Empire, 1780–1914', *Transactions of the Royal Historical Society*, 6th ser., 10 (2000), pp. 378–80.

[52] Cannadine, *Decline and Fall*, pp. 13–15; Bentley, *Lord Salisbury's World*, pp. 65–92.

[53] Mackinnon, 'Colonialism and the Highlands', pp. 22–5.

[54] For instance, G. Campbell, 'The tenure of land in India', in Probyn (ed.), *Systems of Land Tenure in Various Countries*, pp. 125–196; Dewey, 'Celtic agrarian legislation', pp. 30–70; Vaughan, *Landlords and Tenants*, p. 5.

[55] Dewey, 'Images of the village community', pp. 291–328; J. McLaren, A. R. Buck and N. E. Wright, 'Property rights in the colonial imagination and experience', in J. McLaren, A. R. Buck and N. E. Wright (eds), *Despotic Dominion: Property Rights in British Settler Societies* (Vancouver: UBC Press, 2004), pp. 1–22.

levels. It reminds us that even in Canada, regarded by many prospective European emigrants as a land-rich utopia where the dead hand of landlordism could be escaped, land issues were not entirely clear-cut, with competing definitions of the rights and responsibilities of property.[56] Even Lord Dufferin, in his many speeches encouraging migrants to Canada, would often stress as one of its advantages that of 'the prospect of independence, of a roof over his head for which he shall pay no rent, and of ripening cornfields around his homestead which own no master but himself'.[57] He admitted privately that expectations of land rights were necessarily different in Canada to those in Britain, acknowledging: 'Proprietorial rights, in the sense in which they exist in England, are very unsuitable to the atmosphere of this country.'[58] In the settlement colonies, this narrative excluded indigenous peoples, whose rights, lives and societies were being broken apart by the actions of settlers, but ironically, the popular image encouraging European settlement made great play that these were lands that were empty, free from the landlordism of the *ancien régime*.[59] An opportunity to right a social and historical wrong was being given to settlers, facilitated by the crushing of indigenous rights.[60]

That land issues were translated across the world was due in no small part to the mobility and transnational movement of people and ideas.[61] Land was not just a historical, cultural or legal construct, it was an economic and social reality. It was framed in the nineteenth

---

[56] Bitterman, 'Upholding the land legislation', pp. 4–5.

[57] Public Record Office of Northern Ireland (PRONI), D1071, H/H/9/10, speech by Lord Dufferin to members of the Toronto Club, 2 September 1874.

[58] PRONI, D1071 H/H/6/2, fo. 51, Dufferin to Holland, C.O., 9 June 1874.

[59] J. Belich, *Replenishing the Earth: The Settler Revolution and the Rise of the Anglo-World* (Oxford: Oxford University Press, 2009); M. Harper, *Adventurers and Exiles: The Great Scottish Exodus* (London: Profile Books, 2004); J. C. Weaver, *The Great Land Rush and the Making of the Modern World, 1650–1900* (Montreal: McGill-Queen's University Press, 2003).

[60] E. Wolf, *Europe and the People without History* (Berkeley: University of California Press, 2010); J. Darwin, *Unfinished Empire: The Global Expansion of Britain* (London: Penguin, 2012); for a more specific case study see F. Vernal, 'Discourses of land use, land access and land rights at Farmerfield and Loeriesfontein in nineteenth century South Africa' in Laidlaw and Lester, *Indigenous Communities and Settler Colonialism*, pp. 102, 106–8, 132.

[61] Including via newspaper reporting in Britain, Ireland and the imperial territories. A. Tindley, 'All the arts of a Radical agitation': transnational perspectives on British and Irish landowners and estates, 1800–1921', *Historical Research*, 91 (2019), p. 254.

century as the bedrock of all economies, despite (indeed, because of), the rapid industrialisation underway in Europe, America and elsewhere. This created a situation where modernity seemed to be running in parallel with the past; industrial and imperial Britain represented the future, while rural and agricultural regions such as Highland Scotland, Ireland or India represented the primitive past. The early nineteenth century had been characterised by efforts to enforce or impose various forms of modernity on these 'backward' areas; by the 1870s a significant and influential section of legislators and thinkers argued that this was the wrong approach.[62] Instead, they suggested that historical traditions should be respected and reinstituted, as modernity was a jacket that simply did not fit.[63] The fluctuating importance of history versus progress, rights versus responsibilities, and the changing contexts of industrialisation, growing democracy and modernity were shared via a global feedback loop fuelled by the communications revolution and the increasing mobility of both people and ideas.[64]

ACTION ON LAND REFORM – LANDED AND STATE RESPONSES

The fact is, the first principles of Government have been shaken in every quarter, and new forces, new principles, new men, are governing the country.[65]

What was landlordism *for* in the nineteenth century? Old certainties were being challenged everywhere, and within this trend the periodic eruptions of rural agitation seen in Scotland were not unusual in the wider context.[66] This section will place the changing nature of landlord–tenant relations in Scotland in their wider context, to understand how these changes influenced landed and government responses. This is not

---

[62] See Richards, *Highland Clearances*, pp. 41–62; D. Lockhart (ed.), *Scottish Planned Villages* (Edinburgh: Constable, 2012).

[63] For example, Mill, *England and Ireland*, pp. 7–10.

[64] Frie and Neuheiser, 'Introduction', pp. 438–41; A. Mackillop, 'A Reticent People'? The Welsh in British Asia, 1700–1815', in H. V. Bowen (ed.), *Wales and the British Overseas Empire, 1680–1830* (Manchester: Manchester University Press, 2011) p. 145; A. Kirk-Greene, *Britain's Imperial Administrators, 1858–1966* (Basingstoke: Palgrave Macmillan, 2000), pp. 7–11, 202–9; Smith, 'Second Slavery, Second Landlordism', pp. 222–4.

[65] British Library, F130/24b, fo. 206, G. Goschen to Dufferin, 16 October 1886.

[66] Indeed, Scotland was often favourably compared to sites of more striking violence, principally Ireland: Cannadine, *Decline and Fall*, pp. 8–25; F. Campbell, *The Irish Establishment, 1879–1914* (Oxford: Oxford University Press, 2009), pp. 2, 19–20.

a new approach; there is a well-established historiography that compares the Scottish land question to that of its near neighbour, Ireland.[67] By looking specifically at the role of landowners in society and their relations with their tenantry, we can track how far Scotland's radical tradition on land issues was unusual or not in the global context.[68]

How landowners in Scotland understood their traditional social, political and economic functions was under pressure by the mid nineteenth century. Older understandings of leadership, paternalism and service were being undermined internally as well as challenged externally, as the political structures of British society shifted beneath the twin pressures of growing democracy and economic revolution. Rather than being a service aristocracy, providing rule by the best for the benefit of all, they were increasingly seen as parasitic, absentee blockages on political liberties, monopolisers of wealth and anachronistic, often immoral, dead wood.[69] 'No country, however rich, can permanently afford to have quartered upon the revenue a class which declines to do the duty which it was called upon to perform since the beginning,' as David Lloyd George argued in his famous Limehouse speech of July 1909.[70] They were under pressure to justify their inherited privileges in the face of a rising meritocracy, although different parts of Britain and Ireland saw these pressures grow at different rates.[71] In Scotland, criticism coalesced around two issues. First was the concentration of very large landed estates into a relatively small number of hands.[72] The figures became

[67] A. G. Newby, '"Scotia Major and Scotia Minor": Ireland and the birth of the Scottish land agitation, 1878–1882', *Irish Economic and Social History*, 31 (2004); J. Hunter, 'The Politics of Highland Land Reform, 1873–1895', *Scottish Historical Review*, 53 (1974).

[68] Cameron, 'Communication or separation?' pp. 633–66; Newby, *Ireland, Radicalism, and the Scottish Highlands*.

[69] I. Packer, *Lloyd George, Liberalism and the Land: The Land Issue and Party Politics in England, 1906–1914* (London: Boydell and Brewer, 2001); Vaughan, *Landlords and Tenants*, pp. 3–4.

[70] *The Budget and the people. A speech delivered for the Budget League at the Edinburgh Castle, Limehouse, London on July 30th 1909 [. . .] by the Rt. Hon. David Lloyd George, M.P.*, available at <https://www.parliament.uk/about/living-heritage/evolutionofparliament/houseoflords/house-of-lords-reform/from-the-collections/peoples-budget/limehouse/>.

[71] F. Byrne, 'Estate management practices on the Wentworth-Fitzwilliam core estates of Ireland and Yorkshire: a comparative study, 1815–65', unpublished PhD thesis (Maynooth University, 2017); Dooley, *The Decline of the Big House in Ireland*, pp. 3–10; O. Purdue, *The Big House in the North of Ireland: Land, Power and Social Elites, 1878–1960* (Dublin: University College Dublin Press, 2009), pp. 1–12.

[72] Exposed firstly by J. Bateman, *The Return of Owners of Land* (London, 1876)

oft-quoted: the dukes of Sutherland owned over one million acres in Scotland alone, and the dukes of Argyll, Atholl and Buccleuch each held estates of well over 100,000 acres each.[73] Second, and particularly from the 1870s, criticism built around the growing trend of turning much of this land over to the pursuit of commercial sport. Growing political and public anger developed around a narrative of the unproductive monopoly of huge swathes of land. In Tom Johnston's famous words: 'our Old Nobility is not noble, that its lands are stolen lands – stolen either by force or fraud: show people that the title-deeds are rapine, murder, massacre, cheating or Court harlotry.'[74] Of course, this shift in land use was productive for the landowners who raked in fat rents from keen sportsmen. The trend for sport saw no sign of slacking off well into the twentieth century, and land reform campaigners targeted it on both economic and moral grounds.

Scottish landowners were not alone in facing intensifying criticism; their Irish peers were under even greater pressure, their situation heightened by their 'Anglo' status, symbols of British power and the target of both nationalists and land reformers.[75] Landowners in the empire were not immune from these pressures either, although the autocratic nature of imperial power structures supported their privileges in many cases. Although in Britain and Ireland land reform was reluctantly granted to stave off further crisis, in the empire the British authorities sought social stability and cohesion and were unwilling to risk destabilising colonial structures by undermining traditional landed power.[76] This

and emphasised again by Bateman in his *The Great Landowners of Great Britain and Ireland* (London: Harrison, 1883); Cannadine, *Decline and Fall*, pp. 8–11, 710.

[73] Cannadine, *Decline and Fall*, pp. 3–25; Tindley, *The Sutherland Estate*, pp. 1–13. See E. Rothschild, *The Inner Life of Empires: An Eighteenth-Century History* (Princeton: Princeton University Press, 2011), pp. 1–11 for an example of the transnational activities of a minor Scottish gentry family.

[74] Johnston, *Our Scots Noble Families*, p. xxxv.

[75] R. C. D. Black, *Economic Thought and the Irish Question, 1817–1870* (Cambridge: Cambridge University Press, 1960), pp. 51–70; J. S. Donnelly, *The Land and the People of Nineteenth-Century Cork* (London: Routledge and Kegan Paul, 1975); A. Shanks, *Rural Aristocracy in Northern Ireland* (Aldershot: Gower Publishing Co., 1988), pp. 111–29; W. E. Vaughan, *A New History of Ireland, volume 5: Ireland under Union, 1801–1870* (Oxford: Oxford University Press, 1989); Vaughan, *Landlords and Tenants*, pp. 173–99; J. S. Donnelly, 'The Irish Agricultural Depression of 1859–64', *Irish Economic and Social History* (1976), pp. 33–54; H. Brasted, 'Indian nationalist development and the influence of Irish Home Rule', *Modern Asian Studies*, 14:1 (1980), pp. 37–63.

[76] C. Dewey, 'Cambridge Idealism': Utilitarian revisionists in late nineteenth

caveat aside, declining rural deference, and in some places outbreaks of violent agitation, were part of the imperial picture.[77] Those landed gentlemen who took a leading political or imperial role connected the hot spots of rural and land agitation to calls for self-government. Lord Dufferin labelled this the 'germ theory' – that agitation for land rights spread like a contagion across the world, and slippage in one place acted as the thin end of the wedge elsewhere.[78] Landed Scots had long played a role in empire, particularly India, and so were well positioned to take a comparative view of their situation and lobby government accordingly.

In this they were not always successful, as the relationship between the landed classes and the British government was changing. Whether in the Highlands of Scotland, the rural Punjab or the Canadian Maritimes, landowners could be less and less sure of governments supporting their interests over others.[79] The Third Reform Act 1884 was the moment of sea-change in Scottish rural society, when the majority of male rural labourers got the vote for the first time, and thanks to the Secret Ballot Act 1872, they were able to vote without fear of reprisal, which they did overwhelmingly at the 1885 election, putting in place radical Liberal MPs in five out of the six Highland counties, replacing the landowners and sons of landowners that had held those seats as almost a right.[80] Morally, politically and even economically, governments were beginning to abandon landed interests in favour of those of the majority. Witness Lord Dufferin's outrage when first made aware of a potential land act for Prince Edward Island: his language was certainly not that of compromise, and spoke of a growing paranoia about the international threat to landed power: 'There has also come up from the Local Legislature

century Cambridge', *Historical Journal*, 17 (1974), pp. 63–78; I. J. Catanach, 'Agrarian disturbances in nineteenth century India', in D. Hardiman (ed.), *Peasant Resistance in India, 1858–1914* (Oxford and New Dehli: Oxford University Press, 1993), pp. 184–6, 191–2.

[77] PRONI, D1071, H/H/1/2, Dufferin to Lord Carnarvon, 29 May 1874; see also a similar comparison made between civil order in Ireland and Canada, H/H/1/3, Dufferin to Carnarvon, 29 October 1875; Steele, 'Ireland and the Empire in the 1860s', pp. 64–5; Bitterman and McCallum, 'Upholding the land legislation', pp. 16–19.

[78] Although leading intellectuals disagreed: John Seeley, for instance, argued against 'germ theory'. See Behm, 'Settler colonialism', pp. 792–5.

[79] Bentley, *Lord Salisbury's World*, pp. 94–101; B. Knox, 'The Earl of Carnarvon, empire and imperialism, 1855–90', *Journal of Imperial and Commonwealth History*, 26:2 (1998), pp. 48–9.

[80] A. Tindley, 'The Sword of Avenging Justice: politics in Sutherland after the Third Reform Act', *Rural History*, 19:2 (2008), pp. 179–99.

of Prince Edward Island a Bill expropriating land owners in the Island under very unfair conditions. I have told my Government that I could not consent to it becoming law.'[81] This was not a revolutionary process, and well into the twentieth century the House of Commons, cabinets and even prime ministers remained strikingly landed in character.[82] However, government policies from taxation to town planning and land reform from the 1880s increasingly put pressure on landed, heritable interests. In this Scotland was not strikingly unusual; increasingly governments were curbing landed power as they themselves became less landed in complexion, and shifting the balance of that power away from landed to plutocratic and professional interests.[83]

This pattern replicated itself across the empire; indeed, was even more striking in imperial contexts, where the power of the British state was imposed autocratically to maintain imperial security.[84] This security was by some distance the most important imperial priority; the privileges and priorities of landed families and individuals in the colonial territories much less so, except where they were seen to contribute to that security. From the late 1860s, Gladstone had moved towards a historicist position as regards land ownership and tenancy, as first evidenced in the Irish Land Act 1870, and firmly established by the Land Law (Ireland) Act 1881 and the Crofters Holdings (Scotland) Act 1886.[85] This view was predicated on a belief in the superiority of ancient village communities, communal systems of land occupancy and moral rights to land so occupied, which horrified those who, like Lord Salisbury or the duke of Argyll, based their views on the principles of contract.[86] 'For the future the relation between landlord and tenant ought to rest upon contract, and upon contract only,' Argyll had insisted (futilely), as early as 1854.[87] The historicist view was influential in Indian policy, and the government

[81] He does in the end, however; PRONI, D1071, H/H/1/2, Dufferin to Carnarvon, 29 May 1874; see also H/H/6/2, fo. 21, Dufferin to Herbert, C.O., 7 May 1874; Bitterman, 'Upholding', pp. 3, 11–12.

[82] M. Bentley, *Politics Without Democracy, 1815–1914* (Oxford: Oxford University Press, 1984), pp. 97, 118.

[83] Thompson, 'English Landed Society in the Twentieth Century': 'IV: Prestige without power?' *Transactions of the Royal Historical Society*, 6th ser., 3 (1993).

[84] C. Bayley, 'Ireland, India and the empire', pp. 380–8.

[85] G. R. G. Hambly, 'Richard Temple and the Punjab Tenancy Act of 1868', *English Historical Review*, 79:310 (1964), pp. 47–66.

[86] See for comparison M. Chase, *The People's Farm: English Radical Agrarianism 1775–1840* (Oxford: Oxford University Press, 1988).

[87] House of Lords, Debates, 3rd ser., vol. 135, cc. 157–8, 13 July 1854; Bentley, *Lord Salisbury's World*, pp. 94–101.

of India passed a series of tenancy acts which interfered in the relationship between indigenous landowners and their tenants on a historicist basis, in part to justify British conquest in the subcontinent.[88] Given the centrality of land ownership to political power, it is unsurprising that any reforms made to land tenure anywhere would be deeply controversial and for some politicians – such as the duke of Argyll and the 1881 Act – represented an uncrossable Rubicon.[89] Despite their fears, taking the long view, what is surprising about government attempts to curb landed power is how relatively unsuccessful they were, particularly in the (re)distribution of land ownership.

Overall, the later nineteenth century saw a significant increase in the role the state played in British society, in education, health and welfare, housing and employment.[90] Its increasing 'interference' in property – as landowners saw it – was part and parcel of this expansion of responsibilities, both moral and political-economic. Landowners were willing to tolerate some interference as a route back to 'normality', particularly in those places affected by major rural and tenant agitation and disturbance. It was also the case that the expansion of autocratic imperial governance in the British colonial territories fed back into understandings of state power in Britain itself, of what governments could do and the level of interference they could justify, even into the sacrosanct principles of property and contract.

CONCLUSIONS

The nineteenth-century history of land reform in Scotland is shared with the history of land reform in the rest of Britain, Ireland and the imperial territories. Unsurprisingly, in an age where the political classes were made up by a tiny social – often landed – elite, usually interrelated,

---

[88] Dewey, 'Images of the village community', p. 294; K. Mulhern, 'The Intellectual Duke: George Douglas Campbell, 8th Duke of Argyll', unpublished PhD thesis (University of Edinburgh, 2006), pp. 131–4; Bayly, *Birth of the Modern World*, pp. 299–300.

[89] Argyll resigned from Gladstone's cabinet in 1881 in protest over the Irish Land Act; Bentley, *Lord Salisbury's World*, pp. 94–101; Mulhern, 'Intellectual Duke', pp. 85, 93–4, 123; D. Omissi, 'A most arduous but a most noble duty': Gladstone and the British Raj in India, 1868–98', in *Gladstone, Ireland and Beyond* (eds), M. E. Daly and K. T. Hoppen (Dublin: Four Courts Press, 2011), pp. 179–99.

[90] Cannadine, *Decline and Fall*, pp. 14–16, 27–31, 182–235; A. Tindley, '"Actual pinching and suffering': estate responses to poverty in Sutherland, 1845–86', *Scottish Historical Review*, 90:2 (2011), pp. 236–56.

certainly sharing the same educational culture and expectations, attitudes towards the role of landowners, social structures and land reform were replicated across the political and imperial establishment. Local factors meant differing responses and any transnational comparison must be anchored in the local contexts, not least due to the power of historical and cultural memory over land reform agendas and justifications.[91] That said, Scotland's land reform history is not particularly exceptional when placed into the wider context. Approaches to land reform sometimes emphasised the principles of dual ownership and sometimes land purchase; infrastructural investment and the promotion of emigration were often pushed forward in tandem with land reform, whether in Canada, Scotland or India. These policies were often dependent on whether the Liberal or Conservative parties were in the ascendant at Westminster, not the local conditions and demands.

Scottish land reform influenced, and was influenced by, trends from across the world, facilitated by the transnational movement of people and ideas across place and time. Rather than seeing Scottish land reform or the underpinning structures of land ownership patterns as unique, historically speaking it is more helpful to see them contextualised much more widely. It was the case that the level of concentration of land ownership in Scotland was somewhat unusual in the European (though not the Russian) context, but this was one extreme of a spectrum of European landed power which remained significant until well into the twentieth century.[92] Scotland's and Britain's landed classes retained much of their power in this period precisely because of the success of the agricultural and industrial revolutions, not in spite of them. They were at the vanguard of economic change and benefited from it accordingly, securing their economic and political foundations more effectively than many of their European neighbours. It took the power of the changing state to curb these powers in the later nineteenth century, across a range of different fronts, of which land reform was only one.

---

[91] N. Whelehan, 'Playing with scales: transnational history and modern Ireland', in N. Whelehan (ed.), *Transnational Perspectives on Modern Irish History* (London, Routledge, 2015), pp. 7–8.

[92] See Vaughan, *Landlords and Tenants*, pp. 1, 6.

5

Still on the Agenda? The Strange Survival of the Scottish Land Question, 1880–1999

Ewen A. Cameron

THIS CHAPTER ANALYSES THE historical background to the current debates on land reform in Scotland. Since the creation of the Scottish Parliament in 1999 the discussion of land reform – always present in the bloodstream of Scottish politics – acquired a new context. Devolution meant that it was now possible to contemplate legislation on this vexed question in Scottish politics and culture. This aim was realised under a Labour–Liberal Democrat coalition Scottish government in 2003 and then, further, by an SNP minority government in 2016. The debates on these bills were suffused by historical reference, mostly to the Highland Clearances.[1] The chapter will look at earlier debates on the Scottish land question and consider the ideas that emerged from those discussions. The way in which the Scottish land question 'survived' in the post-1918 period, when the conventional view is that from that date land ceased to be a major issue in British politics, will be considered.[2]

The 'land question' conjures images of the Victorian and Edwardian period when politicians faced issues arising from Ireland and, to a lesser extent, the Highlands of Scotland. It is also redolent of a time in which the Liberal party was one of the leading parties of the state and dominant in Scotland. Questions over the ownership and distribution of land exercised radical Liberals, as did the models of tenure and the way in which these technical questions related to wider social ills, such as overcrowded housing or rural poverty. These politics were energised by the

---

[1] *Scottish Parliament, Official Report*, 24 November 1999, cols 863, 867, 871; 27 September 2000, col. 700; 20 March 2002, cols 10388–93; 16 March 2016, cols 241, 244, 246.

[2] F. M. L. Thompson, 'The strange death of the English land question' in Matthew Cragoe and Paul Readman (eds), *The Land Question in Britain, 1750–1950* (Basingstoke: Palgrave Macmillan, 2010), pp. 257–70.

publication in the UK in 1880 of Henry George's *Progress and Poverty* which asked profound social questions and placed land reform, through 'the single tax', at the heart of their solution.[3] George did not want to empower the state to confiscate or purchase land, as that would be too disruptive and would extend overmuch the machinery of government. Instead, he argued that rent, that is, the share in wealth produced by the mere ownership of land, should be appropriated through a new tax. The yield from this tax would be such that all other taxes could be abolished, hence the 'single tax'.[4] George visited Scotland on many occasions and debated the land question with the 8th duke of Argyll, the most vocal contemporary defender of landed property. In common with many land reformers, George saw the Scottish case as key to understanding the iniquities at the heart of private land ownership.[5] The 'land question' was not only a technical matter of tenure, settlement and resources but also a moral question.

Even for those Liberals who felt that a 'single tax' on the economic rent of land was extreme, the underlying principle of Georgite ideas appeared in the land campaign of the Edwardian period when the valuation and taxation of land was central to the ideas of David Lloyd George as Chancellor of the Exchequer. Land and politics were not merely a Liberal fad, however. The emerging Labour movement, drawing on the Liberal heritage, also placed matters of land and property near the top of their agenda. This was not a straightforward matter; there was much disagreement within the Labour movement about the different strands of land reform. Many on the left in Scotland argued for land nationalisation (as opposed to Georgite 'land restoration'). The key text was by Alfred Russel Wallace.[6] In common with other authors in

[3] Charles Albro Barker, *Henry George* (Oxford and New York: Oxford University Press, 1955), pp. 378–416; Elwood P. Lawrence, *Henry George in the British Isles* (East Lansing, MI: The Michigan State University Press, 1957), pp. 42–3, 45, 58; John R. Frame, 'America and the Scottish Left: the Impact of American Ideas on the Scottish Labour Movement from the American Civil War to World War One', PhD thesis (University of Aberdeen, 1998), pp. 77–118.

[4] Henry George, *Progress and Poverty*, 4th edn (London: Kegan and Paul, 1881), pp. 149, 364.

[5] Henry George, 'The "Reduction to Iniquity"', *Nineteenth Century*, 16 (1884), p. 139; Duke of Argyll, 'The Prophet of San Francisco', *Nineteenth Century*, 15 (1884), pp. 537–58.

[6] Alfred Russel Wallace, *Land Nationalisation* (London: Trübner & Co., 1882). This volume went through several editions in the author's lifetime, in 1883, 1892, 1896 and 1902. Other important texts on the subject included Harold Cox, *Land Nationalization and Land Taxation* (London: Methuen and Company, 1906); Robert

this period, including George, Wallace noted the contrast between the seemingly exponential increase of national wealth and the proliferation of poverty, crime and disease. In Wallace's view, the prevailing system of land tenure – which gave wide latitude to the private owner, however large or small his estate or however virtuous his personality – lay at the heart of the problem. Although he gave particular prominence to the iniquity of land ownership in Ireland, Scotland had also attracted his attention, as would befit a disciple of Robert Owen.[7] He regarded the Highlands as an example of 'that terrible power over their fellow creatures which absolute property in land gives to individuals who possess large estates'.[8] Wallace's solution was 'the abolition of private property in land and its complete nationalisation – undoubtedly a measure of radical if not of revolutionary character, but the evils to be cured are so gigantic and so deeply-rooted that any less searching remedy would be powerless to effect a cure of the disease'.[9] H. M. Hyndman's Democratic (later Social Democratic) Federation, an organisation that regarded the nationalisation of land as a necessary, but not sufficient, measure for social reform, was also active in Scotland.[10]

These ideas were current during the period from the 1880s to the 1920s when the land question was a matter of protest and conflict as well as a question of print and ideas. The 'land war' of the 1880s projected the Scottish land question onto a wide stage. Political elites were worried that a region of virtue had been polluted by dangerous ideas from Ireland. Although George and other radicals – Michael Davitt for example – were present in the Highlands during the 1880s, their ideas were not particularly influential in practical terms. The principal objective of land reformers was security of tenure and access to more land for grazing. This is clear from the evidence given to the Royal Commission, chaired by Lord Napier, which investigated the grievances of the crofters

Blatchford, *Land Nationalisation* (London: Clarion Press, 1906); A. Emil Davis and Dorothy Evans, *Land Nationalisation: The Key to Social Reform* (London: Parsons, 1921), the authors were leading figures in the 'Land Nationalisation Society'.

[7] Owen was a utopian socialist whose ideas were an inspiration to many on the left in the Victorian and Edwardian period. In 1799 he purchased the New Lanark cotton mill from his father-in-law and attempted to run it on non-commercial lines.

[8] Wallace, *Land Nationalisation*, pp. 29, 95–6

[9] Ibid., p. 134.

[10] 'Land Nationalisation', *Justice*, 11 November 1884; Henry George and H. M. Hyndman, 'Socialism and rent-appropriation: a dialogue', *Nineteenth Century*, 17 (1885) pp. 369–80.

in 1883–4.[11] The first objective was achieved with the Crofters Holdings (Scotland) Act 1886 but it provided only weak provisions for making more land available to the crofters. Napier's more adventurous proposals, drawn from his Indian experience, for the creation of self-regulating townships had, like George's, provoked the easily irked duke of Argyll into a defence of landed property and a vindication of his own estate management. For all the intellectual fireworks, this debate proved academic. The Liberal government resorted to repackaging for Scottish conditions the Irish Land Act of 1881. The limitations of this approach was evident from the crofters' testimony to the 'Deer Forest Commission' in the early 1890s.[12] Successive pieces of legislation in 1897, 1911 and 1919 went some way towards dealing with the latter grievance. These Acts had different ideological objectives and historical contexts. That of 1897 was introduced by a Conservative government with the aim of releasing landlords from the burden of dealing with small tenants and offering them the opportunity, at the price of their crofter tenure, to become owners of their own land; they were uninterested in this.[13] The only exception was the tenants of the Glendale estate on the west side of the island of Skye, who in 1904 accepted the offer of the Congested Districts Board and contracted fifty-year loans to acquire the ownership of their crofts, which then ceased to be crofts. A contrasting history was provided by the equally disputatious tenants of the Kilmuir estate in the north end of the island. They resisted the blandishments of the Congested Districts Board and the Ministers of the Liberal government and the estate was effectively nationalised, although that language was not used, other than by mischievous journalists.[14]

The Act of 1911 was motivated by short-term political gain on the part of a Liberal government elected after strident rhetoric on the land question. Its hasty drafting, and the fact that it became a pawn in the

---

[11] Report of the Commissioners of Inquiry into the Condition of the Crofters and Cottars in the Highlands and Islands of Scotland, 1884. C. 3980.

[12] Royal Commission (Highlands and Islands) 1892, 1895. C. 7668, C. 7681.

[13] E. A. Cameron, Land for the People? The British Government and the Scottish Highlands c.1880–c.1925 (East Linton: Tuckwell Press, 1996), pp. 83–101.

[14] Charles Stewart, The Highland Experiment in Land Nationalisation (London, 1904); National Records of Scotland (NRS), AF42/4903, Memo by Reginald MacLeod, 3 April 1908; similar events took place in Vatersay, in this case the estate management applied pressure to 'nationalise', see NRS, AF42/5871, Narrative of proceedings leading up to the purchase of Vatersay, 19 February 1909; NRS, AF42/5991, Notes of a conference held in Edinburgh, 13 March 1909; Ben Buxton, The Vatersay Raiders (Edinburgh: Birlinn, 2008), pp. 118–40.

battle with the House of Lords, delayed its passage and compromised its effectiveness.[15] The final piece of legislation in this first phase of land reform – the Land Settlement (Scotland) Act of 1919 – was a product of the drive to build a 'land fit for heroes' in the aftermath of the Great War. It was passed with broad support by an all-powerful coalition government, it had substantial funding, and it provided for land nationalisation in the Highlands.[16]

The long-term effect of land settlement is ambiguous. On the ground it has been very important as these estates have provided a different model of land ownership with 'The Department' (of Agriculture and Fisheries for Scotland and its successors) regarded as an effective landowner. During the Taylor Commission on Crofting Reform in the early 1950s, a minority report argued for an extension of the model. This was not adopted, however, and the idea of land nationalisation was marginalised in policy terms, although it remained part of the debate on the land question in Scotland.[17] Much of the period saw frustration for activists from different political traditions, especially socialist and nationalist, who sought to advocate it. At the time of the Knoydart 'land raid' of 1948 this was very clear, as the Labour government declined to yield to pressure to purchase an estate that had been brought into the public eye by the raiders and their advocates, including in song by Hamish Henderson.[18] By the 1980s the context had changed again.

[15] Cameron, *Land for the People?*, pp. 102–64 ; L. Leneman, *Fit For Heroes? Land Settlement in Scotland After World War I* (Aberdeen: Aberdeen University Press), pp. 5–19.

[16] Leneman, *Fit for Heroes?*, pp. 20–52; Bob Chambers, 'For want of land: a study of land settlement in the Outer Hebrides, Skye and Raasay between the two world wars', PhD thesis (University of Aberdeen, 2013).

[17] 'Note of Dissent by Mrs Margaret H. Macpherson', *Commission of Enquiry into Crofting Conditions*, Cmd 9091, 91; NLS, Gunn MSS, Dep. 209/22/5, Matthew Campbell to Gunn, 2 February 1954. She was still extolling the virtues of public land ownership nearly forty years later: see letter to *West Highland Free Press*, 6 July 1990.

[18] NRS, CS275/1952/4, Court of Session proceedings against the raiders; NRS, SEP12/7/1, Advisory Panel on the Highlands and Islands: Report to the Panel by the Agriculture and Forestry Group: Knoydart Estate; NRS, SEP12/7/3, Memorial to the Rt Hon Arthur Woodburn, M.P. Secretary of State for Scotland regarding Family Holdings on Knoydart Estate; H. Henderson, 'Ballad of the men of Knoydart', in R. Ross (ed.) *Collected Poems and Songs* (Edinburgh: Polygon, 2000), pp. 128–30; Timothy Neat, *Hamish Henderson: A Biography, Volume 1: The Making of the Poet (1919–1953)* (Edinburgh: Polygon, 2007), pp. 230–2, Neat notes that Henderson's ballad was not published or broadcast for many years and was awkward politically because of its mixture of nationalistic and socialist ideas.

When government-owned property, especially the public housing stock, was being considered for privatisation, the Scottish estates came under scrutiny. In 1979 DAFS was being urged to sell the land settlement estates. The principal grounds for this pressure that they were loss-making (between £1.26 million and £1.53 million annual losses in the years 1975–6 to 1978–9), were surplus to state requirements and that there was a need to make staff cuts. The plans to dispose of them ran into complications imposed by the technicalities of crofting tenure but this official discussion was suggestive of a political atmosphere that was not propitious for land reform. This was not only the result of the election of a Conservative government in 1979 but also the result of growing financial pressures in the UK from the mid 1970s.[19]

For the land reformers of the 1880s, sporting estates were an egregious moral transgression on the part of landowners. Here were vast acreages set aside for the questionable leisure activities of the rich and powerful, while crofters and cottars subsisted on marginal land. Liberal politicians continually returned to this issue. In 1892, a Royal Commission was established to look into the question. Known as the 'Deer Forest Commission' it was largely composed of critics of sport and its recommendations were spun to suggest that there were untapped land resources under deer.[20] Lloyd George made this a theme of his 'land campaign' just before the Great War and returned to it during his post-war premiership. These were attempts to use a classical Liberal issue to hold the fissiparous party together, something that was more difficult after 1918.[21] There were, broadly, two responses to this line of argument. The first asserted that sporting estates provided employment for the local population and business for local suppliers of food and other goods. It has been argued that this is a doubtful proposition in that sporting estates were markedly non labour-intensive, even compared to sheep farms, and that rich sporting tenants tended to bring considerable quantities of supplies with them on the vast trains that rumbled north

---

[19] The National Archives (TNA), HLG29/2134, T. M. Brown (DAFS) to C. P. Thomas (Treasury), 13 December 1979; Thomas to Brown, 18 January 1980.

[20] *Royal Commission (Highlands and Islands) 1892*, Report; Cameron, *Land for the People?*, pp. 77–81.

[21] *Royal Commission (Highlands and Islands) 1892*; *Report of the Departmental Committee ... with Regard to Lands in Scotland Used as Deer Forests*, 1922, Cmd 1636; B. Short, *Land and Society in Edwardian Scotland* (Cambridge, 1997), pp. 313–14; Annie Tindley, '"The system of landlordism supreme": David Lloyd George, the 5th duke of Sutherland and Highland land sales, 1898–1919', *British Scholar*, 3 (2010), pp. 24–42.

from London Euston in August.[22] The second argument was that they were located on land useless for other purposes. Considerable ingenuity was deployed to articulate this argument. The most indefatigable defender of the deer forest was George Malcolm, a manager of sporting estates. His advocacy was central to pushing aside attacks on commercialised sport from Liberal governments from the 1880s to the 1920s.[23] In 1909 the marquis of Tullibardine, heir to the dukedom of Atholl, attempted to draw attention to this issue by inviting nine working men, five Liberal and four Conservative, to inspect his deer forests. His point was that there had been so much radical propaganda on the subject that he wanted to demonstrate that the land used for sport could not be put to more productive use. Clearly, this was not an objective or scientific review but it was effective politics.[24]

Issues concerned with the ownership of, access to and redistribution of land have remained more important in Scotland than in other parts of the United Kingdom.[25] The politics of the land question are reflected in many areas of Scottish culture.[26] Significant works of twentieth-century Scottish literature, in both Gaelic and English, are concerned with the histories and geographies, communities and places, grievances and aspirations, associated with land.[27] The clearances and the Crofters War of

[22] Willie Orr, *Deer Forests, Landlords and Crofters: The Western Highlands in Victorian and Edwardian Times* (Edinburgh: John Donald, 1982), pp. 90–118.

[23] Malcolm's works included: *The Population, Crofts, Sheep Walks, and Deer Forests of the Highlands and Islands* (Edinburgh: William Blackwood and Sons, 1883); *Deer Forests: Past, Present and Future* (Edinburgh: William Blackwood and Sons, 1890); *Local Migration of Crofters: Is it Feasible or Desirable?* (Edinburgh and London: William Blackwood and Sons, 1883, 1894); *Lists of Deer Forests in Scotland, with Remarks on Shootings, Sheep Farms, Small Holdings and Afforestation in Scotland* (Edinburgh: William Blackwood and Sons, 1912).

[24] Parliamentary Archive, Andrew Bonar Law MSS, 28/1/39, 'Atholl Forest Report'; *The Scotsman*, 23 August 1909, p. 4; 26 August 1909, pp. 6, 9; 28 August 1909, p. 10; 30 August 1909, p. 8; 31 August 1909, p. 6; 20 September 1909, p. 9; 25 September 1909, p. 8; 27 September 1909, p. 9.

[25] Ewen A. Cameron, 'Setting the heather on fire: the land question in Scotland', in Cragoe and Readman, *Land Question in Britain*, pp. 109–25; Ewen A. Cameron, 'Unfinished Business: The Land Question and the New Scottish Parliament', *Contemporary British History*, 15 (2001), pp. 83–114.

[26] Andrew Noble, 'Urbane silence: Scottish writing and the nineteenth-century city', in George Gordon (ed.), *Perspectives of the Scottish City* (Aberdeen: Aberdeen University Press, 1985), p. 64.

[27] George Bruce and Frank Rennie (eds), *The Land Out There: A Scottish Land Anthology* (Aberdeen: Aberdeen University Press, 1991); C. W. J. Withers, '"The Image of the Land": Scotland's geography through her languages and literature',

the 1880s are prominent in this body of work.[28] This engagement with the history of the land question continues throughout the twentieth century. It is evident in the work of Aonghas MacNeacail, especially in his poem '*oideachadh ceart*' ('a proper schooling'). In this poem MacNeacail asserts that a series of incidents from the life of the township of Idrigill, Skye, are not events from history but part of the memory of the township: they are alive and connected to the present, rather than being past and archived.[29] Perhaps the most sustained piece of writing to explore themes relating to the wider social and cultural impact of the land question is Sorley MacLean's '*An Cuilithionn*'. This poem attempts to relate the island of Skye to themes in European and global history in the 1930s, the period in which most of the poem was written, although it was not published in full until the 1980s.[30] The clearances and the crofters' response in the 1880s are at the centre of the Skye history from which themes of global relevance emanated.[31]

Writers in English also produced important works centered on the clearances and the land question. Neil M. Gunn's *Butcher's Broom* (1934) contained an extended discussion of the impact of the clearances on a community in Sutherland. *The Silver Darlings* followed in 1942, a sequel to *Butcher's Broom* in the sense that it looked at the fishing communities of the Moray Firth in the aftermath of the Napoleonic Wars. Gunn was concerned with the history of the land question in his fiction and carried out detailed historical research.[32] Gunn was a pragmatic nationalist and this comes through from one of his later novels,

---

Scottish Geographical Magazine, 100 (1984), pp. 81–95; David McCrone, 'Land, democracy and culture in Scotland', *Scottish Affairs*, no. 23 (Spring 1998), pp. 73–92.

[28] Samuel MacLean, 'The Poetry of the Clearances', *TGSI*, 38 (1937–41), pp. 293–324; D. Meek (ed.), *Tuath is Tighearna: Tenants and Landlords* (Edinburgh: Scottish Gaelic Texts Society, Scottish Academic Press, 1996), pp. 13–40; Silke Stroh, *Uneasy Subjects: Postcolonialism and Scottish Gaelic Poetry* (Amsterdam: Rodopi, 2011), pp. 214–32.

[29] Aonghas MacNeacail, *dèanamh gàire ris a' chloc, dàin ùra agus thaghte: laughing at the clock, new and selected poems* (Edinburgh: Birlinn, 2012), pp. 162–5; for the events at Scuddaburgh see Donald Shaw, *The Idrigill Raiders* (Ullapool, 2010); Ewen A. Cameron, '"They Will Listen to no Remonstrance": Land Raids and Land Raiders in the Scottish Highlands, 1886 to 1914', *Scottish Economic and Social History*, 17 (1997), pp. 43–64.

[30] Christopher Whyte (ed.), *An Cuilithionn 1939 and Unpublished Poems of Somhairle MacGill-Eain/Sorley MacLean* (Glasgow: ASLS, 2011).

[31] Whyte (ed.), *An Cuilithionn 1939*, p. 4.

[32] NLS, Dep. 209/22/7, Gunn to Duncan Gollan, 6 May 1964.

The Drinking Well (1946). This book deals with economic conditions in the central Highlands during the 1930s. It is full of set-piece scenes where characters debate nationalism and agricultural problems.[33] Not so heralded as Gunn, but perhaps the first novelist to deal directly with the clearances, was Ian MacPherson. Better known for his *Shepherds' Calendar* and his dystopian *Wild Harbour*, MacPherson drew on his father's knowledge of the sheep-farming industry to write two novels, *Land of Our Fathers* (1933) and *Pride in the Valley* (1936), about the clearances and their aftermath. These novels were the starting point for MacPherson's ideas about economic development in the post-clearance and contemporary Highlands, an important theme of his journalism. Like Gunn, MacPherson was drawing on history to inform contemporary debates about the land question.[34] Later works that touched on these themes included Fionn MacColla's *And the Cock Crew* (1945) and Iain Crichton Smith's *Consider the Lilies* (1968). These were important novels, although slightly distinct from those considered above in that they concentrated on the theme of the 'betrayal' of the people by the clergy of the Church of Scotland and, compared to the work of Gunn or MacPherson, were less concerned with historical chronology and 'accuracy'.

These are important works in the history of Scottish literature but they are important in a history of the Highland land question for other reasons. In the period from the 1930s to the 1970s these and other works did much to keep the issue alive in the minds of a wider public who may not have been directly affected by the grievances associated with Scotland's systems of land ownership and tenure. The most important work, however, was *The Cheviot, the Stag and the Black, Black Oil*, first performed in 1973. This play dealt with the ways in which the Highlands had been exploited by sheep farmers, landlords, sporting tenants and, in the later twentieth century, the forces of international capitalism represented by the oil industry. The text also dealt with the ways in which the people of the Highlands fought back against such

---

[33] Richard Price, *The Fabulous Matter of Fact: The Poetics of Neil M. Gunn* (Edinburgh: Edinburgh University Press, 1991), pp. 42–61, 90–102, 134–49; Margery McCulloch, *The Novels of Neil M. Gunn: A Critical Study* (Edinburgh: Scottish Academic Press, 1987), pp. 45–61, 119–31; Maurice Walsh, *Trouble in the Glen* (Edinburgh: W. & R. Chambers, 1950).

[34] Douglas F. Young, *Highland Search: The Life and Novels of Ian MacPherson* (Kinloss: Librario, 2002); John Manson, 'Mearns to Strathspey: the novels of Ian MacPherson (1905–44)', *Cencrastus* (Spring/Summer 1996), pp. 23–6; *Aberdeen University Review*, 31 (1944–5), pp. 127–8.

forces.[35] In combination with the new and assertive *West Highland Free Press*, the reaction to *The Cheviot* helped to raise the profile of the land question in Scottish politics at a particularly interesting moment when mainstream politics provided few fresh ideas on the matter.

Nevertheless, Scottish politics began to open up in the 1960s. Political debates in the 1940s and 1950s had been conducted within narrow limits and the Scottish Unionists, as the Conservatives were called north of the border, and Labour had dominated elections. In the 1960s, however, the Liberal party and the SNP began to take some small steps onto the Scottish political stage. These developments had an effect on the main political parties, especially the Labour party. In the Highlands the Unionists were worried about the Liberal advance and by the late 1960s had developed an awareness that they were identified as the party of the landed class. Attempts to craft a local appeal in the Highlands failed to prevent the Liberals winning several seats in 1964 and 1966.[36] The Labour party had a strong tradition of anti-landlord rhetoric but had not tackled the land question during its periods of government.[37] During the 1930s the party had become centralised in its organisation and centralist in its economic thinking.[38] During the 1960s, however, the party did open its mind to land reform in a way that had not been evident for a generation. Partly this was rhetorical. In proposing what became the Highlands and Islands Development Board (HIDB) the Secretary of State for Scotland, William Ross, allowed his public oratory to soar and in private had argued that the Board should deal with the

[35] John McGrath, *Six-Pack: Plays for Scotland* (Edinburgh: Polygon, 1996), pp. 139–99; John McGrath, 'The Year of the Cheviot', in John McGrath, *The Cheviot, the Stag and the Black, Black Oil*, revised, illustrated edition (London: Bloomsbury, 1993), pp. v–xxix.

[36] Oxford, Bodleian Library, Conservative Party Archive, CCO 500/50/1, Surveys of Scottish, Welsh and West Country Nationalism, 1967–8, John Davidson, Scottish Conservative & Unionist Research Officer, to R. Webster, Conservative & Unionist Central Office, 4 August 1966.

[37] Leading land reformers such as Gavin Clark and John Murdoch had been involved in the formation of the SLP in 1888. Johnston's anti-landlord articles in *Forward* were edited by him in book form as Thomas Johnston, *Our Scots Noble Families* (Glasgow: Forward Publishing, 1909), with an introduction by J. Ramsay MacDonald; for Johnston's later ambivalence to this book see his *Memories* (London: Collins, 1952), p. 35, where he called it 'unnecessarily wounding'.

[38] W. W. Knox and A. MacKinlay, 'The re-making of the Scottish Labour in the 1930s', *Twentieth-Century British History*, 6 (1995), pp. 174–93; NRS, DD15/12, Memo concerning Highland development commissioner, no date but c.1938.

land question. As constituted in 1965, however, the Board had few real powers to deal with entrenched inequalities in land ownership.[39]

More prosaically, the Labour government returned to the question of crofting reform. Many of the problems of crofting tenure that had dogged the system since 1886 were unresolved. In 1968 leading figures in the Crofters Commission[40] argued for a mass conversion of crofting tenure to owner-occupation. They suggested that the new context supplied by the establishment of the HIDB and the Agriculture Act of 1967 made many aspects of crofting tenure 'obsolete'. In particular, there were substantial disincentives to enterprise and a chronic lack of capital in the crofting economy. The Commission advised that conversion to owner-occupation would unlock the potential of the crofting counties.[41] This provoked a long debate that ended with the Crofting Reform (Scotland) Act 1976, which permitted individual crofters to become owner-occupiers and provided some facilities for crofters to share in economic development but did not address the issues laid out in 1968. These seemingly technical issues revealed the capacity of the land question to stimulate heated debate. Perhaps sensing a rare political opportunity, the Western Isles Conservatives hailed this as an example of the way in which a 'property-owning democracy' could bring positive benefits to society.[42] More interesting politics took place, however, in the Labour party. Leading activists, such as Margaret MacPherson, Allan Campbell MacLean, Brian Wilson and Roderick MacFarquhar – advocates of land nationalisation – were horrified by the proposals, which they felt were driven by bureaucratic aims, undermined crofting and set back wider land reform.[43] They argued that owner-occupation for crofters would damage the crofting system and leave the interests of

[39] *Parliamentary Debates*, 5th series, vol. 708, cols 1079–80, 1095, 16 March 1965; TNA, D4/1740, HIDB, draft memo by the Secretary of State for Scotland, 30 November 1964; see also TNA, T224/1115.

[40] This body should not be confused with the Crofters Commission established by the 1886 Crofters Act, which was the forerunner of the Scottish Land Court of 1912; *No Ordinary Court: 100 Years of the Scottish Land Court* (Edinburgh: Avizandum, 2012).

[41] NRS, CRO3/3/2, Crofters Commission: Recommendations for the Modernisation of Crofting, 17 October 1968; Donald J. MacCuish, 'The case for converting crofting tenure to ownership', *TGSI*, 46 (1969–70), pp. 89–113.

[42] *Stornoway Gazette*, 3 May 1969.

[43] A. K. Bell Library, Perth (AKBLP), John McEwen Papers, MS 5/517, Brian Wilson to John McEwen, 15 January 1976; James N. McCrorie, *The Highland Cause: The Life and Times of Roderick MacFarquhar* (Regina, Saskatchewan: University of Saskatchewan Press, 2001), pp. 200–10.

landowners largely untouched. The reforms fell with the Labour government in 1970 and were remodelled by the new Conservative government but had not reached the statute book when that government fell in 1974. Labour returned to the task with a bill that was passed in 1976 as the Crofting Reform (Scotland) Act and gave individual crofters the right to purchase their holdings at fifteen times the annual rent; granted a 50 per cent share in the development value of land taken out of crofting and sold for such purposes as housing, and gave greater powers to grazing committees in crofting townships.[44] This was, at one level, a small episode confined to the crofting areas but it touches on wider issues that had been current in the debates on the land question since the 1880s. The key issue was the extent to which changes in tenure, such as the introduction of crofting, could work to alter in a more fundamental sense the social and economic relationships between those who owned the land and those who lived on it. Most governments, whether Liberal, Conservative and, later, Labour, believed that this was sufficient but there had always been a group – represented here by MacFarquhar and his colleagues – who wanted land nationalisation.

Another way in which the land question clung to the political agenda was through the activities of a small band of dedicated land reformers. These people were working outside the structures of political parties, although they retained connections with the Labour movement and the SNP. Their principal work was to identify who owned Scotland. Cadastral work had a history going back to the 1870s, when most land was in the hands of individuals, often well-known aristocrats and leading gentry, and information was relatively easy to discern, although labour-intensive to present. Until the 1870s little was known about land ownership in Britain. An official *Return of Owners of Land* in 1876 was followed in the late 1870s and early 1880s by successive editions of John Bateman's enumeration of landed proprietors.[45] It became clear that Scottish land was in remarkably few hands: landowners with more than 1,000 acres owned 92 per cent of the total area of land. The figure in England was 56.1 per cent, 60.8 per cent in Wales and 78.4 per cent in Ireland. By the post-1945 period it was clear that gaining information on this question was difficult and there was official reluctance to provide it. In 1965, for example, the Labour MP Willie Hamilton asked

---

[44] James Hunter, *The Claim of Crofting: The Scottish Highlands and Islands, 1930–1990* (Edinburgh: Mainstream, 1991), pp. 125–48.
[45] John Bateman, *The Great Landowners of Great Britain and Ireland*, 4th edn (London: Harrison, 1883).

parliamentary questions seeking information about who owned what in
the Highlands. In advising Ministers on the answer, civil servants were
very reluctant to have details disclosed. They argued that 'there seems
little doubt that many owners of large estates would resent being named
in Hansard'.[46]

Pre-eminent among those who attempted to fill this gap in knowledge
in the later part of the twentieth century was the remarkable figure of
John McEwen. McEwen had published his groundbreaking book *Who
Owns Scotland?* in 1977, having trailed some of his ideas in 1975 in *The
Red Paper on Scotland* and been coaxed into the public eye by its editor,
Gordon Brown.[47] In his correspondence with McEwen, Brown cited the
support of John McGrath for McEwen's work and McGrath contributed
a foreword to *Who Owns Scotland?*[48] McEwen's ultimate objective, as
he told Brown, was 'to effect a complete change of ownership (by the
state) of these 10m acres'.[49] McEwen recalled that he was regarded as
something of an eccentric by the Labour establishment as he pursued his
'gowk's errand'. His aim was not only the completion of the empirical
task implied by his book's title but also to emphasise the 'terrific mess
into which landlords in Scotland have landed us'.[50] His answer was
state ownership and he printed 'clause 4' of the 1918 constitution of the
Labour Party at the start of his book.[51] McEwen's long-term influence
is important, as shall be shown below, but there is also evidence that his
work and the response to it had an effect in the Scottish Office. When the

---

[46] NRS, SEP12/273, Memo on landholdings in the Highlands, April 1965;
Parliamentary Debates, vol. 711, col. 61w, 28 April 1965; Jim Sillars, 'Land owner-
ship and land nationalisation', in Gordon Brown (ed.), *The Red Paper on Scotland*
(Edinburgh: EUSPB, 1975), p. 255; see questions by the Labour MP for Dundee
West, Peter Doig, *Parliamentary Debates*, vol. 870, cols 1019–20, 20 March 1974.

[47] John McEwen, *Who Owns Scotland?* (Edinburgh: EUSPB, 1977); John
McEwen, 'Highland landlordism', in Brown (ed.), *The Red Paper on Scotland*,
pp. 262–9.

[48] AKBLP, John McEwen Papers, MS 164/5/524, Gordon Brown to John
McEwen, 29 October 1974.

[49] AKBLP, John McEwen Papers, MS 164/5/524, McEwen to Brown, 24
November 1974.

[50] McEwen, *Who Owns Scotland?*, 7; Roger Millman, 'The marches of Highland
estates', *Scottish Geographical Magazine*, 85 (1969), pp. 172–81; Roger Millman,
'The landed properties of northern Scotland', *Scottish Geographical Magazine*, 86
(1970), pp. 186–203.

[51] He also printed a verse ('Ye see yon birkie ca'd a Lord') from Robert Burns'
'For a' that an' a' that'; there was a long history of Burns being used in the land
reform cause, see Christopher A. Whatley, *Immortal Memory: Burns and the
Scottish People* (Edinburgh: John Donald, 2016), p. 166.

government was considering the bill that became the Land Registration (Scotland) Act 1979, they contemplated inserting a clause (clause 4, ironically) that would have demanded information about land ownership, including those who benefited from corporate land ownership. Ultimately the clause was not included in the bill that went forward, lest it be too controversial and threaten its passage. Perhaps a technical bill on an aspect of conveyancing was not the correct place for this measure but the evidence seems to show that politicians and civil servants were motivated by the way in which McEwen's book had focused attention on the questions about land ownership that he posed.[52]

McEwen's work was taken on by Robin Callander who began to publish in the 1980s when, although the wider political environment might have been unpropitious, there was a slightly wider group of activists working on the land question.[53] The Labour party was more interested in the question and even the SNP had moved to the left and deepened its concern with the land issue. In 1986 Callander sent a copy of one of his publications to McEwen, citing it as evidence that 'land is still on the agenda – just!' This stimulated a furious response from McEwen, arguing that land had never been off the agenda and criticising Callander for engaging in mere intellectual activity that was bound to be inadequate to deal with the depth of injustice around the land question.[54] McEwen's work has been taken on by the redoubtable Andy Wightman, now an MSP for the Green Party. Since the 1990s Wightman has been continuing the task that McEwen began. He has refined the methodology of earlier researchers and reached more nuanced conclusions. Like McEwen his objective was not merely empirical but also political, as he stated in the introduction to one of his early publications:

> It is thus a contribution to stimulating and informing interest in a subject which lies at the very heart of how the people of Scotland relate to their country and how they will enter the next millennium – as a society with a

[52] Kenneth Reid, 'Beneficial Interest and the Land Registration Act of 1979', in Andrew J. M. Steven, Ross G. Anderson and John MacLeod (eds), *Nothing So Practical as a Good Theory: Festschrift for George L. Gretton* (Edinburgh: Avizandum, 2017), pp. 194–209. I am grateful to Malcolm Combe for this reference.

[53] Robin Callander, *A Pattern of Landownership in Scotland with Particular Reference to Aberdeenshire* (Finzean: Haughend Publications, 1987); Robin Callander, *How Scotland is Owned* (Edinburgh: Canongate, 1988).

[54] AKBLP, John McEwen Papers, MS 164/5/354, Callander to McEwen, 30 July 1986; McEwen to Callander, 2 August 1986; Callander to McEwen, 8 August 1986. The book that sparked this exchange was Robin Callander and John Hulbert (eds), *Land: Ownership and Use* (Longforgan: Andrew Fletcher Society, 1986).

firm grip over its future or as a society drifting past the kind of opportunities that could transform the lives of everyone fortunate to live in a country of immense potential.[55]

This point of view is in a clear line of descent from the Victorian and Edwardian period but more important is the fact that in this pre-devolution period Wightman was engaged in the task of trying to push land reform onto the political agenda.

An important model for land reform emerged in the early 1920s but was barely noticed at the time. This was the idea of community ownership. It is striking that most of the debate on the Scottish land question in the period since the 1880s has involved legislative proposals, rather than ideas that have emerged from the grass roots. Community ownership has, to a degree, broken this cycle. Since the early 1990s this approach appears to have broken the logjam of Scottish land reform. As we have seen, since the 1920s, land nationalisation has no longer been a realistic option; no government, of any political hue, has shown interest in using the land settlement powers that remained on the statute book. Community ownership emerged in the early 1990s in the cases of attempts, many of them realised in time, to purchase estates from private landowners. In the cases of Assynt, Eigg, Knoydart and Gigha the precise models that were followed were different from each other in subtle ways but each of them sought a release from the capriciousness of the private landowner to avoid the suffocating embrace of the state.[56] There are, however, historical precedents. When Lord Leverhulme abandoned his estates in the island of Lewis in 1923 he claimed that he wanted to pass all of his land to the community that lived on it. Given the economic circumstances of the time and dormant state of the land market, this was less altruistic than it might seem. Nevertheless, although this offer was

---

[55] Andy Wightman, *Who Owns Scotland?* (Edinburgh: Canongate, 1996), p. xi; see also his *Scotland: Land and Power, the Agenda for Land Reform* (Edinburgh: Luath Press, 1999) and *The Poor Had No Lawyers* (Edinburgh: Birlinn, 2010).

[56] Cameron, 'Unfinished Business', pp. 83–114; J. MacAskill, *We Have Won the Land* (Stornoway: Acair, 1999); Isobel MacPhail, 'Land, crofting and the Assynt Crofters Trust: a post-colonial geography', PhD thesis (University of Wales, Lampeter, 2002); Alistair McIntosh, *Soil and Soul: People Versus Corporate Power* (London: Aurum Press, 2001), pp. 131–47, 170–95, 262–78; Camille Dressler, *Eigg: The Story of an Island* (Edinburgh: Polygon, 1998), pp. 147–93; A. Fiona D. MacKenzie, *Places of Possibility: Property, Nature and Community Land Ownership* (Oxford: Wiley Blackwell, 2013); Catherine Czerkawska, *God's Islanders: A History of the People of Gigha* (Edinburgh: Birlinn, 2006); Brian Wilson, 'At last Gigha is freed from the petty power of the big house', *West Highland Free Press*, 21 March 2002.

rejected by the representatives of those who lived beyond Stornoway, 70,000 acres in and around that town was passed to a trust elected by the residents of the town and its surroundings. Although the Stornoway Trust has been in existence for nearly a century its development has been difficult and for much of the period since 1923 the environment has been as unsupportive of community ownership as of land nationalisation.[57] There was an attempt to use the concept of community ownership to deal with the 'problem' of the government-owned crofting estates in the early 1990s but despite quite advanced plans and some support from the Scottish Crofters Union, the idea was not taken forward.[58]

In conclusion, if we consider the history of the debate on the Scottish land question from the high point of interest in the period from 1880 to 1920 to the advent of the devolved Scottish Parliament in 1999, there is a certain level of continuity. The land question has remained in the bloodstream of Scottish politics and in the cultural memory of Scotland. Partly this is related to a seemingly continual need to adopt the rhetoric of atonement for the Clearances. The land question survives in the political traditions represented by the modern Labour, Scottish National and Liberal Democrat parties. Further, the survival of crofting tenure keeps a technical aspect of the issue on the political agenda. Before the 1930s, however, land reform was seen as a way of effecting comprehensive social reform through taxation and redistribution. It is worth remembering, although it has been largely forgotten, that the coalition government of the early 1920s redistributed substantial areas of land in the Highlands, taking much of it into public hands. By this period the transformational capacity of land reform was not so much emphasised. In the post-1945 period the land question drifted to the edges of Scottish political debate but it did not disappear and when Scottish politics became reanimated in the 1960s it emerged from the shadows. Interesting new ideas, such as community ownership (discussed in detail in Chapter 7), have developed and have been implemented but the land question has not quite recovered its centrality to comprehensive social reform in the way that would have been understood in the years before the Great War.

[57] James Hunter, *From the Low Tide of the Sea to the Highest Mountain Tops: Community Ownership of Land in the Highlands and Islands of Scotland* (Kershader: Ravenspoint, 2012), pp. 31–6; MacAskill, *We Have Won the Land*, pp. 177–98; Roger Hutchison, *The Soap Man: Lewis, Harris and Lord Leverhulme* (Edinburgh: Birlinn, 2003), pp. 181–218.

[58] *West Highland Free Press*, 9 March 1990, 3 August 1990, 6 December 1990, 12 April 1991, 19 April 1991, 21 June 1991.

PART II

Law

6

Earth and Stone: History, Law and Land through the Lens of Sasine*

Andrew R. C. Simpson

IN EARLY AUGUST 1317, a seventeen-year-old woman named Ada appeared before a court of the burgh of Aberdeen.[1] The court was made up of the burgesses, those who held privileges to trade in the town, and presiding over the court were the bailies, who had been elected from amongst their number.[2] In the presence of the bailies and the burgesses, Ada asserted that she had a claim in relation to some lands in the Gallowgate. She told a long story, reconstructed here from the fragmentary court roll, of how her family had once undoubtedly held good title to those lands. She then explained how her family had fallen on hard times. Consequently, they had borrowed money from one Master Roginald of Buchan to pay their debts. Roginald, doubting the ability of Ada's family to repay the loan, asked them to put up some land as security for the debt. The mechanism used to achieve this was relatively simple. One member of Ada's family transferred land he owned in the Gallowgate to Roginald,

---

* I am grateful to George Gretton and to Hector MacQueen for their comments on this chapter. Any errors remain my own.

[1] For this dispute, see W. Croft Dickinson, *Early Records of Aberdeen 1317, 1398–1407* (Edinburgh: Scottish History Society, 1957), pp. 3–7; reference has been made to an unpublished translation of the court roll of 1317 found in ibid., pp. 3–17, which is being prepared for publication by the author of the current chapter and Dr Jackson Armstrong of the University of Aberdeen. The case is discussed in P. Chalmers, 'Remarks on the Law of Burghs concerning Delivery of Lands within Burgh', in John Stuart (ed.), *Spalding Club Miscellany Five* (Aberdeen: Spalding Club, 1852), p. 49–55. The surviving account of the case is fragmentary, nonetheless, the reconstruction given here seems to be supported by the evidence. This will be discussed further in the introduction to the transcript to be published by the present author and Dr Armstrong.

[2] For the governance of the medieval burghs, see, for example, Croft Dickinson, *Early Records of Aberdeen*, pp. xxxii–xl, pp. lxxvii–xc; see also E. Patricia Dennison, *The Evolution of Scotland's Towns* (Edinburgh: Edinburgh University Press, 2018), p. 31–8.

but the grant was made subject to a power on the part of the debtors (Ada's family) to recover them once the debts were paid.

Ada's story then took a rather dramatic turn. She explained that Roginald had subsequently forfeited the lands he held in security due to his rebellion against the king, Robert I (r.1306–29). This probably meant that Roginald had been aligned with some of the king's most powerful political enemies, the Comyn earls of Buchan. Their defeat at the battle of Inverurie in 1308 enabled the king to carry out reputedly ferocious reprisals against the Comyns' former supporters.[3] Following those reprisals, Roginald probably lost the lands given to him by Ada's family in security for the debts owed to him. Once they had been forfeited, the king granted the lands to one of his own supporters, William of Lindsay, rector of Ayr.

Ada's family had left Aberdeen during these conflicts, but now she, the heiress of the lands, had returned, and was asserting her claim. However, it seems that she could not pay the remaining family debt that would have allowed her to redeem the lands. In order to extinguish her claims to the lands in the Gallowgate completely, William of Lindsay decided to buy Ada out. She consented to this, and so she declared her wish to transfer the lands to William before the burgesses of Aberdeen. At Ada's request, the court of the burgh then rose, leaving their place of meeting – perhaps the old tolbooth by the Shiprow[4] – and headed for the lands in the Gallowgate themselves. There, in the presence of the assembled burgesses of the town, Ada and William of Lindsay engaged in a ceremony to give him the same entitlement to the lands that Ada's ancestors had once held. How this was achieved is described in some detail in the record. First, Ada handed a silver penny *de uttoll* to the bailie of the burgh, one Thomas, son of Reginald. Simultaneously, William handed a similar penny *de intoll* to the same official; these were payments made to enter into burgh property.[5] Second, and still in the presence of the full court, William was formally put into possession of the lands by Bailie Thomas, perhaps by symbolically giving him earth and stone lifted from

[3] On this conflict, see G. W. S. Barrow, *Robert Bruce*, 4th edn (Edinburgh: Edinburgh University Press, 2005), p. 227–8.

[4] E. Patricia Dennison, Anne T. Simpson and Grant G. Simpson, 'The Growth of Two Towns', in E. Patricia Dennison, David Ditchburn and Michael Lynch (eds), *Aberdeen Before 1800: A New History* (East Linton: Tuckwell Press, 2002), p. 13–43 at p. 19–21.

[5] For this aspect of the ceremony, see Joanna Kopaczyk, *The Legal Language of Scottish Burghs: Standardization and Lexical Bundles 1380–1560* (Oxford: Oxford University Press, 2013), p. 130–1.

the lands themselves, as was required in the ceremony of sasine at a later date.[6] Here Bailie Thomas was acting on behalf of the feudal superior of the burgh, who was, of course, the king, Robert I.[7] Simultaneously, as the record attests, Ada handed over a written charter making a grant of the lands in favour of William of Lindsay. The clerk of the burgh recorded that the transfer was done 'according to that law of the burghs, through which it is said, delivery of lands in burghs ought to be made with charters and with acclamation'.[8]

The story comes from the first entry in one of the earliest surviving court rolls detailing a transfer of lands in Scotland. It also draws attention to the topic that will be discussed in this chapter. Legally speaking, the possession of the lands which was given in 1317 by Bailie Thomas to William of Lindsay was described in the burgh court roll as *sasine* of the lands. As one legal historian has put it, '[t]o have sasine was to have been put into possession of land by the grantor, typically although not invariably the lord of whom the lands were to be held.'[9] As this implies, at this time sasine was essentially a state of fact, that is to say possession given on the authority of the feudal lord of the lands (also known as the 'superior'). In giving sasine to another, the lord would either act personally, or through an officer who would act on his command or 'precept'.[10] In the case of the burghs, the lord – the king himself – gave authority to the burgh bailies to act on his behalf in granting sasine.[11] Next, in all instances where a lord or his representative sought to fulfil the precept or decision to give sasine, two additional things had to be done. In the first place, the lord or his representative had to adhere to the forms required by law to give sasine. The burgh records discussed here indicate that the payment of the pennies of *intoll and uttoll,* the public investiture of the grantee in the lands and the equally public acts of the handing over of a charter and acclamation, were such formal requirements in the burgh

---

[6] George L. Gretton, 'The Feudal System', in Kenneth G. C. Reid, *The Law of Property in Scotland* (Edinburgh: Butterworths, 1996), para. 90; at an early date, earth and stone, rather than 'hasp and staple' as mentioned here by Gretton, could be used in the burghs – see Kopaczyk, *Legal Language*, p. 130–1.

[7] Croft Dickinson, *Early Records of Aberdeen*, pp. xxii–xl.

[8] Ibid., p. 7.

[9] Hector L. MacQueen, *Common Law and Feudal Society in Medieval Scotland*, classic edn (Edinburgh: Edinburgh University Press, 2016), p. 140.

[10] Gretton, 'Feudal System', para. 89.

[11] Note that the bailies' authorisation to give sasine of burgh lands was implied – see Gretton, 'Feudal System', para. 65.

of Aberdeen.[12] In the second place, contemporary practice indicates that the charter was required to outline certain things to explain the nature of the sasine conferred. In any age, delivery of possession is a bare act, unless one has some way of determining the quality of possession given. So, the charter might have narrated that sasine had been given for a fixed period of time, for life for example. Alternatively, the charter might have narrated that the grantee had received sasine *in feudo et hereditate* – in fee and heritage. Strictly speaking, this meant that when the original grantee died, his heirs were entitled to receive sasine of the lands from their lord on the terms outlined in the original grant.[13] Thus, for a valid transfer of lands or claims in land at this time, first there had to be authority from the lord of the lands to give sasine; second, there had to be a public act of sasine; and third, there had to be a charter explaining the intended legal consequences of the sasine.[14]

Why is this of any relevance to the present volume, which is concerned with land reform in contemporary Scotland? If a historical overview is desired in order to contextualise modern discussions on the topic, then one might be forgiven for thinking that the relevant overview would simply be concerned with the development of 'land law'. The difficulty is that the *category* of land law has existed for a relatively short time in Scottish legal history, and so any history of that *category* of law would simply be anachronistic. Alternatively, one might suggest that a history of land *ownership* would be suitable here. Again, the difficulty is that the modern concept of 'ownership' has changed radically since the medieval period. [15] By contrast, one legal institution which *has* been developed continuously in relation to claims affecting land for the last 850 years or so is that of sasine. Giving of sasine came to be seen as an essential element in the constitution of any *right* in land; and the effects of that doctrine, often pithily stated as '*nulla sasina, nulla terra*', continue to

[12] On the ceremony, see, for example, Gretton, 'Feudal System', para. 89–90; as regards the ceremony in the burghs, see also Kopaczyk, *Legal Language*, p. 130–1.

[13] See, for example, MacQueen, *Common Law*, pp. 113–14; Gretton, 'Feudal System', para. 63–70: for some important contextualised comments on the development of the term '*feudum*' in twelfth-century Scotland, see Alice Taylor, *The Shape of the State in Medieval Scotland* (Oxford: Oxford University Press, 2016), p. 45–53.

[14] This analysis follows that found in G. Donaldson, 'Aspects of Early Scottish Conveyancing', in Peter Gouldesbrough (ed.), *Formulary of Old Scots Legal Documents* (Edinburgh: Stair Society, 1985), pp. 153–86 (particularly at pp. 165–75).

[15] For shifting concepts of '*dominium*' over the centuries, see David L. Carey Miller, 'Transfer of Ownership', in Kenneth Reid and Reinhard Zimmermann (eds), *A History of Private Law in Scotland* (Oxford: Oxford University Press, 2000), vol. 1, p. 269–304.

reverberate today.[16] As a result, by studying the history of sasine one can address many questions that those interested in the historical development of claims and rights in land might wish to pose.

Writing a comprehensive history of sasine would require at least one book-length study; the present chapter is necessarily highly selective. It will proceed by discussing individual disputes or cases which illustrate key developments in the history of sasine. The first section will consider medieval mechanisms used to regulate disputes relating to grants of sasine. The second section will explore one way in which the medieval process of giving sasine was reconceptualised in light of the influence of Roman law and canon law during the early modern period. The third section will consider how the formalistic processes of feudal conveyancing were extensively reformed during the nineteenth and twentieth centuries.

As the story develops, it will be shown that the development of the Scottish system of *transfer* of land gradually came to be the province of legal experts and, ultimately, professionals. They drew on their expertise to develop and adapt that system to contemporary needs. If it is hoped that this area of Scots law shall continue to show such flexibility, such an expectation will probably continue to be directed first and foremost towards the profession. For the purposes of this book, one point that emerges from the discussion of more recent history is that any proposed reforms to the law relating to transfer of land that do not extensively engage the views of legal practitioners are unlikely to sit easily with Scottish legal culture as it has developed – for good or ill – over the past few hundred years. Of course, any judgement on the merits and drawbacks of that culture is beyond the scope of the present chapter.

DISPUTES OVER SASINE: THE ROLE OF THE BRIEVES AND THE SCOTTISH COMMON LAW

The ways in which disputes relating to grants of sasine were regulated can be introduced by considering a grant of lands made more than a century before Ada appeared before the bailies and burgess of Aberdeen in relation to her claim to lands in the Gallowgate. Seen in context, the grant must have involved a giving of sasine by the lord of the lands of Balfeith in the Mearns in 1197. While the charter granting the lands is not, in itself, particularly interesting for the present study, what is interesting is that other evidence reveals the grant of sasine had only been

---

[16] Gretton, 'Feudal System', para. 89 (discussed further below).

made possible following the resolution of a dispute. The dispute also serves to introduce many of the key legal actors who were charged with the administration of justice, and indeed with making and enforcing grants of sasine.[17]

a) Transferring the lands of Balfeith

The act whereby the lands of Balfeith were transferred seems to have followed the pattern already identified, as can be seen from the text of a charter confirming the transfer. The charter was granted by Humphrey de Berkeley, a prominent nobleman in the Mearns, in favour of Arbroath Abbey. The document can be approximately dated to 1197, and it is preserved today in a cartulary that was once kept by the Abbey. It narrates that Humphrey de Berkeley had established the boundaries of his lands of Balfeith after they had been 'perambulated . . . according to the assize of the realm, in front of the lord Matthew, bishop of Aberdeen and Earl Gilbert, earl of Strathearn' by 'men of standing of the lord king in Angus and the Mearns'. [18] This had been done so that Humphrey, who seems to have held the lands from the king *in feudo et hereditate*, could give sasine of the same lands to God, St Thomas Becket and the monks of the Abbey. While evidence is lacking on the point, the act of giving sasine itself may have involved the handing over of earth and stone; in a later period, different symbols were used depending on the nature of heritable property being handed over – to name a few examples, net and coble were used for fishings, an oar and some water were used for rights of ferry and for an annualrent – a right to an annual income from the property – earth, stone and a coin.[19]

In giving sasine, Humphrey seems to have followed the three steps

---

[17] The account given here of the dispute draws on G. W. S. Barrow, *The Kingdom of the Scots*, 2nd edn (Edinburgh: Edinburgh University Press, 2003), p. 57–67; Dauvit Broun, 'The king's brithem (Gaelic for "judge") and the recording of dispute-resolutions', Feature of the month no. 11, *Paradox of Medieval Scotland 1093–1286*, April 2010, <http://paradox.poms.ac.uk/feature/april10.html> (last accessed 1 April 2019); and Taylor, *Shape of the State*, pp. 312–13. Note the word 'sasine' does not feature in the original documents, but Broun, 'The king's brithem', draws on internal evidence to argue convincingly that the conclusion of the dispute over the lands was immediately followed by a ceremonial transfer of the lands – i.e. with the ceremony of 'sasine', albeit that Broun does not use the word himself. Reproducing Broun's argument in full is beyond the scope of the present article, but the present chapter assumes it is correct.

[18] Broun, 'The king's brithem'.

[19] Gretton, 'Fedual System', paragraph 90 (see paragraph 112 for the annualrent).

necessary to give sasine outlined above. First, he had clearly authorised the transfer; indeed, he may have been present at the time of the
perambulation to carry it out personally. Second, Broun has argued
convincingly that he, or his representative, had carried out the formal
ceremonial transfer of the lands to the Abbey following the conclusion of
the perambulation, once the boundaries of the lands were clear. In other
words, he formally gave sasine of the lands to the Abbey at this point.
Third, he declared the nature of the grant in a charter. He explained that
the monks were to hold Balfeith from Humphrey 'in free and pure and
untroubled alms'.[20] This was a different form of holding from that mentioned above, *in feudo et hereditate*, and indeed from a holding of lands
in burghs ('burgage' lands), commonly described as holdings '*in feudo
et hereditate ac in libero burgagio*'. Grants *in feudo et hereditate* were
often made in exchange for some military service to the granter, while
grants *in feudo et hereditate ac in libero burgagio* were often made for a
very nominal return of 'watch and ward' (the defence of the burgh).[21] By
contrast, in exchange for a grant 'in free and pure and untroubled alms',
the monks had to fulfil a different condition of service in order to hold
the lands perpetually. Typically, as in this case, the granter required the
grantee to say masses for his soul, the souls of his family and the souls
of the royal family of Scotland. It was believed that this sort of gift could
help those for whom the masses were said, in that those services might
expedite the beneficiaries' exit from purgatory after death.[22]

b) An underlying dispute

For present purposes, what is intriguing here is that the three steps of
authorising transfer, giving sasine and declaring what had been done
in a charter were *preceded* by the process known as 'perambulation'.
As already stated, this had established the boundaries of the lands in
which Humphrey de Berkeley himself had been saised by the king; and
that, in turn, revealed how much land Humphrey had at his disposal
to give to Arbroath Abbey.[23] A little more about the dispute can be
gleaned from a remarkable document preserved in another cartulary

[20] Broun, 'The king's brithem'.

[21] See, for example, Gretton, 'Feudal System', paragraphs 64–5; MacQueen,
Common Law, pp. 34–5.

[22] Gretton, 'Feudal System', paragraph 66 (see paragraph 66, n. 1 for the phrase
'tenure by alms').

[23] On perambulation, see now above all Taylor, *Shape of the State*, pp. 312–5.

of Arbroath Abbey. This records a declaration made on 11 November 1221 before Alexander II (r.1214–49) and the royal court assembled at Forfar, perhaps in the old royal castle there. The declaration was made by a man named Mael Brigte, who described himself as a *judex* of the lord king. The statement given by the *judex* was reduced to writing in a brief document, to which the *judex* added his seal 'for the greater security of this business for the future'; this document was subsequently copied into a cartulary of Arbroath Abbey.[24]

Standing before the king and his courtiers, the *judex* declared that he recalled how he had helped to resolve a dispute between Humphrey de Berkeley and Walter, son of Sibbald. He remembered that the dispute was about the boundaries of certain lands, specifically the lands of Balfeith in the Mearns. This had been resolved by means of a perambulation carried out 'according to the assize and custom of the realm'; note that a similar phrase can be found in the charter of 1197.[25] The *judex* then narrated that following this procedure had made it necessary to enlist the help of various men local to the Mearns. These were individuals who knew the boundaries of the lands well, and all had Gaelic names. Mael Brigte the *judex* assured the king and his advisers that this had been done with great care. He stated that he had produced holy relics in the presence of the men who were to declare the boundaries, who may be termed here the 'perambulators'. He had then asked the perambulators to swear an oath on the relics that they would declare the boundaries of the lands truthfully, according to their knowledge. Furthermore, they had been asked to swear that they would do this 'neither on account of any gift nor on account of fear of Humphrey de Berkeley, who was sheriff at that time'.[26] Why was Humphrey's role as a sheriff significant here? In brief terms, the sheriff was a royal officer who possessed a range of roles in relation to royal governance and administration. By the 1220s, and indeed earlier than that, sheriffs presided over territorial units known as sheriffdoms. Within those areas, the sheriff was a powerful figure, responsible for the administration of the king's laws and for the collection of revenues due to the monarch. Much of the kingdom was divided into sheriffdoms by this point; and yet large areas remained outwith the sheriffdoms too, as will be explained shortly.[27] The point that should be

[24] Broun, 'The king's brithem'.
[25] Broun, 'The king's brithem'.
[26] Ibid.
[27] On contemporary sheriffs and sheriffdoms, see Taylor, *Shape of the State*, pp. 195–210.

noted is that it is not difficult to imagine why the perambulators might have been afraid of, and biased towards, Humphrey de Berkeley.

The act of walking around the lands was also to be carried out in the presence of one of the justices of Scotland, Gille Brigte, earl of Strathearn. The justice – later known as the justiciar – came to have a role in supervising the work of the sheriffs. Perhaps as early as the 1220s, the justiciar's ayres were becoming established, in the course of which the justiciar would go from sheriffdom to sheriffdom, hearing serious disputes and auditing the work of the sheriffs. In this case, the presence of Gille Brigte the justice may have been meant to provide some added oversight that everything was done properly in the resolution of a dispute in which a powerful local royal official had a direct interest.[28]

Mael Brigte then recalled how the perambulators had walked around the lands of Balfeith. Presumably it was the case that he and the justice, Earl Gille Brigte, walked with them. In this way, Mael Brigte the *judex*, the justice and the perambulators established the boundaries of Humphrey de Berkeley's lands. As a result, the dispute between him and Walter, son of Sibbald was resolved, facilitating Humphrey's grant of sasine of the lands of Balfeith in favour of Arbroath Abbey. The detailed list of perambulators given in 1221 by Mael Brigte the *judex* is remarkably similar to that in the list of 1197, right down to the level of the order in which the names of perambulators was given. This has led one historian to suggest that Mael Brigte had kept his own written records of the dispute of 1197, on the basis of which he gave his declaration before the king in Forfar in 1221.[29] While the role and figure of the *judex* is shadowy, it is clear that in Gaelic-speaking Scotland the *judices* were, among other things, trusted to uphold procedures used in the resolution of disputes and to know and remember matters relating to boundaries of lands.[30]

c) Dispute resolution and standardised procedures in medieval Scotland

For present purposes, what matters most is that a pattern can probably be identified here which is undoubtedly visible in other near-contemporary records. The pattern is as follows: a command to give sasine of lands

---

[28] Literature on the justice is evaluated critically in Taylor, *Shape of the State*, pp. 210–44.

[29] Broun, 'The king's brithem'.

[30] Taylor, *Shape of the State*, pp. 114–35.

could be coupled with a perambulation, where the boundaries of the lands were unclear or disputed. The establishment of the boundaries by perambulation would then be followed by the act of sasine. In turn, that act of sasine would precede, or occur simultaneously with, the delivery of a charter explaining the nature of the sasine. In fact, this pattern had been established, at least for use *in some cases*, for several decades. So in one charter, dated between 1173 and 1214, the king confirmed a gift of lands made to Dryburgh Abbey, stating that this was land 'which Robert son of Werenbald, my Sheriff of Lanark . . . perambulated and saised by my command'.[31] In other words, the king had commanded his sheriff to establish the boundaries of the lands in question, and then to give sasine of the lands. The charter also made it clear that sasine *had*, in fact been given, and then went on to narrate the basis on which this had happened. Similarly, in a charter dated sometime between 1165 and 1173, William I (r.1165–1214) confirmed grants of land that royal officers had 'perambulated and saised' in favour of Newbattle Abbey in 1162.[32]

What was perhaps a little different in 1197 was one of the points that Mael Brigte the *judex* restated in his declaration of 1221. The perambulation, he maintained, had been carried out 'according to the assize and custom of the realm'.[33] In other words, it seems that at some point a Scottish monarch had laid down a law governing how perambulations were to be carried out. The text of this law is not known to have survived. What did survive was a standardised procedure of perambulation, which could, where boundaries of lands were unclear, precede the giving of sasine of those lands.[34] That standardised procedure came to be articulated in a royal writ known as a brieve.[35] The brieve would be addressed by the king to a royal officer, in landward areas the sheriff or the justiciar, and in the burghs the provost and bailies, and instruct that officer to resolve the particular dispute at hand. Early formularies, or collections of standard forms, of brieves, survive from the fourteenth century, and these contain the text of the brieve of perambulation;

---

[31] G. W. S. Barrow, *Regesta Regum Scottorum II: The Acts of William I* (Edinburgh: Edinburgh University Press, 1971), pp. 294–5.

[32] Barrow, *Regesta II*, pp. 161–2.

[33] Broun, 'The king's brithem'.

[34] See Taylor, *Shape of the State*, pp. 312–5 (which discusses the dispute considered here). The insight relating to fact that perambulation often preceded sasine was noted by Donaldson, see Donaldson, 'Aspects', pp. 167–8.

[35] For the medieval brieves, see MacQueen, *Common Law*; see also now Taylor, *Shape of the State*, pp. 266–348.

early-fourteenth-century evidence shows that this brieve had also been known as the brieve of sasine, perhaps because perambulation was so closely linked to the giving of sasine of disputed lands.[36] An early version of the brieve of perambulation may have been used to commence proceedings in the dispute between Humphrey of Berkeley and Walter, son of Sibbald.[37]

The formulary that makes reference to the brieve of sasine, which is contained in an important manuscript of standardised royal letters and brieves known as the Ayr Manuscript, is dated between 1323 and 1346.[38] This reveals that Scottish monarchs had developed a wide range of standardised procedures to deal with questions or disputes relating to sasine during the course of the thirteenth century. One standardised procedure that was commonly used in practice was outlined in a brieve known as a brieve of inquest. In this, the king addressed the sheriff, instructing him to convene an assize – effectively, an inquest set up to discover the truth of a matter – consisting of good and faithful men of the sheriff's locality. They would not have been dissimilar from the 'men of standing of the lord king' who had perambulated Balfeith. According to the terms of the brieve, the assizers were then required to answer certain questions concerning a deceased person, on the one hand, and an individual claiming to be his or her heir, on the other. For example, the assizers were asked to determine whether or not the deceased had held lands of the king heritably, and they were asked whether or not the deceased had died a loyal subject of the monarch. The sheriff then had to return the finding of the inquest to the king. Depending on the findings, the king might then issue a subsequent *breve de saisina post inquisicionem*, instructing the sheriff to give sasine of the lands to the heir.[39]

Other brieves, also attested in the Ayr Manuscript, dealt with more contentious matters. These, like the brieve of perambulation, came to be directed to the justiciar, or to those holding special commissions to act with the powers of justiciars in specific disputes. An important example is the brieve of novel dissasine, which was introduced through a law promulgated by Alexander II in 1230. This applied where an individual had once been saised of lands, and had then subsequently

[36] See A. A. M. Duncan, *Scottish Formularies* (Edinburgh: Stair Society, 2011) on the brieve of sasine, and its link with the brieve of perambulation, compare no. A9 (p. 14) with E73 (p. 90).

[37] Taylor, *Shape of the State*, p. 313.

[38] Duncan, *Scottish Formularies*, p. 9; the Ayr MS formulary is given at p. 11–36.

[39] Duncan, *Scottish Formularies*, p. 19 (A22), p. 53 (E11), p. 62 (E27). For the brieves of inquest, see, above all, Taylor, *Shape of the State*, pp. 323–43.

lost sasine unjustly and without a judgement. The individual in question, on proving his claim before an assize, was entitled to be immediately re-saised of his lands.[40] Slightly different was the brieve of mortancestry, which may also have been introduced in 1230, and which was operational by the 1250s at the latest. Suppose an individual claimed that to be the heir of a close relative, and that the close relative had died vest and saised of lands *as of fee*, in this instance meaning on a heritable basis. Suppose too that the same individual claimed that the lands were now unjustly withheld from him by a third party. In that case, the brieve of mortancestry provided an immediate remedy; if he could prove his case before an assize of the good men of the locality, then he would be entitled to be re-saised of the lands immediately.[41] A third brieve, the brieve of right, enabled the courts to look into the deeper question of who was actually *entitled* to sasine, without making direct reference to who actually *had* been saised in the recent past.[42]

d) The emergence and scope of the brieves explained

Therefore, by the early fourteenth century, Scottish monarchs had developed an elaborate system of brieves. Many articulated procedures designed to protect the grants of sasine of land that they, and indeed others, within the realm had made. It might be asked what had generated the impetus to develop procedural protections for grants of sasine in the late twelfth and thirteenth centuries. Indeed, it might also be asked where the procedures governing the giving of sasine had come from. It is well-known that the Scottish brieves, and the system of transfer of lands that they protected, were couched in and adapted from the legal procedures and language of contemporary England. The brieve of novel dissasine is modelled on the writ of novel disseisin; the brieve of mortancestry is modelled on the English writ of mort d'ancestor; the whole Scottish concept of sasine was originally modelled on the English seisin; and Scottish charters drew inspiration from English feudal grants of land.[43] Yet this does not explain *why* these procedures and mechanisms

---

[40] Duncan, *Scottish Formularies*, p. 14 (A9), p. 18 (A21); MacQueen, *Common Law*, pp. 136–66; Taylor, *Shape of the State*, pp. 285–93, p. 308.

[41] Duncan, *Scottish Formularies*, p. 18 (A20); MacQueen, *Common Law*, pp. 167–87; Taylor, *Shape of the State*, pp. 308–9.

[42] Duncan, *Scottish Formularies*, p. 17 (A18–A19); MacQueen, *Common Law*, pp. 188–214; Taylor, *Shape of the State*, pp. 315–18.

[43] See MacQueen, *Common Law*, pp. 24, 136–7, 167–8, 188–9, 252–3; see also the conclusions drawn in Taylor, *Shape of the State*, pp. 438–55.

for granting lands were adapted to be used in Scotland at this time. Briefly, the answer that makes best sense of the available evidence stems from the fact that William I (r.1165–1214) and his son Alexander II (r.1214–49) wished to consolidate their political position against internal dynastic rivals and the external threat of domination by successive monarchs of England. To do this, they decided to give extensive gifts of land to their supporters to secure their loyalty. In addition, they made gifts of land to the church and to the new burghs in order to advance spiritual and economic reforms that they were promoting within the kingdom at the time. Yet to articulate and protect those gifts of land, appropriate legal language and procedures were required. Neither seem to have been developed in the customs of Gaelic-speaking Scotland; and so, mechanisms for making and protecting grants of land were borrowed and adapted from contemporary England for use in Scotland.[44]

This desire to protect grants of land led them to develop the framework of remedies found within the brieves. It has been argued in the past that the brieves were commonly available to the subjects of the Scottish king, and that as a result they were used to enforce a Scottish 'common law'. However, this last claim is disputed, and rehearsing the parameters and current state of the debate is beyond the scope of the present chapter. Nonetheless, two things ought to be made clear. First, in geographical terms, there is considerable discussion over whether or not the common law was, in fact, actually common at all. It was stated above that the surviving brieves were addressed to Scottish royal officers, who operated in and through the sheriffdoms and the burghs. It was also stated that large territories within the kingdom lay *outwith* the sheriffdoms. These were the great provincial lordships of earls and others who came to hold land in what was known as 'regality'. Grants of land in regality often conferred extensive jurisdiction upon the grantees, to such an extent that the royal officers of justice – the sheriffs and the justiciars – were often excluded from hearing disputes in those territories. That meant, in turn, that brieves addressed to the sheriffs and the justiciars could have no effect within the regalities, which by the fourteenth century covered about half of the kingdom. For the purposes of the present article, this raises serious questions about whether or not the surviving evidence tells us much about the giving and protection of sasine across vast swathes of the realm.[45]

[44] See Taylor, *Shape of the State*, pp. 26–83, pp. 438–55.

[45] See MacQueen, *Common Law*; Taylor, *Shape of the State*; David Carpenter, 'Scottish Royal Government from an English Perspective', in Matthew Hammond

Legal historians debate the question of whether or not the king also addressed brieves that mirrored those addressed to the sheriffs and justiciars to the great territorial earls and lords of regality.[46] Regardless of the answer, what is clear is that these lords were expected to *replicate* the brieves and procedures used in the king's courts within their own jurisdictions. What is also clear is that from the late twelfth century onwards, territorial lords who held jurisdictional privileges were required to invite the local sheriff or his representative to attend their courts so as to ensure that those courts were conducted properly. In other words, the sheriffs and the justiciars may not have had any *direct* jurisdiction within the great lordships; but they did possess a *supervisory* jurisdiction there. Furthermore, if the great lords were found wanting in their administration of justice, they would face disciplinary consequences. Given that this is so, there may be some reason to believe that there would have been broad consensus across the kingdom concerning the nature of sasine, and how it was to be protected and enforced, during the medieval period.[47]

One rule that was articulated with reference to the concept of sasine was, in principle, commonly applicable by 1318 at the latest. This rule, promulgated in statute by Robert I, was to the effect that no one could be ejected from land of which he claimed to have been vest and saised as of fee without the king's pleadable brieve or some similar brieve – perhaps a reference to brieves issued by lords of regality in imitation of those issued by the king. This exemplifies the point that a Scottish common law had come into being. The perceived need to give protection to those who had been justly saised of lands lay close to its heart.[48]

(ed.), *New Perspectives on Medieval Scotland 1093–1286* (Woodbridge: Boydell and Brewer, 2013), pp. 117–59; and Andrew R. C. Simpson, 'Foreword: Common Law and Feudal Society in Scholarship since 1993', in MacQueen, *Common Law*, pp. xxix–lxi. On the regalities, see Alexander Grant, 'Franchises north of the border: baronies and regalities in medieval Scotland', in Michael Prestwich (ed.), *Liberties and Identities in the Medieval British Isles* (Woodbridge: Boydell and Brewer, 2008), pp. 155–99.

[46] See Taylor, *Shape of the State*, pp. 326–32; MacQueen, *Common Law*, p. 194.

[47] The point, developed in Taylor, *Shape of the State*, is summarised at ibid., pp. 346–7. See also Alice Taylor, 'Crime without punishment: medieval Scotland in comparative perspective', in D. Bates (ed.), *Anglo-Norman Studies 35: Proceedings of the Battle Conference 2012* (Woodbridge: Boydell and Brewer, 2013), pp. 287–304. On the replication of the king's brieves by the great feudal lords, see MacQueen, *Common Law*, pp. 112–13.

[48] For the 1318 brieves rule, see, for example, MacQueen, *Common Law*, pp. 105–35; the statute of 1318 can be found at K. M. Brown, et al. (eds), *The Records of the Parliaments of Scotland to 1707 (RPS)* (St Andrews, 2007–19), <http://www.rps.ac.uk/> (last accessed 1 April 2019), 1318/27.

SASINE TRANSFORMED: THE INFLUENCE OF EXPERT LAWYERS

The legal world of the bailies who heard Ada's claim to the lands in the Gallowgate in 1317 operated on certain basic assumptions. Trusted royal servants, noblemen and clergymen administered justice across the realm. In so doing, they did not generally draw on any formal education as such – raising obvious questions about how uniform their work actually was – but rather on their extensive experiences of operating the mechanics of the system. It should be emphasised that the implementation of the system over which they presided, and the resolution of disputes thrown up by it, was heavily dependent on the input, involvement and – above all – collective memory of reputedly good and trustworthy men within each locality. Under the supervision of experienced bailies, sheriffs, justiciars and the like, it was they who determined the boundaries of lands in perambulations, they who sat on inquests to determine the suitability of an heir to receive sasine of lands, they who determined whether or not a dissasine had been wrongful, and they who decided where ultimate feudal title lay in disputes initiated by brieve of right. The effectiveness of the system depended, on the one hand, on such individuals' knowledge of the legal position of their neighbours, and, on the other, on the experience of the officials who operated the procedures of the common law.[49]

This legal world was transformed in the fifteenth, sixteenth and seventeenth centuries. The experience of the royal officers and the knowledge of those who sat on the assizes came to be seen by litigants as insufficient guarantors of justice. It came to be felt that the increasingly complex legal world of late-medieval Scotland could only be handled by those with some legal expertise and formal training.[50] This, in turn, fundamentally reshaped the law relating to the transmission and protection of sasine. Such changes to the law, and their deeper causes, can be introduced through the lens of another dispute which was heard in 1587.

---

[49] I am grateful to Graeme Small, and also to John Ford, for first helping me to formulate this point in relation to another study on the extent to which it is appropriate to speak of 'men of law' in medieval Aberdeen; see Andrew R. C. Simpson, 'Men of Law in the Aberdeen Council Register? A Preliminary Study, ca.1450–ca.1460', *Juridical Review* (2019), 136–59. Any errors in this regard remain my own. See also Andrew R. C. Simpson, 'Men of Law in the Aberdeen Council Register? A Preliminary Study Revisited, c. 1450–1460', in J. Armstrong and E. Frankot (eds), *Cultures of Law in Urban Northern Europe: Scotland and its Neighbours c. 1350–c. 1700* (Routledge, forthcoming).

[50] See note 49 above.

a) A dispute over warrandice

On 29 July 1587, an expert lawyer and advocate, Thomas Craig of Riccarton, presented a supplication to parliament in Edinburgh on behalf of his client, Elizabeth Stewart, countess of Moray.[51] The dispute was over the countess's duty to honour an obligation in relation to certain lands in which she had 'infeft' another, Sir John Wishart of Pittarow. To explain, she had formally given sasine and entered him into the lands as the superior – she had infeft him in the lands.[52] Now she wished to dispute her duty to honour an obligation she owed him known as 'warrandice', by which she was required to uphold his infeftment in the face of a contrary claim.[53] The lands in question lay within the earldom of Mar, which had reverted to the Crown during the fifteenth century. The Crown transferred large territories within the earldom to different individuals, including James Stewart, earl of Moray, and Elizabeth Stewart's father. Moray had, in turn, granted some of the lands he had received from the Crown to his own vassal: Sir John Wishart of Pittarow. So Pittarow was infeft in lands he held from Moray as Moray's vassal, which Moray, in turn, held from the Crown as the Crown's vassal. Nonetheless, a difficulty arose in the mid sixteenth century. The heir to the old earldom of Moray, John, Lord Erskine, pursued a successful claim to be given the title of earl of Moray in 1565. While he was thereafter John Erskine, first earl of Moray, at that stage he did not simultaneously recover any of the old lands of the earldom. But in 1587 his son, John, second earl of Moray, petitioned Parliament to be served heir to the extensive territories of the earldom of Mar. He was, ultimately, going to succeed. At a stroke, Parliament was about to leave all of those recipients of grants of territories from the earldom of Moray over the past century with no legal basis for retaining the lands.[54]

---

[51] See *RPS*, 1587/7/94; the dispute is discussed in Andrew R. C. Simpson, 'Legal Learning and the Prescription of Rights', in Harry Dondorp, David Ibbetson and Eltjo Schrage (eds), *Limitation and Prescription: A Comparative Legal History* (Berlin: Duncker and Humblot, 2019), pp. 263–95 at pp. 276–7. Some points about the dispute have been clarified here.

[52] On the meaning of infeftment, see Gretton, 'Fedual System', para. 93.

[53] On warrandice in this context, see MacQueen, *Common Law*, pp. 45–7.

[54] On this background to the dispute, see Julian Goodare, 'Erskine, John, eighteenth or second earl of Mar (c.1562–1634), courter and politician', *Oxford Dictionary of National Biography* (Oxford: Oxford University Press, 2004), available at <http://www.oxforddnb.com/view/10.1093/ref:odnb/9780198614128.001.0001/odnb-978 0198614128-e-8867> (last accessed 1 April 2019).

This scenario presented a serious problem for Sir John Wishart of Pittarow, and many others; he had been infeft in lands within the earldom of Mar, but now it was about to be declared by Parliament that his superior – the countess of Moray – had had no right to infeft him in the lands in the first place. In other words, he was going to lose the lands. Once Parliament ratified Erskine's claim, Wishart would not, of course, be left without a remedy. He would be entitled to sue the countess of Moray for breach of her obligation of warrandice – which had passed to her from her father – which required her to uphold his sasine of the lands and his infeftment. Nonetheless, one cannot help but sympathise with the countess. Her father had put Wishart into the lands in good faith, on the basis that the lands were held directly from the Crown, and that they had indeed been held by the Crown for over a century. Surely, a contemporary might have argued, the fact that landholding within the earldom of Mar had been settled for such a long period of time would have made it seem reasonable to conclude that transfers of lands from the earldom would not be disturbed in this alarming manner.

Craig, the countess's expert lawyer, sought to advance such an argument. He maintained that where rights in land had subsisted for a long period of time, this should give rise to *some* legal protections for the holders of the rights in the event that an attempt was made to disturb them. He lamented the fact that once Wishart's infeftment was taken away, this would

> strike upoun the said Countes of Murray contrair all equitie and ressoun, seing hir said umquhile fader wes in *bona fide* the tyme of the alienatioun and resignatioun thairof foirsaid, having ane prescriptioun for sa lang ane tyme for his grund thairanent.[55]

The meaning of the word 'prescription' will be discussed shortly. As a result, he maintained that the countess 'aucht to be relevit of all warrandice of the said alienatioun'. He concluded that if Parliament were to ratify Erskine's right to recover the earldom lands – which it was about to do – then at the end of the act of ratification it should be provided that

> personis quha *bona fide*, groundit upoun the lang prescriptioun of tyme, hes maid ony dispositioun of the saidis landis of the erldome of Mar, or ony pairt thairof . . . be relevit of all warrandice of ony dispositioun of the samin warrandice.[56]

---

[55] *RPS*, 1587/7/94.
[56] Ibid.

In the end, Parliament did not take this course of action, but it did agree to appoint 'amicable compositouris' to adjudicate in the dispute between the countess of Moray and Wishart of Pittarow.[57] What is intriguing for present purposes is Craig's allusion to doctrines of *prescription* as being relevant to the matter at hand. Broadly speaking, doctrines of prescription could entail that rights in things, such as land, could be constituted through long possession – or long *sasine*, in a Scottish feudal context – subject to certain other criteria being satisfied. As will be explained shortly, a specific doctrine of prescription, when combined with developments in the law relating to the giving of sasine, would ultimately have a significant effect on the law relating to feudal landholding in Scotland. It will be seen that Craig's juristic writings on prescription may have been influential in shaping these reforms.

For now, it is important to note that, in attempting to make use of doctrines of prescription, Craig was drawing on his legal expertise *in utroque iure*, or 'both the laws', meaning the learning that had grown up around the surviving texts of ancient Roman law and the canon law of the Roman Catholic Church. Hereafter these legal traditions will be referred to as the learned laws.[58] It is thought that Craig, like many advocates of his time, had studied the learned laws in France. Having acquired this expertise, he then familiarised himself with the laws and 'practick' of Scotland, before being admitted as an advocate to plead before the lords of session in 1563; these lords were judges in a court sometimes called the 'session'.[59] The session had acquired de facto supreme jurisdiction in all Scottish civil matters – including disputes concerning the validity of infeftments, and, consequently, the validity of acts of sasine at some point shortly prior to 1532. In 1532, the court was reconstituted as a College of Justice, and from the outset there was an expectation that the judges and men of law or advocates who staffed it would possess a sophisticated education in the learned laws, and consequently legal expertise.[60] It is necessary to make a few brief comments here concerning the emergence of this court, because its

[57] Ibid.

[58] On the influence of the learned laws, see, for example, Peter Stein, *Roman Law in European History* (Cambridge: Cambridge University Press, 1999), pp. 1–103.

[59] See John W. Cairns, 'Craig, Thomas (1538?–1608), lawyer and jurist', *Oxford Dictionary of National Biography* (Oxford: Oxford University Press, 2004), available at <http://www.oxforddnb.com/view/10.1093/ref:odnb/9780198614128.001.0001/odnb-9780198614128-e-6580> (last accessed 1 April 2019).

[60] John W. Cairns, 'Revisting the foundation of the College of Justice', in Hector L. MacQueen (ed.), *Stair Society Miscellany Five* (Edinburgh: Stair Society, 2006),

members ultimately used their expertise *in utroque iure* to reshape the whole of the Scottish common law, including the law relating to giving of sasine.

b) Fifteenth-century problems in the administration of justice

It was noted earlier that the effective operation of medieval Scots law relied on two things. First, it depended on the extensive (and not necessarily homogeneous) experience possessed by certain officials, such as sheriffs, justiciars and bailies, in the administration of the procedures of the common law. Second, it depended on the knowledge of prominent, trustworthy men in each locality in order to discover the truth of any particular matter, so as to resolve questions or disputes regarding the facts to which the procedures of the law were to be applied. During the course of the fifteenth century, Scottish litigants began to complain that those seeking justice in their disputes could rely neither on the experience of the officials who administered the common law nor on the knowledge of trustworthy men in each locality. There were complaints to the effect that the processes over which the judges and assizers presided were fraught with delay. Perhaps more seriously, it was sometimes argued that the officials who administered the law – who often held office on a hereditary basis – lacked sufficient understanding of the increasingly complex laws that they were required to administer. [61] Indeed, even where the officers did not hold office through hereditary right – as in the burghs – there is evidence from fifteenth-century Aberdeen to suggest that sometimes they felt unable to answer some fairly basic questions.[62]

---

pp. 27–50; Mark A. Godfrey, *Civil Justice in Renaissance Scotland* (Leiden: Brill, 2009), pp. 106–26.

[61] MacQueen, *Common Law*, p. 257–8.

[62] This can be found in the corpus of materials about to be published online as *Aberdeen Registers Online: 1398–1511* at <https://www.abdn.ac.uk/aro> by the Law in the Aberdeen Council Registers (LACR) project, see <https://aberdeenregisters.org> (last accessed 1 April 2019). The LACR project team was led by Jackson Armstrong. A preliminary version of LACR Search, a search tool, was used here to facilitate search within the LACR Corpus. This preliminary tool was based on the application created under the supervision of Adam Wyner by Radostin Stoyanov, Marcel Zak, Cameron Beck, Jack Burn, and Jan Siemaszko, and published in 2017 under licence at <https://github.com/team-charlie/lacr-search/blob/master/LICENSE> (last accessed 18 September 2019). References to the corpus follow those used in the online resoure, they are in the format 'ARO-5-0036-05', 'ARO' being the reference to the Council Registers, volume 5, page 36, entry 5. For the case discussed here, see ARO-5-0602-01, 20 March 1467.

If royal officers, to whom the administration of justice fell, struggled to answer these sorts of questions, it has also been suggested that the problem became more acute as the fifteenth century wore on. Those officers, together with the assizers on whose knowledge they relied, were at the same time finding it difficult to deal with the sophisticated legal documents and devices that were being generated by an increasingly commercial society. As MacQueen has put it, 'by the fifteenth century, cases turned not on what the assizers had seen and heard themselves but on the interpretation of complicated technical documents (which might be forged)'.[63] The range of documentation that might be put before members of assizes seems to have expanded significantly in the fifteenth century. For example, in 1469 Parliament intervened to regulate the situation where the debtor transferred lands to his creditor in security of a debt and subject to a device known as a letter of 'reversion', which bound the creditor – and, from 1469, the creditor's disponees – to return the lands to the debtor on repayment of the debt.[64] The proliferation of technical deeds in practice contributed, in turn, to a related phenomenon also mentioned by MacQueen – namely, anxiety that such documents may have been forged.[65]

c) *Addressing problems in the administration of justice*

For such reasons, it was increasingly felt that the traditional royal officers of justice and the assizes lacked the training and expertise required to do justice. It has been argued in the past that Parliament agreed; in 1496, it required members of the nobility to send their sons – who might go on to administer their fathers' feudal and other hereditary courts – to attend 'sculis of art and jure, sua that thai may have knawlege and understanding of the lawis'.[66] This initiative was consistent with a policy pursued throughout the fifteenth century, which was to make the local courts function effectively through a mixture of education and procedural reform.[67] Yet none of those efforts seem to have satisfied litigants. Through the century, many petitioned the king and his closest advisers in the king's council directly to provide them with justice. The

---

[63] MacQueen, *Common Law*, p. 257.

[64] *RPS*, 1469/17.

[65] MacQueen, *Common Law*, p. 257.

[66] Ibid.; *RPS*, A1496/6/4.

[67] See the discussion and the sources cited in Andrew R. C. Simpson and Adelyn L. M. Wilson, *Scottish Legal History Volume One: 1000–1707* (Edinburgh: Edinburgh University Press, 2017), pp. 115–9.

council had a residual jurisdiction to deal with a range of matters, including complaints from widows, orphans and clergymen and – critically – complaints that royal officers, such as sheriffs, had defaulted in the administration of justice.[68] Over the course of the fifteenth century, probably under pressure from litigants, the jurisdiction of the council was developed and extended by Acts of Parliament. From 1488, the council began to sit more regularly in judicial 'sessions', and gradually the jurisdiction of the conciliar sessions expanded. Again, this probably occurred as a result of pressure from litigants. It has been argued in the past that one of the factors that underpinned the developing jurisdiction of the sessions was that the judges who sat in the sessions – known as 'lords of session' – were frequently senior clergymen who possessed significant expertise in the learned laws. Consequently, they were able to draw upon that expertise in developing the law so as to resolve the increasingly complex disputes that were being thrown up by Scottish society in the late fifteenth century.[69]

Nonetheless, the jurisdiction of the council, and consequently of the lords of session, was limited by two important factors. First, actions initiated by brieves, which were primarily addressed by the king to royal officials such as sheriffs and the bailies of the burghs, could not be heard by the council, in which the king himself sat.[70] Second, the jurisdiction of the lords of session was limited by what was known as the 'fee and heritage' rule. In brief terms, it seems that this meant that *if* two competing titles to heritable property were in dispute, and *if* deciding the dispute would involve a 'final determination of right' between the parties, *then* in that situation the lords of session believed that they were bound to remit the matter in question to the judicial officer who would ordinarily have heard the dispute (often called the 'ordinary judge'). The fee and heritage rule seems to have been a relic of an older and much broader rule, to the effect that council had no jurisdiction over matters where a remedy was available in the ordinary courts of the common law.[71]

During the first two or three decades of the sixteenth century, the lords of session developed their jurisdiction to circumvent such procedural

---

[68] MacQueen, *Common Law*, p. 220.

[69] Godfrey, *Civil Justice*, pp. 40–160; Cairns, 'Revisiting the Foundation'.

[70] Godfrey, *Civil Justice*, p. 21.

[71] MacQueen, *Common Law*, pp. 218–42, which must now be read in conjunction with Godfrey, *Civil Justice*, pp. 268–312, on which the the analysis presented here is based.

barriers. In so doing, they gained supreme jurisdiction over all civil matters in Scotland, including those arising from defective deliveries of sasine, even where competing heritable titles were under consideration. Even in the late fifteenth century, it is clear that they had jurisdiction over what were known as actions of error. Suppose a bailie in a burgh, or a sheriff, and an assize had reached a decision following on from a brieve of inquest to give sasine to, and so infeft, an individual, 'A', in lands as heir to a deceased individual, 'B'. Suppose then a party, 'C', claimed that this had been done in error, for example as a result of partiality on the part of the assize against him. The lords of session had jurisdiction to hear that claim, and to reduce the infeftment in favour of 'B'. The lords' jurisdiction to reduce infeftments in this way – which was at least in part based on a statute of 1471 – expanded over the course of the next few decades to circumvent the fee and heritage rule.[72] This can be seen from a dispute decided in 1531 (*Spittal* v. *Spittal*). Here, two competing titles to heritable property which were asserted by Archibald Spittal and Finlay Spittal. One might have thought that the jurisdiction of the lords would have been barred as a result. Nonetheless, Archibald Spittal did not seek to show that his title was superior to that of Finlay, rather, he focused on attacking Finlay's title, and brought an action to have his infeftment – and so sasine – in the lands reduced. In this, Archibald was successful. This left Archibald as the only individual with any sort of title to the property in question. He then brought an action against Finlay for wrongous occupation of the lands, and had him ejected from them.[73]

Developments like this meant that, before 1532, the lords had acquired de facto supreme jurisdiction over Scottish civil matters, including all matters relating to the validity of deliveries of sasine. That meant that disputes over heritable title, for example, could be brought before the lords.[74] It had also become possible for proceedings taking place in lower courts to be transferred to the lords by means of a process known as 'advocation'. This guaranteed the lords' supervisory jurisdiction over all lower courts.[75] Furthermore, actions like those for error and reduction of infeftment gradually left the old brieves of right, novel dissasine and mortancestry with no useful function in practice, at least in the minds of the lords of session. As a result, they were

---

[72] For the summons of error, see Godfrey, *Civil Justice*, pp. 231–5.
[73] Ibid. pp. 338–40.
[74] Ibid. pp. 313–54.
[75] Ibid. pp. 192–6.

subsequently able to declare with confidence that the brieve of right had fallen out of use.[76]

In 1532, the old conciliar session was reconstituted and placed on a new institutional footing as a College of Justice. Arguably this was done in part to prevent those powerful members of the king's council who lacked legal expertise from trying to influence the decisions reached within the conciliar sessions. From 1532, the advocates and judges who sat in the new College of Justice would generally be expected to possess expertise in the learned laws.[77] They went on to use that learning to reshape and reinterpret the medieval common law of the realm,[78] and concepts such as sasine and infeftment were gradually transformed as a result.

d) Evidential problems and instruments of sasine

This was not the only major shift to take place during this period that affected the development of the law governing deliveries of sasine. During the fifteenth century, there is evidence that suggests litigants began to make more frequent demands for records of their transactions and disputes that would enjoy undoubted authority as being authentic in court. One can probably trace this rise in demand in medieval Aberdeen in the burgh's Council Registers – which survive in a near-continuous run from 1398 – during the 1440s.[79] It was mentioned above that there was a proliferation in the use of technical deeds in fifteenth-century legal practice, and that there was anxiety that some of those documents had been forged. Perhaps there was some direct link between this phenomenon, on the one hand, and the increased demand for documents that would always be deemed authentic, on the other. Regardless, the increasing demand for *authentic* documents or 'instruments' during the course of the fifteenth century generated business for a group of

---

[76] Ibid. pp. 449–53.

[77] Ibid, pp. 94–160; Cairns, 'Revisiting the Foundation'.

[78] For this process, see, for example, J. D. Ford, *Law and Opinion in Scotland During the Seventeenth Century* (Oxford and Portland: Hart, 2007), pp. 181–246.

[79] See ARO-4-0262-02, 8 January 1442; ARO-5-0686-01, 26 October 1444; ARO-5-0699-03, 6 April 1445; ARO-4-0399-05, 16 April 1445; ARO-5-703-01, 14 August 1445; ARO-4-0414-03, 12 September 1445; ARO-4-0444-08, 26 September 1446; ARO-4-0470-09, 23 February 1447; ARO-5-0057-02, 2 August 1449; ARO-5-0753-01, 29 May 1450.

individuals who might have been viewed by contemporaries as 'men of law'; they were the notaries public.[80]

Notaries were appointed on apostolic or imperial authority prior to 1469, when the Scottish monarch James III asserted the right to appoint notaries himself, to the exclusion of the Holy Roman Emperor.[81] Upon being constituted in the role, the notary's basic function was to produce written instruments – often in Latin – that would subsequently be trusted as authoritative records of transactions and disputes. Highly relevant to the present study is that notaries began to produce instruments of sasine, documents attesting the ceremonial giving of sasine.[82] The earliest surviving instruments of sasine date from the late 1300s, and their use became widespread during the 1400s.[83] This development occurred alongside a broader change in conveyancing practice, the full history of which has yet to be reconstructed. It was said earlier in this chapter that medieval transfers of land were frequently achieved in three stages. An oral or written precept might be issued to give sasine (and, more broadly, infeftment) of lands, then the ceremony of sasine would follow, and finally a charter would be granted confirming the giving of sasine and explaining the basis on which the transfer had been made. But during the course of the thirteenth, fourteenth and fifteenth centuries, this process began to change in some cases. Charters might be given *first*, narrating that a particular grant of lands was to be made. Second, a written precept might be given separately from the charter (and ultimately the precept was incorporated *into* the charter), instructing the granter's representative to give sasine. Third, there would follow the ceremony of sasine.[84]

It is important to stress that *both* processes of giving sasine continued to operate in the fifteenth century. For example, charters executed during the 1450s in Aberdeen survive which provided in one single document evidence of *both* the terms of a grant which had already been

[80] See, above all, John Durkan, 'The Early Scottish Notary', in Ian B. Cowan and Duncan Shaw (eds), *The Renaissance and Reformation in Scotland. Essays in Honour of Gordon Donaldson* (Edinburgh: Scottish Academic Press, 1983), pp. 22–40.

[81] Ibid., p. 26; *RPS*, 1469/20.

[82] See Durkan, 'Early Scottish Notary', p. 32.

[83] See W. W. Scott, 'William Cranstoun, Notary Public c.1395–1425, and some contemporaries', in Hector L. MacQueen (ed.), *Stair Society Miscellany Seven* (Edinburgh: Stair Society, 2015), pp. 125–32; Durkan, 'Early Scottish Notary'.

[84] Donaldson, 'Aspects', pp. 165–75.

made and *also* the ceremonial transfer of sasine.[85] Yet the importance of having written evidence of sasine was becoming established. The late-fifteenth-century decision in *Gibson* v. *Monypenie* (1488) required that claimants who alleged they held, or had held, lands in fee and heritage had to be prove their allegation by writ.[86] Furthermore, by the time of the decision of the lords of session in *Laird of Craigiehall* v. *Laird of Glenbervie* (1541), it had been explicitly determined that the formal ceremony of sasine could not be proven by witnesses, but – in general – only by 'autentique writ'.[87] In time, the requirement for an 'autentique writ' to be present in order to prove that the ceremony of sasine had taken place came to be equated with a requirement for a notarial instrument.[88]

The rule that sasine could only normally be proven by writ had important consequences. Sasine was, of course, a necessary prerequisite for infeftment in lands. As one sixteenth-century lord of session put it, quoting a fifteenth-century source, 'the chartour is of nane avail, gif na sasine follow thairupon'.[89] Consequently, if infeftment could not happen without sasine, and if sasine could not be normally proven except by an authentic writ, it followed that such a writ was, in effect, a necessary prerequisite for an infeftment. This may help to explain the later position, which was that the authentic writ or instrument of sasine itself came to be seen as an integral and essential element in the effective transfer of lands.

Instruments of sasine were to enjoy central importance in the development of Scottish feudal conveyancing. Yet their place within that system of conveyancing was about to be fundamentally reconceptualised and transformed in the hands of learned lawyers who were members of the College of Justice. Amongst those lawyers, one of the most influential

---

[85] See, for example, Aberdeen University Library (AUL) Marischal 2/1/6/2/17, 20th February 1450; AUL Marischal/2/1/2/5, 31st May 1451; AUL Marischal/2/1/2/6, 20th May 1454.

[86] Peter G. B. McNeill (ed.), *The Practicks of Sir James Balfour of Pittendreich*, 2 vols (Edinburgh: Stair Society, 1962–63), vol. 2, p. 363, as discussed in James J. Robertson, 'The development of the law', in Jennifer M. Brown (ed.), *Scottish Society in the Fifteenth Century* (London: Edward Arnold, 1977), pp. 136–52 at p. 149.

[87] McNeill (ed.), *Balfour's Practicks*, vol. 2, pp. 363–4.

[88] Gretton, 'Fedual System', paragraph 89.

[89] McNeill (ed.), *Balfour's Practicks*, vol.1, p. 187; for the source, and its date, see J. J. Robertson, *'De Composicione Cartarum'*, in *Stair Society Miscellany One* (Edinburgh: Stair Society, 1971), pp. 78–93.

was the advocate with whom this section of the present chapter began: Thomas Craig of Riccarton.

e) Legal learning and prescription

Prior to his death in 1608, Craig completed his monumental *Jus Feudale in Tribus Libris Comprehensum*. In it, he sought to promote a transfer of authoritative learning from Roman law, canon law and feudal law into Scots law in order to augment the laws of the Scottish realm.[90] His treatment of infeftment provides an example of how that learning was used to develop the law relating to delivery of sasine. It has just been explained that charter alone was insufficient to transfer title to lands; there had to be charter and sasine. Drawing on the work of the contemporary session, Craig rationalised that proposition in terms that were evidently indebted to the learned laws. He explained that 'from the charter, a personal action alone is competent'. By contrast, 'from the sasine is born the real action'. Craig added that this proceeded on the assumption that the sasine had been given in accordance with the will of the feudal lord of the lands.[91]

What did Craig mean when he said that charter without sasine only gave rise to a 'personal action', whilst charter *with* sasine gave rise to a 'real action'? He was alluding to a basic distinction originally drawn in Roman law between the *actio in personam* and the *actio in rem*. The *actio in personam* arose from some obligation, like a contract between two parties. In that case, the pursuer argued that the defender ought to convey something or to do something by virtue of the obligation in question. By contrast, the *actio in rem* arose from some claim the pursuer alleged in respect of a particular piece of property. In that case, the pursuer might argue that the defender was in possession of something which in fact belonged to the pursuer; the claim would be based not on obligation, but on the allegation that the disputed thing was the pursuer's own property.[92] The point that Craig was essentially making was that the charter might potentially give rise to an *actio in*

---

[90] Ford, *Law and Opinion*, pp. 215–46.

[91] Thomas Craig, *Jus Feudale Tribus Libris Comprehenshum* (Edinburgh, 1655), p. 138. In making my own translations of Craig's work I have referred to J. A. Clyde, *Jus Feudale* (Edinburgh: William Hodge, 1934). Clyde's work is not a wholly reliable translation – see J. W. Cairns, 'The *Breve Testatum* and Craig's *Jus Feudale*', *Tijdschrift voor Rechtsgeschiedenis*, 56 (1988), pp. 311–32. An excellent translation is currently being produced by Leslie Dodd and published by the Stair Society.

[92] See, for example, W. W. Buckland, *A Text-Book of Roman Law from Augustus*

personam against the granter to give sasine to the lands granted. By contrast, a charter coupled with sasine of lands would give the grantee a direct claim in the lands, and that would be sufficient to ground an *actio in rem*. Such an *actio in rem* could, for example, be used to recover the lands from one who had wrongfully taken possession. Craig also stated that, according to the custom of Scotland, infeftment would generally only be treated as valid where it could be proven by writ. Taken together with his earlier comments, that meant that such written evidence of sasine would, in his mind, have been required before the *actio in rem* would be available in respect of land.[93]

The use of the ultimately Romanist distinction between the *actio in personam* and the *actio in rem* is only one rather basic example of how Craig drew upon his expertise and legal learning to expound the law of Scotland governing infeftment. A related distinction would go on to have considerable significance in the later law. It is also helpful here to mention one other instance where Craig drew upon his learning to argue that the Scots should be prepared to develop a more radical approach to the law relating to infeftment. In this, he returned to the concept of prescription. It will be recalled that doctrines of 'acquisitive' prescription, which had ultimately been developed from Roman law, permitted the acquisition of property if it had been possessed in certain circumstances over a long period of time. Other doctrines of 'extinctive' prescription could result in the *loss* of certain claims if they had lain unexercised and unenforced over a long period of time.[94]

Craig lamented the limited use of prescription in Scotland in his time. He thought that more extensive use of prescription might have addressed problems that arose from the central importance attributed to written evidence of infeftments in Scotland. He commented that the sons of noble houses frequently lost their inheritance 'by fraud, either of the widow, or of the members of the household, to whom the care of the muniments or written instruments had been entrusted, and the rights of which had been established properly from the beginning'.[95] Such fraudulent destruction of written titles could cost people their lands, sometimes decades after they had taken physical possession of them. Craig advanced learned argumentation to the effect that a doctrine of

---

to *Justinian*, 3rd edn, rev. Peter Stein (Cambridge: Cambridge Unviersity Press, 1963), pp. 674–8.

[93] Craig, *Jus Feudale*, pp. 137–8, 178.

[94] See, for example, Buckland, *Text-Book*, pp. 241–52.

[95] Craig, *Jus Feudale*, p. 125; see generally the discussion at pp. 125–7.

acquisitive prescription ultimately based on Roman law, and on the learned texts on feudal law, could be used to protect vassals and their heirs in these circumstances.[96] Drawing on such sources, he commented that a vassal should be able to acquire feudal title to land if he satisfied three criteria. First, he should have to demonstrate the *animus* or intention to be a vassal to the lord of the lands. If he sought to hold the feu on some other basis – such as pledge, or loan – then he could not, and should not, acquire feudal title by long possession. Second, Craig argued, the vassal should have to possess the feu continuously for thirty or forty years, depending on the nature of the feu in question. Third, he stated that acquisition of title by prescription should only follow if the vassal demonstrated at least one act of feudal service during the thirty- or forty-year period just mentioned. Craig expressly stated that if these criteria were to be satisfied then the vassal should not have to show any title in order to acquire the lands by prescription, because in such a case title would be presumed; this was the approach warranted by the learned laws. Effectively, Craig seems to have been arguing for the use of prescription to provide the courts with a mechanism to presume that the act of infeftment, and so the ceremony of sasine, had been carried out lawfully, even in the situation where relevant written titles had been destroyed. In so doing, he expressly claimed to be proposing a reform to the law that was consistent with the textual learning of the learned laws, which his contemporaries regarded as authoritative guides to the dictates of justice itself.[97]

f) The legislation of 1617

Craig's radical vision for the role of prescription in fortifying title to land never quite came to pass. Nonetheless, in 1594 Parliament did develop a rule that responded to some of Craig's concerns. It addressed the point that some of those who wished to demonstrate feudal title to land might be required to produce in court a fairly extensive 'progress' of titles, a range of documents, including precepts of sasine and other deeds. Parliament responded by providing that where a vassal had possessed land for forty years on the basis of a charter and an instrument of sasine that made reference to the other deeds necessary to establish title, then in that instance there was no

---

[96] Simpson, 'Legal Learning and the Prescription of Rights', pp. 276–82.
[97] Ford, *Law and Opinion*, pp. 215–46.

legal requirement to produce the full progress of writs to defend their position.[98]

This was a sign of things to come. In 1617, arguably acting on the legal advice and expertise of several lords of session, Parliament promulgated an important piece of legislation. This considered 'the gryit prejudice whiche his majesties liegis sustenis in their landis and heretages' as a result of the 'conceilling of thair trew evidentis in thair minoritie and les aige' and 'the injurie of tyme'. The Act continued by noting that the people were 'in a gryit uncertantie of thair heretable rightis and divers pleyis and actiounes ar moved aganes thame efter expyring of threttie or fourtie yearis, whiche nevirtheles by the civill law [i.e. Roman law] and be the lawes of all natiounes ar declaired voyde and uneffectuall'.[99] As a consequence, the Act effectively sought to introduce a type of acquisitive prescription for heritable property. It provided that an individual's heritable infeftment in lands would be established and put beyond challenge in one of two situations. The first was where he could produce a charter and an instrument of sasine relating to the lands which had been *followed* by forty years of continuous possession. The second was where he could produce a series of instruments of sasine of the lands on the basis of which he or his predecessors had possessed the lands, again over a forty-year period.

Simultaneously, the parliament of 1617 introduced a rule establishing a new public Register of Sasines.[100] The aim was to deal with the problems that arose from the fact that the rights in land established by infeftment could not be easily discovered at the time land was to be transferred. Individual notaries had, in the past, kept private collections of copies of instruments of sasine they created, known as 'protocol books'. In addition, past parliaments had attempted to create public registers of some deeds that were designed to evince the establishment of rights in heritable property. Nonetheless, these efforts had had limited success.[101] By contrast, the 1617 Act establishing the Register of Sasines was extremely effective. Part of the reason for this may have been that

---

[98] *RPS*, 1594/4/35.

[99] *RPS*, 1617/5/26.

[100] *RPS*, 1617/5/30.

[101] For registration before 1617, see L. Ockrent, *Land Rights: An Enquiry into the History of Registration for Publication in Scotland* (Edinburgh: William Hodge, 1942), pp. 65–72; K. G. C. Reid, 'From Registration of Deeds to Registration of Title: A History of Land Registration in Scotland', University of Edinburgh Research Paper Series 2015/29, available online at <https://papers.ssrn.com/sol3/papers.cfm?abstract_id=2655598>. See also Richard Rodger and Jennifer Newman,

there were serious consequences for failure to register instruments of sasine – which, as has been explained, were now effectively required to acquire title to heritable property. If an individual were to fail to register an instrument of sasine of lands transferred to him within sixty days, then the instrument would have no effect against a third party who subsequently acquired the lands and completed title to them. In other words, one who held a charter and an instrument of sasine in relation to certain lands might now be open to challenge in his tenure of those lands *unless* he were to record his instrument of sasine in the Register. This gave teeth to what was now evidently a central plank of parliamentary policy, to the effect that instruments of sasine, and so validly constituted rights in land, should be identifiable by the public at large.[102] With hindsight, one can observe that this development antici- pated the later emergence of what modern lawyers term the 'publicity principle'.[103]

g) *The transformative effect of legal expertise*

The legal institution of sasine was transformed during the course of the fifteenth, sixteenth and seventeenth centuries. This took place against a backdrop of deeper changes within contemporary Scottish legal culture. A system that had depended for its effectiveness on the experience of trusted royal administrators and judicial officers, on the one hand, and on the collective memory and knowledge of local 'assizers' on the other, had begun to run into difficulties. These individuals tended to lack the expertise that was sometimes required to make sense of the increas- ingly complex documents and instruments that were being generated to articulate legal transactions. As a result, pressure was placed upon the king and his council – which was staffed in part by senior clergymen with expertise in canon law and Roman law – to resolve such disputes. Gradually, under such pressure from litigants, the jurisdiction of the council – sitting in sessions – expanded to the point where it had acquired supreme jurisdiction in Scottish civil matters. In 1532, the old session was reconstituted as a College of Justice, and the lawyers who resolved dis- putes there drew upon their extensive Romano-canonical legal learning

'Property transfers and the Register of Sasines: urban development in Scotland since 1617', *Urban History*, 15 (1988), pp. 49–57, at pp. 49–50.

[102] *RPS*, 1617/5/30.

[103] See, for example, the discussion in Kenneth G. C. Reid, 'Equity Triumphant', *Edinburgh Law Review*, 1 (1997), pp. 464–9.

to reinterpret and transform the old procedures of the medieval Scottish common law – including the procedures relating to actions of error and reductions of infeftment, which helped to leave the old brieves of novel dissasine, mortancestry and right with no useful application in practice.

If the influence of legal experts reshaped the mechanisms whereby sasines were enforced, the same sort of influence reshaped the rules concerning proof that the ceremony of sasine had actually taken place. At one time, it was at least arguable that this could be established by witnesses. This was rejected in favour of an approach that written evidence was required. That development had only been made possible through the work of notaries public, at least some of whom may have possessed what one might term legal expertise. They met an increasing demand for the production of authoritative documents that would provide authentic records of transactions and disputes. Ultimately it was accepted only a notarial instrument of sasine would be recognised as proof that a ceremony of sasine – and so an infeftment – had actually taken place. Reflecting on such developments, legal experts in the College of Justice maintained that an infeftment could only be completed by charter, precept and sasine, with the latter being established by instrument of sasine. They recast such propositions in Romanist terms, concluding that while charter might, at best, give rise to an *actio in personam*, a charter followed by precept and a ceremony of sasine – if duly recorded in an instrument of sasine – would give rise to an *actio in rem*.

At the same time, at least some of those legal experts gradually came to recognise the problems associated with such a system. The necessity for the presence of a progress of feudal writs to establish title caused problems in practice when those writs were lost, destroyed or forged. It came to be accepted that the solution was twofold. First, the Prescription Act 1617 established that long possession on the basis of some writs – particularly instruments of sasine – should render the possessor's infeftment indefeasible. Second, the Registration Act 1617 established a public Register of Sasines, generating publicity around infeftments in land, and it was established that instruments of sasine that were not registered there within sixty days would be null and void as against third parties. That provided a powerful incentive to register such instruments.

The way in which these points came to be put by expert lawyers was the instrument of sasine, or, if necessary, long possession on the basis of an instrument of sasine gave the possessor what was termed a real *right* in the lands transferred. As one of the most influential jurists of the late seventeenth century, James Dalrymple, Viscount Stair, went on to put it, 'charters, or other writs . . . never become a real right till they be completed by seasin, which imports the taking of possession'.[104] Jurists like Stair also attempted to make greater sense of this last point, again making reference to the learning of Roman law:

> There may be three acts of the will about the disposal of rights; a resolution to dispone, a paction, contract or obligation to dispone, and a present will or consent that that which is the disponer's be the acquirer's. Resolution terminates within the resolver . . . paction does only constitute or transmit a personal right or obligation, whereby the person obliged may be compelled to transmit the real right. It must needs then be the present dispositive will of the owner, which conveyeth the right to any other . . . That the dispositive will is also sufficient to transmit real rights . . . appeareth . . . But, for utility's sake, not only the Romans, but almost all nations require some kind of possession, to accomplish real rights, that thereby the will of the owner may sensibly touch the thing disponed, and thereby be more manifest and sure; so the law saith, *Traditionibus et usucapionibus, non nudis pactis, dominia rerum transferuntur* . . . in property of lands . . . by infeftment . . . the disposition and natural possession makes no real right without seasin.[105]

Such masterly expositions of the law, and of the rationales underpinning it, demonstrate how extensively the legal world of medieval Scotland had been transformed in the hands of legal experts steeped in the learning of Roman law and canon law.

ADAPTATION OF FORM AND THE RE-INFUSION OF CIVILIAN PRINCIPLE

Extending this history to the nineteenth and twentieth centuries is challenging. While excellent work has been produced on specific developments during the nineteenth century in particular, there is still a considerable amount of work to be undertaken before legal historians can claim to understand fully major phenomena of the period, such as the extensive Anglicisation of the law.[106] Such contextual understanding is, of course, essential to any attempt to comprehend specific

---

[104] James Dalrymple, Viscount Stair, *Institutions of the Law of Scotland*, 2nd edn (Edinburgh: the heir of Andrew Anderson, 1693), II.3.16.

[105] Stair, *Institutions*, III.2.3–6.

[106] See, for example, Alan Rodger, 'The Codification of Commercial Law in Victorian Britain', *Law Quarterly Review*, 108 (October 1992), pp. 570–590; on the issue of Anglicisation, see Hector L. MacQueen, 'Pragmatism, Precdepts and Precedents: Commercial Law and Legal History', in Andrew R. C. Simpson, Scott Crichton Styles, Euan West and Adelyn L. M. Wilson (eds), *Continuity, Change and*

developments. For this reason, even providing snapshots in the history of sasine at this time is difficult.

Nonetheless, certain trends can be traced that develop themes already pursued within this article, and these will be discussed here. It has been observed that during the fifteenth, sixteenth and seventeenth centuries, legal experts and notaries public shaped the ways in which the old institutions of the medieval common law were interpreted and developed to meet the needs of the modern era. During the nineteenth and twentieth centuries their successors, who can by this point in time be termed without anachronism legal 'professionals', continued to provide the major impetus for further legal development. This trend found expression in at least two major ways.[107] First, it resulted in the simplification and adaptation of the forms surrounding transfer of sasine and the constitution of infeftments more broadly. Second, as the twentieth century progressed, there was a renewed emphasis in many quarters of the profession – and in particular in the increasingly assertive academic branch of the profession – on articulating the theoretical principles of property law that underpinned and gave meaning to the revised forms. Both points will be considered here briefly.

a) *The mysterious ceremony of infeftment*

By the late nineteenth century, the adherence of earlier generations of notaries and legal professionals more generally to the old forms of feudal conveyancing – ultimately inherited from the medieval period – had become an object of gentle ridicule. The following account of adherence to the forms was published in 1873, but it described the situation as it stood during the second decade of the nineteenth century:

> Another thing of the past, was the mysterious ceremony of infeftment . . . suppose that some fine property had been sold, and that the purchaser wished to be invested in the lands. How was this accomplished? Suddenly five human beings appeared in one of the fields, the leader and sole spokesman being a notary. Two of the band were his clerks, or at least could sign their names. The remaining two were *anything*, generally captured in the vicinity by the notary, only a few minutes previously, and of whom he knew

Pragmatism in the Law: Essays in Memory of Professor Angelo Forte (Aberdeen: Aberdeen University Press, 2016), pp. 10–42.

[107] On the contemporary development of the Scottish legal profession, see John W. Cairns, 'Historical Introduction', in K. G. C. Reid and R. Zimmermann (eds), *A History of Private Law in Scotland* (Oxford: Oxford University Press, 2000), pp. 14–184 at pp. 155–9, pp. 181–2.

nothing whatever. They might have been ... ditchers, packmen, cadgers, weavers, cobblers, herds, colliers ... The notary then, to the amazement of the parties, proceeded to dub, we shall say, a cadger, with the title of 'procurator and attorney', and a ditcher with that of 'bailie' ... The notary next, with a pleased air, pulled from a gaping outside coat-pocket, with flaps as broad as the ears of an elephant, a thickish paper, which he caused the cadger to shuffle to the ditcher, for a moment, uttering at the same time some words, to them perfectly unintelligible; then, snatching the paper from the ditcher, alias the bailie, the notary began to tell in a general way what it was, and, especially, that it contained in the tail of it a 'precept of sasine' ... Next he proceeded to mumble over 'the precept' very fast ... this galloping reading being ended, the notary wildly requested the ditcher, '*qua* bailie', to lift a handful of earth, with as many small stones in it as he could get, and to tear up another handful of grass and stubble; which two handfuls the ditcher was implored to present to the cadger, alias the 'procurator and attorney'. The latter gentleman ... received the dirt, the stones, the grass, and the stubble into his half-closed palms ... They were informed by the notary that these things were 'symbols' ... Suddenly the notary put a shilling into the cadger's hand ... [then] the notary wildly snatched it from him, and coolly replaced it in his own pocket, saying, with a grim smile, that he was 'taking instruments' ... the ditcher and the cadger received each a shilling for their pains ...[108]

This account was evidently written to convey the sense that the whole ceremony had become rather ludicrous, and overly concerned with preservation of form. Much of the old medieval ceremony had survived – the need for the superior to give sasine of the lands through his bailie on the lands themselves; the need for the grantee to receive sasine, in this case through one dubbed his 'procurator', or mandated representative; and, of course, the physical handing over of earth and stone. Yet while the turn of phrase is amusing, it hides a deeper truth. The medieval legal world in which the ceremony on the lands themselves had performed a useful function – which was, presumably, to publicise the fact of the transfer to the wider community – had been superseded by one in which publicity, and indeed the effectiveness of the transfer itself, was fundamentally established by the recording of notarial instruments in the Register of Sasines. What the story really tells the modern reader is that feudal conveyancing had, by the early 1800s, become almost entirely dominated by the work of the notary. In the medieval period, the roles

---

[108] See 'I S', 'Infeftment as it was', *Journal of the Law Society of Scotland*, 25:3 (1980), pp. 90–1; Gretton, 'Feudal System', paragraph 89. On the later history of sasine, see J. M. Halliday, 'The Tragedy of Sasine', *Juridical Review*, 10 (1965), pp. 105–16. I am grateful to Hector MacQueen for referring me to this article.

of the superior's bailies and trustworthy local witnesses was key for the functioning of the whole system of constitution and protection of title. Now the constitution and protection of title largely depended on the written deeds and instruments produced by notaries. Put another way, the importance of the different formal requirements for the constitution of title had shifted, and within the system the ceremony of giving sasine on the lands was left with almost no useful function. It was pure legal theatre, staged by the notaries out of fear that ignoring some aspect of the old ceremony would invalidate the instruments of sasine they produced.

These trends were recognised in the Infeftment Act 1845. This statute proceeded on the assumption just mentioned, namely that the whole system of conveyancing was, in reality, already dominated by notarial practice. Promulgated at the request of senior Scottish lawyers,[109] it established a formal process whereby notaries in possession of all of the writs or 'warrants' required to give sasine of lands in favour of their clients could simply proceed straight to the execution of an instrument of sasine, without having a ceremony of sasine on the lands. The legislation provided that such an instrument would then be treated as a *deemed* sasine, with the same strength and force of a sasine actually given on the lands.

Once this step had been taken, further reforms – again proposed and driven by senior legal professionals working within Scotland – were adopted. Some emerged through landmark decisions of the Court of Session, such as *Young* v. *Leith* (1847), which finally clarified that no real right in lands could be acquired without recording an instrument of sasine in the Register of Sasines.[110] Later examples of reform should be mentioned here briefly. The Titles to Land Consolidation (Scotland) Act 1858 provided that it was no longer necessary to record the instrument of sasine itself. It was possible, instead, to record the dispositive deed (e.g. the charter) that had been directed to the notary to preside over the giving of sasine of the lands, and this was deemed by statute to have the same effect that had formerly been attached to the recording of the instrument of sasine.[111] Under the terms of the Conveyancing

[109] See William M. Gordon, 'George Joseph Bell, Law Commisioner', in William M. Gordon, *Roman Law, Scots Law and Legal History: Selected Essays* (Edinburgh: Edinburgh University Press, 2007), pp. 211–30.

[110] *Young* v. *Leith* (1844) 6 D 370; (1847) D 932, affd (1848) 2 Ross LC 103, HL.

[111] Titles to Land Consolidation Act 1858; see Gretton, 'Feudal System', paragraph 91.

(Scotland) Act 1874 it was no longer necessary to involve the superior in the act of giving sasine of lands. This was important, because in many cases where lands were transferred, they were transferred by one vassal to another who was to become the new vassal of the superior. Involving the feudal superior of the lands had come to be seen as an unnecessary formality, and so this requirement too was dropped.[112] Out of these and other reforms emerged the basic system whereby real rights in land could be constituted by the recording of dispositions in the Register of Sasines. Where the disposition was in some way defective, recording in itself would not confer a real right upon the disponee. Nonetheless, even where this was the case, possession on the basis of the recorded deed could, by virtue of the Prescription Act 1617 and successor legislation, ultimately result in the disponee acquiring a real right in the lands.[113]

b) The law of property in Scotland

In 2004, the House of Lords (at the time the highest ranking civil court for Scots law cases) handed down a much-anticipated judgement in the case of *Burnett's Trustee* v. *Grainger*.[114] Briefly stated, the facts were as follows. Mrs Burnett entered into a contract (missives) to sell a flat to Revd Grainger. He paid the price and took possession. The disposition (that being the term still used for a deed of transfer for land) was delivered shortly after the sale, but Revd Grainger's solicitor failed to record it timeously in the Register of Sasines, as he ought to have done. Mrs Burnett then became bankrupt. Her trustee in bankruptcy was obliged to ingather her estate to distribute it among her creditors. On the orthodox view of Scots property law, she still owned the flat, because a real right in the flat could only have been transferred to Revd Grainger by virtue of the recording of the disposition in his favour. The trustee in bankruptcy then recorded notice of title to the flat. A month later, Revd Grainger's solicitor finally recorded the disposition that had been delivered to him over a year earlier.

The outcome of the dispute was of significant importance to Scottish judges, advocates, solicitors and legal academics. There was a matter of

---

[112] Conveyancing (Scotland) Act 1874; see Gretton, 'Feudal System', paragraphs 94–106.

[113] Kenneth G. C. Reid, *The Law of Property in Scotland* (Edinburgh: Butterworths, 1996), paragraphs 643, 674.

[114] *Burnett's Trustee* v. *Grainger*, 2004 SC (HL) 19.

deep legal principle at stake. This was the fundamental and unbridgeable divide between personal rights and real rights in Scots property law. As just stated, the orthodox position as to how the case ought to have been decided was very clear. At the conclusion of missives, Revd Grainger had nothing but a personal right, a contractual claim against Mrs Burnett alone. On delivery of the disposition, Revd Grainger still had nothing but a contractual claim, albeit that his solicitor now had the document that would, on being recorded in the Register of Sasines, enable his client to acquire a real right of ownership. Yet when Mrs Burnett's trustee in bankruptcy registered title before Revd Grainger, his claim took priority; he won what was called the 'race to the register'. In relation to Mrs Burnett's estate, Revd Grainger had nothing but a claim *in personam* for breach of contract, which was, of course, financially worthless, given that she was bankrupt. The problem was that this orthodox view had been called into question a few years earlier by the decision in *Sharp* v. *Thomson* (1997).[115] There it had been suggested by one senior judge that someone in a position very similar to the Revd Grainger might not have ownership of the property, strictly speaking, but might have what was termed 'beneficial ownership' of the flat. Recognising this intermediate stage between a pure personal right and the acquisition of the full real right of ownership was put forward as a way of doing justice to one who had paid the price for property and taken possession without completing title.[116]

This idea, which was borrowed from English law, was anathema to the basic principles of Scots law as they had been developed since the early modern period.[117] It will be recalled that the medieval system of feudal conveyancing at common law had been developed and interpreted by the legal experts who staffed the College of Justice. As a result, the forms of that system of conveyancing had been given meaning in light of the principles of Roman law and canon law with which they were so familiar. Relying on those principles, learned Scottish lawyers had concluded that neither the contract to acquire land, nor delivery of the charter, could confer a real right in the land. The real right could come only through the delivery of possession, which was achieved through the ceremony of sasine. Furthermore, only the instrument of sasine

---

[115] *Sharp* v. *Thomson*, 1997 SC (HL) 66.

[116] *Sharp* v. *Thomson*, 1997 SC (HL) 66 at 68–77, per Lord Jauncey.

[117] See the literature cited in Scottish Law Commission, *Report on Sharp* v. *Thomson* (Edinburgh: The Stationery Office, 2007), pp. 44–7. I am grateful to George Gretton for this reference.

was accepted as evidence that that ceremony had taken place; and after 1617, the instrument had to be recorded in the Register of Sasines within sixty days to have real effect against third parties. As has been seen, some of these steps were dispensed with in the nineteenth century, allowing the disposition itself to be recorded within the Register of Sasines. Thereafter, by recording the *disposition*, the transferee could acquire a real right. Yet what had not changed was the basic legal meaning attributed to each stage in the conveyancing process. At conclusion of the contract and the delivery of the disposition, the buyer of the land had nothing more than a personal right against the seller. *Only* on the recording of the disposition – which was deemed by statute to be the equivalent of the old ceremony of sasine in law – did the purchaser acquire a real right in the land.

It was that deeper question of the legal *meaning* of the formal devices used to convey land that was at stake in *Sharp* and *Burnett*. Was it the case that those devices would continue to be handled and interpreted in light of the fundamental distinction between personal rights and real rights, which was ultimately derived from Roman Civil law? Or would they be handled in light of a different interpretative framework, which could accommodate itself to English notions of 'beneficial ownership'? Ultimately the House of Lords reasserted the orthodox position in *Burnett's Trustee* v. *Grainger*. Only the act of recording the disposition could give the disponee a real right in the property transferred; before that point, he could have nothing more than a contractual claim against the transferor, in other words, a personal right.[118]

In passing, it is worth noting that many legal academics had passionately advocated the case for reliance on the basic principles derived from Roman law in *Burnett*.[119] They did this for a range of reasons; for example, it was seen as a means of promoting predictability and legal certainty, and in addition the existing authorities of the Scottish legal tradition did point to that being the correct outcome in the cases. Furthermore, the academics in question were arguing from the standpoint of an academic culture in which there had, over several decades, developed a renewed interest in the influence of Roman law in Scots law, and indeed in what could be learnt from other legal systems that were deeply indebted to Roman law, notably South African law and

---

[118] *Burnett's Trustee* v. *Grainger*, 2004 SC (HL) 19. The point of principle is reasserted in the Abolition of Feudal Tenure etc. (Scotland) Act 2000 section 4 and the superseding Land Registration etc. (Scotland) Act 2012 section 50.

[119] See the sources cited in n. 117 above.

German law. This had in part been stimulated by a concern that the survival of a distinctive system of Scots law was challenged by extensive Anglicisation.[120] Regardless, renewed focus on the study of Roman law was a factor that enabled the articulation of the principles of Scots law in systematic and scholarly works, such as Professor Reid's highly authoritative *The Law of Property in Scotland* (1996).[121] Those principles continue to give meaning to the forms used to transfer property, whether it be heritable or moveable.

CONCLUSION

Today, the Register of Sasines is closed to new dispositions.[122] More modern systems of land registration – which continue to respect the principles of property law just mentioned – have been gradually taking its place, as a result of the Land Registration (Scotland) Act 1979,[123] and the Land Registration etc. (Scotland) Act 2012.[124] One reason that these systems have come to enjoy favour is that they have brought with them the key benefit of a state indemnity guaranteeing title (the so-called 'Keeper's Warranty').[125] In addition, the whole feudal structure of Scots property law within which the giving of sasine operated was finally replaced on 28 November 2004, when the Abolition of Feudal Tenure etc. (Scotland) Act 2000 came into force.[126]

What, then, is the relevance of the present study to a book about land reform in Scotland? Fundamentally, it must be that it facilitates understanding of how the law came to be in its present state. On the surface, the article traces important moments in the development of the

[120] For aspects of this movement, see, for example, Kenneth G. C. Reid, 'While One Hundred Remain: T. B. Smith and the Progress of Scots Law', in Elspeth Reid and David L. Carey Miller (eds), *A Mixed Legal System in Transition: T. B. Smith and the Progress of Scots Law* (Edinburgh: Edinburgh University Press, 2005), pp. 1–29.

[121] Reid, *Law of Property*.

[122] Land Registration etc. (Scotland) Act 2012 (asp 5) section 48.

[123] Land Registration (Scotland) Act 1979 c.33.

[124] Land Registration etc. (Scotland) Act 2012 (asp 5).

[125] See Part 2 of the Land Registration (Scotland) Act 1979 c.33 and Part 7 of the Land Registration etc. (Scotland) Act 2012 (asp 5).

[126] Abolition of Feudal Tenure etc. (Scotland) Act 2000 (asp 5); for the date of the coming into force of the relevant provisions of the statute, see the Abolition of Feudal Tenure etc. (Scotland) Act 2000 (Commencement No. 3) Order 2003. On the abolition of feudal tenure, see generally Kenneth G. C. Reid, *Abolition of Feudal Tenure in Scotland* (Edinburgh: LexisNexis UK, 2003).

law regarding transfer of sasine. The formal procedures and ceremonies used in the medieval system of feudal conveyancing were interpreted by expert lawyers in light of legal principles drawn from Roman law and canon law. Forms of conveyancing ultimately descended from the old medieval system continue to operate today, even under the regime of the 2012 Act; there must still be a disposition, and this still must be registered, albeit now in the Land Register. Furthermore, the forms continue to be handled and interpreted in light of fundamental principles ultimately derived from Roman law, such as the unbridgeable divide between personal rights and real rights.

At a deeper level, the present study reveals something else about how the system of Scots property law that we know today has come into being. Since the early modern period, developments in the law have been dominated by what one might term increasing 'professionalisation'. Notaries and expert lawyers in the College of Justice transformed the medieval system of conveyancing in the fifteenth, sixteenth and seventeenth centuries. Subsequent generations of legal professionals succeeded in persuading the British Parliament to simplify the forms of conveyancing; and this was made possible by the fact that the system of transfer was already effectively realised through the work of notaries public, rather than, for example, through the old ceremony of sasine. In the twentieth and twenty-first centuries, there has been a renewed effort to give the revised forms meaning through reliance on Roman principles, and on the principles of legal systems ultimately derived from Roman law. Again, senior practitioners and academics have driven these developments.

Of course, these arguments could be used to overstate the point, and in turn to distort the truth. A range of different factors, such as political and economic pressures, have shaped the reform of land law and property law in the past; one need only think of the crofting reforms of the nineteenth and twentieth centuries to demonstrate that.[127] Yet the very brief introduction to the history of sasine presented here shows that the system of *transfer* of land has long been the province of professionals. Many have enriched it with their expertise, and adapted it to the needs of the society in which they have found themselves. Expectations that the Scottish system will continue to manifest such flexibility, while simultaneously upholding the basic principles of the law, will, in all likelihood, continue to be directed first and foremost towards the profession. Any proposed reform to this area of land law, at least, that does

---

[127] See MacLellan, in this volume.

not fully engage legal practitioners is unlikely to sit easily with the legal culture that has developed in Scotland over the past few hundred years. Of course, making any judgement about the merits or drawbacks of that culture is beyond the scope of this chapter.

7

Legislating for Community Land Rights

Malcolm M. Combe

THE SCOTTISH GOVERNMENT RECENTLY reiterated its commitment to bring one million of Scotland's acres into community ownership by the end of 2020. The policy shift towards community ownership, and the legislation that accompanies that shift, is a relatively new development in the Scottish land law reform process, operating within a mature system of property law that has traditionally afforded a great deal of importance to the entitlements that flow from ownership. Legislative routes for communities to acquire land are set out in the Transfer of Crofting Estates (Scotland) Act 1997, the Land Reform (Scotland) Act 2003, the Community Empowerment (Scotland) Act 2015, and the Land Reform (Scotland) Act 2016. Whilst the 1997 Act is about communities in the Scottish Highlands and Islands acquiring crofting land that happens to be in public sector ownership in a manner that is mutually beneficial, and there are certain similar rights for communities to request assets from a range of public bodies in the 2015 Act, the net effect of the 2003, 2015 and 2016 legislation opens up four methods for a community to acquire land from a private owner, in a manner that (on the assumption the legislation is complied with) either forces that owner to deal only with the community as and when the owner decides to sell or forces that owner to sell to the community as and when the community wishes to acquire.

These are striking and important powers, which are designed to play a role in Scotland's drive towards community ownership. This chapter considers the framework for and the practical impact of this approach to date, with reference to examples of acquisitions which have variously taken place in accordance with such statutory schemes, been driven by the prospect of those schemes as a fallback position, or occurred on ad hoc bases without any apparent reference to the modern legislation.

THE LEGAL LANDSCAPE

Both the Land Reform (Scotland) Act 2003 and the Land Reform (Scotland) Act 2016 contain provisions that are of importance to Scotland's land other than those which can steer or enable a change of ownership. In the case of the 2003 Act, its first Part sets out the scheme for the right of responsible access that allows recreational, educational and in some cases commercial use of the outdoors.[1] The 2016 Act contains provisions about: deer management; the dedicated public body charged with a land reform role known as the Scottish Land Commission; and (of general relevance to Scottish communities) engaging communities in decisions relating to land that may affect them.[2] These provisions are undoubtedly important, but they do not form the focus of this chapter. Instead, it considers the provisions in both statutes that aim to facilitate or, in some cases, compel transfer of land from an existing landowner to a community body. Away from the land reform brand, the Community Empowerment (Scotland) Act 2015 ('the 2015 Act') also introduced new rights of community acquisition that can be deployed against private landowners, by way of legislative amendment to the 2003 Act (introducing a new Part 3A to it). It additionally introduced a scheme that allows communities to take on assets from the public sector. This chapter also analyses these.

None of this analysis should be taken as implying the well-developed system of property law that existed in Scotland before the recent legislation was passed is unimportant. Scots law is generally described as being a 'mixed' legal system, formed of a Civilian (Roman) foundation that has been overlaid by Common Law (English) influence. Its system of property law has retained a Civilian flavour, within which a strong right of ownership gives much autonomy to the owner of a thing. In common with most Civilian traditions, Scots property law is unititular.[3] That is to say, there is only one title of ownership in any thing at any one time. This has not been changed by any of the recent reforms brought in by the

---

[1] Section 1. See generally M. M. Combe, *The ScotWays Guide to the Law of Access to Land in Scotland* (Edinburgh: John Donald, 2018) (with chapter 2 considering the right of responsible access in particular). Much more could be written about the right of responsible access, but for present purposes please see the analysis in Bob Reid's chapter in this volume.

[2] See Parts 8, 2 and 4 of the 2016 Act respectively.

[3] K. G. C. Reid, *The Law of Property in Scotland* (Edinburgh: LexisNexis Butterworths, 1996); G. L. Gretton, and A. J. M. Steven, *Property, Trusts and Succession*, 3rd edn (Haywards Heath: Bloomsbury, 2017).

Scottish Parliament. As we shall see, the land reform measures that communities can benefit from operate within a single-title-per-asset system,[4] allowing community members to associate together into a suitable body and in turn allowing that body to acquire sole title to local assets.

Further, the focus here on the means by which a community can take title to an asset should not be taken as an indication that other means of community participation do not matter. Separately, none of this analysis should be taken as an indication that other land reform measures are unimportant. This is a point that shall be returned to below, but for now it can be noted that community rights to buy do not operate in a bubble and there are other aspects of Scots (land) law that can give communities in various forms certain rights in relation to property. First, the specific examples of traditional commonties, the administration of common good land and crofting common grazings all demonstrate a flavour of community. Next, community involvement in local land decisions might flow from consultations with community councils, the wider planning process, and indeed the accountability of the Crown or public bodies that own or manage land in Scotland. Finally, neighbours may share similar title conditions in relation to land that they own, allowing for a micro-community to regulate land use (within the terms of the Title Conditions (Scotland) Act 2003). All of these rights can be important in particular contexts, but they are discussed elsewhere[5] and this chapter will focus on the new statutory rights. It does so by exploring why new community rights were introduced, then explaining how the rights work. It will conclude by offering some observations about what the rights mean for Scottish communities.

Community rights of acquisition: why is land reform happening in Scotland?

Part 2, Part 3 and Part 3A of the 2003 Act, and Part 5 of the 2016 Act, all offer a means by which a community can acquire land. In general, 'land' is used to mean the ground itself and any buildings on it, but communities can also acquire other rights such as those relating to salmon

---

[4] M. M. Combe, 'Parts 2 and 3 of the Land Reform (Scotland) Act 2003: A Definitive Answer to the Scottish Land Question?', *Juridical Review* (2006), pp. 195–227 at p. 225.

[5] See M. M. Combe, 'Community Rights in Scotland', in T. Xu and A. Clarke (eds), *Legal Strategies for the Development and Protection of Communal Property* (Oxford, Oxford University Press, 2018).

fishing and minerals.[6] Although these four schemes are self-contained, they are similar and an understanding of the structure of one aids understanding of the others. This chapter will analyse these rights of varying strength and application, which will be referred to for simplicity (and simplistically) as the community rights to buy. Before doing that, it will briefly explain why there has been engagement with the issue of land reform by Scottish politicians.

The appetite for reform is investigated elsewhere in this book[7] and beyond.[8] To oversimplify, a crucial factor in this modern land reform story was the establishment of the Scottish Parliament. The Scotland Act 1998 introduced a unicameral legislative forum with the time and the inclination to embrace land law reform when it brought devolution to Scotland. The new Scottish Parliament was spurred on by the formation of the Land Reform Policy Group (LRPG), at the instigation of the majority Labour government that came into power in the 1997 UK general election. Naturally, calls for land reform did not start with devolution,[9] and the very existence of the pre-devolution Transfer of Crofting Estates (Scotland) Act 1997 nicely demonstrates that point, but devolution forms a convenient and not entirely arbitrary date stamp for analysis. The LRPG's recommendations were then taken forward in a variety of legislative measures in the first term of the new devolved administration.[10] The most important of these for present purposes was the 2003 Act, which established two community rights of acquisition. In this first wave of activity, the Scottish Parliament also legislated on matters relating to property law more generally, and specifically in relation to the heavily regulated agricultural holdings sector (as covered by Hamish Lean in Chapter 13 of this volume).

Notwithstanding the 2003 Act, the manner in which the land of contemporary Scotland is owned and organised in the present day as

---

[6] See the Land Reform (Scotland) Act 2003, sections 33(6) and 69. Although minerals are generally included, rights to oil, coal, gas, gold or silver are not.

[7] See M. M. Combe, J. Glass and A. Tindley, 'Introduction' in this volume.

[8] See M. M. Combe, 'The environmental implications of redistributive land reform', *Environmental Law Review*, 18:2 (2016), pp. 104–25 and M. M. Combe, 'The Land Reform (Scotland) Act 2016: another answer to the Scottish land question', *Juridical Review* (2016), pp. 291–313.

[9] As detailed by Ewen A. Cameron at Chapter 5 in this volume.

[10] Land Reform Policy Group, 'Identifying the Problems' (Edinburgh: Scottish Office, 1998); Land Reform Policy Group, 'Identifying the Solutions' (Edinburgh: Scottish Office, 1998); Land Reform Policy Group, 'Recommendations for Action' (Edinburgh: Scottish Office, 1999).

measured against contemporary commitments to sustainability and sound land management for economic, social and environmental goals continued to attract comment. Where previously the human right to property (as protected in Article 1 of the First Protocol to the European Convention on Human Rights, which protects the peaceful enjoyment of possessions and only allows deprivation or control by the state in narrow circumstances) held a certain prominence in the debate,[11] notions relating to food security and shelter have recently emerged as a counterpoint (to the extent that section 98 of the 2003 Act has been amended (by the 2015 Act) to make explicit reference to the International Covenant on Economic, Social and Cultural Rights).[12]

Away from such direct human rights concerns, drivers towards land reform have included arguments about local enterprise or complaints that the pattern of land ownership in Scotland is such that there is dominance by major players in the land market.[13] To make a proper analysis of whether this is a problem for Scotland can be difficult or laborious, owing to the occasionally patchy information about who owns what that is available at present. That patchiness is twofold. First, data that is understandable for non-experts is not always available on public registers for land (albeit this point is being addressed by a move from a deeds registration system that has operated since the Registration Act 1617[14] to a map-based registration of title system that has been phased in since the Land Registration (Scotland) Act 1979); the transition has been slow, but is perhaps nearing completion, with both the Scottish Government and Registers of Scotland committing to a rapid completion

[11] A point discussed and critiqued by Frankie McCarthy in Chapter 9 in this volume.

[12] K. Shields, 'Tackling the Misuse of Rights Rhetoric in Land Reform Debate', Greens Scottish Human Rights Journal, 68 (February 2015), pp. 1–4; Scottish Parliament Information Centre, Briefing 07/01, 'Human Rights in Scotland' (Edinburgh: SPICe, 2017), at <http://www.parliament.scot/ResearchBriefingsAndFactsheets/S5/SB_17-01_Human_Rights_in_Scotland.pdf> (last accessed 18 March 2019); and McCarthy, in this volume.

[13] Land Reform Review Group (LRRG), 'Final Report: The Land of Scotland and the Common Good' (Edinburgh: Scottish Government, 2014): section 24, paragraph 25. And see now S. Glenn, J. MacKessack-Leitch, K. Pollard, J. Glass, and R. Mc Morran, 'Investigation into the Issues Associated with Large Scale and Concentrated Landownership in Scotland' (Scottish Land Commission, 2019) at <https://land-commission.gov.scot/wp-content/uploads/2019/03/Investigation-Issues-Large-Scale-and-Concentrated-Landownership-20190320.pdf> (last accessed 4 June 2019).

[14] The history of this system is more fully explained in Chapter 6 of this volume by Andrew Simpson.

of Land Register coverage to the whole of Scotland in line with the Land Registration etc. (Scotland) Act 2012.[15] The second issue is there can be a lack of clarity about who controls the landholding entity that is registered as owner, a point that Part 3 of the 2016 Act seeks to address. As far as concentration of land ownership is concerned, a paper submitted to the Scottish Affairs Committee at Westminster suggests a figure in the region of 432 landowners own 50 per cent of the privately owned rural land in Scotland.[16] Another driver for reform is about the governance of land, which is particularly seen to be an issue when landowners are termed as 'absentee' (a point which can be compounded when a non-active, non-resident owner is also non-transparent). To simplify, land reformers contend that land is better governed when those who live or work on the land have a stake in its governance. When land is owned by persons who live and work on the land, land reform advocates claim, rural populations stabilise or even grow. Land reform sceptics, in contrast, question whether a community is the best candidate to take on the governance of land, especially when public support in the form of advice and money is being provided.[17] Organisations like Community Land Scotland strongly advocate the case for land reform.[18]

All of this gives a flavour of what has fed into the land reform debate in Scotland. The next consideration is where the community features as a result of that debate.

Community-oriented Scottish land reform

The first real statutory intervention that put communities as land owners to the fore came in the form of the Transfer of Crofting Estates (Scotland)

[15] K. G. C. Reid and G. L. Gretton, *Land Registration* (Edinburgh: Avizandum, 2017). Registers of Scotland is working to a target of migrating all titles to the Land Register by 2024: see <https://www.ros.gov.uk/about/what-we-do> (last accessed 18 March 2019).

[16] J. Hunter, P. Peacock, A. Wightman and M. Foxley, '432:50 – Towards a comprehensive land reform agenda for Scotland: A briefing paper for the House of Commons' (London: Scottish Affairs Committee, 2013) available at <http://www.parliament.uk/business/committees/committees-a-z/commons-select/scottish-affairs-committee/news/land-reform-inquiry/> (last accessed 18 March 2019).

[17] A point touched on by John Lovett in Chapter 8 in this volume. See also J. Lovett and M. M. Combe, 'The Parable of Portobello: Lessons and Questions from the First Urban Acquisition under the Scottish Community Right to Buy Regime' *Montana Law Review* 80:2 (2019), pp. 211–28.

[18] See <https://www.communitylandscotland.org.uk/> (last accessed 18 March 2019).

Act 1997. This legislation provides for the transfer of crofting lands in the Highlands and Islands that are owned by the state to a community body. That community body would then become a crofting landlord, such that it would inherit relationships with the crofting tenants that are *in situ* and take the ownership of the common grazings of the relevant area. The highly regulated crofting scheme that governs such land, which is explained by MacLellan in Chapter 12 in this volume, would mean no particular change of land use could be easily instigated by the incoming owner in the event of a transfer of land ownership, meaning the actual 'on the ground' land reform effect of this measure was always destined to be limited. As it happens, its deployment has been limited anyway, as only one crofting community – West Harris in the Outer Hebrides – has availed itself of the legislative scheme to date.

That being said, a real impact of the 1997 Act was to propel 'community' into the thinking of those framing legislative intervention, but that was not the only factor. Many important examples of community ownership in Scotland came about as a result of community action that did not wait for legislation. The community acquisitions of the islands of Eigg and Gigha (amongst others) pre-dated such developments, and those bellwether communities have generally fared well: both witnessed population increases since transfer to their respective community.[19] That is not to say communities are insulated from all challenges of land management. The Isle of Gigha Heritage Trust has faced some documented issues, particularly in relation to the debt owed by the community landowning entity (and secured on its land) post acquisition,[20] although it can be noted that none have publicly failed in economic terms. In terms of how these organic buyouts have found form, even without any legislative scheme directing them, they have tended to channel that community through one landowning entity. They have been able to do this with a structure and membership that can be tailored to suit them without any particular legal constraints (subject to any stipulations by funders).

Taken together with the 1997 Act, these extra-statutory developments in Scotland and the means by which they were achieved, showcased community models to the Land Reform Policy Group. The

[19] J. Hunter, *From the Low Tide of the Sea to the Highest Mountain Tops: Community Ownership in the Highlands and Islands of Scotland* (Kershader: The Islands Books Trust, 2012).

[20] J. Duffy, 'A tale of two islands as Gigha dream turns sour', *Sunday Herald*, 23 November 2014, at <http://www.heraldscotland.com/news/13190772.A_tale_of_two_islands_as_Gigha_dream_turns_sour/> (last accessed 18 March 2019).

LRPG went on to embrace community models in its work. In passing, it can be noted that it did so without any particular study of comparative models of land reform.[21] From a community land perspective, the culmination of the LRPG's work was the 2003 Act. As already noted, the 2003 Act brought in two rights of community acquisition which were innovative for Scotland. The measures gave rural communities (which were initially classed as those with a population of 10,000 people or less)[22] a right of first refusal over land (Part 2) and crofting communities a right to force a sale of certain crofting land and related assets (Part 3).

After the flurry of activity in Holyrood's first term, land reform did not feature prominently in the second and third terms of the Scottish Parliament. It re-emerged as an issue when the Scottish National Party won an overall majority in the 2011 Scottish parliamentary elections. Shortly thereafter the Scottish Government appointed a group to look at land reform in 2012. This Land Reform Review Group (LRRG) produced its Final Report in 2014, containing sixty-two recommendations as to what the Scottish Government should do,[23] but not before the then First Minister Alex Salmond announced (at the Community Land Scotland Annual Conference in 2013) a commitment to bring one million acres of Scotland under community ownership.[24]

With community having such a central role somewhat pre-judged, the LRRG Final Report considered a number of community-related

---

[21] The lack of comparative research has not continued with more recent studies (see, for example, Scottish Parliament Information Centre, Briefing 15/38, 'International Perspectives on Land Reform' (Edinburgh: SPICe, 2015), at <http://www.parliament. scot/ResearchBriefingsAndFactsheets/S4/SB_15-38_International_Perspectives_on_ Land_Reform.pdf>. (last accessed 18 March 2019); and J. Glass, R. Bryce, M. M. Combe, N. E. Hutchison, M. F. Price, L. Schulz and D. Valero, 'Research on interventions to manage land markets and limit the concentration of land ownership elsewhere in the world' (Scottish Land Commission, Commissioned Report No. 001, 2018) at <https://landcommission.gov.scot/wp-content/uploads/2018/03/Land-ownership-restrictions-FINAL-March-2018.pdf> (last accessed 18 March 2019).

[22] Under the Community Right to Buy (Definition of Excluded Land) (Scotland) Order 2004 (SSI 2004/296).

[23] LRRG, 'Final Report'. The author was appointed as an adviser to the LRRG in 2013.

[24] Scottish Government, 'A million acres in community ownership by 2020', 7 June 2013, <https://news.gov.scot/news/a-million-acres-in-community-ownership-by-2020> (last accessed 18 March 2019), and see now Scottish Government, 'One Million Acre Strategic Implementation Group', at <https://www.gov.scot/groups/one-million-acre-strategic-implementation-group/> (last accessed 18 March 2019).

options. In terms of statutory rights of acquisition, it suggested existing community rights should be made less bureaucratic and expanded to urban areas, and that

> statutory land rights of local communities should include [a] a right to register an interest in land, [b] the existing right of pre-emption over land and a right to buy land, as well as [c] rights to request the purchase of public land and [d] to request Scottish Ministers to implement a Compulsory Purchase Order.[25]

The latter category would have been a narrow one, designed only to be used where a landowner had engaged in some kind of avoidance activity that defeated an otherwise legitimate attempt at community acquisition.[26] It has not been legislated for. Then, a similar but slightly different recommendation also made in section 17 was that communities 'should have the right to request that a local authority exercises a Compulsory Sale Order'.[27] This has also not yet been legislated for, but the Scottish Land Commission has been active in pushing for this.[28]

Not all of the recommendations of the LRRG Final Report made their way into what became the Land Reform (Scotland) Act 2016. Some were destined for the separate but related statute on community empowerment. The Community Empowerment (Scotland) Act 2015 Act amended the 2003 Act, widening the scope of its pre-emptive community right to buy to the whole of Scotland,[29] and finessing the existing scheme to make it more user-friendly. It also introduced provision for communities to make 'asset transfer requests' from public bodies, including their local authority (that is to say, the municipal council), which *must* be considered by that public body in light of a statutory scheme and cannot simply be rejected out of hand. The self-contained

---

[25] LRRG, 'Final Report', section 17, paragraph 27.

[26] LRRG, 'Final Report', section 17, paragraph 25.

[27] LRRG, 'Final Report', section 17, paragraph 33. This has not yet been implemented.

[28] Scottish Land Commission, 'Compulsory Sales Orders – a proposal from the Scottish Land Commission', available at <https://landcommission.gov.scot/wp-content/uploads/2018/08/CSO-Proposal-final.pdf> (last accessed 18 March 2019). Compulsory sale orders have been shelved by the Scottish Government, at least for this Parliament.

[29] By virtue of the 2015 Act, section 36 amended the 2003 Act, section 33. On the first urban buyout, see Lovett and Combe, 'The Parable of Portobello'.

regime for asset transfer requests is found in Part 5 of the 2015 Act and has been in operation since 23 January 2017.[30]

In terms of its impact on private land owners, the 2015 Act introduced a right of community acquisition where land has been 'wholly or mainly abandoned or neglected' or somehow managed in a way that was detrimental to a community's 'environmental wellbeing'.

Then came the most recent Land Reform (Scotland) Act, which was introduced to Holyrood with a 'right to buy land to further sustainable development' for communities. This additional right for communities was not presaged in the LRRG Final Report. The 2016 Act also made separate but related provision for land owners to consult with local communities when making decisions about land.

HOW DOES THIS SUITE OF LEGISLATION WORK?

Having briefly explained how these legal steps came about and what they were designed to achieve, more detail on them follows below. The first wave of community rights – that is to say, the two rights of acquisition in the 2003 Act as originally enacted – will be analysed first, an approach that makes sense chronologically and also because the community body-centric scheme it adopted has been adopted in turn in later waves. The right to buy abandoned, neglected or detrimental land will then be examined as the second wave, with the right to buy land to further sustainable development following as the third wave. Lastly, the similar but different right to make an asset transfer request of a public body will be analysed after the consideration of the four transfer routes that affect private landowners.

First-wave community rights of acquisition

The 2003 Act works by allowing a community body (that is, members of a locality associated together in a suitable juristic persona) to acquire land in certain circumstances. For communities in crofting areas of the Highlands and Islands looking to acquire ownership of land under crofting tenure, common grazings and certain eligible additional land, a sale can be forced on an unwilling seller. For communities seeking to acquire land under Part 2 of the 2003 Act, there are two crucial differences. The right is of first refusal, meaning the owner cannot be

[30] The Community Empowerment (Scotland) Act 2015 (Commencement No. 4 and Transitory Provision) Order 2016 (SSI 2016/363).

forced to transfer and the community right will only trigger when the
owner decides to transfer the land. Relatedly, to acquire this right of
first refusal, a community must first register an interest in the land it
seeks to acquire in a public register, to put the landowner on notice of
its plans.[31] The Register of Community Interest in Land is maintained
by the Keeper of the Registers of Scotland and is available online.[32]

Whilst the owner cannot be forced to sell under Part 2, this right to
register an interest in land and the resulting right of first refusal are still
important powers for the community to have. The pre-emptive right to
buy is stronger than the right to bid that applies in England and Wales
as a result of Part 5 of the Localism Act 2011. That legislation only provides a right to make an offer for a targeted asset of community value,
whereas the Scottish legislation provides that a transferring landowner
must sell to the community at an agreed or set price, if that community
has registered its interest in the aforementioned manner. Whilst the
Scottish regime in Part 2 cannot force a sale to a community, as a
landowner can choose to no longer sell at any point in the transaction,
it does mean a properly constituted community body with a registered
interest cannot be forced to contend with a new landowner for that asset
it has targeted. This is because any transfer that did not first consider
the community could be open to challenge. The moratorium under the
Localism Act 2011 gives communities a (relatively weaker) right to bid
before the owner can transfer to anyone else.[33]

The schemes in Parts 2 and 3 both involve a number of preparatory
steps, the first of which is incorporation of a suitable entity – referred to
as a 'community body' or 'crofting community body' in the legislation[34]
– that serves as its embodiment. This body will then own the land
outright, on a single title. Where the body is a company limited by
guarantee, its articles of association must be tailored to have not fewer
than ten members, provision that at least three quarters of the members
of the company are also members of the local community (with a related
stipulation that those members have control of the company), and provision that any surplus funds or assets of the company are to be applied

[31] The 2003 Act, section 36.

[32] See <https://www.ros.gov.uk/our-registers/register-of-community-interests-in-
land> (last accessed 18 March 2019).

[33] S. Adamyk, *Assets of Community Value: Law and Practice* (London: Wildy,
Simmonds and Hill, 2017).

[34] The 2003 Act, sections 34 and 71. See generally Combe, 'Parts 2 and 3 of
the Land Reform (Scotland) Act 2003: A Definitive Answer to the Scottish Land
Question?'

for the benefit of the community. As originally enacted, the 2003 Act obliged communities to incorporate as a company limited by guarantee, but following the 2015 Act they may form a Scottish charitable incorporated organisation or a community benefit society. Similar rules then apply as regards such an entity's constitution. In all cases, the body must have been recognised by Scottish Ministers as having a commitment to sustainable development.[35] Sustainable development is nowhere defined in the legislation.[36] The community is then left to operate in a suitably sculpted regime under the Companies Act 2006, the Co-operative and Community Benefit Societies Act 2014 or the Charities and Trustee Investment (Scotland) Act 2005 (as applicable).

Whilst more flexibility has undeniably been introduced by allowing these two forms to be adopted by communities as alternatives to a company limited by guarantee, it can be noted that there are more flexible schemes in operation for certain community bodies recognised in other Scottish statutes. A notable comparator is the Transfer of Crofting Estates (Scotland) Act 1997, section 2, which simply needs a body (corporate or unincorporated) to be approved by the Secretary of State, after consultation with the Crofting Commission, that is 'representative of the crofting interests in the property to be disposed of' and 'has the promotion of the interests of persons residing on such property as its primary objective'. There is similar flexibility in the 2015 Act, section 19, which allows a body (again, corporate or unincorporated) with certain simple constitutional requirements to make participation requests of certain public bodies (allowing it to get involved with the delivery of a local service). Whilst there is not complete free rein for the composition of community bodies that can make an asset transfer request of a local authority (a scheme discussed further below), for now it can be noted that 2003 Act community bodies must be referable to a geographical area,[37] whereas asset transfer request community bodies might be a community of interest (i.e. an association of people united by a common cause rather than proximity).[38]

---

[35] The 2003 Act, section 34(4) and section 71(4), as applicable.

[36] A point considered by Andrea Ross in Chapter 10 in this volume.

[37] The 2003 Act, section 34(5).

[38] See the Scottish Government *Community Empowerment (Scotland) Act 2015: Asset transfer guidance for authorities* (2017) at 5.12. A further and similar comparator community scheme now exists in terms of section 6 of the Scottish Crown Estate Act 2019, which might allow for delegation of public (Crown Estate) management functions to a community body but again along slightly different community lines to existing land reform legislation.

Returning to the 2003 Act, once a suitable body has been formed in its terms, there must also be evidence of local support. In terms of the Part 2 right of pre-emption, evidence is needed at the beginning of the acquisition process.[39] Ordinarily, all of this should happen before the land is exposed for sale, although if that is impossible a properly constituted community body can seek to have a 'late' application recognised provided the landowner has not yet finalised a transfer, albeit much stronger evidence of community support for the acquisition is needed.[40]

With regard to approval generally, for both the community right to buy (punctual or otherwise) and the crofting community right to buy, any movement to acquire is followed by a ballot to ensure majority support of the local community before exercise of the right itself.[41] Thereafter, even with that local mandate, acquisition will only be possible with the approval of the Scottish Ministers. That approval will only be forthcoming if the acquisition is in the public interest and compatible with furthering the achievement of sustainable development.[42] The (repeated) role of sustainable development in this statute has been described as a 'primary duty' of the decision-makers which 'has priority over any other duties or objectives',[43] so its application and interpretation are of crucial importance. Assuming a community steers itself through these provisions, the land is then transferred at an agreed or independently valued price.[44] There are provisions that allow the owner to have input into or appeal the overall process throughout.

Second-wave community rights of acquisition

The 2003 Act now has a new Part 3A, introduced by section 74 of the 2015 Act, which enshrines a right which goes beyond pre-emption. This new entitlement has something in common with the crofting community right to buy in that it does not require a willing seller. There is also an overlap with both older community rights in terms of what is a properly constituted community body[45] and conditions for the approval of Scottish Ministers (including the acquisition having sufficient support

[39] The 2003 Act, section 38.
[40] The 2003 Act, section 39.
[41] The 2003 Act, section 52 or section 75, as applicable.
[42] The 2003 Act, section 51(3)(c) and (d), or section 74(1)(j) and (n), as applicable.
[43] A. Ross, *Sustainable Development in the UK: From Rhetoric to Reality?* (Abingdon: Earthscan, 2012), p. 191.
[44] The 2003 Act, sections 59–60A or section 88, as applicable.
[45] The 2003 Act, section 97D.

locally).[46] Assuming those better-known criteria are met, community bodies have the right to acquire 'eligible land' if in the opinion of Scottish Ministers: '(a) it is wholly or mainly *abandoned* or *neglected*, or (b) the use or management of the land is such that it results in or causes *harm*, directly or indirectly, to the *environmental wellbeing* of a relevant community'.[47]

As to what this means, the statute itself lays down certain exceptions (including land being used as someone's home and croft land, the latter already being subject to the crofting community right to buy). Secondary legislation then explains that Scottish Ministers should assess for eligible status on the basis of certain factors.[48] 'Abandoned or neglected land' forms one category, 'detrimental land' is the second category.

For abandoned or neglected land, Ministers must consider the land's (a) physical condition (which might include whether it is a risk to public safety or indeed the wider environment), (b) designation or classification (perhaps as nature reserve or monument, or relative to the local development plan for the area), or (c) use or management (with actual use for any period of time for lawful public recreation, conservation purposes, or something that requires a permit or licence all being relevant, and conversely not being used for any discernible purpose for a period of time would be relevant). For detrimental land, Ministers must again consider use or management of land, and also look at whether harm to environmental wellbeing in a technical sense has in fact occurred, namely is there a 'statutory nuisance' in terms of the Environmental Protection Act 1990 or has there been certain enforcement action under the Antisocial Behaviour etc. (Scotland) Act 2004.

Even where Scottish Ministers are satisfied the targeted area is eligible land, there is more to consider. Before a forced sale can occur, the community must have already tried to purchase the land in question (an attempt which might, but theoretically need not, have involved registration of an interest in land under Part 2).[49] Plus, where the land acquisition turns on environmentally detrimental status, the community scheme must be capable of fixing the problem, and the community must have invited the relevant (environmental) regulator to take suitable

---

[46] The 2003 Act, sections 97H(1)(i) and 97J.

[47] The 2003 Act, section 97C (emphasis added).

[48] See the (snappily titled) Community Right to Buy (Abandoned, Neglected or Detrimental Land) (Eligible Land, Regulators and Restrictions on Transfers and Dealing) (Scotland) Regulations 2018 (SSI 2018/201).

[49] The 2003 Act, section 97H(1)(j).

action in relation to the harm in question.[50] There is then the familiar requirement for Ministers to consent to the exercise of the right, which they will only do if it is both in the public interest and compatible with furthering the achievement of sustainable development.[51] Given how poorly used or managed land must be to be eligible for this forced transfer, it seems fair to say a well-informed community with a viable plan should normally be able to pass the sustainable development criterion when its plan is compared to the existing use. Assuming Scottish Ministers consent, it is for them to appoint a valuer,[52] then the price payable by the community will be based on what this valuer assesses the market value to be. Such price is payable within six months of Ministers granting consent.[53] There is also an accompanying register maintained by Registers of Scotland where information about each right to buy is to be freely available.[54]

These provisions came into force on 27 June 2018.[55] Given their relative youth, there have been no (successful) attempts to use them yet. Given their variegated stipulations, it seems fair to say successful acquisitions will not be everyday occurrences, although these provisions may serve as an effective backstop in some situations (as has been the case with the crofting community right to buy, as noted below).

Third-wave community rights of acquisition

Part 5 of the 2016 Act provides for the fourth legislative route whereby a community can acquire land from a private individual, namely the right to acquire land to further sustainable development. It is not yet in force, but its framework is in place and can be analysed nonetheless. Again, this adopts a community-centric model not unlike Parts 2, 3 and 3A of the 2003 Act with the usual need for a locally accountable community body and local approval of the scheme,[56] but this right to buy is augmented by an onerous process that communities might find difficult

---

[50] The 2003 Act, section 97H(5).

[51] The 2003 Act, section 97H.

[52] The 2003 Act, section 97S.

[53] The 2003 Act, section 97R.

[54] The 2003 Act, section 97F. The Register of Applications by Community Bodies to Buy Land can be found at <https://roacbl.ros.gov.uk> (last accessed 18 March 2019).

[55] The Community Empowerment (Scotland) Act 2015 (Commencement No. 11) Order 2018 (SSI 2018/139).

[56] The 2016 Act, sections 56 and 57.

to negotiate if and when it comes to be used. The reason these tests are onerous is because the prize at the end involves a forced transfer from another individual: assuming the statutory tests are met, and subject to payment of an independently valued price within six months of consent being granted,[57] transfer is compelled.

Where the 2016 Act differs from the earlier rights of acquisition is in asking that more hurdles than public interest and sustainable development are cleared. The transfer of land must also be likely to result in 'significant benefit' to the relevant community, and must be 'the only practicable, or the most practicable, way of achieving that significant benefit'.[58] There is then a further test that 'not granting consent to the transfer of land is likely to result in harm to that community'.[59] Those additional conditions bring the ideas of 'significant benefit' and 'harm' to the fore, both of which are to be determined by an analysis of a community's economic development, regeneration, public health, and social and environmental wellbeing.[60] None of these terms are defined, although environmental wellbeing features in the second-wave right of acquisition. The Scottish Ministers' outlook in relation to sustainable development will be fundamental to the operation of this right to buy (a point considered by Ross in Chapter 10 in this volume). In the event of any disputes between a community body and a landowner in the future, it is likely that this will not be solved by lawyers (or at least not only by lawyers). In applying for consent, the community body must explain why it satisfies the so-called 'sustainable development conditions',[61] at which point anyone affected by the application can put forward their analysis of the same conditions.[62] The potential for a battle of the experts is apparent.

It is worth mentioning at this stage the way Parts 4 and 5 of the Act are tied together, which might offer a tiebreaker in situations where there is disagreement between the existing and aspiring owner about sustainable development, yet the existing owner has been so entrenched so as to make decisions about land without liaising with the local

[57] The 2016 Act, sections 64 and 65.
[58] The 2016 Act, section 56(2)(c). Although there was some sculpting of the provisions about community acquisition to further sustainable development during the legislative process, the general model stayed the same throughout. This provision was one that was amended slightly in the Scottish Parliament, allowing for measurement by way of a 'most practicable' test as opposed to simply 'only practicable'.
[59] The 2016 Act, section 56(2)(d).
[60] The 2016 Act, section 56(12).
[61] The 2016 Act, section 54(6)(a).
[62] The 2016 Act, section 55(2)(b). See further Ross, in this volume.

community. Under section 56(4), Ministers can take into account the extent to which land owners have had regard to guidance issued under section 44 (about engaging a community with decisions affecting land) in determining whether an application to buy land under Part 5 meets the 'sustainable development conditions' for a community buyout. This means the guidance could be important in certain forced-sale contexts, and any landowners wishing to avoid a negative inference should follow relevant guidance,[63] meaning they should consider on what occasions they need to engage the community, who within the community they need to engage with, and how that engagement should manifest itself whenever they make a decision relating to land that might impact on local people.

Finally, attention should be drawn to one innovative feature of Part 5 as compared to the other rights of acquisition, namely that a community may nominate a third-party acquirer to take title instead of the community, albeit the transfer to such a nominee would still need to meet all the tests already mentioned as modified to reflect the third-party acquisition. This novel approach could open up funding and partnership arrangements that have not been possible under existing statutory schemes.

An alternative current: acquisition from the public sector

With regard to the three waves of community rights just mentioned, save for limited exceptions, it generally does not matter who the existing owner of the land is.[64] Normally of greater concern than the ownership status is the status of the land itself, either in law (as croft land) or in terms of what is happening on it. There are two legislative routes to community ownership, though, where it does matter who owns the land. Both are in statutes that have been mentioned already.

The Transfer of Crofting (Estates) Act 1997 was drafted to allow the Secretary of State for Scotland (now the Scottish Ministers) to transfer government-owned crofting assets to local communities. Its scheme does not require a community to register an interest or even request an asset,

---

[63] Scottish Government, *Guidance on Engaging Communities in Decisions Relating to Land* (2018), at <https://www.gov.scot/Publications/2018/04/2478> (last accessed 18 March 2019).

[64] The exceptions are technical, such as the exception to the newer rights where land has fallen to the Crown when the owner has died without any heirs: see the 2003 Act, section 97C(5) and the 2016 Act section 46(2)(d).

but the community would need to be party to and engaged with the scheme as a suitable representative body (in terms of section 2) must be formed to take on the asset.

Of much wider application, on two fronts, are asset transfer requests under Part 5 of the Community Empowerment (Scotland) Act 2015. The first reason this is of wider application is an obvious one, namely that it does not just apply to croft land. The second reason is it does not only apply to land owned by Scottish Ministers. This legislation allows communities (in terms of section 77) to request asset transfers from certain 'relevant authorities'. These are the public sector entities listed in Schedule 3 of the 2015 Act, including arms of devolved and municipal government (i.e. the Scottish Ministers and local authorities) and other entities like the Scottish Environment Protection Agency, the Scottish Courts and Tribunals Service, and Scottish Water.

Communities can use this legislation to seek ownership of land or they might seek a right short of ownership, namely a lease or a right to manage or occupy the land. Where ownership is not sought, there is a statutory requirement to have a written constitution but there is no requirement to incorporate in any particular form (although it seems likely that a public body or any funders would expect a tenant to adopt a suitable form). Where a community body seeks to acquire ownership, section 79(3) requires that it is embodied as a suitable legal personality. As with the community rights that are not restricted to land currently owned by a public sector owner, these include a company limited by guarantee, a Scottish charitable incorporated organisation and a community benefit society, although a noticeable difference is that the legislation asks for twenty rather than ten members.[65] Sensibly, regulations have allowed some bodies to acquire land even if they have less than this floor of twenty members, namely where a community body that has been approved for another right of acquisition then seeks an asset transfer. This means there is no need for a community approved for an earlier acquisition under different rules to reincorporate or form some sort of subsidiary to benefit from this scheme.[66]

The right to request an asset transfer is not triggered by anything in particular and, subject to certain restrictions to (for example) prevent repeated applications for the same asset,[67] a community can expect

---

[65] See also the Scottish Crown Estate Act 2019, section 6.

[66] The Asset Transfer Request (Designation of Community Transfer Bodies) (Scotland) Order 2016 (SSI 2016/361).

[67] The 2015 Act, section 93.

any request to be given due consideration. The community can request ownership or a lease of the land in question, and (on the assumption ownership is sought) the request must state the land to which the request relates, the reasons for making the request, the benefits which the community transfer body considers will arise if the authority were to agree to the request, and the price that the community would be prepared to pay (Section 79). Assuming full compliance, the relevant authority is not allowed to sell the asset until it considers the request (section 84) and it must give due consideration to the application based on the scheme set out in section 82, including whether or not the agreeing to the request would be likely to promote or improve economic development, regeneration, public health, social wellbeing, or environmental wellbeing. Importantly, a relevant authority is also under a reporting obligation to establish and maintain a register of land that it, to the best of its knowledge and belief, owns or leases.[68] This must be accessible to the public and as such it will allow communities to plan for potential acquisitions with reference to that list of assets.

This modern scheme is clearly an innovation, but it should be recalled that local authorities might have decided to offload land in some circumstances prior to this legislation coming into force and it remains competent for them to transact with relevant assets when those assets have not been subjected to an asset transfer request, subject to compliance with local government law generally and any particularly applicable regime, such as procurement and state aid rules and The Disposal of Land by Local Authorities (Scotland) Regulations 2010.[69] Such transfers might well have been instigated by the relevant council rather than a community within its area, although it can be acknowledged that communities could have made these requests anyway, albeit such requests may have met by a refusal or even no response at all. The real innovation, and the real shift in the power balance for community ownership, is that the public sector body *must* agree to a properly made request unless there are reasonable grounds for refusing it, in terms of section 82(5). In this regard, a certain resonance with the new right to buy to further sustainable development found in the 2016 Act is evident: if an application is for a strong purpose, it *must* be granted. Where a community is not satisfied with a decision, there is an appeal and a review mechanism.[70]

Whilst only brief coverage of this statutory scheme is possible here,

---

[68] The 2015 Act, section 94.
[69] SSI 2010/160.
[70] The 2015 Act, sections 85 and 86.

and its associated regulations have not been covered in detail, it is useful to set out the asset transfer scheme as a counterpoint to the other rights of acquisition. As with the right to buy abandoned, neglected or detrimental land, it is perhaps too early to offer bold conclusions about its effects, and the fact it can only apply to land owned by certain bodies will necessarily limit the amount of land it can affect, but it is useful to highlight its terms as an alternative model, not least because of the potential for a community of interest. Further, community asset transfers have already attracted some analysis in terms of the interaction communities have had with them, in a piece of research commissioned by the Scottish Land Commission.[71] No further analysis of the effect of that scheme is offered here, but some brief analysis of the actual effects of the earlier legislation – which has had more time to bed in and be engaged with – will now be offered.

WHAT EFFECT HAVE THE MEASURES HAD SO FAR?

There have been a number of community transfers under the scheme of Part 2 of the 2003 Act, albeit the impact has not been profound in terms of numbers of activated community interests in the Register of Community Interests in Land: only twenty-four community interests have been activated, and even then there have been instances where a number of activations have actually been part of only one scheme. In terms of qualitative rather than quantitative impact, recent Scottish Government-commissioned research seems to indicate positive trends for communities and other benefits across a range of aspects.[72] The scheme is not a one-way street for communities, however: there have been occasions when communities have faced challenge in court, and indeed certain communities who thought they were progressing along

[71] R. Mc Morran, A. Lawrence, J. Glass, J. Hollingdale, A. McKee, D. Campbell, and M. M. Combe, 'Review of the effectiveness of current community ownership mechanisms and of options for supporting the expansion of community ownership in Scotland' (Scottish Land Commission, Commissioned Report, 2018) available at <https://landcommission.gov.scot/wp-content/uploads/2018/11/1-Community-Ownership-Mechanisms-SRUC-Final-Report-For-Publication.pdf> (last accessed 18 March 2019), Chapter 7.

[72] C. Mulholland, G. McAteer, C. Martin, L. Murray, R. Mc Morran, E. Brodie, S. Skerratt and A. Moxey, 'Impact Evaluation of the Community Right to Buy' (Edinburgh: Scottish Government Social Research, 2015) at <www.gov.scot/Publications/2015/10/8581> (last accessed 18 March 2019).

the land reform process (having obtained Scottish ministerial consent for that) have been challenged through litigation.[73]

The impact of the crofting community right to buy, or at least its looming presence, has been more noticeable. This too has been the subject of litigation, but the one buyout which began with community and landowner at loggerheads eventually resulted in a transfer to the relevant community, after the landowner's challenge to the scheme of Part 3 based on the European Convention of Human Rights was unsuccessful.[74] It has also contributed to various transfers of land (particularly in the Western Isles) in the limited area where it operates without the need to resort to litigation.[75] These developments chime with earlier commentary that Part 3 of the 2003 Act marks a 'fairly radical step away from the traditional protection afforded to Scotland's landowners'.[76]

Only brief consideration of the effectiveness of the more developed rights of acquisition has been possible here. Recent research offers further food for thought.[77] For now, that snapshot allows some questions to be considered by way of conclusion.

CONCLUSION

Much has already been said about Scotland's community-centric approach to land reform.[78] This chapter has offered some further analy-

---

[73] Consider *Holmehill Limited* v. *The Scottish Ministers*, 2006 SLT (Sh Ct) 79, *Hazle* v. *Lord Advocate* (Kirkcaldy Sheriff Court (ref B270/07), 16 March 2009), and *West Register (Property Investments) Ltd* v. *Lord Advocate* (Selkirk Sheriff Court (unreported), 11 March 2015), and see further: M. M. Combe, 'No Place Like *Holme*: Community Expectations and the Right to Buy' *Edinburgh Law Review*, 11:1 (2007), pp. 109–16; M. M. Combe, 'Access to Land and to Landownership', *Edinburgh Law Review*, 14:1 (2010), pp. 106–13; and K. G. C. Reid and G. L. Gretton, *Conveyancing 2015* (Edinburgh: Avizandum, 2016), pp. 37–9.

[74] *Pairc Crofters Limited and Pairc Renewables Limited* v. *The Scottish Ministers* [2012] CSIH 96. See further M. M. Combe, '*Ruaig an Fhèidh*: 3', *Journal of the Law Society of Scotland*, 58:2 (2013).

[75] Hunter, *From the Low Tide*.

[76] D. L. Carey Miller and M. M. Combe, 'The Boundaries of Property Rights in Scots Law' *Electronic Journal of Comparative Law*, 10:3 (2006) <http://www.ejcl.org/103/art103-4.pdf> (last accessed 18 March 2019).

[77] Mc Morran et al., 'Review of the effectiveness of current community ownership mechanisms'.

[78] Consider J. Bryden and C. Geisler, 'Community-based land reform: Lessons from Scotland', *Land Use Policy*, 24 (2017), pp. 24–34 and A. F. D. MacKenzie, *Places of Possibility: Property, Nature and Community Land Ownership* (Somerset, NJ: John Wiley & Sons, 2012).

sis, by distilling how the reforms have come to pass, how they work in practice, and noting some of the opportunities, benefits and indeed challenges that have followed from the legislation. Two questions occur, however, as we take stock of the rights that have been introduced at a time when there has been no particular indication that further community rights to acquire will be introduced.

The first question is: why are we here? Did we think this through, or did it just happen because an organic movement which reacted to problems that existed in parts of Scotland caught the imagination of legislators, at just the right time and when there was some precedent for community land ownership on the statute books to adapt (with the 2003 Act following the 1997 Act, to an extent)? A related question is: having developed this framework, why are we aiming for one million acres? Is a metric based on land area the correct one where smaller, strageic urban assets are concerned? This is not to criticise or praise where Scotland sits, but there are times when Scotland seems to be on something of an accidental community land ownership journey which is not really replicated elsewhere, so these questions are worth considering.

This is not to say community ownership is not a legitimate and important pursuit when it comes to vibrant communities.[79] What makes the question especially worth considering is not so much to do with the merits and demerits of community ownership, but rather to wonder whether Scotland has missed a trick when it has been distracted: have other approaches to land reform been somewhat sidelined in comparison to the community-oriented approach? Other approaches to land reform do exist (notably there are some individual rights of acquisition available to certain tenants in Scotland),[80] but even then such rights might not change much on the ground, and (like community or even third-party rights to buy based on a community of place) they are predicated on something happening on or near the ground at the given moment. Perhaps this is something that will be investigated further in the future: interestingly, the Scottish Land Commission has been keen to learn what other jurisdictions are doing in contrast to Scotland's approach to community, and also pushing for the introduction of other devices like the compulsory sale order.

Those heretical questions aside, and even working to the assumption

[79] R. Hopkins, R., *The Power of Just Doing Stuff: How Local Action Can Change the World* (Cambridge: UIT/Green Books, 2013), pp. 58–9.

[80] In terms of sections 13–19 of the Crofters (Scotland) Act 1993 and Parts 2 and 2A of the Agricultural Holdings (Scotland) Act 2003.

that Scotland has stumbled into its particular model of community-oriented land reform, this chapter should provide some detail about how it can work in theory and in reality. The rights of community acquisition introduced to Scots law have provided real opportunities to communities across Scotland without, it is submitted, causing too many issues as regards the rule of law, the protection of private property, and operation of the land market in Scotland. Further analysis about many of these matters now follows in subsequent chapters in this volume, and no doubt further analysis will follow in the future.

8

Towards Sustainable Community Ownership: A Comparative Assessment of Scotland's New Compulsory Community Right to Buy[*]

John A. Lovett

MODERN LAND REFORM ADVOCATES in Scotland have long yearned to bring more land in Scotland under community ownership. In 2013 the Scottish Government embraced this vision by setting an ambitious goal of bringing one million acres of Scotland – more than five per cent of all land in the country – under community ownership by 2020. Incredibly, as of December 2017, 547,691 acres of land – 2.8 per cent of the total land area of Scotland – had already come under community ownership.[1] It is true, of course, that voluntary transfers from private landowners account for a signification portion of this total. Indeed, several prominent transfers – the acquisition of almost 70,000 acres by the Stornoway Trust in 1923 and more than 20,000 acres by the Assynt Crofters' Trust in 1993 – preceded the initial wave of modern land reform legislation that crested in Scotland in the late 1990s and early 2000s.[2] Nevertheless, it is the contention of this chapter that land

[*] The author gratefully acknowledges the many helpful comments and suggestions of editors Malcolm Combe, Jayne Glass, and Annie Tindley. He also expresses his gratitude for the helpful comments received from the participants in the Progressive Property Workshop at Harvard Law School in May 2018, including especially Joseph Singer, Rashmi Dyal-Chand, Bethany Berger, Nestor Davidson and Debbie Becher.

[1] Scottish Government, *Statistics* (18 December 2018), at <https://blogs.gov.scot/statistics/2018/12/18/there-were-547691-acres-in-community-ownership-at-the-end-of-2017> (last accessed 18 September 2019). This figure represents a small decrease from the number reported the previous year. Scottish Government, Department of Agriculture, Environment and Marine, *Estimate of Community Owned Land in Scotland* (7 December 2018), at https://www.gov.scot/publications/estimate-community-owned-land-scotland-2017> (last accessed 18 September 2019).

[2] See A. Wightman, *The Poor Had No Lawyers: Who Owns Scotland (And How They Got It)* (Edinburgh: Birlinn, 2015), table 9, pp. 200–1 (discussed pp. 193–200); A. F. D. Mackenzie, *Places of Possibility* (Malden, MA: Willey-Blackwell, 2013),

reform legislation does matter. Land reform legislation has already had a significant impact on the movement to create more community ownership of land in Scotland and its impact is likely to grow in the future.

A number of recent voluntary transfers of land to community organisations were unquestionably motivated by the community acquisition rights established under the initial wave of land reform legislation. That wave started with the Transfer of Crofting Estates (Scotland) Act 1997, which enabled community groups to acquire crofting lands owned by the State.[3] It concluded with Part 2 of the Land Reform (Scotland) Act 2003, which created a pre-emptive right to buy land if a community group successfully registered such a right and a landowner decided to sell the land, and with Part 3 of the Land Reform (Scotland) Act 2003, which gave crofting communities a true right to buy, that is, a right to force an involuntary sale if certain conditions are met.[4]

A second, and perhaps even more ambitious, wave of land reform legislation arrived in 2015 and 2016 when the Scottish Parliament substantially upgraded the power of community groups to acquire land. In the Community Empowerment (Scotland) Act 2015, the Scottish Parliament enacted a new Part 3A to the Land Reform (Scotland) Act 2003. This 2015 legislation gives a properly constituted community body the right to force a sale of eligible land that is abandoned or neglected or whose use and management by current owners is causing harm to the environmental wellbeing of a community.[5] In the same legislation, the reach of Part 2 of the Land Reform (Scotland) Act 2003 (noted above) is expanded by extending the power of community bodies to assert a pre-emptive right to buy in urban as well as rural areas.[6]

table 1.1, p. 2. For a detailed discussion of the pace of community land acquisition and the size of various holdings, see *Estimate of Community Owned Land in Scotland*, pp. 5, 12, table 1.

[3] For details, see M. M. Combe 'The environmental implications of redistributive land reform', *Environmental Law Review*, 18:2 (2016), p. 118.

[4] See Land Reform (Scotland) Act 2003, section 51(c) and (d) (for the Part 2 community right to buy land, which was actually just a pre-emptive right) and section 74(1)(j) and (n) (for the Part 3 crofting community right to buy). For details on the provisions and impact of Parts 2 and 3 of the LRSA 2003, see Combe, 'The environmental implications of redistributive land reform', pp. 119–21.

[5] See Part 4 of the Community Empowerment (Scotland) Act 2015, section 74 (in force since 27 June 2018) (enacting a new Part 3A of the Land Reform (Scotland) Act 2003, sections 97B–97Z).

[6] Community Empowerment (Scotland) Act 2015, section 36 (in force since 15 April 2016) (amending the Land Reform Scotland Act 2003, section 33). For an exploration of the first acquisition using this expanded pre-emptive right in an urban

Finally, Part 5 of the Land Reform (Scotland) Act 2016 gives a properly constituted community body the right to force a sale of land for the purpose of furthering sustainable development.[7] Significantly, both the 2015 right to force a sale of abandoned, neglected or detrimental land and the 2016 right to force a sale for sustainable development purposes, which I refer to collectively as the New Compulsory Community Right to Buy (NCCRtB), apply not just to rural estates but literally anywhere – in urban as well as rural areas – and they apply not just to land but to all kinds of real property, with a few prominent exceptions.[8] Both of these tools also feature prominently in the Scottish Government's plans to realise the third principle of its new 'Land Rights and Responsibilities Statement': 'More local communities should have the opportunity to own, lease or use buildings and land which can contribute to their community's well-being and future development.'[9]

This chapter examines some of the key features of the NCCRtB using

setting, see J. A. Lovett and M. M. Combe, 'The Parable of Portobello: Lessons and Questions from the First Urban Acquisition Under the Scottish Community Right to Buy Regime', *Montana Law Review*, 80 (2019), p. 211.

[7] See Part 5 of the Land Reform (Scotland) Act 2016, sections 45–73. A community body's right to buy land when the current owner impedes sustainable development is anticipated to come into force at some point in 2019.

[8] I credit the authors of a commissioned report to the Scottish Land Commission for referring to the particular innovations found in Part 2 of the LRSA 2003 as a result of the CESA 2015 and in Part 5 of the LRSA 2016 as either the 'Emergent', 'extended', or '(further) emerging' CRtB. R. Mc Morran, A. Lawrence, J. Glass, A. McKee, D. Campbell and M. M. Combe, 'Review of the effectiveness of current community ownership mechanisms and of options for supporting the expansion of community ownership in Scotland' (Scottish Land Commission, Commissioned Report, 2018), pp. iii, 9, 38, <https://landcommission.gov.scot/wp-content/uploads/2018/11/1-Community-Ownership-Mechanisms-SRUC-Final-Report-For-Publication.pdf> (last accessed 18 September 2019). In coining the initialism 'NCCRtB', I have added the qualifier 'compulsory' to distinguish these two legislative regimes from the pre-emptive community right to buy found in Part 2 of the LRSA 2003. I have substituted 'new' for 'emergent' or 'extended' to acknowledge that Part 3 of the LRSA 2003 had already given a *compulsory* community right to buy to crofting communities.

[9] Part 1 of the Land Reform (Scotland) Act 2016, sections 1–3, mandates that the Scottish Government prepare and publish a land rights and responsibilities statement and requires Scottish Ministers to exercise their functions, as far as reasonably practicable, in a way that promotes the principles of that statement. In September 2017, after extensive consultation, the Scottish Government published the first 'Land Rights and Responsibilities Statement' (LRRS). See <http://www.gov.scot/Publications/2017/09/7869> (last accessed 18 September 2019). For discussion of Principle 3, see LRRS, at pp. 20–4.

the insights of international property law scholars who have analysed – and often criticised – how other legal systems provide for government actors to use the power of eminent domain (which in the UK is called compulsory purchase) to acquire private property and transfer it to another private party (a 'third party') for the purpose of stimulating economic development or providing some other public benefit. One leading German property scholar calls this practice 'third-party transfers for economic development'.[10] Others use the label 'private takings'.[11] Regardless of the name, these expropriations differ from the traditional and generally unproblematic use of eminent domain to acquire land for roads, public hospitals, military bases or schools, in that, after the involuntary acquisition, the condemned property ends up in the hands of a new private actor, rather than being owned and controlled by the government actor itself.

As one insightful pair of commentators observed, an economic development taking is essentially a 'tri-lateral exchange', rather than the typical 'bilateral exchange' found in classic eminent domain, because the expropriator acts as an intermediary facilitating an involuntary transfer of property rights from person A to person B.[12] Although Scottish Ministers never 'take title' to the land or building subject to a proposed community acquisition, the NCCRtB nevertheless involves just such an involuntary third-party transfer.

Because the essential structure of an NCCRtB transfer mirrors an 'economic development taking' or 'private taking', as those concepts are widely understood by property scholars, many stakeholders in Scotland should be interested in how property scholars who have studied these mechanisms in other countries view this exercise of state power. Those stakeholders will include not just private landowners but also Scottish land reform advocates who want the NCCRtB to acquire democratic legitimacy in Scotland, Scottish Ministers who will be charged with implementing the new legislation, and, finally, Scottish lawyers and judges who may have to assert claims and adjudicate disputes under the new legislation.

This chapter examines seven key pressure points found in the

[10] B. Hoops, *The Legitimate Justification of Expropriation* (Claremont: Juta and Co. Ltd, 2017), pp. 3–5. Hoops' recent book is the most comprehensive comparative analysis of such takings ever published.

[11] A. Bell, 'Private Takings', *University of Chicago Law Review*, 76:2 (2009), pp. 517–85.

[12] J. E. Krier and C. Serkin, 'Public Ruses', *Michigan State Law Review* (2004), pp. 859–75, 871–2.

NCCRtB legislation. These pressure points consist of rules, criteria and procedures that provide opportunities for the NCCRtB to gain (or lose) democratic legitimacy in Scottish society. This chapter thus focuses on (1) how the active agents in the NCCRtB process, so called 'community bodies,' are defined and constituted; (2) what kind of land and property is eligible for (or excluded from) a potential NCCRtB acquisition; (3) the crucial criteria for gaining Scottish Ministers' consent to a proposed community acquisition and, in particular, the 'public interest,' 'sustainable development' and 'harm to environmental wellbeing' criteria employed in the new legislation; (4) the role of community ballots in establishing democratic support for a proposed community acquisition; (5) compensation requirements; (6) opportunities for judicial scrutiny; and (7) rules about government funding and third-party purchasers. In analysing each of these pressure points, this chapter draws on the insights of four streams of contemporary property law discourse focused on third-party transfers for economic development.

FOUR STREAMS OF PROPERTY THEORY

Law and economics critique

One prominent stream of property theory that has frequently engaged in the third-party transfer debate could be called the *law and economics critique*. Although some scholars working in this tradition (and also in the often overlapping libertarian tradition) support a categorical rule prohibiting all or most expropriations resulting in a third-party transfer,[13] many law and economics scholars recognise that expropriations carried out explicitly in the name of economic development can sometimes still constitute a legitimate exercise of government power. However, even these scholars who tentatively support such takings worry that the plasticity of the typical 'public interest' or 'public use' requirement for

---

[13] For example, see I. Somin, 'The Limits of Backlash: Assessing the Political Response to *Kelo*', *Minnesota Law Review* 93:6 (2012), pp. 2100–78; J. W. Ely, 'Thomas Cooley, "Public Use" and New Directions in Takings Jurisprudence', *Michigan State Law Review* (2004), pp. 845–57. This view is epitomised by the decision of the Michigan Supreme Court in *County of Wayne* v. *Hathcock*, 684 N.W.2d 765 (Mich. 2004), and builds on nineteenth-century constitutional doctrine espoused by Thomas Cooley. See J. Lovett, 'Somewhat at Sea: Public Use and Third-Part Transfer Limits in Two US States', in B. Hoops et al. (eds), *Rethinking Expropriation I: Public Interest in Expropriation*, The Hague: Eleven International Publishing (2015), pp. 93–124.

the exercise of eminent domain can lead to abuse. Because of excessive judicial deference to the claims of government officials that a proposed transfer will produce significant public benefits, governments will be tempted to overuse the eminent domain power in the service of inefficient or wasteful projects that produce largely *private* (not public) benefits for third-party transferees who have exploited political connections and power through what economists call 'rent seeking'.

Even more frequently, these law and economics scholars worry that the property owners whose land or buildings are acquired for such projects are often undercompensated in important ways. The targeted property owner's individual, subjective interests – personal attachments to property, social capital, ties to jobs, homes and community – are not sufficiently accounted for by the standard 'fair market' valuation metric used by most states and courts to calculate the amount of compensation a condemnee will receive for the involuntary transfer of property.

Law and economics-oriented property scholars tend to propose two types of solutions to these deficiencies in third-party transfers. First, some suggest that courts should scrutinise the proposed economic development projects much more carefully. One influential early voice in this tradition, Lawrence Berger, argued that courts should probe the transactional setting of a proposed third-party transfer to make sure that the targeted property owner actually possesses monopoly power in the relevant local marketplace. Identification of this monopoly power would signal to the court that expropriation is necessary to prevent the property owner from extracting a supra-competitive price for his property and assure that the net aggregate economic gain resulting from the transfer will substantially outweigh the harm inflicted on the condemnee by the involuntary nature of the transaction.[14]

Another seminal contribution to this literature came from Thomas Merrill.[15] Building on Berger, Merrill focused on expropriations in which the state uses its compulsory purchase power to facilitate large-scale urban renewal or economic expansion projects rather than to acquire resources for its own public functions, to create true public goods, or to confront small-scale 'thin market' situations like those involving land-locked parcels. In the former category, which he viewed as more danger-ous, Merrill argued that courts should have discretion to reject 'public

---

[14] L. Berger, 'The Public Use Requirement in Eminent Domain', *Oregon Law Review*, 57 (1978), pp. 204–46, 235–45.

[15] T. W. Merrill, 'The Economics of Public Use', *Cornell Law Review*, 72 (1986), pp. 61–116.

use' justifications whenever (a) the targeted property owner's subjective losses are high, (b) one or a small number of persons will capture the taking's surplus or assembly value, or (c) private condemnees face thin markets because of their own intentional actions or negligence.[16]

In more recent years, property scholars working in the law and economics tradition have grown increasingly sceptical of courts' institutional capacity to make these fine-grained distinctions about the scope of public versus private benefits on the back end of proposed third-party transfers. While some have thus advocated for stringent categorical rules that would completely prohibit or narrowly cabin third-party transfers,[17] others have crafted solutions that focus on making sure that targeted property owners are not systematically undercompensated.

A handful of scholars, such as Berger and Richard Epstein, recommend that compensation awards for third-party transfers should be set *ex ante* at some substantial premium above fair market value (say 150 per cent) to discourage economic development takings in which the net gain in efficiency is only marginal at best.[18] Others argue that courts should protect condemnees by more radically changing the rules of just compensation. James Krier and Christopher Serkin, for instance, argue that when courts value condemned property, they should be required to use projections about the economic benefits that will supposedly flow from the proposed transfer instead of limiting valuation to the economic conditions that exist at the time of the expropriation.[19] Such a future-oriented valuation practice would allow condemnees to share in the economic benefits that the community as a whole will receive and would further induce government proponents of such transfers to 'bear

[16] Merrill, 'The Economics of Public Use', 83–5.

[17] See authors cited at note 13. For the most comprehensive critical account of economic development takings in the US literature that supports a *per se* prohibition on such expropriations, see I. Somin, *The Grasping Hand*: Kelo v. City of New London *and the Limits of Eminent Domain* (Chicago: University of Chicago Press, 2016).

[18] Berger, 'The Public Use Requirement in Eminent Domain', pp. 236–7; R. A. Epstein, *Takings: Private Property and the Power of Eminent Domain* (Cambridge: Harvard University Press 1985), 173–5, 184. A number of US states have adopted this approach when expropriation is used to acquire a person's home or other specific kinds of property. See Lovett, 'Somewhat at Sea', n. 96 (cataloguing statutes). But see B. A. Lee, 'Just Undercompensation: The Idiosyncratic Premium in Eminent Domain', *Columbia Law Review* 113:3 (2013), 593–655, 634–49 (critiquing fixed percentage awards above fair market value).

[19] Krier and Serkin, 'Public Ruses', pp. 868–73.

the costs of undue optimism about the benefits of their programs', and thus produce 'incentives to make realistic assessments'.[20]

Lee Anne Fennell offers her own version of heightened judicial review of the 'public benefits' claimed to result from a third-party transfer and grounds that review in American 'regulatory takings' doctrine.[21] Yet even if a proposed third-party transfer satisfies this invigorated test, Fennell argues that targeted property owners should be able to protect their interest in what she calls 'the uncompensated increment' through 'self-assessment tools'.[22] Her crucial, perhaps mischievous, suggestion is that targeted property owners should be permitted to 'opt-in' to a private taking by setting their own subjective premium above the state's fair market valuation within some specified range in exchange for an annual property tax break. Each year, a property owner opting for self-assessment would effectively grant an option to the state for private takings in exchange for predictable tax breaks.[23]

Finally, Michael Heller and Rick Hills propose that property owners facing a condemnation-assisted development project should be given *voice* to act on their own behalf on a community-wide scale.[24] When any government or private entity is seeking to assemble a number of parcels for an economic development project and the parcels are not uniquely situated (for example, along the route of a proposed highway or next to an expanding airport or harbour), the affected group of property owners should be entitled to form a democratically managed,

[20] Krier and Serkin, 'Public Ruses', p. 869. In extreme cases where the proposed third-party transfer is designed solely to produce a surplus value from land assembly (and no public good or other public benefit), Krier and Serkin suggest that courts should employ 'gain-based' compensation rules, that is, condemnation awards based on the value that the condemned property would have had if the owners had been able to hold out for the anticipated gains resulting from the condemnation. Ibid., pp. 870–1.

[21] L. A. Fennell, 'Taking Eminent Domain Apart', *Michigan State Law Review* (2004), pp. 957–1004, 987–92.

[22] Fennell, 'Taking Eminent Domain Apart', pp. 958–9. Fennell argues that the 'uncompensated increment' consists of three components: (1) the owner's subjective premium, that is, her subjective valuation that exceeds the fair market value and includes personal attachments and social capital; (2) the chance of reaping surplus, post-transfer value; and (3) the value inherent in owner autonomy. Ibid., pp. 962–7.

[23] Fennell, 'Taking Eminent Domain Apart', pp. 995–1002. Fennell's self-assessment compensation scheme draws heavily on an earlier model proposed by Saul Levmore in other contexts. See S. Levmore, 'Self-Assessed Valuation Systems for Tort and Other Law', *Virginia Law Review*, 68 (1982), pp. 771, 779, 784–90.

[24] M. Heller and R. Hills, 'Land Assembly Districts', *Harvard Law Review*, 121:6 (2008), pp. 1465–526.

bottom-up, quasi-governmental entity called a LAD (Land Assembly District). The members of the LAD would be able to decide by ballot whether their neighbourhood will be sold to the land assembler. If the vote were affirmative, elected representatives of the LAD could then negotiate with the assembler and set the selling price and other terms of the property acquisition. Targeted property owners unhappy with the eventual bargain could opt-out, but then their property could be acquired by traditional expropriation measures and their compensation would be limited to market value or by other statutorily defined valuation metrics.[25]

Perhaps the most sophisticated and certainly the most empirically detailed intervention in the law and economics tradition is Yun-Chien Chang's book-length work, *Private Property and Takings Compensation*.[26] Chang's wide-ranging and analytically rigorous study draws on his analysis of thousands of traditional physical takings in Taiwan and New York City and benefits from his four-part typology of assessment methods for condemnation.[27] Chang ultimately concludes that the most efficient, fair and accurate compensation system is one that relies on *ex post* assessment by non-landowners and awards compensation based on the fair market value of condemned properties (the amount a willing buyer would pay a willing seller taking into account not just the current use of the property but all possible uses to which the property might be put other than the use contemplated by the condemnor) and supplements the assessed value with bonus compensation.[28] Crucially, however, the type of bonus compensation that Chang recommends is not a flat premium increase, but rather one based on a schedule of bonus rates that, for example, gives long-term owner-occupants a higher bonus rate to compensate for subjective value and gives owners of non-residential or investment residential property only fair market value compensation.[29] To achieve these ends, Chang also recommends that legal systems utilise a 'hedonic regression model' (essentially an enlarged and more scientific version of comparable sales valuation that takes advantage of 'big data' and factors in many more properties

[25] Heller and Hills, 'Land Assembly Districts', pp. 1448–97.

[26] Y. Chang, *Private Property and Takings Compensation* (Cheltenham: Edward Elgar, 2013).

[27] Chang distinguishes between (1) *ex ante* assessment by landowners, (2) *ex ante* assessment by non-landowners, (3) *ex post* assessment by landowners, and (4) *ex post* assessment by non-landowners. Chang, *Private Property*, pp. 8–12.

[28] Chang, *Private Property*, pp. 4, 55–8, 171–2.

[29] Chang, *Private Property*, pp. 168–70.

and more property characteristics) in eminent domain proceedings to guarantee that landowners obtain no less than fair market value when their property is taken for public use.[30] Although Chang's study does not focus on the special problem of economic development takings, his insights and findings are still highly relevant to the future legitimacy of the NCCRtB.

Progressive property critique

The second stream of contemporary property theory that informs my analysis of the NCCRtB springs from a group of scholars often associated with the *progressive property* movement. Although these theorists are often portrayed as duelling with law and economics property scholars, and particularly with a subset known as 'information theorists' or the 'new essentialists,' the two groups share some common concerns when it comes to economic development takings.

After the United States Supreme Court's controversial decision in *Kelo* v. *City of New London*,[31] several progressive property theorists criticised the majority opinion for its insensitivity to the interests of homeowners who were asked to relinquish their homes for the sake of an economic development project that promised to remake their community in dramatic ways but did not offer the affected homeowners a place in the revitalised community to come. Eduardo Peñalver, for instance, faults the Court for not recognising the 'inherent dignity of home ownership' and not treating homes with an amount of respect that corresponds to the place that this particular form of property has in individual lives.[32] His solution to this judicial failure to honour dignity interests, however, mirrors that of many law and economics scholars. He does not rule out all economic development takings and does not even reject them categorically when they impinge on homeowners. Instead, Peñalver calls for courts to use heightened scrutiny – permitting such

---

[30] Chang, *Private Property*, pp. 29–30, 55–6, 106–66, 171–2. Chang also provides a useful critique of various proposals for determining compensation through landowner self-assessment whether conducted *ex ante* or *ex post*. Chang, *Private Property*, pp. 35–52. Chang provides a succinct summary of his proposed 'hedonic regression models' in Y. Chang, 'Eminent Domain Law in Taiwan: New Law, Old Practice?', in I. Kim et al. *Eminent Domain: A Comparative Prospective*, Cambridge: Cambridge University Press, 93 (2017), pp. 110–13.

[31] 545 US 469 (2005).

[32] E. Peñalver, 'Property Metaphors and Kelo v. New London: Two Views of the Castle', *Fordham Law Review*, 74 (2006), pp. 2971, 2973.

takings only when 'necessary to accomplish important public objectives' – whenever the exercise of eminent domain requires the sacrifice of individual homes.[33]

Laura Underkuffler offers an even more damning critique of *Kelo* and its infamous predecessor *Poletown Neighborhood Council* v. *City of Detroit*,[34] arguing that the failure in those cases stemmed not from the contours of 'public use' doctrine, but rather from the courts' failure to honour 'the principle of equally respected participation' and the courts' 'selective disregard of community'.[35] Underkuffler's critique is particularly important for this chapter because she explains that coercive action taken by a government can only acquire democratic legitimacy if citizens perceive it as 'reasonable and rational'. Yet reasonability and rationality are not purely utilitarian notions for Underkuffler. Instead, they are grounded in something she calls 'moral warrant'.[36] Although most property owners and even most homeowners know that their property is vulnerable to expropriation (according to Underkuffler), they also believe – and are entitled to believe – that it will not be impaired arbitrarily or without their consent or participation. Building on the insights of Frank Michaelman, Underkuffler points out that property – and especially a home – provides the 'material foundation' for social and political self-expression.[37] By allowing the two large-scale expropriation projects to go forward in *Poletown* and *Kelo*, the planners and courts effectively negated residents' opportunities for political participation and subordinated their small-scale community interests to those of the larger community of city, state and nation. Like Peñalver and many of the law and economics scholars, however, Underkuffler essentially recommends more careful judicial oversight, especially when the targeted community is economically and politically vulnerable. Importantly, though, she does not categorically rule out third-party economic development takings.[38]

---

[33] Peñalver, *Property Metaphors*, p. 2975. Peñalver believes that 'large agricultural and mining interests', many of whom he contends are active donors to property rights groups, do not deserve any form of heightened judicial protection when their property is targeted for expropriation. Ibid., p. 2976.

[34] 304 N.W.2d 455 (Mich. 1981) (per curiam), overruled by *County of Wayne* v. *Hathcock*, 684 N.W.2d 765, 787 (Mich. 2004).

[35] L. S. Underkuffler, 'Kelo's Moral Failure', *William & Mary Bill of Rights Journal*, 15:2 (2006), pp. 377, 379–80.

[36] Underkuffler, 'Kelo's Moral Failure', p. 383.

[37] Underkuffler, 'Kelo's Moral Failure', p. 383 (quoting F. I. Michelman, 'Mr. Justice Brennan: A Property Teacher's Appreciation', *Harvard Civil Rights-Civil Liberties Law Review*, 15 (1980): pp. 296, 298–9).

[38] Underkuffler, 'Kelo's Moral Failure', p. 385.

Gregory Alexander, another prominent progressive property theorist, proposes a sophisticated four-step 'purposive' analysis informed by German and South African constitutional law to determine whether a proposed economic development taking should proceed.[39] In the first step, what I call 'scoping', courts must reflect on the core values that underlie property as a constitutionally protected right and contemplate how those values promote human flourishing. In the second step, 'scaling', courts must next identify which of those particular values are placed at risk and measure, in terms of the specific owners involved, the extent to which those values are diminished by the proposed expropriation.[40] In steps three and four, what I call 'timing' and 'looking at both sides', courts must take account of the fact that the roles property can play in individual lives can change dramatically over time, and must acknowledge that an expropriation affects not just the targeted owner but many intended beneficiaries of the expropriation.[41] Although the last step echoes Fennell's call for consideration of the 'average reciprocity of advantage' and the 'character of the governmental advantage' factors from US regulatory takings doctrine, it also evokes Underkuffler's principle of equally respected participation. In the end, Alexander essentially calls for an especially sensitive, highly contextualised 'proportionality' test for third-party takings, one that requires consideration of whether expropriation is the 'only possible means of meeting a particular public need' or is 'strictly necessary' to achieve the particular public ends in view.[42]

The last progressive property theorist whose insights inform my analysis of the NCCRtB may have been the first to address involuntary economic development transfers. In an article that launched much of the progressive property movement in the US and that preceded *Kelo* and even *Poletown*, Joseph Singer famously argued that US courts should recognise that a community consisting of approximately 3,500 employees in Youngstown, Ohio (and their labour union) should have a 'legal

[39] G. S. Alexander, 'The Public Use Requirement and the Character of Consequentialist Reasoning', in B. Hoops et al. (eds), *Rethinking Expropriation II: Context, Criteria, and Consequences of Expropriation* (The Hague: Eleven International Publishing, 2015), pp. 113–35.

[40] Alexander, 'The Public Use Requirement', pp. 124–8.

[41] Alexander, 'The Public Use Requirement', pp. 128–9.

[42] Alexander, 'The Public Use Requirement', p. 132. Alexander has recently updated his proposed purposive analysis for economic development takings in G. Alexander, *Property and Human Flourishing* (New York: Oxford University Press, 2018), pp. 218–29.

right to buy' two steel manufacturing plants owned by US Steel that the company planned to close.[43] Although US courts eventually rejected the employees' claims,[44] Singer contended that US property law should be reconceptualised to account for the moral claims that workers – and the Youngstown community more generally – developed in the continued operation of the plants through their many decades of work and through the broader sacrifices made by the workers, their families and the plants' suppliers to the success of US Steel. Singer specifically argued that the workers' reliance interest claims could be validated either through a judicially supervised buyout, a right of first refusal, or the use of the state or local government's power of eminent domain which would allow for the plants to be transferred either directly to the union or to third parties who would keep them running profitably.[45]

The last two streams of contemporary property discourse addressing third-party transfers, discussed in the next two sections, each have their source in the work of a single scholar, yet their concerns partially overlap with the first two streams. Each of these idiosyncratic critiques has quite specific lessons for the NCCRtB.

Political economy critique

The first idiosyncratic voice is that of William Fischel. In a 2004 article, Fischel re-evaluated the *Poletown* controversy and the dire economic situation facing Detroit, Michigan in the late 1970s that led it and its partner city, Hamtramck, to exercise the power of eminent domain to acquire 1,000 homes and small business, resulting in the removal of 4,200 people, for the purpose of assembling a 465-acre tract of land and then transferring that land to General Motors Corporation (GM) so that it could build a new Cadillac manufacturing plant.[46]

Drawing on the work of several social scientists who studied the crisis,[47] Fischel rejects the narrative that *Poletown* is a story of servile

[43] J. W. Singer, 'The Reliance Interest in Property', *Stanford Law Review*, 40 (1988), p. 614, at p. 617.

[44] Local 1330, *United Steel Workers* v. *US Steel Corp.*, 492 F.Supp. 1, 9–10 (N.D. Ohio 1980); Local 1330, *US Workers* v. *United States Steel Corp.*, 631 F.2d 1264, 1283 (6th Cir. 1980).

[45] Singer, 'The Reliance Interest in Property', pp. 737–8.

[46] W. A. Fischel, 'The Political Economy of Public Use in Poletown: How Federal Grants Encourage Excessive Use of Eminent Domain', *Michigan State Law Review* (2004), pp. 929–55.

[47] B. D. Jones and L. W. Bachelor, *The Sustaining Hand: Community Leadership*

politicians who buckled to the whims of a greedy corporation and sold out a community united in opposition to the project. Instead, Fischel points out that almost every interest group, political leader and institution in Detroit at the time supported the project, including Coleman Young, the city's first African-American mayor, the United Autoworkers Union, the Archdiocese of Detroit and politicians from every party and racial group. Moreover, many local homeowners whose property was acquired for the project cooperated willingly and, in fact, welcomed the generous compensation packages offered by the expropriating municipalities. Despite this, Fischel still recognises that the massive scale of the dislocation eventually approved by the Michigan Supreme Court in *Poletown* was itself problematic and represented a political – though not necessarily an economic – failure.[48]

For Fischel, the real source of failure did not lie in the lack of democratic participation but rather in the fact that neither political decision-makers nor the larger political community had to consider whether the funds used for the involuntary acquisitions could have been put to better use for some other kind of community project. In other words, Detroit taxpayers were not asked to sacrifice anything to fund the project. As Fischel explains, most of the financing for the acquisition came from the US government in the form of a $100 million loan from the US Department of Housing and Urban Development (HUD) that would be paid off over time by taxes on the newly completed GM plant itself

---

and Corporate Power (Lawrence: University Press of Kansas, 1986). See also J. J. Bukowczyk, 'The Decline and Fall of a Detroit Neighborhood: Poletown v. G.M. and the City of Detroit', *Washington & Lee Law Review*, 41 (1984), pp. 49–76.

[48] Fischel, 'The Political Economy of Public Use in Poletown', pp. 936–42, 950–1. Fischel also argues that the most significant factor explaining why some property owners welcomed and others opposed the condemnations was age rather than race or class. Younger homeowners generally welcomed the usually above-fair-market-value compensation packages offered to Poletown property owners and used the awards to buy new homes in other areas whereas older homeowners, particularly older white homeowners, were more reluctant to leave their neighbourhood and foresaw greater disruption in their accumulated social capital. Ibid., pp. 941, 951–2. Fischel refuses to classify the Poletown project as an economic failure because the Cadillac plant was, in fact, constructed and, at the time of publication, was still producing Cadillacs with a workforce of 3,000. Ibid., p. 940. In late 2018, however, General Motors finally announced the closure of the Detroit-Hamtramck manufacturing facility that resulted from the Poletown expropriation. See N. Boudette, 'G.M. to Idle Plants and Cut Thousands of Jobs as Sales Slow', *New York Times*, 26 November 2018, <https://www.nytimes.com/2018/11/26/business/general-motors-cutbacks.html> (last accessed 21 January 2019).

and by block grants from HUD to the City of Detroit. The remainder of the financing came from direct federal and state grants.[49] Further, as the funds used to acquire the land for the GM facility were generally restricted to that particular project, the Detroit community could treat that financing as a non-fungible gift. No one had to consider whether that money could have produced greater benefit to the community if it had been used for public transportation, public health, public schools or police, to name just a few possible alternatives. In short, local decision-makers did not have to calculate 'opportunity costs' for the use of those funds and could insulate local taxpayers from such calculations as well.[50]

Building on these insights, Fischel recommends that courts should continue to defer to local governments' decisions to use eminent domain for traditionally public or even quasi-public uses – for example, to acquire land that will be used for an instrumentality of commerce or to acquire linear or large, contiguous parcels where holdout problems loom. However, when eminent domain is used for non-traditional purposes (pure economic development takings), courts should be required to engage in a more exacting form of review that focuses on the *source* and *fungibility* of the funds being used to acquire the targeted property. If the funds are entirely self-generated by the expropriating authority through taxation of its own constituents, the expropriation should be presumptively legitimate because local voters themselves should, in theory, have strong incentives to ask whether their tax payments should be used for the particular proposed involuntary acquisition. However, if the funds that will finance the expropriation originate from other sources, particularly higher levels of government, courts should require that the expropriating governmental authority prove that it could have used the funds for some other civic purpose but that it intentionally decided to use the funds for the third-party expropriation instead.[51] According to Fischel, the advantage of this internal-versus-external source test (a kind of 'skin in the game' test) and the 'fungibility' assessment for externally generated funds, is that they will allow third-party economic development takings to go forward but only when the active government intermediary puts its own funding at risk or can show that it made a serious 'opportunity cost' assessment. In short, Fischel's political economy approach provides more elasticity than a set of narrow

[49] Fischel, 'The Political Economy of Public Use in Poletown', pp. 943–4.
[50] Fischel, 'The Political Economy of Public Use in Poletown', pp. 944–5.
[51] Fischel, 'The Political Economy of Public Use in Poletown', pp. 949–50.

categorical rules for the public-use inquiry, but it offers the promise of increased constituent accountability.

Ownership as investment

The last critique of contemporary economic development takings comes from Debbie Becher, a US-based sociologist, who has published a striking book-length study revealing her analysis of thousands of expropriations conducted by government redevelopment agencies in Philadelphia, Pennsylvania.[52] Becher argues that property owners and government officials themselves regard such takings as legitimate if the redevelopment project as a whole protects and honours the targeted property owner's 'investment in property'.[53] For Becher, a property owner's 'investment' refers to 'the sacrifice of any kind of value in the hope of obtaining some future benefit' and has two crucial characteristics.[54] First, the sources of values that are sacrificed by the owner must be understood from a pluralistic perspective, that is, a property owner's sacrifice might take the form of money or physical resources, but could just as easily be understood in terms of social capital, skills, career, wisdom or even love. Second, for a property owner's sacrifice to really count as 'investment' it must involve a commitment of time. Thus, an economic development taking must account for the longevity of an owner's sacrifice and commitment to the property at stake.[55]

Translating this insight into practical institutional design, Becher

---

[52] D. Becher, *Private Property and Public Power: Eminent Domain in Philadelphia* (New York: Oxford University Press, 2014). For details of the scope of her research project and its methods, see Ibid., pp. 12-15, and Appendix 1, pp. 259–69.

[53] As Becher continues: 'To secure an investment, government needs, therefore, to protect the value that an individual holds in a property. Government should preserve or help that value grow over time. In addition, an individual's attachment of value to a property gives him or her a claim to the future of the community in which that property is located. Residents who demand a say in how a neighborhood will change and in whether particular changes will enhance or detract from community's value justify this demand through their past sacrifices to the community. In other words, government is expected to protect investment at both the individual and collective level.' Becher, *Private Property and Public Power*, p. 8. Becher defines 'legitimacy' as 'a practical judgment that an action is reasonably justified', and as 'a facet of practice, rather than philosophy or ideology'. Becher, *Private Property and Public Power*, p. 11. For a more detailed elaboration of her theory, see Becher, *Private Property and Public Power*, pp. 225–57.

[54] Becher, *Private Property and Public Power*, p. 8.

[55] Becher, *Private Property and Public Power*, pp. 8, 18–19.

advises that if, for example, an economic development project requires assembly of a large parcel through involuntary acquisitions, those acquisitions will ultimately garner much more public and community support if the planners articulate respect for the multiplicity of sacrifices that owners have made in and for their property and craft compensation remedies that take those sacrifices into account. Consequently, Becher stresses that if an economic development project will require long-term property owners to sacrifice their investment in the short-run, they should be guaranteed some meaningful opportunity to participate in the project's long-run operation and thus re-establish the economic and social connections that developed as a result of their initial 'investments' in their property.[56] Becher is not the only scholar to have made this point. Indeed, in the immediate aftermath of *Kelo*, James Kelly powerfully argued that economic development takings should only be allowed to proceed if expropriating redevelopment agencies used a Homestead Community Consent procedure similar in many ways to the LADs of Heller and Hills, and only if residents in a targeted community are guaranteed an alienable Community Residency Entitlement (CRE), that is, a right to comparable replacement housing in the redeveloped district.[57] Nevertheless, Becher has provided an exceptionally strong empirical case for protecting property owners' sense of investment as a means of securing the long-term success of economic development projects that depend on expropriation.

THE NCCRTB – PRESSURE POINTS AND LEGITIMACY MOMENTS

As noted earlier, the NCCRtB has principally emerged in two Acts of the Scottish Parliament: the Community Empowerment (Scotland) Act 2015 ('CESA 2015'), which enacts a new Part 3A of the Land Reform

---

[56] Becher, *Private Property and Public Power*, pp. 3, 10 (describing success of projects that guaranteed targeted homeowners an opportunity to purchase a new home in planned redevelopment with their compensation payment or other opportunities to reclaim their full social investment in their properties). Conversely, Becher's theory explains why she observed hardly any opposition to economic development takings when a targeted parcel is a vacant or abandoned lot. In those cases, there is no sign of any investment in the resource and, in fact, neighbouring owners often welcome government intervention as securing *their* investments in property. Becher, *Private Property and Public Power*, pp. 7, 9–10.

[57] J. F. Kelly, '"We Shall Not Be Moved", Urban Communities, Eminent Domain and the Socioeconomics of Just Compensation', *St. John's Law Review*, 80:3 (2006), pp. 923–90. See especially Kelly, pp. 982–5.

(Scotland) Act 2003 ('LRSA 2003'), and in Part 5 of the Land Reform (Scotland) Act 2016 ('LRSA 2016'). Several provisions of the Acts are likely to prove particularly challenging for community organisations trying to achieve a community acquisition, for Scottish Ministers who must give their consent for a proposed community acquisition, and ultimately for reviewing courts. These challenging provisions thus constitute pressure points in the legislation. They create opportunities for community acquisitions relying on the NCCRtB to gain or lose democratic legitimacy.

Community bodies

The first key feature of the NCCRtB emerges in the requirements for the formation of a community body that can exercise the right to provoke an involuntary transfer and in the definition of a community itself. A community body can now consist of a wide variety of non-profit organisations, ranging from a company limited by guarantee, a Scottish charitable incorporated organisation, to a community benefit society. The only essential requirements are that the entity's governing rules define the community to which it relates, that the entity have at least ten members, three quarters of whom are members of the community, that these local, community-based members 'have control' of the entity, that surplus funds or assets be applied to the benefit of the community, and, in the case of an organisation being wound-up, that assets be distributed to another approved community body, the government or a chosen charity.[58] All of these rules serve to anchor a community body in the geographical community it aims to represent and guarantee a significant amount of community commitment to the underlying project. At the same time, these requirements provide a great deal of flexibility and allow even a modest group of committed residents of a place to start the process of becoming the actual directors of an organisation that controls a significant amount of community land. These new rules may well help facilitate the process of converting land to community ownership and encourage community acquisitions to bubble up organically from the base of communities rather than originate from a high-level government authority.

---

[58] LRSA 2003, section 97D; LRSA 2016, section 49. These same organisational requirements also appear in section 34 and section 71 of the LRSA 2003, which gives community bodies a preemptive right to buy and crofting communities a right to buy crofting land respectively, as updated by CESA 2015, sections 37, 62.

One interesting aspect of the rules relating to the formation of a community body concerns the definition of a 'community' itself. Both of the relevant parts of the Acts establishing the revitalised CRtB define a 'community' by reference to one or more postcode units *or* a 'prescribed type of area' or an area specified by the Scottish Ministers.[59] In one sense, this definition creates more flexibility than existed in the first incarnation of earlier CRtB legislation, because it allows for a relevant community to be defined by a boundary line on a map, or by various other geographic or political boundaries, rather than an arbitrary postal code.[60] However, the Acts still appear to define a relevant community as a 'community of place' and make no provision for what some social scientists call a 'community of interest'.[61]

This limitation is notable because in Part 5 of the CESA 2015 (titled 'Asset Transfer Requests'), the Scottish Parliament gives a 'community transfer body' the right to request that land owned by the state or some public entity be transferred to the community body by sale or lease and requires Scottish Ministers to consider such a request under a broad range of community development criteria and yet does *not* require that a community transfer body be grounded in any particular community of place.[62] Thus, under Part 5 of the CESA, a community transfer body could comprise any group of people that believe they have something in common and could include, for instance, a faith group, an ethnic or cultural group, people affected by a particular illness or disability, a sports club, a conservation group, or even a clan or heritage group.[63]

[59] LRSA 2003, section 97D(9)(a); LRSA 2016, section 49(9)(b).

[60] Land Reform Review Group (LRRG), 'Final Report: The Land of Scotland and the Common Good' (Edinburgh: Scottish Government, 2014), section 17.1 at p. 98, available at <http://www.gov.scot/Resource/0045/00451087.pdf> or <http://www.gov.scot/Publications/2014/05/2852/0> (both last accessed 18 September 2019). Section 34(5) of the LRSA 2003, as amended by the Community Right to Buy (Scotland) Regulations 2015 (SSI 2015/400), now allows for considerations other than postcode units to be used with the pre-emptive right to buy.

[61] Some land reform advocates suggest that the concept of community should be broadened to include this wider notion of 'community of interest'. LRRG, 'The Land of Scotland and the Common Good', section 15.1, at p. 82. This portion of the Report of the Land Reform Review Group (LRRG) clearly influenced the drafting of the new rules on formation of community bodies.

[62] CESA 2015, sections 77–82. See especially section 80 of the CESA 2015, defining a community transfer body that may make a request for a transfer of land solely in terms of the non-profit status of the organisation and requiring that the company have not fewer than twenty members.

[63] See *A Step by Step Guide for Community Bodies on Asset Transfer as Part*

From the perspective of the four streams of property theory discussed above, this relatively narrow conception of 'community' for the NCCRtB is defensible for now but might require subtle adjustment in the future. In many places in Scotland where the NCCRtB, and its legislative cousin, the preemptive right to purchase land after registration, are most likely to be used, a relevant community may be quite easily identified by a postal code or by a geographic line designated on a map. For example, the community might inhabit an island or a relatively remote portion of the Scottish Highlands. However, if the NCCRtB increasingly gains a foothold in urban or peri-urban areas, geographic lines and postal codes could prove arbitrary and irrelevant in some cases. Further, it may be necessary to widen the scope of a relevant community as was done in Part 5 of CESA 2015 regarding asset transfer requests to allow communities of interest to organise themselves for a community acquisition. Yet if communities of interest do begin to play a greater role in CRtB acquisitions, policy-makers and Scottish Ministers would be well advised to consider whether reliance on communities of interest could lead to the unintended exclusion of some members of a broader social community from participation in a community development project. As Underkuffler and other progressive property theorists warn, for the state's power of eminent domain to remain grounded in 'the principle of equally respected participation', inclusion rather than exclusion must characterise the entire process of expropriation even if the benefits are directed at a local community.

Eligible land

The next important hurdle for a community group seeking to take advantage of the NCCRtB is to demonstrate that the property it seeks to acquire is, in fact, 'eligible land' within the framework of either Act. Two features of the new legislation are crucial in this regard. One feature dramatically expands the scope of property within reach of a community body; the other creates a significant carve-out.

First, under the new Part 3A of the LRSA 2003, eligible land is any land, rural or urban, that is 'wholly or mainly abandoned or neglected' or any land whose current use or management is causing, directly

of the *Community Empowerment (Scotland) Act 2015* (23 January 2017), at <https://beta.gov.scot/publications/asset-transfer-under-community-empowerment-scotland-act-2015-guidance-community-9781786527509/pages/5/> (last accessed 18 September 2019).

or indirectly, 'harm to the environmental well-being of a relevant community'.[64] Harm is defined to include 'any adverse effect on the lives of persons comprising the relevant community'.[65] Recent implementing regulations, however, appear to narrow the scope of abandoned, neglected and detrimental land by instructing that these terms should be understood primarily in the context of the physical condition of the land or buildings at issue, the length of time that the condition has persisted, and the link between the deficient physical condition and threats to public safety, adjacent land or the environment.[66]

The ability of a community body to acquire what US property law scholars would call 'blighted' property is not a surprising development. The influential 2014 report of the Land Reform Review Group (LRRG) to the Scottish Government entitled 'The Land of Scotland and the Common Good' explicitly urged that this kind of neglected or detrimental property be subject to forced sales in the form of auctions and recommended that communities be allowed to participate in these auctions.[67] Property theorists of many stripes would likely support this move. Indeed, Debbie Becher's empirical study of expropriations in Philadelphia reveals that many of the expropriations there were widely welcomed and essentially uncontroversial because owners of blighted property were seen as having effectively disinvested or failed to maintain their investment in property, thus legitimising an involuntary acquisition by redevelopment authorities.[68] Although many property commentators in the US have warned that 'blight' takings can lead to abuse because the statutory definitions of 'blighted' land or buildings are often vague,[69] the CESA 2015 attempts to avoid this problem by specifying that the environmental harm mentioned above must be *more than* 'negligible'.[70] Moreover, the new draft regulations, which aim to circumscribe the category of abandoned, neglected or detrimental land to properties in

---

[64] LRSA 2003, section 97C(2).

[65] LRSA 2003, section 97C(3)(a).

[66] The Community Right to Buy (Abandoned, Neglected or Detrimental Land) (Eligible Land, Regulators and Restrictions on Dealing (Scotland) Regulations 2018 (SSI 2018/208), regulation 3.

[67] 'The Land of Scotland and the Common Good', section 20.1, at p. 121–4.

[68] Becher, *Private Property and Public Power*, pp. 7, 9–10.

[69] I. Somin, 'Let There Be Blight: Blight Condemnations in New York after Goldstein and Kaur', *Fordham Urban Law Review*, 38 (2011), pp. 1193–219; A. Tutt, 'Blightened Scrutiny', *University of California, Davis Law Review*, 47 (2014), pp. 1807–41.

[70] LRSA 2003, section 97C(2).

a physical state of deterioration that are causing immediate health and safety threats or harming adjacent properties, would also be welcomed by US critics of relatively unconstrained blight takings.

Following the approach used to establish the scope of the generally well-received right of responsible access under Part 1 of the LRSA 2003,[71] Part 5 of the LRSA 2016 adopts a universalist approach to the question of what land is within reach of a community body seeking to acquire land through the NCCRtB. Adopting a key recommendation of the LRRG in 'The Land of Scotland and the Common Good', the 2016 legislation defines 'eligible land' to include all rural and urban land in Scotland and even includes bridges and structures built on or over land, inland waters, canals, the foreshore, salmon fishings in inland waters, and mineral rights owned separately from the land.[72] A community body can also apply to acquire a tenancy over eligible land, as long as the tenancy is not a croft tenancy, the tenancy of a dwelling house or any other kind of tenancy that regulations may specify, provided the community body also seeks to acquire the land subject to the tenancy.[73] The only land that is excluded under Part 5 of the LRSA is 'land on which there is a building or other structure which is an individual's home unless the building or structure is occupied by an individual under a tenancy' and 'croft land' within the meaning of the LRSA 2003.[74] The CESA 2015 similarly excludes from the reach of a community acquisition of abandoned, neglected or environmentally harmful property 'an individual's home other than a building or other structure which is occupied by an individual under a tenancy' and 'eligible croft land'.[75]

---

[71] For a detailed study of that legislation and its reception by Scottish courts in light of US property theory, see J. A. Lovett, 'Progressive Property in Action: The Land Reform (Scotland) Act of 2003', *Nebraska Law Review*, 89:4 (2011), pp. 739–818. For a new book on this topic, see M. M. Combe, *The ScotWays Guide to the Law of Access to Land in Scotland* (Edinburgh: John Donald, 2018).

[72] LRSA 2016, section 45.

[73] LRSA 2016, section 48. A possible reason that the Scottish Parliament allows community bodies to use the NCCRtB to acquire all but the specifically exempted tenancies is to prevent hostile landowners from frustrating the purpose of the Act by simply creating a tenancy in favour of a trust, a closely held corporation or even just a friend.

[74] LRSA 2016, section 46(1)–(2). See 'The Land of Scotland and the Common Good', section 17.1 at p. 98 (recommending wider geographic scope for the pre-emptive right to buy). See also Wightman, *The Poor Had No Lawyers*, pp. 357–8 (criticising earlier legislation creating statutory rights for Scotland as too narrow in scope and particularly for excluding urban places).

[75] LRSA 2003, section 97C(5)(a)–(d).

This broad exclusion of owner-occupied homes from the NCCRtB under both Acts goes quite far to put to rest concerns raised by both law and economics scholars and progressive property scholars about the tendency of third-party expropriations to strip homeowners of their subjective premium, to undermine 'the inherent dignity of homeowner-ship', or to weaken the 'material foundation' for social and political self-expression. Some might wonder, though, whether the blanket exclusion of owner-occupied homes from the category of eligible land might take too much property off the table and might unduly discourage a community of homeowners from organising themselves into a structure like a LAD that could negotiate with a developer for a community wide buyout and subsequent redevelopment and relocation initiative. Interestingly, one of the most intriguing proposals in 'The Land of Scotland and the Common Good' suggests that a device known as an 'Urban Partnership Zone' could accomplish this goal.[76] Whether the exclusion of owner-occupied homes from the scope of the NCCRtB would frustrate this kind of initiative is a question for further study.

Admittedly, the ability of a community body to acquire land or build-ings housing residential tenants does seem odd, on first glance, to a non-Scot, particularly one sensitised to the well-documented vulnerabilities of urban tenants in the United States.[77] However, several considerations might explain this. First, the Scottish Parliament may have properly assumed that a proposed community acquisition that would displace a substantial number of residential tenants would never obtain ministerial consent in the first place under the substantive criteria discussed below because it would not be seen as advancing the public interest or the cause of sustainable development. Second, if a community body did succeed in acquiring eligible land on which residential tenancies are located, the 2016 Act specifically prevents the community body from acquiring the tenancies and thus residential tenancies would most likely be unaf-fected.[78] Third, other recent Scottish legislation secures the interests of residential tenants in many situations by giving them the right to remain in their units even at the end of a lease term unless there is cause for evic-tion or some special reason for the landlord to repossess the property.[79]

---

[76] 'The Land of Scotland and the Common Good', section 20.2, at p. 126–8.

[77] The seminal study is M. Desmond, *Evicted: Poverty and Profit in the American City* (Crown Publishers: New York, 2016).

[78] LRSA 2016, section 48.

[79] See generally Private Housing (Tenancies) (Scotland) Act 2016: see also D. Bain, 'Scottish Residential Tenancies' (in this volume).

Fourth, Parliament probably took into account that community-owned and controlled housing associations and trusts, which already provide many affordable residential tenancies and comprise one of the most common types of community bodies in Scotland, are likely to be among the primary beneficiaries of the expanded NCCRtB in Scotland.[80] Finally, Parliament was likely aware that Article 8 of the European Convention on Human Rights, which proclaims a right to respect for private life and the home, provides an additional baseline of residential tenancy protection that would make further express protections in the new legislation unnecessary.

Criteria for consent

Once an official 'community body' is formed and a parcel of 'eligible land' is selected for a community acquisition, the community body can now apply to Scottish Ministers for consent to buy the land and force a sale, rather than just register a pre-emptive right to buy land when it is made available for sale by the landowner as under Part 2 of the LRSA 2003.[81] Although both Acts provide detailed rules on the content of an application and the notice and public comment requirements designed to provide all interested parties with opportunities to engage in the process of deciding whether a community acquisition can go forward,[82] the crucial substantive criteria for ministerial consent are at once multi-faceted and yet open-textured. Rather than establish bright-line rules, the criteria provide many factors for Scottish Ministers to consider and yet those factors still give the Ministers ample discretion to make individualised determinations. The crucial questions from a property theorist's perspective are whether these criteria: (1) narrow discretion in some way that provides predictability; (2) prevent community bodies from using the NCCRtB to bypass the land marketplace too easily when that marketplace would otherwise suffice; and (3) provide any assurance that the use of government funds to finance a community acquisition is cost-justified in light of alternative uses for the funds. Measured against these standards, the substantive criteria for an acquisition under both NCCRtB Acts reveal strengths and weaknesses.

Under the CESA 2015, a NCCRtB application to acquire wholly or

---

[80] 'The Land of Scotland and the Common Good', section 16.1, at p. 86–9.

[81] See Combe, The environmental implications of redistributive land reform', pp. 118–21.

[82] LRSA 2003, section 97G; LRSA 2016 sections 54–5.

mainly abandoned, neglected or environmentally harmful land can go forward if the Scottish Ministers determine that the proposed acquisition (a) is 'in the public interest', (b) is 'compatible with furthering the achievement of sustainable development in relation to land', and (c) 'the achievement of sustainable development in relation to the land would be unlikely to be furthered by the owner of the land continuing to be its owner'.[83] When these criteria – and especially the last one – are construed together with the additional requirement that a community body must demonstrate that it has 'otherwise . . . tried and failed to buy the land',[84] we see the emergence of an inquiry that begins to resemble either Merrill's 'thin market' test or Alexander's 'least invasive means' test for economic development takings.

Although the first two criteria, 'public interest' and 'furthering the achievement of sustainable development in relation to land', are not otherwise defined in the CESA 2015, perhaps the Scottish Parliament assumed that the most important question in community acquisitions under the new Part 3A of the LRSA 2003 would be the more objective question of whether a particular parcel of land or a structure is abandoned, neglected or causing environmental harm. To its credit, the CESA 2015 drills down somewhat further with regard to acquisitions that are proposed as a solution to environmental harm by requiring that a community body show that (a) a proposed community acquisition under this heading will actually remove or substantially remove that harm, (b) the community body requested that 'relevant regulators' take action to abate the harm, and (c) the harm is unlikely to be removed if the current landowner remains as owner.[85] In other words, viewed as a whole, the CESA 2015 substantive criteria seem to require Ministers to ask whether the proposed community acquisition is the only way to avert blight or environmental harm. Whether the still somewhat subjective nature of these criteria would allow owners who have neglected their land or buildings in the past to block proposed acquisitions by implementing some basic maintenance measures at the last instant is an important concern that will require study in the future.[86]

When a community body seeks to acquire eligible land under Part 5 of LRSA 2016, it must convince Scottish Ministers that the proposed

[83] LRSA 2003, section 97H(1).
[84] LRSA 2003, section 97H(1)(j).
[85] LRSA 2003, section 97H(5).
[86] R. Mc Morran, 'Review of the effectiveness of current community ownership mechanisms', section 4.4, p. 39.

transfer (a) 'is likely to further the achievement of sustainable development', (b) 'is in the public interest', (c) 'is likely to result in significant
benefit to the relevant community' and 'is the only practicable, or the
most practicable, way of achieving that significant benefit', and (d) 'not
granting consent to the transfer of land is likely to result in harm to the
community'.[87] Further, section 56(12) of that Act also requires that in
assessing 'significant benefit to the community' and 'harm to the community' Scottish Ministers must attempt to humanise and individualise
the consent determination by considering 'the likely effect of granting
(or not granting) consent to the transfer of land . . . on the lives of the
persons comprising that community with reference to the following
considerations – (a) economic development, (b) regeneration, (c) public
health, (d) social wellbeing, and (e) environmental wellbeing'.[88]

With these open-textured criteria, it appears that the LRSA 2016
urges Scottish Ministers to conduct an inquiry that on one hand borrows
from Berger and Merrill's tests focused on the presence of thin markets,
the availability of other land, and the economic necessity for the involuntary transfer with a kind of human flourishing assessment similar in
scope to what Alexander calls for in his 'purposive analysis' of economic
development takings. One difference between the property scholars'
visions and the LRSA 2016, however, is that the crucial decision-makers
in Scotland will be government officials, not judges interpreting a constitutional text. Another difference is that the LRSA 2016 does not
appear to require, as Alexander would, that the Scottish Ministers 'look
at both sides'. Indeed, the human flourishing assessment embedded in
section 56(12) focuses solely on the interests of the acquiring community, leaving the targeted property owner's subjective interests more or
less off the table. Perhaps, once again, the exclusion of owner-occupied
homes from the category of eligible land explains this omission.

As the reach of the NCCRtB shifts from large rural estates owned by
wealthy, often absentee individual landowners or faceless corporations
or trusts, to urban or peri-urban areas suffering from economic stagnation or decline, the property owners whose land or buildings are subject
to a community acquisition might well turn out to be a more diverse
and, possibly even on occasion, a vulnerable group of individuals.[89] If

---

[87] LRSA 2016, section 56(2).

[88] LRSA 2016, section 56(12). The LRSA 2016 applies the same substantive
criteria when a community body seeks to acquire a non-residential 'tenant's interest'
in land.

[89] My concerns may be overstated if, as was true in the past, the overwhelming

this transpires, the demands of property theorists from both the law and economics and progressive property traditions for more rigorous and heightened judicial scrutiny – and more exacting substantive criteria – could become highly relevant.

Community ballots

Another interesting, though not altogether novel, feature of the NCCRtB under both the 2015 and 2016 Acts is that a proposed community acquisition may not proceed to actual transfer unless the relevant 'community' as defined under the Acts approves the plan through a formal ballot. In this ballot, either at least half of the members of the relevant community must vote, or, if fewer than half vote, 'the proportion that does vote must still be sufficient to justify the community's proceeding to buy the land'. In either case, a majority of those voting must vote in favour of the proposed acquisition.[90]

While this formal ballot mechanism will certainly enhance the democratic legitimacy of any community acquisition, if the 'relevant community' is defined tightly to include just a small community of place, the ballot could perhaps be perceived as a rubber stamp since the immediately benefiting community members will presumably vote in favour of the acquisition.[91] On the other hand, if the community is defined more broadly to encompass a wider political community, then the ballot process could further strengthen the democratic legitimacy of a community acquisition. The risk of casting a wider net in terms of balloting, however, is that the number of low-information voters might increase and thus voters with little knowledge of the potential gains that could be achieved by a proposed community acquisition could prevent it from being realised. Perhaps the most important aspect of the community ballot mechanism, at least as currently formulated, is that it provides a meaningful opportunity for local democratic decision-making

majority of future community acquisitions will be achieved through negotiation with landowners, with the revised NCCRtB only serving as a backstop to motivate reluctant owners to enter into serious sale negotiations. I thank Ian Cooke of Development Trusts Association Scotland for this insight.

[90] LRSA 2003, section 97J(1); LRSA 2016, section 57(1).

[91] It should be noted that in some community acquisitions involving a tightly defined community of place, only a narrow majority initially favoured a community acquisition. For instance, on Gigha only a small majority initially favoured community ownership because historic feelings of powerlessness lead to a lack of community confidence. I thank Ian Cooke for this insight as well.

in a political system that tends to favour centralised authority and that has witnessed a dramatic reduction in the number of local government bodies over the last century.[92] Although the mechanics of community balloting may evolve as Scotland gains even more experience using them to implement the expanded NCCRtB, its continued effort to formally integrate opportunities for democratic participation directly into the process of expanding community ownership and its inclination to give local people a direct voice in shaping the outcome of community acquisition decisions both deserve praise.

Compensation

Perhaps the weakest, or at least the least imaginative, of the NCCRtB provisions concern the processes and criteria used for determining the amount of compensation a private property or tenancy holder will receive if her land, building or tenancy is the subject of an involuntary community acquisition. In contrast to the highly contextualised and human-flourishing oriented criteria that Scottish Ministers must consider before granting consent to a community acquisition, the compensation processes and criteria adopt a singular, market-focused metric to determine the amount of compensation owed to a property owner.

Both Acts first call for the appointment of a third-party appraiser (a 'valuer') and then instruct that the value to be determined by this person is 'the market value of the land at the date the ministers' consent to the proposed acquisition'.[93] The Acts then specify that the 'market value' represents an aggregation of the land's (a) 'open market' value as between a willing seller and buyer, (b) any depreciation in the value of other land or interests belonging to the targeted property owner (severance damages), and (c) 'any amount attributable to any disturbance to the seller which may arise in connection with the transfer' (presumably relocation expenses, lost goodwill, or other economic losses).[94] These provisions do allow for a more particularised, subjective assessment of 'the seller', but only to the extent there exists some person other than

[92] A. Wightman, *Renewing Local Democracy in Scotland*, A Report for the Scottish Green Party (2018), pp. 1–7, at <http://www.andywightman.com/docs/RenewingLocalDemocracy_final_v2.pdf> (last accessed 18 September 2019).

[93] LRSA 2003, section 97S(1), (4); LRSA 2016, section 65(1), (4). The Acts also clarify that 'the valuer' acts on behalf of neither the community body nor property owner and serves only as 'an expert and not as an arbiter'. LRSA 2003, section 97S(2); LRSA 2016, section 65(2).

[94] LRSA 2003, section 97S(5); LRSA 2016, section 65(5).

the community body who might be willing to pay an above-market price 'because of a characteristic of the land which related particularly to that person's interest in buying it'[95] (presumably someone like a member of the seller's family who might be willing to pay a premium to retain the property).

What is striking here is the absence of any mechanism that would allow a targeted property owner to signal her own subjective valuation of the land, as in Fennell's self-assessment procedure, or any mechanism that might allow the targeted property owner to share in the post-acquisition surplus value of the property, as in Krier and Serkin's future-oriented valuation proposal, Heller and Hill's LAD structure for community voice and negotiating power, or Kelly's Consumer Residency Entitlement. Of course, a community body and the prospective 'seller' of land targeted for a community acquisition can always bargain for – and voluntarily enter into – this kind of post-transfer partnership. Indeed, the LRRG suggested just such an 'Urban Partnership Zone' structure in its 2014 report.[96] Yet it remains somewhat surprising, especially given the richly detailed statutory apparatus surrounding the formation of a community body, ministerial consent and community balloting, that the NCCRtB, as currently formulated in the 2015 and 2016 legislation, does not incorporate any more sophisticated compensation and land readjustment tools. Perhaps the explanation for this is the parliamentary assumption that the typical non-neglecting landowner targeted by the NCCRtB (an absentee owner, a corporation or a trust) views the targeted property as a purely fungible investment, or, in the case of abandoned or neglected land, that the landowner has already demonstrated its lack of interest in the land. To the extent these assumptions are borne out, a simple fair market valuation approach may well be, as Chang suggests, the most appropriate valuation mechanism. However, as suggested in the previous section addressing the substantive criteria for ministerial consent, these assumptions may not always be valid in the future as the NCCRtB widens its scope.

Judicial scrutiny

Another surprising feature of both of the NCCRtB statutory regimes is the sparse and strangely bifurcated provision for judicial evaluation of Scottish Ministers' decisions regarding applications to acquire land.

[95] LRSA 2003, section 97S(6); LRSA 2016, section 65(6).
[96] 'The Land of Scotland and the Common Good', section 20.2, at p. 126–8.

Both Acts provide that either the community body or the targeted property owner can appeal the valuation made by the independent 'valuer' to the Lands Tribunal of Scotland, which can then make a complete reassessment of the value of the land.[97]

The two Acts also allow a targeted property owner, a community body, a creditor, and even an individual member of the community affected by a proposed community acquisition to appeal the basic decision of Scottish Ministers to consent (or refuse to consent) to a proposed acquisition. However, these appeals of the merits of an application for consent must go to the sheriff court, from which there is no appeal.[98] In no case does it seem possible to appeal either a compensation or merits decision to the Court of Session.

This structure makes the costs and risks of an appeal particularly burdensome for a targeted property owner who could be forced to make a difficult trade-off between the gains that could be achieved by appealing valuation to the Lands Tribunal against the benefit of challenging the merits of a ministerial grant of consent to the sheriff court, particularly if resources to pay for lawyers are limited. Conversely, a community body that receives permission to go forward with an actual transfer but is unhappy with the valuation determination could still chose to focus all of its resources on an appeal of valuation to the Lands Tribunal. On the other hand, if a community body's application for an acquisition is rejected, it can choose to focus its resources on an appeal of the merits of the ministerial decision in the sheriff court. It seems then that this structure for judicial scrutiny favours the community body, perhaps based on an assumption that the targeted property will have far greater financial resources at the outset.

The other striking feature of the provisions for judicial review is the absence of any indication of the level of judicial scrutiny that a court should employ in the case of an appeal of the ministerial decision to grant or refuse consent to an NCCRtB application. In Scotland, courts are generally constrained in their ability to review ministerial decisions involving the application of legislatively granted discretionary power. Courts can, within narrow boundaries, review acts of ministerial discretion for *illegality*, breach of EU law and ECHR rights (e.g., Protocol 1, Article 1 – peaceful enjoyment of property),[99] legislative compe-

---

[97] LRSA 2003, section 97W; LRSA 2016, section 70.

[98] LRSA 2003, section 97V; LRSA 2016, section 69.

[99] See further F. McCarthy, 'Property Rights and Human Rights in Scottish Land Reform' (in this volume).

tence (e.g., devolution issues), procedural unfairness, and, to a limited extent, can review on substantive grounds.[100] In this last category of judicial review, courts usually engage in what experts call '*Wednesbury* unreasonableness' review, that is, they only inquire whether the ministerial or government action is 'wholly unreasonable or irrational'.[101] Nevertheless, in some cases, particularly when fundamental rights or constitutional principles are at stake, courts will engage in a somewhat more sceptical, or deeper, scrutiny, sometimes described as 'anxious scrutiny'.[102] Whether 'anxious scrutiny', which is typically employed in immigration cases, is the most appropriate form of judicial review for NCCRtB applications is beyond the scope of this chapter. In terms of long-term democratic legitimacy, the legislation might have been stronger had it addressed this important matter.

Government funding and third-party purchasers

The last crucial piece of any prospective community acquisition using the NCCRtB will be funding. Provisions in both the 2015 and 2016 legislation allow Scottish Ministers to pay a grant to an eligible community body if (a) that entity cannot pay all or a part of the final compensation award, (b) the entity has 'taken all reasonable measures' to obtain its own financing, and (c) the Ministers decide that it is 'in the public interest' to pay the grant.[103] At present, most community acquisitions that take place in Scotland (either through voluntary transfer, exercise of a community's registered pre-emptive right to buy or a crofting community's statutory right to buy) have been funded by public grants, primarily through the Scottish Land Fund (SLF), which is funded

---

[100] See generally Sarah Harvie-Clark, Scottish Parliament Information Centre, Briefing – Judicial Review (Edinburgh: SPICe, 8 July 2016) pp. 18–29, at <http://www.parliament.scot/ResearchBriefingsAndFactsheets/S5/SB_16-62_Judicial_Review.pdf> (last accessed 18 September 2019). *Illegality* encompasses actions that are *ultra vires*, failure to consider relevant matters or consideration of irrelevant matters, errors of fact and errors of law within very limited bounds, and decisions by the wrong actor.

[101] SPICe, Briefing – Judicial Review, p. 28 (discussing *Associated Provincial Picture Houses Ltd* v. *Wednesbury Corp.* [1948] 1 K.B. 223).

[102] SPICe, Briefing – Judicial Review, p. 28. For examples of Scottish courts' discussion of and application of 'anxious scrutiny', see *KD Petitioner* v. *SSHD* [2011] CSIH 20, 9 ('the decision letter should demonstrate that no material factor that could conceivably be regarded as favourable to the reclaimer has been left out of account'); *AAQ Petitioner* v. *SSHD* [2012] CSOH 2.

[103] LRSA 2003, section 97U(1)–(2); LRSA 2016, section 68(1)–(2).

directly by Scottish Government budgets and delivered in partnership with Big Lottery and the Growing Community Assets (GCA) fund which draws proceeds only from the sale of lottery tickets.[104]

The open-ended 'public interest' requirement for the payment of a public grant creates yet another opportunity for the NCCRtB to gain public legitimacy. The Scottish Government could use this final 'public interest' standard to address questions raised by Fischel's fungibility critique of economic development expropriations. For instance, it could develop an analytical rubric that tests whether the funds used to pay a grant to a community body could produce a greater return on investment if devoted to some other public project. Alternatively, it could require some portion of a community acquisition grant to come from locally generated tax revenues, thus providing taxpayers in the community with an incentive to make sure that a development project facilitated by a community acquisition is the best, or at least a strong, choice for the use of those locally generated tax revenues.[105] Yet even this potential refinement is subject to an important qualification: many much larger government subsidies in Scotland have historically flowed to existing private property owners, particularly through agricultural subsidies originating in the European Union (though, of course, these will likely soon come to an end with the UK's departure from the EU).[106] Therefore, the relatively modest grants made available through the SLF and GCA Fund are only a small part of government intervention in the private land market in Scotland.

Finally, it should be noted that section 54(1) of the LRSA 2016 allows a Part 5 community body to nominate another person to exercise

---

[104] 'The Land of Scotland and the Common Good', sections 18.1–18.2, at pp. 104–5. Wightman also provides a useful analysis of the funding of community acquisitions through the SLF and the GCA fund, arguing that the source of these funds was not 'public' or 'taxpayers' money as the bulk of the funds came from the sale of lottery tickets. Wightman, *The Poor Had No Lawyers*, pp. 199–200. For details on the Scottish Land Fund and procedures for applying for a SLF grant, see <https://www.tnlcommunityfund.org.uk/funding/programmes/scottish-land-fund> (last accessed 18 September 2019).

[105] Both Acts do allow Scottish Ministers to impose a condition in a grant requiring repayment by the community body in the event of breach, but it is not clear how such a condition would be enforced. LRSA 2003, section 97U(4); LRSA 2016, section 68(4).

[106] According to the LRRG, just one stream of agricultural support payments under the European Union Common Agricultural Policy (CAP) managed by the Scottish Rural Development Programme totalled £1.2 billion for 2007–13. 'Land of Scotland and the Common Good', section 25.2 at p. 174.

its statutory right to buy land and calls this person a 'third-party purchaser'.[107] Although other parts of that Act addressing notice, application, payment and withdrawal procedures also mention this 'third-party purchaser',[108] the Act does not otherwise address the substantive role that this third-party purchaser can play in a community acquisition or the ultimate relationship between the community body and the third-party purchaser.

If the third-party purchaser is simply a non-profit funder or technical service provider, its presence in an NCCRtB acquisition will not materially change the fundamental legitimacy analysis. However, if the third-party purchaser is a development company that is putting its own capital or borrowing capacity into the mix to fund a community acquisition, its participation could signal usefully that the project has realistic revenue-generating potential. At the same time, its participation could also reveal that the NCCRtB mechanism is simply being captured by an opportunistic, rent-seeking private firm. Scottish Ministers and land reform advocates would be wise to give more attention to this ambiguous funding wrinkle in the LRSA 2016.

DISJUNCTIONS

Looking back on this chapter, a reader might rightly question how much relevance the critiques of the property theorists working outside of Scotland have for the NCCRtB given the differences between their respective legal ecosystems and the unique legal and social landscape of Scotland. It should be apparent by now that the paradigmatic case for the largely US-based property theorists involves a municipal redevelopment agency that uses its expropriation power to acquire several, or indeed many, residential or small commercial properties and later combines them into a larger contiguous parcel for subsequent transfer to a private developer or corporation orchestrating a large, mixed-use, commercial or even industrial project. In contrast, the paradigmatic Scottish case justifying the NCCRtB, at least as originally formulated by land reform advocates in Scotland, involves a small, organic, community-based entity challenging a rural, often absentee landowner who refuses to sell all or part of his estate (sometimes an entire island) that could be used to catalyse a local economic development project.

These quite different paradigmatic cases produce an apparent

---

[107] LRSA 2016, section 54(1).
[108] LRSA 2016, sections 54(1)(iv), 60(1)(d), 62(2)–(4), 64(8)–(11), 67(2), 69(9).

misalignment between legitimate fears of exploitation on one hand and ambitious hopes on the other. In the US, large-scale *land assembly* and 'urban renewal' projects have often resulted in mass displacement of the poor and minorities.[109] In Scotland, the potential gains in local community autonomy and sustainability promised by legislatively aided land disassembly inspire many. However, any reader familiar with the recommendations of the Land Reform Review Group or the activities of Community Land Scotland, both of which urge community groups and government to activate underused and undeveloped land all across Scotland, including especially urban land and buildings, may suspect that the broad reach of the NCCRtB as currently developed in the CESA 2015 and the LRSA 2016 could make North American critiques reviewed in this chapter increasingly relevant.[110]

Another potential disjunction between the concerns of the property theorists and the hopes of the land reform advocates in Scotland lies in the very different local government contexts in which expropriations emerge. In the United States, for instance, the government body exercising the power of eminent domain for economic development purposes is typically a local municipality,[111] another local political subdivision such as an airport commission or port authority,[112] or a local redevelopment authority that has been specifically granted expropriation authority under state law.[113] This local, decentralised locus of expropriation authority makes inquiries into the ability of private developers to capture all or most of the benefits of expropriation quite natural. In Scotland and the UK in general, expropriation power tends be far more centralised, and a regional authority can only mobilise that power by

---

[109] For a lucid account of this history, see W. E. Pritchett, 'The "Public Menace" of Blight: Urban Renewal and the Private Uses of Eminent Domain', *Yale Law & Policy Review*, 21 (2003), pp. 1–52.

[110] 'The Land of Scotland and the Common Good', section 20 at pp. 120–30; Community Land Scotland, *Urban Community Landownership in 2018*, at <http://www.communitylandscotland.org.uk/wp-content/uploads/2018/03/Urban_Community-land-full-report.pdf> (last accessed 18 September 2019) (setting forth its agenda for community ownership in urban places).

[111] *Poletown Neighborhood Council* v. *City of Detroit*, 304 N.W.2d 455 (Mich. 1981) (per curiam), overruled by *County of Wayne* v. *Hathcock*, 684 N.W.2d 765, 787 (Mich. 2004).

[112] *County of Wayne* v. *Hathcock*, 684 N.W.2d 765, 787 (Mich. 2004); *St Bernard Port Harbor & Terminal District* v. *Violet Dock Port, Inc., LLC*, 2017-0434 (La. 01/30/2018), 239 So.3d 243.

[113] *Kelo* v. *City of New London*, 545 US 469, 125 S.Ct. 2655 (2005).

obtaining centralised ministerial approval.[114] As the preceding analysis of the NCCRtB demonstrates, however, the expropriation power in Scotland may be shifting to a more localised and decentralised position, at least at the beginning of a community acquisition. This movement, though only partial, could also make the critiques of American property theorists more salient in the years ahead.

One final contrast between the landscape of property theorists surveyed in the beginning of this chapter and the transformative land reform ambitions that animate the NCCRtB lies in the background fears and hopes of their respective broader cultures. When scholars and social critics view the landscape of rural America today, they often see its depopulation, its cultural isolation, its economic decline and, finally, its fear and despair.[115] When they look at US cities, they observe widening social and economic inequality, grounded in the radically disparate experiences that family backgrounds, parenting, educational opportunities, and the structure of communities themselves produce for individuals and families.[116]

When land reform advocates in Scotland look at rural land and communities in their nation and when they turn their attention to urban areas, they tend to be much more optimistic about the benefits that direct intervention in the property regime of Scotland can produce. They see hope, rejuvenation, and the possibility of positive change.[117] This inspiring optimism, which has emerged most recently in the remarkable

[114] T. Allen, 'Controls over the Use and Abuse of Eminent Domain in England: A Comparative View', in R. P. Malloy, *Private Property, Community Development and Eminent Domain* (Aldershot: Ashgate, 2008), pp. 75–100, 85–7.

[115] For a widely read memoir that emphasises the need to escape rural places, see J. D. Vance, *Hillbilly Elegy, A Memoir of a Family and Culture in Crisis* (New York: Harper, 2016). For a robust critique of Vance's dystopian portrait of rural Appalachia, see S. Greenberg, 'Unlearning the Lessons of *Hillbilly Elegy*', *American Prospect*, 8 January 2019, <https://prospect.org/article/unlearning-lessons-hillbilly-elegy> (last accessed 20 January 2019). For an insightful sociological account of how residents of rural Southwestern Louisiana have come to feel culturally and politically alienated from liberal elites in the United States and why they have embraced 'Tea Party' politics, see A. R. Hochschild, *Strangers in Their Own Land: Anger and Mourning on the American Right* (New York: New Press, 2016).

[116] Desmond, *Evicted*; R. D. Putnam, *Our Kids: The American Dream in Crisis* (New York: Simon & Schuster, 2015).

[117] See Mackenzie, *Places of Possibility* (detailing optimism and growing self-confidence in the expansion of community ownership in rural areas); Community Land Scotland, *Urban Community Landownership in 2018* (expressing optimism for community ownership in urban places).

document that the Scottish Parliament mandated that its government produce, the 'Land Rights and Responsibilities Statement', is likely to endure as Scotland's political leadership and civil society have collectively made land reform one of the pillars of Scotland's current national identity. Nevertheless, as the Scottish land reform movement makes further progress in its mission to transform Scottish society, it may well benefit from studying the cautionary tales that property theorists working abroad have told and by considering some of their imaginative property theory solutions to the challenges of economic development takings.

9

Property Rights and Human Rights in Scottish Land Reform

Frankie McCarthy

INTRODUCTION: HUMAN RIGHTS IN THE SCOTTISH LAND REFORM DEBATE

THE REALISATION OF MANY human rights is impossible without land. A cursory glance at Scotland's international human rights obligations, which include protections in respect of health, housing, employment and property itself, makes clear that careful management of this critical and limited resource will be essential for fulfilment of these obligations to the greatest extent possible. The centrality of this relationship is recognised in Scotland's first 'Land Rights and Responsibilities Statement' (LRRS), which sets out in its opening paragraph:

> The overall framework of land rights, responsibilities and public policies should promote, fulfil and respect relevant human rights in relation to land, contribute to public interest and wellbeing, and balance public and private interests. The framework should support sustainable economic development, protect and enhance the environment, help achieve social justice and build a fairer society.[1]

Appendix A to the LRRS clarifies the legal instruments in which 'relevant' human rights are identified, including international, European and domestic sources.[2] The LRRS's Advisory Notes and case studies provide examples of what a 'human rights approach' – in other words, an approach which actualises rights across the spectrum to the greatest extent possible – to land reform might look like.[3] The task for government, public authorities and landowners of every type is to make decisions around land that best support all relevant rights.

---

[1] Scottish Land Rights and Responsibilities Statement (Edinburgh: Scottish Government, 2017), p. 9.

[2] Ibid., pp. 35–40.

[3] Ibid., pp. 13–16.

The emphasis placed by the LRRS on the full range of Scotland's human rights commitments reflects a shift in the land reform conversation. Over the previous twenty years, the discussion seldom engaged with human rights, with one exception, namely the right to peaceful enjoyment of possessions set out in Article 1 of the First Protocol (A1P1) to the European Convention on Human Rights (ECHR). In the Scottish Law Commission's programme of property law reform work in the early part of this century, A1P1 was the only right given detailed consideration.[4] The same approach was taken by the Scottish Executive when introducing draft legislation on land: see, for example, the Policy Memorandum accompanying the first Land Reform (Scotland) Bill, in which two brief paragraphs note the ECHR rights potentially engaged by the Bill with specific reference to A1P1, before concluding that 'the Executive is satisfied that the provisions in the Bill on community ownership and crofting community ownership are compliant with the Convention'.[5]

Increased interest in the role of other human rights in relation to land reform became notable around the time of the publication of the Scottish Human Rights Commission's first Action Plan in 2013. This programme, focused on enhancing awareness and integration of the entire suite of human rights across Scottish public life, specifically referenced the significance of land 'as a key resource for the realisation of a range of human rights' and identified the ongoing land reform process as an opportunity for progressive realisation of those rights.[6] As the land reform conversation moved to focus on the development, enactment and implementation of the Land Reform (Scotland) Act 2016, human rights other than A1P1 received far greater attention than previously. Their significance is now cemented in the LRRS commitment to a human rights approach to reform noted above.

The publication of the LRRS offers an appropriate moment for reflection on how the human rights conversation evolved. In the lead up to

[4] Scottish Law Commission, *Report on Abolition of the Feudal System* (Edinburgh: HMSO, 1999), 5.65–6.58; Scottish Law Commission, *Report on Real Burdens* (Edinburgh: HMSO, 2000), 14.12–14.29; Scottish Law Commission, *Report on Law of the Foreshore and Seabed* (Edinburgh: HMSO, 2003), 1.17; Scottish Law Commission, *Report on Conversion of Long Leases* (Edinburgh: HMSO, 2006), 1.12.

[5] Scottish Parliament, *Policy Memorandum on the Land Reform (Scotland) Bill (SP Bill 44)* (Edinburgh: Scottish Parliament, 2001), pp. 39–40.

[6] Scottish Human Rights Commission, *Scotland's National Action Plan for Human Rights 2013–2017* (Edinburgh, 2013), p. 39.

the 2016 Act, a political and media narrative emerged in which A1P1, representing the claims of existing landowners, was positioned as a barrier to reform. Scholars noted that it was being used as a 'red card' to obstruct debate about land reform and deployed as a 'trump card' over competing interests in land.[7] Media commentators suggested it was 'by far the biggest hurdle' and provided a 'constraint' by which the SNP government found 'its hands partially bound'.[8] The authority of other human rights instruments, particularly the International Convention on Economic, Social and Cultural Rights (ICESCR), was called upon to overcome this barrier, implying an opposition between the (A1P1) rights of landowners, and the (ICESCR) rights of the rest of society in relation to land. Two comments bookending the 2016 Act debates illustrate the perceived conflict. First, in the Report of the Land Reform Review Group, the document instigating and delineating the conversation which eventually produced the 2016 Act, compliance with fundamental human rights was defined as part of the 'common good' towards which all land reform measures should be aimed, with the observation:

> The traditional focus in discussion in Scotland about human rights and land reform has been the balance to be struck between private property rights and the public interest under Article 1 of the European Convention on Human Rights First Protocol . . . However, as the work of the Scottish Human Rights Commission demonstrates, the relationship between human rights and land in Scotland is not only about the principle in that Protocol.[9]

Then, in the final debate in the Scottish Parliament, immediately preceding the vote which passed the Act into law, Mike Russell MSP commented:

> Land reform in Scotland is hard to do at this time because of the European Convention on Human Rights. I am not in any sense against the ECHR, but

---

[7] A. Miller, 'Land, owned privately or otherwise, is a national asset that should serve the public interest', *The Herald*, 10 April 2015, <https://www.heraldscotland.com/opinion/13209283.land-owned-privately-or-otherwise-is-a-national-asset-that-should-serve-the-public-interest/> (last accessed 27 May 2019); K. Shields, 'Tackling the misuse of rights rhetoric in land reform debate', *Scottish Human Rights Journal* 68 (2015), pp. 1–4.

[8] A. Tickell, 'Land reform: through the looking glass', *Lallands Peat Worrier*, 24 June 2015, <http://lallandspeatworrier.blogspot.com/2015/06/land-reform-through-looking-glass.html> (last accessed 27 May 2019); A. Massie, 'The SNP's land reform fantasy world', *The Spectator*, 20 August 2016, <https://www.spectator.co.uk/2016/08/the-snps-land-reform-fantasy-world/> (last accessed 27 May 2019).

[9] Land Reform Review Group, 'The Land of Scotland and the Common Good' (Edinburgh: Scottish Government, 2014), p. 23.

as we heard at the start of the debate, land reform post-ECHR tends to be focused on individuals' property rights. There are other rights, and those rights are expressed in a range of documentation, including the [ICESCR and further instruments now identified in Appendix A to the LRRS].[10]

In this chapter, I argue that the political and media positioning of A1P1 as a barrier to land reform is a mischaracterisation. A1P1 may have been cast in this role partly because of successful legal challenges to earlier land reform legislation under its auspices, but doctrinal analysis of the limited available case law demonstrates little support for construction of A1P1 as a landowner's right. Drawing on a theoretical model developed by US constitutional property scholar Joseph Singer, I argue that A1P1 understood correctly provides a valuable framework for ensuring *all* interests in land are given due consideration. I also argue that, as the only directly justiciable right available, A1P1 can provide an essential tool for enforcing the LRRS commitment to land reform informed by all relevant human rights.

The chapter is in four parts. First, an outline of Scotland's human rights framework is provided, so that the constellation of potentially competing claims on land and their interaction can be understood. Second, an analysis of the A1P1 case law on land reform reveals the attenuated nature of the protection it provides to landowners. Third, Singer's citizenship model of property rights protection is explained, and the case is made for it as an appropriate interpretation of A1P1. The final section will draw the threads together and argue for a revised understanding of A1P1 as a key enforcement mechanism for all human rights within land reform.

SCOTLAND'S HUMAN RIGHTS FRAMEWORK

International and European human rights obligations

Scotland and the United Kingdom are subject to an interlocking framework of global, European and domestic human rights obligations.[11] At the global level, the United Nations is the key proponent of international human rights standards, developed post Second World War through

---

[10] Scottish Parliament, Official Report, 16 March 2016, cols 50–1.

[11] For a detailed exploration of this complex area, see P. Alston and R. Goodman, *International Human Rights* (Oxford: Oxford University Press, 2012); J. L. Murdoch, *Reed and Murdoch: Human Rights Law in Scotland*, 4th edn (Edinburgh: Bloomsbury Professional Ltd, 2017).

the International Bill of Rights and subsequent treaties (such as the Convention on the Rights of the Child).[12]

Rights contained within these instruments can be split into two broad categories. The first are civil and political rights, contained primarily within the Universal Declaration of Human Rights (UDHR) and the International Covenant on Civil and Political Rights (ICCPR). Murdoch describes rights within this category as grounded in the Western liberal democratic tradition, stressing protection for personal integrity, procedural propriety in the determination of civil and criminal actions, protection for democratic processes and the promotion of religious tolerance and plurality of belief.[13] Freedom from arbitrary deprivation of property is included within this category.

UDHR rights were implemented in the European legal order by way of the ECHR, and its protections also overlap significantly with those in the ICCPR.[14] The protection provided to property in A1P1 of the ECHR is as follows:

> Every natural or legal person is entitled to the peaceful enjoyment of his possessions. No one shall be deprived of his possessions except in the public interest and subject to the conditions provided for by law and the general principles of international law.
>
> The preceding provisions shall not, however, in any way impair the right of a State to enforce such laws as it deems necessary to control the use of property in accordance with the general interest or to secure the payment of taxes or other contributions or penalties.

At the time of writing, the UK's continued adherence to the ECHR is not beyond doubt, although the process of withdrawing from the Convention would be legally complex.[15] Since predictions as to the

---

[12] Alston and Goodman, *International Human Rights*, pp. 139–44.

[13] Murdoch, *Reed and Murdoch*, 2.03.

[14] W. A. Schabas, *The European Convention on Human Rights: A Commentary* (Oxford: Oxford University Press, 2015), pp. 1–2.

[15] J. Wadham, H. Mountfield, E. Prochaska, and R. Desai, *Blackstone's Guide to the Human Rights Act 1998*, Seventh Edition (Oxford: Oxford University Press, 2015), pp. 16-21; A. McHarg, 'Will devolution scupper Conservative plans for a "British" bill of rights?', *UK Human Rights Blog*, 2 October 2014, <https://ukhumanrightsblog.com/2014/10/02/will-devolution-scupper-conservative-plans-for-a-british-bill-of-rights/> (last accessed 27 May 2019); C. Gearty, 'The Human Rights Act should not be repealed', *UK Constitutional Law Association Blog*, 17 September 2016, <https://ukconstitutionallaw.org/2016/09/17/conor-gearty-the-human-rights-act-should-not-be-repealed/> (last accessed 27 May 2019); K. Boyle and E. Hughes, 'Identifying routes to remedy for economic, social and cultural rights', *The International Journal of Human Rights*, 22:1 (2018), p. 46.

eventual resolution of these issues are highly speculative at present, this chapter assumes the ECHR will continue to apply to the UK for the foreseeable future. Whilst a member of the European Union, the UK is also signatory to the Charter of Fundamental Rights of the European Union. Since the land reform legislation in Scotland has not generally been introduced in pursuance of underlying EU regulation,[16] the Charter is unlikely to have much significance and will not be considered further here.

The second broad category of rights applicable in the UK and Scotland are economic and social rights, contained primarily within the International Covenant on Economic, Social and Cultural Rights (ICESCR). Murdoch describes these as forming the basis of socialist conceptions of human rights, and the extent to which they can or should be recognised as legal obligations is the subject of considerable debate.[17] ESC rights fall within seven headings: workers' rights; the right to social security and social protection; protection of and assistance to the family; the right to an adequate standard of living; the right to health; the right to education; and cultural rights.[18] Similar protections are set out at European level in the European Social Charter (1961).

The Scottish land reform programme, with its focus on sustainable development across economic, social and environmental spheres (see Ross, Chapter 10), has intersections across the full range of these entitlements.[19]

UK and Scottish human rights obligations

Under section 35 of the Scotland Act 1998, the Westminster government may prohibit a Scottish Parliament Bill being submitted for Royal Assent if it is incompatible with the UK's international obligations, which include those contained in the UN and European instruments described above. Section 58 contains an equivalent provision for delegated legislation and acts or omissions of members of the Scottish Government.

The rights contained within the ECHR have also been directly

[16] *Aklagaren* v. *Hans Akerberg Fransson*, Case C-617/10; [2013] EUECJ C-617/10
[17] Murdoch, *Reed and Murdoch*, 2.03; Alston and Goodman, *International Human Rights*, pp. 291–310.
[18] Office of the United Nations High Commissioner for Human Rights, *Frequently Asked Questions on Economic, Social and Cultural Rights* (Geneva: United Nations, 2008), p. 2.
[19] K. Shields, 'Human Rights and the Work of the Scottish Land Commission: A Discussion Paper' (Inverness: Scottish Land Commission, 2018).

incorporated into UK domestic legislation by the Human Rights Act 1998 (HRA), with additional Convention-related obligations in the Scotland Act 1998. The combined effect of these pieces of legislation in Scotland is that, first, any purported legislation of the Scottish Parliament which cannot be given effect in a way compatible with Convention rights will be considered *ultra vires* the Parliament and therefore 'not law' (Scotland Act, section 29(1)). Secondly, any public authority act (defined to include omissions) which is not compatible with Convention rights will be unlawful (HRA, section 6; Scotland Act, section 57).

Enforcing human rights

The mechanisms available for enforcement of our human rights obligations vary depending on the source of the right in question.

Rights contained within the ECHR can be directly enforced against Scottish or UK public authorities, including both governments, through court action. The UK first recognised the jurisdiction of the European Court of Human Rights in Strasbourg in 1966, and once the HRA came into force in 2000, it was competent for these proceedings to be raised in the domestic courts (HRA, section 7).[20] Where a court or tribunal in the UK is faced with a Convention rights question, it is obliged to 'take account of' relevant jurisprudence of the Strasbourg court (HRA, section 2(1)). Domestic jurisprudence has interpreted this obligation to mean that a Strasbourg decision should be followed unless there is a strong reason to deviate from it.[21]

Rights contained within the ICESCR and other UN Conventions are not directly justiciable. In other words, it is not possible for a person to raise an action in a domestic or international court in respect of a contended violation of these rights by the state. Compliance is enforced instead through various international law mechanisms, chief amongst which is a UN monitoring process.[22] In respect of each Convention, a scrutiny committee has been established, composed of international experts in the field. Member state governments are obliged to report to each committee at regular intervals (usually once every five years)

---

[20] Wadham et al., *Blackstone's Guide*, p. 24.

[21] *R (Anderson)* v. *Secretary of State for the Home Department* [2002] UKHL 46; [2003] 1 AC 837; *R (on the application of Ullah)* v. *Special Adjudicator* [2004] UKHL 26; [2004] 2 AC 323 HL.

[22] For an overview, see Alston and Goodman, *International Human Rights*, pp. 691–3.

in respect of progress with implementing the relevant Convention. The committee scrutinises the report and produces Concluding Observations, commending good practice where appropriate and highlighting areas of concern where state compliance with its obligations is lacking. The committee has no power to compel a state to take (or refrain from) action. However, criticism in the Concluding Observations is a form of political censure intended to motivate states to improve their practices. Rights under the European Social Charter are enforced in a similar fashion. At domestic level, monitoring of this kind is carried out by the Joint Committee on Human Rights at Westminster and the Equality and Human Rights Committee at Holyrood. Other non-judicial domestic enforcement mechanisms can also be identified.[23]

This distinction between the direct justiciability of ECHR rights and the enforcement mechanisms available in respect of UN Convention rights may create an impression that the former category of rights is more 'real'. Since the ECHR rights are largely civil and political, it is the social and economic rights set out the ICESCR which are at risk of being perceived to have a lower status. If the human rights of primary relevance to the land reform debate are the right to property and the social and economic rights outlined above, and if A1P1 is the only one of those rights that can lead directly to legal action against the government, it may be understandable that A1P1 is the right with which stakeholders – including government, landowners and others – have historically been preoccupied.

Although ICESCR rights cannot be directly enforced in court, they may nevertheless have an influence on domestic judicial decision-making. In the Supreme Court decision in R *(on the application of JS)* v. *Secretary of State for Work and Pensions*,[24] Lord Hughes noted that an international treaty which has not been incorporated into domestic law may nevertheless be relevant to the court in three ways, two of which are relevant to the land reform discussion. First, if the construction of domestic legislation is in doubt, the court may conclude that it should be construed so as to adhere to the UK's international obligations. Secondly, where claims are brought under the HRA, and there is a sufficiently close connection between the Convention right under consideration by the court and an international treaty obligation, international law requires the court to have regard to that obligation in interpreting the Convention right.[25] In

[23] Boyle and Hughes, 'Identifying routes', pp. 52–4.
[24] [2015] UKSC 16; [2015] 4 All England Reports 939 at paragraph [137].
[25] See also *Moohan, Petitioner* [2014] UKSC 67; [2015] AC 901: [63]-[64] and [78].

R (JS), the petitioners argued that the introduction of a benefit cap in the UK unjustifiably discriminated against women in contravention of their rights under A1P1 together with Article 14 of the ECHR, which provides for freedom from discrimination in relation to exercise of any other Convention right.[26] The petitioners sought to rely on provisions relating to child welfare within the United Nations Convention on the Rights of the Child as an aid to interpretation of Article 14 of the Convention. The Supreme Court was not satisfied that freedom from discrimination was sufficiently closely connected to protection of child welfare for the UN Convention to be relevant in this case. However, it is possible to imagine ICESCR rights becoming relevant to an interpretation of the public interest requirement of A1P1 in a land reform context. This proposition remains untested, but the possibility is important in understanding A1P1's potential value as a tool for rights-compliant land reform, discussed further below.

A1P1 IN THE COURTS – A SIGNIFICANT HURDLE TO LAND REFORM?

A1P1's reputation as a barrier to land reform presumably emerged in part from challenges to pre-2016 Act legislation by landowners who contended their property rights had been violated. As the second ever case in which Scottish Parliament legislation had been found to contravene the ECHR, *Salvesen* v. *Riddell*[27] attracted particular attention. One Edinburgh law firm reported that

> the Scottish Parliament was left with something of a bloody nose by the courts declaring one of its flagship provisions non-compliant with human rights.[28]

Land reform campaigner Lesley Riddoch suggested there was subsequent timidity by the Parliament around agricultural land reform 'because it feared further legal challenge'.[29]

---

[26] *R (on the application of JS)* v. *Secretary of State for Work and Pensions* [2015] UKSC 16; [2015] 4 All England Reports 939.

[27] *Salvesen* v. *Riddell* [2013] UKSC 22; 2013 *Scots Law Times* 863.

[28] A. Drane and L. Tainsh, 'Scottish Government Agricultural Holdings Review – Final Report 2015', *Davidson Chalmers: News and Insight*, 28 January 2015, <https://www.davidsonchalmers.com/news-and-insights/scottish-government-agricultural-holdings-review-%E2%80%93-final-report-2015> (last accessed 27 May 2019).

[29] L. Brooks, 'Campaigners call for land reform as Scottish farmer faces eviction', *The Guardian*, 10 November 2015, <https://www.theguardian.com/politics/2015/

A finding that Scottish Parliament legislation is contrary to human rights should always be significant, of course, and will inevitably impact on the public and political perception of land reform. However, the extent to which A1P1 has hindered land reform from a *legal* perspective should not be overblown. In fact, there have only been three litigated cases to date. The scope of the cases has been limited – no case yet has offered a central challenge to a land reform measure, with the focus instead on procedural aspects or exceptions to the general rules. The findings against Parliament have been more limited still. An analysis of each case serves to make the point.

Pairc Crofters Ltd *v.* Scottish Ministers

The first human rights challenge to land reform concerned the crofting community right to buy provided by Part 3 of the Land Reform (Scotland) Act 2003. The crofting community represented by the Pairc Trust had made a successful application to buy the ownership and tenancy of land in south-east Lewis. Pairc Crofters Ltd and Pairc Renewables Ltd – the owner and tenant respectively of the land in question – challenged the outcome of the application as contravening their rights under A1P1 and Article 6 of the ECHR. No argument was made that the introduction of a right to buy was in itself a violation of A1P1. The litigation concerned the procedure by which the right was exercised.[30]

The petitioners' complaint centred on the requirement for property rights holders to be given a reasonable opportunity to put their case to the decision-maker when deprivation of those rights was at issue. Deprivation of property through state action can only be justified under A1P1 where it is lawful, pursues a legitimate aim in the public interest and strikes a fair balance between the needs of the state and the right of the applicant without imposing an individual and excessive burden.[31] Meeting those conditions requires respect for due process when determining that the deprivation should occur. The petitioners argued that the relevant provisions of the 2003 Act, and the accompanying Crofting Community Right to Buy (Ballot) (Scotland) Regulations 2004, failed to respect due process at four stages in the procedure, including during the

---

nov/10/campaigners-protest-at-farmers-eviction-due-to-land-reform> (last accessed 27 May 2019).

[30] *Pairc Crofters Ltd* v. *Scottish Ministers* [2012] CSIH 96; 2013 *Scots Law Times* 308.

[31] *James* v. *UK* (1986) 8 EHRR 123 at paragraph [50].

crofting community ballot on whether an application to buy should be made, and when Ministers were making their determination on whether to grant or refuse an application.

The Inner House of the Court of Session found no violation of Convention rights. In broad terms, the court was satisfied that the extent of landowners' opportunities to participate in the process was sufficient for the requirement of due process, and that the obligation on Ministers to make decisions 'in the public interest' throughout the procedure necessarily required Ministers to take landowners' interests into account. Lord Gill noted:

> Section 72(4) ... provides that the public interest includes the interests of any sector of the public, however small, which in the opinion of Ministers would be affected by the exercise of the right to buy. That plainly includes the interests of the landowner.[32]

Any decision taken by Ministers in a specific case would be open to challenge by a landowner if it were manifestly unreasonable.

The A1P1 challenge represented by *Pairc* was therefore limited and ultimately unsuccessful. There is little here to support the perception of A1P1 as a significant barrier to reform.

Salvesen *v.* Riddell

The background to *Salvesen* is legally and factually complex but must be understood to contextualise the significance of the decision. Salvesen owned a farm in East Lothian which was subject to a tenancy agreement. The tenant was a limited partnership comprised of the Riddell family (who occupied the farm) as general partners, and an agent of the landlord as limited partner. The creation of a limited partnership composed of the landlord and the intended occupiers of the land had become a common mechanism for circumventing the security of tenure provided by the Agricultural Holdings (Scotland) Act 1991 in the years following its introduction. Where the tenancy was held by limited partnership, although the tenancy itself was secure against the landlord, the *tenant* could be dissolved relatively easily, achieving the same end goal of terminating tenants' rights over the land. The Scottish Government sought to neutralise the effect of this mechanism which undermined the policy ambitions pursued through the security of tenure regime. Section 72 of the Agricultural Holdings (Scotland) Act 2003 accordingly

---

[32] *Pairc Crofters Ltd* v. *Scottish Ministers*, at paragraph [37].

provides that, where a limited partner seeks to terminate a limited partnership prior to the agreed end date of the tenancy, the general partners may send a notice asserting their intention to continue the tenancy nevertheless, holding as tenants in their own right.

The clause which became section 72 was not included in the Bill which became the 2003 Act when it was introduced into Parliament by the Scottish Government on 16 September 2002. A proposed amendment to the Bill incorporating this provision was published on 3 February 2003. Anticipating that many landlords might seek to avoid its effects by taking steps to dissolve affected limited partnerships before the Act came into force, the amendment specified that the provision would apply to any attempted termination from 4 February 2003 until a later date to be determined. Actions taken during the remaining hours of 3 February 2003 were not covered, however, and landlords including Salvesen took steps to dissolve affected limited partnerships before close of business on that day. A subsequent amendment published on 10 March 2003 backdated the provision to apply to any attempted termination from the date of the Bill's introduction on 16 September 2002. Accordingly, although Salvesen's actions were not caught by the provision when he took them on 3 February 2003, they were retroactively caught by the provision following the amendment of 10 March 2003.

The March amendment also introduced a new provision which became section 73 of the 2003 Act. Section 73 enables a landlord in a tenancy which had been continued under section 72 to terminate the tenancy on its agreed end date through service of a notice. This provision was, however, only available to landlords who took steps to dissolve affected limited partnerships from 1 July 2003 onwards. Landlords who had acted between 16 September 2002 and 30 June 2003 had no power to terminate the tenancy.

Following Salvesen's steps to dissolve the partnership on 3 February 2003, the Riddell family asserted their right to continue the tenancy under section 72. Salvesen raised a court action contending, amongst other things, that section 72 of the Act was contrary to A1P1. The argument, though not pressed in the initial round of litigation in the Scottish Land Court, was successful in the Inner House of the Court of Session, which found section 72 as a whole to contravene A1P1.[33] The Supreme Court made a narrower finding, upholding the Inner House's decision only to the effect that section 72(10) – the subsection that prevented

---

[33] *Salvesen v. Riddell* [2012] CSIH 26; 2012 *Scots Law Times* 633.

landlords in Salvesen's group benefiting from section 73 – contravened A1P1.[34]

The decision focused on the difference in treatment between landlords like Salvesen who took steps to terminate limited partnerships between 16 September 2002 and 30 June 2003, and those who took steps from 1 July 2003 onwards. The latter group benefited from section 73; the former did not. The interference with the property rights of landlords in the former category was therefore significantly greater. Based on ministerial statements at the time the March amendment was introduced and the circumstances surrounding its introduction, Lord Hope noted that it was hard not to see section 72(10) as having been designed to penalise landlords who acted to terminate limited partnerships on 3 February. He did not consider this punitive justification fair, or reasonably related to the aim of the legislation as a whole, which was focused on enhancing the security of agricultural tenants and streamlining the operation of the sector. Accordingly, the interference with the rights of landlords in the former category was disproportionate. Lord Hope also noted that the former category was not composed solely of landlords who acted on 3 February, and since no justification was offered for the differential treatment of other landlords caught within this group, their inclusion seemed arbitrary, again in contravention of A1P1.

The detail of the Supreme Court's finding is critical to understanding its significance for the overall land reform programme. The subsection of the 2003 Act which violated A1P1 applied only to agricultural landlords who had taken steps to dissolve limited partnership between 16 September 2002 and 1 July 2003, and concerned only the circumstances in which such landlords could terminate the secure 1991 Act tenancies which may have been acquired by general partners as a result. By far the greater part of the 2003 Act, including the key provisions creating a preemptive right to buy for agricultural tenants and strengthening security of tenure in the sector, was not called into question. Moreover, the reason why the subsection contravened A1P1 was that it was intended to have a punitive effect on the landlords concerned. The current land reform programme pursues a complex set of policy objectives, but punishment of property rights holders is nowhere to be found within them. Any precedent set by the case is extremely narrow in scope, and it seems difficult to imagine how a similar set of circumstances could emerge.

Accepting this argument does not deny that the *Salvesen* decision is significant. Most obviously, it was of critical importance to every person

---

[34] *Salvesen* v. *Riddell* [2013] UKSC 22; 2013 *Scots Law Times* 863.

in a relevant limited partnership in the relevant period. The impact of the decision on the lives of people affected was unarguably profound. This argument also does not concede that the *Salvesen* decision was correct. Arguments can and have been made that the court's application of A1P1 was misguided.[35] The point I make is simply that the scope of the *Salvesen* decision is so limited that it cannot support a characterisation of A1P1 as a significant hurdle to land reform. Far from being struck down, the major reforms brought about by the 2003 Act were not even in question.

McMaster *v.* Scottish Ministers

If *Salvesen* was limited in scope, the decision in *McMaster* which resulted directly from it was even more so. The Agricultural Holdings (Scotland) Act 2003 Remedial Order 2014 was enacted to address the aspects of section 72 of the 2003 Act which *Salvesen* had found to contravene A1P1. One effect of the Order was that landlords in Salvesen's category – those who had acted to terminate limited partnerships between 16 September 2002 and 30 June 2003 – were no longer barred from making use of section 73 of the 2003 Act to terminate a tenancy on its agreed end date. Allowing this category of landlords to make use of section 73 resolved the A1P1 issue in *Salvesen*. However, it created a new A1P1 issue for tenants under the continued leases.

The petitioners in *McMaster* were former general partners who had become tenants through section 72. Under the law apparently in force at the time they asserted their rights, they had acquired secure tenancies in respect of which section 73 did not apply. Following the finding in *Salvesen* that section 72(10) was 'not law', and the resulting enactment of the Order, the petitioners continued to hold those tenancies. However, section 73 now did apply, meaning the security of their tenure was much reduced. In the cases of many of the petitioners, landlords had already exercised their rights under section 73, meaning the tenancies were at an end. The Order contained no scheme for compensation related to its effects on tenants, and where individual petitioners had sought compensation from the government, their claims had been

---

[35] M. M. Combe, 'Human rights, limited competence and limited partnerships: *Salvesen* v. *Riddell*' *Scots Law Times (News)*, 32 (2012), pp. 193–200; A. McHarg and D. Nicolson, 'Salvesen v Riddell' in S. Cowan, C. Kennedy and V. Munro, *Scottish Feminist Judgments: (Re)creating the Law from the Outside In* (Oxford: Hart, 2019).

refused. The petitioners contended that their rights under A1P1 had been violated.

In the first judicial consideration of the dispute, in the Outer House of the Court of Session, Lord Clarke found that the Order effected a control of the use of the tenancies by changing the conditions under which they could be terminated.[36] It was not in dispute that the control was lawful and pursued a legitimate aim in the public interest. However, if the reduction in security of tenure had resulted in loss to the petitioners which had not been compensated, this would amount to a disproportionate interference with the petitioners' A1P1 rights. It was not possible to say whether loss had been suffered in any specific case because the relevant facts had not been placed before the court. Lord Clarke indicated that, to ensure A1P1 compliance, compensation should be provided where petitioners could demonstrate specific losses directly caused as a consequence of their reasonable reliance on the pre-Order level of security of tenure, and for associated frustration and inconvenience. However, the value of that compensation should be offset against the windfall benefit to the petitioners of the security of tenure enjoyed in the period between their acquisition of the tenancy and the enactment of the Order. Should there be a case where application of these principles demonstrated an overall loss to a person in the petitioners' position, and no compensation was paid by the government, that person's rights under A1P1 would likely be violated. This analysis was approved by the Inner House on appeal.[37]

Again, there may be arguments about the approach taken to A1P1 in this case. However, as with *Salvesen*, the decision's scope in relation to the broader land reform programme is very limited. Successive findings of A1P1 contraventions by the Scottish Parliament are no doubt embarrassing politically and may influence the opinion of the public, but from a legal perspective, A1P1 has done little to stand in the way of reform. The idea reiterated in parliamentary debates that the ECHR makes land reform 'hard to do' is not, in my submission, borne out by the jurisprudence. Based on the case law to date, A1P1 has proved very little hindrance to land reform.

---

[36] *McMaster v. Scottish Ministers* [2017] CSOH 46; 2017 *Scots Law Times* 586.

[37] *McMaster v. Scottish Ministers* [2018] CSIH 40; 2018 *Scots Law Times* 982.

RECONSTRUCTING A1P1 – THE CITIZENSHIP MODEL

Reported cases cannot, of course, tell the whole story. If Parliament suspects legislation will contravene A1P1, it should not pass it in the first place, after all. Perhaps the challenge presented by A1P1 is best represented not by the flaws which have been found in the legislation introduced so far, but the restrictions it has placed on the development of land reform legislation in the first place.

It is impossible to know exactly how A1P1 concerns have influenced the land reform programme pursued by government to date. In this section of the chapter, however, I argue that A1P1 need not prove a barrier to broad scale and radical land reform. This argument draws on insight from US scholarship, particularly the work of Joseph Singer. The misconstruction of A1P1 that has dominated the 2016 Act discussion encapsulates what Singer terms the 'castle model' of human rights protection of property. He argues that a 'citizenship model' is a better way of understanding how this protection is meant to operate. I transplant this argument to the European context, arguing that the citizenship model is an accurate interpretation of the text of A1P1 and its jurisprudence. I go on to argue that this citizenship model approach to A1P1 helps us to understand how ESC rights, far from being contradicted by A1P1, can actually be enforced *through* A1P1. Employing the citizenship model suggests that, far from inhibiting an LRRS-style human rights approach to land reform, A1P1 is actually the only mechanism by which individuals can ensure it takes place.

Singer and the citizenship model

Protection of property rights against unjustified interference by the state is a common provision in constitutional documents and Bills of Rights throughout the world.[38] At its heart, this protection recognises that, because land is fundamental to the fulfilment of basic human needs such as food and shelter, secure rights in property (not necessarily ownership rights, it should be noted) are a prerequisite to independent political participation. If state authorities have the power to dispossess citizens at will, dissent becomes dangerous, and debate may be stifled or absent. Expropriation of dissenting voices is a common tactic of

[38] G. S. Alexander, *The Global Debate Over Constitutional Property: Lessons for American Takings Jurisprudence* (London: University of Chicago Press, 2006), pp. 1–26.

dictatorial regimes. Protection of property rights is therefore essential to democracy.[39] The nature of property rights and the extent to which they should be protected to meet this democratic need is a central question in political and legal debate.[40]

In recent decades, the richest source of legal scholarship on this issue has been the 'takings clause' of the Fifth Amendment to the United States constitution, which simply states: 'nor shall private property be taken for public use, without just compensation'. As the number of decisions handed down by the US Supreme Court in respect of this clause has grown, concern has developed amongst scholars as to the coherency of the emerging doctrine, with one commentator pointedly describing the jurisprudence as 'a muddle'.[41] The extensive literature suggests the roots of the confusion lie in a debate, poorly articulated within the jurisprudence, as to the values which property law was created to protect in the first place.[42] Numerous underpinning values can be suggested for a property rights system, such as the protection of individual liberty, the maximisation of preference-satisfaction or the promotion of human flourishing. The contended incoherency in the takings jurisprudence is said to result from the Supreme Court implicitly accepting different underpinning values for property rights in different situations, which inevitably leads to different findings about the extent

[39] F. I. Michelman, 'Property as a constitutional right', *Washington & Lee Law Review*, 38 (1981), pp. 1097–114.

[40] For an overview see G. S. Alexander and E. M. Peñalver, *An Introduction to Property Theory* (New York: Cambridge University Press, 2012).

[41] Carol M. Rose, '*Mahon* Reconstructed: Why the Takings Issue is Still a Muddle', *S. California Law Review*, 57 (1984), p. 561.

[42] G. Calabresi and A. D. Melamed, 'Property rules, liability rules and inalienability: one view of the cathedral', *Harvard Law Review*, 85 (1972), pp. 1089–128; R. A. Epstein, *Takings: Private Property and the Power of Eminent Domain* (Cambridge, MA: Harvard University Press, 1985); J. Nedelsky, *Private Property and the Limits of American Constitutionalism: The Madisonian Framework and Its Legacy* (London: University of Chicago Press, 1990); C. M. Rose, '"Takings" and the practices of property: Property as wealth, property as "propriety"' in C. M. Rose, *Property and Persuasion: Essays on the History, Theory, and Rhetoric of Ownership* (Boulder, CO: Westview Press, 1994), pp. 49–71; G. S. Alexander, *Commodity & Propriety: Competing Visions of Property in American Legal Thought 1776–1970* (London: University of Chicago Press, 1997); J. W. Singer, *Entitlement: The Paradoxes of Property* (New Haven and London: Yale University Press, 2000); L. Underkuffler, *The Idea of Property: Its Meaning and Power* (Oxford: Oxford University Press, 2003); R. A. Epstein, *Supreme Neglect: How to Revive Constitutional Protection for Private Property* (New York: Oxford University Press, 2008).

to which state action impinging on those rights for the benefit of others can be justified.[43]

Singer's work does not deny the existence of these competing justificatory values for property rules, nor does he argue for one justification over others. Instead, he suggests we accept that property is a contested concept, with the property law rules in place in any society at a given time representing nothing more than the current compromise as to the weight various values should be accorded. In his view, ongoing alteration of property rules is not only inevitable, but a healthy indication of a society that continues to address and readdress the compromise it has struck as circumstances change.[44]

In Singer's paradigm, the court plays an essential role by providing a forum in which compromises around property rules can continue to be negotiated, with the judiciary holding the other branches of government to account if they stray too far.[45] Performing this role effectively requires the court to ask the correct questions which, in Singer's view, the US Supreme Court does not always do. The difficulty here comes back to the court's implicit acceptance of property as a coherent concept referable to one underlying value. Singer identifies two models of decision-making commonly employed by the US Supreme Court.[46] In the first, the claimant's property is her castle, within which she has absolute dominion, and any government interference with that freedom must be justified. The castle model has obvious resonance with the libertarian understanding of property. In the second model, property rights are legitimised by the investment the owner has made in the property, and are protected so long as that expectation of protection is justified by the investment made. This model resonates with economic understandings of property. In both cases, the concept of ownership is considered fundamentally incompatible with the idea of obligation, and the burden is placed on the state to justify limits on the presumed absolute power of owners.[47]

The problem with these models, in Singer's view, is their failure to acknowledge obligations as inherent to ownership. They suggest that property rules do no more than delineate the entitlements of individual

[43] Rose, '"Takings" and the practices of property'; Alexander, *Commodity & Propriety*.

[44] Singer, *Entitlement*, pp. 19–55; 197–216.

[45] Singer, *Entitlement*, pp. 215–16.

[46] J. W. Singer, 'The ownership society and takings of property: castles, investments and just obligations', *Harvard Environmental Law Review*, 30 (2006), pp. 314–16.

[47] Singer, 'The ownership society', p. 329.

rights holders – entitlements with which the state should not interfere. This description of property law rules does not acknowledge the full extent of their effect. For Singer, property law rules structure the society in which we live. This is a consequence of the fact that property, particularly land, is a finite resource. For many civil and political rights, such as the right to a fair trial or to freedom of speech, upholding my rights does not deny anyone else – every person can enjoy the right to the maximum extent possible. Where land is concerned, however, upholding my ownership rights necessarily denies the rights of other people over that land. Another way of expressing this is to say that property rules involve allocation of scarce resources. Since land is a resource every human being needs to survive, the allocations we choose to make through our property law system affect everyone. This structuring effect of property law explains why it is legitimate to expect owners and other rights holders in land to undertake responsibilities towards the rest of society.[48]

To perform its function effectively in takings cases, the court must take the systemic effect of property rules into account. By denying that social obligation is inherent to ownership, the castle and investment models hinder that process. Singer therefore develops an alternative framework – the citizenship model – that is better adapted for consideration of property's systemic effects.

Singer's citizenship model starts from the assumption that obligations are inherent to property rights. The liberty that property secures for me is only legitimate to the extent that the same liberty can be secured for you. He explains:

> The citizenship model seeks to confer freedom and equality on all persons, spreading rights to all, but it simultaneously places owners in the role of guardians of social order. This position of guardianship entails duties to refrain from actions that endanger the underpinnings of a free and democratic society that treats all individuals with equal concern and respect ... Property serves social as well as individual functions.[49]

Accordingly, the core of constitutional property is not protection from *any* obligation at all, as the castle and investment models might suggest. Rather, constitutional property provides protection from obligations that are *unjust* in the sense that they go beyond those that a reasonable citizen should be expected to undertake. Framing the question in this

[48] Singer, *Entitlement*, 144–78; see also Underkuffler, *The Idea of Property*, pp. 132–49.
[49] Singer, 'The ownership society', pp. 329–38.

way focuses attention on identifying the correct obligations, and prevents a construction of constitutional property that ignores the responsibilities that must result from property's systemic effects. It also forces a conversation in which the values which are being given preference within the property law system must be articulated, and a compromise acknowledged. As Singer suggests, the citizenship model

> invites debate about what obligations we have as citizens in a free and democratic society, bound to laws adopted by elected officials, but protected by certain basic constitutional rights. Further it asks us what kind of property regime we want the law to support.[50]

The citizenship model cannot tell us which obligations are just and which are unjust. Making this determination is the essence of the compromise that property law must always represent. However, Singer notes that, in a democratic country bound by the rule of law, we must start with the presumption that lawful obligations are both legitimate and reasonable as well as fair and just.[51] Legislation passed by a democratically elected parliament represents the compromise currently acceptable to society, in other words. A constitutional property right is designed to protect against obligations that, despite being acceptable to society as represented by Parliament, fail to respect certain minimum standards. Constitutional jurisprudence helps us to understand what those standards are.

The citizenship model and A1P1

Singer developed the citizenship model to deal with constitutional protection of property rights in a context where the values underpinning those rights were a matter of debate. It is this aspect of Singer's model that makes it so suitable for use in relation to A1P1. Some constitutional documents set out in clear terms the purpose of the protection they provide, with section 25 of the Constitution of South African perhaps the most well-known example. By contrast, the drafters of the ECHR were keen to avoid framing the property protection in a way that enshrined a particular political or economic understanding of property's purposes. At the time of the ECHR's drafting, European governments occupied a range of points on the political spectrum from right to left. Consensus on some minimum level of protection appropriate for

---

[50] Singer, 'The ownership society', p. 336.
[51] Singer, 'The ownership society', p. 659.

property rights proved impossible. The text which became A1P1 was a long-negotiated compromise, within which states were intentionally given considerable freedom to pursue the economic and political policies around property that their elected legislatures viewed as appropriate. Minimum standards would, it was hoped, emerge through the case law.[52]

To date, the European Court of Human Rights jurisprudence has maintained a wide margin of appreciation for states in this respect. The standards which have emerged generally focus around the *processes* by which property rights are impacted by the state, rather than the purposes of state action. A1P1 jurisprudence separates state actions into three categories. In a deprivation of possessions, a person loses ownership of their property, whether through legal loss of title or through restraint of their rights so severe that their legal rights lose all practical meaning. A control of use involves a less dramatic regulation of property rights. An interference with the peaceful enjoyment of possessions covers state action which does not fit easily into the other two categories.[53] Regardless of the category of the interference, state action must meet three conditions. It must be lawful, in the sense of meeting the usual rule of law guarantees of legitimacy, foreseeability and non-arbitrariness. It must pursue a legitimate aim in the public interest, in relation to which the court allows a very wide margin of appreciation to states – no A1P1 violation under this head has ever been found in a case where the state has presented an objective of any kind for their actions. Finally, the interference must be proportionate, in the sense of striking a fair balance between the effect on the person concerned and the public interest.[54] The only rule as such that can be discerned in respect of proportionality is that, outwith exceptional circumstances, fair compensation must be provided for a deprivation of possessions or it will not be proportionate.[55] Beyond that, it is possible to identify a number of factors that the court will consider in reviewing proportionality, which include the opportunity for the person concerned to put their case to the relevant public authority, the significance of the public interest objective pursued,

---

[52] F. McCarthy, 'Protection of Property and the European Convention on Human Rights' *Brigham-Kanner Property Rights Conference Journal*, 6 (2017), pp. 317–18.

[53] *Sporrong and Lönnroth* v. *Sweden* (1983) 5 EHRR 35 at paragraph [61]; *James* v. *United Kingdom* (1986) 8 EHRR 123 at paragraph [37].

[54] *James* v. *UK* at paragraph [50].

[55] *Lithgow* v. *United Kingdom* (1986) 8 EHRR 329 at paragraph [120]; *Jahn* v. *Germany* (2006) 42 EHRR 49 at paragraph [94].

and the level of compensation available if any, with the weight placed on these factors varying from case to case.[56]

Faced with this explanation of the protection of property provided by the text of A1P1 and the Strasbourg jurisprudence, the utility of the citizenship model is obvious. A1P1 *necessitates* the discussion of property's justificatory values that the citizenship model is designed to elicit. In its recognition that the public interest may override peaceful enjoyment of possessions, A1P1 *incorporates* the idea of obligation as inherent to ownership on which the citizenship model is based. In its refusal to set safeguards beyond concern for appropriate process and compensation for deprivation, A1P1 jurisprudence *requires* discussion of justificatory values to take place at domestic level. The citizenship model of constitutional property protection makes perfect sense for the protection provided by A1P1.

THE CITIZENSHIP MODEL, A1P1 AND SCOTTISH LAND REFORM

Reflecting on the debates around the 2016 Act with the benefit of the analysis above offers some insight on the way A1P1 has been charac-terised. The idea of A1P1 as a landowner's right, an obstacle to land reform, relies on a 'castle model'-type conceptualisation of ownership, in which obligations on owners are alien. This characterisation is not supported by the case law, in which the highly limited scope of A1P1 challenges to date has resulted in minimal restriction on the ongoing land reform programme. This characterisation also conflicts with the text of A1P1 and the jurisprudence of the Strasbourg court, in which the obligations inherent in ownership are clearly recognised and the margin of appreciation given to states to pursue projects around property is wide.

I have focused on the citizenship model here in the hope of disrupting this prevailing characterisation of A1P1. In my argument, disruption would be desirable first because the prevailing characterisation is incor-rect as a matter of law. As my analysis above indicates, the citizen-ship model is a much better fit for the protection offered by A1P1. It emphasises that the role of the court is to identify *unjust* obligations on owners, a determination that can only be reached through consideration of the values underlying our system of property law. Those values have been the subject of sustained debate in this country for decades, and the current consensus is now encapsulated within the LRRS. A correct

[56] McCarthy, 'Protection of Property', pp. 309–15.

understanding of A1P1 allows us to both recognise and expect that the court will take these values into account when determining when an obligation on a landowner goes too far.

In addition, far from undermining the significance of ESC rights in relation to land reform, reconstruing A1P1 in line with the citizenship model has the benefit of providing a clear framework within which those rights can be taken into account by a court. The appeal to international human rights instruments has clearly influenced government and Parliament in the recent land reform discussions, and that influence is to be welcomed. However, our ability to enforce continued adherence to those commitments on the part of our public authorities is restricted by the fact they are not directly justiciable. Adopting a citizenship approach to A1P1 enables its justiciability to be used in the service of the whole constellation of human rights. These rights, and the commitment to them within the LRRS, encapsulate the values that the court must address when determining the correct balance between the public interest and the needs of the landowner. Within the citizenship framework, a close connection between the directly justiciable A1P1 and the non-incorporated ICESCR – a connection, it will be recalled, that it is necessary to show before an unincorporated instrument can be relied upon by the court – will be easier to establish. A1P1 becomes an enforcement tool for ESC rights, rather than a barrier to their realisation.

Publication of the LRRS represents a significant milestone in Scotland's land reform journey. Its commitment to the full range of Scotland's human rights obligations might be seen by some as a victory over the impediment of A1P1. By reconstruing A1P1 in line with Singer's citizenship model of constitutional property protection, I hope that the property right may come to be seen as an integral and complementary aspect of the human rights approach to land reform, rather than a hurdle.

10

The Evolution of Sustainable Development in Scotland: A Case Study of Community Right to Buy Law and Policy, 2003–18*

Andrea Ross

OVER THIRTY YEARS HAVE passed since the World Commission on Environment and Development defined sustainable development as 'development that meets the needs of the present without compromising the ability of future generations to meet their own needs' ('the Brundtland definition').[1] Since then sustainable development has become a significant objective worldwide and the Brundtland definition its most widely accepted iteration. The Brundtland definition encourages discourse by bringing together different and conflicting interests but it also allows a wide range of different interpretations (and hence, outcomes) to be considered legitimate.[2] To that end, states, international organisations, businesses, and individuals have tried various ways of moving beyond the rhetoric provided by the broad parameters of Brundtland to deliver the transformational change needed to address modern challenges such as poverty, climate change and biodiversity. During this time, law and policy, like other tools, have been used to varying degrees of success. Effective ownership, management and access to land are central for sustainable development and can impact significantly on the opportunities for local enterprise.[3] In 1998, Scotland's Land Reform

---

* With the kind permission of Edinburgh University Press and the editors, a version of this chapter appears in a special issue of *Sustainability* entitled 'Environmental Law for Sustainability 2018', T. Koivurova, V. Mauerhofer (eds), available at <https://www.mdpi.com/journal/sustainability/special_issues/Environmental_Law> (last accessed 22 September 2019).

[1] World Commission on Environment and Development, *Our Common Future* (the 'Brundtland Report') (Oxford: Oxford University Press, 1987).

[2] A. Ross, 'Why legislate for sustainable development? An examination of sustainable development provisions in UK and Scottish statutes', *Journal of Environmental Law*, 20:1 (2008), at p. 39.

[3] Land Reform Policy Group (LRPG), 'Identifying the Problems' (Edinburgh: Scottish Office, 1998), para. 2.5.

Policy Group concluded that 'Land reform is needed on the grounds of fairness and to secure the public good'[4] and following on from this, Scotland has introduced various schemes that facilitate or, in some cases, compel the transfer for land from an existing landowner to a community body. Sustainable development is a primary objective of all of these regimes. This chapter critically explores how the law and policy relating to sustainable development in the context of the various community right to buy regimes in Scotland have matured and evolved from their introduction in 2003 to the present. Importantly, it uncovers a new era in sustainable development policy in Scotland that has the potential to move well beyond the rhetoric of sustainable development to deliver transformational outcomes.

The Land Reform (Scotland) Act 2003 (LRSA 2003) gives certain community bodies a pre-emptive community right to buy land (that is to say, a right of first refusal) where there is a willing seller.[5] The same Act also creates a right for crofting community bodies to compulsorily acquire crofting land in certain circumstances.[6] More recently, the Community Empowerment (Scotland) Act 2015 (CESA 2015) introduces Part 3A into LRSA 2003 which creates a right for community bodies to compulsorily acquire land that has been abandoned or neglected or somehow managed in a way that is detrimental to a community's 'environmental wellbeing'.[7] Also, the Land Reform (Scotland) Act 2016 (LRSA 2016) Part 5 introduces community rights to compulsorily acquire land to further the achievement of sustainable development.[8] This chapter refers to these rights collectively as the community right to buy regimes. The regimes all share an express requirement that communities wishing to

---

[4] Ibid., para. 2.2.

[5] Part 2, section 33. Initially only rural communities with populations of less than 10,000 were included. This was extended to cover all of Scotland (Community Empowerment (Scotland) Act 2015, section 36 which amends section 33).

[6] Part 3. Crofting is a form of small landholding mainly found the north and west of Scotland, which gives the crofter (tenant) almost absolute security of tenure. Crofts and crofters are now defined under the Crofters (Scotland) Act 1993. An individual crofter's right to compel a sale of a house and croft land has existed since 1976. See M. M. Combe, 'Community Rights in Scots Property Law', chapter 5, in T. Xu and A. Clarke (eds), *Legal Strategies for the Development and Protection of Communal Property* (Oxford: Oxford University Press, 2018), p. 86; E. I. M. MacLellan, 'Crofting Law', Chapter 12, this volume.

[7] The community right to buy abandoned, neglected or detrimental land under Part 3A came into force on 27 June 2018.

[8] As of July 2018, Part 5 is not yet in force.

exercise any of the rights to buy must have sustainable development at the heart of their community body and of their proposals for the land.[9]

Arguably, sustainable development is a poor champion for any of its component parts whether economic, social or environmental. Rather, as Ross contends, it is most usefully viewed as a framework or forum for sometimes complementary, but often conflicting, factors to be raised and the best solution found.[10] Even within its own parameters, this view of sustainable development requires a balancing of factors. States often define sustainable development for their own purposes by simply referring to the Brundtland definition which offers little assistance in relation to the priority afforded to different factors.[11] Occasionally, states, usually in policy statements, adapt the Brundtland definition to reflect needs and priorities relevant to their own circumstances, or the political priorities of the current government in power. The detail on what factors should be considered and the priority among them may be set out as a tailored interpretation of sustainable development or as a defined process for assessing what is considered sustainable development for that particular state.[12] The conventional wisdom is that having a common understanding or clear vision of sustainable development across government is helpful for delivering sustainable development outcomes.[13]

Alternatively, the balancing can occur outside the interpretation of sustainable development, where sustainable development is expressly balanced against other factors. This wider decision-making process can usefully be described as the 'sustainable development equation'.[14] These are usually set out in the enabling legislation itself. Decisions about what factors should be raised and the priority afforded to each in any

[9] For more detail about the operation of the rights more generally see M. M. Combe, 'Legislating for Community Land Rights' Chapter 7, this volume.

[10] A. Ross, 'It's Time to Get Serious – Why Legislation Is Needed to Make Sustainable Development a Reality in the UK' *Sustainability*, 2 (2010), p. 1101 at p. 1105.

[11] A. Ross, *Sustainable Development Law in the UK – From Rhetoric to Reality?* (Abingdon: Earthscan/Routledge, 2012), chapter 4.

[12] For example: Wellbeing of Future Generations (Wales) Act 2015.

[13] Organisation for Economic Co-operation and Development (OECD) *Improving Policy Coherence and Integration for Sustainable Development: A Checklist* (Paris, 2002); P. Hardi and T. Zdan (eds), *Assessing Sustainable Development: Principles in Practice* (Winnipeg: IISD, 1997), <https://www.iisd.org/pdf/bellagio.pdf> (last accessed 11 December 2018).

[14] A. Ross and A. Zasinaite, 'The use of presumptions and duties in sustainable development equations: promoting micro-renewables and preserving historic buildings', *Environmental Law Review*, 19:2 (2017), 93–112.

given sustainable development equation can vary significantly among regimes.[15] Often, within these equations, sustainable development appears as a secondary obligation to be considered in the exercise of a primary function or obligation. For example, under the Climate Change (Scotland) Act 2009, section 92(1) the Scottish Ministers must take into account the need to exercise their functions in a way that contributes to the achievement of sustainable development.

In contrast, all of Scotland's community right to buy regimes have sustainable development as a primary duty and it equates to or has priority over the other duties or objectives within the various decision making provisions or sustainable development equations.[16] Additionally, the more recent 2015 and 2016 regimes include provisions that tailor the interpretation of sustainable development for their specific purposes by narrowing its scope and setting out conditions for assessing what is sustainable. The combination of this regime-specific tailoring of sustainable development and its status as a primary objective make Scotland's community right to buy provisions exceptional in UK and global terms and worthy of in-depth examination.

The chapter begins by examining sustainable development as a policy goal within Scotland to uncover three distinct eras of sustainable development policy. It then briefly explains the background to sustainable development within the community right to buy provisions introduced in the LRSA 2003 Parts 2 and 3 as well as the policy that details how sustainable development is to be defined and assessed within these regimes. This section reveals a gap between current Scottish Government policy on sustainable development and that used to assess sustainable development for the purposes of Parts 2 and 3 of the LRSA 2003. The chapter then explores how the interpretation of sustainable development itself and the process of assessing what is sustainable development has developed and been specifically tailored to the particular context of compulsory acquisition by community bodies within the more recent community right to buy regimes established by the CESA 2015 (in Part 3A LRSA 2003) and Part 5 of the LRSA 2016. Next, the chapter analyses how the relationship between sustainable development and the public interest and human rights within sustainable development equations has evolved from 2003 to 2016. The chapter concludes that the new community right to buy regimes herald the beginning of a fourth era in sustainable development policy in Scotland which moves away from a

[15] Ross, *Sustainable Development Law in the UK*, chapter 8.
[16] See discussion on Parts 2 and 3 LRSA 2003 below.

single 'one size fits all' approach for the whole of Scotland to one where both sustainable development itself and wider sustainable development equations are tailored to the specific requirements of individual regimes and contexts.

SUSTAINABLE DEVELOPMENT IN SCOTLAND

Most statutory provisions that refer to sustainable development leave defining sustainable development and even the process of assessing what is sustainable development to policy, to allow flexibility reflecting changing times and different political ambitions. This is certainly the case in Scotland where since 2003 there have been three significant eras of sustainable development policy. Each reflects the political priorities of the governments in power at that time and for that time.

When the LRSA 2003 was passed, the Scottish Government (known then as the Scottish Executive) policy on sustainable development was set out in a Statement published in 2002 entitled *Meeting the Needs ... Priorities, Actions and Targets for Sustainable Development in Scotland*.[17] The Statement described sustainable development as combining economic progress with social and environmental justice. It endorsed the widely accepted Brundtland definition of sustainable development yet also recognised the need to define the term further. It set out a vision based on the following principles:

> have regard for others who do not have access to the same level of resources, and the wealth generated
> minimise the impact of our actions on future generations by radically reducing our use of resources and by minimising environmental impacts
> live within the capacity of the planet to sustain our activities and to replenish resources which we use[18]

The vision resonates with the aims of the right to buy regimes enacted the following year, especially its reference to environmental justice which it defined as 'fundamentally ... ensuring that people do not live in degraded surroundings and it means not making unrealistic demands on the environment to absorb waste and pollution'.[19]

---

[17] Scottish Executive, *Meeting the Needs ... Priorities, Actions and Targets for Sustainable Development in Scotland* (Edinburgh, 2002), <https://www.webarchive. org.uk/wayback/archive/20180514194918/http://www.gov.scot/Publications/2002 /04/14640/4040> (last accessed 1 October 2018).

[18] Ibid., p. 3.

[19] Ibid., p. 4.

While quite progressive in its vision, the language in the statement is weak ('have regard to') and thus was aspirational rather than driven by outcomes. Moreover, the statement's scope was limited to three priority areas – resource use, energy and travel instead of working across all aspects of government and governance.[20]

The second era began in 2005 when the UK, Scottish, Welsh, and Northern Ireland administrations, jointly produced *One Future – different paths: the UK's shared framework for sustainable development*, which set out five principles:

> living within the Earth's environmental limits
> ensuring a strong, healthy and just society
> achieving a sustainable economy
> promoting good governance
> using sound science responsibility[21]

Importantly, the previous focus on high economic growth in sustainable development across the UK was replaced by a goal of a sustainable economy. This change, combined with the explicit acknowledgement of the Earth's environmental limits, demonstrated a deeper commitment to ecological sustainability.[22] The *Framework* received global acclaim and is held out as good practice.[23] In late 2005 Scottish Executive published *Choosing Our Future – Scotland's Sustainable Development Strategy* which closely followed the *Framework*.[24] It was more committed to economic growth than the UK *Framework*, but throughout, environmental objectives and actions are listed ahead of social and economic goals, thus reinforcing a vision based on limits rather than tradeoffs.

The third era followed the Scottish National Party's (SNP) success in the Scottish Parliament election in May 2007. The SNP government

---

[20] Ibid., p. 5–6.

[21] HM Government, Scottish Executive, Welsh Assembly Government, and Northern Ireland Office, *One future – different paths: the UK's shared framework for sustainable development* (Norwich: The Stationery Office, 2005), p. 8, <https://www2.gov.scot/resource/doc/47121/0020703.pdf> (last accessed 11 December 2018).

[22] 'Ecological sustainability' emphasises the need to operate within the carrying capacity of the Earth. See K. Bosselman, *The Principle of Sustainability* (Aldershot: Ashgate, 2008), pp. 5, 162–9.

[23] D. Swanson and L. Pinter, 'Governance strategies for national sustainable development strategies' in *Institutionalising Sustainable Development* (Paris: OECD, 2007), p. 34.

[24] Scottish Executive, *Choosing our Future – Scotland's Sustainable Development Strategy* (Edinburgh, 2005).

replaced the previous government's sustainable development strategy with its own *Economic Strategy* and *National Performance Indicators*.[25] While recent Scottish policy continues to state the Scottish Government's support for the five principles in the 2005 UK *shared framework for sustainable development*[26]it is clear that the Scottish Government's focus is on economic growth rather than sustainable economy.[27]

The *Economic Strategy* defines sustainable development using the Brundtland definition, however, since 2007 the Scottish Government largely avoided using the term.[28] Instead, the emphasis is on the Scottish Government's adopted overall objective: 'To focus government and public services on creating a more successful country, with opportunities for all of Scotland to flourish, through increasing sustainable economic growth'.[29] 'Sustainable economic growth' is left undefined in the *Economic Strategy* although the approach is characterised by four key priorities: sustainable investment in people, infrastructure and assets; innovation and openess; inclusive growth; and international outlook.[30] The Strategy was updated in 2011 and 2015, however, the overall approach to sustainable development has remained largely constant.[31] The 2015 *Economic Strategy* added two key pillars to the approach to sustainable economic growth: increasing competitiveness and tackling inequality.

As will be discussed below, the LRSA 2003 does not define sustainable development so current policy on sustainable development is very influential in terms of the delivery of the statutory aims.

---

[25] Scottish Government, *Economic Strategy* (Edinburgh, 2007), <https://www2.gov.scot/Publications/2007/11/12115041/0> (last accessed 11 December 2018).

[26] Scottish Government, *Scottish Planning Policy* (Edinburgh, 2014), para. 25, <https://www.gov.scot/publications/scottish-planning-policy/> (last accessed 11 December 2018).

[27] A. Ross, 'The future Scotland wants – Is it really all about sustainable economic growth?' *Edinburgh Law Review* 19:1 (2015), pp. 66–100.

[28] Ross, 'The future Scotland wants', p. 82.

[29] Scottish Government, *Economic Strategy* (Edinburgh, 2015), p. 13, <https://www.gov.scot/publications/scotlands-economic-strategy/> (last accessed 11 December 2018).

[30] Ibid., p.36.

[31] Scottish Government, *Economic Strategy* (Edinburgh, 2011), <https://www2.gov.scot/Publications/2011/09/13091128/0> (last accessed 11 December 2018). Scottish Government, *Economic Strategy* (2015).

SUSTAINABLE DEVELOPMENT AND THE LAND REFORM (SCOTLAND) ACT 2003, PARTS 2 AND 3

Despite Scotland's unsettled history surrounding land ownership and use, the main emphasis of the LRSA 2003 was not about righting any past wrongs but rather on increasing the opportunities for local enterprise and addressing concerns about the concentration of land ownership in Scotland among a few large estates some of whom had non-resident or absentee owners.[32] As Combe explains it was only after the passage of the Scotland Act 1998 and the creation of the Scottish Parliament that there was a legislative forum with the time and the inclination to address land reform issues in Scotland.[33] With devolution imminent, the Scottish Office established the Land Reform Policy Group (LRPG) in 1997 to study the system of land ownership in Scotland. It reported in 1998 that 'the overriding objective of rural policy and thus land use should be to foster the sustainable development of rural communities and remove land-based barriers to development'.[34] This established a strong link between sustainable development and issues of fairness associated with the balancing of the public interest with private property rights.

Interestingly, in 1998 the LRPG provided a contextualised definition of sustainable development: 'development that is planned with appropriate regard for its longer term consequences and is geared towards assisting social and economic advances, that can lead to further opportunities and a higher quality of life for rural people whilst protecting the environment'. The definition continues, stating that 'in this context sustainable development requires an integrated approach to be taken in the key areas of economic, social and environmental policy'.[35] However, as the Land Reform (Scotland) Bill passed through Parliament in 2002, legislators chose to drop the definition of sustainable development to leave the term undefined.[36]

As originally passed, Part 2 of the LRSA 2003 creates a pre-emptive right for community bodies to acquire rural land in certain prescribed circumstances. Part 3 creates a right to compel a sale of crofting land in certain prescribed circumstances for crofting communities. The

---

[32] Combe, 'Community Rights in Scots Property Law', p. 89.
[33] Ibid., p. 88.
[34] LRPG, 'Identifying the Problems', para. 2.2 and para. 2.5.
[35] Ibid., para. 2.4–2.6.
[36] A. Pillai, 'Sustainable rural communities? A legal perspective on the community right to buy', *Land Use Policy*, 27 (2010), pp. 898–905, 899.

provisions in Part 2 were extended to include urban land by CESA 2015 but remain otherwise largely unchanged.

Consistent with the drafting of UK legislation generally, and despite its importance, sustainable development does not feature as the overall aim of Parts 2 and 3 of the LRSA 2003. Instead, sustainable development is set out as an objective for the acquiring community body regarding its proposals for the land, and as a duty for the Scottish Ministers supported by strict administrative procedures. Section 34(4) provides that a body is not a community body unless Ministers are satisfied that the main purpose of the body is consistent with furthering the achievement of sustainable development. The same rule applies to crofting community bodies under Part 3, section 71(4). Section 38(1) provides that 'Ministers shall not decide that a community interest is to be entered in the Register[37] unless they are satisfied . . . that the acquisition of the land by the community body to which the application relates is compatible with furthering the achievement of sustainable development'.[38] The strong substantive provisions relating to sustainable development are supported by serious procedural consequences for noncompliance in administrative law and company law. The project cannot proceed unless the community interest is registered. Indeed, research by Fox and later Pillai found several applications have been rejected because either the community's purposes were not consistent with sustainable development or because the community's proposals for the land were not compatible with sustainable development.[39]

Parts 2 and 3 create obligations on both sides of the regulatory equation. On one hand, they require bodies and community interests to have a sustainable development objective that is enforceable by procedures, and on the other hand, they impose a substantive duty on the Scottish Ministers. For example, the LRSA 2003 section 51(3) provides that

[37] The Register of Community Interests in Land is maintained by the Keeper of the Registers of Scotland.

[38] While the terms 'consistent' and 'compatible' are often treated as synonymous, here the use of compatible as opposed to consistent likely reflects the direct relationship of the interest with the particular piece of land and community. The Collins dictionary provides a useful distinction: if one *fact* or *idea* is consistent with another, they do not *contradict* each other; compatible means to work *well* together or to exist together successfully, <https://www.collinsdictionary.com/dictionary/english/consistent> (last accessed 11 December 2018).

[39] A. Fox, 'Update on the Right to Buy Land' Proceedings from Rural Law Conference Glasgow CLT (2007), at 47; Pillai 'Sustainable rural communities?', p. 901.

Ministers shall not consent [to a proposal by a community to buy land] 'unless ... Ministers are satisfied that [among other things] what the community body proposes to do with the land is compatible with furthering the achievement of sustainable development'.[40] The mandatory language not only creates a strong obligation but also creates a legal rule as it sets out how the Scottish Ministers are actually to make the decision. This combination of a strong substantive purpose focused on sustainable development backed up by administrative procedures arguably creates a powerful legislative partnership in relation to sustainable development with real potential to deliver transformational change.[41]

That is not to say that no other objectives or duties are relevant to the community right to buy regimes in Parts 2 and 3. On the contrary, several other obligations play an important part of the decision-making processes or wider sustainable development equations. First, the Scottish Ministers are subject to certain general obligations. For example, under the Scotland Act 1998 the Scottish Ministers must not do anything that is incompatible with the European Convention on Human Rights (ECHR) (section 57(2)) or the UK's international obligations (section 58(3)). Moreover, the Climate Change (Scotland) Act 2009 places a duty on public bodies, including the Scottish Ministers, to exercise their functions in the way best calculated to contribute to the delivery of climate change targets and deliver any climate change programmes. These duties are put in a wider context by an additional obligation to act in a way that it considers is most sustainable.[42] Likewise, Scottish Ministers are under an obligation in exercising any functions, to further the conservation of biodiversity so far as is consistent with the proper exercise of those functions.[43] While symbolic, these obligations remain outside the specific decision making equation set out in a regime's enabling legislation and as shown by Ross and Zasinaite, this may limit their influence in practice especially in court.[44] A full analysis of the impact of these general obligations in community right to buy regimes is beyond the scope of this chapter.

Within the provisions of Parts 2 and 3 of the LRSA 2003 themselves, several requirements exist that operationalise certain values within

[40] The same language used in Part 3, section 74(1).
[41] Ross, *Sustainable Development Law in the UK*, chapter 8.
[42] Section 44(1) (a)–(c).
[43] Nature Conservation (Scotland) Act 2004, section 1.
[44] Ross and Zasinaite, 'Presumptions and duties in sustainable development equations'.

property, administrative and company law. These relate mainly to the ownership of land, its location, the interests of tenants, its connection with and proximity to the community', and notice requirements, forming conditions precedent that are considered important for ensuring the regime operates as it is intended. It is not the aim of this chapter to explore these procedural obligations in any more detail.

More substantively, the public interest is also a key objective and duty in Parts 2 and 3. The LRPG in 1998 argued that 'the public interest in securing sustainable rural development may justify a range of public sector intervention measures to bring about outcomes which would not happen if development was left solely to market forces'.[45] While the LRPG quote above seems to indicate that sustainable rural development would always be in the public interest, as enacted the LRSA 2003 provisions in Parts 2 and 3 seem to address the possibility at least that a proposal could arguably be consistent with sustainable development but not be in the public interest. To this end, the public interest is considered alongside but separately from sustainable development in the relevant sustainable development equation. Section 51(3) provides that Ministers shall not consent to the exercise of a community right to buy (the preemptive right) unless they are satisfied that the proposed purchase of the land is in the public interest. The Act does not define public interest any further nor does it consider its relationship with private interests.

The Scottish Ministers have been willing to enforce this requirement and Pillai found that applications had been rejected for failing to be in the public interest.[46] In *Holmehill Ltd* v. *The Scottish Ministers and Anor* the court held that

> As sustainable development clearly underlies the Act, an ambition to prevent development is a factor that may be taken into account in construing public interest. The guidance at para 30 makes it clear that applications which aim to subvert the planning process are not considered to be in the public interest.[47]

The guidance referred to by the court is discussed in detail below.[48]

---

[45] LRPG, 'Identifying the Problems', para. 2.6.

[46] Pillai, 'Sustainable rural communities?', p. 901.

[47] 2006 SLT (Sh Ct) 79 at 101. M. M. Combe, 'No Place like Holme: Community Expectations and the Right to Buy' *Edinburgh Law Review*, 11 (2007), pp. 109–16.

[48] Scottish Government, *Part 3 of the Land Reform (Scotland) Act 2003 Community Right to Buy, Guidance for applications made on or after 15 April 2016* (Edinburgh, March 2016), <https://www.gov.scot/publications/community-right-buy-guidance-applications-made-15-april-2016/> (last accessed 8 January

The influence and impact of the right to buy provisions in terms of both the community body's aims and the suitability of community interests clearly depend on the interpretation given to sustainable development at any given time. Yet, the LRSA 2003 provides no definition of sustainable development or its relationship with the public interest which, as noted above, is also left undefined. By failing to do so, much of the balancing process is moved into the political arena. The approach taken to sustainable development will decide not only what factors are to be taken into account in decision making but also the weight to be afforded to each. The result is that sustainable development at any given time is what the Scottish Government says it is and, as discussed above, that can change significantly over time and for different contexts.

It is unsurprising that more detailed policies exist that specify how sustainable development is to be assessed under Parts 2 and 3 of the LRSA 2003. The Guidance for the Part 2 Community Right to Buy (CRBG) and Part 3 Crofting Community Right to Buy (Crofting Guidance) provide specific instructions on the objectives, operation and processes of the two regimes. While Parts 2 and 3 of the LRSA 2003 are now fifteen years old, the policy in relation to both is relatively recent. There have been three iterations of the CRBG in 2004, 2009 and 2016 and two sets of Crofting Guidance in 2004 and 2009.[49] Interestingly, there is no perceptible change in the sustainable development guidance in these versions to reflect each of the Scottish three different eras of sustainable development policy in Scotland since 2003. Indeed, even the latest 2009 Crofting Guidance and 2016 CRBG continue to describe the Scottish Government's approach to sustainable development as being set out in the 2002 document *Meeting the Needs – Priorities, Actions and Targets for Sustainable Development in Scotland*[50] relying on the policy that dates back to when the two regimes were introduced. Nowhere in either Guidance is reference made to the *Economic Strategy*, or the Scottish Government's central purpose of 'increasing sustainable economic growth'. Clearly, the reasons for producing detailed updated policy in 2009 and 2016 was not to reflect changes in overall Scottish Government sustainable development policy despite this being very

2019); Scottish Government, *Guidance on the Crofting Community Right to Buy under Part 3 of the Land Reform (Scotland) Act 2003* (Edinburgh, June 2009), <https://www.gov.scot/publications/crofting-community-right-buy-under-part-3-land-reform-scotland/> (last accessed 8 January 2019).

[49] Scottish Government (March 2016); Scottish Government (June 2009).

[50] Scottish Government (March 2016), para. 87 and Scottish Government (June 2009).

much the case. One can only speculate why such important central policy has been largely ignored by those responsible for drafting the detailed policy on an important aspect of the government's land reform agenda. Pillai describes the result in practice as the regime 'generating its own rhetoric largely based on CRB guidance'.[51]

Indeed, the CRBG and Crofting Guidance provide significant detail as to what type of information is needed to satisfy Ministers in relation to sustainable development. Recall that under Part 2, Ministers must be satisfied that the registration of a community interest (and also the exercise the community body's right to buy) is compatible with 'furthering the achievement of sustainable development'.[52] Part 2 is a pre-emptive right and requires a willing seller. In contrast, Part 3 creates a right to force a sale of crofting land to a crofting community. Despite their differences, the two sets of guidance in relation to sustainable development policy are very similar.

Paragraph 85 of the CRBG provides that 'Applications to register a community interest in land have the best chance of success if they explicitly address the likely overall impacts of land registration in terms of environmental, economic and social benefits . . .' Interestingly, it goes on to indicate that 'The Act does not require that every element of any planned development be compatible with the achievement of sustainable development, but that the acquisition of the land as a whole should be compatible with furthering sustainable development'. The 2004 CRBG stopped at this point. In contrast, more recent 2009 and 2016 versions continue: 'Proposals for developments that might result in lasting significant environmental damage are likely to fail to meet this legislative requirement.'[53] Thus, projects such as community renewable energy projects may be very positive for the community but this needs to be balanced with any impact they may have on water, land and the environment. Moreover, the guidance provides that 'proposals to prevent any development or those that aim simply to maintain the status quo . . . will be construed as not being compatible with furthering sustainable development'.[54] These new paragraphs show an evolution in the interpretation of sustainable development within the right to buy guidance. The first prioritises the prevention of significant environmental

[51] Pillai, 'Sustainable rural communities?', p. 904.
[52] Sections 38(1) and 51(3)(c).
[53] Scottish Government (March 2016), para. 85.
[54] Scottish Government (March 2016), para. 85 and Scottish Government (June 2009), para. 100.

damage and the second discourages action aimed at stifling innovation and positive change. These policy changes create a bespoke approach to sustainable development tailored to the needs of these specific regimes.

The CRBG also suggests community bodies set out the positive economic, social and environmental consequences of their aspirations. It suggests community bodies produce a long-term plan to demonstrate how they would achieve sustainable development.[55] The long-term element of sustainable development is very clear and the guidance states there is an expectation that 'the exercise of a community right to buy *deliver lasting benefits* to your community'.[56]

Unlike previous guidance and the current Crofting Guidance 2009, the CRBG 2016 also provides very detailed advice in relation to what the actual proposals should contain to demonstrate compatibility with furthering the achievement of sustainable development and advises the use of separate headings for social, environmental and economic development. Social development could, for example, include: clear community benefits; the direct improvement or creation of specified local services; and infrastructure in the short term. The examples given as environmental development include: the improvement or provision of new amenity for locals and visitors in terms of access, interpretation and education; the enhancement of natural resources, wildlife or habitats; and short-term negative impacts that are outweighed by longer-term advantages to the community. Examples of economic sustainability include: the creation of new jobs or protection of existing local jobs; and the diversification of the economic base of the area.[57]

Both the CRBG 2016 and the Crofting Guidance 2009 also influence how the wider sustainable development equations operate for Parts 2 and 3 of the LRSA 2003 respectively. Both provide advice in relation to what is the public interest stating that community bodies should show how the proposed acquisition would bring real benefits to the whole of the community and not just the community body itself. Likewise, the community body should consider and show that such benefits are not outweighed by any disadvantages to the wider community, the environment or the economy, or are not disproportionate to the degree of any harm to private interests as a result of the registration and the exercise

---

[55] Scottish Government (March 2016), para. 86 and Scottish Government (June 2009), para. 101.

[56] Scottish Government (March 2016), para. 89 and Scottish Government (June 2009), para. 103.

[57] Scottish Government (March 2016), para. 89.

of the right to buy.[58] These provisions acknowledge the need to consider the impact on the private property rights of the existing owner in the decision-making process.[59]

Thus, over the years the various versions of the detailed guidance on the two original community rights to buy (CRBG and Crofting Guidance) have failed to respond and reflect changes in wider Scottish Government policy on sustainable development and instead refer to 2003 Scottish Government policy on sustainable development which has a strong emphasis on social and environmental justice. However, the policy has not stood still, rather it has evolved independently of Scottish Government policy on sustainable development to, for example, increase the emphasis on preventing significant environmental harm, and acknowledging wider interests. The result has been a widening gap between the approach taken to sustainable development under the community right to buy regimes and Scottish Government policy more generally.

This inconsistency can cause difficulties for the right to buy regimes which are so dependent on the definition of sustainable development to function. If applicants and decision-makers are unsure of what sustainable development means in the context of land reform they will be reluctant to move away from the status quo. This slows down the land reform process. Moreover, those investing in change need some certainty that it will continue to be acceptable and viable as sustainable development in years to come. The result is a need for consensus about the meaning of sustainable development in the context of land reform. There is also a need for more practical, and arguably bespoke, iterations of sustainable development, its component parts and its relationship with other interests within wider sustainable development equations.

EVOLUTION OF THE DEFINITION OF SUSTAINABLE DEVELOPMENT IN THE COMMUNITY RIGHT TO BUY REGIMES

Allowing more tailored, regime-specific approaches to sustainable development may be a means of bridging the policy gap that currently exists. Historically, little attempt has been made to contextualise sustainable development within a state for different sectors such as education, forestry or health. This is likely partially due to a resistance from defining

---

[58] Scottish Government (March 2016), para. 90 and Scottish Government (June 2009), para. 108.
[59] See discussion on human rights below.

sustainable development in any detail at all and also perhaps due to concerns that different approaches would lead to inconsistent decision-making and confuse regulators and the regulated alike.[60] Yet, regulatory regimes, often very appropriately, are designed to champion a particular aspect of sustainable development, whether that is cultural heritage, community engagement, biodiversity or a low-carbon economy.[61] As such, the tensions and connections within sustainable development itself vary in different contexts and may need to be treated differently. Both law and policy can be used to do this.

To this end, there appears to have been an acceptance by both Government and Parliament that land use requires a more bespoke approach to sustainable development. This acceptance is visible both in the interpretation of sustainable development used in the new community right to buy regimes and also in the sustainable development equations used for decision-making in these regimes. It is also visible in what can be referred to as 'bridging policies' that aim to show how land reform and the community right to buy fit within wider Scottish Government sustainable development policy.

The Scottish Government's *Economic Strategy* sits in the middle of its policy framework. Its overall purpose is 'To focus government and public services on creating a more successful country, with opportunities for all of Scotland to flourish, through increasing sustainable economic growth'.[62] The purpose is to guide all government action and, consequently, policy produced for different sectors and jurisdictions should, arguably, be largely consistent and aimed at delivering that purpose. Several high-level policies have connections with land use and management.[63] Of these, the *Land Use Strategy* is likely the most important and is a key commitment of the Climate Change (Scotland) Act 2009.[64] Its purpose is to promote long-term, well-integrated, sustainable land use

---

[60] Ross, 'It's Time to Get Serious'.

[61] Ross and Zasinaite, 'Presumptions and duties in sustainable development equations'.

[62] Scottish Government, *Economic Strategy*, p. 13.

[63] For example: Scottish Government, *Scottish Planning Policy*; Scottish Government, *The National Planning Framework* (Edinburgh, 2014), <https://www.gov.scot/publications/national-planning-framework-3/> (last accessed 11 December 2018); Scottish Government, *2020 Challenge for Scotland's Biodiversity* (Edinburgh, 2013), <https://www.gov.scot/publications/2020-challenge-scotlands-biodiversity-strategy-conservationenhancement-biodiversity-scotland/> (last accessed 11 December 2018).

[64] Section 57.

delivering multiple benefits for all in society.[65] It uses the Brundtland definition of sustainable development and has three key objectives:

> Land-based businesses working with nature to contribute more to Scotland's prosperity
> Responsible stewardship of Scotland's natural resources delivering more benefits to Scotland's people
> Urban and rural communities better connected to the land, with more people enjoying the land and positively influencing land use[66]

The approach to sustainable development in the *Land Use Strategy 2016* (and its 2011 predecessor) is aligned with that of the *Economic Strategy* in so much as it focuses on prosperity. It also contextualises the Scottish Government's approach to sustainable development for land use by adding an emphasis on stewardship and promoting an ecosystem services approach to land use[67] and in this regard provides a bridge between the *Economic Strategy* and the detailed community right to buy guidance, albeit an implicit one.

Law can also be used to set out a more bespoke interpretation or approach to sustainable development which acknowledges and perhaps prioritises certain factors and recognises how the tensions inherent in sustainable development are likely to play out in any given context. While the LRSA 2003 is silent as to the meaning of sustainable development, the public interest and their relationship to one another, the drafting of the newer legislation is more ambitious.

Part 3A was added to the LSRA 2003 by the CESA 2015 and creates a right for community bodies to compulsorily acquire land that has been abandoned or neglected or somehow managed in a way that is detrimental to a community's 'environmental wellbeing'. Unsurprisingly, given the more interventionist nature of this right and its impact on the landowner, more protection is afforded to the current owner and the consent process is more detailed. Pursuant to section 97H Ministers

---

[65] Scottish Government, *Getting the best from our land – A Land Use Strategy for Scotland 2016–2021* (Edinburgh, 2016). Producing the *Land Use Strategy* was a key commitment under the Climate Change (Scotland) Act 2009. The first *Strategy* was laid in Parliament on 17 March 2011. The *Strategy* must be reviewed every five years. <https://www.gov.scot/publications/getting-best-land-land-use-strategy-scotland/> (last accessed 11 December 2018).

[66] Ibid., p. 6.

[67] Ibid., p. 14. 'The ecosystem approach is a strategy for the integrated management of land, water and living resources that promotes conservation and sustainable use in an equitable way.' Convention on Biological Diversity <https://www.cbd.int/ecosystem/> (last accessed 11 December 2018).

must not consent to an application unless they are satisfied among other things that the exercise of the right to buy is compatible with furthering the achievement of sustainable development in relation to the land. Importantly, this provision slightly redefines the meaning of sustainable development for this particular right to buy so that it differs even from the right to compel a sale of crofting land as set out in Part 3 of the LRSA 2003. Notably, the Scottish Ministers must be satisfied that the proposal is compatible with furthering the achievement of sustainable development of the land as opposed to sustainable development more generally. This arguably creates a narrower interpretation of sustainable development that is focused on land. In the context of these decisions, this will include the land subject to the buyout, its surrounding areas, its characteristics, its use in the short and longer term as well as the sustainable development of land more generally in Scotland and elsewhere.

Also under Part 3A, where there is evidence that the existing arrangements are resulting in harm to the environmental wellbeing of the relevant community (so-called 'detrimental land'), the decision-making process or sustainable development equation is adapted. Under section 97H(5) Ministers must not consent to the application unless they are satisfied (a) that the exercise by the community body of the right to buy is compatible with removing, or substantially removing, the harm to the environmental wellbeing of the relevant community; (b) that community body has, before the application is submitted, made a request to the relevant regulator(s) (if any), to take action to remedy or mitigate the harm; and (c) (regardless of the above) that the harm is unlikely to be removed, or substantially removed, by the owner of the land continuing to be its owner.

This decision-making process specific to detrimental land[68] prioritises removing harm to the environmental wellbeing of a relevant community within the meaning of sustainable development. Its procedural requirements then set standards that ensure the harm is significant and that the current owner has been given the opportunity to resolve the problem.

The LRSA 2016 also introduces new right to compulsorily acquire land – this time to further sustainable development. To access this right, community bodies must show their proposals and aims are more than simply consistent or compatible with the furtherance of sustainable development, they must satisfy Ministers that their proposal will further sustainable development. This is a more onerous test. The rules for this regime (once they are in force) will be the most comprehensive

---

[68] It is not applicable to abandoned or neglected land.

and given the emphasis on sustainable development, it is unsurprising that law-makers have decided to include more detail about how sustainable development is to be interpreted. Section 56 provides that Ministers must not consent to an application to buy land unless they are satisfied that application meets the sustainable development conditions and certain procedural requirements.[69] The introduction of sustainable development conditions in statute is a unique development for Scotland, where the definition and interpretation of sustainable development has up until now been left to policy and guidance and allowed to change with new governments and political priorities.[70]

There are four sustainable development conditions set out in section 56(2):

(a) the transfer of land is likely to further the achievement of sustainable development in relation to the land
(b) the transfer is in the public interest
(c) the transfer of land is likely to result in significant benefit to the community and is the only practicable, or most practicable, way of achieving that benefit
(d) that not granting consent to the transfer is likely to result in significant harm to the community

Interestingly, the public interest has changed from being a factor to be balanced with sustainable development in the wider sustainable development equation to now being within the assessment of what is sustainable development itself. Moreover, as discussed below, the meaning of public interest is expanded in subsequent provisions. This is also true for some of the other sustainable development conditions. For example, section 45(10) provides that in determining what constitutes significant benefit

---

[69] The procedural requirements set out in section 56(3) include (among other things): the community body has made a written request to the owner of the land to transfer the land to it and the owner has not responded or agreed to the request; the land is eligible land; all those with relevant interests have been correctly identified; the owner is not prevented from selling the land; a significant number of the members of the community have a connection with the land or the land is in or sufficiently near to the area comprising the community; the community has approved the proposal to exercise the right to buy.

[70] Conditions or principles of sustainable development are present elsewhere for example Wellbeing of Future Generations (Wales) Act 2015, available at <http://www.legislation.gov.uk/anaw/2015/2/contents/enacted> (last accessed 12 December 2018). Quebec's Sustainable Development Act 2006 section 6 D-8 1.1. Available at <http://legisquebec.gouv.qc.ca/en/ShowDoc/cs/D-8.1.1> (last accessed 12 December 2018).

to the community or harm to the community, the Scottish Ministers must consider the likely effect of granting (or not granting) consent to the transfer of land or tenant's interest on the lives of the persons comprising that community with reference to the following considerations:

(a) economic development
(b) regeneration
(c) public health
(d) social wellbeing
(e) environmental wellbeing

The conditions differ significantly from the Scottish Government's goal of 'increasing sustainable economic growth' and add substantial detail to the wider parameters of the Brundtland definition to prioritise: sustainable development of land; significant benefits to the community; and the avoidance of harm to the community as well as bringing the public interest explicitly back into the definition of sustainable development.

Thus, while the definition of sustainable development within the guidance on the original community right to buy regimes has evolved, it has not been in line with wider Scottish Government sustainable development policy. The *Land Use Strategy* makes some inroads in bridging that gap and demonstrates an acceptance within the Scottish Government to tailor sustainable development to the particular needs of land use but unfortunately this is not reflected in the most recent iterations of the guidance for Parts 2 and 3. The more recent community right to buy legislation shows a willingness on the part of legislators to provide more contextualised interpretations of sustainable development within the law itself tailored to the needs of those specific regimes.[71]

EVOLUTION OF THE ROLE OF THE PUBLIC INTEREST AND ITS RELATIONSHIP WITH SUSTAINABLE DEVELOPMENT IN THE COMMUNITY RIGHT TO BUY REGIMES

While it is difficult to imagine an interpretation of sustainable development that does not include some element of public interest at least on paper, as noted above, the public interest is considered separately from the factors considered inherent in sustainable development itself in the sustainable development equations and relevant guidance for the community right to buy regimes in the LRSA 2003. In contrast, as one of

---

[71] This bespoke approach to drafting sustainable development provisions is also evident in the Scottish Crown Estate Act 2019, sections 7(2) and 11(2).

the sustainable development conditions in LRSA 2016 the public interest is explicitly part of the assessment of what is or is not sustainable
development. Whether the public interest is considered inside or outside
the approach to sustainable development likely makes little impact on
actual decision-making. Rather, its value is more symbolic. Whereas
previously, sustainable development was considered separately from the
public interest, in the context of Part 5, sustainable development by
definition must be in the public interest.

Part 5 also sets criteria that must be considered in assessing what is or
is not in the public interest. Section 56(10) provides that in determining
whether a transfer of land is in the public interest the Scottish Ministers
must take into account any information given under section 55(2)(a)
which relates to the owner's or any tenant's views on the likely impact
on themselves of the community body's proposals for the land as well
as their own current or intended use for the land. Ministers must also
consider the likely effect of granting or not granting consent to the
transfer on land use in Scotland. Thus, in assessing the public interest,
Ministers must consider the broader interests of land use in Scotland,
the private interests of the current owner or tenant and the likely impact
of the community body's proposals on those private interests. This then
informs what is or is not considered sustainable development.

The public interest thus plays a crucial role in balancing the conflict between the community interests and those of the individual. The
balancing of these is subject to the ECHR which has its own jurisprudence on public interest[72] and the next section examines changes in
the relationship between human rights, public interest and sustainable
development since 2003.

EVOLUTION OF THE RELATIONSHIP BETWEEN HUMAN RIGHTS AND SUSTAINABLE DEVELOPMENT IN SCOTLAND'S COMMUNITY RIGHT TO BUY REGIMES

The 2003 community right to buy regimes were largely predicated on
the grounds of fairness and securing the public good. More specifically,

---

[72] A discussion of the relevant theories relating to the public interest is beyond the
scope of this chapter. See A. McHarg, 'Reconciling Human Rights and the Public
Interest: Conceptual Problems and Doctrinal Uncertainty in the Jurisprudence of the
European Court of Human Rights', *Modern Law Review*, 62:5 (1999), 671–696.
F. McCarthy, 'Property Rights and Human Rights in Scottish Land Reform', chapter
9, this volume.

the vision developed by the LRPG for the pattern of land ownership in the future in Scotland sought to increase diversity in the way land is owned and used, encourage the fullest possible exploitation of rural development opportunities, and increase community involvement in land ownership and use to ensure that local people would not be excluded from decisions which might affect their lives.[73]

At the time, these community interests were promoted and protected through the objectives of furthering sustainable development and being in the public interest as well as certain procedural obligations such as those to ensure sufficient community proximity and community approval.[74] These original right to buy provisions are silent in relation to the human rights of the wider community or those of individual land owners and tenants. However, the power to force or direct a sale from a private individual to a community body does not sit comfortably with the right to enjoy peaceful enjoyment of possessions under A1P1 to the ECHR.[75]

While the A1P1 to the ECHR has been used to challenge various land reform measures that deprive individuals of certain property rights or control their use of property,[76] it has also been used to impose positive obligations on states to ensure individual welfare for all citizens by creating a process for balancing private property rights with the public interest.[77] The European Court on Human Rights has taken the view that the national authorities are best placed to appreciate what is 'in the public interest' both in relation to the existence of a problem of public concern warranting measures of deprivation of property and of the remedial action to be taken.[78] In *Pairc Crofters Ltd* the Court of Session held that Part 3 of the LRSA 2003 was compatible with both the

---

[73] LRPG, 'Identifying the Solutions', p. 3.

[74] For example: LRSA 2003 section 38(1)(2).

[75] See Scotland Act 1998, section 29(2) for limits on the competence of the Scottish Parliament and section 57(2) for limits on powers of Scottish Ministers in relation to the ECHR.

[76] Salvesen v Riddell [2013] UKSC 22.

[77] M. M. Combe, 'The Land Reform (Scotland) Act 2016: another answer to the Scottish land question' *Juridical Review* (2016), pp. 291–313 at 299. See *Codona* v. *United Kingdom* (485/05) Unreported European Court of Human Rights 7 February 2006, admissibility decision.

[78] *James v. United Kingdom* (1986) 8 EHRR 116 at 41. See also: *Handyside* v. *United Kingdom* (app. no. 5493/72) [1976] ECHR 5 (7 December 1976); *Silver and others* v. *United Kingdom* (app. nos 5947/72, 6205/73, 7052/75, 7061/75, 7107/75, 7113/75 and 7136/75), 25 March 1983, Series A, No. 61; *Lingens v. Austria* (1986) 8 EHRR 407. See also *AXA General Insurance Company Ltd* v. *Lord Advocate No 5* [2011] UKSC 46; 2012 S.C. (UKSC) 122.

landlord's and interposed tenant's rights under the ECHR Article 6(1) (fair hearing) and A1P1.[79]

Beyond the jurisprudence, there has also been a noticeable trend in the Scottish land reform debate to move away from using human rights solely as a means of preventing change to one that supports and promotes change.[80]

Indeed, both the CESA 2015 and the LRSA 2016 promote a 'human rights based approach to land reform'[81] which in turn, is reflected in the sustainable development equations for these regimes. The influence is evident in several respects.

First, perhaps in response to the *Pairc* case, the balancing of the public interest and private interests of the land owners and occupiers is more expressly set out in the sustainable development equations within the new legislation, albeit differently in each. The sustainable development equation set out in section 97H of Part 3A of the LSRA 2003 (the right for community bodies to compulsorily acquire land that has been abandoned or neglected or somehow managed in a way that is detrimental to a community's 'environmental wellbeing') requires Ministers to actively compare the capacity and desire to further the achievement of sustainable development of the proposer to that of the current owner in the decision as to whether or not to force a sale.

In contrast, under section 56 in Part 5 of the LRSA 2016 the public interest is included as one of the sustainable development conditions and is now part of the assessment of what is or is not sustainable development. As discussed above under section 56(10) the views of existing owners and tenants on the likely impact of the proposal on them as well as the likely impact of the proposal on land use in Scotland more widely are expressly part of the public interest and in turn, part of the assessment of what is or is not sustainable development.

The LRSA 2016 also contains two provisions that move human rights to the forefront of land use policy in Scotland. Firstly, section 1 imposes a duty on the Scottish Ministers to prepare and publish a land rights and

[79] [2012] CSIH 96.

[80] See, for example, Land Reform Review Group, 'Final Report: The Land of Scotland and the Common Good' (Edinburgh: Scottish Government, 2014) p. 235. <https://www.gov.scot/publications/land-reform-review-group-final-report-land-scotland-common-good/> (last accessed 11 December 2018).

[81] K. Shields, 'Human Rights and the Work of the Scottish Land Commission – A Discussion Paper' (Scottish Land Commission, 2018) <https://landcommission.gov.scot/wp-content/uploads/2018/05/Land-Lines-Human-Rights-Kirsten-Shields-May-20182.pdf> (last accessed 11 December 2018).

responsibilities statement (LRRS) setting out principles for land rights and responsibilities in Scotland and then section 3 imposes a duty on the Scottish Ministers, in exercising their functions and so far as reasonably practicable, to promote the principles set out in LRRS. The first LRRS was produced in 2017 and goes some way to addressing the policy gap described earlier and in sharp contrast to the CRBG 2016 and Crofting Guidance 2009, it explicitly states in Annex B that it is to sit alongside the *Land Use Strategy* in the Scottish Government's policy framework.[82] It also makes reference to current Scottish Government policy on sustainable development noting that 'sustainable development is strongly linked to inclusive growth, a long-term aim of the Scottish Government which means 'growth that combines increased prosperity with tackling inequality; that creates opportunities for all and distributes the dividends of increased prosperity fairly'. It requires managing the land sustainably so that it can continue to deliver these benefits over time.'[83] Importantly, the LRRS also provides guidance as to the relevance of various international human rights treaties and to international principles including the ECHR, the International Covenant on Economic, Social and Cultural Rights (ICESCR) and others.[84]

The LRSA 2016 also requires the Scottish Ministers under section 44(1) to issue guidance about engaging communities in decisions relating to land which may affect communities. This section requires the Scottish Ministers to have regard to the desirability of promoting respect for and observance of relevant human rights and internationally accepted principles and standards for responsible practices relating to land.[85] It is not a strongly worded obligation but symbolic nonetheless. In turn, Part 5 of the Land Reform (Scotland) Act 2016 provides: 'In determining whether an application to buy land meets the sustainable development conditions [. . .] the Scottish Ministers may take into account the extent to which, in relation to the relevant community, regard has been had to guidance issued under Section 44.' Thus, the guidance is part of the assessment process for determining sustainable development under Part 5. The first guidance issued under section 44(2) is expressly set out as part of the Scottish Government's policy framework, aligned with the

[82] Scottish Government, 'Scottish Land Rights and Responsibilities Statement' (2017) <https://www.gov.scot/publications/scottish-land-rights-responsibilities-stat ement/> (last accessed 11 December 2018).
[83] Ibid., p. 14.
[84] Ibid., p. 36.
[85] Section 44(2)(a) and (b).

LRRS[86] and paragraph 15 provides that the guidance supports a change across all of urban and rural Scotland, so that engagement and collaboration with local communities about significant issues is the norm and local cities and land owners see each other as partners in achieving sustainable development.[87]

These two final provisions and the statutory guidance produced pursuant to them herald a new era for the way sustainable development is interpreted in land use decisions that is much more tailored as to how it relates to other obligations (notably human rights) in decisions about land. Moreover, the content of the policy fits within Scotland's wider policy framework on sustainable development while also addressing specific needs relevant to land ownership, management and use.

ANALYSIS AND CONCLUSIONS

The pre-emptive community right to buy regime under Part 2 and the right of crofting communities to force a sale of crofting land in Part 3 of the LRSA 2003 were created to promote the furtherance of sustainable development predicated on fairness and the public good. The LRSA 2003 left defining sustainable development to policy to allow the flexibility to accommodate changing times and political priorities. Since then there have been three different eras of sustainable development policy in Scotland, however, interestingly, the community right to buy policy on sustainable development has failed to reflect these changes and instead has evolved independently resulting in a divergence between it and in wider Scottish Government policy. Scotland's *Land Use Strategy* goes some way towards bridging this gap but even its aims and objectives have yet to be properly incorporated within the specific guidance on Parts 2 and 3 of the LRSA 2003.

Moreover, while the LRSA 2003 expressly requires consideration of the 'public interest' in the decision-making process, it is silent about the human rights justifications for the land reforms it creates as well as their impact on the human rights of existing owners and tenants. Unsurprisingly, this silence has led to uncertainty and a challenge under the ECHR. The introduction of new and arguably more interventionist

---

[86] Scottish Government, *Engaging Communities in Decisions Relating to Land: Guidance* (Edinburgh, 2018), p. 4, <https://www.gov.scot/publications/guidance-engaging-communities-decisions-relating-land/> (last accessed 11 December 2018).

[87] Ibid., Annex A, para. 24.

community right to buy regimes in 2015 and 2016 seem to have provided an opportunity to address some of these shortcomings.

Interestingly, much of the change has been instigated using legislation. Some of the legislation applies to land use decisions generally. Other legislative change is only relevant to the new, more interventionist, right to buy regimes. Some of the legislative change is directed at the meaning and interpretation of sustainable development itself in the context of community right to buy decisions while others address how sustainable development relates to other factors within wider decision-making processes or sustainable development equations, notably, human rights.

The newer legislation provides more detail on how sustainable development is to be interpreted and interestingly, this differs in different contexts. For example, the right for community bodies to compulsorily acquire land that has been abandoned or neglected or somehow managed in a way that is detrimental to a community's 'environmental wellbeing' limits the scope of sustainable development to the sustainable development of land. Moreover, where land management may cause environmental harm additional weight is given to reducing that harm within the interpretation of sustainable development. Under Part 5 of the LRSA 2016 (the right to compel a sale to further the achievement of sustainable development) Ministers are to be satisfied that certain statutory sustainable development conditions are met before granting consent. While an always important part of the sustainable development equation for community right to buy regimes, under Part 5 the public interest is explicitly included in the list of sustainable development conditions and thus, expressly part of the process for assessing what is considered sustainable development.

The new regimes also expressly include the interests and plans of the current owner's or any tenant's interests within the decision-making process, thus, expressly acknowledging the potential impact of these regimes on A1P1 to the ECHR right to property. Legislation has also been used to introduce a 'human rights approach' to land reform that expressly refers to rights beyond the ECHR such as those under the ICESCR. This has been made operational mainly through the introduction of statutory guidance incorporated into the wider sustainable development equations for all land use decisions including the community right to buy regimes.

All of this equates to a move away from relying on policy to define sustainable development to an increased use of binding legislative conditions and rules to inform decision making on sustainable development. Legislation is also being used to impose obligations to produce policy on particular land use and public engagement matters and to have regard to that policy in the right to buy sustainable development equations.

These changes herald a fourth era for sustainable development in Scotland which moves away from a single centralised approach to one that is tailored to the context of land in Scotland and then further tailored to the needs of each of the different community right to buy regimes. There clearly has been a recognition that the generic objective of 'increasing sustainable economic growth' set out in the *Economic Strategy* needs some refinement for land use purposes particularly given the obvious tensions created by community right to buy regimes between public and private interests and their potential to stop or prevent environmental harm. To this end, the public interest and human rights, especially in relation to community engagement and the rights of the current owner, have clearly defined roles in the decision-making processes relating to land. These developments show a significant evolution in the implementation and delivery of sustainable development in Scotland. It takes time for a country to move away from rhetoric and it takes experience to acknowledge that a 'one size fits all' approach may not be suitable in all cases. It then takes time for that country to develop suitable and genuinely sustainable, bespoke solutions that use legislation and policy to best effect.

11

Scottish Residential Tenancies

Douglas Bain

Of all the areas of Scots Law, the law of leases is the one which least lends itself to in-depth academic study.[1]

S O BEGINS THE PREFACE to Robert Rennie's 2015 Scottish Universities Law Institute (SULI) volume on *Leases*, suitably downplaying its topic. Rennie explains that this assessment – that the Scots law of leases is unconducive to academic study – is due to two reasons in particular. Firstly, any lease is itself the source of the rights and obligations under that lease; and, secondly, that

> [W]here statute has intervened to alter the rights and obligations of the parties such as in residential or agricultural leasing, the reasons for such intervention are generally social, environmental or economic. Changes in the law in these areas tend to alter the bargaining or commercial power of the two parties rather than alter or modify any deep legal principles.[2]

In the foreword to the volume,[3] Lord Drummond Young[4] identifies many statutory reforms (amending the law 'almost beyond recognition' over the last forty years) and developments in the common law in relation to leases. Thus, if the Scots law of leases is insusceptible to academic study, it is at least not static; and, indeed, it is arguable that the reforms of the last forty years – of the last century, in fact – have had a far greater effect on the Scots law of leases than is generally recognised. For example, the new private residential tenancy regime introduced under the Private Housing (Tenancies) (Scotland) Act 2016 is one in which statutory regulation is imposed from the very beginning

---

[1] Robert Rennie, with Mike Blair, Stewart Brymer, Frankie McCarthy and Tom Mullen, *Leases* (Edinburgh: W. Green, 2015), p. vii.

[2] Ibid., p. vii.

[3] Ibid., p. v.

[4] Author of the judgement in *Advice Centre for Mortgages Ltd* v. *McNicoll*, 2006 SLT 591, one of the most interesting commercial leasing cases of the last decade.

of the tenancy,[5] in consequence rendering core elements in the classic Scots common law lease redundant, to an extent that might suggest that much of the old Scots language of the lease may no longer be fit for purpose. Or does it? Writing in the *Journal of the Law Society of Scotland* in 2007, Ian Quigley made the provocative comment that 'in modern commercial property practice there is no such thing as "a lease", and that there are many different types of leases depending on the commercial circumstances of each case'.[6] Statutory developments in respect of residential leasing make a similar point, only more forcefully; and the period from the beginning of the twentieth century to the present date has seen a great deal of statutory intervention in relation to the law of leases in Scotland, with only now, post 2017, the legislators pausing to draw breath.

The Scots law of leases is broken down into various elements, reflecting the realities of leasing. First come the general body of principles underpinning the law, then the different broad species of the lease are divided into three main categories – commercial, agricultural and residential (with odds and ends making up a residual class, for example, fishings). This chapter concerns itself with the residential lease in Scots law. Residential leasing in Scotland has been the subject of considerable statutory reform (since the early twentieth century), as has agricultural leasing (since 1883).[7] Commercial leasing has been less affected comparatively, though it would be wrong to say that statute has completely bypassed the sector.[8]

The lease in Scots law is an institution of some antiquity. Bell[9] and Hunter,[10] writing in the first half of the nineteenth century, offer fanciful accounts tracing the institution back to the tenth and eleventh centuries, when the distinction between the lease and the feu was not sharply

[5] Adrian Stalker, 'The Private Housing (Tenancies) (Scotland) Bill', *SCOLAG*, 457 (2015), pp. 226–8 at p. 226. In the social rented sector, the Housing (Scotland) Act 2001 provides a similarly statutory regime.

[6] Quigley, Ian, 'On the wrong track', *Journal of the Law Society of Scotland*, 52:2 (2007), pp. 48–50.

[7] The Agricultural Holdings (Scotland) Act 1883. See Lean, in this volume.

[8] Important statutory provisions of particular relevance to commercial leasing include the Law Reform (Miscellaneous Provisions) (Scotland) Act 1985, the Tenancy of Shops (Scotland) Acts 1949 and 1964, the Land Tenure Reform (Scotland) Act 1974, and the Registration of Leases (Scotland) Act 1857.

[9] Robert Bell, *Treatise on Leases*, 4th edn (Edinburgh: Archibald Constable & Co., 1825), pp. 2–30.

[10] Robert Hunter (edited by William Guthrie), *A Treatise on the Law of Landlord and Tenant*, 4th edn (Edinburgh: Bell and Bradfute, 1876), I, p. 1.

observed,[11] though the institutional writer Stair[12] is content to begin his treatment of the lease (or Tack) with the Leases Act 1449.[13] Rennie rather inclines to regard the 1449 Act as being overhyped:

> Most authors regard the enactment of the Leases Act 1449 [. . .] as a pivotal piece of legislation changing the juristic nature of a lease. That is perhaps something of an exaggeration. The Act was simply a piece of social legislation, designed to protect poverty-stricken agricultural tenants.[14]

However, the Act does at the very least tell us that the lease was already well embedded in Scots law in the mid fifteenth century and that the relative balance of power between the landlord and tenant was by that period a matter for some concern.

Shorn of complexities and specialities the lease in Scots common law is simply a species of contract, giving rise to a personal right as between the parties.[15] The word 'lease' carries a double meaning, encompassing the underlying contract and the right flowing from that contract.[16] This double meaning flags up at an early stage the possible issues in respect of the language of the lease. Rennie offers eight different definitions of the word 'lease' at pp. 3–7 in his recent SULI volume,[17] and there are others. One useful recent definition quoted in Rennie is that of Angus McAllister:

> A lease is a contract by which a person, known as a tenant, is allowed to occupy someone else's heritable property for a finite period. In return for this

---

[11] G. Paton, H. Campbell and Joseph G. S. Cameron, *The Law of Landlord and Tenant in Scotland* (Edinburgh: W. Green & Son Ltd, 1967), p. 3; *Stair Memorial Encyclopaedia Reissue*, 'Landlord and Tenant', para. 1. Note that Lord President Cooper's analysis of the lease in *Millar v. McRobbie*, 1949 SC 1 was predicated upon feudal analogy.

[12] James Dalrymple, Viscount Stair, *Institutions of the Law of Scotland*, 2nd edn (Edinburgh: 1693), II.3.16.

[13] 18–19 A.P.S. c.6.

[14] Rennie, *Leases*, p. 7. For an illustrative historical example, consider '[t]he *Magna Charta* of the Scots tenant's security, is of the Scots Parliament 1449', per *General Report of the Agricultural State, and Political Circumstances, of Scotland, Drawn Up for the Consideration of the Board of Agriculture and Internal Improvement, Under the Direction of the Right Hon. Sir John Sinclair, Bart. the President, Volume 5* (Edinburgh: Archibald Constable & Co, 1814), p. 262.

[15] William Murray Gloag, *The Law of Contract*, 2nd edn (Edinburgh: W Green & Son Ltd, 1929), p. 233; George L. Gretton and Andrew J. M. Steven, *Property, Trusts and Succession*, 3rd edn (Haywards Heath: Bloomsbury, 2017), p. 286; Paton and Cameron, *The Law of Landlord and Tenant in Scotland*, p. 5.

[16] *Stair Memorial Encyclopaedia Reissue*, 'Landlord and Tenant', para. 3.

[17] Rennie et al., *Leases*.

he pays to the person granting the right (i.e. the landlord) a periodic payment known as rent. Rent usually takes the form of money, but may also (though not commonly) be paid in goods.[18]

This definition sums up the 'contract' aspect of the lease. From it, one can discern the four necessary elements; parties, property, period and price. 'Heritable property' in this context means land (including any buildings).

The important fifth element in the lease, the one which through the intervention of statute transmutes the common law lease (a personal right, enforceable between the parties to the contract only) into a right enforceable against strangers to the contract (generally termed a real right) is possession, actual or constructive.[19] This was the innovation of the Leases Act 1449, subsequently augmented by the Registration of Leases (Scotland) Act 1857 (as amended) and the Land Tenure Reform (Scotland) Act 1974.[20]

Of course, protection against a landlord's successor in title may well enable a tenant three years into a five-year lease to sit tight during the remaining two years of the lease where the new landlord wants early possession of the property for her own purposes, but it does nothing to protect the tenant beyond year five where that successor landlord has taken the necessary steps to terminate the tenancy and to recover possession. The ability of the tenant to do so is an incident of another class of right entirely, generally termed security of tenure, and is invariably the result of statutory intervention.[21] Such intervention invariably

---

[18] Angus McAllister, *Scottish Law of Leases*, 4th edn (London: Bloomsbury, 2013), para. 1.1.

[19] As discussed by Lord President Cooper in *Millar* v. *McRobbie*, 1949 SC 1.

[20] In relation to the three currently extant statutory private residential tenancy regimes in Scotland, the statutes of 1449, 1857 and 1974 are irrelevant. The statutory definition of 'landlord' in the Rent (Scotland) Act 1984 section 115 and the Housing (Scotland) Act 1988 section 55 'includes any person from time to time deriving title from the original landlord . . .', whilst the Private Housing (Tenancies) (Scotland) Act 2016 states at section 45, '[w]hen ownership of a property let under a private residential tenancy is transferred, the landlord's interest under the tenancy transfers with it.' Thus, each regime enacts anew provisions approximately analogous with the '. . . suppose the lordis sel or analy thai landis [. . .] quhais handis at euir thai landis cum to . . .' provision in the 1449 Act.

[21] See note 20 above for the three current private residential sector statutory tenancy regimes. In the social rented sector – formerly the public sector, before which council housing – the main statute is now the Housing (Scotland) Act 2001. Statutory security came late to the social rented sector (in 1980) whereas in the private sector it was introduced in 1915. This is discussed below.

reflects the social, environmental or economic agenda identified in Rennie.[22]

If this agenda is viewed as being something apart from the law of leases – stated most extremely, a contaminant upon the purity of the Scots law lease – then it is a contaminant that has been around for a very long time; and, indeed, whatever its origins, the lease is a social, environmental, economic and political invention with social, environmental, economic and political roots and consequences.[23] Alternatively it can be viewed as an aspect of *all and haill* the law of leases. This is the view advanced in this chapter.

A QUESTION OF BALANCE

In respect of leases generally there is an issue of power balance between the landlord and the tenant. Where rented properties are scarce, the balance will generally favour the landlord. In times of plenty, the tenant may be in the stronger position, but historically, famine is more common than feast.

To the beginning of the First World War the residential rented sector in Scotland was largely unregulated by statute. The public policy agenda from 1449 to the latter part of the nineteenth century was to protect tenants from landlords' creditors and successors in title, and to ensure procedural fairness and effectiveness in eviction; but beginning in the early twentieth century statute increasingly intervened to level the playing field. Sometimes it went too far and required to be reined in by new statute. Sometimes that counterbalancing statute went too far in the other direction, and so on. This has been the pattern of the last century: a seesaw.

As at the beginning of the twentieth century in Scotland, private renting was king. In 1914 private tenancies accounted for approximately 90 per cent of the housing stock.[24] In 1921 the percentage was reduced

---

[22] Rennie et al., *Leases*, p. vii.

[23] The early history of the lease is discussed in Hunter, *Landlord and Tenant*, I, p. 1; Bell, *Treatise on Leases*, pp. 2–30; Walter Ross, *Lectures*, 2nd edn (Edinburgh: Bell & Bradfute, 1822), p. 457ff. None of these are particularly enlightening.

[24] Peter Robson, *Residential Tenancies: Private and Social Renting in Scotland*, 3rd edn (Edinburgh: W. Green, 2012), p. 5; Peter Robson, 'Housing' in Elaine E. Sutherland, Kay E. Goodall, Gavin F. M. Little and Fraser P. Davidson (eds), *Law Making and the Scottish Parliament* (Edinburgh: Edinburgh University Press, 2011), pp. 141–56.

to 80 per cent and in 1931 70 per cent.[25] By 2016 that figure stood at 15.4 per cent, this actually representing an increase from 7.3 per cent in 2002.[26] As the private rented sector declined, owner-occupation and the public sector grew, with by 1981 the public sector accounting for 55 per cent of the housing stock, owner-occupation accounting for 35 per cent, and private renting 10 per cent.[27] In 1991 the percentages had swapped round, with 38 per cent of housing stock in the public sector and 52 per cent in owner-occupation, in consequence of the political innovation of the right to buy (discussed below). Figures published in 2017 show that of Scotland's 2,567,000 dwellings, 57.7 per cent were owner-occupied, 15.4 per cent privately rented, 12.3 per cent rented from local authorities/New Towns/Scottish Homes, 10.8 per cent rented from housing associations and 3.8 per cent being vacant private dwellings and second homes.[28] The low point in terms of the residential private rented sector in Scotland was during 1998–2000 when it fell to 6.7 per cent,[29] and its resurgence since 2000 has been consistent and steady. The Scottish residential private rented sector is now larger than what formerly used to be known as the public sector, as in the council or 'corporation', a turnaround in the position of the 1950s forward. This is not a flash in the pan, and the Scottish Government has recognised the important role of the residential private rented sector in Scotland.[30] With housing demand outstripping supply, it cannot afford not to.

The process of law reform in relation to residential leasing in Scotland from the beginning of the last century can be divided into four phases: stage 1, 1911–79; stage 2, 1980–99; stage 3, 2000–13; and

[25] Duncan Maclennan, 'Owner Occupation; New Patterns, Policies and Parliament' in Colin Jones and Peter Robson, *Health of Scottish Housing* (Aldershot: Ashgate Publishing Ltd 2001), p. 152.

[26] Ibid.

[27] Ibid.

[28] Scottish Government, 'Housing Statistics for Scotland – Stock by Tenure' (Edinburgh, 2 October 2017). Available at <http://www.gov.scot/Topics/Statistics/Browse/Housing-Regeneration/HSfS/KeyInfo> (last accessed 2 April 2019).

[29] Ibid.

[30] See Scottish Government, *A Place to Stay, a Place to Call Home: A Strategy for the Private Rented Sector in Scotland* (Edinburgh, 30 May 2013) <https://beta.gov.scot/publications/place-stay-place-call-home-strategy-private-rented-sector -scotland/pages/8/> (last accessed 2 April 2019) and the many documents preceding it, some of which will be available via the web archive at <https://www.webarchive.org.uk/wayback/archive/20170106175317/http://www.gov.scot/Topics/Built-Envi ronment/Housing/privaterent/government/Tenancy-Review> (last accessed 2 April 2019).

stage 4, 2014 onwards. During stages 1 and 2, Westminster was the legislature, with Holyrood taking up the reins from 1999–2000. During the Westminster era the trend was for new legislation to apply on an all-UK basis, though from the late 1960s the trend became 'for there to be separate but parallel legislation' in relation to tenancy matters, with, from 1986 forward, different rules beginning to emerge north and south of the border.[31] During stage (3), in the private rented sector the emphasis was upon improving housing standards and landlord practice, and the social rented sector concentrated on finding a proper place for the housing associations and providing means for regulating tenant behaviour. Stage (4) inaugurated a new private residential sector tenancy regime and introduced a new judicial forum for private tenancy cases.

STAGE 1: 1911–79

The first comprehensive investigation into the state of housing conditions in Scotland was commenced in 1912 and led to the 1917 publication of the *Report of the Royal Commission on the Housing of the Industrial Population of Scotland Rural and Urban*.[32] The findings of the detailed enquiry – of housing shortage, gross overcrowding,[33] affordability issues[34] and squalid housing conditions – prompted the amazement of the Commission:

> If it is to be asked how this enormous accumulation has occurred, one answer is; that the conditions of Scottish housing have never been adequately investigated [. . .] it is only now that the nation has the means of discovering how far Scotland has been left behind, and by what poor standards the housing

[31] Robson, 'Housing' in Sutherland et al., *Law Making and the Scottish Parliament*.

[32] Cmd 8731, available at <https://archive.org/details/reportofroyalcom00sco trich> (last accessed 2 April 2019).

[33] Ibid., p. 7, Tables I and II. A shortfall of 113,430 houses was identified. The concerns in respect of overcrowding were supported by the finding of the 1911 census – see Census of Scotland 1911: Report on the twelfth decennial census of Scotland, volume II (1913) (Cmd 6896) at pp. c–ciii, available at <https://archive. org/stream/b28039920_0002#page/n112/mode/1up> (last accessed 2 April 2019): 54.9 per cent of the population of Scotland was living in accommodation of two rooms or fewer, with 52.2 per cent of the houses in Scotland containing two rooms or less.

[34] See Annette O'Carroll, 'Historical Perspectives on Tenure Development in Urban Scotland' in Hector Currie and Alan Murie, *Housing in Scotland* (Coventry: Chartered Institute of Housing, 1996), pp. 20–1.

of her working classes has been measured. Our report, and the evidence it rests upon, will carry conviction to every disinterested person.[35]

While the report of the Royal Commission was to prove highly influential in the longer term, 1915 saw an important intervention of the State into Scotland's residential private sector in the form of the Increase of Rent and Mortgage Interest (War Restrictions) Act 1915. The Act was intended to deal with war profiteering on the part of private landlords which was threatening the war effort. In areas where key war industries (armaments, shipbuilding) were located (and in which landlord and tenant antipathy was already strong),[36] the influx of workers to service those industries had the effect of increasing the demand for an already scarce resource, that is, housing, with the law of supply and demand kicking in. As noted by Robson: 'Soon after the outbreak of the First World War landlords throughout Britain took advantage of their market position and responded to the increase in demand for housing in industrial areas by raising rents.'[37]

The 1915 Act also followed on from the Glasgow rent strikes of 1915, and Robson notes that:

> The impact of the decision to introduce rent controls in 1915 had an impact all out of proportion to what those debating the issue could have imagined. Although this has been characterised as 'legislation to protect the poor' it is fairer to say it was simply a knee-jerk reaction to a clear and present threat.[38]

The 1915 Act operated quite simply by fixing rents and landlords' mortgage rates at their August 1914 levels. In relation to the rent, it meant that a landlord could not exploit scarcity (i.e. the lack of availability of other like properties) to make a profit by terminating an existing tenancy and then creating a new one at a higher rent as there was no higher rent that could be charged. The Act did not extend to furnished lets or tenancies where there was board or attendance provided and there was an upper cap based upon the rateable value of a property above which the Act did not apply (initially thirty pounds for a house in Scotland, 'house' including part of a house let as a separate dwelling).

In a Court of Session decision in 1952, Lord Patrick observed that

---

[35] Ibid., p. 347. A fuller statement may be found at p. 346. It is lengthy but worth searching out.

[36] Ibid., p. 23.

[37] Robson, *Residential Tenancies*. A new edition of *Residential Tenancies* was published in 2019: Peter Robson and Malcolm M. Combe, *Residential Tenancies: Private and Social Renting in Scotland*, 4th edn (Edinburgh: W. Green, 2019).

[38] Ibid., pp. 8–9.

[o]ne main purpose of the Rent Acts is to mitigate the hardships inherent in a period of shortage of dwelling-houses. This mitigation is achieved by abrogating the common law rights of the landlords of dwelling-houses to which the Acts apply and maintaining the tenants in possession.[39]

Whilst innovatory, the 1915 Act was not revolutionary. It did not prohibit completely landlords from seeking recovery of possession. Landlords were not barred from seeking recovery of possession on the ground of rent arrears or non-performance of other conditions of the tenancy, or

on the ground that the tenant has committed waste or has been guilty of conduct which is a nuisance or an annoyance to adjoining or neighbouring occupiers, or that the premises are reasonably required by the landlord for the occupation of himself or some other person in his employ, or in the employ of some tenant from him, or on some other ground which may be deemed satisfactory by the court making such order.[40]

The common law right of the landlord in a lease alluded to by Lord Patrick was the landlord's right of eventual recovery of possession, a lease being a right subject to a duration. True, there were other older protections for the tenant in the form of a requirement for a minimum of forty days' notice ahead of the scheduled end of a lease to recover possession,[41] with the doctrine of tacit relocation operating to penalise the dilatory landlord by allowing a lease to roll over after the intended end date on the legal assumption that this is what parties would have wished, but neither these or the 1915 Act (nor the statutes which followed it) did anything to bar the landlord's ultimate right to recover possession. They did not turn a tack into a feu.

The 1915 Act was intended to be a temporary measure, to end six months after the conclusion of hostilities,[42] but it continued beyond this period by the Increase of Rent and Mortgage Interest (Restrictions) Act 1919. It was then expanded by the Increase of Rent and Mortgage Interest (Restrictions) Act 1920, which began, at section 5, to put in place grounds for the recovery of possession in what begins to look like the modern form.

The period 1920–79 is a long period that is best summarised in abbreviated form, and is well discussed in Robson's *Residential Tenancies*

---

[39] *Cowan & Sons* v. *Acton*, 1952 SC 73 at 91.

[40] The 1915 Act, section 1(3).

[41] *Stair Memorial Encyclopaedia Reissue*, 'Landlord and Tenant', para. 387.

[42] Increase of Rent and Mortgage Interest (War Restrictions) Act 1915, section 5(2).

and (in more detail) Paton and Cameron's *Landlord and Tenant*.[43] The succession of statutes was protean, and as Professor Sir Thomas Broun Smith noted:

> [a] mass of statute law now regulates the letting of certain categories of premises or subjects, and it is both impossible and undesirable to expound the detail of the various statutory 'codes' in an introductory treatise [. . .] the general reader and student should recognise the great importance of statutory leases in the law of Scotland today . . .[44]

The main effects of the Rent Acts regime were (1) that in qualifying tenancies rent charges and increases became subject to statutory regulation, originally by means of nationally fixed standard rents but from 1965 through a mechanism known as the 'fair rent', in the calculation of which scarcity was excluded; (2) the landlord's right to recover possession was made subject to statutory grounds for possession many of which were subject to the discretion of the court or linked to the provision of suitable alternative housing being secured; (3) statutory rights of succession were created; (4) the distinction was introduced between the contractual tenancy and the statutory tenancy, the former being what was entered into by the parties and thereafter continued by agreement or through tacit relocation, with the latter popping into existence in the event of the landlord giving notice. One practical consequence of this was that initial rents might well reflect the state of the market but that an application for a fair rent (which might be done by the landlord or the tenant or both) would create a rent limit which would remain in force for three years and thereafter until a new fair rent was applied for, and that would run notwithstanding that one tenant leaves and is replaced with a new tenant. Optimising rents without becoming subject to a fair rent was a matter for fine consideration.[45]

Between 1923 and 1938 there were limited decontrols, with full control resuming in 1939, for the same reasons as in 1915. Controls were removed by the Conservative government in 1957 but reintroduced by Labour in 1965. By 1957 the private rented sector was in decline and rent controls were seen as deterring private landlords

---

[43] Robson, *Residential Tenancies*, pp. 8–11; Paton and Cameron, *The Law of Landlord and Tenant in Scotland*, chapter XX generally and in particular pp. 496–9.

[44] Thomas Broun Smith, *A Short Commentary on the Law of Scotland* (Edinburgh: W. Green & Son Ltd, 1962), p. 519.

[45] The 1947 Central Office of Information short documentary film *Fair Rent*, set in Aberdeen, may be seen online in the British Film Institute collection at <https://player.bfi.org.uk/free/film/watch-fair-rent-1947-online> (last accessed 2 April 2019).

from investing in new housing and improving their existing stock. The means by which decontrol was effected – by cushioning the impact of decontrol through extending transitional protection to existing sitting tenants – contributed towards the emergence of the phenomenon known, after the notorious landlord, as Rachmanism. Sitting rent-controlled tenants were induced to leave their tenancies (a process known as 'winkling')[46] through financial inducements, threats of harm and full-on terror tactics, prompting Harold Wilson's famous observation 'the plain fact is that rented housing is not a proper field for private profit.'[47] A practical consequence of the transitional protection was that when the Rent Act 1965 resumed statutory protection there remained a group of 1957 Act controlled tenancies. These two statutory regimes ran in parallel until 1980. It is worth noting that the introduction of new statutory tenancy regimes can – but not always – be *prospective*, leaving withering earlier regime tenancies in place to decline and die out. Thus, for example, Rent Act fair rent cases can still call in the Inner House of the Court of Session nearly thirty years after the statutory regime was superseded.[48]

Under the Rent Act 1974, full protection was extended to furnished tenancies and tenants with resident landlords were granted some protection by means of Part VII contracts (named after the relevant Part of the legislation). The group that was not protected was Scotland's largest group of tenants, namely the tenants of public landlords. As noted by Peter Robson and Paul Watchman:

> Prior to the Tenants' Rights, etc. (Scotland) Act 1980 (c. 52), public sector tenants had scant protection against eviction [. . .] the justification for the difference in treatment between public and private tenants being that public sector landlords were regarded as being responsible whereas private sector landlords were not and that it was essential that the management powers of local authorities should be unhindered.[49]

---

[46] The character of the Winkler turns up in 'Get 'em Out by Friday', a song by Genesis from the 1972 album *Foxtrot*.

[47] Quoted in J. Barry Cullingworth, *Essays on Housing Policy* (Hemel Hempstead: Allen and Unwin, 1979), at p. 61.

[48] *Wright* v. *Elderpark Housing Association*, 2017 SLT 995.

[49] Peter Robson and Paul Watchman, 'Housing (Scotland) Act 1987' in *Scottish Landlord and Tenant Legislation* (Edinburgh: W. Green/Sweet & Maxwell, 1999) at A.202.1.

STAGE 2: 1980–99

While the Labour government had by 1977 accepted the case for extending statutory security to public sector tenants, it was Margaret Thatcher's Conservative government that enacted the necessary legislation, in the shape of the Tenants' Rights, etc. (Scotland) Act 1980, subsequently consolidated in the Housing (Scotland) Act 1987, then superseded by the Housing (Scotland) Act 2001. In the residential private rented sector the Rent Acts were consolidated by the Rent (Scotland) Act 1984 and then superseded by the Housing (Scotland) Act 1988. The housing associations during this period went from being in the unusual position of (1) not having Rent Act regulated status[50] but nevertheless being covered by the fair rent provisions in the Rent Act,[51] to (2) qualifying as secure tenancies, but still being covered by the Rent Act fair rent provisions whilst also not having the secure tenancy right to buy until 1986,[52] then (3) being *prospectively* shifted back out of the public sector and into the assured tenancies regime, with old rights including fair rent eligibility being continued for pre-2 January 1989 tenancies or root tenancies (as where a pre-1989 tenant transfers on or post-2 January to another property let by the same association),[53] before (4) ultimately (in 2001) being repositioned into the social rented sector.

The Housing (Scotland) Act 1988 assured tenancy regime was the last tenure reform of the Westminster Parliament. The Housing (Scotland) Act 2001 and Private Housing (Tenancies) (Scotland) Act 2016 are Acts of the Scottish Parliament.

Section 1 of the Tenants' Rights, etc. (Scotland) Act 1980 concerns the secure tenant's right to purchase the dwelling house they occupy. Right to buy – in pursuit of a 'property-owning democracy' – was introduced in 1980, around which time, as discussed above, public housing was the majority tenure in Scotland. While proposals for the extension of security of tenure to public sector tenants in Scotland predated and were unconnected with right to buy it is hard to conceive of right to buy flourishing in an environment in which council tenants did not have security and an application to purchase might be met by way of return with a notice to quit. The other major statutory reform of the

---

[50] Rent (Scotland) Act 1971, section 5.

[51] Housing (Financial Provisions) (Scotland) Act 1972, section 61.

[52] Tenants' Rights, etc. (Scotland) Act 1980 section 1(3), amended by the Housing (Scotland) Act 1986, section 1(1).

[53] See Housing (Scotland) Act 1988, section 43.

1980s – the Housing (Scotland) Act 1988 – had a connected agenda, namely diminishing the large institutional public landlords.

Unlike tenancies under the Rent Acts (in which the contractual/statutory distinction was made, as would also be the case in respect of tenancies under the Housing (Scotland) Act 1988), secure tenancies under the 1980 Act (and subsequently the 1987 Act) were governed by statute from the very outset, and such common law concepts as notice to quit to prevent the operation of tacit relocation become irrelevant.[54] Under the secure tenancy regime, tenants were granted security of tenure, the right to a written lease, the right to sub-let, the right to carry out minor repairs and improvements, succession rights, rights restricting the variation of the tenancy, the right to buy, and rights in relation to the recovery of possession by the landlord. As with the Rent Acts, recovery of possession was made subject to notice and specified grounds for possession, some of which being mandatory and others being subject to the discretion of the court, and yet more being mandatory but subject to the provision of suitable alternative accommodation to the tenant. However, landlords were not subject to 'fair rent'-type rent controls, and were given powers under Part XI of the 1987 Act to charge and vary rents, taking no account of the personal circumstances of the tenants, driven by the exigencies of the Housing Revenue Account.

The right to buy provisions were contained in Part III of the 1987 Act, and were extended so as to increase the maximum discount for flats to 70 per cent of the market value price as determined by the district valuer or an agreed qualified valuer (for non-flats it was 60 per cent), and the scheme put in place provisions (at section 216) for the local authority to act as a lender of last resort. Over and above these provisions the Act was amended by the Leasehold Reform, Housing and Urban Development Act 1993 to introduce a form of staircased right to buy through a procedure known as 'rent to loan' or 'rent to mortgage', which operated by allowing the tenant to purchase on the basis of an initial capital payment subject to a deferred financial contribution – predicated upon repayment following some future sale of the property – and a monthly payment around the level of the rent. This opened up home ownership to people who previously could not afford it.

---

[54] Save, post 2001, in relation to Short Scottish Secure Tenancies under the Housing (Scotland) Act 2001, which extends tacit relocation to SSSTs. See *City of Edinburgh Council* v. *Smith*, 2016 SLT (Sh Ct) 343. See also Robson, *Residential Tenancies*, pp. 360–2 and Adrian Stalker, 'Housing Law Update', *SCOLAG*, 467 (2016), pp. 181–6 at 182–3 for discussion of this difficult topic.

In the private rented sector the Rent Acts had their final consolidation in the Rent (Scotland) Act 1984, but major change was to follow within four years with the Housing (Scotland) Act 1988. The 1988 Act is divided into four Parts, the fourth of which is a miscellaneous and general Part. The first three, whilst ostensibly appearing unconnected, are in fact very closely connected. Part I dissolves the former Scottish Special Housing Association, and transfers its housing stock and the regulatory functions of the former Housing Corporation to a new body called Scottish Homes. Part III contains provisions on 'Change of Landlord: Secure Tenants', promoted as 'pick a landlord' but in reality 'pick a tenant'. Part II creates a new form or tenancy, the assured tenancy, and its short form/reduced rights variant, the short assured tenancy. Scottish Homes became a major new public landlord but was disbanded in 2008. In the intervening years 75,000 homes are transferred to housing associations and cooperatives, not as secure tenancies but as assured tenancies (and in some cases not even that, as in the case of the fully mutual housing cooperatives), but with preserved right to buy.

The 1988 Act took new Housing Association lets out of the secure tenancy regime and into the assured tenancy regime. It abolished fair rents for post-1 January 1989 tenancies, with rents resetting to what the market might bear, with rent increases being subject to a requirement of notice and timing and further increases within a year being prohibited.[55] In relation to recovery of possession, the model of the later Rent Acts and secure tenancy regime was followed, with requirements of notice and specified grounds for possession and so on. One novel ground for possession was introduced in the form of mandatory Ground 8, '[b] oth at the date of the service of the notice under section 19 of this Act relating to the proceedings for possession and at the date of the hearing, at least three months' rent lawfully due from the tenant is in arrears.'[56] This mandatory ground was controversial but it was also, in respect of classic private letting, largely irrelevant as most private landlords took the opportunity offered in the Act to let out using the form of tenancy known as the short assured tenancy (SAT). Ground 8 was relevant in relation to housing associations as they used the full form of the assured tenancy, but in relation to private landlords the use of the SAT was an obvious default position. This is because, while a species of the assured tenancy, the SAT, properly created with proper notice to the tenant, did not carry any security of tenure-type rights beyond the point of its

---

[55] Housing (Scotland) Act 1988, section 24(4).
[56] Ibid., section 18 and sched. 5, Ground 8.

proper termination. In short, if the paperwork was right, the tenant has no defence against an eviction action, and might as well leave when the landlord desired rather than incurring the cost an action for recovery of possession of heritable property (and any other consequences of having a court order against her).[57] The 1988 Act accordingly shifted the balance of power back in favour of the private landlord. By the late 1980s the private residential sector was at a numerical low point in Scotland, accounting, in 1990, for 9.1 per cent (including housing associations) of the housing stock, and it was part of the policy agenda behind the 1988 Act to revitalise the private rented sector,[58] assisting in mobility where people 'got on their bikes' in search of work in other parts of the country, and also, with homelessness growing in Scotland, the prospects of a revived private rented sector contributing to a solution would have appealed to a Conservative government.[59]

In relation to the housing associations, new tenancies from 2 January 1989 were assured tenancies under the 1988 Act, with no fair rent rights.[60] Tenants of Scottish Homes remained secure tenants,[61] but Scottish Homes' agenda was one of offloading its tenants through right to buy and stock transfer (in which case the transferred tenancies would be assured). The excepted class in all of this was that of the cooperative housing associations, which were excluded from all statutory regimes on the basis of the control they provided to their tenants, although the lack of statutory protection left those tenants vulnerable to eviction.[62]

---

[57] There had been a short form of the Rent Act tenancy – the short tenancy under section 9 of the 1984 Act (though introduced by the Act of 1980). It was not popular, being subject to a minimum period of a year and a maximum of five years, and subject to a far rent (which, presumably, would have reflected the short nature of the tenancy).

[58] Alan Murie, 'Housing Tenure and Housing Policy' in Hector Currie and Alan Murie, *Housing in Scotland* (Coventry: Chartered Institute of Housing, 1996), p. 64.

[59] But note that the 1988 Act also introduced (at section 70) a new function for rent officers – whose principal tasks had hitherto included fixing Rent Act fair rents – in setting indicative rent levels for Housing Benefit and housing subsidy purposes, the idea being that rent deregulation should not amount to a free-for-all against the public purse. Thus began a process that has ended up in Universal Credit. Deregulation and a suspicion of the market make uneasy bedfellows. A second initiative of the era – John Major's 'rent a room' tax incentive scheme for encouraging homeowners with a spare room to become resident landlords by means of a rental income tax disregard still exists.

[60] Section 12 and sched. 4.

[61] Ibid.

[62] Douglas Bain, 'Eviction of Housing Co-operative Tenants', *SCOLAG*, 267 (2000), pp. 5–6. The 2001 Act brought such tenants within the umbrella of the

Landlord choice was a policy driven by a critique of the central-ist and monopolistic nature of 'over-large council empires',[63] which in pursuit of low-rent policies had delivered poor-quality housing stock and services, and in so doing had hindered social and labour mobility.[64] To quote the 1987 White Paper *Housing: The Government's Proposals for Scotland*:

> [the] unreasonable control and unnecessary deprivation of many people's opportunity for any choice or control over such vitally important aspect of their lives has impoverished the quality of those lives and hindered Scotland's capacity to respond to economic problems and challenges.[65]

While Scottish Homes had succeeded in halving its housing stock by 1996,[66] and had even facilitated some local authority-to-housing asso-ciation stock transfers,[67] transfers were not fully embraced until after the introduction of the single social tenure under the Housing (Scotland) Act 2001. Changing landlord would have been a hard sell to those housing association tenants with the right to a fair rent and the right to buy as, whilst the latter might be preserved by means of contract, any transferred tenancy would be an assured tenancy, and hence not subject to the fair rent regime. Also, a contractually preserved right to buy might be good as between the parties to the contract while the contract subsisted, but that contract might be terminated, bringing into existence a statutory tenancy but with the loss of the contractual right. It should be noted that local authority tenants transferring their tenancies to housing associations following the commencement of the 1988 Act

---

Scottish Secure Tenancy regime. The story of the fully mutual co-ops is a fascinating one.

[63] Tom Begg, *Housing Policy in Scotland* (Edinburgh: John Donald Publishers Ltd, 1996), p. 185.

[64] Ibid., p. 185ff.

[65] Scottish Development Department, 'Housing: The Government's Proposals for Scotland' (1987), p. 1. It is worth remembering here the findings of the 1917 Royal Commission. In Scotland the trade-off between housing quality and lower rents saw tenants favouring the latter over the former, hence the popularity of overcrowded single-room accommodation. Large public landlords had been seen as a means of remedying this by delivering good-quality affordable accommodation, but by the late 1980s those public landlords had come to be seen as being a cause of the problem of poor-quality housing.

[66] Alice Belcher and Vikki Jackson, 'Housing association governance in Scotland and England', *Juridical Review* (1998), pp. 104–18.

[67] Ibid.

would have been considered to have lost their secure tenancy by virtue of now having a tenancy under the 1988 Act assured tenancy regime.[68]

By the end of the 1990s the 'public landlord' housing stock (25.3 per cent) was diminishing with owner-occupation (62.3 per cent) rising on a cause and effect basis. The traditional private rented sector was stagnant at 6.7 per cent of the housing stock, with the housing associations accounting for 5.7 per cent.[69] In the traditional private rented sector the default tenancy type was the 1988 Act short assured tenancy, whereas the housing associations had some secure tenants with new tenancies from 2 January 1989 being assured (subject to the qualification that some housing association tenants were excluded from statutory security regimes generally, that is, the cooperative housing associations).

STAGE 3: 2000–13

The Scotland Act 1998 legislated for the establishment of a devolved Scottish Parliament and a Scottish Executive, later renamed Scottish Government. Scots property law fell within the competence of the new legislature. During the period 2001–13 the Parliament was to prove an indefatigable legislature. The Housing (Scotland) Act 2001 updated the 1987 Act secure tenancy, creating a new form or tenancy called the Scottish secure tenancy (SST). The SST extended to houses let as separate dwellings by local authorities, water or sewerage authorities, and 'registered social landlords' (RSL).[70] The housing associations fell under the RSL banner, thus council and housing association tenancies were brought under a single tenancy type. This extended statutory rights to the tenants of the co-ops and removed housing association tenants from the ambit of the 1988 Act 'three months rent arrears' mandatory ground for possession, but the Housing (Scotland) Bill preceding the 2001 Act had its critics. Heralding it as 'packaging for the death of local authority housing' Mike Dailly wrote: 'The Housing Bill has all the markings of a Trojan Horse designed to smooth the way for large scale stock transfers. The single social tenancy represents a sugar coated pill which seeks to remove traditional barriers to stock transfer.'[71]

---

[68] But the argument was made that at least some such tenants could have retained secured tenancy status – see Mike Dailly, 'Can stock transferees remain secure tenants?', *SCOLAG*, 253 (1998), pp. 104–6.

[69] See Scottish Government, 'Housing Statistics for Scotland'.

[70] 2001 Act section 11(1).

[71] Mike Dailly, 'Single social tenancy – the demise of local authority housing?', *SCOLAG*, 268 (2000), pp. 28–9 at p. 28.

Dailly's article was at least partially prophetic, as in March 2003, following a ballot in which 58 per cent of tenants who voted said 'yes' to a stock transfer proposal, the entire housing stock of Glasgow City Council (approximately 85,000 properties) was transferred to a newly created Glasgow Housing Association.[72]

The 2001 Act reformed but preserved the right to buy, and it introduced a variant 'special circumstances' form of the SST, as in the short Scottish secure tenancy (SSST), which was for use as a tool in tackling antisocial behaviour and also for temporary housing/special purpose social rented-sector tenancies (for example, temporary housing for homeless people, decant housing, housing for essential workers).[73] While an exceptionally important piece of statutory reform, overall, in terms of the housing stock and access to housing issues, the 2001 Act was generally passive, though the right to buy was to be more significantly limited under the Housing (Scotland) Act 2010 and ultimately abolished, with no new applications accepted after 1 August 2016, by means of provisions in the Housing (Scotland) Act 2014.

The other major reforms of the period 2000–13 for the residential private rented sector included:

The commencement of the provisions in the Civic Government (Scotland) Act 1982 for the licensing of Houses in Multiple Occupation

The introduction of a private landlord registration scheme under Part 8 of the Antisocial Behaviour etc. (Scotland) Act 2004

Amendments to the repairing standard in relation to private tenancies by the Housing (Scotland) 2006 and the establishment of the Private Rented Housing Panel as a free means for enforcing a landlord's duty to repair

---

[72] Ade Kearns and Louise Lawson, 'Housing Stock Transfer in Glasgow – the First Five Years: A Study of Policy Implementation', *Housing Studies*, 23:6 (2008), pp. 857–78; Kim McKee, 'Learning lessons from stock transfer: the challenges in delivering second stage transfer in Glasgow', People, Place & Policy Online, 3:1 (2009), pp. 16–27, available at <https://extra.shu.ac.uk/ppp-online/learning-lessons-from-stock-transfer-the-challenges-in-delivering-second-stage-transfer-in-glasgow/> (last accessed 2 April 2019).

[73] 2001 Act, sections 34–7 and sched. 6. Interestingly, although the SSST is a species of the SST, the SST is statutory from commencement, whereas the statutory provision creating the SSST recognises such common law concepts as the ish and tacit relocation (section 34(5)(a) and (b)), rendering it necessary for the service of a notice to quit in addition to a section 36 notice by the landlord prior to raising an action for recovery of possession. This is similar to 1988 Act model in which notice to quit so as to terminate a tenancy is required plus formal statutory notice, per section 33 of the 1988 Act. It is hard to reconcile this survival of the common law in what is in otherwise a wholly statutory regime.

The introduction of tenancy deposit schemes under Part 4 of the Private
Rented Housing (Scotland) Act 2011
The introduction of tenancy information packs under the same Act

Thus, while the main form of tenancy remained the short assured
tenancy, the expectation of professionalism on the part of the landlords
was steadily ratcheted up. However, simultaneous with this, as Robson
notes, 'the private rented sector had grown significantly since the introduction of the assured and the short assured tenancy regimes in the
Housing (Scotland) Act 1988'[74] – the sector was beginning to bounce
back, from 7.5 per cent in March 2001 to 15.4 per cent in March
2016 (figures exclusive of and, ultimately, outstripping the housing
associations).[75]

In October 2007 the Scottish Government published the discussion
paper *Firm Foundations: The Future of Housing in Scotland.*[76] This
was followed by the establishment of a Private Rented Sector Strategy
Group,[77] leading to a consultation on a strategy for the private rented
sector,[78] ultimately leading to the publication of the Scottish Government
strategy document *A Place to Stay, A Place to Call Home: A Strategy for
the Private Rented Sector in Scotland.*[79] In that document's foreword,
the then Minister for Housing and Welfare, Margaret Burgess, said:

[74] Peter Robson, 'Reviving tenants' rights? The Private Housing (Tenancies)
(Scotland) Act 2016', *Juridical Review* (2018), pp. 108–14 at p. 108.

[75] Scottish Government, 'Housing Statistics for Scotland', 'Key Information and
Summary Tables'.

[76] Available via an archive website at <https://web.archive.org/web/2013020218
0430/http://www.scotland.gov.uk/Publications/2007/10/30153156/2> (last accessed
2 April 2019).

[77] The minutes of the group meetings are available via an archive website at
<https://web.archive.org/web/20140706072506/http://www.scotland.gov.uk:80/
Topics/Built-Environment/Housing/privaterent/government/prsreview/strategy/Mee
tings> (last accessed 2 April 2019).

[78] Available via an archive website at <https://web.archive.org/web/2014022507
4127/http://scotland.gov.uk:80/Publications/2012/04/5779/0> (last accessed 2 April
2019).

[79] Available   at   <https://www.gov.scot/Publications/2013/05/5877/0>   (last
accessed 2 April 2019). The Scottish Government pages cited in the three preceding
notes are accessible via <archive.org> – a United States non-profit digital archive.
The current Scottish Government website is a beta version, at <www.gov.scot> with
the old site being at <www.scotland.gov.uk>, but in the process of changing over it
seems that some important older documents can only be found in what is in effect
an overseas charitable website, and others nowhere at all unless privately saved or
printed in hard copy. This is a worrying trend.

We want to make the Private Rented Sector in Scotland an attractive and affordable housing option for anyone who wishes to live in it. The flexibility and affordability it can offer a range of households is a key strength. [...] To ensure standards continue to rise, the Scottish Government is determined to support the development of a more targeted and effective framework. We want to work with good, professional landlords to help them prosper, but we are determined to tackle the practices of landlords who do damage to the image of the sector and undermine the cohesion of communities.

The report stated that 'the Scottish Government is committed to taking a tenure neutral approach to housing and promoting mixed tenure communities, seeking sustainable choices for all rather than encouraging one particular tenure' and identified three strategic aims:

to improve the quality of property management, condition and service
to deliver for tenants and landlords, meeting the needs of the people living
   in the sector consumers seeking accommodation; and landlords committed
   to continuous improvement
to enable growth, investment and help increase overall housing supply

A Place to Stay, A Place to Call Home heralded the next tranche of residential tenancies law reform in Scotland.

STAGE 4: 2014–PRESENT

The period 2014–16 saw the enactment of three important new statutes, the Housing (Scotland) Act 2014, the Tribunals (Scotland) Act 2014 and the Private Housing (Tenancies) (Scotland) Act 2016. The 2016 Act emerged out of the A Place to Stay, A Place to Call Home strategy, with the Acts of 2014 being consistent with it. While the Housing (Scotland) Act 2014 contains important provisions in respect of the right to buy (that is, its final abolition) and the allocation of social housing, as well as provisions in respect of the regulation of letting agencies and private sector housing provisions, it is the provisions in Part 3 of the Act that are of greatest interest. Part 3 of the Act transfers the sheriff's jurisdiction in relation to regulated and assured tenancies to the First–tier Tribunal for Scotland (except in relation to criminal offences). The First-tier Tribunal for Scotland and its appellate chamber, the Upper Tribunal for Scotland were established by the Tribunals (Scotland) Act 2014. Private Residential Tenancies under the Private Housing (Tenancies) (Scotland) Act 2016 also fall within the jurisdiction of the new tribunal structure. The statutory change of jurisdiction became effective on 1 December 2017.[80]

The First-tier Tribunal for Scotland is organised into a structure of chambers and the relevant chamber in respect of the sheriff's transferred jurisdiction herein discussed is the Housing and Property Chamber, in terms of the Housing and Property Chamber (First-tier Tribunal for Scotland (Chambers) Regulations 2016.[81] It is worth noting that while sheriffs sat alone the First-tier Tribunal for Scotland may consist of a legal member, a legal member and an ordinary member, or a legal member with two ordinary members (as per the First-tier Tribunal for Scotland Housing and Property Chamber and Upper Tribunal for Scotland (Composition) Regulations 2016).[82] The rules for the new chamber are stated in the First-tier Tribunal for Scotland Housing and Property Chamber (Procedure) Regulations 2017.[83] The new Tribunal has now taken over the sheriff's civil jurisdiction in relation to private residential lets, including tenancies under the Rent (Scotland) Act 1984, the Housing (Scotland) Act 1988, and the Private Housing (Tenancies) (Scotland) Act 2016, and also some tenancies excluded from those statutory regimes (for example, resident landlords), and the class of right known as the licence or residential licence. Scottish secure tenancies and short Scottish secure tenancies remain within the bailiwick of the sheriff court.

The Private Housing (Tenancies) (Scotland) Act 2016 creates a new residential private rented sector tenancy regime for Scotland, the Private Residential Tenancy (PRT). The PRT applies to leases created after the new regime's commencement date of 1 December 2017. Existing assured and short assured tenancies, and protected tenancies, continue to exist, being left to wither over time. However, as no new Rent Act tenancies could be created after 2 January 1989 and given that the vast majority of full assured tenancies were Housing Association tenancies (which were shifted, with retrospective effect, into the Scottish Secure Tenancies regime, in consequence of the 2001 Act), the surviving vestiges of the earlier regimes will not last overlong.

The new tenancy applies where (1) a property is let to a 'tenant' – which must be at least one 'individual', though other 'individuals'

---

[80] The 2016 Act, section 71.
[81] SSI 2016/341, regulation 2(b).
[82] SSI 2016/340, regulation 2.
[83] SSI 2017/328.

and persons[84] may share a tenancy as a separate dwelling, and (2) the property or any part of it, is or has been occupied by that tenant as the tenant's only or principal home. As with the earlier Acts relating to residential tenancies – for example, the Acts of 1986, 1987 and 1988 – there are certain categories of tenancy which are excluded from the PRT regime. There is no requirement for a written lease in order to bring into existence a PRT. A verbal contract will suffice,[85] with section 3 of the Act specifying that any lack of writing may be cured by way of an application to the First-tier Tribunal, with powers of sanction being granted to the Tribunal in relation to defaulting landlords. Furthermore, the lack of an ish – that is to say, a definite end date – does not bar the creation of a tenancy, per section 4(1) of the 2016 Act. The distinction between contractual and statutory tenancies, as made in the Rent Acts and the 1988 Act does not apply under the PRT. The Act renders many of the established common law principles of the lease irrelevant.

The 2016 Act stated that the Scottish Ministers may by regulations prescribe various tenancy terms – 'statutory terms' – which will apply to PRTs generally,[86] with further powers to make regulations to allow for such statutory terms to be disapplied in particular circumstances, and, in fact, the Scottish Government has published a model tenancy agreement that can be used in respect of PRTs.[87]

Sections 10–14 of the Act (Part 3) require the landlord in a PRT to supply the tenant with a written tenancy agreement and also other specified information such as may be prescribed by regulations.[88] Failure by the landlord to do so allows the tenant to request that the First-tier Tribunal draw up the terms of the tenancy, with, as noted above, the

---

[84] The distinction between 'individual' and 'person' is an interesting one. 'Individual' tends to suggest a natural person, but 'person' might bear a wider meaning. Under section 25 of the Interpretation and Legislative Reform (Scotland) Act 2010, in an Act of the Scottish Parliament or a Scottish Statutory Instrument the words and expressions used are to be construed according to Schedule 1 of that Act. Schedule 1 defines 'person' as including a body of persons corporate or unincorporated and a partnership constituted under the law of Scotland. Thus, although a legal person could not be a sole tenant under a PRT, it might be a joint tenant.

[85] Section 3 disarms section 1(2) of the Requirements of Writing (Scotland) Act 1995 and gives rise to a statutory form of *rei interventus*.

[86] Sections 7 and 8.

[87] See the Private Residential Tenancies (Statutory Terms) (Scotland) Regulations 2017 (SSI 2017/408). The document was published on 18 October 2017 and is available at <https://beta.gov.scot/publications/scottish-government-model-private-residential-tenancy-agreement/> (last accessed 2 April 2019).

[88] Sections 10–11.

PRT having come into existence when the tenant commenced occupation of the subjects. The Tribunal has the further power to financially sanction the landlord's failure to provide information.[89]

Sections 18–34 and 35–43 (comprising Part 4 of the Act) provide a comprehensive statutory code in relation to rent increases under a PRT. The model of the rent is the 'open market rent', as per section 32 of the Act, but the Act introduces the idea of 'rent pressure zones', to be designated by the Scottish Ministers, in which rent increases may be subject to limitation. Thus, the Act proceeds on the basis of the 1988 Act rent model with a nod in the direction of the Rent Act model going back to 1915. Sections 44–61 (Part 5) provide an equally comprehensive statutory code in relation to the termination by the parties of a PRT.[90] A PRT is not terminated when the original landlord's interest in the let property is ended, as in such circumstances that outgoing landlord's interest is by statute transferred to the new proprietor.[91] Thus, the Leases Act 1449 is replicated and superseded by a new statutory provision. With proper notice, a tenant may bring a PRT to an end at any point after the expiry of a minimum notice period, which, where there is no agreement to the contrary, means twenty-eight days.[92] This period may be extended by (valid) agreement of the parties.[93]

A PRT may come to an end on the basis of mutual agreement of the parties where the landlord has issued and the tenant has received a notice to leave (which must state an eviction ground per section 62 of the Act), and the tenant in consequence ceases to occupy the subjects,[94] but where the tenant remains in occupation, the landlord, having given proper notice in proper form, has to apply to the First-tier Tribunal

---

[89] Section 16.

[90] Section 44.

[91] Section 45.

[92] Sections 48–9.

[93] The twenty years statutory maximum term for residential tenancy in Scotland (Land Tenure Reform (Scotland) Act 1974 section 8) was disapplied in respect of PRTs by the insertion of a subsection (3ZA) into section 8 of the 1974 Act. The amendment was effected by means of sched. 4 para. 1 of the 2016 Act. This prompts the question as to whether the parties to a PRT might 'validly' agree a minimum notice period of, say, thirty years. For further considerations in respect of tenant notice, see Mitchell Skilling and Douglas Bain, 'Choose your friends wisely, choose your co-tenants very carefully: joint tenants and the private residential tenancy' (6 September 2018), University of Aberdeen, Law School blog, <https://www.abdn.ac.uk/law/blog/choose-your-friends-wisely-choose-your-cotenants-very-carefully-joint-tenants-and-the-private-residential-tenancy/> (last accessed 2 April 2019.

[94] Section 50.

for an eviction order.[95] Where the tenant has not ceased to occupy the subjects, in order for the First-tier Tribunal to award an eviction order, the landlord needs to be able to satisfy it that one or more of the eviction grounds specified in Schedule 3 of the Act applies.[96] There are two notice periods, and these are:

> 28 days if the tenant's occupancy of the subjects has been for not more than six months, or if the ground for eviction or one of the grounds for eviction being founded upon is any of Grounds 10–15 in the Act, these being the 'tenant's conduct' grounds[97]

or

> A longer notice period of 84 days applies if the tenant has been entitled to occupy the property in excess of six months, or where the notice to leave does not found exclusively on any one or more of the 'tenant's conduct' grounds for eviction.[98]

Schedule 3 lists eighteen eviction grounds. Some of these are mandatory, meaning the Tribunal will grant an order if the ground is established, others are discretionary. One ground (Ground 12 – rent arrears of three or more consecutive months) is mandatory but with a discretionary strand, reflecting the reality of benefit reform and Universal Credit. Overall, the grounds are broadly in line with the grounds for possession in the Housing (Scotland) Act 1988 and other comparable statutory regimes. The Act contains no equivalent of the automatic ground for recovery of possession that existed in respect of short assured tenancies at section 33 of the Housing (Scotland) Act 1988; i.e. that the tenancy was a properly created short assured tenancy which had been properly terminated by means of proper notice given in the correct form subject to the correct notice periods with no tacit relocation operating.

The Private Housing (Tenancies) Scotland Act 2016 concludes a century of law reform in relation to residential tenancies in Scotland. It is the first residential tenancy regime to be created by the Scottish Parliament, the SST model in the social rented sector being more of the nature of an adaptation of a 1980 prototype, notwithstanding the creation of its short variant form, the SSST. One might now expect the Scottish legislature and executive to sit back awhile and take stock as their changes play out; the Scottish Government needs the 2016 Act

---

[95] Sections 51–6.
[96] Section 51.
[97] Section 54(2)(b)(i) and (3).
[98] Section 54(2)(b)(ii) and (3).

to succeed, and the risk for it is that private landlords, deprived of the comfort blanket of the short assured tenancy, will vote with their feet. The policy's success or failure will take some years to become clear.

CONCLUSIONS

With effect from 1 December 2017 Scotland has a new private residential sector tenancy regime which will be tried and tested in a new judicial forum. In the social rented sector the Scottish secure tenancy and the short Scottish secure tenancy apply across all Registered Social Landlords, with the sheriff retaining legal jurisdiction. Similar principles will apply across the two sectors but there are also differences, and in each sector the classic Scots common law lease is modified and enhanced and transformed. Revolutionary though the reforms of 1915 may have seemed at the time, in retrospect they appear modest. The process of reform from pre-1915 to the present day has been one in which attempts have been made to strike a fair balance of power between the landlord and tenant. The Rent Acts arguably went too far in one direction, and the residential private rented sector went into stagnation, but the 1988 Act regime, and, in particular, the short assured tenancy model, equally arguably, went too far in the opposite direction, and required the corrective remedies of the 2016 Act. This is in broad brush the story of the last century in terms of residential leasing, but similar points can be made in respect of agricultural holdings. So what can we conclude from all of the foregoing?

It would be useful here to return to the text from Rennie's recent SULI volume on leases quoted at the beginning of this chapter: 'Changes in the law in these areas tend to alter the bargaining or commercial power of the two parties rather than alter or modify any deep legal principles.'[99] This is undoubtedly correct, at least up to the volume's date of publication (2015). Statutes may have qualified landlords' rights to increase rents and bring leases to an end. Succession rights may have been secured for tenants. Rights in relation to housing conditions enhanced. The regulation of landlords may have been stepped up to professionalise the economic activity of private leasing and improve housing standards in the private rented sector. But none of these reforms changed the basic nature of the lease as a bilateral contract granting time-limited rights to the possession of land in return for a consideration, in respect of which there must be a landlord and a tenant, specified subjects, a rent and a

---

[99] See note 3 above.

duration. In relation to the latter two elements, Scots common law has been willing to remedy gaps to give rise to some form of recognisable right. 'Rent' and 'duration' might be interpreted liberally to allow for a lease, albeit not infinitely so, and words have been less liberally interpreted when it comes to making that lease unduly onerous against the landlord's singular successors. With nineteen years being the common historical duration of an agricultural lease, but one year encompassing a growing cycle, an inferred one-year term protects the tenant to an extent but does not unreasonably incommode the landlord.[100] The Acts of 1984 and 1988 did nothing to affront this. In the public sector, the 1987 Act still paid lip service to the concepts of the ish, tacit relocation and notice to quit, as does the 2001 Act, by implication in relation to SSTs and expressly in relation to SSSTs.[101]

The 2016 Act seems to establish a complete statutory code in relation to Private Residential Tenancies, effective from day one. The PRT is literally an ishless tack – it is open-ended from the very outset (section 4). Furthermore, as long as there is an initial rent, it is 'to continue to be regarded as giving rise to a tenancy despite the term of the agreement requiring the tenant to pay rent subsequently being removed from the agreement or otherwise ceasing to have effect' (section 4).[102] Two of the essentials of the common law lease are disapplied, yet still there is a tenancy. One way to deal with this would be to adopt the position that the 2016 Act private residential tenancy has departed so far from the classic Scots law lease so as to no longer be one, but, rather, a form of statutory-enhanced 'not a lease' tenancy. This is an extreme position

[100] Compare Paton and Cameron at pp. 6–7 with pp. 107–10 to see the step-up. In respect of inferred period and rent the *locus classicus* is *Gray* v.. *Edinburgh University*, 1962 SC 157. Also *Shetland Islands Council* v. *BP Petroleum Development Ltd*, 1990 SLT 82.

[101] In fact, one can still find a model Scottish Secure Tenancy agreement in the old Scottish Government website at <https://www.gov.scot/Publications/2002/09/15391/10797> (last accessed 2 April 2019), which includes the following text at 1.4: 'The tenancy will start on [This Agreement will take effect from] .... (the entry date). This is regardless of the date on which this Agreement is signed. This Agreement will continue from the entry date until .... and after that on a [weekly/fortnightly/four weekly/calendar monthly] basis. There are different ways of ending the tenancy and these are described in Part 6 of this Agreement.'

[102] This echoes, over two centuries later, Lord Bankton's words 'that which is validly constituted must continue tho' matters have come to a state wherein it could not have had a beginning', *Institute of the Laws of Scotland* (Edinburgh: A. Kincaid and A. Donaldson, 1752), IV.XLV. 42, 43.

predicated upon linguistic purity. And, as a matter of common sense, an impractical position also; it is implausible that for so long as the 2016 Act private residential tenancy continues to exist that it will not receive extensive consideration in future editions of such works as McAllister's *Scottish Law of Leases* and Rennie's *Leases*.

Another view is that the 2016 Act, whilst apparently disapplying the common law, in fact preserves it[103] – the common law is tenacious. For example, the requirement at common law for a lease to have a duration is there to distinguish the lease – a time-limited right in land – from the feu, a right without limit of time. Similarly, the requirement for a rent distinguishes the lease once again from the feu but also from lesser rights amounting to precarious possession. The 2016 Act does not invert any of this – the right under a PRT is not without limit of time and the landlord's right to a rent is not snatched away.

The Scots law lease is not static. It has not survived so long as to have outlasted the feudal system through inertia. It is a living, dynamic institution, protean in its nature. Quigley's observation[104] that there is no such thing as the single definitive 'lease', only many different species of the lease, is insightful, and, it is submitted, correct. Imagine, then, the Scots law lease not as a fortress under siege, but rather as something in the form of a Venn diagram, in which several circles overlap; four perhaps. One represents the lease at common law, a personal contract. A second, the lease made effective, through the intervention of statute, against a landlord's singular successors, something 'invested by statute with the quality of a real right'.[105] A third circle would represent the statutory regimes conferring security of tenure and other important rights. A fourth circle may be necessary to accommodate specialities and oddities, such as licences.

The four circles in the Venn diagram would interact and overlap but not inevitably to a fixed and equal extent. The circles would not be the same size, and the overlaps would not be fixed once and for all time, but would vary as law, society and policy changed. While some circles

---

[103] This point was made to me by one of the students in my 2017–18 Scottish Law of Leases honours class, Finn O'Neill, and I give him due credit for it. The same student also coined the term 'matrix of rights', used in this chapter. I have been fortunate to have a number of excellent students in my Leases honours class.

[104] See note 6 above.

[105] Paton and Cameron, *The Law of Landlord and Tenant in Scotland*, p. 5. See also John Rankine, *A Treatise on the Law of Leases in Scotland*, 3rd edn (Edinburgh: W. Green & Son, 1916), p. 1: 'The contract is in its essence purely personal; in certain circumstances it gives rise to what is substantially a real right.'

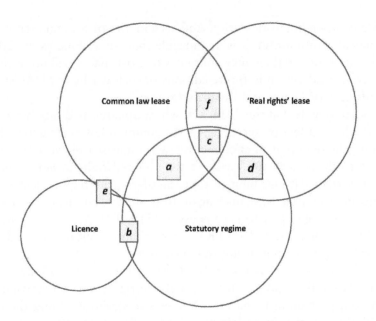

Figure 11.1 But note that the circles will not all be the same size nor will they be true circles, or even regular in shape, and that the two and three-circle overlap will, depending upon the facts and degree, be shifting territory.

might overlap with others to a very high degree – for example, a housing association tenancy would satisfy the requirements for a common law lease, while falling within the ambit of the Leases Act 1449 and the Housing (Scotland) Act 2001, whereas, contrawise, case law has given us the example of a 2001 Act SST which would *not* have satisfied the requirements under the common law and the 1449 Act to be a lease at all due to there being no rent,[106] making it a licence, yet still the tenant had the right to buy.

Such a Venn diagram, illustrating what might be described as a matrix of rights, might look like that shown in Figure 11.1.

Consider the three-way interaction in this model of the bare contractual 'common law' lease, the 'real rights' lease, and the lease under a statutory regime conferring security of tenure. In most cases the three main circles will overlap almost completely – for example, a tenant of a Registered Social Landlord will generally have a contractual lease which will qualify as a real right by virtue of the Leases Act 1449, and the

---

[106] See *Kinghorn* v. *City of Glasgow District Council*, 1984 SLT (Lands Tr) 9 and *Andrew* v. *North Lanarkshire Council* 4 May 2011, Lands Tr.

tenancy will be a Scottish Secure Tenancy under the Housing (Scotland) Act 2001.

In this model:

a Attempts have been made to locate occupancy agreements in this overlap territory – i.e. to take contracts granting time-limited rights to the possession of land in return for a consideration which have been held not to give rise to a real right on the grounds of property law confusion (for example, where co-owners A, B and C grant a lease to A), and to seek to passport them into statutory security. The cases here are *Clydesdale Bank plc* v. *Davidson*[107] and *Serup* v. *McCormack & Ors*.[108] The question has prompted some academic debate,[109] but the Scottish Law Commission seems minded to shut the gate.[110]

b Depicts the overlap territory in, for example, the case of *Andrew* v. *North Lanarkshire Council*,[111] or illustrates the inclusion of licences in the deposit guarantee schemes under the Housing (Scotland) Act 2006 and the Tenancy Deposit Schemes (Scotland) Regulations 2011.[112] Two recent Sheriff Appeal Court (Civil) cases, *Gray* v. *MacNeil's Executor* and *Devon Angling Association* v. *Scottish Water*, suggest that overlap areas *a* and *b* remain viable topics for judicial debate.[113]

c Generally accommodates RSL tenants.

d The overlap illustrated here is probably misleading, as before a lease can be 'real' it must firstly, as a minimum, be valid at common law; given which the *d* territory in Figure 11.1 probably better illustrates its deviser's limited drawing skills.

e There are cases in which the necessary elements for a common law lease

---

[107] 1998 SC 51 (HL).

[108] Scottish Land Court, 18 April 2012.

[109] See Catherine Bury and Douglas Bain, 'A, B and C to A, Revisited' *Juridical Review*, 2013, pp. 77–89; B. Gill, 'Two Questions in the Law of Leases' in F. McCarthy, J. Chalmers and S. Bogle (eds), *Essays in Conveyancing and Property Law in Honour of Professor Robert Rennie* (Cambridge: Open Book Publishers, 2015), pp. 255–78, also at <http://dx.doi.org/10.11647/OBP.0056> (last accessed 2 April 2019); Mitchell Skilling, 'The Fifth Element: Should Exclusive Possession Be Considered an Essential Requirement for the Constitution of a Contract of Lease in Scots Law?', *Aberdeen Student Law Review*, 7 (2017), pp. 1–26; and Peter Webster, 'The Continued Existence of the Contract of Lease' in A. J. M. Steven, R. G. Anderson and J. A. MacLeod (eds), *Nothing So Practical as a Good Theory: Festschrift for George L. Gretton*. (Edinburgh: Avizandum, 2017), pp. 119–35.

[110] Scottish Law Commission Discussion Paper No. 165, *Discussion Paper on Aspects of Leases: Termination* (May 2018).

[111] 4 May 2011, Lands Tr.

[112] SSI 2011/176.

[113] *Gray* v. *MacNeil's Executor* [2017] SAC (Civ) 9, 2017 SLT (Sh Ct) 83; *Devon Angling Association* v. *Scottish Water* [2018] SAC (Civ) 7, 2018 SC (SAC) 35.

are present but the result is nevertheless deemed to be a licence, e.g. where the extent of possession is too limited, or short-term lets (commonly associated with the modern Airbnb brand), and these might fall here.

f Accommodates those commercial leases not covered by the Tenancy of Shops Acts.

It is respectfully submitted that each of these intersection areas lends itself very well to in-depth academic study. The Scots law lease is not dry as dust or done to death. How could it possibly be?

12

Crofting Law

Eilidh I. M. MacLellan

IT IS NOT NECESSARY to read much of the Napier Report (as it became known) to understand why the law governing rights to land in nineteenth-century Scotland required to be reformed. The report, being the final outcome of the *Inquiry into the Condition of the Crofters and Cottars of the Highlands and Islands of Scotland* (which will be referred to throughout this chapter as 'the Napier Commission'), makes for painful reading, as the gross inequality between landlord and tenant is repeatedly demonstrated. The response of Gladstone's Liberal government was illustrative of the wider political, social and economic changes taking place throughout Scotland. Land reform was by this time well established on the political agenda in Scotland. Its time had come, in part, due to the breakdown of the relationship between clan chiefs and those who had once been clansmen and women, or with those who acquired land from traditional owners. Together with new economic challenges such as the decline in the price of cattle, overpopulation, the failure of the potato crop and the end of the kelp industry, that shift in societal structure resulted in clearance, resettlement, famine and widespread social deprivation. These hardships led directly to the agitation of the mid to late nineteenth century, which in turn led to the Napier Commission.[1]

This chapter aims, firstly, to summarise the development of crofting law from 1886 to 2019. It is fair to say that a few elements of the current framework could scarcely have been predicted 133 years ago. However, as Sir Crispin of Agnew of Lochnaw, Bt QC has observed, 'many of the

---

[1] Scottish Records Office, *The Crofters* [further details to be supplied], p. 15; J. Hunter, *The Making of the Crofting Community* (Edinburgh: John Donald, 1976); E. A. Cameron, *Land for the People? The British Government and the Scottish Highlands, c.1880–c.1925* (East Linton: Tuckwell Press, 1996).

sections of the 1993 Act can be found in the wording of the 1886 Act'.[2] The backbone of the system has always been the principles of (1) security of tenure, (2) controlled rents, and (3) compensation for improvements carried out to the land. Despite demonstrable current appetite for the reform of crofting law, there have been remarkably few calls to remove the original protections. The chapter will go on to identify and analyse some of the challenges which face crofting in the modern era, namely: (1) the state of crofting legislation itself, (2) crofting law and its arguably dysfunctional relationship with the wider land reform movement, (3) the conflicting objectives of the crofting system, and (4) the market in crofts and croft tenancies.

DEVELOPMENT OF CROFTING LAW

Very few practitioners will ever have cause to consult anything other than their copy of the Crofters (Scotland) Act 1993, and perhaps, if they have a specific query relating to the (new) Crofting Register, they may have to resort to the Crofting Reform (Scotland) Act 2010. However, there are a further twenty Acts of Parliament concerning crofting law, some entirely obsolete.[3] Development can be conveniently broken down into six phases.

1886–1911

Despite the weight of evidence gathered by the Napier Commission, the Crofters Holdings (Scotland) Act 1886 did not deliver the measures which some had hoped for, particularly in relation to the restoration of lands lost during the clearances.[4] Rather, the 1886 Act protected

---

[2] C. H. Agnew, *Crofting Law* (Edinburgh: T. & T. Clark, 2000), p. 1.

[3] Crofters Holdings (Scotland) Act 1886, Crofters Holdings (Scotland) Act 1887, Crofters Commission (Delegation of Powers) Act 1888, Crofters Common Grazing Regulation Act 1891, Congested Districts (Scotland) Act 1897, Crofters Common Grazing Regulation Act 1908, Congested Districts (Scotland) Act 1897, Small Landholders (Scotland) Act 1911, Land Settlement (Scotland) Act 1919, Small Landholders and Agricultural Holdings (Scotland) Act 1931, Crofters (Scotland) Act 1955, Crofters (Scotland) Act 1961, Crofting Reform (Scotland) 1976, Crofter Forestry (Scotland) Act 1991, Crofters (Scotland) Act 1993, Scottish Land Court Act 1993, Transfer of Crofting Estates (Scotland) Act 1997, the Land Reform (Scotland) Act 2003 (Part 3 thereof), Crofting Reform (Scotland) Act 2007, Crofting Reform (Scotland) Act 2010, Crofting Amendment (Scotland) Act 2013.

[4] D. Flyn and K. Graham, *Crofting Law* (Edinburgh: Avizandum, 2017), p. 5; Cameron, *Land for the People?*

any person who at the passing of this Act is tenant of a holding from year to year, who resides on his holding, the annual rent of which does not exceed thirty pounds in money, and which is situated in a crofting parish, and the successors of such a person in the holding, being his heirs or legatees.[5]

In addition to security of tenure[6] and compensation for improvements,[7] these newly defined crofters were also given the right to bequeath their tenancy to a family member,[8] the right to renounce their tenancy,[9] and the right to have a fair rent fixed every seven years.[10] Notably, there was a requirement that tenants should be resident on their holdings, although this was part of the definition of 'crofter',[11] rather than a statutory condition. There was no right to assign the tenancy and, importantly, if the crofter renounced and the land became vacant, the protection no longer applied. The protected status applied to the crofter, rather than the croft; a marked difference to the current position whereby once designated as a croft, the land remains such unless a formal process of removal (e.g. decrofting[12] or resumption[13]) is undertaken. Landlords, for their part, could remove a crofter who was in breach of the statutory conditions of tenure. They also enjoyed reserved rights to mine, quarry, shoot, make roads, take access, and resume all or part of the croft for the good of the estate. These reservations can still be found in Schedule 2 to and section 20 of the Crofters (Scotland) Act 1993. The 1886 Act also established the first Crofters Commission, which was at that time a quasi-judicial body.[14] Common grazings did not feature in the 1886 Act, but were subject to regulation by way of the Crofters Common Grazings Regulation Acts 1891 and 1908. These Acts introduced the still-familiar concept of common grazings committees to manage the grazings.

The 1886 Act did bring some relief. The *Report of the Royal Commission of the Highlands and Islands*, published in 1892, remarked that fair rents, combined with the security of tenure now enjoyed by

---

[5] Crofters (Scotland) Act 1886, section 34. In territorial extent, crofting law applied to the former counties of Argyll, Inverness, Ross and Cromarty, Sutherland, Caithness, Orkney and Shetland.

[6] Ibid., section 1.

[7] Ibid., section 8.

[8] Ibid., section 16.

[9] Ibid., section 7.

[10] Ibid., section 6.

[11] Ibid., section 34.

[12] Ibid., sections 24 and 25.

[13] Ibid., section 20.

[14] Agnew, *Crofting Law*, p. 1.

crofters, resulted in improved cultivation and better morale.[15] However,
the same report also identified that there had been little improvement in
agricultural production in the crofting counties,[16] and the later Taylor
Report published over sixty years later criticised the Act's failure 'to
promote the consolidation of holdings or to restrict their subdivision',[17]
and furthermore noted that the 1886 Act differed widely from the recommendations of the Napier Commission. There was a sense, by 1954,
that the 1886 Act had been a missed opportunity, and MacCuish and
Flyn, writing in 1990, observed that it 'fell far short of what crofters
had been demanding, especially by reason of failure to provide for
restoration of lands lost in the Clearances'.[18] They further note that
cottars – those with no access to land for subsistence agriculture – were
particularly disappointed.[19]

1911–55

The next stage in the development of crofting legislation extended the
protection given to crofters across the whole of Scotland (rather than
simply the crofting counties), by way of the Small Landholders (Scotland)
Act 1911. It provided that the protected person was called a small
landholder rather than a crofter. This measure also formed the Scottish
Land Court to replace the Crofters Commission, and the Department of
Agriculture to replace the Congested Districts Board. The 1911 Act also
introduced such familiar provisions as the requirement upon a crofter to
cultivate the croft by himself or his family with or without hired labour
and also the concept of putting a croft to a subsidiary or auxiliary use.[20]
These alternative uses, at this stage, were not permitted to prejudice the
agricultural use of the croft. The 1955 Act was amended by the Crofters
(Scotland) Act 1961, which provided for the creation of new crofts, and
a method of calculating compensation for permanent improvements.[21]

---

[15] *Report of the Royal Commission of the Highlands and Islands*, 1892, cited in
the later Taylor Report (see note 17), chapter II, p. 13 paragraph 23.

[16] Ibid.

[17] 'Report of the Commission of Inquiry into Crofting Conditions', (HMSO,
April 1954), chapter 2, p. 12, paragraph 22.

[18] D. J. MacCuish and D. Flyn, *Crofting Law* (Edinburgh: Butterworths/Law
Society of Scotland, 1990), paragraphs 1.03 and 1.04.

[19] Ibid.

[20] Agnew, *Crofting Law*, p. 4.

[21] Agnew, Crofting Law, p. 5.

1955–76

The Crofters (Scotland) Act 1955 can be seen from a modern perspective as the beginnings of the modern crofting framework. The 1955 Act was passed in the wake of the 'Report of the Commission of Inquiry into Crofting Conditions', which became known as the Taylor Report. The Commission had been charged with reviewing 'crofting conditions in the Highlands and Islands with special reference to the secure establishment of a small holding population making full use of agricultural resources and deriving the maximum economic benefit therefrom'. [22] The Commission therefore proceeded on the assumption that agricultural activity in crofting areas was to be encouraged. The key features of the 1955 Act were the restriction of crofting tenure to the crofting counties (leaving the Small Landholders Acts to apply to relevant holdings in the rest of Scotland), the establishment of a new Crofters Commission, and the return of purely administrative functions from the Scottish Land Court. The Register of Crofts was also established. Crofters were given enhanced rights of assignation, bequest and decrofting,[23] and retiring crofters were given the option of obtaining a title deed to their house and garden ground if they passed on their crofts to a new (invariably younger) crofter.[24]

1976–93

Reforms introduced by the Crofting Reform (Scotland) Act 1976 transformed the crofting system by bestowing upon crofters an absolute right to purchase a croft house and garden ground, together with a qualified right to purchase croft land, and an entitlement to share in the value of any land taken for development.[25] The focus on agricultural production, so prevalent in the 1950s, was by 1976 fading. It was thought that economic development ought to be prioritised over agriculture,[26] and the 1976 Act certainly facilitated that. There has been discussion, in crofting circles, of a causal link between the 1976 reforms and the current

[22] 'Report of the Commission of Inquiry into Crofting Conditions', chapter 1, p. 7.
[23] MacCuish and Flyn, *Crofting Law*, paragraphs 1.16 and 1.17.
[24] MacCuish and Flyn, *Crofting Law*, paragraph 1.17.
[25] Crofters (Scotland) Act 1993, section 21.
[26] 'Final Report of the Committee of Inquiry on Crofting', paragraph 2.1.4, available at <https://www.webarchive.org.uk/wayback/archive/20150404100646/http://www.croftinginquiry.org/> (last accessed 28 March 2019).

deficiencies of the crofting system. Certainly, the 1976 Act introduced free-market principles to a system which originally protected *against* an emerging free-market economy, and allowed crofters to view their land as development land rather than agricultural land.

The case of *Whitbread* v. *Macdonald*[27] conferred further rights upon crofters, allowing them to seek a title deed to the croft or any part of it in the name of an unrelated third party. This led to a proliferation of house plots on the open market, with crofters receiving market value for the same, and the owners of the land receiving crofting (that is, nominal) value. This practice was brought to an end by the joint operation of the Crofting Reform (Scotland) Act 2010 which closed the loophole created by the case, and the financial crash of 2008, after which self-build mortgages became virtually unavailable for a time.[28]

The 1976 Act also had the effect of creating a new type of person affected by crofting legislation. A 'crofter' is defined[29] as 'the tenant of a croft'. There was no defined term to describe a crofter who purchases his croft. That person is no longer a crofter, because the tenancy is extinguished upon registration of the conveyance in his favour. [30] Such persons were accepted to be, in law, landlords of a vacant croft. They were commonly called 'owner-occupiers', although that term was not defined until much later,[31] and even then it was defined inadequately and has arguably caused more problems than it resolved.[32]

Common grazings were another casualty of the 1976 Act. A tenanted croft commonly includes a right or share in common grazings, held as a pertinent of the tenancy. If the tenancy is assigned by the crofter, so is the grazings share (and any other pertinent of the tenancy, for example a right to use the foreshore or cut peat). However, when a crofter acquires the title deed to a croft, the link between croft and share is severed, leaving the grazing share in tenancy. Coupled with the wider decline

[27] 1992 SC 479; 1992 SLT 1144.

[28] M. M. Combe, 'Crofting, nominee sales and the separation of powers', *Edinburgh Law Review*, 14 (2010), pp. 458–63; J. MacAskill, *We have Won the Land* (Stornoway: Acair, 1999) pp. 50–4 for discussion of the relevance of this decision in the purchase of the North Assynt Estate by the Assynt Crofters Trust.

[29] Crofters (Scotland) Act 1993, section 3(3).

[30] *Cameron* v. *Bank of Scotland* 1989 SLT (Land Ct) 38.

[31] Crofters (Scotland) Act 1993 (as amended by the Crofting Reform (Scotland) Act 2010 section 19B.

[32] E. MacLellan, 'The Curse of s. 19B', 15 September 2017, <http://camus.scot/curse-s-19b> (last accessed 28 March 2019).

in the use of common grazings, this has resulted in numerous grazing shares being lost.

In 2012 the Crofting Commission made a reference to the Scottish Land Court under section 53 of the 1993 Act,[33] asking the Court to answer thirty interrelated questions pertaining in one way or another to common grazings.[34] In a paper presented to the Faculty of Solicitors of the Highlands and Islands in 2012 by the advocate Iain F. MacLean (now deputy chair of the Scottish Land Court), the reference was described as being 'like a particularly nasty examination paper'.[35] (MacLean appeared in the hearing on the matter as *amicus curiae*.)[36] With the benefit of hindsight, it is now obvious that the 1976 reforms, coupled with the *Whitbread* v. *Macdonald* case, advanced the rights of the individual crofter to an unsustainable degree. The predictable consequence has been that the pendulum on the spectrum of individual versus collective rights has now moved away once again from the former towards the latter.

1993–97

The Crofters (Scotland) Act 1993 consolidates the 1955, 1961 and 1976 Acts. As is the norm for consolidation statutes, it did not make substantive changes to the law, rather it organised previously disparate statutes into one piece of legislation. It has been subsequently amended by the 2007, 2010 and 2013 Acts.

1997–2019

After the 1976 Act there followed a period of around two decades before there was any word of new crofting legislation.[37] The Land Reform Policy Group, formed after the Labour Party swept to power in Westminster in 1997, identified a vision for crofting in the future.

[33] Reference by the Commission under section 53 of the 1993 Act (Application RN SLC/121/11 – Order of 3 August 2012).

[34] B. Inkster, 'Common grazing shares – where are we now?', *The Journal Online* 58:1, 21 January 2013, <http://www.journalonline.co.uk/Magazine/58-1/1012083.aspx> (last accessed 28 March 2019).

[35] I. F. MacLean, 'Recent Developments in Crofting Law', paragraph 36, available at <http://www.terrafirmachambers.com/articles/RecentDevelopmentsInCroftingLaw.pdf> (last accessed 28 March 2019).

[36] 'friend of the court'.

[37] MacLean, 'Recent Developments in Crofting Law', paragraph 8.

The vision included simplified legislation, more sustainable crofting communities, more local involvement and accountability, more active crofters, and allowing crofts to be utilised for activities other than agriculture.[38] Although crofting law did not feature in the Land Reform Policy Group's *Proposals for Legislation* the following year,[39] a draft crofting bill was published by the Scottish Parliament in 2002. However, the draft bill failed to catch the public's imagination, and by 2005 it was almost unrecognisable as the Crofting Reform etc. Act 2007. Many of the more controversial clauses of the draft bill had been shelved pending the report of the Committee of Inquiry on Crofting, chaired by Professor Mark Shucksmith. Professor Shucksmith's remit was to identify a vision for the future of crofting and to suggest legislative and administrative changes to realise that vision. The 'Shucksmith Report'[40] was published on 12 May 2008 and proposed thirty recommendations, some of them radical.

The draft bill which followed the Shucksmith Report contained many proposals which were widely criticised and ultimately dropped, including (1) the concept of using a croft tenancy as security for a mortgage, and (2) an occupancy requirement relating to all land decrofted since 12 May 2008, which demanded that any house built on such land be used 'as a main residence' by either owner or tenant. These mechanisms are of a particularly technical nature and are not well suited to the purposes suggested by the Committee, which led to some scepticism from the legal community. The 2010 Act that eventually followed all of this reorganised and reconstituted the Crofters Commission as the Crofting Commission and also provided for a majority of elected Commissioners. The Act introduced a new, map-based Crofting Register and also contains measures of a regulatory nature designed to allow crofters who do not fulfil their various obligations to be regulated more effectively.

The 2007 and 2010 Acts, while no doubt well intentioned, have done crofting no favours, and crofting legislation is generally accepted to be in desperate need of restating, redrafting, and/or consolidation. The Crofting Law Group[41] has been pushing for change, with members

[38] Land Reform Policy Group, 'Identifying the Solutions' (Edinburgh: Scottish Office, September 1998), at p. 78.

[39] Land Reform Policy Group, 'Proposals for Legislation' (Edinburgh: Scottish Executive, July 1999).

[40] 'The Final Report of the Committee of Inquiry on Crofting'.

[41] An organisation to promote the knowledge and understanding of crofting law, with membership open to all <http://www.croftinglawgroup.org> (last accessed 28 March 2019).

Derek Flyn (retired solicitor) and Keith Graham (retired principal clerk to the Scottish Land Court) heading the Crofting Law Sump,[42] a project to identify and prioritise areas in need of attention.

In April 2018, the Scottish Government[43] confirmed that it will, within the current parliamentary term, reform the more urgent aspects of crofting law. There is a further commitment to a more strategic review of crofting law commencing now, but being delivered by a subsequent Parliament.

CHALLENGES FOR THE CROFTING SYSTEM

Crofting legislation

The statutory framework of crofting is cumbersome, to say the very least, yet until the Crofting Amendment (Scotland) Act 2013 there appeared to be no appetite for reform of crofting law. That legislation was deemed necessary due to a perceived problem with the decrofting provisions contained in the Crofting Reform (Scotland) Act 2010. It was the further layer of complexity provided by the 2013 Act which prompted many to call publicly for the reform of crofting legislation, whether in the form of consolidation, fresh legislation, or redrafting. It was, and remains, clear that crofting law must be improved, and it is no exaggeration to claim that the greatest challenge faced by the crofting system in 2018 is the legislation itself. The Crofting Law Sump talks[44] of 'the present impenetrability of crofting law, caused by the "layering" of amendments, one after the other, without refining the accumulated mass of legislation'. This 'impenetrability' is illustrated particularly well by the succession procedures, where multiple paper versions of the legislation are required, preferably laid out in hard copy on the floor, together with rulers and highlighter pens, to establish what the law is.

The impenetrability creates hazardous professional risks for solicitors, and the increased complexity creates substantial costs for clients. Crofting conveyancing transactions are now complex and protracted as a matter of course, which is unsustainable for both solicitors and clients.

---

[42] The Crofting Law Sump is a project undertaken by members Derek Flyn and Keith Graham, to identify areas of crofting law in need of reform. The Final Report can be found at <http://www.crofting.org/uploads/news/CLGreport.pdf> (last accessed 28 March 2019).

[43] Available at <https://blogs.gov.scot/rural-environment/2018/04/12/crofting-update/> (last accessed 14 March 2019).

[44] Crofting Law Group Sump, p. 7 paragraph 2.1.1.

As MacLean remarked in his 2012 paper to the Faculty of Solicitors of the Highlands and Islands, the old joke that the definition of a croft is an area of land surrounded by a sea of legislation 'has never been both less funny or more true, as those of us who have had to grapple with the legislation in recent times would readily confirm'.[45]

Crofting law versus land reform

Although the reform of crofting law is a type of 'land reform' in that it relates to the reform of laws affecting land, it has arguably been developed in a vacuum, separated from concepts of community ownership, community engagement, and all other elements of wider land reform. Furthermore, crofting law affects a statutorily defined group of people, and therefore is restrictive in nature, whilst the movement for wider land reform is, at heart, inclusive rather than exclusive.[46] In some circumstances, crofting law operates in opposition to the wider land reform agenda. Crofters may belong to the wider non-crofting community as well as the crofting community, but the extra rights enjoyed by crofters are sometimes found to be the cause of tension and discord.[47] For example, in circumstances where a community body purchases a crofting estate, either via the specialist crofting community buyout legislation[48] or otherwise,[49] it purchases only the landlord's interest in any tenanted crofts, and rights to purchase do not extend to crofts which have been acquired by crofters under the crofting Acts. Furthermore, crofters who have a community body as their landlord can still exercise their rights under sections 12–19 of the 1993 Act to acquire their croft land and the site of their house and garden ground. Similarly, other rights held by crofters under the crofting Acts are unaltered by a change of landlord. In some cases, community bodies are surprised to be held to the same standards as any other landlord when approached by a crofter looking to exercise a right to purchase. Some request a 'top up' payment to reflect the fact that land is to be removed from community ownership.

[45] MacLean, 'Recent Developments in Crofting Law', p. 1.

[46] For further discussion of the separateness of crofting law, see J. MacAskill, 'The crofting community right to buy in the Land Reform (Scotland) Act 2003' *Scottish Affairs*, 49 (Autumn 2014), pp. 104–33.

[47] M. M. Combe, 'Parts 2 and 3 of the Land Reform (Scotland) Act 2003: A Definitive Answer to the Scottish Land Question?', *Juridical Review* (2006), pp. 195–227.

[48] Land Reform (Scotland) Act 2003, Part 3.

[49] The Transfer of Crofting Estates (Scotland) Act 1997.

Others suggest rights of pre-emption or other onerous title conditions and servitude rights, none of which a crofter is obliged to agree to.

These matters relate only to the acquisition of land by a crofter. Landlords (whether private, public or community body) have, in addition, rights in relation to tenanted crofts, such as the right to construct roads and tracks, to quarry for minerals, and to shoot deer.[50] These are generally exercised so infrequently that crofters often forget they exist. More proactive community landlords may take a different approach. There is no provision in the crofting Acts for a community landlord to be treated differently to a private landlord, and it remains the case that the crofting system is an onerous system when viewed from a landowner's perspective. The crofting Acts, despite their many flaws, still deliver unrivalled protection to crofters, and this can act in opposition to the rights held by communities, acquired via land reform legislation. The body of landlord and tenant law has developed because as the rights of one are advanced, so the rights of the other must necessarily be tempered. This principle applies regardless of whether the landlord is a private individual, a company, a community organisation, or a trust.[51] The conflict between land reform law and crofting law may be brought into focus when the Scottish Government's strategic review of crofting law is undertaken. The solution from a community perspective is to amend the crofting Acts to confer different rights on different types of landlord, but that is likely to be energetically resisted by the crofting lobby, who could be expected to view it, correctly, as an infringement of their historical and hard-won rights.

The conflicting priorities of the crofting system

It is self-evident that to enjoy any success whatsoever, and to allow any perceived success to be measured, crofting legislation must have a

---

[50] Schedule 2, Crofters (Scotland) Act 1993.

[51] See *MacDonald & Others* v. *South Uist Estates Limited* RN/SLC/37/08 – <http://www.scottish-land-court.org.uk/decisions/SLC.37.08.rub.html> (accessed 14 March 2019) – this case serves as a reminder that (1) a community landlord is still a landlord, and (2) that a crofter's rights in a common grazing differ very much from a crofter's rights in and to their own croft. A right in common grazing is simply a right to graze a certain number of livestock, and as long as the landlord's plans do not infringe the crofter's ability to do so, then the land can be developed. If the landlord requires to remove land from the crofters, thus reducing the livestock which can be grazed, then the landlord must resume, or enter into a scheme for development, and in either case the crofters would be compensated.

clear purpose, and must be fulfilling that purpose. The justification for
bestowing special rights upon a small group of people has changed over
the course of history, and currently is rather confused. This confusion
is causing, or at least exacerbating, some of the systemic difficulties
experienced over recent years. The 1886 Act was passed to address some
historical wrongs, and to protect those who were essentially peasant
farmers against landlords who, for various reasons, could not or did not
wish to continue to relate to their tenantry as they previously had. At its
heart, the 1886 Act was designed to improve the desperate standard of
living amongst those in the crofting counties at the time.

The Shucksmith Report contains a helpful analysis[52] of the differing
policy objectives which crofting law has been used to promote over
the years. Shucksmith agreed that in 1886 the priority was to improve
the standard of living amongst crofters. The report goes on to say that the
Great Depression of the 1930s, and specifically the lack of employment
in industrial centres, caused many to return to the crofting counties, and
from 1939 the focus was on economic development to provide employment for this increasing population, to allow them to supplement their
crofting income. In the post-war period, food shortages caused a change
in focus towards agricultural production, and the Taylor Committee's
remit was to facilitate greater agricultural production in the Highlands
and Islands.[53] The 1955 and 1961 Acts were therefore designed with
agricultural production in mind, and over the next two decades there
was much amalgamation of crofting units as crofters attempted to form
viable agricultural units. The new Crofting Commission was given the
objective of reviving agriculture along with what the Shucksmith Report
calls 'a tortuous burden of administration and regulation'.[54] There was
at this time no regional economic development agency, illustrating that
the move towards agriculture was also a move away from economic
development.

The pendulum swung back in 1965, when the Highlands and Islands
Development Board (HIDB, the predecessor of Highlands and Islands
Enterprise (HIE)) was established. The objective of the HIDB was to
promote economic development in the Highlands and Islands, and this

[52] 'Final Report of the Committee of Inquiry on Crofting', p. 14; J. Hunter, *The
Claim of Crofting: the Scottish Highlands and Islands 1930–1990* (Edinburgh:
Mainstream, 1991).
[53] 'Report of the Commission of Inquiry into Crofting Conditions', chapter 1,
p. 7.
[54] 'Final Report of the Committee of Inquiry on Crofting', p. 14, paragraph 2.1.3.

objective was to be enhanced by the rights to acquire their crofts which crofters were given by the 1976 Act. The theory behind that, Shucksmith notes, was that to obtain the loans necessary for diversification, crofters required to own their land. The argument 'has raged ever since between those who argue that this is necessary to allow crofters to diversify their enterprises and those who see this as creating a free market in crofts which will lead to the demise of crofting'.[55]

It is now common knowledge (not to mention settled law) that in order to obtain commercial loans on croft land, the land must be *both* decrofted (removed from the scope of the crofting Acts) *and* purchased by the crofter. The decrofting element invariably requires planning per-mission[56] to be obtained before an application will be seriously consid-ered. The consequences are that (1) only diversified uses which require planning permission are assisted by the 1976 rights, thus a myriad of uses which do not require planning permission cannot be facilitated by way of acquiring the landlord's interest in a croft; and (2) land is not merely purchased by the crofter but also removed entirely from the crofting system, which in turn contributes to the conflict (explained later in this chapter) experienced by the Crofting Commission between the need to consider population retention (enhanced by a crofter successfully diversifying and thus being able to remain on their croft) and the need to consider the effect of land being removed from the crofting system (not enhanced because land is being decrofted). Although the right to purchase may have been originally justified by the need for crofters to raise finance to diversify, the reality is that the right to purchase alone does not meet this objective effectively.

An indication that economic development has, since 1965, remained king, was the transfer (by administrative function) in February 2010 of the Commission's development function to Highlands and Islands Enterprise.[57] This is widely accepted not to have been a productive reform, and there have been calls for it to be reversed. However, despite the aforementioned transfer to HIE, the Commission still has statutory functions, in addition to (1) regulating and (2) reorganising crofting, of (3) promoting the interests of crofting and (4) keeping under review

[55] Ibid., p. 15, paragraph 2.1.4.

[56] Town and Country Planning (Scotland) Act 1997 and the Planning etc (Scotland) Act 2006. See also R. McMaster, A. Prior and J. Watchman, *Scottish Planning Law* (Haywards Heath: Bloomsbury Professional, 2013).

[57] The transfer was underpinned by section 2 of the Crofting Reform (Scotland) Act 2010, which repealed the old section 1(2), and replaced it with a new section 1(2).

matters relating to crofting. It must be tricky for the Commission to fulfil these functions whilst not having any development function per se (nor indeed the resources relating thereto). It must also be challenging for the Commission to fulfil two objectives which, on the face of it, are in direct conflict with each other. The Commission is currently required[58] to have regard, in the exercising of their functions, to (a) the desirability of supporting population retention, and (b) the impact of changes to the overall area of land held in crofting tenure on the sustainability of crofting.

In practical terms, this is a dilemma between, on the one hand, allowing decrofting of land to facilitate housebuilding, and on the other hand, protecting crofting land and retaining it as such, rather than as development land.[59] It has often been suggested that common grazings land can and should be used for building, but the qualities which make land attractive for development are the same qualities which make it for good agricultural land: good drainage, reasonably flat topography and good access to roads and services. Doubtless, many areas of common grazing land could be developed, but there will be a cost to that, and if there is a choice then the more financially attractive route will be followed. The current conflict between the Commission's objectives are therefore reflective of the long-standing historical conflict between prioritising agricultural use on the one hand, or economic development on the other hand.

If the historical conflict between agricultural use versus diversification and economic development has led us to the current impasse, then perhaps history can also teach us the value of balance and compromise. It is not necessary for the crofting system to be solely focused on either of those objectives to the exclusion of the other, but if both objectives *are* to be fulfilled, then the legal and funding frameworks need to change, and must change in ways which complement each other. It is possible to put a croft to either agricultural use or a diversified use (currently described as 'another purposeful use'.)[60] However, the only crofting-specific land-use funding which is available is for agricultural use. The Crofting Counties Agricultural Grant Scheme (CCAGS) is valued by

[58] 1993 Act, section 1(2A)(a).

[59] See N. King, 'MacGillivray v Crofting Commission – were the 2010 changes to the decrofting process necessary?' *Juridical Review* (2017), pp. 107–12, for comparison of pre and post 2010 provisions.

[60] 1993 Act, section 5C(2)(a)(ii) for tenant crofters and section 19C(2)(c)(ii) for owner-occupier crofters.

crofters, yet not fully utilised, and its future is under threat as a result. There is currently no crofting-specific funding for diversified uses.

The Shucksmith Commission noted that between 1982 and 2007, on holdings of less than 30 hectares in the crofting counties, the area of cropped land fell by 49 per cent, the area planted for oats fell by 83 per cent, barley by 46 per cent, the area planted for potatoes fell by 79 per cent, and stock feeding crops by 51 per cent. On the other hand, the land being used for grazing increased by 47 per cent, and for mowing by 24 per cent.[61] The Report goes on to explain that 'the agricultural trends described . . . have been driven by changes in agricultural subsidies and grants, fluctuating exchange rates and a fall in prices'.[62] If the support system and the legal framework complemented each other more effectively than they do at present, and were both designed to fulfil a specific set of non-contradictory objectives, the crofting system could arguably offer greatly enhanced benefits to both crofters and also the wider community.

The impossibility of purchase

According to the Crofting Commission's figures,[63] 87 per cent of crofters are aged 41 years or above, with only 10 per cent in the 21–40 age range. One factor undoubtedly affecting this statistic is that crofts on the open market (whether owned or tenanted) are exclusively available to cash purchasers. Even agricultural lenders will not lend on croft land or croft tenancies. Whilst there are (theoretically) support mechanisms available to those who already own or tenant a croft, the only support mechanisms[64] available to assist in purchasing the land itself are hopelessly oversubscribed and are withdrawn for 2018/2019. Furthermore, these schemes are not crofting-specific. To purchase a croft, even of modest size and productivity, without any improvements or planning permission and not particularly close to a population centre, might costs tens of thousands of pounds. If planning permission has been obtained, then the price will escalate. It is possible that these values are inflated

[61] 'Final Report of the Committee of Inquiry on Crofting', p. 31, paragraph 3.1.4.
[62] Ibid., p. 33, paragraph 3.2.1.
[63] Available at <http://www.crofting.scotland.gov.uk/facts-and-figures> (accessed 14 March 2019).
[64] Young Farmers Start-Up Grant Scheme and New Entrants Start-Up Scheme, detailed at <https://www.ruralpayments.org/publicsite/futures/topics/all-schemes/new-entrants/young-farmers-and-new-entrants-start-up-grant-schemes/> (last accessed 28 March 2019).

by the possibility of development introduced by the 1976 Act. The Shucksmith Committee proposed measures to encourage commercial lenders to provide conventional mortgages to allow prospective crofters to purchase land. They proposed (1) a map-based Crofting Register to be introduced to establish boundaries in order to give lenders a clear idea of what they were lending on, and (2) that the Registration of Leases (Scotland) Act 1857 should be amended so that a crofting lease could be registered, thus making it possible to grant a standard security against it.

No headway seems to have been possible in relation to the funding element, despite a 2009 Scottish Government consultation paper which accepted, in general terms, that crofters should be able to obtain loan finance without having to decroft an area of land to do so. The Scottish Government also agreed to consult with the Scottish Committee of Clearing Bankers and the Council of Mortgage Lenders with a view to moving forward with the idea of obtaining private sector mortgages over croft land, but the results of those discussions (if they took place) were not made public. Reaction to the consultation paper was generally negative, and ultimately, when the draft Crofting Reform (Scotland) Bill 2009 was published, the mortgage provisions had been dropped. A common concern seemed to be that lenders simply would not agree to lend, there being simply too many variables to satisfy the lender's understandable requirement for certainty in all matters.[65] Until the market in crofts no longer requires a lump cash sum, the age demographic will not improve. Healthy communities need people of all ages, backgrounds and abilities, and the lack of loans means that as land prices rise and wages continue to stagnate, there will be a decreasing number of young people entering communities in crofting areas.

Professor Shucksmith and his Committee noted that although the population of the Highlands and Islands has generally grown since the 1960s, particularly between 2001 and 2006 when there was an increase of 1.7 per cent across the region (more than three times that of Scotland as a whole), the growth is spread unevenly, and those moving into the area tend to be older.[66] Furthermore, the Report noted[67] that in a survey of

---

[65] On this point, in his 2012 paper, MacLean remarked, 'I was deeply sceptical about this even before the turmoil in the banking world which has seen such a sharp brake being applied to lending, and I remain to be convinced that prudent lenders will be prepared to advance significant sums on the strength of such a dubious security.' *Recent Developments in Crofting Law*, paragraph 32.

[66] 'Final Report of the Committee of Inquiry on Crofting', p. 17, paragraph 2.2.3.

[67] Ibid., p. 20, paragraph 2.4.4.

crofters and non-crofters, the most important characteristic in making a thriving crofting community was said to be having younger crofters.

Young people generally require loans to enable them to purchase crofts. If the Scottish Government is serious about encouraging young people into crofting, then creative solutions must be engineered to open up the market in crofts and croft tenancies. The Scottish Government has recently announced,[68] as part of its crofting reform package, a dedicated new entrant scheme for crofters, which is a very welcome development indeed. However, the detail of that is not yet clear, and that is where the devil can usually be found.

CONCLUSION

The system of crofting desperately needs direction and reform. Historically, the focus has moved between agricultural production and diversification for economic development. There is no need necessarily for a focus on one to the exclusion of the other, and it is entirely possible for both to be supported and encouraged. The Shucksmith Committee felt that 'crofting is about so much more than simply agriculture'.[69] The Committee carried out a survey which found that on average, 70 per cent of the average crofting household income came from non-croft sources.[70] Of course, this figure includes those who make much more than that from their crofts, and those who make nothing at all, but it does suggest that ongoing agricultural support *must* be coupled with wider economic development to ensure the availability of employment in crofting areas. However, there remains a strong cultural attachment to crofting as an agricultural activity. Furthermore, as the United Kingdom prepares to leave the European Union, there is more of a focus on domestic food production, to which the crofting system contributes generously. Agriculture is likely, therefore, to remain at the heart of the crofting system, together with the many diversified uses which are now possible.

In whatever ways crofts are utilised, there is something more elemental which is a common experience amongst many crofters and their families, to do with a connection to the land and landscape, as well as

---

[68] Available at <https://blogs.gov.scot/rural-environment/2018/04/12/crofting-update/> (last accessed 14 March 2019).

[69] 'Final Report of the Committee of Inquiry on Crofting', p. 41, paragraph 3.4.1.

[70] Ibid., p. 41, paragraph 3.4.1.

a cultural, environmental and linguistic heritage. For all its focus on agriculture, the Taylor Committee recognised this too, and

> thought it right, however, to record our unanimous conviction, founded on personal knowledge and on the evidence we have received, that in the national interest the maintenance of these communities is desirable, because they embody a free and independent way of life which is worth preserving for its own intrinsic quality.[71]

That free and independent way of life, whether sustained by agriculture or diversification, is currently at risk as a result of the many and varied deficiencies of the legal and financial framework of the crofting system. The lack of clarity around why *specifically* governments should support crofting, the conflicting functions of the regulator and objectives of the legislation, the inaccessibility of crofts to all but cash purchasers, all of these factors contribute to the failure of the system, but it is the complex condition of the legislation and the failures of successive governments to properly reform it, which is the greatest threat of all.

---

[71] 'Report of the Commission of Inquiry into Crofting Conditions', p. 9, paragraph 12.

13

Agricultural Tenancy Legislation and Public Policy Considerations in Scotland

Hamish Lean

AGRICULTURAL TENANCIES HAVE LONG played an important part in the fabric of rural Scotland. According to the results from the Scottish Government's June 2018 Scottish Agricultural Census, the total area of land in Scotland used for agriculture was 6.2 million hectares. Of that total, 1.28 million hectares was rented.[1] The aim of this chapter is to review the part that public policy considerations have had to play in the development of agricultural tenancy law in Scotland. It is useful to set out the historical context, albeit briefly, before doing so.

One starting point for a legal history of agricultural tenancies in Scotland might be an Act of the Scottish Parliament promulgated in the fifteenth century. The Leases Act 1449 is still current law. It provides that:

> it is ordanit for the sauftie and fauour of the pure pepil that labouris the grunde that thai and al vthiris that has takyn or sal tak landis in tym to cum fra lordis and has termes and yeris thereof that suppose the lordis sel or analy thai landis that the takaris sall remayn with thare takis on to the ische of thare termes quhais handis at euir thai landis cum to for sic lik male as thai tuk thaim of befoir.

Essentially, the Act protects tenants under existing leases from being forced to give up vacant possession simply because the original landlord has sold or transferred ownership of the land to a third party.[2] Although

---

[1] Scottish Government, Results from the June 2018 Scottish Agricultural Census, available at <https://www.gov.scot/publications/results-june-2018-scottish-agricultural-census/> (last accessed 28 March 2019).

[2] For a more detailed discussion in a wider historical context see Paul J. Du Plessis, 'Historical evolution of the maxim "sale breaks hire"' in Cornelius van der Merwe and Alain-Laurent Verbeke (eds), *Time-Limited Interest in Land – The Common Core of European Private Law* (Cambridge: Cambridge University Press, 2012), pp. 19–32 and the discussion in that book under the heading 'Case 2: What

the following discussion reviews historical developments that are more recent in nature, the legal regulation of relations between landowners and tenants of land for agricultural purposes has been with us in Scotland for a very long time indeed.

In the great era of agricultural improvement during the eighteenth century, the granting of agricultural tenancies, with suitable obligations on the part of the tenant concerning cultivation and fixed equipment, was a deliberate policy measure on the part of landed estate proprietors to promote and encourage improvements.[3] The duke of Buccleuch, for example, issued a general declaration in 1768 to the tenants of his south country estates. It made clear that tenants who made 'improvements on their let farms by building, inclosing, or other ways cultivating their possessions' would be allowed to hold their leases upon reasonable terms and for such period of years that would be sufficient not only to indemnify them of the expenses they incurred in carrying out works of improvement on the farm 'but to reward their industry for improving and cultivating, according to the worth and extent thereof'.[4] The duke further provided that if any tenants so improving were to be removed or dispossessed from any cause whatsoever before they had been indemnified by the length of their possession, the succeeding tenant would be obliged to compensate them to an amount decided by mutually chosen arbiters. This was an early attempt to give confidence to agricultural tenants to invest in the productivity of the let farm, not only for their own benefit but also for the benefit of the estate. It did so by encouraging them to make the investment in the knowledge that either they would be in occupation for a sufficient length of time to recoup the value of their investment or they would be entitled to be compensated by the incoming tenant if forced to give up possession before then. The general declaration also sought to reassure prospective tenants that they would not be charged excessive rents.

The agricultural tenant's desire for security of tenure over a reasonable period of time, to receive compensation for their own investment on the let farm and to pay an economic rent are themes that we see appearing repeatedly over the following 250 years. These tenants were

happens if land subject to a time-limited interest is conveyed to a third party', with Scotland discussed at pp. 149–52. The Scottish contributor to this comparative book was Peter Webster.

  [3] See B. Bonnyman, *The Third Duke of Buccleuch and Adam Smith: Estate Management and Improvement in Enlightenment Scotland* (Edinburgh: Edinburgh University Press, 2014).

  [4] Quoted in Bonnyman, *The Third Duke of Buccleuch and Adam Smith*, pp. 74–5.

not subsistence farmers but had access to capital to invest on the farm and they expected to make a profit from that investment. As we have seen, some landed estates recognised the need to incentivise their tenants whilst of course protecting their own interests and increasing the value of their own possessions. In many ways, the benefit to the tenant was incidental to the landlord's principal aim, which was the improvement of the productivity, profitability and capital value of the estate.

Agricultural tenancies during and after the age of improvement remained a matter of private contract between landlord and tenant, the terms reflecting the relative bargaining strengths of the parties. It remained the case that most farmers were tenants on large landed estates. The great agricultural depression of the last quarter of the nineteenth century, however, led to political pressure for legislative intervention to protect the lot of the tenant farmer. Although the Corn Laws had been repealed in 1846, there was no immediate drop in grain prices despite many commentators at the time predicting the ruin of British agriculture. It was not until the end of the American Civil War, the opening up of the American prairies to agricultural cultivation and the vast increase in imported grain into the United Kingdom that for domestic farmers prices for grain began to fall. The price of wheat dropped by approximately 50 per cent in the period between 1867 and 1898.[5] The impact on farming was dramatic. For example, during that period, rents on large farms in Banffshire fell by up to 36 per cent and in Moray by at least 25 per cent.[6] Ironically, the rental values of much smaller subsistence farms retained their value. One of the reasons was the availability of family labour at little or no cost as compared to the substantial labour costs of larger farms, which required a large workforce.

The resulting political pressure, from what Carter has described as the class of capitalist farmers, achieved mainly through the efforts of the Liberal Party, resulted in a series of Acts of Parliament in the 1880s that greatly ameliorated the position of such farmers.[7] Firstly, the tenant farmer gained the protection of the Ground Game Act 1880, which allowed the tenant to control rabbits and game on the farm. Secondly, the Hypothec Abolition (Scotland) Act 1880 abolished the landlord's right of hypothec for the rent of land let exceeding two acres in extent.

[5] T. W. Fletcher, 'The Great Depression of English Agriculture 1875–1896' in P. J. Perry (ed.), *British Agriculture 1975–1914* (London: Methuen, 1973), pp. 30–55.

[6] See Ian Carter, *Farm Life in Northeast Scotland, 1840–1914: The Poor Man's Country* (Edinburgh: John Donald, 1979), p. 90.

[7] Carter, *Farm Life in Northeast Scotland, 1840–1914*, p. 90.

Prior to the Act coming into force a landlord was entitled to use this security right to seize all or any of the tenant's assets as security for unpaid rent in a way which could bring about the immediate ruin of the tenant. Thirdly, the Agricultural Holdings (Scotland) Act 1883 introduced a statutory right for the first time to tenant farmers to be compensated for their improvements on the let farm. The 1883 Act also allowed the tenant to remove the tenant's fixtures at the end of the tenancy and introduced a right of bequest on the part of the tenant to family members, subject to a right of reasonable objection by the landlord.

Parliament had recognised that the conduct of farming was a matter of crucial national importance and that legislative intervention in the private contracts of agricultural landlords and tenants was desirable and appropriate in the national interest. This was apparent from the outset. In a review of the legislation in the case of *Earl of Galloway* v. *M'Clelland*,[8] Lord Salvesen explicitly pointed out that the legislation was 'really in the interests of both landlord and tenant, as well as of the community at large, to whose advantage it is that the arable land of Scotland shall be cultivated to the best advantage'.[9] As we shall see, it is this public policy consideration that has driven agricultural tenancy legislation ever since.

---

[8] *Galloway (Earl of)* v. *McClelland*, 1915 SC 1062.

[9] This quote features in a discussion of the Agricultural Holdings (Scotland) Act 1908, a statute which consolidated and built upon the earlier legislation. This had the effect removing the deterrent to invest in improving a holding in a way that (at common law) would primarily benefit the landlord, by offering compensation to the tenant in appropriate circumstances. The fuller quote is as follows: 'While the Act . . . innovated on the common law it did so without inflicting any injustice on either party. The tenant was encouraged to make beneficial expenditure on the farm by the circumstance that so far as it constituted an improvement to the incoming tenant he should receive the full value of such improvement; while the landlord was not prejudiced by having to pay (to the extent to which he derived benefit) for something which he received through expenditure which the tenant was under no obligation to make, and in the ordinary case would not have made. While the Act therefore constituted an interference with freedom of contract in certain respects it did not, as I think, infringe any principle of equity, but was really in the interests of both landlord and tenant as well as of the community at large, to whose advantage it is that the arable land of Scotland shall be cultivated to the best advantage.'

A GRADUAL INCREASE IN THE TENANT'S STATUTORY PROTECTION

Additional legislation over the following sixty years further enhanced the rights of the agricultural tenant. This included the Agricultural Holdings (Scotland) Act 1908, which introduced freedom of cropping and disposal of produce, a right to compensation for damage to crops by game, a right to call for the making of a record of condition of the fixed equipment on the holding and a right to compensation for disturbance where the tenancy was terminated unreasonably. The jurisdiction of the Scottish Land Court was extended to disputes between agricultural landlords and tenants in 1931 by Part II of the Small Landholders and Agricultural Holdings (Scotland) Act 1931.

As a matter of clear public policy in the public interest, at the outset of the Second World War, special measures under the Emergency Powers (Defence) Acts of 1939 and 1940 were introduced. Where a landowner had purchased a farm after the outbreak of the war, a notice to quit served on an agricultural tenant could not be acted upon without ministerial consent (for notices which would be effective after the end of 1941).

At the end of the war and at a time when food rationing was still in place, the then Labour government introduced the Agriculture (Scotland) Act 1948 with retrospective effect whereby, except in very limited circumstances, a notice to quit an agricultural holding could not be acted upon by the landlord if the tenant served a counter notice requiring that the Land Court gave consent to the operation of the notice to quit. The purpose was to ensure continuity of production as part of a wider effort to create an efficient agricultural sector.[10] The 1948 Act and previous agricultural holdings Acts were then consolidated in the Agricultural Holdings (Scotland) Act 1949. The radical nature of the introduction of security of tenure should not be underestimated, cutting across as it did with retrospective effect many contractual relationships still current when the Act came into force and where the landlord had fully expected to be able to recover vacant possession at the end of the tenancy. In many ways it might be said that this change has coloured landlord and tenant relationships ever since. Many tenancies granted prior to 1948 for fixed periods became secure tenancies in the tenant's favour. Wide-ranging rights of succession were granted to such tenancies. Many of those tenancies continue to exist, the tenancy being inherited

[10] See Lord Gill, *Agricultural Tenancies*, 4th edn (Edinburgh: W. Green, 2017).

by succeeding generations within the same family. A lease of land for grazing or mowing for a period of less than a year however did not attract the protection of the Acts and a tenant in such a tenancy did not acquire security of tenure. Grazing and mowing leases have continued to be exempt from the protection of the legislation to the current day.

A series of Acts followed after 1949 further regulating amongst other things inheritance of tenancies and rent reviews. These Acts and the 1949 Act were consolidated in the Agricultural Holdings (Scotland) Act 1991 and agricultural tenancies where the tenant enjoys security of tenure are usually referred to as traditional tenancies or 1991 Act tenancies. As a result of the introduction of security of tenure, agricultural tenancies became increasingly litigious. Given that, for most practical purposes, an agricultural tenant had security of tenure for the whole of the tenant's life and generous opportunities to transfer the tenancy after death, so potentially locking up a farm within a tenancy for the foreseeable future, landlords became increasingly willing to take opportunities to terminate such tenancies.

By the early 1970s, an effective means of avoiding security of tenure had been devised. This was the limited partnership tenancy. In Scots law a partnership is a separate legal person distinct from the individual partners who enter into it.[11] A limited partnership formed in accordance with the provisions of the Limited Partnerships Act 1907 protects the limited partner from joint and several liability for the debts of the partnership except for the amount of the limited partner's original capital contribution, which could be a relatively nominal sum. Accordingly, a landlord or his nominee acting as the limited partner entered into a limited partnership with a farmer who became the general partner. A lease was then granted to the limited partnership. By controlling the duration of the limited partnership, the landlord was able to control the duration of the tenancy. The lease was otherwise subject to the provisions of the 1991 Act but could not survive the termination of the limited partnership. Such tenancies became the predominant means of letting out agricultural land in Scotland and it became rare to see a tenancy granted to an individual tenant. The limited partnership tenancy had become a de facto fixed duration tenancy and some general partners regarded them as a device or sham to avoid security of tenure under the 1991 Act.

One such general partner challenged the mechanism unsuccessfully

---

[11] Partnership Act 1890, section 4(2).

in Court. In the case of *MacFarlane* v. *Falfield Investments Ltd*,[12] the Court held that the intention of Parliament was that it was in the public interest that tenants of agricultural holdings should have the degree of security of tenure which the statutory provisions secured for them, but the arrangement in this case did not constitute an attempt to contract out of the statutory security of tenure provisions, for in each instance the tenant was a limited partnership and, so long as the lease endured, the limited partnership was entitled to the statutory protection afforded by the Act.

LEGISLATION UNDER THE SCOTTISH PARLIAMENT

Fixed duration tenancies were introduced in Scotland by the Agricultural Holdings (Scotland) Act 2003.[13] This was the first intervention by the new Scottish Parliament into agricultural tenancy law. The 2003 Act introduced the short limited duration tenancy of up to a maximum of five years and the limited duration tenancy of a minimum of fifteen years, later reduced to ten years.[14] The Act was designed to encourage landlords to let out land. It also introduced reforms to existing secure tenancies including the introduction of a right of assignation to a family member, the removal of clauses requiring the tenant to reside personally on the holding and the introduction of a right to diversify away from agricultural activity should the tenant so wish.[15] Claiming compensation for improvements was made easier and tenants were given a right to opt out of arrangements where they had agreed to take on the landlord's renewing obligations in respect of fixed equipment. Part 2 of the Act also introduced a pre-emptive right to buy for secure tenants whereby subject to the registration of an interest in the Agricultural Tenants Register, which is part of the Register of Community Interests in Land, the landlord could not take steps to sell the farm without first of all giving the tenant an opportunity to buy it.

The 2003 Act also made important changes in respect of limited partnership tenancies. As the Agricultural Holdings Bill progressed through the Scottish Parliament there was lobbying from a group of

[12] 1998 SC 14.

[13] For detailed examination of the background to the introduction of the Act, see Sam Read-Norrie, 'Agricultural Tenancies: Making Room for Generation Y – Will Only the Land Endure?' *Aberdeen Student Law Review*, 7 (2017), pp. 27–55.

[14] Public Services Reform (Agricultural Holdings (Scotland) Order 2011 (SS1 2011/232)).

[15] Agricultural Holdings (Scotland) Act 2003, sections 37–43.

agricultural tenants who formed the Scottish Tenant Farmers Action Group[16] seeking the introduction of an absolute right to buy for existing agriculture tenants including general partners in limited partnership tenancies.[17] Ultimately, these efforts were unsuccessful but as the Bill was reaching its final stages in the Scottish Parliament many landlords served notices terminating limited partnership tenancies regardless of the fact that the limited partnership itself might have a considerable time yet to run before its expiry. These notices were motivated by fears of the introduction of an absolute right to buy. Notoriously, on the night of 3 February 2003, estate managers up and down the length of Scotland were visiting general partners in limited partnership tenancies, serving them with termination notices.[18] As a result, a late amendment was made to the Bill by introducing what would become sections 72 and 73 of the 2003 Act to provide that where a general partner received a notice terminating the limited partnership between September 2002 and July 2003, the purpose of which was to deprive the general partner from acquiring rights under the 2003 Act, the general partner was entitled to serve a notice which would convert them into a fully secure agricultural tenant in their own right. A property owner could avoid this consequence if he could prove to the Land Court's satisfaction that the notice terminating the limited partnership was served for a reason other than to deprive the general partner of rights under the Act. General partners who received termination notices after September 2003 were given substantially less protection. By serving a counter notice, they too could become tenants in their own right but landlords were given the right to terminate that tenancy, effectively on three years' notice.[19]

These specific provisions gave rise to important constitutional questions about the legislative competence of the Scottish Parliament. The Parliament derives its legislative authority from the Scotland Act 1998, an act of the Westminster Parliament. The 1998 Act constrains the powers of the Scottish Parliament by inhibiting it from acting in a manner incompatible with the European Convention on Human Rights

---

[16] See now the website of the Scottish Tenant Farmers Association, which notes, 'The STFA has evolved from the Scottish Tenant Farmers Action Group which was formed in 2001 in response to the Scottish Executive's tenancy reform proposals . . .' <http://www.tfascotland.org.uk/> (last accessed 28 March 2019).

[17] Read-Norrie, 'Making room for Generation Y', p. 33.

[18] Read-Norrie, 'Making room for Generation Y', p. 37.

[19] For an overview of the parliamentary process and the circumstances of it, see Malcolm M. Combe, 'Human rights, limited competence and limited partnerships: *Salvesen v. Riddell*', *Scots Law Times (News)* (2012), pp. 193–200 at p. 194.

or European Union law (in the latter case, for at least as long as the United Kingdom remains a member of the EU).[20] In the case of *Salvesen* v. *Riddell*, an agricultural landlord, Salvesen, appealed against a decision of the Scottish Land Court declaring that a general partner in a limited partnership tenancy had become a fully secure 1991 Act tenant by virtue of a 3 February 2003 limited partnership termination notice and subsequent counter notice. The Court of Session, acting as the appeal court from the Land Court, upheld the landlord's appeal that the relevant provisions of the 2003 Act, by breaching the landlord's ECHR rights in respect of property, were outwith the legislative competence of the Scottish Parliament.[21]

The Scottish Government subsequently appealed that decision to the United Kingdom Supreme Court. In its decision,[22] the Supreme Court found that the relevant provisions within the 2003 Act were excessive in their effect and that they were also arbitrary. In a detailed discussion of the proper application of the European Convention of Human Rights, the Court commented that not every infringement of a right under the Convention will result in a breach of the Convention and that Parliament has a broad area of discretion in the exercise of its judgement as to social and economic policy when pursuing a legitimate aim in the general interest. As the Court put it, the question to be answered was whether the general interest demands in the case of *Salvesen* v. *Riddell* were sufficiently strong to justify the extent of the prejudice suffered by Salvesen. Ultimately, the Supreme Court found that the justification did not exist because of the arbitrary treatment of landlords who had served termination notices between 16 September 2002 and 1 July 2003 compared with landlords who had served notices after that date.[23] In the latter case, landlords were able to secure vacant possession of the farm, albeit three years after the end of the limited partnership whereas in the former case, landlords were at risk of creating a fully secure tenancy in favour of the general partner capable of being inherited by succeeding generations without any prospect of being able to recover possession.

As a result of a direction by the Supreme Court, the Scottish Government introduced the Agricultural Holdings (Scotland) Act 2003 Remedial Order 2014.[24] This brought those general partners who had

---

[20] See generally Frankie McCarthy's chapter in this volume.
[21] *Salvesen* v. *Riddell* [2012] CSIH 26.
[22] *Salvesen* v. *Riddell* [2013] UKSC 22, paragraphs 36–42.
[23] See McCarthy, this volume, page 000.
[24] SSI 2014/98.

been served notices during the relevant period back into the double
notice procedure.[25] Many of those people, some of whom who had
thought that they were now secure tenants received notices of removal
and some have been forced to vacate their holdings. This effect on the
erstwhile tenants occasioned further (unsuccessful) litigation on human
rights grounds, as analysed elsewhere in this volume.[26]

HOLDING BACK THE TIDE

There was a slow but steady take-up of the new forms of limited duration tenancy after their introduction in 2003 while the number of secure
tenancies continued to decline.[27] Many of those secure tenancies were
sold to the sitting tenant at a discount. Some tenancies were given up
and were returned to the landlord either to be let out on a limited duration basis or to be farmed in hand by the landlord or made subject to
contract farming agreements. Secure tenancies remained controversial.
In particular rent reviews were the subject of much dissatisfaction. Many
agricultural rents had remained static since the mid 1990s but a spike
in commodity prices in 2007 provoked a rash of rent review notices.
By the time those rent reviews were taking place in 2008 commodity
prices had declined but the cost of inputs had increased. There was
much confusion about the application of the open-market test provided
for in the 1991 Act where in fact no open market had existed in respect

[25] Much has been written about the saga, including the following by M. M.
Combe: 'Human rights, limited competence and limited partnerships: *Salvesen* v.
Riddell' *Scots Law Times (News)* (2012), pp. 193–200; 'Peaceful enjoyment of
farmland at the Supreme Court', *Scots Law Times (News)* (2013), pp. 201–3; and
'Remedial works in agricultural holdings', *Scots Law Times (News)* (2014), pp. 70–1
and by D. J. Carr: 'Not law' *Edinburgh Law Review*, 16 (2012), pp. 410–14; and
'Not law (but not yet effectively not law)', *Edinburgh Law Review*, 17 (2013),
pp. 370–6.

[26] See F. McCarthy, Chapter 9 in this volume. See also M. M. Combe, 'Human
rights and limited partnership tenancies, again', *Scots Law Times (News)* (2017),
pp. 79–82; K. Shields, '*McMaster* v. *Scottish Ministers* – the tenant farmers case',
Juridical Review 2017, pp. 113–21; and D. S. K. Maxwell, 'Mistaken rights to property, agricultural tenancies, and good governance: *McMaster* v. *Scottish Ministers*',
Journal of Planning and Environment Law, 10 (2018), pp. 1076–89.

[27] Scottish Government, Results from the June 2016 Scottish Agricultural
Census, available at <https://www.gov.scot/binaries/content/documents/govscot/
publications/statistics/2016/10/results-june-2016-scottish-agriculture-census/docu
ments/00508460-pdf/00508460-pdf/govscot%3Adocument/00508460.pdf>   (last
accessed 28 March 2019).

of such tenancies for at least forty years. Some very high-profile Land Court cases took place, conducted at great expense to both landlord and tenant.[28] There was concern about the lack of agricultural land being made available for let and the lack of opportunities for new entrants into the industry.

It was against this background that the Scottish Government established the Agricultural Holdings Legislation Review Group which reported in 2015.[29] Chaired by the then Cabinet Secretary Richard Lochhead, it was made up of a number of agricultural lawyers, an academic and a working farmer.[30] The Group's Report formed the basis of Part 10 of the Land Reform (Scotland) Act 2016.[31] The remit of the Group was to determine what legislative, policy and fiscal changes were required to enable the achievement of the Scottish Government's vision of a Scottish tenant farming sector that is dynamic, getting the best from the land and the people farming it and providing opportunities for new entrants forming part of a sustainable future for Scottish farming. The Report concluded that if the tenanted sector was to thrive and grow then 'while we need to hold on as far as possible to the existing supply of secure 1991 Act tenancies for the time being, we must substantially increase the supply of new long term limited duration tenancy type vehicles'. On one view, Part 10 of the 2016 Act can be seen as further enhancing the rights of existing secure tenants whilst loosening regulation in relation to fixed duration tenancies.

THE 2016 REFORMS – AN OVERVIEW

A key innovation of the 2016 Act (in Part 2 of the legislation) was the establishment of the Scottish Land Commission and the creation the new office of Tenant Farming Commissioner. The Commissioner is obliged to exercise his or her functions with a view to encouraging good relationships between landlords and tenants of agricultural holdings.

---

[28] *Morrison-Low* v. *Paterson's Executors* [2012] CSIH 10; *Capital Investment Corporation of Montreal Ltd* v. *Elliot*, 2014 SLCR 19.

[29] Scottish Government, *Review of Agricultural Holdings Legislation Final Report* (Edinburgh, 2015), available at <https://www.webarchive.org.uk/wayback/archive/20170701074158/www.gov.scot/Publications/2015/01/5605> (last accessed 28 March 2019).

[30] The writer was one of the members of the Group.

[31] For a more detailed examination of the background to the introduction of the 2016 Act see Read-Norrie, 'Making room for Generation Y', pp. 44–54.

Those functions include preparing Codes of Practice[32] and enquiring into breaches. The Commissioner has certain enforcement powers[33] with regard to failure to cooperate with an inquiry, including the ability to impose a fine, but has no power to impose a sanction on any party should it be established that in fact they were in breach. The Scottish Ministers must review the Commissioner's functions before the end of three years after the Commissioner is established, and government is given the power to amend, remove or confer new functions on the Tenant Farming Commissioner.

Returning to Part 10 of the 2016 Act, where the substantive amendments to agricultural tenancy law reside, Chapter 5 changes the basis for rent review in respect of 1991 Act tenancies so that the focus shifts from the open-market test to one where the productive capacity of the holding is given prominence but also takes into account the potential rental value of surplus housing and diversified activities on the holding. Chapter 3 provides that there will no longer be a requirement for secure tenants to register their pre-emptive right so that it arises automatically should the landlord take steps to sell all or part of the farm. Chapter 8 introduces a time-limited amnesty, due to expire on the 13 June 2020, for tenant's improvements whereby a tenant can ensure that compensation can be obtained at the end of the tenancy for improvements which have been carried out without the necessary advance notice procedures having been followed. Chapter 9 introduces a right to object to a landlord's proposed improvement. Chapter 6 substantially expands succession and inheritance rights for both 1991 Act tenancies and fixed duration tenancies. The provisions are complex but suffice to say that the expansion of the range of eligible family members who are entitled to inherit to include the tenant's parents, siblings, descendants and spouses and civil partners of siblings and descendants means that in most cases, should the family desire, a secure tenancy will remain within the tenant's family for the foreseeable future.

In order to encourage elderly tenants to retire and to allow an opportunity for new entrants to acquire an agricultural tenancy, the Agricultural Holdings Legislation Review Group recommended that a tenant of a secure 1991 Act tenancy should be allowed to convert the tenancy into a modern limited duration tenancy with a term of thirty-five years and then be given the right to transfer that agricultural

---

[32] Codes of practice and related guidance can be found online: <https://landcommission.gov.scot/tenant-farming/codes-of-practice/> (last accessed 28 March 2019).

[33] Land Reform (Scotland) Act 2016, sections 29–35.

tenancy on the open market to any suitably qualified person for value. In one of the more controversial aspects of the 2016 Act, the Scottish Government departed from this recommendation and introduced, in Part 10, Chapter 7, a right of relinquishment for secure tenants. Under this procedure, a secure 1991 Act tenant can offer to sell the tenancy back to the landlord and if the landlord chooses not to buy it, the tenant is then able to sell it for value on the open market as a secure tenancy to a new entrant or a progressing farmer. The Act sets out a valuation formula to assess the price which the landlord has to pay which is one half of the difference between the open-market vacant possession value of the farm and the value of the farm subject to the agricultural tenancy, disregarding the tenant's rights of assignation and succession, together with the value of the tenant's claims for compensation for improvements and the normal waygoing claims. These provisions have been met with hostility by landowners.[34]

Part 10, Chapter 4 provides that in certain circumstances where a landlord has failed to comply with their obligations under the tenancy the tenant has a right to apply to the Scottish Land Court for an order that the landlord sell the holding. The detailed provisions quite properly contain a number of protections for the landlord. The landlord must first have failed to remedy a material breach of his or her obligations despite having been ordered to do so by the Land Court or at arbitration. The Land Court may only make an order for sale if it is satisfied that the landlord has failed to comply with the award in a material regard and that the failure substantially and adversely affects the tenant's ability to farm the holding in accordance with the rules of good husbandry, that greater hardship would be caused by not making the order than by making it and that in all the circumstances it is appropriate.

Part 10, Chapter 1 introduces a modern limited duration tenancy with a minimum ten-year term and an optional break after five years where the lease is in favour of a new entrant and with significant freedom of contract in respect of rent review and fixed equipment obligations. Chapter 2 also introduces a modern full repairing limited duration tenancy where a tenant takes full responsibility for all repair, renewal and replacement of fixed equipment on the holding in return for a minimum term of thirty-five years and subject to a productive capacity test in respect of rent. The short limited duration tenancy introduced by the Agricultural Holdings (Scotland) Act 2003 survives unscathed. Grazing leases are still permissible.

---

[34] Read-Norrie, 'Making room for Generation Y', pp. 52–3.

At the time of writing, the new rules concerning rent review, relinquishment, forced sale on the part of the landlord, abolition of the need to register a pre-emptive right to buy and the introduction of full repairing limited duration tenancies have yet to be brought into force.

CONCLUSION

Public policy remains the driver behind agricultural tenancy legislation in Scotland, as it has been for almost 150 years. The main concern of the current legislature remains the continuing decline in tenanted land in Scotland.[35] However, commentators have been highly critical of the legislative measures which have been introduced. For example, a former Lord President of the Court of Session, Lord Gill, author of the leading textbook on agricultural tenancies in Scotland and formerly the pre-eminent member of the Scottish Bar acting in respect of agricultural tenancy disputes delivered a historical perspective on agricultural tenancy legislation in Scotland at the 2019 Annual General Meeting of the Scottish Agricultural Arbiters and Valuers Association.[36] He was highly critical of the piecemeal and reactive nature of the legislation which has taken place regulating Scottish agricultural tenancies since the statutory introduction of security of tenure in 1948. The legislation reacted to particular problems within the sector and did not necessarily take proper stock of the overall needs of the sector. It was akin to a doctor treating the symptoms but not the underlying cause of a debilitating illness. Critics have also deplored the complicated and fragmentary nature of the legislation. Those providing legal advice on agricultural tenancy law must have a comprehensive knowledge of the 1991 Act, the 2003 Act and the 2016 Act and the complicated interplay between all three pieces of legislation. The legislation requires urgent consolidation. The complicated nature of the legislation and its retrospective effect is itself a deterrent on the part of landlords who may wish to let out their land.

---

[35] A. McKee, L. A. Sutherland, J. Hopkins, S. Flanigan, and A. Rickett, 'Increasing the Availability of Farmland for New Entrants to Agriculture in Scotland' (Inverness: Scottish Land Commission, 2018), <https://landcommission.gov.scot/wp-content/uploads/2018/05/McKee-et-al.-Final-report-to-SLC-Increasing-land-availability-for-new-entrants-2.5.2018.pdf> (last accessed 28 March 2019).

[36] Alex Maule, 'Law lord calls for review of 2016 Land Reform Act', *The Courier*, 14 March 2019, <https://www.thecourier.co.uk/fp/business/farming/farming-news/848628/law-lord-calls-for-review-of-2016-land-reform-act/> (last accessed 28 March 2019).

It is likely that agricultural tenancy legislation in Scotland will continue to generate political controversy. Recent statutes have increased protections for tenants who have tenancies regulated by the 1991 Act whereas those tenants with fixed duration tenancies find there is an increasingly lighter regulatory touch, for example in respect of substantial freedom of contract for fixed equipment obligations and rent. The creation of the Scottish Parliament has introduced a new dynamic. It remains apparent however that government continues to regard legislative intervention in relations between agricultural landlords and tenants to be in in the public interest.

PART III

Policy

14

Planning and Rights: Are there Lessons for Town Planning We Can Borrow from Land Reform?

Robert G. Reid

TOWN PLANNING HAS BECOME accustomed to being a focus for significant criticism, but in recent years it has intensified.[1] From green belts
to the housing crisis and affordability, planning is seen as the problem or
the solution dependent upon whose perspective one views these issues
from. The financial crisis of 2008 and consequential housing crisis have
sparked many column inches suggesting that the planning system needs
further amendment. The Adam Smith Institute even suggested in 2016,
'Just blow up, repeal in their entirety, the Town and Country Planning
Acts. Job done.'[2] This chapter draws on a practitioner's eye-view to
consider the impact of land reform upon planning and whether issues
within planning (and housing) could be addressed by borrowing a leaf
from the land reform agenda in Scotland.

SEVENTY YEARS OF PLANNING – THE BACKGROUND

The Town and Country Planning Act 1947 and its sister Scottish statute
the Town and Country Planning (Scotland) Act 1947 form the basis
for town and country planning in the United Kingdom. The Scottish
and English versions of planning legislation formed a centrepiece of the

---

[1] See K. Barker, *Review of Housing Supply 2004* (Norwich: HMSO, 2004):
<https://webarchive.nationalarchives.gov.uk/+/http://www.hm-treasury.gov.uk/bar
ker_review_of_housing_supply_recommendations.htm> and K. Barker, *Housing:
Where is the Plan?* (London: London Publishing Partnership, 2004). See also P.
Cheshire, 'Turning houses into gold: the failure of British planning' in *CentrePiece*,
19:1 (2014), <http://cep.lse.ac.uk/pubs/download/cp421.pdf> (last accessed 18
March 2019).

[2] T. Worstall, 'Quite so, let's blow up the Town and Country Planning Acts',
Adam Smith Institute Blog, 2 May 2016, <https://www.adamsmith.org/blog/quite-
so-lets-blow-up-the-town-and-country-planning-acts> (last accessed 18 March
2019).

radical post-war Attlee government agenda which also brought us the New Towns Act 1946, the National Insurance Act 1946, the National Health Service Act 1946 and very many more. Seventy years later there is a growing tension between the original core purpose of planning, and an ever-increasing plethora of amending legislation, perhaps 'tinkering with' or 'tweaking' the planning system, beyond its capacity to deliver. One commentator recently expressed this point in the following terms: 'In pulling resources towards regulation, tick box exercises and additional duties, we may miss the potential that planning has to dream big, co-ordinate, and importantly to deliver.'[3]

In spite of this heated debate, the fundamental pillars of planning legislation, as set down in 1947, have remained an almost unchanged constant. These pillars are:

That planning is a democratic system
That planning is done in the public interest
That you need planning permission to develop
That decisions about planning should be made on the basis of a plan and
That there is a right of appeal should your proposals be refused permission.

That there has been so little variation in these fundamentals over that seventy-year period is not only remarkable but is also testament to the original vision of the radical post-war government. Most of the planning legislation since has tended to adapt and modify at the edges, without discarding these fundamentals. However, the system did not arrive as a fully fledged thoroughbred. It was rather the result of a knockabout political process at Westminster, where debate was conducted between the elected politicians in the House of Commons, including the executive of the day which was pushing for reform, and the reviewing upper house, the House of Lords. The character of that political process also led to certain measures being removed, as they were regarded as being politically unacceptable in 1947. Those wanting to look at these omissions in depth need do no more than look at the 1942 Uthwatt Report.[4] It had postulated a system that dealt with land values and compensation necessitated by, in effect, the nationalisation of the development rights in land. This momentous change took its first steps on the 'appointed day' – 1 July 1948 – after which development rights over land were

---

[3] 'Repositioning the Planning System', *Heads of Planning Scotland Blog*, 13 February 2019, <https://hopscotland.org.uk/2019/02/13/repositioning-the-planning-system/> (last accessed 18 March 2019).

[4] 'The Final Report of the Expert Committee on Compensation and Betterment', Cmd 6368 (London: HMSO, 1942).

'vested' in the state, thus necessitating planning permission to develop. The fundamental pillars had arrived but some of the superstructure may have been too controversial to make it through the legislature, or only survived for a short period. Most notably, the unresolved compensation and betterment issue has reverberated down the decades and remains unresolved to this day, despite several legislative attempts to implement.[5] Planners have come to know these historic issues as 'the fault lines' in planning, tracing all the way back to the 1947 legislation. Those arguing for these fault lines to be fixed are, in effect, carrying forward a land reform argument which can be traced even further back to pre-1920 and to the work of land reformers such as Henry George.[6]

However, it is another of the fault lines which is causing the most heated debate in Scotland in 2019, as we consider yet more planning legislation. The right to appeal a refusal of planning permission was never an intended part of the original configuration of the planning system. It was not a clearly formed concept that had emerged over the preceding interwar period, as a necessary component of the emerging planning framework. The political and socio-economic context played a far more important role in the genesis of rights of appeal. 'An Englishman's home is his castle' was something of a backdrop. And, in contrast to the liberal and social concerns of the Attlee government, the House of Lords tended to be more concerned about property matters, given it had traditionally been the home of landed interests and was comparatively more aligned with such interests than the elected House of Commons.

The Labour government actually led the right of appeal as an accommodating amendment in order to secure Royal Assent for the 1947 Acts. Amidst clauses enabling compulsory purchase, development charges and nationalising development rights, it is hardly surprising from our perspective in the twenty-first century that politicians would seek to protect the right to develop their own land. The archives of the Ministry of Town and Country Planning and successors: National Parks and Countryside are now available online at the National Archives.[7] The detailed rough and tumble, to and fro, back and forth of the political

[5] See J. Corkindale, 'Fifty Years of the Town and Country Planning Acts Time to Privatise Land Development Rights?' *IEA Studies on the Environment*, 11 (1997) <http://www.iea.org.uk/sites/default/files/publications/files/upldbook383pdf.pdf> (last accessed 18 March 2019).

[6] For background, see the website of The Henry George Foundation <https://www.henrygeorgefoundation.org> (last accessed 18 March 2019).

[7] Available at <https://discovery.nationalarchives.gov.uk/details/r/C8787> (last accessed 18 March 2019).

moves and motivations would be fertile ground for study in the context of today's property and planning debates surrounding an imminent Planning (Scotland) Act[8] and a potential third-party right of appeal ('TPRA'). Thus, the genesis of planning appeals has clear relevance today in Scotland, not only during parliamentary consideration of the second planning statute of this century, but also because of the parallels to the ongoing land reform debate.

DOES LAND REFORM OFFER A TEMPLATE?

Several legislative land reform steps have now been taken in Scotland since devolution and the formation of the Scottish Parliament, which crucially substituted the United Kingdom's House of Lords as a revising legislature with a committee system drawn from a unicameral parliament elected using some elements of proportional representation. In 2016, Professor Ewen Cameron observed that 'issues concerned with the ownership of, access to, and redistribution of land have remained more important in Scotland than in other parts of the United Kingdom'.[9] It is worth noting that he also observes that land reform and the land question declined in legislative importance from the 1920s onward until their re-emergence in the newly formed Scottish Parliament. It may be observed that this same period (1920–2000) coincides with the significant advance of town planning in legislative terms. Could one have supplanted the other in the public discourse? And did one or the other benefit as a consequence? By the millennium, the question of 'rights' within planning was certainly coming to the fore, as the two strands of debate began to overlap.

It was during the lead-up to the Planning etc. (Scotland) Act 2006 that the notion of a third-party right of appeal started to emerge. Did the discussions surrounding 'responsible access' in the Land Reform (Scotland) Act 2003 ('LRSA 2003') play a part in influencing the direction of the TPRA debate? This may seem like an obscure question, but many people were involved in both sets of discussions. Without going into the full detail of the right of responsible access that is found

---

[8] See the passage of this legislation here: Planning (Scotland) Bill: <https://www.parliament.scot/parliamentarybusiness/Bills/106768.aspx> (last accessed 18 March 2019).

[9] See E. A. Cameron, 'The strange survival of the Scottish land question', University of Aberdeen, School of Law Conference, 25–26 August 2016. And see now Cameron, in this volume.

in Part 1 of the LRSA 2003,[10] it is important to remember that much of the work connected with access to the countryside across Scotland would have been carried out within planning departments. Even when the notion of the 'access authority' began to emerge (a term which now denotes the relevant local authority or where applicable national park authority), it was and remains likely that there would be a close working relationship with the 'planning authority'.

Indeed, the LRSA 2003 even borrowed a well-established part of planning practice, namely local plans, to help overcome one key aspect of countryside access. Whilst England's common law had ensured many miles of rights of way south of the border, the same could not be said in Scotland. Work done in 1993 for Scottish Natural Heritage by Peter Scott Planning Services had estimated that there were approximately 60,000 kilometres of paths and tracks extant, on the ground, in Scotland.[11] But crucially less than 100 kilometres were fully formed, fully asserted rights of way upon which the ordinary member of the public had the right to be there. After approximately 150 years of routes being waymarked by the third sector, the rights of way system, for a variety of reasons, was failing Scotland. This is not to say public rights of way were historically unimportant, but rather an alternative methodology was urgently needed for paths in modern Scotland.

The recipe had to be a simple, speedy, administrative system which could designate these important paths to protect them. What evolved into legislation, policy and practice was for access officers in local authorities to prepare plans setting out the existing and desired path networks on Ordnance Survey base maps, and then using tried and tested local plan methodologies to secure them. It would be a statute-based, administrative route as opposed to a court-based, prescription-proof route.[12] The approach would be called Core Path Plans, and the routes mapped on such plans would be called core paths. The process would take what had been described as 'chopped-up spaghetti', that is, the disjointed, unworkable and disappearing paths of Scotland and turn them into 'meaningful networks'. These networks would be based upon the most important, serviceable and popular path routes in the

[10] See generally M. M. Combe, *The ScotWays Guide to the Law of Access to Land in Scotland* (Edinburgh: John Donald, 2018).

[11] Peter Scott Planning Services, *Footpaths and Access in Scotland's Countryside 1993* (Edinburgh: Scottish Natural Heritage, 1993).

[12] Public rights of way can be lost by twenty years' non-use, in terms of the Prescription and Limitation (Scotland) Act 1973. See further Combe, *The ScotWays Guide*, pp. 122–3.

network, supplemented by new links. The plans were called Core Path Plans because these paths formed the 'core' of the wider path networks. They were the more important paths where maintenance of some form, by some authority, would be required.

There is a strong temptation to celebrate the fact that, as of 31 March 2016, there were 21,602 km of core paths in Scotland, secured by thirty-four separate Core Path Plans, all of which had been through an adoption procedure not dissimilar to the one used for Local Plans/Local Development Plans.[13] We should remember that as a matter of course, Local Plans also designate green belts, conservation areas and allocate land for various land uses. It is thus more significant with hindsight that this logical and rational approach to paths took so long to appear. Existing systems have an inherent inertia within them which augers against change, something that the town planning profession should reflect upon. There is now little doubt that having overcome initial minor teething problems Core Path Plans have become an astonishing success story.[14] In the context of active travel, health debates[15] and our need to overcome transport paralysis, Core Paths will become even more important in the future.

ACCESS RIGHTS AND RIGHTS WITHIN PLANNING

What relevance, beyond borrowing a planning technique, does this have for our planning system? One hopes that the relevance of path networks is clear when considering town planning, given the importance of movement and transport to land use. However, perhaps less obvious is the link which is apparent when one considers the underlying question of 'rights', which connects this apparent digression into access legislation with TPRA. The connection simply derives from the way 'rights' per se were so germane to the LRSA 2003 framework and how such ordinary,

---

[13] 'Scotland's networks of paths and trails: key research findings' (Inverness: Scottish Natural Heritage, 2018. <https://www.nature.scot/sites/default/files/2018-09/Research%20Consolidation%20Report.pdf> (last accessed 18 March 2019).

[14] See Combe, *The ScotWays Guide*, pp. 79–81 for details of the law.

[15] The current Scottish context can be seen in the publication 'Everyday walking for a happier, healthier Scotland. Strategy 2017–2020' produced by the charity Paths for All, available at <https://www.pathsforall.org.uk/resources/resource/everyday-walking-for-a-happier-healthier-scotland-strategy-2017---2020> (last accessed 31 March 2019). See also E. Dinnie, K. Brown and S. Morris, 'Community, cooperation and conflict: Negotiating the social well-being benefits of urban greenspace experiences', *Landscape and Urban Planning*, 112 (2013), pp. 1–9.

everyday rights for citizens should now be fundamental to any legislative framework in the twenty-first century. The right to be on land was *the* most fundamental matter in the whole LRSA 2003 formulation. Many commentators have made the link to *allemansrätt* (every man's right [to roam]), the Scandinavian tradition upon which most northern European access systems are based. Indeed, those involved in authoring the LRSA 2003 always saw the rural and especially the mountainous lands of Scotland as having more in common with Norway or Sweden than with northern England. With this ideal in mind they came up with a statutory right of access to all land based on *allemansrätt*.

From an American perspective, Professor John Lovett speaks of post-devolution Scotland, 'where a small band of recreational access advocates, enlightened landowners, law reformers, legislators, and jurists have done something remarkable'.[16] He was, of course, referring to the new right of access created by the LRSA 2003 legislation. Different commentators have drawn different significance to what came into being. At the time it did not seem particularly radical or even remarkable to many of those involved, just hard fought and long overdue. Rational and logical, the right of access was what was required to make the whole access system operational, irrespective of whether it would be viewed as controversial. In particular, it was the underlying motive force that would make Core Path Plans fully effective. Knowing that folk had the right to be on land, no one should legitimately see their presence as a reason to block access, but instead a rationale for managing access. Their behaviour and responsibility were clearly codified in a new Scottish Outdoor Access Code,[17] along with the responsibilities of land managers (backed up in statute by section 2 on responsible access and section 3 on responsible management in the LRSA 2003). It was clear that the principal management 'device' where there was such a right of access would be 'the path' itself. Not an outmoded keep-to-the-path philosophy, but a recognition that many people simply prefer to walk on paths, a predictable behaviour that enables management. Core Paths coupled with the Access Code formed a potent means to manage this new right of access.

There is some irony that mountain access may well have been the talisman to many involved in the land reform debate in 2003, but very few

---

[16] J. A. Lovett, 'Progressive Property in Action: The Land Reform (Scotland) Act of 2003', *Nebraska Law Review*, 89:4 (2011), pp. 739–818, 741.

[17] Available at <https://www.outdooraccess-scotland.scot/> (last accessed 31 March 2019).

mountaineers, if they were being honest, would have owned up to there being a serious mountain-access issue. That particular debate, dating back to James Bryce MP (Liberal MP for Tower Hamlets, 1880–5, and for South Aberdeen, 1885–1907) and his series of Mountain Access Bills (none of which were passed) had largely been won by dint of folk simply voting with their feet. The actual, no-go areas in Scotland were the more populated areas in and around our villages, towns and cities. The fact that access to our hills is now based upon a statutory right of access is undoubtedly significant, beneficial and even remarkable. However, the really radical element of this formulation is the way the LRSA 2003 fully enables path planning in our more populated areas. Path networks have burgeoned not just through our Core Path Plans, but also leaflet by leaflet, village to village. It is an unheralded, unsung, small-scale revolution and all the more remarkable for being so. It also evidences admirably the radical aspects of the legislation Professor Lovett mentions: that it was 'rights' based.[18]

A PUTATIVE THIRD-PARTY RIGHT OF APPEAL

The foregoing account concerning access demonstrates the way in which small communities were beginning to view rights and the way they could extend to town planning. In particular they have come to realise that the right to appeal a planning decision only accrued to the developer or landowner and not to the neighbours or community at large who were arguably the main customers of the planning system. There is nothing so challenging as a section of society who perceive their rights thwarted. Community councils, who already have a statutory role in planning (in terms of Part IV of the Local Government (Scotland) Act 1973), and our amenity societies began to point out the obvious, apparent imbalance in the positions of applicant and objector, protagonist and antagonist. New campaigning groups even emerged to push for a third-party right of appeal, one of them called, in suitably emotive fashion, Planning Democracy. Having witnessed at close hand all the debate about Part 1 of the LRSA 2003 the logic seemed persuasive to say the least. However, it remains significant that this chapter's author was also the only Director of Planning in Scotland who supported a TPRA in the early 2000s, as we moved toward a new Planning Act in 2006. All of the opposition to TPRA believed – and it does indeed seem a question

---

[18] Lovett, 'Progressive Property in Action', p. 741, and see the discussion at p. 752.

of belief, even an article of faith – that communities should be satisfied and grateful for upfront involvement in the so-called plan-led system.[19] They are not to have their own equivalent right of appeal. This whole question depends in large degree upon whether planning, in the public interest, is for its customers – i.e. those who make planning applications – or for its beneficiaries in wider society.

The planning profession looks to higher sources for reference points on such fundamental matters, a recent example of which is the bidecennial cycle of Habitat conferences (1976, 1996 and 2016). 'Habitat' is an international standing conference of the UN which has been pursuing the rationale of planning since the 1970s, the last of which, Habitat III[20] took place in Quito in 2016. It is purposed with reinvigorating the global commitment to sustainable urbanisation and particularly focused upon the implementation of a 'New Urban Agenda' for planning. Key outcomes focused upon communities and their 'rights'. A prominent commitment maintains the fundamental importance of 'integrating equity into the development agenda. Equity becomes an issue of social justice, ensures access to the public sphere, extends opportunities and increases the commons.' The relevance to a rights-based view of planning is plain to see. As the purposes of planning evolve and become ever more codified as delivering sustainability, perhaps it is the inertia in our own system which remains the key issue. This perspective started with the 1947 legislation setting up the fundamental pillars for town planning, much of which has since travelled across the globe. So, it ill behoves us in Scotland to be seen procrastinating over the modernisation of our own planning system to finally encompass equal rights and recognise that we *all* have a stake in what we plan, not just the developers.

This debate could not have been more graphically evidenced than by the way senior echelons of the property and planning professions in Scotland recently opposed TPRA once again in a letter to the broadsheet

---

[19] For more information on the plan-led system see House of Commons Library Briefing Paper 7459, 'Comparison of the planning systems in the four UK countries' (20 January 2016), p. 3, available at <https://researchbriefings.parliament.uk/ResearchBriefing/Summary/CBP-7459> (last accessed 31 March 2019): 'All four countries have a planning system that is "plan-led". "Plan-led" means that national and local planning policy is set out in formal development plans which describe what developments should and should not get planning permission, how land should be protected and seeks to ensure a balance between development and environmental protection in the public interest.'

[20] See UN Habitat III Conference <https://www.un.org/sustainabledevelopment/habitat3/> (last accessed 18 March 2019).

Scottish newspapers in July 2018.[21] All of the signatories purport to represent their members as opposing TPRA. This may well be true for some of the business representative signatories. However, it is not beyond the realms of possibility that if the grass-roots membership of the professional bodies was canvassed, views would be evenly balanced between support and opposition for TPRA. In such circumstances a far more nuanced stance would have been seemlier from the officers. Nevertheless, the assembled weight of the Royal Town Planning Institute Scotland, Heads of Planning Scotland, the Institution of Civil Engineers Scotland, the Royal Incorporation of Architects in Scotland, the Royal Institution of Chartered Surveyors in Scotland, Homes for Scotland, the Scottish Property Federation, Scotland's Towns Partnership, and (most significantly to this writer) Planning Aid Scotland all oppose the introduction of a TPRA in Scotland. Should anyone be surprised that such a group of professional and property organisations would combine and unite to oppose TPRA? To the lay person, a move to equalise rights would appear to be obvious and in the best, wider public interests of the community at large. It seems a peculiarly professional, almost closed-shop view to oppose TPRA.

These organisations state that the 2018 Planning Bill is an 'opportunity to put communities at the heart of planning through ensuring that they are engaged early and meaningfully'.[22] The organisations go on to suggest that they want to see a system that is 'inclusive, respected, ambitious and works in the public interest. [They] want to empower communities so that they can influence how their place changes over time with a planning system that fosters participation, collaboration and co-production.'[23] These are words that are hard to gainsay or criticise and fully in line with the Habitat III commitments referenced above. Town planners aspire to such a well-formed and inclusive arena in which to plough this sustainable furrow. Yet this grouping asserts that 'third party or equal rights of appeal will not support these ambitions'.[24] System inertia is discussed above; at best, this could be an example of it. In support of their position the organisations also assert that TPRA will lead to more decisions being made by government. This disregards

---

[21] 'Influencing the Scottish Planning Bill', Royal Town Planning Institute letter (also published as a letter in the Scottish press), 2 July 2018, available with a cover explanation at <https://www.rtpi.org.uk/briefing-room/news-releases/2018/july/influencing-the-scottish-planning-bill/> (last accessed 18 March 2019).

[22] Ibid.

[23] Ibid.

[24] Ibid.

the arrangements put in place in the Planning etc. (Scotland) Act 2006 to devolve many appeal decisions back to local authorities.[25] The launch of Local Appeal Panels to make appeal decisions in the locality where the refusal took place brings decision-making on many appeals back to the local level, away from the reporters. Over 500 planning appeals a year have been dealt with at the local level since these measures were introduced, halving the number which proceed to Ministers. The organisations go on to suggest that competing commercial interests would frustrate development and 'potentially pit one part of a community against another'.[26] Notwithstanding the fact that commercial competition is not a material consideration in planning, if any interest did stoop to such depths, it would not only be outed but would also have deleterious implications for the way they were viewed the next time they engaged with planning or made a planning application.

The resourcing difficulties cited by the organisations as being exacerbated by TPRA chime with anyone who has been a hard-working desk officer in this system. However, this ignores the highly probable effect TPRA would have in deterring speculative applications, often contrary to the development plan, presently submitted as a 'punt' with the full intention of appealing the decision, perhaps not even waiting for a local democratic decision. In other words, the front loaded, plan-led system would only be reinforced by TPRA.

There is a suggestion that TPRA would undermine democratically elected planning authorities' responsibility to ensure planning decisions are taken locally, in the public interest. This is hard to comprehend since *any* appeal to a higher authority, no matter from whom, be they developer or objector, will have this effect. If 'localism' is to be advocated and mean anything in this context then the only logical step would be to remove appeals altogether. Democratic elections come around regularly; councillors can be voted in and voted out. This is a perfectly reasonable way for local democracy to be manifest within planning fully in line with Habitat III.

Perhaps most controversial of all is the suggestion from the organisations that TPRA would 'weaken constructive early engagement'.[27] Nothing undermines local engagement more than the knowledge that at the end of the planning process, when faced with a refusal, any applicant

---

[25] See A. Ferguson and J. Watchman, *Local Planning Reviews in Scotland* (Edinburgh: Avizandum, 2015).

[26] Ibid.

[27] Ibid.

can simply appeal. The whole narrative of planning and its interaction with democracy is scattered with cases where both good planning practice and good engagement are dashed, in the final stage, by an appeal decision. There is no guarantee that good engagement is going to result in the outcomes that those engaged or engaging would prefer. Having taken part in many Pre-Application Consultation (PAC) exercises (in line with the Town and Country Planning (Scotland) Act 1997, section 35A, which was introduced by the Planning etc. (Scotland) Act 2006) there is a danger of wasting people's time and energy until the matter of TPRA is resolved. Communities of interest are collectively intelligent and not easily fooled. Without equal rights of appeal, PAC is completely undermined. There is also a throwaway and immensely patronising suggestion from the organisations that it will only be the articulate, well-heeled communities that will benefit. This is a fairly sad indictment on our assembled professions and should not be condoned in any way, let alone cited as a reason for maintaining the appeals status quo. It is not hard to work out who most of our present day 'appellants' actually are; namely those doing development rather than those affected by it.[28]

Lastly, the professional bodies suggest that public trust in the planning system must be a priority. Our standing as planners is at a low ebb; as low as I can remember in over forty years of involvement in the profession. There are no more Directors of Planning, just third-, fourth-, even fifth-tier, so-called Heads of Planning. Planning consultancies work hand in hand with lobbyists, political pundits and the media to achieve their ends. Planning is branded as the 'drag anchor on growth'[29], an accusation that I continue to work against, but that feeling that the profession has shot itself in the foot over TPRA has never figured so large. A first step going forward would be to open up, face up, even own up to the possibility that there is indeed a glaring issue over 'rights', which will get in the way of all other reform until it is properly addressed.

This personal perspective is consistent with prescriptions I advocated

---

[28] A full breakdown of appeals decided is available in the Department of Planning and Environmental Appeals annual reports the latest of which is available at: <https://www.gov.scot/binaries/content/documents/govscot/publications/corporate-report/2017/07/planning-and-environmental-review-annual-review-2017-2018/documents/fce99557-ec2d-49e1-9086-40aeaf364909/fce99557-ec2d-49e1-9086-40aeaf364909/govscot%3Adocument> (last accessed 18 March 2019).

[29] P. Swinney, 'Statsblog: Planning must support growth, not restrict it', *The Guardian*, 10 August 2011, <https://www.theguardian.com/local-government-network/statsblog/2011/aug/10/statsblog-planning-must-support-growth> (last accessed 27 May 2019).

for the Planning etc. (Scotland) Act 2006. I remain open to the adoption of TPRA simply because I have seen the galvanising effect that resolving 'rights' issues can have as illustrated earlier in respect of Core Path Plans. That does not necessarily mean abandoning appeals. There are many circumstances where cross-examination, in a Public Local Inquiry-type arena, are absolutely necessary. Nuclear power stations, incinerators, spaceports, wind farms, the list is an easy one to compile – yet even then we abandon a significant proportion of the approval of these developments to lightweight assessment, often carried out by the applicant, based upon policy and legal frameworks which were put in place in an earlier era. However, I remain equally open to the suggestion that there should be no rights of appeal at all, provided scrutiny is detailed and thorough. Only our elected local planning authority decisions are properly in line with the Habitat III aspirations. Democratic process means that if you do not like the decisions you can vote out the decision-makers at the next election. It certainly has its attractions.

WOULD ADOPTION OF RIGHTS WITHIN PLANNING HAVE A WIDER APPLICABILITY?

In the face of so many intractable problems facing society one might question the value of such detailed debates about the complex machine that is our Scottish planning system. Why does it matter so much and why should we care, especially about our fundamental rights? The final part of this perspective will focus on some of the practical planning dimensions of our housing crisis and whether the 'rights' issues which sit at the heart of that crisis – so tragically manifest in the Grenfell Tower disaster[30] – offer fertile ground for policy development in line with Habitat III.

There are many claimed rights associated with one's home: a right to light, a right to a view; a right to peace and quiet; a right to amenity; a right to be consulted as a neighbour when a development comes along next door; and perhaps even a right to object. The European Convention on Human Rights even provides a right to a private, family life. All of these are ephemeral to a degree and not necessarily a guarantee of a house to live in (although an existing owner of a house is protected through the provision that guarantees peaceful enjoyment of

[30] The full details of the Grenfell Inquiry can be found at <https://www.grenfell towerinquiry.org.uk> (last accessed 18 March 2019).

possessions).[31] Future residents and the homeless (in planning terms at least) have little or no say in such matters, other than through exercise of their ballot at elections. It is salutary that local council elections have such a pitiful turnout.[32]

In the context of our housing crisis, the planning professions at large should be justifiably frustrated at the repeated political assaults on the planning system, as if it was the 'only' root cause of the housing crisis.[33] In the public mind it is easy to equate 'not building enough' houses with how difficult it is to get planning permission for housing development. Those fault lines in planning tracing all the way back to 1947 are in plain sight here and point to solutions far wider than planning, though you might not think this when reading contemporary news media. It should be recalled that council housing remains 'permitted development'.[34] The rationale behind this stems from the fact that the planning system was not intended to provide housing for the nation but was designed to control and limit the use of land. One might question in such light why the planning profession repeatedly assumes the mantle of white knight in the face of one of the biggest problems facing contemporary Britain; namely, our housing crisis.

Housing authority professionals smile at the suggestion that the planning authority deals with housing. It is in the very nature of the planning professional to shoulder the many and various problems, environmental, economic, or societal that we face. When planners train, they often own up and reflect nostalgically that they did so to save the planet. Planners always step up to the plate. They give planning permission to housing developments, they zone additional housing land, they use planning agreements to secure planning gain and affordable housing contributions,[35] all done with gravitas and sense of priority. It

[31] The two ECHR rights at issue here are Article 1 of the First Protocol (peaceful enjoyment of property) and Article 8 (right to a home and family life), as discussed in Frankie McCarthy's chapter in this volume.

[32] For detail on election turnouts, see N. Dempsey, House of Commons Briefing Paper 8060 (2017), <https://researchbriefings.parliament.uk/ResearchBriefing/Summary/CBP-8060%23fullreport> (last accessed 18 March 2019).

[33] See Cheshire, 'Turning houses into gold'.

[34] See the Town and Country Planning (General Permitted Development) (Scotland) Order 1992, Schedule 1, Class 33 (SI 1992/223).

[35] These are known as 'Section 75 Agreements' in Scotland, owing to the relevant section under the Town and Country Planning (Scotland) Act 1997 (and as Section 106 Agreements in terms of the equivalent legislation in England and Wales) and can be used to bind the landowner and indeed a later landowner into doing something. As such, they have a role in relation to making some kind of developer contribution

is therefore more than curious that planners rarely argue 'why aren't we building council houses again, like councils did during the severe post-war housing crisis?'[36]

HOUSING AND PLANNING – A LOCAL CASE STUDY

It is instructive to reflect upon the immediate history of planning and housing in north-east Scotland, which acts as a microcosm to illustrate the tensions within the housing and planning debate. A number of very large housing sites between Inverness and Aberdeen now enjoy planning permission for over 20,000 houses. Many would think this a good thing, given current need. Sadly, this is a misapprehension based upon the conventional wisdom which assumes that the housing will be built the moment the consents are granted. It is a triumph of hope over reality. Glen Bramley describes developing housing by this, essentially private-sector route, as being akin to 'pushing string'.[37] How did we end up in this cul-de-sac?

A well-meaning, competitive initiative from government designed at promoting sustainable communities was announced in the late 1990s where success (that is, successfully being zoned for development in the relevant local development plan) depended at least in part upon that imperative 'go large'.[38] A lot of houses were needed (but, ironically, still are) and sites were successful at Aviemore (An Camas Mòr – 1,500 houses), Inverness (Tornagrain – 5,000 houses), Aberdeenshire (Chapelton of Elsick – 8,000 houses) and Aberdeen (Grandholm – 7,000 houses).

Any of these sites can be scrutinised in full detail on the Planning Portal in Scotland where the planning system can be witnessed, in

to reflect 'planning gain' (that is to say, the value uplift that might follow from a planning permission).

[36] See R. Reid, 'Housing Crisis? What Crisis?'; *Scottish Planning and Environmental Law Journal*, 167 (January 2015), pp. 8–9.

[37] 'Planning for New Housing: housing need, economic growth and evidence base for local strategies', conference presentation by Professor Glen Bramley (Heriot-Watt University) given at the South West Observatory Bristol Conference, 26 February 2013. The full quote is: 'Getting developers to build is like pushing string. You can give them permission but they don't have to take this up and can determine the rate of build out.'

[38] See Scottish Government, *Scottish Sustainable Communities: Initiative – Report* (Edinburgh, 2009), available at <https://www2.gov.scot/resource/doc/27 3506/0081710.pdf> (last accessed 18 March 2019).

action, in real time, on the internet.[39] These 'Sustainable Communities' went through local plan processes, scrutiny and then subsequent, successful selection. Many other shovel-ready sites, often already under the control of housebuilders, were overlooked as a result. These four new towns, for that is what in reality they are, have more in common than just their size. The scale of the landholdings, close to our major cities, was unlikely to be found in a single site other than those already controlled by major landowners. Each of these four development proposals warrant detailed, close scrutiny, in terms of their contribution to solving our housing crisis, an issue no less prevalent in north-east Scotland than elsewhere in the UK. I will focus on one of these new towns in more detail, namely Chapelton of Elsick. The chief protagonist behind this particular development is the duke of Fife.

To quote the duke of Fife (speaking, as he then was, as the earl of Southesk), he stated in 2013 that the Elsick masterplan

> offered the local politicians a solution as to where to put 4,000 houses in the short term without annoying everyone in the area. The existing communities were the biggest supporters because they didn't want further development. Places like Portlethen are a lesson to anyone on how not to develop – there are no facilities and it has just been bolt-on developments through the years. By taking a number of 100 -unit developments away to a single place you remove the problem from these communities but it also provides the critical mass to create something that is big enough to be sustainable.[40]

Construction commenced at Elsick in 2013, but the several thousand houses that were supposed to have been completed by 2018 have not remotely materialised; delivery has barely exceeded 200 houses (as noted in the *Aberdeen and Aberdeenshire Housing Land Audit*).[41] At these build-out rates it will take over twenty years to deliver this particular new town. Added to this, existing infrastructure provision such as railway stations, motorway junctions, major drainage facilities and school provision were somewhat ignored. Our capacity within the planning system of compounding problems rather than solving them is writ

---

[39] Scottish ePlanning Portal, <https://www.eplanning.scot/ePlanningClient/> (last accessed 18 March 2019).

[40] Aberdeen and Grampian Chamber, 'Business Bulletin' March 2013, p. 2 at p. 3.

[41] Aberdeen City Council and Aberdeenshire Council, Aberdeen and Aberdeenshire Housing Land Audit 2018, (Aberdeen, 2018), available at <https://www.aberdeen-city.gov.uk/sites/default/files/2018-07/Housing%20Land%20Audit%202018.pdf> (last accessed 18 March 2019).

large in this one example. The underlying issue is that consenting such schemes cannot be accompanied by any form of performance obligation – leaving it to the landowner to judge when to open or close the tap.

HOUSING AND PLANNING – THE WIDER PICTURE

Pre-1970, housing was not worth very much at all as an asset, and in the late 1960s and early 1970s, £2,500 would secure a perfectly reasonable family home. To prove why such affordability prevailed will always be difficult, but the significant provision of council housing at that time would have been a principal component of any rational explanation.

Sadiq Khan, at time of writing mayor of London, is faced with perhaps the most daunting housing problem in the UK. It is a 'wicked' problem doubly relevant to all of us because of the impact the London housing market has upon the rest of the country. Analysts are often heard commenting upon the many local housing markets operating in the UK, perhaps evidenced by the tale of 20,000 houses not being built in Grampian. It is a self-evident truth that a house in the far north of Scotland will cost far less than a house in Chelsea, but the mortgage rates remain the same. It is fundamental to any understanding of the housing crisis to recognise the culpability of our financial (credit) markets as well as our land and property markets. They are inextricably linked and the subject of numerous treatises explaining the culpability of economists and the economic theories they espoused from 1980 onwards, leading through to the financial crisis experienced around the globe in 2008.[42] Indeed as we just pass the tenth anniversary of the financial crisis there is much being written to revisit what transpired.[43] Perhaps useful for the purposes of this perspective is to focus on the distortions that have developed post-1980 in the planning system and highlight how they have helped fuel our housing crisis. In 2015, the average price of a

---

[42] See, for instance, M. Wolf, The Shifts and the Shocks: What We've Learned – and Have Still to Learn – From the Financial Crisis (London: Penguin Books, 2014); L. Ahamed, The Lords of Finance: 1929, The Great Depression, and the Bankers who Broke the World (London: Windmill Books, 2010); or M. Lewis, The Big Short: Inside the Doomsday Machine (New York: W. W. Norton and Co., 2010). One is inclined to comment that few of these authorities/writers predicted the crash. One who is most notably recognised for having 'called it right' is Nouriel Roubini, Crisis Economics: A Crash Course in the Future of Finance (London: Penguin Books, 2010).

[43] See J. Lanchester, 'After the Fall', London Review of Books, 40:13, 5 July 2018, pp. 3–8, for a decade-on perspective of the financial crisis.

house in London passed £500,000. In contrast, at the same time, the average price of a house in Scotland was less than 40 per cent of that price, at £175,000.[44] The abandonment of an interventionist regional planning system and simultaneous lack of commitment to an industrial policy fuelled an overheating of the south-east England economy beyond anything that could have been brought about by design. Many will actually applaud this as the direct result of what has become known as neoliberalism which saw the market as the answer to everything. They do so whilst ignoring the unintended consequences of what has transpired leaving the younger, aspiring generations struggling to gain a foothold on the housing ladder, or not, as the case may be.

Khan is clearly aware of the size and seriousness of this problem. He has publicly stated that 66,000 houses are needed to be built per annum in London to solve the problem.[45] It is not only a wicked problem, it is also a 'ticking time bomb' problem. Every year that the target is not met fuels the crisis even further. There is considerable irony in the fact that London City Hall planners are so skilful in assessing the size and scale of the problem. In previous generations, town planners and town planning skills have been far more central, even pivotal to that effort. Comprehensive redevelopment featuring significant numbers of council houses has shaped much of London and continues to have significant utility today.[46] But the UK planning profession has moved so far beyond its earlier modus operandi, as to be almost unrecognisable and its ability to solve the housing crisis has to be questioned. Any Scottish first-year student of planning will point out that the core legislative framework is set out in the Town and Country Planning (Scotland) Act 1997. It is a 300-page tome which would deter any but the determined, but in reality, the crucial regulatory sections are confined to the first sixty pages. Significantly, the rest includes 'powers' designed to allow planning authorities to 'intervene' but they are rarely used. The sister New

---

[44] See Office of National Statistics monthly publications of house price information. The September 2014 bulletin was of particular significance because the average price of a London house went over £500,000 for the first time – a fact covered widely in the media at the time.

[45] See R. Booth, 'Sadiq Khan: London needs to build 66,000 new homes a year, up from 29,000', *The Guardian*, 27 October 2017, <https://www.theguardian.com/uk-news/2017/oct/27/sadiq-khan-to-raise-target-for-affordable-housing-in-london> (last accessed 18 March 2019).

[46] See S. Broughton, *Municipal Dreams: The Rise and Fall of Council Housing* (London: Verso Books, 2018).

Towns legislation empowered further intervention and delivered the not-insignificant achievement of our UK new towns.

TO BUILD COUNCIL HOUSES AGAIN

So how does this relate to our housing crisis and delivering a sea change in housebuilding? The first lesson is to recognise that you cannot regulate your way out of this housing crisis. Politicians, especially, seem to think that speeding up consents, allocating more land or breaching the green belt will solve the crisis, yet these are all regulatory measures. Whilst the UK needs all the houses that the present system can build, focusing reliance on these existing approaches is to ignore the bigger issues, given the scale of procurement that will now be required. Not only is it misguided, it actually fuels the problem even further, focusing attention and effort onto levers that are incapable of finding a higher level of performance. There will even be some who will continue to advocate our current 'predict and provide' approach simply because it allows a private-sector housing industry to control delivery and maintain high price levels. Such behaviours are perfectly understandable in terms of a conventional economic view but why is it that our planning system seems so blind to this? These are normal money-making, share-price-aware, business activities, but hardly logical if your planned outcome was to flood the housing market, making houses more affordable. To make this all realign we have to do something very different indeed.[47]

The second lesson is that we have actually solved a housing crisis before. We have dealt with chronic housing shortages after two World Wars, a worldwide economic depression in the 1930s and the consequential global upheaval. In the 1950s and 1960s the UK managed to build up to 400,000 homes per annum, sustaining such levels of output year on year, providing homes for all. What was the key to this approach? The answer is simple: council housing. It is an approach we have all-but-forgotten today; instead we have so-called affordable housing and social housing. Affordable housing (provoking the observation that all other housing is 'unaffordable') is planning jargon that we

---

[47] See J. Ryan-Collins, T. Lloyd and L. Macfarlane with the New Economics Foundation, *Rethinking The Economics of Land and Housing*, (London: Zed Books, 2017) or The Land Reform Review Group, 'Final Report: The Land of Scotland and the Common Good' (Edinburgh: Scottish Government, 2014), Part 5, Land Development and Housing, <https://www.gov.scot/publications/land-reform-review-group-final-report-land-scotland-common-good/pages/50/> (last accessed 18 March 2019).

were all complicit in promoting. Through the use of a legal planning device, never intended for such use, we invented 'planning gain' and all that it has now spawned. Planning gain is a cul-de-sac, in truth, born of a vanity that we could substitute Nye Bevan's great dream of building council housing with a regulatory tax on housebuilding, to fund construction of affordable housing. How did we get here? And when the public at large ask why we cannot build enough houses today, the simple answer is because we stopped building council houses. Why? Because the then prime minister Margaret Thatcher decided to allow a 'right to buy' to win votes.[48] It is an interesting variant of the 'rights' debate in planning. Politicians across the political spectrum are beginning to recognise the scale of this mistake and the way that it will reverberate down the generations. Politicians are less united regarding their favoured prescriptions for solving the consequences, though few would disagree about the scale of intervention now required.

The third lesson we should learn is very simple indeed. If we can agree that we have only ever succeeded in procuring sufficient housing when we built council housing in numbers to match the private sector, then we must ask what we can do to recreate the most favourable conditions to do so again. There are three aspects to this. First, to make the acquisition of land by public authorities in the public interest, compulsory if necessary, as straightforward efficient and economic as possible. This means making sure that land acquisition or procurement should be at existing-use value, and not some hope value based upon future expectation of development. It fully operationalises the planning mantra 'right development, right place'. Some would say the land should come into public ownership first – as part of that process, allowing public interest-led development to take place, with significantly higher standards of design and procurement.[49] This is what happens in other European nations in places we visit and admire but seem unable to replicate in the UK, for want, I would submit, of sufficient ambition. However, it is a topic that the Scottish Land Commission has recently begun to explore.[50] We

[48] See Broughton, *Municipal Dreams*, chapter 7, 'Rolling back the frontiers of the state: 1979 – 91' for insight on right to buy. For the policy's impact as regards residential leases, see Bain in this volume.

[49] See the Land Reform Review Group, 'Final Report', Part 5, Land Development and Housing – for an explanation of Public Interest-Led Development.

[50] S. Tolson and A. Rintoul, 'Public Interest Led Development in Scotland: a discussion paper' (Inverness: Scottish Land Commission, 2018), <https://landcom mission.gov.scot/wp-content/uploads/2018/03/Land-Lines-Public-Interest-Led-Deve lopment-Steven-Tolson-March-2018.pdf> (last accessed 31 March 2019). See also

also need to ensure that funding the procurement of new homes does not recreate the substantial debt overhang that so handicapped housing management in recent decades. The debt write-offs brought about by the Inquiry into Glasgow's Housing led by Sir Robert Grieve (former Chief Planner Scotland)[51] enabled new and innovative practices, but did not galvanise new council housebuilding. Housing associations, their organisation and modus operandi preoccupied that inquiry. Finally, we should remember what Nye Bevan said in 1946 about housing numbers. 'We must not only build quickly, we must build well. In the next year or so we will be judged by the number of houses we have put up. But in ten years we will be judged by the quality of those homes.'[52]

FINAL THOUGHTS

Can we see a connection between TPRA and housing development? Both are clearly *not* Habitat III compliant in Scotland and they should be. Rights issues and equity are still to be resolved, principally because our professional and system inertia don't allow us to make progress. Other places in the world are now stealing a march in housing and planning practice. It is highly significant that some Western states, replete with planning systems based upon our own, are beginning to introduce a rights-based housing system based upon the UN Covenant on Economic, Social and Cultural Rights.[53] Most recently, Canada has adopted housing policy which overtly declares that it will approach housing as a human right and develop policy in that direction. The Canadian government stated in 2017 that its Housing Strategy will be a

---

'Delivering Better Places in Scotland: A guide to learning from broader experience' (Edinburgh: Scottish Government, 2010), available at <https://www.webarchive. org.uk/wayback/archive/20170701174255/http://www.gov.scot/Publications/2010 /12/31110906/0> (last accessed 31 March 2019).

[51] Sir Robert Grieve, *Inquiry into housing in Glasgow* (Glasgow: Glasgow District Council, 1986).

[52] See L. Hanley, *Estates: An Intimate History* (London: Granta Books, 2007), which quotes Nye Bevan's 1946 speech.

[53] See the UN International Covenant on Economic, Social and Cultural Rights: Adopted and opened for signature, ratification and accession by General Assembly resolution 2200A (XXI) of 16 December 1966, Article 11(1) of which provides 'The States Parties to the present Covenant recognize the right of everyone to an adequate standard of living for himself and his family, including adequate food, clothing and housing, and to the continuous improvement of living conditions.' See also the discussion by McCarthy, in this volume.

first step in a larger effort to 'progressively implement the right of every Canadian to access adequate housing'.[54]

In the context of Habitat III and a generation of young folk coming along who will be excluded from housing (and will blame baby boomers),[55] a more detailed examination of the rights issues in planning would be timely and instructive. This policy direction, based upon rights, is the one that we should all follow if we are ever to solve not only the housing crisis we are facing but perhaps a wider range of developmental and environmental problems affecting us all. The lessons from land reform in Scotland are that solving the rights issues leads to practical solutions on the ground becoming the norm.

* * *

The Planning (Scotland) Bill 2018 discussed in this chapter became an Act when it received Royal Assent on 25 July 2019. It will take some time for all the measures in the Act to come into effect through secondary legislation, probably well into 2021. The fundamental pillars of planning, set out above, remain unchanged. Most of the provisions are process-focused. Of greatest significance has been the political decision taken not to include a third-party right of appeal. It was debated at length in the final reading of the Bill, with the case led by Andy Wightman MSP and Monica Lennon MSP, but in the end defeated. The debate is worth reading. We do, however, now have a legal requirement for a Director of Planning to be appointed by each Scottish Planning Authority. Full details of the Act and the Parliamentary proceedings are available on the respective websites.[56]

[54] See 'Canada's National Housing Strategy: A Place to Call Home', at <https://www.placetocallhome.ca/pdfs/Canada-National-Housing-Strategy.pdf> (last accessed 18 March 2019).

[55] David Willetts, *The Pinch – How the Baby Boomers Took Their Children's Future – and Why They Should Give It Back* (London: Atlantic Books, 2010).

[56] Scottish Parliament, Meeting of the Parliament 19 June 2019, 'Official report', <http://www.parliament.scot/parliamentarybusiness/report.aspx?r=12195&i=1101 60#ScotParlOR> (last accessed 26 November 2019). Also see Scottish Government, 'Planning: post-bill work programme', 30 September 2019, <https://www.gov.scot/publications/transforming-planning-practice-post-bill-work-programme/> (last accessed 26 November 2019).

15

Crofting Policy and Legislation: An Undemocratic and Illegitimate Structure of Domination?

Iain MacKinnon

CROFTING IS A FORM of land tenure given statutory recognition by the Crofters Holdings (Scotland) Act 1886. This Act gave enduring land rights to landholders in north and west Scotland, an area which became known as 'the crofting counties'. For generations before the Act was passed these landholders had been subject to arbitrary removals in a process of social change that has earned the area's landlords lasting opprobrium.[1] Although crofting tenure has been reformed repeatedly since the 1886 Act, the fundamental rights of security of tenure, fair rents and compensation for improvements have been retained. However, it is generally agreed that the crofting system in the early twenty-first century is in a bad way: its legal system 'a morass', common grazings significantly underused, many crofters absent from their holdings, and significant numbers of crofts unused or in poor condition.[2]

Recent efforts to take legislative action on crofting have proved contentious with some actors implicating Scottish Government policy and legislation in its decline. Moreover, there have been related accusations that when government forms policy and legislation for crofting, it does not engage with crofters in good faith. For instance, during the consultation processes examined in this chapter, the main crofting representative organisation, the Scottish Crofting Federation (SCF), called into question the integrity of the Scottish Government's commitment to constructive engagement by implying that the Scottish Government is willing to

---

[1] J. Hunter, *The Making of the Crofting Community* (Edinburgh: John Donald, 1976); E. Richards, *The Highland Clearances* (Edinburgh: Birlinn, 2000).

[2] C. Agnew, 'Crofting: A clean slate', *Northern Scotland*, 6 (2015), pp. 84–97; G. Jones, *Trends in Common Grazings: first steps towards an integrated need strategy* (European Forum on Nature Conservation & Pastoralism, 2011), pp. 5, 11; Crofting Commission, *Crofting Commission Annual Report and Accounts* (Inverness, 2018), p. 15.

'shaft' crofters when forming agricultural policies, is 'two-faced' in its dealings with crofters, and holds a 'colonial attitude' towards crofting.[3]

This chapter is a preliminary study which tries to understand these extreme expressions of mistrust and disempowerment by critically examining two recent processes of crofting policy formation. Firstly, it analyses changes made to crofting tenure regulation following the 2008 Committee of Inquiry on Crofting (CoIC); secondly, it analyses the Scottish Government's response to a consultation on crofting support while it was developing the Scottish Rural Development Programme (SRDP) for 2014–20.[4] Respectively, these two processes exemplify the two main political debates related to crofting: tenure regulation and agricultural support. The results of these case studies will inform a second-order analysis that considers the extent to which the development of crofting policy and legislation in Scotland meets an emerging set of normative national and international standards for guiding the ways in which legitimate processes of political change should occur in modern democratic societies.[5]

The chapter begins by discussing underlying principles that guide processes of political change in constitutional democracies, and outlining some of the normative decision-making standards. It then moves on to the legislative case studies, discussing, firstly, the post-CoIC legislative process that imposed a new statutory obligation on some crofters, and, secondly, a proposal to discard a crofting-specific funding scheme as part of the SRDP reform. Each case study is then compared with the national and international standards and principles. Finally, a concluding section calls into question the nature of the underlying social and political relationship between the Scottish national legislature and what is often called 'the crofting community'.

---

[3] Scottish Crofting Federation (SCF), 'SCF warn that Government register plan could rob crofters of their rights', SCF news release, 14 May 2010; SCF, '"Hands off the crofters' scheme" says the crofting federation', SCF news release, 11 February 2014; SCF, 'Crofters warned to speak up or get shafted', SCF news release, 14 February 2014.

[4] The inception, reception and legislative outcomes of CoIC are complex and have had far-reaching consequences for crofting politics and practice. Much in the political processes surrounding CoIC is relevant to this chapter's focus. However, for the purpose of this preliminary investigation, the focus here has been narrowed to one particularly contentious legislative change.

[5] A brief version of case study 1 appeared in the *West Highland Free Press* in November 2012. A shorter version of the second case study was submitted in 2014, with the author's approval, by the Scottish Crofting Federation to the Scottish Parliament committee scrutinising the SRDP reform proposals.

BACKGROUND PRINCIPLES OF LEGITIMACY FOR DECISION-MAKING IN CONSTITUTIONAL DEMOCRACIES

The guidelines and standards on decision-making processes that this article outlines are part of a wider shift that has occurred over much of Europe during the last thirty years, according to the Council of Europe's (CoE) constitutional advisory group, the Venice Commission. It argues that the direction of constitutionally inscribed changes in the relationship between the citizens (*demos*) of many European states and their governments (*nomos*) has redrawn this relationship in ways 'such as to reduce executive power (and strengthen parliament)' and 'improve human rights'.[6]

Regardless of whether these changes to decision-making processes are formally ascribed in constitutional orders, or take the form of 'voluntary guidelines' or 'standards' by which decision-making processes should proceed, they can be understood as a rebalancing of the relationship between two underlying principles of legitimacy for guiding political associations and processes of political change in modern constitutional democracies. These have been termed the principle of constitutionalism (or the rule of law) and the principle of democracy (or popular sovereignty) and are said to be co-equal in status as 'the basic law implicit in modern constitutions'. The principle of constitutionalism requires the rule of law as a general system of principles, rules and procedures to apply to the exercise of political power in the whole and in every part of any constitutionally legitimate process of political, social and economic cooperation. The principle of democracy requires that the *demos* – those who are subject to the constitutional system – impose it upon themselves.[7][8]

The Canadian political philosopher James Tully, who was an adviser to the Canadian government's Royal Commission on Aboriginal Peoples

---

[6] Venice Commission, *Report on Constitutional Amendment*, <http://www.venice.coe.int/webforms/documents/?pdf=CDL-AD(2010)001-e> (last accessed 11 May 2018).

[7] J. Tully, *Public Philosophy in a New Key, Volume II: Imperialism and Civic Freedom* (Cambridge: Cambridge University Press, 2008), pp. 92, 94.

[8] See also the exchange on this topic between John Rawls and Jürgen Habermas in the 1990s: J. Rawls, *Political Liberalism* (New York: Columbia University Press, 1996), p. 137 and J. Habermas, *Between Facts and Norms: Contributions to a Discourse Theory of Law and Democracy* (Massachusetts: MIT Press, 1996), pp. 110, 112; and the work of Quentin Skinner: Q. Skinner, *Liberty Before Liberalism* (Cambridge: Cambridge University Press, 1998), p. 74.

and has published a series of groundbreaking books on modern constitutionalism, has argued, 'If someone else imposes the rules by which the
demos are governed, and even if they have a range of freedoms within
this other-imposed regime, they are not self-governing, self-determining,
or sovereign and are thus unfree.' He emphasises that it is an indispen-
sable condition of being

> free democratically . . . not only to be able to participate in various ways in
> accordance with the principles, rules and procedures of the constitutional
> system, as important as this is, but also to be able to take one step back,
> dissent, and call into question the principles, rules, or procedures by which
> one is governed and to enter into (rule-governed) deliberations over them, or
> usually a subset of them, with those who govern.[9]

That is, the ability of citizens to participate in a political process can be
compromised at two levels. On one level the quality of their participation can be limited by the actions of those who govern a particular decision-making process; on the other level the background constitutional
procedures which coordinate citizens' involvement in decision-making
processes generally can also act to limit participation.

Tully concludes that if members of a political association 'do not
have a voice in the way in which political power is exercised, and thus
power is exercised over them without their say "behind their backs", as
in the market or bureaucratic organisations, then they are, by definition,
subjects rather than citizens' and experience the political association 'as
[an alien and imposed] structure of domination that is both "unfree"
and "illegitimate"'.[10]

The case studies will examine how the constitutional rules and
procedures that coordinate legislative processes in Scotland act on the
abilities of crofters as political actors to participate in and influence
decision-making processes that affect them. The emerging national and
international framework of decision-making principles and standards
acts as a normative basis for analysing the democratic legitimacy of the
legislative processes in the case studies. This examination may serve
to illuminate both a background rationale behind crofters' extreme
complaints previously mentioned, and, also, whether the relationship
between government and crofters as a collective should be considered
free and legitimate, or whether it is structured, instead, as a relationship
of domination.

---

[9] Tully, *Public Philosophy in a New Key, Volume II*, pp. 93–4.
[10] J. Tully, *Public Philosophy in a New Key, Volume I: Democracy and Civic
Freedom* (Cambridge: Cambridge University Press, 2008), pp. 161, 165.

SOME NORMATIVE NATIONAL AND INTERNATIONAL DECISION-MAKING STANDARDS THAT APPLY TO SCOTLAND

The Scottish Government's 'National Standards for Community Engagement' (NSCE) are described as key principles for effective practice in community engagement and are intended to support 'more influential community participation in policy, strategy and planning processes'. Although their preamble does not explicitly apply the standards to government, they do say they are for elected representatives and public sector bodies 'to help them . . . make sure that the community engagement is fair and effective'. According to the NSCE, in an engagement process 'communication between all participants [should be] open, honest and clear' and based on 'trust and mutual respect'. The decisions taken as a result of the engagement should 'reflect the views of participants in the . . . process'. During the process participants should commit to 'two-way communication with the people they work with or represent' and all affected parties should be 'involved at the earliest opportunity'.[11]

The NSCE represents one local expression of a wider movement of governance in Europe which has sought to improve civil participation in the decision-making process, as evidenced by the CoE's 'Guidelines' on this subject which were adopted in 2017. The Guidelines conclude that enabling conditions for civil participation in decision-making 'requires all involved to honestly and sincerely exchange viewpoints to ensure that the positions of civil society are effectively taken into consideration by public authorities with decision-making powers'. Its principles include 'mutual respect', 'openness, transparency and accountability', and 'responsiveness, with all actors providing appropriate feedback'.[12]

Land governance is an area where particular emphasis has been placed on states to apply these kinds of decision-making principles in order to ensure more effective and meaningful citizen involvement. In 2012 the UN published its Voluntary Guidelines on the Responsible Governance of Tenure (VGGTs) which outline internationally accepted principles and standards of responsible practices for the use and control of land, fisheries and forests. Although not binding on states, the Guidelines have

[11] Scottish Government, *National Standards for Community Engagement* [revised version] (Scottish Government and Scottish Community Development Centre: Edinburgh, 2016), <http://www.voicescotland.org.uk> (last accessed 11 May 2018).

[12] Council of Europe (CoE), *Guidelines for civil participation in political decision-making* (Strasbourg, 2016) <https://search.coe.int/cm/Pages/result_details.aspx?ObjectID=09000016807509dd> (last accessed 17 May 2018), sections III(3), III(4)(a,d,e).

been produced using a human-rights based approach and endorsed by more than 100 countries. The VGGTs offer a wide range of guidance to states on responsible governance, including recommendations about good-faith and meaningful consultations based on 'full and effective participation of all members or representatives of affected communities . . . when developing policies and laws related to . . . customary tenure systems'. The Guidelines also recommend that states should 'delegate tenure governance in transparent, participatory ways . . . and anyone who could be affected should be included in the consultation, participation and decision-making processes'.[13]

Scottish land reform legislation states that when issuing guidance on engaging communities in decisions which may affect them relating to land, the government 'must have regard to the desirability of promoting respect for internationally accepted principles and standards' including those of the VGGTs.[14] When the Scottish Government issued such guidance in 2018, it said it 'expect[ed] all those with control over land in Scotland to engage with local communities in an open and effective way'. Describing the NSCE as principles of good practice, the land guidance reflects the standards set out in earlier documents, emphasising, for instance, that '[e]ngagement should be carried out in good faith, with a view to genuinely listening to the ideas put forward by members of local communities' who 'can reasonably expect their views to be heard and taken into account when decisions are reached'.[15] This body of standards can now be used to assess the democratic legitimacy of recent decision-making processes directly affecting crofters in Scotland.

Case study 1: The introduction of a 'duty-to-report'

In September 2006, in a move described at the time as 'the biggest and most embarrassing legislative climb-down since devolution', the Scottish Executive was forced to remove key sections of its crofting reform bill

---

[13] United Nations, *Voluntary Guidelines on the Responsible Governance of Tenure of Land, Fisheries and Forest in the Context of National Food Security*, available at <http://www.fao.org/3/a-i2801e.pdf> (last accessed 11 May 2018), sections 3b(6), 8.7, 8.9, 9.7, 9.9.

[14] Land Reform (Scotland) Act 2016, available at <http://www.legislation.gov.uk/asp/2016/18/section/44/2016-06-28?view=plain> (last accessed 11 May 2018), section 44.

[15] Scottish Government, *Guidance on Engaging Communities in Decisions Relating to Land* (Edinburgh, 2018), section 21, section 64.

only a week before the bill was due for parliamentary debate.[16] This was
the result of intense, unresolved criticism of the way the bill dealt with
crofting regulation and the market in croft land. In an effort to resolve
the impasse, the Executive appointed the Committee of Inquiry on
Crofting (CoIC) with a remit to 'identify a vision for the future of crofting' contributing to the goals of 'sustaining and enhancing population
across rural Scotland, improving economic vitality, safeguarding landscape and biodiversity and sustaining cultural diversity'.[17] On the basis
of this vision CoIC was empowered to identify necessary regulatory and
incentive changes. CoIC's wide-ranging recommendations included proposals to democratise and localise tenure regulation, reinforce support
for crofter housing, reshape the agricultural support system, and create
new rules to diminish the market in croft land. However, some of these
recommendations were subject to criticism and efforts made by some
crofters to reject CoIC entirely.[18] The Scottish Government's official
response accepted only some of the recommendations, and many of
those were also reshaped during the legislative process.[19]

One of the more controversial aspects of the new law has been the
creation of a 'duty-to-report' for crofters which was neither a CoIC
recommendation nor one of the Scottish Government's own proposals
for legislation. The 'duty-to-report' imposed an obligation on members
of every crofting common grazings committee to report on the condition of their grazings and of every croft sharing in the grazings, and in
particular to report on whether crofters in the township were neglecting
their land or were absent from the croft.[20]

---

[16] 'Crofting Climb-down by Executive', *The Scotsman*, 23 September 2006,
<https://www.scotsman.com/news/politics/crofting-climb-down-by-executive-1-114
1866> (last accessed 19 April 2018).

[17] *Committee of Inquiry on Crofting, Final Report*, 2008, <https://consult.
gov.scot/agriculture-and-rural-communities/crofting-consultation-2017/supporti
ng_documents/Shucksmith%20Report.pdf> (last accessed 11 May 2018), p. 76.

[18] Scottish Parliament/Pàrlamaid na h-Alba, Rural Affairs and Environment
Committee agenda, 2 March 2010, <http://archive.scottish.parliament.uk/s3/com-
mittees/rae/papers-10/rup10-05.pdf> (last accessed 10 October 2018), pp. 13–16.

[19] Scottish Government, 'Committee of Inquiry on Crofting, Government
Response', 2008.

[20] Crofting law requires that crofters live on or within 32 kilometres of their
croft, and do not neglect the croft; that is, they should manage it to meet standards
of good agricultural and environmental condition (Crofters (Scotland) Act 1993,
sections 5AA, 5B, 19C); Crofting Reform (Scotland) Act 2010, available at <http://
www.legislation.gov.uk/asp/2010/14/pdfs/asp_20100014_en.pdf> (last accessed 10
October 2018), section 38.

The introduction of the 'duty-to-report' can be delineated in relation to the Scottish Parliament's legislative process which consists of three stages. Following pre-legislative consultation, in the first stage a draft government bill is sent to a parliamentary committee which reports back on the general principles of the bill, and Parliament then votes on whether or not the bill should proceed to stage two. During stage two the committee scrutinises in much greater detail the proposals for law that are laid out in the bill. At this committee stage MSPs have the power to propose amendments to the draft legislation. Stage three then follows, when Parliament debates and votes to pass or fail the bill. The 'duty-to-report' provision was introduced during the Rural Affairs and Environment Committee's stage two deliberations as it dealt with the post-CoIC crofting legislative reforms. At this stage a single MSP, albeit one representing a crofting area, was able to introduce the 'duty-to-report' provision as an amendment which was then passed into law without any formal consultation process with those it affected. Its proponent argued that it would 'provide an opportunity for people who live in the crofting communities to take responsibility' and a 'mechanism to allow people to discuss' the way forward.[21] However, crofting representatives did not share this view. The measure provoked a furious response, described by SCF as 'an unreasonable and unwelcome obligation on crofters to shop each other to the commission'.[22] The factor of the community-owned Stornoway Trust estate, Iain MacIver, condemned it as an attempt to oblige a few individuals working in a voluntary capacity 'to police croft land that isn't even theirs'.[23]

MacIver's 'policing' observation draws attention to the fact that the 'duty-to-report' provision appears to delegate an aspect of crofting tenure governance to local grazings committees. In such circumstances, the VGGT standards call for delegation to occur 'in transparent, participatory ways' ensuring that those affected are 'included in the consultation, participation and decision-making processes'.[24] As no formal or systematic effort was undertaken to ascertain the views of those who

[21] Scottish Parliament/Pàrlamaid na h-Alba, Meeting of the Parliament, 1 July 2010, <http://www.parliament.scot/parliamentarybusiness/report.aspx?r=5633& mode=pdf> (last accessed 11 May 2018), cols 28081, 28082.

[22] 'The commission' here refers to the Crofting Commission which regulates crofting tenure. For the Commission's role, see chapter 12 in this volume.

[23] 'Fury as crofters are told to spy on their neighbours', West Highland Free Press, 26 October 2012, pp. 1–2; 'Trust factor expresses his concern over croft "spies"', West Highland Free Press, 2 November 2012, p. 3.

[24] United Nations, Voluntary Guidelines, sections 8.7, 8.9.

would be affected by the 'duty-to-report' before it passed into law, it appears that in this case the affected population was excluded from, rather than included in, these processes. Moreover, it seems clear that the decision-making process behind the 'duty-to-report' is in breach of the VGGT implementation principle (6) which says that states should ensure 'active, free, effective, meaningful and informed participation of individuals and groups in decision-making processes'. The UN considers this principle 'essential' for responsible land tenure governance.[25]

Furthermore, the means by which the 'duty-to-report' was passed into law appears to disclose that the Scottish legislative process does not meet the Scottish Government's own NSCE during decision-making processes. Although the NSCE recommends that affected parties should be 'involved at the earliest opportunity' in the decision-making process, the affected parties do not appear to have been involved in the creation of the 'duty-to-report' at all. The 'duty-to-report' was created in such a way that meant it did not 'reflect the views of participants in the ... process', as the NSCE also recommends; the condemnation with which it was received is a reflection of the failure to involve those affected by it. There was no process of 'two-way communication with the people ... [that the legislators] work with or represent'. According to the NSCE, in an engagement process 'communication between all participants [should be] open, honest and clear' and based on 'trust and mutual respect'. However, in this case no procedurally valid communication took place, and the response of crofting representatives appears to make clear that the cost of the legislators not giving those affected a say on the 'duty-to-report' was a loss of trust and mutual respect.[26]

The legislature's use of the amendment process to impose the 'duty-to-report' without significant involvement of those affected by the new law discloses how the standard procedure of the Scottish legislative system can enable law-makers to achieve policy aims without the need for reference to anyone beyond the law-makers themselves. To adopt the language of the Council of Europe Guidelines for good decision-making, it appears that the 'recourse to ... procedures involving a limited number of actors' which 'should be made only in exceptional circumstances and for which reasons are given' is in fact enabled as part of the standard procedures of the Scottish legislative system.[27]

[25] United Nations, *Voluntary Guidelines*, section 3B(6).

[26] Scottish Government, *National Standards for Community Engagement*.

[27] CoE, *Guidelines for civil participation in political decision-making*, section VI(16).

Cumulatively, the framework of decision-making principles and standards suggests that the Scottish legislature may need to revisit, not only the particular 'duty-to-report' provision that was created, but also the background legislative procedure by which it creates law in general, as the amendment process appears to enable law-makers to bypass what is internationally recognised as an 'essential' principle of responsible democratic governance.

There is another, additional, consideration here. The CoE participation guidelines assume that its standards for civil participation operate within political systems of 'representative democracy, based on the right of citizens to freely elect their representatives at reasonable intervals', and that these systems are 'part of the common heritage of member States'.[28] However, the bodies that legislate for crofting – the Scottish Parliament, and its committee which scrutinises crofting legislation – are made up of a majority of representatives who are not crofters, and who do not represent the crofting counties. Of course, on many issues that relate to crofting, such as for agricultural support, crofters are one stakeholding interest among many. However, on the issue at stake here – that of tenure regulation – crofters are the main, and it could be argued the only, group affected by the decisions that are made.

The fact that some of those who legislate for crofting say they do not have significant understanding of crofting tenure and society may aggravate the situation.[29] However, the underlying dilemma, in terms of the inherited European assumption that citizens have a right to elect representatives who will make decisions on the issues that concern them, is that the crofting population in Scotland does not elect the majority of people who then make decisions on issues that specifically concern crofters and crofting. In this sense crofters do not share in the common democratic heritage of European states and may, as a result, be more

---

[28] CoE, *Guidelines for civil participation in political decision-making.*

[29] Scottish Parliament/Pàrlamaid na h-Alba, Rural Affairs and Environment Committee Report, col. 2380, 10 February 2010, <http://www.parliament.scot/parliamentarybusiness/report.aspx?r=5099&mode=pdf> (last accessed 11 May 2018); Scottish Parliament/Pàrlamaid na h-Alba, Rural Affairs, Climate Change and Environment Committee, Official Report, col. 2189, 13 May 2013, <http://www.parliament.scot/parliamentarybusiness/report.aspx?r=8332&mode=pdf> (last accessed 11 May 2018); Scottish Parliament/Pàrlamaid na h-Alba, Rural Economy and Connectivity Committee, Official Report, 9 November 2016, cols. 12, 18–22, <http://www.parliament.scot/parliamentarybusiness/report.aspx?r=10620&mode=pdf> (last accessed 11 May 2018).

appropriately considered a subaltern society without the means, in principle or practice, to determine their future.

Case study 2: Removing support for crofting

The second case study analyses the Scottish Government's reform proposals for crofting support as part of the 2014–20 Scottish Rural Development Programme (SRDP), the means by which it implements the rural development pillar of the European Union's Common Agricultural Policy. The reform proposals included one to replace an existing Crofting Counties Agricultural Grant Scheme (CCAGS) – which provided capital grants to crofters for a limited range of agricultural operations – with a scheme operating on the same basis but open to all Scottish farms and small holdings under 50 hectares. The government stated it was proposing the change 'on the basis of the feedback from the stage 1 consultation'.[30]

However, the Scottish Government's claim that stage one feedback could provide a basis for the plan to replace CCAGS with a Scotland-wide scheme is questionable. The claim was justified in paragraph 169 of the stage two 'final proposals' document. Here is paragraph 169 in full:

> With respect to eligibility considerations, consultees were asked whether support for crofting currently provided under the CCAGS should extend to small land holders of like status. 60% of those responding to the question agreed and there was a strong consensus that support should extend to the whole of Scotland on the basis that small scale low-intensity farms play an important role in supporting rural employment and maintaining the social fabric of rural areas.[31]

Paragraph 169 therefore asserted as fact that 60 per cent of consultees responded positively to a question that asked whether CCAGS provisions should be extended to non-crofters. This stage one question had asked:

> Do you agree or disagree on whether support for crofting should extend to small land holders of like economic status who are situated *within crofting counties*? [author's emphasis][32]

---

[30] Scottish Government, 'Consultation on Scotland's Rural Development Programme (SRDP) 2014–20, Stage 2: Final Proposals' (Edinburgh, 2013a), paras 170–2, 177, <http://www.scotland.gov.uk/Resource/0044/00440079.pdf> (last accessed 12 February 2014).

[31] Scottish Government, 'Consultation, Stage 2: Final Proposals', para. 169.

[32] Scottish Government, 'Consultation on Scotland Rural Development

This question shows that in the stage one consultation, the idea of extending CCAGS throughout Scotland was not an option. However, it is impossible to discern this fact from the particular choice of words subsequently used by the Scottish Government in paragraph 169 of its final proposals. Indeed, the paragraph implies that it was this wider question that was asked.

Paragraph 169 then took the argument for extension further, claiming that the consultation revealed 'a strong consensus that support should extend to the whole of Scotland'. 'Consensus' is defined as a 'general or widespread agreement among all the members of a group'. The government's evidence of 'strong consensus' for the extension of support beyond the crofting counties is likely to be derived from the following statement in the analysis of responses to the stage one consultation:

> A strong theme in the responses to Question 12 was that small landowners of like economic status should be eligible for funding . . . *irrespective of whether they were situated in crofting counties.* As stated above, if small scale, low-intensity farms can deliver the Government's priority outcomes, there is no reason to limit ring-fenced support to crofting counties only [emphasis in original].[33]

Therefore, in order for government to justify its proposal to replace CCAGS, it must demonstrate that a strong 'general or widespread agreement' existed among stage one respondents that a Scotland-wide scheme should replace CCAGS. However, only 60 per cent of respondents agreed with the proposal to include non-crofters *within* the crofting counties in a new crofting programme. The other 40 per cent did not state their agreement to this proposal. The stage one analysis states that 27 per cent disagreed with the proposal – including all crofting representative groups. The position of the other 13 per cent was not fully explained.[34]

If 27 per cent of respondents believed that non-crofters from *inside* the crofting counties should not qualify for support, then it would seem to follow that this 27 per cent would also believe that non-crofters from *outside* the crofting counties should not qualify for support. Therefore, the analysis appears to show that at least 27 per cent – and potentially

Programme (SRDP) 2014–2020 Stage 1: Initial Proposals' (Edinburgh, May 2013b), p. 28.

[33] D. Griesbach, J. Waterton and A. Platts, 'Scotland's Rural Development Programmes Consultation on Stage 1 Proposals. An Analysis of Responses' (Edinburgh: Scottish Government, 2013), section 6.53, <http://www.scotland.gov.uk/Resource/0043/00432421.pdf> (last accessed 12 February 2014).

[34] Griesbach et al., 'Scotland's Rural Development Programmes', section 6.51.

at least 40 per cent – of respondents were not part of the strong 'general or widespread agreement' that the Scottish Government reported it had found for extending crofting support throughout Scotland. Furthermore, in order to demonstrate that even half of all stage one respondents were in favour of extending crofting support throughout Scotland, the stage one analysis would have had to provide evidence that around 85 per cent of all responses which supported extension to non-crofters within the crofting counties also supported extension beyond the crofting counties. This evidence was not presented.

However, it is not only the weight of support for the proposal that is questionable. The government's argument in paragraph 169 also failed to disclose that stage one respondents were not giving their views to a direct replacement for CCAGS. Instead, they were responding to proposals for a Crofting Support Scheme [CSS], a far more comprehensive scheme to fund 'all types of grants relevant to crofting', including agri-environment schemes as well as capital grants.[35] Although the Scottish Government presented the consultation feedback as justification to open up CCAGS beyond the crofting areas, this feedback was actually on a qualitatively different scheme.

Therefore, the government used a questionable interpretation of the consultation feedback on this new extensive scheme to justify the replacement of a different, more limited scheme already in existence. Its final proposals appear, *prima facie*, to have misrepresented the consultation feedback in order to implement a different political agenda regarding crofting support.

One uncontroversial and relatively strong consensus that did emerge from the consultation was that 73 per cent of respondents supported establishing the CSS, with only 8 per cent disagreeing. All responding crofting and farming organisations favoured the CSS.[36] Despite the high level of consensus this proposal attracted, the Scottish Government did not take on board the views of the majority because 'a number of respondents . . . did not believe that a single scheme could fund all the requirements crofters might have, and did not think the Government should seek to create a scheme that would do this'. It thus came to the conclusion that such a scheme 'would be complex and would add a disproportionate administrative burden'.[37] The Scottish Government did not state who the negative respondents were and why their views

---

[35] Scottish Government, 'Consultation, Stage 1: Initial Proposals', p. 28.

[36] Griesbach et al., 'Scotland's Rural Development Programmes', section 6.36.

[37] Scottish Government, 'Consultation, Stage 2 Final Proposals', para. 175.

were considered more important than the eight crofting and farming organisations who were unanimously in favour. Neither did it explain why a comprehensive crofting scheme was included as a possibility in the stage one consultation in the first place, given the government's opposition to it in principle.

The Scottish Government rejected the CSS proposal despite 73 per cent of respondents supporting it. In this regard it is worth recalling that the stage one analysis report showed that 73 per cent appears to have been the highest possible proportion of respondents in favour of opening crofting support beyond the crofting areas.[38] The government therefore appears to have rejected a strong consensus in favour of the CSS while, at the same time, proposing replacement of CCAGS on the basis of what is likely to have been a less robust 'consensus' that was based on responses to a question that did not directly relate to CCAGS.

In conclusion, multiple omissions underpinned the Scottish Government's proposed replacement of CCAGS with a Scotland-wide scheme. The government omitted the fact that the 60 per cent of consultees who favoured extending crofting support to non-crofters were responding to a question which was specific to a limited extension within the crofting counties. The government also omitted the fact that their claimed 'strong consensus' for extending CCAGS support beyond the crofting counties was actually made in response to a question about a different scheme, the comprehensive CSS. Furthermore, the government rejected the proposal for the CSS, despite the CSS having, at the very least, the same level of support as the claimed 'strong consensus' for the proposal to extend CCAGS. Indeed, at stage one, it also omitted the fact that it was already opposed, in principle, to the comprehensive CSS that it was proposing. In none of the above examples of policy-making did the consultation evidence justify the Scottish Government's final proposal. It can therefore be argued that the government consistently shaped the SRDP consultation process on crofting support in order to pursue policy

---

[38] The consultation feedback states that 60 per cent of respondents were in favour of extending support *within* the crofting counties, but this figure could possibly be as high as 73 per cent because there is a constituency of 13 per cent whose views are not explained. However, we don't know what the views of respondents were to extension *beyond* the crofting counties, because this question wasn't asked. If everyone who was in favour of extension *within* the crofting counties was also in favour of extension *beyond* (which is a big assumption) then the very maximum proportion that could be in favour of the government's proposal to replace CCAGS is 73 per cent. This is the same as the proportion favouring the CSS which the Scottish Government rejected out of hand.

objectives that did not reflect the evidence that government had received from the public about how crofting support should be taken forward. Following strong representation from SCF and the National Farmers Union of Scotland the Scottish Government dropped the proposed replacement scheme and agreed to retain a separate CCAGS.

In terms of the Scottish National Standards for Community Engagement, it is questionable that the Scottish Government's engagement with respondents on crofting support can be considered 'fair and effective' or that the proposal to replace CCAGS accurately reflected the views of consultation participants.[39] Perhaps more fundamentally, the SRDP case study calls into question whether the Scottish Government 'honestly and sincerely' – in the words of the CoE Guidelines – considered the views of civil society when arriving at the decision to replace CCAGS, and treated those views in a respectful, open and transparent way.[40]

CROFTING POLICY AND LEGISLATION: AN UNDEMOCRATIC AND ILLEGITIMATE STRUCTURE OF DOMINATION

The political relationships disclosed in these two case studies can be considered in light of the earlier discussion of citizens' democratic freedom in modern states. This discussion distinguished two related but distinct ways in which citizens' freedom to participate in decision-making processes can be compromised. The first level relates to the power of those governing a particular decision-making process to limit or to shape citizen participation. This first level is important when considering whether consultees in the SRDP reform case study had 'a voice in the way in which political power was exercised'. The second level relates to the background constitutional procedures and principles that coordinate the ways in which decision-making processes take place. This level draws our attention to the ways in which these systems of rules constrain or enable different voices to inform the negotiations that lead to political change. This second level is important in considering the process by which the legislature successfully governmentalised grazings committees through the 'duty-to-report', questioning whether this was achieved without crofters having a say and, therefore, as Tully puts it, 'behind their backs'.

---

[39] Scottish Government, *National Standards for Community Engagement.*

[40] CoE, *Guidelines for civil participation in political decision-making*, sections III (3), (4)(a)(d).

The discussion on the conditions for legitimacy in modern political orders also offers a way to understand the apparently extreme expressions of mistrust and disempowerment made by crofting representatives quoted at the start of this chapter. For instance, if the governors of a decision-making process promise to treat civil society contributions honestly and sincerely, but then misrepresent consultation evidence to propose an outcome that the evidence, at face value, does not support (as appears to have happened in the SRDP reform), such actions by governors might reasonably lead to the accusation – such as the one made by the SCF – that the governors are 'two-faced'. Equally, if governors claim to be committed to ensuring meaningful involvement of citizens in legislative changes that directly affect them, but then establish a law and those affected by that law are given no opportunity to participate in its creation (as appears to be the case in the 'duty-to-report'), such actions might reasonably lead those affected to believe that they are in a relationship with their governors that can accurately be described as 'colonial', as the SCF have asserted. In both instances the people affected might legitimately consider their interests to have been 'shafted'.

This chapter's analysis suggests that the political relationship between Scotland's government and the country's crofting population repeatedly fails to meet national and international standards and principles which should protect crofters' ability as citizens to engage in political decision-making upon matters that affect them. In consequence, it is hard to consider that the framework of conventions guiding the legislative process of Scottish constitutional democracy consistently places crofters in the normative position of being citizen members of civil society. Instead, the evidence of the SRDP reform and the post-CoIC legislation suggests that, as a social and political entity, the crofting community of the twenty-first century may more accurately be considered subaltern: the collective subject of an undemocratic and illegitimate structure of domination that appears to be eroding their landholding traditions while, at the same time, undermining their right to meaningfully participate in political life.

As stated at the outset, this is a preliminary investigation. A fuller understanding of the democratic deficit that helps to define the relationship between crofting and government in contemporary Scotland would require, in addition to a more comprehensive contemporary analysis, a critical historical survey of the subaltern heritage of the modern crofting community and the political processes and languages of description by which the form of un-freedom faced by crofters today came into being. This history would include the pre- and post-Culloden 'domestic colonisation' of the area that became known as the 'crofting counties'.

It would also include an analysis of the idea that crofting tenure was a legislative response to an ethnic rising – rather than a class rising – in the late nineteenth century, and that crofting tenure can therefore be considered, in its origins at the least, as belonging to a 'Celtic' *ethnos*, buried below the imperial constitutional norms of a British *demos*.[41]

---

[41] PP, XXXVI: *Report of the Commissioners of Inquiry into the Condition of Crofters and Cottars in the Highlands and Islands of Scotland*, 1884, p. 111.

16

Does Size Really Matter? Sustainable Development Outcomes from Different Scales of Land Ownership

Jayne Glass, Steven Thomson and Rob Mc Morran

LAND USE IN RURAL Scotland falls within several overlapping policy spheres (for instance, agriculture, forestry, energy) and is subject to a range of policy instruments. Although Scottish policy toward land ownership is increasingly rooted in concerns about fairness, equality and the fulfilment of human rights,[1] there are still relatively few measures in place in Scotland focused on the type of landowner or the scale of land ownership. This contrasts with some other countries, where there are specific policy targets and/or land market interventions that relate to who can own land and how much land can be owned by one individual.[2]

Despite the lack of policy targets or controls in relation to who can own land in Scotland (and how much they can own), the concentrated pattern of land ownership in rural Scotland that has perpetuated over several centuries continues to be a central focus of contemporary debate. As a result, the 'Land Rights and Responsibilities Statement' published by the Scottish Government in 2017 seeks 'a more diverse pattern of land ownership and tenure, with more opportunities for citizens to own, lease and have access to land'.[3] In this chapter, we present and reflect on the findings of research carried out between 2015 and 2016 to assess the impacts of differing scales of rural land ownership on local social, economic and environmental outcomes in six Scottish parishes.[4]

---

[1] McCarthy: this volume.

[2] J. Glass, R. Bryce, M. M. Combe, N. E. Hutchison, M. F. Price, L. Schulz, and D. Valero, 'Research on interventions to manage land markets and limit the concentration of land ownership elsewhere in the world' (Scottish Land Commission, Commissioned Report No. 001, 2018).

[3] Scottish Government, 'Land Rights and Responsibilities Statement', Principle 2, <https://www.gov.scot/publications/scottish-land-rights-responsibilities-statement/> (last accessed 31 March 2019).

[4] S. Thomson, A. Moxey, A. Wightman, A. McKee, D. Miller, E. Brodie, J. Glass, J. Hopkins, K. Mathews, K. Thomson, R. Mc Morran, and R. Bryce, 'The impact

SCOTLAND'S CONCENTRATED PATTERN OF RURAL LAND OWNERSHIP

From the seventeenth century into the second half of the nineteenth century, there was an increasing concentration of land ownership in rural Scotland into fewer and fewer private estates.[5] Changes in land ownership and the objectives of owners in this period were some of the reasons that many landlords cleared people from the land,[6] often to capitalise on the more profitable nature of sheep farming, which emerged because of agricultural improvements and industrial needs for food and fibre.[7] The Scottish Clearances,[8] which involved the displacement and eviction of communities across rural Scotland (particularly in the century from 1760), continue to generate debate among historians, reformers and policy-makers.[9] However, there is no doubt that this period of history had the greatest impact on communal memory in the Highlands and Islands, retaining powerful historical symbolism today and contributing to negative sentiments about private land ownership.[10]

In the mid nineteenth century, large tracts of land were bought up by the newly rich industrial magnates of the Victorian era, and existing landlords who sought to expand their holdings.[11] Many sheep farms were converted to sporting estates managed for the shooting of deer and grouse as the primary land use.[12] The collapse of sheep prices in the 1870s made land available at relatively low values for sporting

of diversity of ownership scale on social, economic and environmental outcomes: Exploration and case studies', Report to Scottish Government (Edinburgh: Scottish Government, 2016).

[5] Robin F. Callander, *A Pattern of Landownership in Scotland* (Finzean: Haughend Publications, 1987).

[6] There were many factors leading to the Clearances: the changing nature of landed power, a significant population boom and the impact of the new industrial and imperial economies. See Chapters 1, 2 and 5 in this volume for further context.

[7] A. F. D. Mackenzie, 'The Cheviot, The Stag . . . and the White, White Rock? Community, identity and environmental threat on the Isle of Harris', *Environment and Planning D: Society and Space*, 16 (1998), pp. 509–32.

[8] T. M. Devine, *The Scottish Clearances* (Penguin: London, 2018).

[9] See Chapters 1, 2 and 5 in this volume for further context.

[10] A. McKee, C. Warren, J. Glass and P. Wagstaff, 'The Scottish private estate', in J. Glass, M. F. Price, C. Warren and A. Scott (eds), *Lairds, Land and Sustainability: Scottish Perspectives on Upland Management* (Edinburgh: Edinburgh University Press, 2013), pp. 63–85.

[11] Ibid.

[12] D. C. MacMillan, K. Leitch, A. Wightman and P. Higgins, 'The Management and Role of Highland Sporting Estates in the Early Twenty-First Century: The

use, which subsequently led to some 60 per cent of Scotland becoming sporting estates.[13] A government survey in 1872 found that 90 per cent of Scotland's 7.9 million hectares was owned by 1,380 private landowners.[14] By 1873, half of Scotland's land was owned by 118 people, and 50 per cent of the Highlands was in the hands of fifteen landowners – this peak of concentrated land ownership continued for several decades.[15]

From the 1890s, land settlement – the breaking up of large farms or estates into small holdings – began to take place in Scotland in response to the rural overcrowding, landlessness and deprivation that had developed in many parts of the Highlands and Islands.[16] Following the Napier Commission (1884) and the Crofters Holdings (Scotland) Act 1886, the Highlands and Islands Royal Commission recommended in 1895 that land used as deer forest or large sheep farms was suitable for subdivision into holdings for crofters and other small tenants, and for creating moderate-sized farms. The Congested Districts Board (CDB) acquired land (by agreement, under the auspices of the Congested Districts (Scotland) Act 1897) for settlement and to help create 252 new holdings for crofters on private estate land and 388 holdings on state-owned land between 1897 and 1912 (when it was replaced by the Board of Agriculture in terms of the Small Landholders (Scotland) Act 1911).[17] Despite the small scale of early land settlement, there was some evidence of intensification of land use. However, the land settlement process at this time had inadequate funding and the powers of the CDB were very limited.[18]

Between 1912 and 1956, 1,661 holdings were created on private estate land and 3,010 on state-owned land across the country.[19] In this era, the geographic specificity of crofting was removed and unique

Owner's View of a Unique But Contested Form of Land Use', *Scottish Geographical Journal*, 126 (2010), pp. 24–40.

[13] W. Orr, *Deer Forest, Landlords and Crofters: the Western Highlands in Victorian and Edwardian Times* (Edinburgh: John Donald, 1982).

[14] Callander, *A Pattern of Landownership in Scotland*.

[15] A. M. Armstrong, A. S. Mather, *Land Ownership and Land Use in the Scottish Highlands*. (Aberdeen: University of Aberdeen, Department of Geography, 1983).

[16] A. S. Mather, 'The rise and fall of government-assisted land settlement in Scotland', *Land Use Policy*, 2 (1985), pp. 217–24.

[17] Ibid.

[18] L. Leneman, 'Land Settlement in Scotland after World War I', *The Agricultural History Review*, 37 (1989), pp. 52–64; See Cameron: this volume.

[19] Mather, 'The rise and fall of government-assisted land settlement in Scotland', pp. 217–24.

rules were applied across Scotland to small-scale tenanted landholdings defined and governed by the Small Landholders (Scotland) Acts 1886 to 1931.[20] After the First World War, small landholdings were created through compulsory purchase via the Land Settlement (Scotland) Act 1919, principally to enable ex-servicemen to secure access to land. The Crofters (Scotland) Act 1955 reintroduced separate geographical regulation for the Highlands and Islands.[21] By the 1970s, most of the small landholdings had been sold to sitting tenants or amalgamated into larger units,[22] and the Scottish Government estimate that currently only about sixty-eight remain.[23]

Other important changes in the pattern of land ownership occurred in the twentieth century as a result of external economic and socio-political factors. These included a reduction in the area held by larger estates, often as a result of increased death duties in the first half of the twentieth century which led to the sale of landholdings, wider economic recession, and unprofitable land ownership.[24] There was also a major expansion in the extent of land owned by state and public agencies. For example, from 1919 until the 1970s, there was a considerable increase in the amount of land managed by the Forestry Commission, which now

[20] Whilst there is significant and easily accessible legislation and regulation available on the other holding types in Scotland (e.g. crofting, agricultural tenancy), small landholdings have not been specifically legislated for since the Small Landholders and Agricultural Holdings (Scotland) Act 1931, meaning data on small landholdings is relatively inaccessible, fragmented and dated – a position that led to the Scottish Government Small Landholdings Legislative Review in 2017. It can also be noted that there are – theoretically – two types of landholder with special tenancy rights, namely 'small landholder' and 'statutory small tenant', with the latter being afforded less protection owing to the fact that any fixtures on the land were provided by the landowner rather than the occupier. It is understood, as at 25 September 2018, no one in Scotland claims to have a statutory small tenancy. See C. Agnew, 'Small landholdings legislation: guide to the law in Scotland' (Edinburgh: Scottish Government, 2018), <https://www.gov.scot/publications/small-landholdings-legislation-guide-law-scotland/> (last accessed 31 March 2019).

[21] A system that is explained by MacLellan in this volume.

[22] Mather, 'The rise and fall of government-assisted land settlement in Scotland'; Leneman, 'Land Settlement in Scotland after World War I'.

[23] A. Tindley, M. Gibbard and M. M. Combe, 'Small Landholdings: Landownership and Registration', Scottish Government commissioned report, Project SG/RESAS/004/17 (Edinburgh: Scottish Government), <https://www.gov.scot/publications/small-landholdings-landownership-registration-project-report/> (last accessed 31 March 2019).

[24] For an overview of this see D. Cannadine, *The Decline and Fall of the British Aristocracy* (New Haven: Yale University Press, 1990), pp. 3–24.

makes up Scotland's National Forest Estate.[25] In the 1980s and early 1990s, the total area of land owned by charitable environmental organisations such as the National Trust for Scotland also rose by 146 per cent to reach 133,500 hectares.[26] Nonetheless, land ownership in Scotland continues today to be dominated by just over 400 private owners (0.008 per cent of the population) who have been estimated to own 50 per cent of privately owned rural land.[27] Moreover, there is a long-term pattern of low turnover in the estate land market, which is unlikely to change in the near future, and most owners, regardless of whether they inherit or purchase their estates, wish to pass their estate to an heir.[28]

A national survey of private landowners carried out in 2013 returned 228 responses, which were used alongside other public and private 'estates' databases to estimate that 1,125 owners held 4.1 million hectares (70 per cent of Scotland's rural land) in 'estates' (landholdings with a range of interests that may include in-hand farming, let farms, sporting interests, forestry, residential property, workspaces, tourism and community facilities).[29] Of these estates, 87 were estimated to be larger than 10,000 hectares (67 of these are in the Highlands), 667 were 1,000–10,000 hectares in size, and 371 were smaller than 1,000 hectares. There are a range of factors that influence the scale of any individual landholding (now and historically), including: inheritance tax relief, capital gains tax (and capital gains tax rollover relief), income tax relief, agricultural subsidies, forestry grants, succession laws, divorce settlement, gifts to family members, debts that can be settled through the sale of landholdings, and the lotting of landholdings to maximise potential sale value.[30] These factors influence new purchases of land, as well as sales of land and succession of land.

[25] Land Reform Review Group, 'The Land of Scotland and the Common Good' (Edinburgh: Scottish Government, 2014), p. 52.

[26] R. Mc Morran and J. Glass, 'Buying Nature', in Glass et al., *Lairds, Land and Sustainability*, pp. 173–88.

[27] J. Hunter, P. Peacock, A. Wightman and M. Foxley, '432:50 – Towards a comprehensive land reform agenda for Scotland', Briefing Paper for the House of Commons Scottish Affairs Committee (2014).

[28] McKee et al., 'The Scottish private estate', pp. 63–85.

[29] R. Hindle, S. Thomson, S. Skerratt, R. Mc Morran and P. Onea, 'Economic Contribution of Estates in Scotland: An Economic Assessment for Scottish Land & Estates' (Musselburgh: Scottish Land and Estates, 2014). The survey received 228 responses.

[30] For a more comprehensive list of these factors, see Thomson et al., 'The impact of diversity of ownership scale on social, economic and environmental outcomes', pp. 89–90, Appendix 5.

DIVERSITY OF OWNERSHIP IN SCOTTISH POLICY

In 1998, the Land Reform Policy Group concluded that the existing system of land ownership in Scotland was inhibiting development in rural communities and causing degradation of the natural heritage because of poor land management.[31] This conclusion ultimately led to the adoption of the main objective of Scottish land reform policy, which remains relevant today: to remove the land-based barriers to the sustainable development of rural communities.[32] The Group argued that this could only be achieved through increasing diversity in land ownership, between private, public, not-for-profit and community sectors, and via increasing community involvement in local decision-making about how land is owned and managed.

Nearly ten years after the Land Reform (Scotland) Act 2003, the Scottish Government's Rural and Environment Science and Analytical Services (RESAS) department suggested that there remained a lack of clarity over the rationale and remit of land reform surrounding the land-based barriers to the sustainable development of communities.[33] There was uncertainty about the form this 'sustainable development' should take, or what features should be prioritised. They also questioned whether the land-based barriers mentioned in the policy rhetoric related to ownership or stewardship, since both are likely to be important for sustainable development, with different measures required for each (the potential benefits are unlikely to be accrued through changing ownership alone). They further suggested that, in certain circumstances, other approaches (for example, land leasing, changes to land and asset management) may be at least as effective as land reform policy in achieving sustainable development in rural communities. It is against this backdrop that the RESAS division of the Scottish Government commissioned a study to provide evidence-based conclusions to address the hypothesis that 'diverse (scale of) land ownership leads to better social, economic and environmental outcomes'.[34]

[31] Land Reform Policy Group, 'Identifying the Problems' (Edinburgh, Scottish Office, 1998).

[32] Land Reform Policy Group, 'Recommendations for Action' (Edinburgh, Scottish Office, 1999).

[33] Scottish Government Rural and Environment Science and Analytical Services, 'Overview of Evidence on Land Reform in Scotland'. Rural and Environmental Science and Analytical Services (Edinburgh: Scottish Government, 2012), <http://www.gov.scot/Publications/2012/07/3328/0> (last accessed 31 March 2019).

[34] Thomson et al., 'The impact of diversity of ownership scale on social, economic and environmental outcomes', p. 9.

The remainder of this chapter presents and discusses the results of that project, which the authors of this chapter completed for the Scottish Government in 2016 (with the assistance of other researchers in our project team, who are listed at the end of this chapter).[35]

FORMS OF 'SUSTAINABLE DEVELOPMENT'

Despite being a notoriously difficult concept to pin down, sustainable development highlights the importance of equity with a focus on development that meets the needs of the present without compromising the ability of future generations to meet their own needs.[36] The political rhetoric of the sustainable development agenda has become embedded in land reform legislation, most notably through the 'right to buy land to further sustainable development' for communities in the Land Reform (Scotland) Act 2016, and the requirement for community bodies seeking to purchase land or other assets to have a commitment to sustainable development.[37] Sustainable development remains undefined in the legislation,[38] although in a 2012 court case Lord Malcolm's opinion was that the term is readily understood by legislators, Ministers and the Scottish Land Court.[39]

Academic research has sought to define and measure sustainable development outcomes, as applied to the context of land ownership in rural Scotland[40] and in terms of rural socio-economic outcomes.[41] The National Upland Outcomes (developed for English uplands by the UK Government's Department for Environment, Food and Rural Affairs) also provide a framework for partnership working to deliver sustainable land use.[42] We reviewed these existing outcome measurement frameworks alongside the Scottish Government's National Performance

---

[35] Ibid.

[36] Ross: this volume.

[37] Combe: this volume; Lovett: this volume.

[38] Ross: this volume.

[39] *Pairc Crofters* v. *The Scottish Ministers* [2012] CSIH 96, at paragraph [101], <https://www.scotcourts.gov.uk/search-judgments/judgment?id=dc7586a6-8980-69d2-b500-ff0000d74aa7> (last accessed 31 March 2019).

[40] J. H. Glass, A. Scott and M. F. Price, 'The power of the process: Co-producing a sustainability assessment toolkit for upland estate management in Scotland', *Land Use Policy*, 30 (2013), pp. 254–65.

[41] A. Copus and J. Hopkins, 'Mapping Rural Socio-Economic Performance', Report for Rural Communities Team, Food Drink and Rural Communities Division (Edinburgh: Scottish Government, 2015).

[42] Department for Environment, Food and Rural Affairs, 'National Upland

Table 16.1 Sustainable development outcomes for rural communities

	Sustainable development outcomes
Economic development	Economic self-reliance, financial reliability
	Diverse, plentiful, high quality employment opportunities
	Favourable population structure
Social development	High quality, available, affordable homes
	Communities benefit from the outdoors
	Strong rural social fabric and infrastructure
	Empowered and confident communities
Environmental enhancement	Public benefits from sustainable ecosystems
	Enhanced biodiversity
	Contribution to climate change mitigation

Framework to identify ten outcomes that we deemed important for sustainable development in rural communities (see Table 16.1).

We also developed a framework of numerous other factors that may influence local development for application within the research. These include: *geographic factors*, such as land capability and climate; *infrastructure and technology factors*, such as digital connectivity; *economic factors*, such as market prices and fuel prices; *policy factors*, such as income and business taxation; and *social and demography factors*, such as demographic change, political influence and motivations for owning land.[43]

UNDERSTANDING OUTCOMES IN SIX SCOTTISH PARISHES

To understand the extent to which the scale of land ownership influences the outcomes we deemed important for sustainable development in local communities (henceforth referred to as 'local outcomes'), we identified six rural parishes[44] to study in detail, from an initial list

Outcomes: A framework to help develop local partnership outcomes' (London: Defra/Natural England, 2013).

[43] The motivations of private landowners have been considered in some depth by Macmillan et al., 'The Management and Role of Highland Sporting Estates in the Early Twenty-First Century', pp. 24–40; and P. Wagstaff, 'What motivates private landowners?', in Glass et al., (eds), *Lairds, Land and Sustainability*, chapter 4.

[44] In Scotland, civil parishes are units of local government which were abolished by the Local Government (Scotland) Act 1929. The geographical area is still referred to for statistical purposes, particularly when data is available at the parish scale (as

of twenty-eight parishes where current land ownership patterns were known. The parishes were organised into fourteen pairs, with one parish in each pair having been fragmented (that is, historically under the control of one private estate or a small number of large estates which had been broken up into smaller landholdings) and the other having remained substantially intact (largely remaining under the control of one estate or a small number of large estates). Each of the paired parishes were in relatively close geographic proximity and we used Geographic Information System (GIS) mapping in the selection process to allow an impartial and scientific approach to selecting pairs of parishes that were broadly comparable in terms of their physical geography (altitude/topography, land capability, land cover and peripherality) and land use, but each had different land ownership patterns.

The three selected paired parishes were located near each other (generally within the same local authority region) and spread across different agricultural land capabilities[45] and a range of distances from major urban centres to reflect different types of estate and differing degrees of peripherality. Table 16.2 provides more information about each parish that was selected (parish names are not revealed to preserve the anonymity of participants). It is important to note at this point that, at the direction of Scottish Government, this project excluded crofting areas and areas under community land ownership as potential case studies. Crofting land was excluded due to the existing fragmentation of crofting land management (ownership being less of a factor due to crofting legislation) and community ownership was in its relative infancy.

We created quantitative profiles for each of the six parishes to provide a timeline of land ownership changes and other key outcomes (for example, demography, housing) over the last century. The profiles included data from a range of sources, including the June Agricultural Census, environmental GIS datasets and population census data. The

was the case in this research), and the term also occurs regularly in land transfer documentation.

[45] The Land Use Capability system is based on a series of guidelines that allows soil maps and other landscape and climatic information to be interpreted into land classification maps. There are seven classes (Class 1 has the highest potential flexibility of use and Class 7 is of very limited agricultural value), <https://www.hutton.ac.uk/learning/exploringscotland/land-capability-agriculture-scotland> (last accessed 1 March 2019).

Table 16.2 Descriptions of the case study pairs (anonymised)

'Unfragmented' parish Landholding scale maintained	'Fragmented' parish Landholding scale not maintained
Parish 1A • Accessible rural area • Six villages and two smaller hamlets • Largely owned by a single private estate	Parish 1B • Accessible rural area • Two towns • Main estate sold and broken up after the First World War
Parish 2A • Relatively accessible rural area • Partly urban and several small villages • Majority of the parish under the ownership of a private estate	Parish 2B • Remote coastal area 40 mins from urban centre • Four villages and popular tourist destination • One of the main estates was split up in the 1920s and 1940s
Parish 3A • Remote rural area • Two main villages and cluster of hamlets • Majority of the parish under the ownership of a private estate	Parish 3B • Remote rural area • One main village and several small villages/hamlets • Principal estate largely broken up in the 1920s creating numerous smaller holdings

Sasine Register[46] was used to identify changes in the ownership of estates on sub plots more than one hectare in size.[47]

We also conducted fieldwork in each parish to understand key 'drivers' of changes and outcomes in each place over the last fifty years. We carried out interviews and focus groups with a range of landowners, land managers, local heritage groups, historians, local business representatives and other community members to enable us to develop a more detailed understanding of parish history and how these 'drivers' affected change. There was a tendency to contact and receive information from older community members due to the historical focus of the work, and we recognise that younger and newer community members may have offered different perspectives in some cases.

[46] See Simpson: this volume. The Sasine Register is searchable via the Scotland Search website, <https://scotlandsearch.org.uk/sasine-register> (last accessed 1 March 2019). The register itself is maintained by Registers of Scotland, <https://www.ros.gov.uk/our-registers/general-register-of-sasines> (last accessed 1 March 2019). It is gradually being replaced by the map-based Land Register of Scotland, with a target closing date for the Sasine Register of 2024.
[47] Otherwise, the exercise would have taken much longer. We focused on the first and second major changes in ownership.

UNDERSTANDING FRAGMENTATION

Searching the Sasine Register and talking to local people in the interviews and focus groups revealed that the break-up of landholdings in the fragmented parishes had occurred for several reasons. In the first fragmented parish, the 'selling off' of land took place in the interwar period because the then owner of one large estate experienced financial difficulties during the 1920s Depression. This led to the existence of more owner-occupied farms, small agricultural holdings and private house plots. Since then, there have only been limited changes to land ownership scale in that parish, although land has been bought and sold between owners, as well as farmland being sub-let, typically as seasonal lets. In the second fragmented parish, which was historically owned between three large estates, fragmentation into sixty different ownership units occurred between the 1920s and 1980s, partly as a result of economic problems in the 1930s when leasing land was uneconomic. Additionally, one of the large estates had been broken up due to a need to raise funds to pay 'death duties' which were levied on the property following the death of the owner, with the inheriting owner paying the duties by selling land to ex-servicemen upon their return to their tenancy as a form of reward after the First World War.

The principal estate in the third fragmented parish was almost entirely split up by 1950, with the solitary estate broken into seventy-seven new landholdings over the century since 1900. Whilst parts of the controlling estate had been sold off to pay for mounting debts in the early 1900s, the main fragmentation within the parish was a result of death duties. In this case, land value inflation has been a significant factor in recent years, driven in part by income from sales for housing development being reinvested and partly by support from the Common Agricultural Policy (CAP) being capitalised into land values. To explain briefly, CAP was a form of European Union (EU) support payable in relation to rural land, and in addition to driving land-use choices (to ensure eligibility for support) the very fact of eligibility also affected the value of land.

The total area of agricultural holdings[48] also differed somewhat between the parishes due to differences between farming systems (which relate to land capability) and the extent of ownership fragmentation.

---

[48] Agricultural holdings are all holdings listed in the June Agricultural Census, ranging from large estates to small paddocks and covering 6.2 million hectares of Scotland, <https://www2.gov.scot/Topics/Statistics/Browse/Agriculture-Fisheries/PubFinalResultsJuneCensus> (last accessed 31 March 2019).

In the unfragmented parishes, which remain under one ownership or a small number of ownerships, the number of agricultural holdings had fallen by 7 per cent between 1982 and 2012.[49] In at least one parish, this was a direct result of the amalgamation of smaller holdings to create more viable units for tenants, or due to holdings being taken back 'in hand' (that is to say, managed directly) by the estate. In contrast, there were 7 per cent more agricultural holdings over the same period in the fragmented parishes, perhaps because of the subdivision of holdings through the sale of land. In all the parishes, participants identified a trend towards the amalgamation of farm units over time to create larger, more economic farms that benefit from economies of scale. Coupled with amalgamations, there was a general trend (in five of the six parishes) for the number of small 'hobby' holdings to stay stable or rise – this was often associated with sales of housing with paddocks.

In five of the parishes, there was a sudden decrease in land farmed under agricultural tenure between 2002 and 2012. This was largely due to the 2003 reform of the CAP, which decoupled agricultural support (by removing the link between the receipt of a direct payment from the EU and the production of a specific product) and introduced the area-based Single Farm Payment.[50] In one of our focus groups, land managers (who were mostly owner-occupiers) described that over the last decade there has been a notable reduction in estate investment in tenant farms. There had been a trend to bring tenanted holdings back 'in hand' where possible and this has been followed by seasonal letting of the land, thereby avoiding security-of-tenure issues[51] and allowing the landowner access to area-based CAP payments.

ECONOMIC OUTCOMES – ECONOMICS, EMPLOYMENT AND POPULATION

The motivations of landowners were considered important by participants in our interviews and focus groups. While landowner absenteeism (not being resident on the estate) was not a key concern, it was evident that even different generations of owners from the same families had

---

[49] These calculations were made using holding-level data from the annual June Agricultural Census.

[50] C. Morgan-Davies, T. Waterhouse and R. Wilson, 'Characterisation of farmers' responses to policy reforms in Scottish hill farming areas', *Small Ruminant Research*, 102 (2012), pp. 96–107.

[51] See Lean: this volume.

invested to differing degrees in the development of estate infrastructure, businesses and other assets such as housing stock. In all the unfragmented parishes, participants felt that the estate(s) still had an important influence over the area.

There had been a reduction in the number of full-time occupiers of agricultural holdings in all but one of the parishes between 1982 and 2012. This was attributed to amalgamations enabled by the mechanisation of farming activities, a general need to develop additional off-farm income streams to help maintain the farming business, and the purchase of farms by new entrants to the sector who see the farm as secondary to their main employment. Part-time farming had become more prevalent in all parishes, with the reliance on off-farm income commonplace over the last twenty to thirty years. In terms of agricultural productivity, standard output per hectare[52] in 2014 was considerably higher in all the fragmented parishes than in their unfragmented counterparts. In the second and third pairs of parishes, there were also higher Standard Labour Requirements[53] and numbers of livestock units in fragmented parishes when compared to the unfragmented parishes. These figures suggest that there tended to be a greater economic intensity to agricultural activities in the fragmented parishes, although these findings should be interpreted with caution as agricultural Gross Value Added and profitability are not solely dependent on output levels.

The CAP was seen as a key driver of farming activity in all parishes since the late 1970s, through measures such as intervention pricing, coupled support payments, Less Favoured Area support, and the Scottish Rural Development Programme.[54] Participants also described important investment in farm buildings, fencing, roads, and so on, that was facilitated by older government schemes such as the Farm and Horticultural Development Scheme in the 1970s and 1980s. However, feedback from participants in all parishes described how farm diversification (adding additional income streams to the business) is an important strategy for

[52] Standard Output represents the estimated farm gate worth of crops and animals using standardised output factors, without taking any account of the costs incurred in production. For more detail, see <https://www.webarchive.org.uk/wayback/archive/20170701074158/www.gov.scot/Publications/2013/06/5219> (last accessed 1 March 2019).

[53] Standard Labour Requirements represent the notional amount of labour required by a holding to carry out all its agricultural activity; it is used as a measure of farm size.

[54] C. Warren, *Managing Scotland's Environment* (Edinburgh: Edinburgh University Press, 2009).

helping land-based businesses to remain economically viable, unless they invest significantly in specialisation. There has also been a significant decrease in the number of farm workers in the last forty years, due to mechanisation, with this decline in on-farm employment evident in the parishes studied in the research.

It was also noted in the unfragmented parishes that there had been a significant decline in the number of estate workers since the 1980s. This had noticeable social impacts locally, such as closures of schools and/or shops, although this decline had freed up some tied housing[55] for private rental or sale. Large estates in two of the three unfragmented parishes were relying increasingly on a network of self-employed contractors for land and property maintenance. This means that there are now fewer year-round land-based jobs than there once were (although jobs and economic benefits still arise from expenditure on contractors), and there has been a loss of connection with land management within the local resident population.

Beyond agriculture and other land-based businesses, participants reported that urban-based economic development and the centralisation of public services had led to a general lack of industry and small businesses within the parishes. In all parishes (including the first pair which had recent, large population increases), stories were told about declines in local shops, trades and services over time, particularly because of improved population mobility and the rise of internet shopping. In the third pair, there had been a significant increase in the number of tourism-related enterprises to capitalise on demand from visitors to a popular, scenic area.

Population change was regarded as an important driver of change in all parishes. Population census data for the three fragmented parishes suggested that they were each more likely to have experienced population growth between 1991 and 2011 than their unfragmented counterparts. For example, in the unfragmented parishes, the population of parish 1a declined by about 18 per cent, whilst in 2a it was static, and in 3a there was a modest growth of 4 per cent. This compared with the fragmented parishes, where there was a 63 per cent increase in 1b, a 14 per cent increase in 2b and a 13 per cent increase in 3b. The working-age population (16–74 years) changed by a similar proportion to the total population in each parish. However, these changes occurred during a period when rural communities across Scotland had experienced demographic change. All six parishes had an increase in the over-65-year-old

---

[55] Housing provided to estate employees as part of their employment terms (not owned).

grouping in the same time period and, with the exception of one parish (1b), saw a rise in the proportion of 45–64-year-olds. The proportion of 25–44-year-olds fell in all of the parishes except one (also 1b).

In general, the research participants did not equate land ownership factors with changes in populations, instead suggesting that change occurred because of wider economic and societal changes. All the parishes experience out-migration of young adults as they seek education and employment opportunities[56] and most businesses in the parishes struggle to recruit young workers. Instead, they are reliant on transient/ migrant labour, which may present additional challenges in the light of the result of the 2016 referendum on the UK's membership of the EU.[57] The influence of land ownership on these changes is unlikely to be simple and/or direct. However, population growth reflects employment and housing opportunities and the latter may be affected by the willingness of landowners to release land for new housing, but also by existing residents' and planning authorities' willingness to accept housing.

SOCIAL OUTCOMES – HOMES AND COMMUNITY CONFIDENCE

Interviewees and focus group participants described to us how the quality of housing standards in all the parishes had improved dramatically, particularly in the last forty to fifty years. The introduction of electricity, phones, insulation, central heating, modern appliances, etc., in most households, coupled with a reduction in overcrowding of housing were reported as having helped in significantly improving the quality of life of householders. Nonetheless, it was acknowledged that the pace of improvement has often been at the behest of the landlord, whether private or public.[58]

---

[56] This was also reported to be the case in wider rural Scotland in M. Woolvin and D. Skerratt, 'The third sector and civil society in rural Scotland: present and future?' in S. Skerratt, J. Atterton, C. Hall, D. McCracken, A. Renwick, C. Revoredo-Giha, A. Steinerowski, S. Thomson, M. Woolvin, J. Farrington and F. Heesen (eds), *Rural Scotland in Focus* (Edinburgh: Rural Policy Centre, SRUC, 2012).

[57] For example, the potential impacts of Brexit were found to have affected the confidence of a proportion of seasonal workers in Scottish agriculture, and their expectations about returning to Scotland in the future. See S. Thomson, R. Mc Morran, J. Bird, J. Atterton, L. Pate, E. Meador, P. De Lima and P. Milbourne, 'Farm Workers in Scottish Agriculture: Case Studies in the International Seasonal Migrant Labour Market', Commissioned report for the Scottish Government, Project No. CR2016/25 (Edinburgh: Scottish Government, 2018).

[58] See Cameron in Chapter 5 of this volume for consideration of this in the urban context.

In all parishes, the sale of former estate housing and the sale of buildings for conversion to housing or industrial development was an important driver of change. The sale of these types of assets had led to different outcomes depending on the location. Land sales for housing development were regarded as important in the more accessible locations, while the negative impacts of high numbers of second homes or tourism accommodation were more important in the less accessible case studies (where this type of home ownership was more common). Participants' concerns related to a lack of affordable housing stock for locals and an ageing population (although the latter was not always seen negatively with, for example, a highly skilled group of older people engaged in important volunteering activities in one parish).

Residents of the unfragmented parishes had much higher reliance on private rented accommodation than those in the fragmented parishes and participants suggested that where there had been a reduction in estate or farm workers, the vacated housing was generally used for private rental or holiday lets, although there was still some tied housing provision for retired estate workers in one parish (1a). A lack of affordable housing (to buy or rent) was one of the main factors that participants felt led to out-migration of younger families. There was difficulty finding affordable housing for locals in several parishes (for example, only six out of a total of seventy houses built in a village in parish 1a were 'affordable'). This lack of affordable housing is normally due to demand pressures from commuters and second-home owners. In one parish, where affordable housing existed, there were no local employment opportunities available for potential new residents. It was interesting to note that in one parish (3b) a smaller village had retained its 'affordable' status because plots of land had deliberately not been sold by the landowner to second-home owners or developers. This had led to the village having more permanent residents and younger families than elsewhere in the parish. In another parish (1b), where there had been rapid housing development, the growth was attributed to the willingness of farmers around the village to make option agreements with developers, Local Development Plan[59] decisions and demand due to a growing population.

Other discussions about social outcomes focused on schools, transport, local healthcare provision, village hall closures and broadband coverage. Patterns of land ownership were not generally regarded as significant in determining social outcomes relative to these other factors.

[59] A Local Development Plan is required for each council area across Scotland under the Town and Country Planning (Scotland) Act 1997.

We heard accounts of how, in the unfragmented parishes, landowners played an active community role through support for and participation in local projects and events (for example, the funding of some community activities and provision of land for agricultural shows). In general though, any changes relating to these outcomes were not attributed directly by participants to the decisions and actions of landowners.

ENVIRONMENTAL OUTCOMES – NATURAL HERITAGE AND CLIMATE CHANGE

In the first case-study pair, land is used for a mixture of purposes: cropping, pasture and a relatively small proportion of rough grazing. Very little land in these parishes is under environmental designation. In the second pair, there is very little cropping land, with about half of agricultural land used as pasture and the other half as rough grazing. Here, there is a higher proportion of the land under designation (around 31 per cent in 2a and 7 per cent in 2b). The third pair is largely dominated by rough grazing and both parishes have a number of environmental designations covering between 15 per cent and 20 per cent of the land.

Land ownership was mentioned infrequently in relation to environmental quality in the six parishes, with the potential for landowners with large landholdings to coordinate across large areas noted in some cases. There were some concerns that absentee landlords might neglect some aspects of land management. Environmental designations, aspects of the CAP, forestry grants and taxes were all identified as more important drivers of change of how the landscapes have been managed in the parishes over the past fifty years.

THE INFLUENCE OF LAND OWNERSHIP SCALE ON SUSTAINABLE DEVELOPMENT OUTCOMES

In the last twenty years, there has been considerable rhetoric about the scale of land ownership and how it may impact on the development of local communities. The Final Report of the Land Reform Review Group noted in 2014 that:

> The concentrated ownership of private land in rural communities places considerable power in the hands of relatively few individuals, which can in turn have a huge impact on the lives of local people and jars with the idea of Scotland being a modern democracy. The Group considers that a less concentrated pattern of land ownership would open up increased economic and

social opportunities in many parts of rural Scotland, helping create stronger and more resilient rural communities.[60]

The research that we have presented in this chapter found that land ownership scale is one of many factors that influence the economic, social and environmental development of communities. In the six parishes that were selected for this study, the complexity of ownership motivations and societal, policy and economic interactions in driving community development made it too challenging to conclude that scale of land ownership has been the main factor in determining the sustainable development of the communities we studied. There was a wide range of land ownership scales and degrees of land ownership fragmentation within the parishes, and different local community development pathways resulted in different local outcomes. Whilst it may have been tempting to conclude that these differing local outcomes were related to land ownership factors, the research found that interactions between other factors have a very strong bearing on local development.

The key historical (and current) forces of change in the parishes were often described by participants as not directly related to land ownership. Instead, a range of general socio-economic factors were at play, including regional economic growth; mechanisation; reductions in the size of the land-based workforce; increased mobility, commuting and connectivity; housing developments; tourism growth; second homes; and ageing populations. The accessibility of urban areas was a key factor, with changes in land-based employment, demography and housing development influenced by proximity to larger settlements. The more remote parishes experienced less population growth, higher shares of employment in farming and forestry, a growing reliance on the tourism sector, and higher proportions of housing stock used as second homes and tourism accommodation, when compared to their more accessible counterparts. Nonetheless, in all of the unfragmented parishes, land ownership scale was seen as providing owners with important influence over some outcomes, particularly the supply of land and housing (a finding which chimes with other research on this topic).[61] In contrast, ownership change, and fragmentation of landholdings, offered

---

[60] Land Reform Review Group, 'The Land of Scotland and the Common Good', p. 165.

[61] For example, R. Mc Morran, S. Thomson, R. Hindle and H. Deary, 'The economic, social and environmental contribution of landowners in the Cairngorms National Park', <https://cairngorms.co.uk/uploads/documents/Look%20After/CNP_Landowner_Survey_-_FINAL_REPORT.pdf> (last accessed 31 March 2019).

opportunities to several existing farm tenants to develop their businesses further.

Historic fragmentation of large landholdings generally resulted in the emergence of a wide range of sizes of landholdings, from houses with a small paddock to small estates. As agriculture has become increasingly mechanised and businesses have sought economies of scale, evidence from the fieldwork suggests that, as within the tenancy sector, there has been considerable (re)amalgamation of units in the last fifty years. The analysis of June Agricultural Census data suggests that there is currently greater agricultural intensity in those parishes where fragmentation occurred, but (as explained earlier in this chapter) this needs to be interpreted cautiously since agricultural performance is determined by a multitude of factors and standard output coefficients may overestimate or underestimate actual output levels. Even where fragmentation had occurred, the current owners of farms in one parish could not conclude that fragmentation had led to positive outcomes for the wider rural communities in their area, despite the clear individual benefits derived, with fragmentation of land ownership being described as the most important driver of change from their families' perspectives.

The analysis of population census data also suggests that there has been greater population growth in the case studies where fragmentation occurred, but the influence of land ownership on population growth is unlikely to be simple or direct. Indeed, participants did not tend to equate land ownership with changes in populations and referred instead to wider societal changes. The significant decline since the 1980s in the number of estate workers in the unfragmented parishes was, however, linked with local social impacts such as shop closures.

This study developed a transferable method that can be used to assess sustainable development pathways and outcomes in comparative studies of rural areas.[62] We focused on six case-study parishes under private land ownership – we were not able to examine other forms of large-scale land ownership (e.g. ownership by public bodies or conservation charities), or parishes in crofting counties, due to the scope of the research project and specification from the funders. Whilst the process of collating historical information was problematic at times (due to boundary changes, data consistency and data availability) and the processes of recruiting case-study participants (with latent knowledge of change factors) difficult, the methodical approach worked well in enabling comparative analysis of the case studies.

---

[62] For example, McKee et al. use this method in Chapter 17 of this volume.

We write this chapter at a time when the Scottish Land Commission – the body created by the Land Reform (Scotland) Act 2016 with statutory functions relating to land reform – has published the results of its public call for evidence in 2018 of the experiences of people living and working in parts of Scotland where the majority of land is owned by either a single individual or organisation, or a very small number of individuals or organisations.[63] The results of that report show that the concentration of decisions about land use being in the hands of a small number of people (as compared to other countries) remains an ongoing concern that will no doubt attract further political and academic scrutiny. The evidence we have presented in this chapter suggests that scale of land ownership, and land ownership change, can have an influence on the sustainable development of rural communities. However, these are only two of many drivers of change that make up a complex policy landscape in rural areas.

Acknowledgements

The research presented in this chapter was conducted by Steven Thomson, Andrew Moxey, Andy Wightman, Annie McKee, Dave Miller, Ellie Brodie, Jayne Glass, Jon Hopkins, Keith Mathews, Ken Thomson, Rob Mc Morran and Rosalind Bryce. The research was funded by the Scottish Government.

[63] Scottish Land Commission, 'Addressing Scotland's pattern of land ownership can unlock economic and community opportunities', <https://landcommission.gov.scot/2019/03/addressing-scotlands-pattern-of-land-ownership-can-unlock-economic-and-community-opportunities/> (last accessed 20 March 2019).

Agricultural Models in Scotland and Norway:
A Comparison

Annie McKee, Heidi Vinge, Hilde Bjørkhaug and Reidar Almås

IT IS ARGUED THAT the scale and concentration of private land owner-ship in Scotland maintains historical inequalities and injustices, and that alternative models of land occupancy and a greater diversity of landowner type could lead to more productive land use and associated socio-economic benefits.[1] Contemporary land reform in Scotland aims to redress these historical inequalities and injustices, and ensure that land ownership and management is in the public (and private) interest. The stated objective of the recent land reform process by the Scottish Government is that 'Scotland's land must be an asset that benefits the many, not the few',[2] and that rights to land must promote 'fairness and social justice'.[3] This chapter aims to provide insights for Scottish land reform policy through examining the pattern of land tenure, in conjunction with rural and agricultural policies, in Norway. It may be argued that much of what the Scottish Government aspires to achieve through land reform processes – in terms of greater equality and trans-parency in land ownership, as well as sustainable and empowered rural communities – already exists in the so-called 'Norwegian model' of social democracy in land governance.[4]

This chapter will draw on the timelines of two parishes in rural Norway to offer reflections on how the Norwegian agricultural model can provide insight for Scottish land reform and the implications of

[1] See Chapters 5 and 16 in this volume for further analysis of land ownership concentration.

[2] Scottish Government, 'A Consultation on the Future of Land Reform in Scotland' (Edinburgh, 2014), p. 6.

[3] Scottish Government, Results from the June 2016 Scottish Agricultural Census, 25 October 2016.

[4] J. Bryden, L. Riddoch and O. Brox, 'Conclusions' in J. Bryden, O. Brox and L. Riddoch (eds), *Northern Neighbours: Scotland and Norway since 1800* (Edinburgh: Edinburgh University Press, 2015), pp. 282–6.

an alternative land tenure regime. A review of relevant legislation and policy change in Norway reveals an increase in renting in the agricultural sector, and how the Norwegian subsidy system encourages farmers to expand unit size and invest in technology. Reflections are made on the nature of the relationship between landowner and tenant and how this underpins rural sustainable development, again seeking to draw lessons for the Scottish land question.

AN OVERVIEW OF THE STRUCTURE OF NORWEGIAN AGRICULTURE

Rural Norway is characterised by a pattern of small farms and multifunctional agriculture, with most farms incorporating both privately owned and privately managed 'in fields' (*innmark*) and communally managed 'out fields' (*utmark*, which may be uncultivable or too upland for crops), as well as areas of forestry, waters, and land with hunting rights.[5] In its natural and economic structure, landholdings are relatively small.[6] Small private landowners collaboratively manage game species and ecosystem services, as well as communal grazing areas beyond the treeline. The community basis of family farming in Norway, and the value of reciprocity to neighbouring farm businesses, are also endorsed.[7]

The so-called 'Norwegian model' of agriculture (i.e. the pattern of land tenure, in conjunction with rural and agricultural policies) is often revered internationally, in particular due to the small scale of farms yet profitability of agriculture in Norway. Only 3 per cent of the land in Norway is suitable for arable cropping, with an average farm size of 23.9 hectares in 2016.[8] Of critical importance to the Norwegian model of

[5] W. E. Dramstad and N. Sang, 'Tenancy in Norwegian agriculture', *Land Use Policy*, 27 (2010), pp. 946–56.

[6] A. Anderssen, 'The Land Tenure System in Norway, and Local Democracy in Relation to Land Issues', Presentation to the Highlands and Islands Forum, Inverness, March 1998; R. Almås, 'From state-driven modernisation to green liberalism 1920–2000', in R. Almås (ed.), *Norwegian Agricultural History* (Trondheim: Tapir Academic Publishers, 2004), pp. 296–357.

[7] V. H. Hausener, G. Brown and E. Lægreid, 'Effects of land tenure and protected areas on ecosystem services and land use preferences in Norway', *Land Use Policy*, 49 (2015), pp. 446–61; Anderssen, 'The Land Tenure System in Norway'; S. Gezelius, 'Exchange and Social Structure in Norwegian Agricultural Communities: How Farmers Acquire Labour and Capital', *Sociologia Ruralis*, 54 (2014), pp. 206–26.

[8] Statistics Norway, 'Structure of agriculture, 2016, preliminary figures', <https://

agriculture is the support received from the national production subsidy system (differentially allocated according to geography, commodity and farm size), production and sales cooperatives (who participate in legally guaranteed market regulations), a politically powerful farming voice, and a regulated land market.[9] Norwegian farm structure has played a key role in maintaining communities in remote rural areas,[10] in conjunction with a high level of pluriactivity.[11] Agricultural policies in Norway advocate multifunctional agriculture, with associated social and environmental sustainability outcomes.[12] Nonetheless, it is highlighted: 'Norway's agriculture still emerges as an advanced state-planned market economy'.[13]

As in Scotland, the history of land ownership underpins the structure of the agricultural system in Norway.[14] Key historical points of departure within the history of land ownership in Norway from that of

www.ssb.no/en/jord-skog-jakt-og-fiskeri/statistikker/stjord> (last accessed 28 June 2017); S. S. Prestegard and A. Hegrenes, 'Agriculture and Rural Development Policy in Norway', in A. K. Copus (ed.) *Continuity or Transformation? Perspectives on Rural Development in the Nordic Countries*, Nordregio Report (2007), vol. 4, pp. 123–35.

[9] Almås, 'From state-driven modernisation'; Prestegard and Hegrenes, 'Agriculture'; Gezelius, 'Exchange'.

[10] 18.5 per cent of the Norwegian population in 2017 live in a rural area, with a decline of 0.8 per cent since 2016, see Statistics Norway, 'Population and land area in urban settlements', <https://www.ssb.no/en/befolkning/statistikker/beftett/aar> (last accessed 30 January 2018). In contrast, in Scotland, 17 per cent of the total population live in rural areas (6 per cent in remote rural and 11 per cent in accessible rural), with an increase in rural population between 2016 and 2017 of 0.4 per cent. An increase in the Scottish population overall between 2016 and 2017 is attributed to positive net migration see Scottish Government, 'Rural Scotland Key Facts 2018', Rural and Environment Science and Analytical Services, Scottish Government, October 2018.

[11] Gezelius, 'Exchange'.

[12] H. Bjørkhaug and C. A. Richards, 'Multifunctional agriculture in policy and practice? A comparative analysis of Norway and Australia', *Journal of Rural Studies*, 24 (2008), pp. 98–111; P. Lombnæs, O. A. Bævre and N. Vagstad, 'Norwegian Agriculture: Structure, Research and Policies', *The European Journal of Plant Science and Biotechnology*, 5 (Special Issue 1, 2011), pp. 1–4.

[13] R. Almås and M. Haugen, 'Norwegian Gender Roles in Transition: the Masculinization Hypothesis in the Past and the Future', *Journal of Rural Studies*, 7 (1991), pp. 79–83.

[14] cf. M. R. G. Goodale and P. K. Sky, 'A comparative study of land tenure, property boundaries, and dispute resolution: case studies from Bolivia and Norway', *Journal of Rural Studies*, 17 (2000), pp. 183–200; Almås, 'From state-driven modernisation'.

Scotland, may be recognised in the 1928 Land Act (*Jordloven*) in which the Norwegian government granted an 'absolute right to buy' to the *Husmenn* (which may be equated to the Scottish crofters, who gained a 'right to buy' in 1976; see Chapter 12), which consequently led to the demise of the *Husmann* class (that is, small tenant farmers) and rise of the small owner-occupier farmer.[15] Today, land ownership and farming in Norway are regulated according to three key laws, translated as the Allodial Act, the Concession Act, and the Land Act.[16] Firstly, the 'Odel law' (*Odelsrett*), has been in place since the Middle Ages in Norway, and historically permits the oldest male child to inherit the farm. The new Allodial Act (legislated in 1974) revised this historic principle and granted men and women equal rights when taking over farms. Today it remains that close family members in direct descending line of the landowner have pre-emptive rights of farm purchase, with non-relatives requiring a licence for land purchase.[17] This distinctive legislative instrument maintains land in family ownership and avoids the fragmentation of properties in generational shifts,[18] thus mirroring Scottish succession law and the historical impact of primogeniture[19] coupled with the contemporary ability to bequeath land freely on death rather than in a way that enforces division amongst heirs.[20] The fundamental principle of the *odel* maintains strong connections to rural areas by much of the population. This law and other public policies in Norway thus promote continuity in farm ownership and conservation of farm size, which protect community structure, retaining social ties between family members and neighbouring farmers.[21]

In Norway the owners of farmland must be resident on their

---

[15] This is in contrast to the picture of small holdings in Scotland, due in part to the later individual right to buy for crofting (introduced comparatively later in 1976), and the fact that crofters have had little incentive to buy their own crofts, for example due to the loss of access to grant funding, and the lack of desire to gain title given security of tenure; Almås, 'From state-driven modernisation'.

[16] S. Pollock, 'International Perspectives on Land Reform', SPICe Briefing, 10 July 2015 (Edinburgh: SPICe, 2015).

[17] Gezelius, 'Exchange'.

[18] Almås, 'From state-driven modernisation'; M. Forbord, H. Bjørkhaug and R. J. F. Burton, 'Drivers of change in Norwegian agricultural land control and the emergence of rental farming', *Journal of Rural Studies*, 33 (2014), pp. 9–19.

[19] cf. S. Harvie-Clark, 'Succession (Scotland) Bill', SPICe Briefing 15/48, 26 August 2015 (Edinburgh: SPICe, 2015).

[20] M. I. Rudd, 'Reform of Legal Rights in Succession: Retaining Viable Agricultural Units', *Juridical Review*, 2018, pp. 172–90.

[21] Gezelius, 'Exchange'.

landholding, and they must undertake 'active' farming on the land, which limits farm expansion through land purchase.[22] The Concession Act regulates the transfer of farm property ownership, unless an exemption has been granted, for example, through the sale to close family, for transfer to those with *odel* rights, or where a property is below minimum size of 0.25 hectares.[23] Concessions will only be granted if it is the buyer's intention to live on the farm (for a five-year minimum), and based on their plans for farm management. As Forbord and colleagues explain:

> The Concession Act regulates the purchase of land by legal persons (e.g. limited companies) by providing preference to potential purchasers whose stated occupation is farming . . . this means that where land is taken over by a company, at least one person must be an active farmer.[24]

In some cases, conditions for concession include sale of land to a neighbour for agricultural purposes, and research findings indicate that concession obligations may be exempted by the local political majority.[25] Nonetheless, without a concession (or exemption) the owner must sell the land in its entirety within the timescale and at a price set by the municipality (*kommune*).

Finally, the Land Act aims to ensure that all land resources are best used for society and farmers, though promoting rural settlement, employment and agricultural development.[26] This key legislation confirms that it is the landowners' responsibility that land is 'actively farmed' and that land is maintained in good condition. Farmland rental arises as an option for landowners who do not wish to be active farmers. The Land Act controls land renting and requires written ten-year contracts between landowner and tenant, which are submitted to the municipality.[27]

---

[22] To compare, in Scotland, owner-occupier crofters (but not farmers) are subject to a duty to live within 32 km. Not doing so can lead to sanctions, such as requiring that the croft be let out (but ownership would remain unchanged).

[23] cf. F. Flemsæter, 'Geography, Law and the Emotions of Property – Property enactment on Norwegian smallholdings', PhD thesis (Trondheim: NTNU, 2009).

[24] Forbord et al., 'Drivers of change', p. 12.

[25] M. Forbord and O. Storstad, 'Praktisering av regelen om boplikt på landbrukseiendommer. En analyse basert på saker i utvalgte kommuner', Report 02/08 (Trondheim: Centre for Rural Research, 2008).

[26] H. Vinge, 'Food Security, Food Sovereignty, and the Nation-State: Historicizing Norwegian Farmland Policy', in A. Trauger (ed.), *Food Sovereignty in International Context. Discourse, Politics and Practice in Place* (New York: Routledge, 2015), pp. 87–105.

[27] Landbruksdirektoratet, 'Driveplikt og jordleie', <https://www.landbruksdirekto

Dramatic increases in areas of rented farmland have been attributed to a shift in Norwegian agricultural and rural policy, towards supporting larger-scale and more efficient agricultural production units.[28] Forty per cent of farmland is now rented farmer-to-farmer (or non-resident *odel* to 'active farmer')[29], with implications for land management practices and underpinning social structures within the farming community.[30] Indeed, it has been stated that the predominant management system for a large proportion of the total agricultural area is farmland tenancies, which reduces land abandonment and permits farm expansion whilst avoiding complicated land sales.[31] Norway is not exempt from the shift to neoliberalism[32], not least with regard to agricultural policies,[33] and a debate is emerging regarding changes to the concession laws, in order to increase competitiveness in global production markets.[34] The implications of this debate around the role of market forces – and the counter-lessons evident from Scottish land reform – are discussed later in this chapter.

THE NORWEGIAN MODEL IN PRACTICE: INSIGHTS FROM TWO FARMING COMMUNITIES

Case-study methodology

Two former parishes in the Melhus municipality of Sør-Trøndelag, central Norway,[35] were examined in order to understand the lived experience

---

ratet.no/no/eiendom-og-skog/eiendom/driveplikt/driveplikt-og-jordleie#utleie-av-jord> (last accessed 16 May 2017).

[28] Dramstad and Sang, 'Tenancy'; Forbord et al., 'Drivers of change'.

[29] Forbord et al., 'Drivers of change'.

[30] Dramstad and Sang, 'Tenancy'.

[31] Dramstad and Sang, 'Tenancy'.

[32] Defined as 'a modified form of liberalism tending to favour free-market capitalism' (Oxford English Dictionary, 2018; see also Thorsen and Lie, 2006, below). Oxford English Dictionary, 'Neo-liberalism', <https://en.oxforddictionaries.com/definition/neo-liberalism> (last accessed 3 May 2018); D. E. Thorsen and A. Lie, 'What is Neoliberalism?' Working paper, Department of Political Science, University of Oslo, 2006, <http://folk.uio.no/daget/What%20is%20Neo-Liberalism%20 10-11-06.pdf> (last accessed 3 May 2018).

[33] R. Almås and H. Campbell, 'Rethinking Agricultural Policy Regimes: Food Security, Climate Change and the Future Resilience of Global Agriculture', *Research in Rural Sociology and Development*, 18 (2012) (Bingley: Emerald Insight).

[34] J. Bryden, 'Land Reform proposals in Norway and Scotland – BBC debate', <https://johnmbryden.wordpress.com/2016/02/12/land-reform-proposals-in-norway-and-scotland-bbc-debate/> (last accessed 12 February 2016).

[35] The case-study parishes are referred to as 'Melhus central' and 'Melhus rural',

of the Norwegian model of agriculture. The case-study parishes were selected due to their close proximity to an urban centre (Trondheim), which had influenced population and land-use changes in the case-study parishes over the past century.[36] The case-study locations were also familiar to the researchers, therefore supporting accessibility to interviewees and insights into local issues. Semi-structured, biographical interviews were undertaken (largely in English) with members of the farming community in the Norwegian parish case studies in March and April 2016. Sixteen people participated in the interviews, comprising a purposive sample of owner-occupier farmers (and family members) located throughout the two parish case studies, including two interviewees that also self-defined as community representatives (i.e. former local politicians and community group leaders). These community representatives were also resident farmers.[37]

Interviewees were invited to describe the history of their farm and the surrounding parish (or community) area over the past century, to identify the key events and changes that had happened in their lifetime, and those recounted by previous generations. Critically, the interview sought to understand the views held by the farmers of the social and economic drivers for these changes, and the consequences of those drivers for their farm, the local community, and the future of the Norwegian agricultural system. This interview data provides an insight into the Norwegian agricultural model and the implications of an alternative (and changing) land tenure regime to that found in Scotland. These insights are illustrative of underpinning features of the Norwegian model and changes necessary in order to achieve this model in Scotland.

The key drivers of change emerging from the interview analysis are presented in the following section, in addition to a summary of interviewee views on the social consequences of the historic and potential future changes to their farm and the Norwegian agricultural model more broadly. These consequences provide the basis for reflection on necessary cultural change required in Scotland to accompany the implementation of land reform policy.

---

with the latter located in a more remote area of the Melhus municipality than the former.

[36] Specifically, this allowed comparison with existing parish case studies close to Aberdeen, which were explored in Chapter 16 of this volume. The methodology presented in this chapter is based on the work of Thomson et al., see Chapter 16.

[37] Specific case-study locations (below municipality scale) and participants' names remain anonymous.

Economic drivers of change

The history of land ownership and land-use change in the Norwegian case studies is characterised by the establishment and expansion of small-scale owner-occupied farms.[38] The primary drivers of change across the previous century are considered to be economic in nature,[39] including the influence of the market (i.e. production prices, cooperatives, and supermarket contracts) and market-driven policies, government incentives, mechanisation, and the availability of off-farm employment opportunities.[40]

In detail, the influence of the 'channelling policy' (*kanaliseringspolitik-ken*) from the 1960s onwards, which zoned specific geographic regions for different production types, led many farmers to cease livestock (and grass) production in Melhus 'central', shifting to grain, or seeking off-farm work, at least part-time. Similarly, the arrival of production quotas for milk, and concessions for chicken, led some farmers to consider whether or not to continue with the scale of their main production. Changes to the milk quotas at the end of the 1990s resulted in changes in local agricultural practices, as well as structural changes in farm sizes and the number of active farms in Melhus 'rural'. Critically, milk quotas are based on historical production, as well as the amount of farm land available for grazing and to spread manure. Therefore, changes that encouraged an increased dairy herd size required an associated increase in landholding scale, through land purchase or renting. The current system allows farmers to buy or rent quota to expand production, and many farmers in both Melhus 'central' and 'rural' are reported to have 'built bigger and bought quotas', although this can be expensive in the short term. The interviewees described historic subsidy schemes for the cultivation of 'new' farmland, and improvements to allow/extend cultivation (drainage, levelling, etc.), that are no longer available today. The

---

[38] cf. Almås, 'From state-driven modernisation'; O. Brox, 'Reflections on the Making of Norway', in J. Bryden, O. Brox and L. Riddoch (eds), *Northern Neighbours: Scotland and Norway since 1800* (Edinburgh: Edinburgh University Press, 2015), pp. 154–63.

[39] The influence of natural conditions (e.g. landscape and land capability), as well as the unreliability of weather and climate change were mentioned by interviewees as further drivers of change, but are not central to the focus of this chapter.

[40] cf. Dramstad and Sang, 'Tenancy'; H. Bjørkhaug, 'Exploring the sociology of agriculture: Family farmers in Norway – future or past food producers?' in D. Ersaga (ed.) *Sociological landscape: Theories, realities and trends* (InTeck, 2012), pp. 283–303; Gezelius, 'Exchange'.

interviewees also stated that it is very difficult to become a new entrant dairy farmer today (unlike in previous generations) due to the high cost of milk quotas, amongst other costs.

Furthermore, a key driver of change has been the influence of the production market and market demands (for example, for Norwegian chicken and local food developments), interconnected with the influence of government production subsidies (such as encouraging organic conversion, and increasing concessions for chicken production). Interviewees also noted that government subsidised loans[41] are not allocated to farms below a certain scale, as described: 'You don't get the subsidies if you don't "build large enough", so you have to build much larger than you have possibilities with your own land.'

Farmers increasing their production must have access to available farmland in order to receive building/development subsidies, as well as sufficient area for the spreading of livestock manure; the consequences of this driver are discussed in terms of property rights later in this chapter. Declines in production prices are further highlighted as a driver of change; one interviewee explained that solely producing grain would be economically unsustainable in Melhus 'rural' due to low grain prices, despite farming full-time. Key economic drivers of change also include the influence of external agencies (e.g. the Norwegian food agency), supermarket contracts ('they do with us what they want'), production cooperatives (for example, milk prices paid by TINE,[42] the Norwegian dairy cooperative; chicken overproduction mitigated through cooperative payments – farmers paid to stop production, etc.), and other local farmers (for example, joint farming enterprises, and local farmers copying the success of pioneer farmers into chicken production).

The availability of alternative employment sources and the proximity to Trondheim may be considered economic drivers of change in the

---

[41] Subsidised loans have been available from 'Innovation Norway' to eligible farmers over a minimum scale since 2013. However, in April 2017 the Norwegian Parliament voted in favour of a new policy that gives priority to small and medium-sized farms when it comes to government support for investment. Hence, the farmer quoted above would now be eligible for subsidised loans.

[42] The milk price is set by the Agricultural Agreement after annual negotiations between the farmers' unions and the Norwegian Government. TINE, as a cooperative but also a private actor, is required to pay that price to the individual farmers. This process is understood by all Norwegian dairy farmers, although they might describe the price-fixing actor as 'TINE'. A *tine* (pronounced 'teeneh') is a traditional Norwegian wooden container to keep butter and cheese fresh (TINE, 2018). TINE, 'About TINE', <https://www.tine.no/english/about-tine/about-tine> (last accessed 29 October 2018).

Norwegian case studies. Post-1945 farm workers largely disappeared from farms, shifting to salaried jobs rather than seasonal farm work. The availability of off-farm work in the city and suburbs, as well as the arrival of the oil industry and consequential higher wages in other industries, contributed to an out-migration of young people from farms in the case studies, whilst others established their own businesses (carpentry, painting, etc.). It was reported that many farms went from full- to part-time management during the 1970s and 1980s, with farm work undertaken predominantly in the evening and at weekends.

Mechanisation during the mid twentieth century also contributed to declining farm employment, as well as a reduction in forestry work available off-farm; manual labour could not compete in terms of efficiency. Interrelated with a mechanised and more automated farming system (with the introduction of robotic milking, for example) are the high costs of renewing production equipment, consequently driving increases in farm scale. As one interviewee explained: 'For instance, in grain production, investment in a new harvester is so large, you need more area to defend this investment.'

The challenge of farmland preservation is mentioned by interviewees, including the impact of infrastructure developments, such as road construction, in breaking up small land units. The consequences of these economic and political drivers on farm scale and tenure are further considered in the following sections.

Social drivers of change

Many of the economic drivers of change described by the interviewees were interrelated with social drivers, and have had consequences for the social structure of the farming community in the Norwegian case studies. Overall, the interviewees noted that quality of life has improved over the previous century for the farming community across the case-study region, with higher income levels and less requirement for long working hours, especially after shifts from livestock to grain production (as in Melhus 'central'), and in relation to increasing subsidy levels since the mid 1970s. However, the shift from 'grass to grain' (that is, the end of animal and hay production), compounded by the impact of mechanisation, has led to predominantly 'solo farming'. Some interviewees believed that historically the farming community in this part of Norway had a 'better life' because they were not alone on the farm, and they had people around in the 'good and the bad'. Farming was a shared livelihood, neighbours worked at home, and therefore met regularly: '[It is] difficult to compare being a farmer when I was a young farmer than now. Before, it was a way of life, it was the farm, it was the neighbours.'

As described, historically the majority of residents in the case-study parishes were farmers, thus they were 'on the same level'; with fewer farmers there may be social imbalances in the community. Therefore, social changes are related to the consequences of drivers of change in land management.

Nonetheless, the high price of machinery has contributed to increasing cooperation between farmers, and due to the decreasing numbers of farmers, the 'culture of helping each other' was thought to be increasingly important. Joint farming was considered conducive to increasing production, overcoming individual challenges through communication and interaction, as well as improved land management practice (e.g. soil conservation through limiting compaction). However, previous joint farming experiences demonstrated to interviewees that amalgamation and efficiency drivers can lead to further declines in farming employment, as described:

> They thought that if you put four farms together it would be work for all of us, and income for all of us, but it's much more efficient, and it was not income for four people anymore, so someone has to get out!

Furthermore, the interviewees described challenges of maintaining agreements, relationships, and shared responsibilities in joint farming operations, and noted experiences where partners failed to spend time at the outset of their joint enterprise building trusting relationships and agreeing governance structures.

Social drivers of change may be considered to also include individual farmer decision-making, for example regarding changes to production, or developing on-farm diversification activities; whilst these decisions were also influenced by gaining additional income, the choice of diversification reflected the interviewees' personal interests. Examples include one interviewee who 'chose community vegetable garden use of farmland because they like to be with people', and another who described themselves as a 'pragmatic organic farmer', driven by the use of their own resources on the farm. Furthermore, the perceived limit to individual farmer capacity was noted by interviewees. As described, the decision whether to build a new cow barn (or to stop farming), for example, and the scale of the barn, is determined by the extent that the farmer believes they can manage the additional workload, their future plans and the plans of the next generation.

Shifting farm ownership and management between generations is noted as a window for change in production. Furthermore, automatic succession to the oldest child was believed to no longer be the norm, as the children must be interested in farming, and the farm may be handed down to other children. The interviewees also explained that a change to historic family connection with a farm would be a social driver, with, for example, new farm owners possessing 'less interest' (or perhaps less likelihood of long-term investment, both social and economic) in farm management.

A final, critical driver of change – or arguably of preservation – is that of the interviewees' own defined limits to farm scale, i.e. the maximum farm scale that they considered to be optimum/ideal, as explained:

> Yes, we can rent more land; we could manage more land. But we don't need it! . . . This is the proper size for a farm.

> I think it was a little bit needed that we had to get bigger. But I think . . . now we are pushing the limit.

This self-imposed farm scale limit may be related to the egalitarian culture in Norway, and historic farm equality.[43] However, contrasting views on limits to farm scale arose between interviewees, which gives an insight into wider tensions within the Norwegian agricultural system, in particular concerns regarding the implications of continued farm expansion and so-called 'farm cannibalism'. Whilst the earlier quotes describe the view that farm scale should remain small and within the management capability of a farming family, others explained that due to policy changes and government incentives (as described earlier regarding the minimum scale for building subsidy allocation), the only option was to expand the scale of farm businesses, thus: 'I think honestly that every farmer in Norway wants this, because they can see that economies of scale make sense, to a point.'

Increasing farmer competition over land and resource access is a concern arising from the trend of farm amalgamation and decreasing farmer numbers in the case studies.[44] As the interviewees explained, with increasing farm scale, farmers are required to compete for available land, which in turn can raise land prices, exacerbated by the removal of land price restrictions. This perceived competition was of concern to the

---

[43] The basis for the channelling policy was that it provided a corporatist, partnership model for agriculture, with negotiations between state and farm organisations in order to balance conflicts, and to divide gains and losses between regions and farmer groups (see Almås, 'From state-driven modernisation').

[44] See also Dramstad and Sang, 'Tenancy'.

case-study interviewees, with regard to maintaining positive relations, thus: '. . . still we can work together and we meet in the social areas, and talk . . . But maybe if there is a lot of competition we start to get more unfriendly! . . . Because instead of working together we have to fight with each other.'

The importance of maintaining good relations was exemplified by interviewees whose scale of production is reliant on the use of land or machinery owned by neighbouring farmers. One interviewee described 'collaborating' with neighbours regarding crop rotations, with another describing the 'flexibility' of their relationship with neighbours as central to their future plans for farm expansion.[45] The role of 'good relations', and therefore social capital as a key feature of the Norwegian model, is considered later in this chapter.

CONSEQUENCES OF CHANGE TO PROPERTY RIGHTS

Key changes and drivers of change have had consequences for land ownership and governance in the Norwegian case studies. The interviewees described the implications of the changes over the previous century, in particular that farm amalgamation and increased scale of production, has led to considerable increases in rented farmland.[46] One interviewee stated that 45 to 50 per cent of farmland in the overall municipality of Melhus is now rented; this is considered high, having increased from 20 per cent in 2011.[47] In addition to production increases, the rise of renting is also associated with the high costs involved in the renewal of production equipment (as mentioned, for example, more land is required to repay the investment of a combine harvester), and landowners stopping active farming for alternative employment sources, therefore offering land to neighbouring farmers or 'entrepreneurs'. There is both demand for land by expanding farm businesses ('with more and more Angus [cattle] I must have more land'), and supply from those who are moving out of farming livelihoods, but retaining farm ownership. The increase in renting, however, is also related to a lack of farmland for sale, partly due to Norwegian legislation that prohibits the sale of arable land separate from the farmhouse on properties over 2.5

---

[45] See also the findings of Gezelius, 'Exchange'.

[46] As earlier reported by Dramstad and Sang, 'Tenancy', and Forbord et al., 'Drivers of change'.

[47] This interviewee quoted figures produced by the agricultural department of the Melhus municipality.

hectares.[48] There is also considerable place attachment, as described by the interviewees, therefore many landowners are reluctant to part with family landholdings, and wish to retain farming as an option for future generations. Furthermore, the rise of farm 'entrepreneurship' (including renting land across significant distances and undertaking contracted agriculture) represents a move away from owner-occupiers with inter-generational connection to and in-depth knowledge of the land; this was perceived negatively by some interviewees.

Rental agreements are for a minimum of ten years, with manda-tory municipality oversight. The interviewees described the simplicity and flexibility (including break clauses) of 'ordinary' rental agreements, and the underpinning principles including maintaining soil health and the tenant farmer's responsibility to pay for improvements. It was considered easier to have different plots of land rented from different landowners, because this allows for competition in rental prices that the tenant can favourably negotiate, and retains a 'communal attitude' (for instance, a bigger landowner might rent land for a higher price). Others noted, however, that rental land prices (as well as milk quota prices) are increasing due to the increasing demand for rented land:

> So now in this area there is no free land – if you want some you have to bid higher – and some do that. So not everyone is thinking it is for the community – they think 'I need more, I have to bid higher'.

Furthermore, the existence and uncertainty of break clauses in tenancy agreements, in contrast to historic, informal land 'borrowing' (without formal agreements or financial transactions, thus: 'no longer will a farmer hand over land to an active farmer') means that some interview-ees considered it financially uncertain to base expansion on rented land, as explained:

> I will have more land and more grass, then I must go to my neighbour – he will rent the land to me. But you have contract maybe 10 years, then yes – maybe you don't have that for the next 10 years.

Whilst some interviewees who are responding to drivers of change and are seeking to increase production described their approach of renting land from part-time neighbouring farms 'when needed', others described the impact on their business of losing rented ground due to the landowner wishing to return to farming or change the land use (for development, for example). Renting depends on 'being in the right place

---

[48] See also Flemsæter, 'Geography, Law and the Emotions of Property'.

at the right time' and divides landholdings due to distances between rented fields.

The farmers interviewed emphasised the importance of 'personal' (or private) ownership of the land that allows control and farmer decision-making in the long term. Personal ownership supports collaborative farming approaches, thus: 'if you have your own farm you can work together with other farms'. As one interviewee explained, the political trend in Norway towards market liberalism and the potential for the open sale of farm property will lead to increasing competition and the potential for farmers to again become 'tenants', as they were in the eighteenth century:

> This development will be important. You can risk that farmers end up as *leilendinger* – tenants – as they were in the crofter system back in the 1700s. Back then the farms were transferred to the farmers, and now we may risk going the other way.

The interviewees asserted that it is important to retain their identity as 'free farmers'. Fundamentally, the shift in property rights with farm rental expansion is in turn changing power relations within and between the farming communities in the case studies. The value of equality to the key features of the Norwegian model is considered in the following discussion section.

IMPLICATIONS OF A CHANGING MODEL: NORWEGIAN AND SCOTTISH PERSPECTIVES

A key feature of the land governance model in Norway is the relative equality of property owners and there has existed a tradition of informal renting (referred to as 'borrowing' by interviewees), between neighbouring farms. The underpinning governance and institutions (both formal and informal) are strongly communal in nature.[49] There also exists a long history of collective land management, both for farm business survival (for instance, the role of forestry work in subsidising farm income) and for wider environmental and community benefit such as the interviewees' participation in the local skiing and hunting clubs. An important feature of the Norwegian model described by the interviewees was the self-imposed limits to farm scale, which may be considered an example of the application of 'virtue ethics' with regards to land

---

[49] Almås, 'From state-driven modernisation'.

ownership, as detailed by Peñalver (2009),[50] and reciprocity detailed by Gezelius (2014).[51]

However, it may be argued that the model of social cooperation and progressive property rights is challenged by the drivers of change and consequences described by the interviewees in the previous section. In particular, the findings highlight the challenge of good governance in joint farming arrangements and the undermining of communal attitudes with increasing land competition, which are related to the drive for efficiency within Norwegian land policy developments such as possible removal or relaxation of the concession laws.[52] Nonetheless, as expressed by the farming interviewees, the shift to a system based on economies of scale rather than state support was accepted by some, who also described the influence of global production trends/commodity prices and the perceived limitations of national policies, such as regarding pesticide use. Others interviewed were concerned with the realities of farm 'cannibalism', increasing land rental prices (in conjunction with relatively short-term rental contracts), and the loss of social infrastructure with declining farmer numbers: 'if you eat up the land of your neighbour you can enlarge, but that is not good for the community, because then in the end you are alone'.

This debate in Norway reflects the Lockean principle of 'limits to equality', and generates 'consequential geographies' with a land tenure system increasingly based on formal renting.[53] It is noted by the interviewees that the management of disparate landholdings by a declining number of farmers is likely to have social, economic and environmental consequences, not least through increasing carbon emissions with transport between field locations, limited land management on marginal units, and reduced time for family life and community participation. The significant increase in renting and farm unit expansion in Norway raises questions of sustainability, and the possible necessity of land consolidation. There also exists the potential for creating social imbalance and inequalities, with tenants (rather than landowners) holding power in the

---

[50] The three main virtues in land use decision-making are explained as industry (which may be equated to efficiency), justice and humility; See also J. A. Lovett, 'Progressive Property in Action: The Land Reform (Scotland) Act 2003', *Nebraska Law Review*, 89 (2011), pp. 739–818.

[51] Gezelius, 'Exchange'

[52] cf. Bryden et al., 'Conclusions'.

[53] B. Ilbery, D. Maye, D. Watts and L. Holloway, 'Property matters: Agricultural restructuring and changing landlord-tenant relationships in England', *Geoforum*, 41 (2010), pp. 423–34.

land market.[54] However, it is unreasonable to suggest that a rural elite will emerge in Norway, given the relatively small size of farms that are offered for rent by non-active farmers.

The model is arguably further threatened with reported challenges to associated Norwegian institutions, including the *odel* and the *kårfolk*. The latter is described as the tradition of the older generation continuing to live on the farm, shifting to a smaller dwelling house (the *kårstue*), and continuing to provide knowledge and practical support to the next-generation farmer. As the case studies illustrate, due in part to the rise of part-time farming and increasing rural house prices, the transition between generations may be determined increasingly by economic factors rather than considerations of family or inheriting farming knowledge. Interviewees explain that retired farmers today are more interested in securing their own property rights, which can threaten the *kårfolk* institution. As is the case across Europe, farm succession is increasingly delayed, the average age of farm owners is rising, and there are limited routes into farm management for younger people and new entrants.[55] The interviewees also mentioned tensions arising in farm succession planning, with inheritance based on the wishes of the next generation to continue to farm, and the influence of off-farm, higher-waged employment options as well as economic drivers such as replacing machinery or building infrastructure increase scale of production. The risk related to a decline in function of the *Odelsrett*, the Allodial Act, and the Concession Act, would be the opening of possible land speculation and increasing land prices. However, the former appears relatively unlikely in Norway in the short term, due to the factors inhibiting farm land sales, as well as due to transgenerational ownership practices, and strongly held place attachment or 'land memory'.[56] Nonetheless, this tension illustrates the need for coherence between property enactments and policy interventions

[54] cf. S. M. Cashin and G. McGrath, 'Establishing a modern cadastral system within a transition country: Consequences for the Republic of Moldova', *Land Use Policy*, 23 (2006), pp. 629–42.

[55] See review by L. Zagata and L. A. Sutherland, 'Deconstructing the "young farmer problem in Europe": towards a research agenda', *Journal of Rural Studies*, 38 (2015), pp. 39–51.

[56] Flemsæter, 'Geography, Law and the Emotions of Property' and see also M. Skår, G. Swensen, B. K. Dervo and O. Stabbetorp, 'Diversity in a Norwegian agrarian landscape: Integrating biodiversity, cultural and social perspectives into landscape management', *International Journal of Biodiversity Science & Management* 4 (2018), pp. 15–31; E. M. Peñalver, 'Land Virtues', *Cornell Law Faculty Publications*, Paper 104 (2009), pp. 821–88.

that adopt a liberal view of property ownership.[57] Indeed, possible future neoliberal shifts in land policies in Norway may undermine the model of social cooperation, leading to a necessary formalisation of property rights, such as increasing security of tenure for farm land tenants and *kårfolk*.[58]

It is clear that the Norwegian case studies provide many insights into the underpinning features of and challenges to a model of socio-democratic land governance. Scotland seeks to shift to a model of social cooperation and obligation in land use decision-making, and to a certain extent, the ongoing process of land reform creates the necessary institutional framework.[59] What is missing from the Scottish situation, and is evident in the case studies in Norway, is a historical legacy of social obligation, communal land management, and property-owner behaviour, which is embedded in national agricultural institutions, with high levels of legitimacy. The critical point of departure was Norway's Land Act of 1928 which abolished the landless *Husmann* class and thus generated more landowner equality. Subsequent legislative advancements in Norway have maintained farm units on the scale of family ownership and institutional management, which have restricted farm land sales through market interventions.[60] This is in stark contrast to the market-based system in Scotland and the concentrated power of private land ownership. It is also important to recognise that the cultural practices of land ownership and land management in Scotland are intertwined with social class and historical privileges; this is not the case in Norway, again due to divergent histories that have supported the maintenance of an egalitarian land tenure system.[61]

Nonetheless, the positive change anticipated by the Land Reform (Scotland) Act 2016 may be supported by adopting the underpinning features of the Norwegian model, not least seeking greater equality and

[57] Flemsæter, 'Geography, Law and the Emotions of Property'.

[58] cf. E. Ostrom and E. Schlager, 'The Formation of Property Rights', in S. S. Hanna, C. Folke and K-G. Mäler (eds), *Rights to Nature: Ecological, Economic, Cultural, and Political Principles of Institutions for the Environment* (Washington: Island Press, 1996), pp. 127–56.

[59] See for instance Chapters 7 and 8 in this volume.

[60] cf. J. Glass, R. Bryce, M. M. Combe, N. E. Hutchison, M. F. Price, L. Schulz and D. Valero, 'Research on interventions to manage land markets and limit the concentration of land ownership elsewhere in the world' (Scottish Land Commission, Commissioned Report No. 001, 2018).

[61] cf. H. Newby, C. Bell, D. Rose and P. Saunders, *Property, Paternalism and Power: Class and Control in Rural England* (London: Hutchinson University Library, 1978).

partnership-working between property owners. The increasing formality of farm tenant rights may be seen as one route to readdress the balance between landowner and tenant, but as this analysis illustrates, this system of property rights must be supported by positive social relations.[62]

Insights from sociological research suggest that interactions and 'communicative interactivity' form the basis for human relationships, that human agency is enacted through interactions, and that this can create social capital.[63] Social capital may be defined as 'the structure of relations between actors and among actors that facilitates productive activity ... a structure in which others may be contacted, obligations and expectations can be safely formed, information can be shared and sanctions can be applied',[64] or, as Putnam explains, 'features of social organisation, such as trust, norms, and networks, that can improve the efficiency of society by facilitating coordinated actions'.[65] Interactions that foster trust and reciprocity are considered to enhance social capital. Understanding micro-level interactions and processes of exchange provides insight into the power relations that permeate such spaces of interaction.[66] It may be inferred that private land ownership, both in Scotland and worldwide, has an influence on the generation of trust and, in turn, social capital, including the potential to deplete it through changes to land management that cause fragmentation in interaction, and perhaps inherently through power differentials between landowners, tenants, and the wider rural community.[67]

As the Scottish Government seeks to increase diversity of land

---

[62] cf. H. Lean, 'Scottish Perspective: Land Reform (Scotland) Act 2016', *Agricultural Law Association Bulletin*, 85 (2016), pp. 13–14; S. Read-Norrie, 'Agricultural Tenancies: Making Room for Generation Y – Will Only the Land Endure?', *Aberdeen Student Law Review*, 7 (2017), pp. 27–55. And arguably communicative action, see A. J. McKee, 'Legitimising the Laird? Communicative Action and the role of private landowner and community engagement in rural sustainability', *Journal of Rural Studies*, 41 (2015), pp. 23–36.

[63] I. Falk and S. Kilpatrick, 'What is social capital? A study of interaction in a rural community', *Sociologia Ruralis*, 40 (2000), pp. 87–110.

[64] M. Shucksmith, 'Endogenous development, social capital and social inclusion: perspectives from LEADER in the UK', *Sociologia Ruralis*, 40 (2010), pp. 208–18 (p. 210).

[65] R. Putnam, *Making Democracy Work* (Princeton: Princeton University Press, 1993), p. 167.

[66] E. Jupp, 'The feeling of participation: Everyday spaces and urban change', *Geoforum*, 39 (2008), pp. 331–43.

[67] See E. Kemp-Benedict, 'Inequality, Trust, and Sustainability', Stockholm

ownership through land reform, there are further lessons to learn from supporting good governance in co-management and collaborative farming arrangements, as illustrated in the Norwegian case studies, not least the need to build institutions and trusting relationships between land managers, and to reach early agreement on governance structures. Many involved in the Scottish land sector describe the need for more flexibility in farm tenancies, to encourage greater access to land for young farmers and new entrants, and there may be lessons to learn from the approach to land leasing based on neighbourliness and coopera- tion evident in the Norwegian case studies.[68] This model would allow owners of smaller-scale properties in Scotland to achieve the economies of scale required for efficient production, whilst sharing the benefits of land ownership. However, the Norwegian interviewees emphasised the importance of 'personal' ownership in maintaining collaborative farming arrangements, therefore emphasising the continued relevance of private (rather than community or state) land ownership. Nonetheless, the support mechanisms of farmer-to-farmer equality and positive social relations can be undermined by competition for land access/acquisition, as described by the Norwegian interviewees, therefore raising the ques- tion in Scotland regarding the possibility of market interventions as in Norway, to enable optimum land use and diversity of ownership.

CONCLUSION

The Norwegian model is presented as a system of equitable land owner- ship and sustainable agriculture to which Scottish policy-makers and land reform campaigners aspire.[69] Unlike in Scotland, the question of land reform does not appear to feature in public or political discourse in Norway, although there is some consideration of the need for land consolidation due to the distances between rental units managed by 'solo farmers' (and resulting environmental impacts, in terms of trans- port fuel emissions and marginal land abandonment). In contrast to Scotland, there exists a much greater proportion of the population with access to land, due to the scale of landholdings and extent of close

Environment Institute, Working Paper, September 2011, and Newby et al., *Property, Paternalism and Power*, and McKee, 'Legitimising the Laird?'.

[68] cf. Read-Norrie, 'Agricultural Tenancies', and A. McKee, L. Sutherland, J. Hopkins, S. Flanigan and A. Rickett, 'Increasing the Availability of Farmland for New Entrants to Agriculture in Scotland', Report for the Scottish Land Commission, 2018.

[69] Bryden et al., 'Conclusions'.

farming connections within family histories. The Norwegian model may be proposed as a suggested policy solution for Scotland. However, in order to achieve this aspiration, several potential changes in Scotland would allow greater alignment with the institutions and governance of land in Norway. These changes may include greater influence of local communities and local authorities in the allocation of land for rent and perhaps also tenancy length, replicating the role of the municipality in Norway, and seeking to overcome barriers to new agricultural tenancies in Scotland.[70] Scottish policy-makers could review guidance regarding succession and inheritance to promote equality of land ownership between claimants on inheritance.[71] Furthermore, it is important that the Scottish policy-makers seek to maintain social networks (and hence, social capital) between members of the local farming community, and between the farming and non-farming rural community, as exists in Norway through strong rural connections, and recreational activities.

Time will tell whether the Land Reform (Scotland) Act 2016 leads to effective change and fulfilment of the Scottish Government's land reform intentions. Nonetheless, the exploration of the lived experience of farmers in the Norwegian case studies presented illustrates the value of international comparison to gain insights and experiences from alternative perspectives and institutional settings. Indeed, learning from the Norwegian experience indicates that the Scottish policy goal of land reform may require:

(1) Support for underpinning networks and developing social capital between rural actors (i.e. owners and managers of land, and those who live and work in rural areas).

(2) Mechanisms that create opportunities for equality in land access (e.g. through succession and inheritance), to avoid competition between landowners and countering trends of farm 'cannibalism', through building cooperation and new business models.[72]

---

[70] cf. Scottish Government, June 2016 Scottish Agricultural Census.

[71] See S. Shortall, L.-A. Sutherland, A. McKee and J. Hopkins, 'Women in Farming and the Agriculture Sector', Report for the Environment and Forestry Directorate, Rural and Environment Science and Analytical Services (RESAS) Division, Scottish Government, 9 June 2017, <http://www.gov.scot/Publications/2017/06/2742> (last accessed 17 March 2019).

[72] It should be noted that in Scotland, the Land Reform (Scotland) Act 2016 also brought the Scottish Land Commission (SLC) into existence. The Commission's remit is focused on four strategic priorities, including land for housing and development, diversity of land ownership, land use decision-making, and agricultural holdings (i.e. including reinvigorating the tenanted sector in Scotland). According to the

To conclude, this chapter also provides an insight into Norwegian land policies, to highlight the consequences of potential future changes to the Norwegian model. Similar to Scotland, Norway is not exempt from the pressures of neoliberalism, not least with regard to agricultural policies, and dramatic increases in areas of rented farmland have been attributed to a shift in Norwegian agricultural and rural policy, towards supporting larger-scale and more efficient agricultural production units.[73] A debate is emerging regarding policy changes intended to increase competitiveness in global production markets.[74] Such legislative reform in Norway would have consequences for land prices, increasing the rate of land sales and land speculation, as well as influencing traditional rural community structures. In this regard, it is opportune for Norwegian policy-makers to consider and reflect on alternative land systems which are governed more directly by market forces, such as in Scotland.[75]

Acknowledgements

We are very grateful to all the interviewees for their time, openness and hospitality. Annie McKee acknowledges the receipt of a fellowship from the OECD Co-operative Research Programme: Biological Resource Management for Sustainable Agricultural Systems in 2016, and staff time supported by the Rural and Environment Science and Analytical Services Division of the Scottish Government through the Strategic Research Programme, 2011–16 and 2016–21.

remit of the SLC, it appears that they can progress these mechanisms, and support a change of culture in the relationship of landowners with other rural actors.

[73] Almås and Campbell, 'Rethinking Agricultural Policy Regimes'; Dramstad and Sang, 'Tenancy', and Forbord et al., 'Drivers of change'.

[74] Bryden, 'Land Reform proposals in Norway and Scotland'.

[75] cf. Bryden et al., 'Conclusions', and Bryden, 'Land Reform proposals in Norway and Scotland'.

Index

abandoned land, 163, 167, 178, 196–8, 237, 252–3, 261
Aberdeen, 24–5, 113–16, 131, 135, 136–7
Abolition of Feudal Tenure etc. (Scotland) Act (2000), 4, 151
absentee landlords, 59, 67, 88, 159, 202, 243, 379, 384
absolute right to buy, 4, 318, 391
academic research, 2–3, 47–8; *see also* knowledge production; universities
access rights, 4, 18, 155, 295, 332–6
acquisitive prescription, 139–40, 141
actio in personam, 138–9, 143–4, 148–50, 152
actio in rem, 138–9, 143–4, 147–50, 152
actions of error, 134, 143
Adam Smith Institute, 329
affordable housing, 200, 329, 345, 347–8, 375, 383
afforestation, 35
Agnew, Sir Crispin, of Lochnaw, 293–4
agrarian radicalism, 13, 56–73, 81, 87–90, 96, 100–1
Agricultural Enlightenment, 12, 39–55
Agricultural Holdings Legislation Review Group, 321, 322
Agricultural Holdings (Scotland) Act (1883), 314
Agricultural Holdings (Scotland) Act (1908), 315
Agricultural Holdings (Scotland) Act (1949), 315
Agricultural Holdings (Scotland) Act (1991), 16–17, 223, 225, 316
Agricultural Holdings (Scotland) Act (2003), 223–7, 317–20
agricultural improvement, 10, 12, 23, 35–6, 39–55, 312, 314, 317, 322, 369; *see also* land improvement
agricultural labour, 28–9, 34–5, 53, 60, 381, 385
agricultural publications, 50
agricultural science, 35, 47–8
agricultural shows, 49
agricultural societies, 35–6, 49–50
agricultural subsidies, 8, 19, 208, 307, 361, 372, 378, 379, 380, 390, 395–6
agricultural technology, 36
agricultural tenancies
  and agricultural improvement, 12, 51–5, 312, 314, 317, 322
  assignation rights, 317

break clauses, 401
case law, 223–7, 314, 317, 319
and the Common Agricultural Policy, 379
compensation for crops damaged by game, 315
compensation for improvements, 312, 314, 317, 322
compensation for unreasonable termination of tenancy, 315
competitive bidding for, 28, 401
complexity of legislation, 324
diversification, 317, 322
farm valuation, 323
fixed equipment obligations, 312, 317, 323
forced sale of landlord's holding, 323
freedom of cropping and disposal of produce, 315
improving leases, 52
informal land borrowing, 401, 402
in Ireland, 13, 56–73
landlord–tenant relations, 12, 13, 42, 223–7, 313, 315, 321–2
leases, 51–2, 264, 288, 311–25
limited duration tenancies, 317, 320, 321
limited partnership tenancies, 223–7, 316–20
long leases, 51
market for, 28, 320–1
modern limited duration tenancies, 322–3
new entrants, 17, 321, 322–3, 407, 408
in Norway, 389, 392–3, 400–2, 403, 405, 407–8, 409
policies on, 311, 314, 315, 321, 324
and public interest, 314, 315, 317
rents, 26, 30, 32, 37, 52, 312, 313, 316, 320–1, 322
repairing limited duration tenancies, 323–4
retirement of tenants, 322
right to buy, 17, 317–18, 322
scale of holdings, 386
secure tenancies, 315–16, 317, 319, 320–1, 322–3
security of tenure, 16, 33, 51, 223–7, 312–13, 315–21, 379, 401, 405
short limited duration tenancies, 317, 323
single-tenant farms, 26, 27, 33–4, 35, 51, 52–3
small landholdings, 16, 296, 297, 361–2
statutory reform, 264
subtenants, 53
succession rights, 314, 315–16, 322
tenants-at-will, 42, 51

termination through service of notice, 224–7, 318–20
written leases, 51
see also crofting
Agricultural Tenants Register, 317
Agriculture Act (1967), 104
Agriculture (Scotland) Act (1948), 315
Alexander II, 120, 123, 125
Alexander, Claud, 35
Alexander, Gregory, 188, 201, 202
allemannsrätt, 335
Allodial Act (Norway), 391, 404
allotments, 27
American Civil War, 313
Americas, 23, 24, 26, 29–30, 31, 37, 81; *see also individual countries*
And the Cock Crew (MacColla), 102
Andrew v. North Lanarkshire Council, 291
Anglicisation (of the law), 144, 151
Anglo-Irish War, 76
Annexed Estates, 33, 35, 50
antisocial behaviour, 167, 280
Antisocial Behaviour etc. (Scotland) Act (2004), 167, 280
anxious scrutiny, 207
arable farming, 26, 27–8, 40–1, 384, 389, 395, 397
Arbroath Abbey, 118–20
Arch, Joseph, 60
Argyll, dukes of *see* Campbell, Archibald, 3rd duke of Argyll; Campbell, George, 8th duke of Argyll
aristocracy
agriculture as aristocratic ideal, 45
declining power of, 76, 80–1, 88–92
service aristocracy, 80–1, 88
see also private landowners
Arkwright, Richard, 35
asset-stripping, 32
asset transfer requests, 154, 162–3, 165, 171–3, 195
assignation rights, 295, 297, 317
assizes, 123–4, 127, 131–2
assured tenancies, 274, 276–9, 283
Assynt, 108, 177
Attlee, Clement, 330, 331
Australia, 81, 84
Ayr Manuscript, 123

backwardness, 78, 81, 87
bailies, 113–15, 122, 127, 131, 133, 146–7
Balfeith, 117–23
Ballinasloe Tenant Defence Association, 67–8
banditry, 25, 32
bands of surety, 28
Bank of Scotland, 29, 30–1
banking, 29, 30–1, 33, 37, 308
Bateman, John, 5, 105
Becher, Debbie, 192–3, 197
Belgium, 80
Bell, Patrick, 36
Bell, Robert, 264
beneficial ownership, 149, 150
Bengal Tenancy Act (1885), 74–5

Berger, Lawrence, 182, 183, 202
Bessborough Commission, 64
Bevan, Nye, 348, 349
Big Lottery, 208
biodiversity, 236, 245, 251, 357, 375
Black, Joseph, 48
Blackwood, Frederick Hamilton Temple, Lord Dufferin, 75, 78–9, 86, 90–1
Board for the Annexed Estates, 50
Board of Trustees for the Encouragement of Fisheries, Arts, and Manufactures of Scotland, 50
boundaries, 118–23, 127, 308
Bramley, Glen, 343
Brazil, 37
break clauses, 401
Brexit, 20, 208, 218, 309, 382
brieve of inquest, 123, 134
brieve of mortancestry, 124, 134, 143
brieve of novel dissaine, 123–4, 134, 143
brieve of perambulation, 122–3
brieve of right, 124, 127, 134–5, 143
brieves, 122–6, 127, 133–5, 143
Brigte, Gille, 121
Brigte, Mael, 120–1, 122
British Columbian, 79
British empire, 12, 23, 26, 31–2, 34, 36–8, 75–81, 84–7, 89–92
British Society for Fisheries, 35
British Wool Society, 50
broadband coverage, 383
Broun, Dauvit, 119
Brown, Gordon, 106
Bruce, Edward, Lord Kinloss, 25
Brundtland definition, 236, 238, 240, 242, 252, 255
Bryce, James, 336
Buccleuch, duke of *see* Scott, Henry, 3rd duke of Buccleuch
building subsidies, 396, 399
built environment, 23, 35
Burgess, Margaret, 281–2
burghs, 113–16, 119, 122, 125, 131
Burnett's Trustee v. *Grainger*, 148–50
Butcher's Broom (Gunn), 101

Callander, Robin, 5, 107
Cameron, Ewen, 332
Cameron, Joseph G. S., 272
Campbell, Archibald, 3rd duke of Argyll, 31, 33
Campbell, Colin, of Glenure, 32
Campbell, George, 8th duke of Argyll, 66, 91, 92, 95, 97
Campbell, John, 1st marquess of Breadalbane, 37
Campbell clan, 25
Campbells of Glenorchy, 37
Canada, 13, 26, 75, 81, 83–4, 85–6, 90–1, 349–50
Cannadine, David, 80–1
canon law, 117, 130–1, 133, 138, 142–4, 149
capital repatriation, 12, 23, 32, 37
capitalism, 12, 36–7, 58, 102, 313
carbon emissions, 403, 407
Caribbean, 23, 29, 31, 37

Carnegie, David, 4th duke of Fife, 344
carrying trade, 24, 30
Carter, Ian, 313
castle model (property rights), 228, 230–1, 234
casual labour, 28, 34
Catholic Church, 65, 67–8, 130; see also canon law
cattle, 26, 28, 34, 293; see also dairy farming; livestock
centralisation (public services), 381
ceremony of sasine, 114–16, 118–19, 136–7, 143, 145–7, 149–50
Chang, Yun-Chien, 185–6, 205
Chapelton of Elsick, 344
charities, 10, 372, 386
Charities and Trustee Investment (Scotland) Act (2005), 165
charitable incorporated organisations, 165, 171, 194
Charles I, 26–7
Charles II, 27
Charter of Fundamental Rights of the European Union, 218
charters, 115–16, 118, 119–20, 122, 136–9, 141, 142, 143, 147
Chartism, 59, 60
Chartist Land Plan, 60
Cheviot, the Stag and the Black, Black Oil (McGrath), 102–3
Choosing Our Future policy statement, 241
church lands, 23, 24–5
Church of Scotland, 67, 102
citizenship model (property rights), 216, 228–35
Civic Government (Scotland) Act (1982), 280
civil wars, 23, 27, 76
clan expropriations, 25
Clark, Samuel, 59
clearances
    Highlands, 14, 23, 33–4, 56, 57, 83, 94, 100–2, 109, 294, 296, 369
    literary depictions, 14, 100–2
    Lowlands, 12, 14, 23
climate change, 6, 10, 236, 239, 245, 375
Climate Change (Scotland) Act (2009), 239, 245, 251
Clydesdale Bank plc v. Davidson, 291
coal, 24, 25
collective memory, 127, 142, 369
College of Justice, 130–1, 135, 137, 142–3, 149, 152
Combe, Malcolm, 243
commercial leases, 264, 292
commercial sport, 60, 64, 83, 89, 99–100, 102, 369–70
commercialism, 26, 28–9, 43, 55
Commission for Securing the Peace of the Highlands, 28
Committee of Inquiry on Crofting (CoIC), 18, 352, 357
Common Agricultural Policy (CAP), 361, 378, 379, 380, 384
common law, 125–6, 131, 133, 143, 155, 263–6, 275, 284, 287, 288–91, 333

commonties, 8, 42, 54, 156
communities
    centrality to land reform debate, 7–10, 154, 159–63, 174–6
    communities of interest, 19, 165, 173, 195, 196, 340
    cooperation, 9
    crofting communities see crofting
    defining, 3, 7–8, 19, 194–6
    economic development, 169, 172, 202, 249, 255, 375, 379–82
    empowerment of, 10, 19, 162–3, 375
    environmental wellbeing, 163, 167, 169, 172, 178, 181, 197, 202, 237, 252–3, 255, 261, 375, 384
    involvement in decision-making, 155, 156, 163, 169–70, 257, 259–60, 261, 355–6, 373
    and land management, 8–9, 156, 159, 373
    landownership see community landownership
    participation of private landowners, 384
    and the planning process, 156, 336–41
    public health, 169, 172, 202, 255, 383
    regeneration, 7, 169, 172, 202, 255
    and rural development, 8, 257
    social wellbeing, 169, 172, 202, 255, 375, 382–4
    sustainable development, 373, 375–87
communities of interest, 19, 165, 173, 195, 196, 340
community ballots, 166, 181, 203–4, 222–3
community benefit societies, 165, 171, 194
community bodies, 156, 160, 163, 164–6, 171, 179, 181, 194–6, 244
Community Empowerment (Scotland) Act (2015), 5, 19, 154, 155, 162–3, 165, 166, 171–3, 178, 193–212, 237, 239, 244, 252–3, 258, 261
Community Land Scotland, 159, 210
community landownership
    abandoned or neglected land, 163, 167, 178, 196–8, 237, 252–3, 261
    appeal and review mechanisms, 172, 206
    asset transfer requests, 154, 162–3, 165, 171–3, 195
    ballots on local support, 166, 181, 203–4, 222–3
    centrality to land reform policy, 154, 159–63, 174–6
    community body formation, 156, 160, 163, 164–6, 171, 179, 181, 194–6, 244
    community landlords, 302–3
    compensation for forced transfers, 181, 182, 183–6, 204–5
    crofting communities see crofting
    democratic legitimacy, 180–1, 187, 194, 203, 207
    detrimental land, 163, 167–8, 178, 196–8, 237, 252–3, 261
    emergence of idea, 108–9
    in England and Wales, 164
    forced transfers, 15, 163, 166–70, 177–212, 237, 252–5, 260, 261
    government funding, 4, 181, 207–8

in the Highlands and Islands, 108–9, 159–60, 163, 174, 177
judicial scrutiny, 181, 205–7
and land management, 8–9, 159
land valuation, 166, 168, 169, 182, 183–6, 204–5, 206
litigation challenging, 173–4
and property theory, 15, 180–212
and public interest, 15, 166, 168, 181–4, 201–2, 207–8, 222–3, 243, 246–7, 249, 254–62
registration of interest, 162, 164, 173, 244, 248
right to bid, 164
right to buy, 4, 15, 19, 154–76, 177–212, 222–3, 236–40, 243–62, 374
and sustainable development, 15, 163, 165–6, 168–70, 179, 181, 201–2, 236–40, 243–62, 374
target of one million acres, 154, 161, 175, 177
third-party purchasers, 170, 181, 208–9
in urban areas, 3, 19, 162, 178, 196, 210, 244
Community Residency Entitlement (CRE), 193, 205
Community Right to Buy Guidance (CRBG), 247–50, 259
Companies Act (2006), 165
companies limited by guarantee, 164–5, 171, 194
company law, 165, 244, 246
Company of Scotland, 29
comparative analyses, 2, 12–13, 19, 56–73, 74–93, 388–409
compensation
  to agricultural tenants for crops damaged by game, 315
  to agricultural tenants for improvements, 312, 314, 317, 322
  to agricultural tenants for unreasonable termination of tenancy, 315
  to crofters for improvements, 16, 74, 294, 295, 296, 351
  to private landowners for forced transfer of land, 181, 182, 183–6, 204–5
  and property rights, 229, 233–4
compulsory purchase, 75, 162, 180–93, 331, 348; see also forced transfers
compulsory purchase orders, 162
compulsory sale orders, 162, 175
concentration of ownership, 5–6, 7, 10, 41, 82–4, 88–9, 93, 105, 158–9, 243, 368–87, 388
Concession Act (Norway), 391, 392, 403, 404
conciliar sessions, 130–1, 132–5, 142–3
Congested Districts Board, 97, 296, 370
conservation organisations, 10, 372, 386
Conservative Party, 66, 69, 93, 97, 99, 100, 103, 104, 105, 272, 274, 277
Consider the Lilies (Crichton Smith), 102
consolidation of holdings, 42, 296, 304, 379, 403, 407
constitutionalism, 353–4

Constructive Unionism, 66
contractual tenancies, 272, 275, 278, 284
Convention on the Rights of the Child (UN), 217, 221
conveyancing
  crofts, 301
  feudal conveyancing, 113–17, 137, 145–7, 149, 152
  nineteenth-century reforms, 147–8
  role of notaries public, 146–7, 152
  twentieth- and twenty-first-century reforms, 151–2
  see also sasine
Conveyancing (Scotland) Act (1874), 147–8
cooperation, 9, 389, 390, 398, 402–3, 405, 407
Co-operative and Community Benefit Societies Act (2014), 165
Core Path Plans, 333–4, 335, 336
core paths, 18, 333–6
Corn Laws, 313
Cosgrove, Patrick, 71
cottars, 53, 54, 296
cotton, 35; see also textiles
council housing, 342–3, 345–9; see also housing: public sector provision
Council of Europe, 353, 355, 359, 360, 365
Council of Mortgage Lenders, 308
Court of Session, 42, 147, 206, 223, 224, 227, 270–1, 273, 319
Covenanting movement, 27, 28
Craig, Thomas, of Riccarton, 128–30, 138–40
Crichton Smith, Iain, 102
Crofters Commission (established by 1886 Act), 65–6, 73, 74, 295–6; see also Crofting Commission (regulatory body)
Crofters Common Grazings Regulation Acts (1891; 1908), 295
Crofters Holdings (Scotland) Act (1886), 8, 13, 64, 65, 72–3, 74, 91, 97, 294–6, 304, 351, 370
Crofters Party, 69
Crofters (Scotland) Act (1955), 297, 371
Crofters (Scotland) Act (1961), 296
Crofters (Scotland) Act (1993), 294, 295, 299
Crofters War, 11, 14, 58, 66–8, 96, 100–1
crofting
  age profile of crofters, 307–9
  and agrarian radicalism, 56–73, 96, 100–1
  agricultural land use, 296, 297, 304, 306–7, 309
  agricultural support, 306–7, 352, 361–5
  assignation rights, 295, 297
  case law, 298
  common grazings, 96–7, 105, 156, 160, 295, 298–9, 306, 351
  community body formation, 160, 164–5, 171, 244
  community landlords, 302–3
  community landownership, 109, 154, 159–61, 163, 166, 170–1, 174, 178, 222–3, 237, 243–50, 260, 302–3
  compensation for improvements, 16, 74, 294, 295, 296, 351

crofting (*cont.*)
  complexity of legislation, 301–2, 351
  conflicting objectives of crofting system, 16, 294, 303–7
  consolidation of holdings, 296, 304
  conveyancing transactions, 301
  creation of new crofts, 296
  crofters absent from holdings, 351, 357
  crofting counties, 4, 16, 74, 104, 296–7, 304, 306–7, 351, 361–4, 366, 386
  crofts as security for borrowing, 300, 305, 308
  cultural aspects, 309–10
  decrofting, 295, 297, 300, 301, 305, 306
  defining, 8, 295
  development land use, 297–8, 304–6
  diversified land use, 296, 300, 304–7, 309
  'duty-to-report' provision, 356–61, 365–6
  and economic development, 297–8, 304–7, 309
  funding, 305, 306–7, 352, 361–5
  grazings committees, 105, 295, 357–8, 365
  holdings created by Congested Districts Board, 370
  involvement of crofters in policy decision-making, 18, 351–67
  land improvement, 16, 74, 294, 295, 296, 351
  landlord rights over crofting land, 295, 303
  landlord–tenant relations, 56–73, 91, 293, 302–3, 351
  market for crofts and croft tenancies, 16, 294, 298, 307–9, 357
  media representations, 59, 64
  new entrants, 307–9
  owner-occupation, 97, 104–5, 298–9
  policy formation, 18, 351–67
  political representation, 64–5, 69, 360–1
  population retention, 305–6, 357
  registration of crofts, 294, 297, 300, 308
  relation of crofting law to general land reform measures, 16, 294, 302–3
  relationship between crofting community and government, 352, 360–1, 365–7
  relocation to crofts after clearances, 34, 83
  renouncement of tenancies, 295
  rent strikes, 68
  rents, 16, 65–6, 74, 294, 295–6, 351
  restoration of land lost during clearances, 294, 296
  retirement of crofters, 297
  right to buy, 4, 105, 154, 159–61, 163, 166, 174, 178, 222–3, 237, 243–50, 260, 297–9, 302–3
  security of tenure, 4, 16, 74, 96–7, 294, 295–6, 351
  standard of living, 304
  subdivision of holdings, 296
  succession rights, 295, 297
  tenure regulation, 352, 356–61, 365–6
  title deeds to crofts, 297, 298
  see also agricultural tenancies
Crofting Amendment (Scotland) Act (2013), 301

Crofting Commission (regulatory body), 104, 165, 297, 299, 300, 305–6, 397; *see also* Crofters Commission (established by 1886 Act)
Crofting Community Right to Buy (Ballot) (Scotland) Regulations (2004), 222–3
Crofting Community Right to Buy Guidance (Crofting Guidance), 247–50, 259
Crofting Counties Agricultural Grant Scheme (CCAGS), 306–7, 361–5
Crofting Law Group, 300–1
Crofting Law Sump, 301
Crofting Reform etc. Act (2007), 300
Crofting Reform (Scotland) Act (1976), 104, 105, 297–8, 305
Crofting Reform (Scotland) Act (2010), 294, 298, 300, 301
Crofting Register, 294, 297, 300, 308
Crofting Support Scheme (CSS), 363–4
Croke, Thomas, 65
Cromwell, Oliver, 27, 56
crop rotation, 35, 52, 400
Crown Estate lands, 4
'*Cuilithionn, An*' (MacLean), 101
Cullen, William, 48
Culloden, battle of, 57
customary tenure, 42
customs and excise duties, 30

Dailly, Mike, 279–80
dairy farming, 395–6
Dale, David, 35
Dalrymple, James, Viscount Stair, 143–4, 265
Darien expeditions, 29–30
Davitt, Michael, 62–3, 64, 68, 96
death duties, 371, 378
debts, 25, 27, 30, 32, 33, 113–14, 132, 160, 372, 378
decision-making processes
  community involvement, 155, 156, 163, 169–70, 257, 259–60, 261, 355–6, 373
  national and international standards, 355–6, 358–60, 365, 366
  principles for legitimate decision-making, 352, 353–4, 365–6
  representation of crofters' interests, 18, 351–67
decrofting, 295, 297, 300, 301, 305, 306
deemed sasine, 147
deer forest, 64, 99–100, 370; *see also* sporting estates
Deer Forest Commission, 97, 99
deer management, 155
deference, 58, 81, 82, 90
democracy, 6, 64–5, 68–72, 82, 87, 88, 90–1, 203–4, 228–9, 339–42, 352–4, 360–1, 365–6
Democratic Federation, 96
democratic legitimacy, 180–1, 187, 194, 203, 207, 353–4, 365–6
demographic change, 308, 375, 381–2, 385, 386
Denmark, 40

Department of Agriculture and Fisheries for Scotland (DAFS), 98, 99, 296
detrimental land, 163, 167–8, 178, 196–8, 237, 252–3, 261
Detroit, MI, 187, 189–91
devolution, 4, 6, 94, 157, 243, 279, 332
Devon Angling Association v. *Scottish Water*, 291
digital connectivity, 375, 383, 385
direct jurisdiction, 126
Disposal of Land by Local Authorities (Scotland) Regulations (2010), 172
dispossession, 9, 58, 60; *see also* clearances; evictions; expropriations; indigenous land rights; land forfeitures; land sequestrations
dispute resolution, 117–26, 127
distilling, 34, 35
diversification, 10, 12, 35, 249, 296, 300, 304–7, 317, 322, 380–1, 398
diversity of ownership, 4, 10–11, 257, 373–4, 406–7
Division of Commonty Act (1695), 42, 54
Division of Runrig Act (1695), 42
documents *see* legal documents
Dooley, Terence, 71
Drinking Well, The (Gunn), 102
droving, 26, 27–8, 30
Drummond, John, of Quarrel, 31
Drummond Young, James, Lord, 263
Dryburgh Abbey, 122
dual ownership, 93
Duff, William, Lord Braco and 1st earl of Fife, 32
Dufferin, Lord *see* Blackwood, Frederick Hamilton Temple, Lord Dufferin
Dutch Republic, 24, 26, 30
'duty-to-report' provision, 356–61, 365–6

Earl of Galloway v. *M'Clelland*, 314
East India Company, 29, 31
East Indies, 29
economic development, 82, 102–4, 169, 172, 180–93, 202, 210, 249, 255, 297–8, 304–7, 309, 375, 379–82
economic growth, 45–6, 241, 242, 247, 251, 262, 385
economic liberalism, 46, 402
Economic Strategy policy statement, 242, 247, 251–2, 262
economic sustainability, 241, 242, 247, 249, 251, 262
economies of scale, 379, 386, 399, 403, 407
ecosystem services, 252, 389
Edinburgh, 25, 29, 37, 48, 49, 50
Edinburgh Society for Encouraging Art, Science, Manufactures and Agriculture, 49
egalitarianism, 399, 402–3, 405
Eigg, 108, 160
Emergency Powers (Defence) Acts (1939; 1940), 315
emigration, 28–9, 34, 58, 79, 86, 93; *see also* migration
eminent domain, 180–93, 210; *see also* compulsory purchase; forced transfers

employment, 249, 304, 309, 375, 381, 382, 383, 385, 392, 395, 396–7, 400, 404; *see also* labour
enclosure, 27, 35, 40, 42–3, 52, 54, 58
energy production, 10, 241, 248
England
  agricultural improvement, 44
  agricultural labour, 60
  agricultural societies, 50
  banking, 31
  community right to bid, 164
  concentration of ownership, 105
  customary tenure, 42
  grain market, 36
  housing crisis, 345–6
  industrialisation, 36, 77–8
  land hunger, 83
  livestock market, 27–8, 36
  manufacturing, 24
  National Upland Outcomes, 374
  planning law, 329–30
  public rights of way, 333
  Scotland's economic disparity with, 44–5
  and the Treaty of Union, 23, 30–2, 36
  urbanisation, 24, 77–8
Enlightenment, 12, 23, 34, 39–55, 59
Entail Acts, 42, 47
entails, 42, 47
entrepreneurship, 24, 26, 34–5, 38, 400, 401
environmental designations, 384
environmental development, 249, 375, 384
environmental justice, 240, 250
Environmental Protection Act (1990), 167
environmental wellbeing, 163, 167, 169, 172, 178, 181, 197, 202, 237, 252–3, 255, 261, 375, 384
Equality and Human Rights Committee, 220
Erskine, John, 1st earl of Moray, 128
Erskine, John, 2nd earl of Moray, 128–9
Established Church *see* Church of Scotland
estate management *see* land management
estate workers, 381, 383, 386
European Convention on Human Rights (ECHR), 9, 158, 174, 200, 214–35, 245, 256–61, 318–19, 341–2
European Court of Human Rights, 219, 233–4
European Social Charter, 218, 220
European Union, 20, 208, 218, 309, 319, 361, 378, 379, 382
evangelical revival, 67
eviction orders, 286
evictions, 34, 58, 70, 267, 285–6, 369
existing-use value, 18
experimental methods, 47–8
expropriations, 25, 26, 91, 181–93, 197, 199, 208–11, 228–9
extinctive prescription, 139

fair hearing, right to, 222–3, 257–8
fair rents, 272, 273, 274, 276, 278, 295–6, 351
famine, 26, 29, 31, 44, 71, 78
Farm and Horticultural Development Scheme, 380
farm cannibalism, 399, 403, 408

farm entrepreneurship, 400, 401
Farmers Magazine, 41
fee and heritage rule, 133–4
Fenian movement, 61, 62, 64, 67–8
Fennell, Lee Anne, 184, 188, 205
feudal conveyancing, 113–17, 137, 145–7, 149, 152; *see also* sasine
feudal jurisdiction, 47, 125–6
feudal superiors, 4, 115, 148
feudal tenure systems, 4, 26, 46–7, 67–8
Fife, duke of *see* Carnegie, David, 4th duke of Fife
financial crisis (2008), 298, 329, 345
financial markets, 345–6
Firm Foundations: The Future of Housing in Scotland, 281
First-tier Tribunal for Scotland, 282–3, 284–6
First World War, 76, 98, 270–1, 371, 378
Fischel, William, 189–92, 208
fishing, 25, 26, 33, 34–5, 54, 59, 156–7, 198
fishing rights, 156–7, 198
fixed equipment, 312, 317, 323, 397, 400
Flyn, Derek, 296, 301
food production, 304, 309, 315
food rationing, 315
food security, 158, 228
Forbord, Magnar, 392
forced transfers, 15, 163, 166–70, 177–212, 237, 252–5, 260, 261; *see also* compulsory purchase
forestry, 10, 35, 37, 54, 371–2, 384, 389, 397, 402
Forestry Commission, 371–2
Forfeited Estates, 11; *see also* land forfeitures
forgery, 132, 135, 143
Fox, A., 244
fragmentation of ownership, 376, 378–9, 385–6; *see also* subdivision of holdings
France, 24, 76, 80, 84, 130
franchise, 69, 90
Free Church of Scotland, 64, 67–8
Freeman's Journal, 63, 65
French Revolution, 76
furnished tenancies, 270, 273

Gaelic poetry, 14, 101
Geary, Laurence, 70
General Motors Corporation (GM), 189–91
General View of the Agriculture of the County of Dumfries (Johnston), 54
Geographic Information System (GIS) mapping, 376
George, Henry, 62–3, 64, 77, 95–6, 331
German law, 151, 188
Germany, 26, 30, 76, 80
Gezelius, Stig, 403
Gibson v. *Monypenie*, 137
Gigha, 108, 160
Gill, Brian, Lord, 324
Gladstone, William E., 64, 68, 72, 74, 83, 91, 293
Glasgow, 3, 29 ,48, 270, 280, 349
Glendale estate, Skye, 97
gold, 23, 24, 29

governance, 13, 75, 77, 79–81, 85, 355–6, 361–5
government funding
  for community land purchase, 4, 181, 207–8
  for crofting, 306–7, 352
  see also subsidies
Graham, Keith, 301
grain, 29, 36, 40–1, 313, 395, 396, 397
Gray v. *MacNeil's Executor*, 291
grazing land, 27–8, 54, 71, 96–7, 105, 156, 160, 295, 298–9, 306, 351, 384, 389, 395
grazing leases, 316, 323
grazings committees, 105, 295, 357–8, 365
Great Famine (Ireland), 71, 78
green belts, 329, 334, 347
Green Party, 107
Grenfell Tower disaster, 341
Grieve, Sir Robert, 349
Ground Game Act (1880), 313
Growing Community Assets (GCA) fund, 208
Guidelines for civil participation in political decision-making (Council of Europe), 355, 359, 360, 365
Gunn, Neil M., 101–2

Habitat III conference, 337, 338, 339, 341, 349, 350
Habsburg empire, 76
Hamilton, Willie, 105–6
Harris, Matt, 63
health, 169, 172, 202, 255, 383
Heller, Michael, 184–5, 193, 205
Henderson, Hamish, 98
Heritable Jurisdictions (Scotland) Act (1746), 47
Highland and Agricultural Society, 36
Highland Land Law Reform Association, 60, 69
Highland News, 64
Highland societies, 50, 59
Highland Society of Scotland, 50
Highlands and Islands
  agrarian radicalism, 13, 56–73, 96, 100–1
  agricultural improvement, 12, 35–6
  Annexed Estates, 33
  clan expropriations, 25
  clearances, 14, 23, 33–4, 56, 57, 83, 94, 100–2, 109, 294, 296, 369
  community landownership, 108–9, 159–60, 163, 174, 177
  concentration of ownership, 370
  Crofters War, 11, 14, 58, 66–8, 96, 100–1
  crofts *see* crofting
  economic development, 102, 104, 304–7
  emigration, 34, 58
  emphasis upon in land debates, 3
  and historicism, 81, 91
  impact of civil war, 27
  infrastructure, 34, 36
  land hunger, 83
  land nationalisation, 98
  land redistribution, 109, 370–1
  landlord–tenant relations, 56–73, 91
  literary depictions, 14, 100–3

livestock farming, 28
perceived backwardness, 78, 81, 87
planned villages, 34–5
political representation, 64–5, 69, 103
population growth, 308
poverty, 63, 370
rent strikes, 68
sporting estates, 60, 64, 83, 89, 99–100, 102
Highlands and Islands Development Board (HIDB), 103–4, 304–6
Highlands and Islands Enterprise (HIE), 304–6
Highlands and Islands Royal Commission, 370
Hills, Rick, 184–5, 193, 205
historicism, 2, 6–7, 8, 75, 81, 82, 85–6, 91–2
'hobby' holdings, 379
holiday lets, 383, 385
Holmehill Ltd v. The Scottish Ministers and Anor, 246
home ownership, 186–7, 190, 198–200, 268, 275, 279
Home Rule (Ireland), 64, 66, 69, 72
homelessness, 277, 280, 342
Homes, Henry, Lord Kames, 47, 48
Homestead Community Consent, 193
Honourable Society of Improvers of Agriculture in Scotland, 44–5, 46, 50
House of Lords, 148, 150
housing
    affordable housing, 200, 329, 345, 347–8, 375, 383
    construction of, 343–5, 347–9, 383
    council housing, 342–3, 345–9
    holiday lets, 383, 385
    home ownership, 186–7, 190, 198–200, 268, 275, 279
    homelessness, 277, 280, 342
    housing associations, 200, 268, 269, 274, 276, 277–80, 283, 290, 349
    housing crisis (current), 18, 329, 341–50
    housing crisis (post-war), 343, 347
    and human rights, 341–2, 349–50
    make-up of housing sector, 267–8, 279
    market for, 345–6, 383
    overcrowding, 94, 269, 382
    and planning, 18, 329, 341–50, 382
    private sector provision, 267–8, 270–7, 279, 280–91
    public sector provision, 18, 99, 268, 273–6, 279–80, 287, 342–3, 345–9
    quality of, 7, 269–70, 278, 287, 349, 375, 382
    scarcity of supply, 18, 267–8, 269, 270–2, 341–50, 383
    second homes, 383, 385
    stock transfers, 276, 277–8, 279–80
    surveys of conditions, 269–70
    and sustainable development, 343–4, 382–3, 385
    tenancies see residential tenancies
    tied housing, 381, 383
Housing: The Government's Proposals for Scotland, 278
Housing and Property Chamber, 283

Housing and Urban Development (HUD) department, 190–1
housing associations, 200, 268, 269, 274, 276, 277–80, 283, 290, 349
Housing (Scotland) Act (1987), 274, 275, 288
Housing (Scotland) Act (1988), 274–5, 276–9, 283, 285, 286, 287, 288
Housing (Scotland) Act (2001), 274, 278, 279–80, 288, 290
Housing (Scotland) Act (2006), 280, 291
Housing (Scotland) Act (2010), 280
Housing (Scotland) Act (2014), 280, 282
human flourishing, 188, 202, 204, 229
human rights
    as basis for land reform, 7, 9–10, 15, 257–8
    case law, 216, 220–7, 233–4, 257–8, 319
    civil and political rights, 217–18, 220, 231
    economic and social rights, 218, 220, 228, 235, 349
    enforcement, 219–21
    European Convention, 9, 158, 174, 200, 214–35, 245, 256–61, 318–19, 341–2
    European Court of Human Rights, 219, 233–4
    fair hearing, 222–3, 257–8
    and food security, 158, 228
    freedom from discrimination, 221
    and housing, 341–2, 349–50
    human rights law, 15, 216, 219–27
    media and political representations, 15, 215–16, 234
    peaceful enjoyment of property, 158, 206, 214–16, 217, 220–35, 257–8, 261, 341–2
    private, family life, 341
    and property rights, 7, 9–10, 15, 158, 174, 213–35, 256–60, 261, 318–19
    protection for residential tenancies, 200
    and public interest, 213, 215, 217, 222–3, 227, 233–5, 239, 256–60, 319
    respect for private life and the home, 200
    right to shelter, 7, 158, 228
    Scottish and UK obligations, 218–19
    Scottish human rights framework, 216–21
    and sustainable development, 239, 256–61
    Universal Declaration, 217
Human Rights Act (1998), 219, 220
Hume, David, 46
Humphrey de Berkeley, 118–23
Hunter, Robert, 264
hunting, 54–5, 389, 402
Husmann class, 391, 405
Hutton, James, 48
Hyndman, H. M., 96
Hypothec Abolition (Scotland) Act (1880), 313–14

imperialism, 12, 13, 23, 31–2, 75–81, 84–7, 89–92; see also British empire
improvement culture, 12, 39–55, 312; see also agricultural improvement; land improvement
improvement literature, 44, 50
improvement societies, 44–5, 49–50
improving leases, 52

in feudo et hereditate landholdings, 116, 118, 119
in feudo et hereditate ac in libero burgagio landholdings, 119
in free and pure and untroubled alms landholdings, 119
in regality landholdings, 125–6
Increase of Rent and Mortgage Interest (Restrictions) Act (1919), 271
Increase of Rent and Mortgage Interest (Restrictions) Act (1920), 271
Increase of Rent and Mortgage Interest (War Restrictions) Act (1915), 270–1
India, 8, 13, 31, 35, 74–5, 78, 81, 84–5, 87, 90, 91–2
indigenous land rights, 79, 81, 84, 86
industrial labour, 23, 33, 34–5, 53
industrial technology, 35
industrialisation, 13, 35, 36, 76, 77–8, 87
inequality, 104, 211, 242, 259
infeftment, 128–30, 134–41, 143, 145–8; *see also* sasine
Infeftment Act (1845), 147
inflation, 12, 23, 24, 53
infrastructure, 34, 93, 242, 344, 375, 397
inquest, brieve of, 123, 134
instruments of sasine, 135–7, 139–42, 143–4, 146–8, 149–50
intellectual classes, 48–9
International Bill of Rights, 217
International Covenant on Civil and Political Rights (ICCPR), 217
International Covenant on Economic, Social and Cultural Rights (ICESCR), 158, 215, 218, 219, 220, 259, 349
international law, 217, 219–20, 235
internet shopping, 381
intervention pricing, 380
investment model (property rights), 192–3, 230–1
Ireland
    agrarian radicalism, 13, 56–73, 89
    agricultural tenancies, 13, 56–73
    Catholic Church, 65, 67–8
    Civil War, 76
    concentration of ownership, 105
    Constructive Unionism, 66
    emigration, 58
    evangelical revival, 67
    Famine, 71, 78
    Fenian movement, 61, 62, 64, 67–8
    and historicism, 81, 91
    Home Rule, 64, 66, 69, 72
    Jacobitism, 29
    Land Acts, 13, 64, 54, 71–2, 74, 91, 97
    land hunger, 83
    Land League, 57, 60–3, 65, 68–70, 72
    Land War, 58, 60–3, 67–72
    landlord–tenant relations, 56–73, 88, 89, 91
    media reporting, 59, 63, 65
    nationalism, 59, 60–1, 63, 70–1, 89
    Parnell split, 57, 70–1
    perceived backwardness, 78, 81, 87
    Plan of Campaign, 69–70
    plantation of Ulster, 25
    political representation, 68–72
    poverty, 64, 72
    rent strikes, 68
    Scottish mercenaries, 25
    War of Independence, 76
Irish Civil War, 76
Irish Land Act (1870), 74, 91
Irish Land War, 58, 60–3, 67–72
Irish National Land League, 57, 60–3, 65, 68–70, 72
Irish Parliamentary Party, 68–71, 72
Islands *see* Highlands and Islands; *and individual islands*
Isle of Gigha Heritage Trust, 160

Jackson, Alvin, 57
Jacobite rebellions, 4, 32–3, 45
Jacobitism, 4, 29, 31–3, 45
Jamaica, 37
James III, 136
James VI and I, 25
James VII and II, 28, 29
job creation, 249
Johnston, Tom, 89
Joint Committee on Human Rights, 220
joint farming, 396, 398, 403
joint-stock companies, 29
judices, 120–1, 122
judicial review, 181, 205–7
jurisdiction
    of conciliar sessions, 130, 133–5
    direct jurisdiction, 126
    of feudal lords, 47, 125–6
    First-tier Tribunal, 283
    of justiciars, 125–6
    Scottish Land Court, 315
    of sheriffs, 125–6, 282–3, 287
    supervisory jurisdiction, 126, 134
justiciars, 121, 122, 123–4, 125–6, 127, 131

kårfolk, 404, 405
Keeper's Warranty, 151
Keir, William, 52
Keith, George, 5th Earl Marischal, 24–5
Kelly, James, 193, 205
Kelo v. *City of New London*, 186–7, 193
kelp production, 34, 293
Khan, Sadiq, 345, 346
Kilmuir estate, Skye, 97
Kirk *see* Church of Scotland
kirklands, 23, 24–5
knowledge production, 39, 47–8
knowledge transfer, 39, 48–51
Knoydart, 98, 108
Krier, James, 183–4, 205

labour
    agricultural, 28–9, 34–5, 53, 60, 381, 385
    casual, 28, 34
    estate workers, 381, 383, 386
    female workers, 28
    industrial, 23, 33, 34–5, 53
    job creation and protection, 249

labour market, 28–9, 30
migrant labour, 382
mobility of, 12, 34–5, 381, 385
and planned villages, 34–5, 53
rise of wage labour, 26, 28–9
seasonal, 28, 34, 53, 397
self-employed contractors, 381
Standard Labour Requirements, 380
and trade unions, 60
wages, 28–9, 53
see also employment
Labour Party, 94, 95, 103–7, 109, 157, 272,
274, 299, 315, 331
Laird of Craigiehall v. *Laird of Glenvervie*, 137
land acquisition
and agrarian radicalism, 66, 71, 75
asset transfer requests, 154, 162–3, 165,
171–3, 195
by communities *see* community
landownership; right to buy
compulsory purchase, 75, 162, 180–93, 331,
348
by crofters *see* right to buy
at existing-use value, 18
forced transfers, 15, 163, 166–70, 177–212,
237, 252–5, 260, 261
land grabbing, 71
and property theory, 15, 180–212
by public authorities, 18, 348–9
from public authorities, 154, 162–3, 165,
170–3, 195
right to buy *see* right to buy
third-party purchasers, 170, 181, 208–9
Land Act (Norway), 391, 392–3, 405
Land Assembly Districts (LADs), 185, 193, 205
land forfeitures, 27, 29, 32–3, 114
land grabbing, 71
land hunger, 82, 83–4
land improvement, 10, 12, 16, 54, 74, 294,
295, 296, 351; *see also* agricultural
improvement
Land Law (Ireland) Act (1881), 13, 64, 65, 74,
91, 97
land management
and access rights, 335
and the Agricultural Enlightenment, 12,
39–41, 51–2
and agricultural tenancies, 51–2
commonties and common grazing, 156, 295
and communities, 8–9, 156, 159, 373
co-operative approaches, 9, 389, 402
detrimental management, 163, 167–8, 178,
196–8, 237, 252–3, 261
ecosystem services approaches, 252
and improvement *see* land improvement
and landlords, 26, 34, 51–2
and lease conditions, 52
in Norway, 389, 393, 398, 402, 403
policies on, 251–2
and private landowners, 23, 34, 51–2, 159,
379–81
and public authorities, 156
soil management, 398, 401
and stewardship, 252, 373

and sustainable development, 236, 251–2,
253, 259, 373
see also land use
land market, 23, 31, 37, 372, 378, 390, 405
land nationalisation, 62–3, 69, 95–6, 98–9,
104–5, 108
Land of Our Fathers (MacPherson), 102
'Land of Scotland and the Common Good'
report, 197, 198, 199, 205, 215
land purchase *see* land acquisition
land reclamation, 28, 52
land redistribution, 7, 14, 71, 100, 109, 370–1
land reform associations, 60
Land Reform Policy Group (LRPG), 4, 6, 157,
161, 236–7, 243, 246, 257, 299–300, 373
Land Reform Review Group (LRRG), 5, 6,
161–2, 197, 198, 205, 210, 215, 384–5
Land Reform (Scotland) Act (2003), 4, 8, 18,
154–8, 161, 163–8, 173–4, 178–9,
193–212, 222–3, 237, 239, 243–50,
252–3, 255, 257–8, 260, 332–6, 373
Land Reform (Scotland) Act (2016), 5, 154–7,
159, 162, 163, 168–70, 179, 194–212,
214–15, 228, 234, 237, 239, 253–5, 256,
258–60, 261, 321–4, 374, 387, 405–6,
408
Land Register, 152, 158–9
land registration, 107, 141–2, 143, 146,
147–52, 158–9, 294, 297, 300, 308
Land Registration (Scotland) Act (1979), 107,
151, 158
Land Registration etc. (Scotland) Act (2012),
151, 159
Land Rights and Responsibilities Statement
(LRRS), 179, 212, 213–15, 216, 234–5,
258–60, 368
land sequestrations, 27, 32
land settlement, 370–1
Land Settlement (Scotland) Act (1919), 98, 371
land speculation, 404
Land Tenure Reform (Scotland) Act (1974),
266
land transfer *see* conveyancing; sasine
land use
and the Agricultural Enlightenment, 12,
39–55
changes driven by private landowners, 10,
12, 41, 43
crofting land, 296, 297–8, 300, 304–7, 309
detrimental use, 163, 167–8, 178, 196–8,
237, 252–3, 261
diversification of, 10, 12, 296, 300, 304–7,
380–1, 398
ecosystem services approaches, 252
environmental designations, 384
influence of Common Agricultural Policy,
378, 380
intensification of, 370, 380, 386
and planning, 334
policies on, 251–2, 255, 258–62
and stewardship, 252, 373
and sustainable development, 236, 251–2,
253, 255, 258–62, 373
see also land management

Land Use Strategy policy statement, 251–2, 255, 259, 260
land valuation, 33, 95, 166, 168, 169, 182, 183–6, 204–5, 206, 323
land wars *see* Crofters War; Irish Land War
landholding size, 18–19, 368–87
Landlord and Tenant (Ireland) Act (1870), 64
landlords
  absentee landlords, 59, 67, 88, 159, 202, 243, 379, 384
  community landlords, 302–3
  duty to repair, 280
  forced sale for failure to comply with obligations, 323
  and land management, 26, 34, 51–2
  leasing policies *see* leases
  mortgage rates, 270–1
  professionalism, 281, 282, 287
  profiteering by, 34, 270
  and property rights, 42–3, 65, 223–7
  Rachmanism, 273
  recovery of possession, 266, 271, 272, 275, 276–7, 285–6, 295
  recovery of rent arrears, 65, 271, 276, 286, 313–14
  registered social landlords, 279–80, 290–1
  registration of private landlords, 280
  rents paid to *see* rents
  resident landlords, 273, 283
  right of hypothec, 313–14
  rights over crofting land, 295, 303
  sanctions applicable to, 284–5
  serfdom imposed by, 24
  successors in title, 266, 267, 288, 289
  see also agricultural tenancies; crofting; private landowners; residential tenancies
landownership
  changes in patterns of, 10–11, 18–19, 24–6, 27, 369–72
  by charitable and conservation organisations, 10, 372, 386
  by communities *see* community landownership
  concentration of, 5–6, 7, 10, 41, 82, 83–4, 88–9, 93, 105, 158–9, 243, 368–87, 388
  consolidation of holdings, 42, 296, 304, 379, 403, 407
  diversity of, 4, 10–11, 257, 373–4, 406–7
  dual ownership, 93
  fragmentation of, 376, 378–9, 385–6
  indigenous land rights, 79, 81, 84, 86
  as investment, 192–3, 230
  and power, 12, 41, 77, 80–1, 88–92
  private *see* private landowners
  right to buy *see* right to buy
  rights and responsibilities of, 82, 84–5, 86, 230–2, 234
  scale of landholdings, 18–19, 368–87, 389, 393, 395, 396, 397, 399, 400, 402–3, 407
  and social prestige, 41, 43
  by the state and public authorities, 10, 18, 98–9, 109, 156, 162, 370, 371–2, 386
  subdivision of holdings, 296, 370, 379

surveys of, 5, 105–8, 372
and sustainable development, 15, 18–19
see also home ownership; property rights
Lands Tribunal of Scotland, 206
landscape, 6, 12, 35, 53–4, 357
landscaping, 26, 36
Law of Property in Scotland (Reid), 151
learned laws *see* canon law; Roman law
Leasehold Reform, Housing and Urban Development Act (1993), 275
leases
  agricultural leases, 12, 51–2, 264, 288, 311–25
  and asset transfer requests, 171–2
  case law, 291
  commercial leases, 264, 292
  and common law, 263–6, 275, 284, 287, 288–91
  conditions and covenants, 52
  definitions of, 265
  grazing leases, 316, 323
  improving leases, 52
  and land management, 52
  long leases, 51
  and personal rights, 265–6
  and real rights, 266, 289–91
  residential leases, 16, 263–92
  tacit relocation, 271, 272, 275, 288
  written leases, 51, 275, 284
Leases Act (1449), 265, 266, 285, 290, 311
Lee, J. J., 66
legal documents
  authenticity of, 135–7, 143
  complexity of, 132, 142
  instruments of sasine, 135–7, 139–42, 143–4, 146–8, 149–50
  loss or destruction of, 139–40, 143
  and notaries public, 136, 141, 143, 145–7
  potential forgery of, 132, 135, 143
legal expertise, 117, 127–44
legal professionals, 117, 145, 152–3
legal training, 127, 132
Less Favoured Area support, 380
letters of reversion, 132
letting agencies, 282
Lever, William, Lord Leverhulme, 108–9
Lewis, 25, 108–9, 222
Liberal Democrat Party, 94, 109
Liberal Party, 74, 83, 90, 93, 94–5, 97–8, 99–100, 103, 105, 293, 313
liberalism
  economic, 46, 402
  political, 7–8, 68, 75, 81, 85, 99
  see also neoliberalism
libraries, 50
Liebig, Justus von, 48
light plough, 36
limited duration tenancies, 317, 320, 321
Limited Partnerships Act (1907), 316
limited partnership tenancies, 223–7, 316–20
linen, 31, 33, 35, 46; *see also* textiles
literary societies, 49
literature, 1–2, 14, 100–3
Lithuania, 24

livestock
  commercial farming of, 34, 369, 370, 395, 397
  droving of, 26, 27–8, 30
  grazing for *see* grazing land
  market for, 27–8, 29, 36, 293
  numbers of units, 380
  theft of, 28, 32
  see also cattle; sheep
Lloyd, Clifford, 61
Lloyd George, David, 88, 95, 99
Local Appeal Panels, 339
local authorities *see* public authorities
Local Government (Scotland) Act (1973), 336
local plans, 333–4, 383
Localism Act (2011), 164
Lochhead, Richard, 321
London, 27–8, 31, 32, 37, 345–6
long leases, 51
long possession, 129–30, 139–41, 143
Lovett, John, 335, 336
Lowlands
  and the Agricultural Enlightenment, 12, 39–40, 51
  agricultural improvement, 12, 39–40
  Annexed Estates, 33
  banditry, 25, 32
  clearances, 12, 14, 23
  importance of inclusion in land debates, 3
  industrialisation, 78
  landscape, 12
  single-tenant farms, 51
  urbanisation, 78

McAllister, Angus, 265–6, 289
MacColla, Fionn, 102
MacCuish, Donald J., 296
MacDonald, Alexander, 66
MacDonald clan, 25
McEwen, John, 106–7
MacFarlane v. *Falfield Investments Ltd*, 317
MacFarquhar, Roderick, 104, 105
McGrath, John, 102–3, 106
MacGregor clan, 25
McHugh, Edward, 63
MacIain clan, 25
MacIver, Iain, 358
MacKenzie clan, 25
MacLean, Allan Campbell, 104
MacLean, Iain F., 299, 302
MacLean, Sorley 101
MacLeod clan, 25
McMaster v. *Scottish Ministers*, 226–7
MacMillan, John, 64
MacNeacail, Aonghas, 101
MacPherson, Ian, 102
MacPherson, Margaret, 104
MacQueen, Hector, 132
MacRae, James, 31
Malcolm, George, 100
Malcolms of Poltalloch, 36–7
manufacturing, 23, 24, 26, 29, 33, 35
map-based land registration, 158–9, 300, 308

markets
  for agricultural tenancies, 28, 320–1
  for crofts and croft tenancies, 16, 294, 298, 307–9, 257
  as drivers of agricultural change, 36
  failure of, 7
  financial markets, 345–6
  for grain, 29, 36, 313
  for housing, 345–6, 383
  influence on Norwegian system, 393, 395, 386, 409
  for labour, 28–9, 30
  for land, 23, 31, 37, 372, 378, 390, 405
  for livestock, 27–8, 29, 36, 293
  for residential tenancies, 270, 272, 276
  thin markets, 182–3, 201, 202
mechanisation, 36, 80, 380, 381, 385, 386, 395, 397
media representations
  of agrarian radicalism, 59, 63, 64, 65
  of crofters, 59, 64
  of human rights, 15, 215–16, 234
  in Ireland, 59, 63, 65
  of planning, 340, 342
Meeting the Needs policy statement, 240–1, 247
Meikle, Andrew, 36
memory, 58, 71, 82–3, 85–6, 93, 101, 127, 142, 369
Menteith, James, 35
mercantilism, 23, 27, 29, 46
mercenaries, 25
Merrill, Thomas, 182–3, 201, 202
Mexico, 24, 29
Michaelman, Frank, 187
migrant labour, 382
migration, 26, 27, 29, 30, 34, 58, 79, 86, 93, 382, 383, 397
military tenure, 47
mineral resources, 32, 33, 157, 198
mining, 25, 34, 295
modern limited duration tenancies, 322–3
modernisation, 59, 84, 87
money rents, 26, 266
Moody, T. W., 62–3
mortancestry, brieve of, 124, 134, 143
mortgages, 270–1, 298, 300, 308, 345
mountain access, 335–6
Mulvagh, Conor, 69
multifunctional agriculture, 389, 390
Murdoch, Jim, 217, 218

Napier, Francis, 64
Napier Commission, 65, 72, 74, 83, 96–7, 293, 294, 296, 370
Napoleonic Wars, 37
National Farmers Union of Scotland, 365
National Forest Estate, 372
National Performance Indicators, 242, 375
National Standards for Community Engagement (NSCE), 355, 356, 359, 365
National Trust for Scotland, 372
National Upland Outcomes, 374

nationalism
  Irish, 59, 60–1, 63, 70–1, 89
  Scottish, 69, 98, 101–2
Navigation Acts, 27
neglected land, 163, 167, 178, 196–8, 237,
  252–3, 261
neoliberalism, 346, 393, 405, 409
new entrants
  agricultural tenancies, 17, 321, 322–3, 407,
    408
  crofting, 307–9
  in Norway, 396, 404
New Lanark, 35, 96
New Model Army, 27
new towns, 333–4
New Towns Act (1946), 330, 346–7
New Zealand, 81
Newbattle Abbey, 122
'No Rent Manifesto', 65
Norway
  active farming requirement, 392
  agricultural renting, 389, 392–3, 400–2, 403,
    405, 407–8, 409
  arable farming, 389, 395, 397
  collaborative approaches, 389, 396, 398,
    400, 402–3, 405, 407
  comparative analysis with Scotland, 13, 19,
    388–409
  competition over land, 399–400, 401, 403,
    407
  dairy farming, 395–6
  diversification, 398
  egalitarianism, 399, 402–3, 405
  farm cannibalism, 399, 403
  farm entrepreneurship, 400, 401
  forestry, 389, 397, 402
  grazing, 389, 395
  hunting, 389, 402
  Husmann class, 391, 405
  influence of market forces, 393, 395, 396,
    409
  informal land borrowing, 401, 402
  joint farming, 396, 398, 403
  kårfolk, 404, 405
  landowner–tenant relations, 19, 389, 403–4
  land legislation, 19, 391–3, 400–1, 403, 404,
    405
  land management, 389, 393, 398, 402, 403
  land market, 390
  land policy, 19, 389–93, 395–6, 403, 404–5,
    409
  mechanisation, 395, 397
  multifunctional agriculture, 389, 390
  new entrant farmers, 396, 404
  off-farm employment, 395, 396–7, 400, 404
  part-time farming, 397, 404
  place attachment, 401, 404
  production cooperatives, 390, 396
  production quotas, 395–6, 401
  property rights, 400–2, 404–5
  right to buy, 391
  scale of holdings, 389, 393, 395, 396, 397,
    399, 400, 402–3, 407
  security of tenure, 401, 405

social structures, 397–400, 403–4
subsidies, 19, 389, 390, 395–6, 399
succession practices, 391, 398–9, 404
sustainable development, 389, 390, 404
notaries public, 136, 141, 143, 145–7, 152
Nova Scotia, 26
novel dissasine, brieve of, 123–4, 134, 143

Oban Times, 64
O'Brien, William, 70–1
odel law (Norway), 391, 392, 404
'oideachadh ceart' (MacNeacail), 101
oil industry, 102, 397
One Future – different paths policy statement,
  241, 242
open-ended tenancies, 16, 199
open-market test, 320–1, 322
organic farming, 396, 398
Orkney, 25–6
Ottoman empire, 76
overseas trade, 23, 24, 27, 29, 30–2, 46
Owen, Robert, 96
ownership see landownership

Pairc Crofters Ltd v. Scottish Ministers, 222–3,
  257–8
Parnell, Charles Stewart, 69–71
Parnell split, 57, 70–1
part-time farming, 380, 397, 404
Partnership Act (1890), 316
paternalism, 28, 88
Paton, George C. H., 272
patriotism, 33, 44–5
peaceful enjoyment of property, 158, 206,
  214–16, 217, 220–35, 257–8, 261, 341–2
Peñalver, Eduardo, 186–7, 403
pennies de uttoll and de intoll, 114, 115
perambulation, brieve of, 122–3
perambulations, 118–23, 127
personal rights, 138–9, 143–4, 148–50, 152,
  265–6
Peru, 24, 29
Philadelphia, PA, 192–3, 197
Philosophical Society, 50
Pillai, Aylwin, 244, 246, 248
place attachment, 401, 404
Place to Stay, A Place to Call Home strategy
  document, 281–2
Plan of Campaign, 69–70
planned villages, 12, 33, 34–5, 53
planning
  appeals, 330, 331–2, 336–41, 349
  and access rights, 18, 332–6
  and communities, 156, 336–41
  and democracy, 339–40, 341
  designation of land use, 334
  fundamental principles, 330–1, 337
  and housing, 18, 329, 341–50, 382
  and infrastructure, 344
  and land reform models, 332–4
  Local Appeal Panels, 339
  local plans, 333–4, 383
  media representations, 340, 342
  nationalisation of development rights, 330–1

new towns, 333–4
planning gain, 348
planning law, 17–18, 156, 329–33, 336, 338–41, 346–7
planning permission, 305, 307, 330–2, 336–41, 343, 349
Planning Portal, 343–4
political representations, 340, 342
Pre-Application Consultations (PACs), 340
and public interest, 18, 330, 337, 339, 348
and public trust, 340
speculative applications, 339
and sustainable development, 337, 343–4
third-party right of appeal (TPRA), 332, 336–41, 349
town planning, 17–18, 91, 329–30, 332, 334, 337, 346
Planning etc. (Scotland) Act (2006), 332–3, 336, 339, 340, 341
Planning (Scotland) Act (2019), 332, 338
plantations
  Americas, 26, 29–30, 37
  Scotland, 24–5, 26
  Ulster, 25
poaching, 54
Poland, 24
Poletown Neighbourhood Council v. City of Detroit, 187, 189–91
political economy, 23, 30, 34, 45–6, 52, 63, 189–92
political participation, 187–8, 190, 204, 228, 353–6, 365–6
political representations
  of human rights, 15, 215–16, 234
  of planning, 340, 342
pollution, 240
population growth, 308, 381–2, 385, 386
poverty, 63, 64, 72, 94, 96, 236, 370
Pre-Application Consultations (PACs), 340
precepts of sasine, 115, 119, 136, 140, 143, 146
pre-emptive right to buy, 4, 19, 162, 164, 166, 178, 196, 237, 243–4, 260, 317, 322
prescription, doctrines of, 129–30, 139–41, 143
Prescription Act (1617), 140–1, 143, 148
Pride in the Valley (MacPherson), 102
Prince Edward Island, 75, 90–1
Private Housing (Tenancies) (Scotland) Act (2016), 16, 263–4, 282–7, 288–9
private landowners
  and agricultural improvement, 35–6, 39–55
  community participation, 384
  compensation for forced transfer of land, 181, 182, 183–6, 204–5
  consultation with local communities, 163, 169–70, 356
  as drivers of land use changes, 10, 12, 41, 43
  as dominant form of landownership, 10, 41
  financial resources, 43
  forced transfers of land from, 15, 163, 166–70, 177–212, 237, 252–5, 260, 261
  housing provision, 267–8, 270–7, 279, 280–91, 383

and land management, 23, 34, 51–2, 159, 379–81
  perceived incompetence, 78–9
  planned village creation by, 34–5, 53
  power and influence, 12, 41, 77, 80–1, 88–92
  powerful landowning families, 10, 66–7, 89
  relationship with the state, 79, 82, 90–2
  rights and responsibilities, 82, 84–5, 86, 230–2, 234
  social prestige, 41, 43
  and sustainable development, 18–19, 368–87
  wealthy industrialists and financiers, 83, 369
  see also aristocracy; landlords; property rights
Private Rented Housing Panel, 280
Private Rented Sector Strategy Group, 281
Private Residential Tenancies (PRTs), 283–7, 288–9
production cooperatives, 390, 396
production quotas, 395–6, 401
productive capacity test, 322, 323
productivity, 40–1, 296, 312, 313, 380, 386
progress, 2, 46–7, 58, 78, 81, 82, 87
progressive property movement, 186–9, 196, 199
property rights
  and allocation of scarce resources, 231
  case law, 221–7, 233–4, 257–8
  castle model, 228, 230–1, 234
  citizenship model, 216, 228–35
  and compensation, 229, 233–4
  competing underlying values, 229–30, 232, 234–5
  constitutional protection of, 188, 228–35
  and control of trespassing and poaching, 54
  and democracy, 228–9
  and enclosure of land, 42–3, 54
  and human rights, 7, 9–10, 15, 158, 174, 213–35, 256–60, 261, 318–19
  investment model, 192–3, 230–1
  and landlords, 42–3, 65, 223–7
  and the market, 7
  in Norway, 400–2, 404–5
  and public interest, 213, 215, 217, 222–3, 227, 233–5, 243, 256, 319
  and responsibilities, 82, 84–5, 86, 230–2, 234
  restriction and qualification of, 4
  see also landownership
property theory, 15, 180–212
Proposals for Legislation (Land Reform Policy Group), 300
proprietary runrig, 42
Protestant Reformation, 23
Protestantism, 23, 67
provender rents, 26
Prussia, 80; *see also* Germany
public authorities
  accountability, 156
  acquisition of land from, 154, 162–3, 165, 170–3, 195
  and asset transfer requests, 154, 162–3, 165, 171–3, 195

public authorities (*cont.*)
  housing provision, 18, 99, 268, 273–6, 279–80, 287, 342–3, 345–9
  land acquisition, 18, 348–9
  land management, 156
  landownership, 10, 18, 156, 162, 371–2, 386
  see also state, the
public health, 169, 172, 202, 255, 383
public interest
  and agricultural tenancies, 314, 315, 317
  balancing with property rights under ECHR, 213, 215, 217, 222–3, 227, 233–5, 243, 256–60, 261, 319
  and community right to buy, 15, 166, 168, 181–4, 201–2, 207–8, 222–3, 243, 246–7, 249, 254–62
  defining, 3, 254–5
  and human rights, 213, 215, 217, 222–3, 227, 233–5, 239, 256–60, 319
  and planning, 18, 330, 337, 339, 348
  and sustainable development, 237, 239, 243, 246–7, 249, 254–62
publicity principle, 142
public rights of way, 333–4; *see also* access rights; core paths
Putnam, Robert, 406

quarrying, 26, 34, 37, 295, 303
Quigley, Ian, 264, 289
quotas, 395–6, 401

R (JS) v. *Secretary of State for Work and Pensions*, 220–1
Rachmanism, 273
rack-renting, 52
ranching, 72, 83
real rights, 138–9, 143–4, 147–50, 152, 266, 289–91
Red Paper on Scotland (Brown), 106
reductions of infeftment, 134, 143
Reformation, 23
regeneration, 7, 169, 172, 202, 255
Register of Community Interests in Land, 164, 173, 317
Register of Sasines, 18, 141–2, 143, 146, 147–51, 377, 378
registered social landlords (RSLs), 279–80, 290–1
Registers of Scotland, 158–9, 164, 168
Registration Act (1617), 141–2, 143, 158
registration of interest, 162, 164, 173, 244, 248, 317
Registration of Leases (Scotland) Act (1857), 266, 308
Reid, Kenneth, 151
renewable energy, 10, 248
Rennie, Robert, 263, 265–6, 267, 287, 289
Rent Act (1957), 272–3
Rent Act (1965), 272–3
Rent Act (1974), 273
rent pressure zones, 285
Rent (Scotland) Act (1984), 274, 276, 283, 288
rent strikes, 3, 68, 270
rent to loan, 275

rents
  agricultural tenancies, 26, 30, 32, 37, 52, 312, 313, 316, 320–1, 322
  arrears, 65, 271, 276, 286, 313–14
  controls on, 16, 270–3, 275, 285, 294, 295–6
  crofts, 16, 65–6, 74, 294, 295–6, 351
  fair rents, 272, 273, 274, 276, 278, 295–6, 351
  fixed rents, 272
  levels of, 26, 30, 32, 37, 52, 65–6, 270–3, 275, 276, 285, 294, 295–6, 351
  money rents, 26, 266
  'No Rent Manifesto', 65
  paid to clan gentry in exile, 32
  provender rents, 26
  rack-renting, 52
  renegotiation of, 26
  rent pressure zones, 285
  rent reviews, 316, 320–1, 322
  rent strikes, 3, 68, 270
  residential tenancies, 3, 16, 270–3, 275, 276, 285
  sliding scales of, 52
repairing limited duration tenancies, 323
repairs, 275, 280
resident landlords, 273, 283
residential licences, 283, 289–92
residential tenancies
  assured tenancies, 274, 276–9, 283
  case law, 291
  and common law, 263–6, 275, 284, 287, 288–91
  contractual tenancies, 272, 275, 278, 284
  deposits schemes 281, 291
  fair rent, 272, 273, 274, 276, 278
  furnished tenancies, 270, 273
  housing association tenancies, 200, 268, 269, 274, 276, 277–80, 283, 290
  housing standards, 269–70, 278, 287, 382
  landlord–tenant power relations, 16, 267–9, 270, 277, 287
  leases, 16, 263–92
  letting agencies, 282
  make-up of rental sector, 267–8, 279
  and the market, 270, 272, 276
  multiple occupation, 280
  not excluded from community right to buy, 198–200
  notice requirements, 271, 275, 276, 285–6
  open-ended tenancies, 16, 199
  Private Residential Tenancies (PRTs), 283–7, 288–9
  private sector tenancies, 267–8, 270–7, 279, 280–91, 383
  protection against landlords' successors in title, 266, 267, 288, 289
  protection under European Convention on Human Rights, 200
  public sector tenancies, 268, 273–6, 279–80, 287
  and real rights, 266, 289–91
  recovery of possession, 266, 271, 272, 275, 276–7, 285–6

rent strikes, 3, 270
rents, 3, 16, 270–3, 275, 276, 285
repairs, 275, 280
resident landlords, 273, 283
residential licences, 283, 289–92
right to buy, 268, 274, 275, 276, 278, 280, 282, 290, 348
scarcity of supply, 267–8, 269, 270–2, 383
Scottish secure tenancies (SSTs), 279, 280, 283, 286, 287, 288, 290–1
secure tenancies, 274–5, 276, 277, 278–9
security of tenure, 266–7, 274–5
short assured tenancies (SATs), 276–7, 279, 281, 283, 286, 287
short Scottish secure tenancies (SSSTs), 280, 283, 286, 287, 288
statutory tenancies, 272, 275, 278, 284
subletting, 275
succession rights, 272, 275, 287
tacit relocation, 271, 272, 275, 288
tenancy agreements, 284–5
tenancy information packs, 281
tenant behaviour, 269, 271, 280, 286
see also housing
Restoration, 27
retirement, 297, 322, 404
Return of Owners of Land (1876), 105
reversion, letters of, 132
revolutions, 27, 76
Riddoch, Lesley, 221
right, brieve of, 124, 127, 134–5, 143
right to bid, 164
right to buy
abandoned or neglected land, 163, 167, 178, 196–8, 237, 252–3, 261
absolute, 4, 318, 391
agricultural tenancies, 17, 317–18, 322
appeal and review mechanisms, 172, 206
asset transfer requests, 154, 162–3, 165, 171–3, 195
ballots on local support, 166, 181, 203–4, 222–3
communities, 4, 15, 19, 154–76, 177–212, 222–3, 236–40, 243–62, 374
compensation for forced transfers, 181, 182, 183–6, 204–5
council houses, 348
crofts, 4, 105, 154, 159–61, 163, 166, 174, 178, 222–3, 237, 243–50, 260, 297–9, 302–3
democratic legitimacy, 180–1, 187, 194, 203, 207
detrimental land, 163, 167–8, 178, 196–8, 237, 252–3, 261
forced transfers, 15, 163, 166–70, 177–212, 237, 252–5, 260, 261
government funding, 4, 181, 207–8
guidance documents, 247–50, 255, 259, 260
judicial scrutiny, 181, 205–7
land with owner-occupied homes excluded, 198–200
land valuation, 166, 168, 169, 182, 183–6, 204–5, 206
litigation challenging, 173–4

in Norway, 391
pre-emptive, 4, 19, 162, 164, 166, 178, 196, 237, 243–4, 260, 317, 322
and property theory, 15, 180–212
and public interest, 15, 166, 168, 181–4, 201–2, 207–8, 222–3, 243, 246–7, 249, 254–62
registration of interest, 162, 164, 173, 244, 248, 317
residential tenancies, 268, 274, 275, 276, 278, 280, 282, 290, 348
and sustainable development, 15, 163, 165–6, 168–70, 179, 181, 201–2, 236–40, 243–62, 374
third-party purchasers, 170, 181, 208–9
rights *see* access rights; human rights; personal rights; property rights; real rights; right to buy
roads, 34, 36, 295, 303
Robert I, 114, 115, 126
Robson, Peter, 270, 271–2, 273, 281
Roginald of Buchan, 113–14
Roman law, 117, 130–1, 133, 138–40, 142–4, 149–51, 152, 155
Ross, William, 103–4
Royal Bank of Scotland, 31
Royal Commission on the Housing of the Industrial Population of Scotland, 269–70
Royal Society of Edinburgh, 50
rum, 31, 37
runrig, 27, 42, 51
rural amenities, 381, 383, 386
Rural and Environment Science and Analytical Services (RESAS), 373
rural development, 8, 18, 257, 352, 361–5, 373
Russell, Mike, 215–16
Russia, 13, 76, 80, 84, 93

Salmond, Alex, 161
salt, 24, 34
Salvesen v. *Riddell*, 221, 223–6, 319
sasine
actions of error, 134, 143
and brieves, 122–6, 133–5, 143
ceremony, 114–16, 118–19, 136–7, 143, 145–7, 149–50
charters, 115–16, 118, 119–20, 122, 136–9, 141, 142, 143, 147
and common law, 125–6, 131
deemed sasine, 147
dispute resolution, 117–26, 127
historical development, 14, 113–53
influence of Roman and canon law, 117, 130–1, 133, 138–40, 142–4, 149–51, 152
instruments of sasine, 135–7, 139–42, 143–4, 146–8, 149–50
and legal expertise, 117, 127–44
modelled on English procedures, 124–5
nineteenth- and twentieth-century reforms, 117, 144–51
and perambulations, 118–23, 127
precepts, 115, 119, 136, 140, 143, 146
and prescription, 129–30, 139–41, 143
reductions of infeftment, 134, 143

sasine (*cont.*)
  Register of Sasines, 18, 141–2, 143, 146, 147–51
Scandinavia, 335; *see also* Denmark; Norway; Sweden
schools, 180, 191, 344, 381, 383
science, 35, 47–8, 241
Scotland Act (1998), 157, 219, 243, 245, 279, 318–19
Scott, Henry, 3rd duke of Buccleuch, 312
Scott, James C., 56
Scott, Peter, 333
Scottish Affairs Committee, 5, 159
Scottish Agricultural Census, 311, 376, 386
Scottish Committee of Clearing Bankers, 308
Scottish Courts and Tribunals Service, 171
Scottish Crofters Union, 109
Scottish Crofting Federation (SCF), 351–2, 358, 365, 366
Scottish Crown Estate Act (2019), 165, 171, 255
Scottish Environment Protection Agency, 171
Scottish Homes, 276, 277
Scottish Human Rights Commission, 214, 215
Scottish Land Commission, 5, 6, 18, 155, 162, 172, 175, 321, 348, 387
Scottish Land Court, 224, 296, 297, 299, 315, 318, 319, 321, 323, 374
Scottish Land Fund, 4, 207–8
Scottish Land Reform Alliance, 60
Scottish Law Commission, 214, 291
Scottish National Party (SNP), 94, 103, 105, 107, 109, 161, 215, 241–2
Scottish nationalism, 69, 98, 101–2
Scottish Natural Heritage, 333
Scottish Outdoor Access Code, 335
Scottish Parliament
  agricultural tenancy legislation, 16–17, 317–25
  community right to buy legislation, 154–76, 177–81, 193–212, 237, 239, 243–50, 252–62
  crofting legislation, 16, 299–302, 308, 351–67
  human rights obligations, 218–19, 245
  land reform legislation generally, 42, 44, 94, 214–15, 221–7, 234–5, 252–62, 374, 405–6, 408
  legislation challenged on human rights grounds, 221–7, 257–8, 318–19
  legislative processes, 6, 332, 354, 358–60, 366
  planning legislation, 332–3, 338–41, 346–7
  re-establishment on devolution, 4, 6, 94, 157, 243, 279, 332
  residential tenancy legislation, 16, 263–4, 269, 274, 279–87
  unicameral structure, 6, 157, 332
Scottish Rural Development Programme (SRDP), 18, 352, 361–6, 380
Scottish secure tenancies (SSTs), 279, 280, 283, 286, 287, 288, 290–1
Scottish Tenant Farmers Action Group, 318
Scottish Water, 171
seasonal labour, 28, 34, 53, 397

second homes, 383, 385
Second World War, 315
Secret Ballot Act (1872), 69, 90
secularisation, 23, 24–5
secure tenancies, 274–5, 276–9, 315–17, 319, 320–1, 322–3; *see also* Scottish secure tenancies (SSTs)
security against borrowings, 113–14, 132, 300, 305, 308
security of tenure
  agricultural tenancies, 16, 33, 51, 223–7, 312–13, 315–21, 379, 401, 405
  crofting, 4, 16, 74, 96–7, 294, 295–6, 351
  in Norway, 401, 405
  residential tenancies, 266–7, 274–5
Select Society, 49
self-assessment (of land value), 184, 205
self-employed contractors, 381
self-improvement, 46, 49
serfdom, 24, 35
Serkin, Christopher, 183–4, 205
Serup v. *McCormack & Ors.*, 291
service aristocracy, 80–1, 88
sessions *see* College of Justice; conciliar sessions; Court of Session
Seven Years War, 33
Sharp v. *Thomson*, 149–50
Shawe-Taylor, John, 71
sheep, 26, 34, 369, 370; *see also* livestock; wool
shelter, right to, 7, 158, 228
Shepherd's Calendar (MacPherson), 102
sheriff court, 206, 283, 291
sheriffdoms, 120–1, 125
sheriffs, 120–1, 122, 123, 125–6, 127, 131, 133, 282–3, 287
Shetland, 25–6
shipbuilding, 37
shipping insurance, 37
shops, 28, 58, 381, 386
short assured tenancies (SATs), 276–7, 279, 281, 283, 286, 287
short limited duration tenancies, 317, 323
short Scottish secure tenancies (SSSTs), 280, 283, 286, 287, 288
Shucksmith, Mark, 300, 304, 305
Shucksmith Report, 300, 304, 307, 308–9
silver, 23, 24, 29
Silver Darlings, The (Gunn), 101
Sinclair, Sir John, 42, 51
Singer, Joseph, 188–9, 216, 228–35
Single Farm Payment, 379
single-tenant farms, 26, 27, 33–4, 35, 51, 52–3
Skye, 62, 68, 97, 101
Skye Vigilance Committee, 62
slave trade, 37
Small, James, 36
Small Landholders (Scotland) Act (1911), 296, 297, 370
Small Landholders and Agricultural Holdings (Scotland) Act (1931), 315
small landholdings, 16, 80, 296, 297, 361–2, 370–1; *see also* agricultural tenancies; crofting

Smith, Adam, 46, 47, 48
Smith, Sir Thomas Broun, 272
Smout, T. C., 50–1
social capital, 400, 405, 408
social development, 249, 375, 382–4
social justice, 6, 213, 240, 250, 337
social prestige, 41, 43
social wellbeing, 169, 172, 202, 255
socialism, 98, 218
Society of Improvers see Honourable Society of
    Improvers of Agriculture in Scotland
societies see agricultural societies; Highland
    societies; improvement societies; land
    reform associations; literary societies
soil chemistry, 48
soil management, 398, 401
South African law, 150, 188, 232
South Sea Bubble, 30
South Uist, 66
Spain, 23, 24, 29, 32
Special Resident Magistrates, 61
Spittal v. Spittal, 134
sporting estates, 60, 64, 83, 89, 99–100, 102,
    369–70
Stafford, Lord see Sutherland-Leveson-Gower,
    Cromartie, Lord Stafford
standards of living, 218, 304
state, the
    and agricultural improvement, 39
    definitions of sustainable development, 238,
        239, 243, 254–5, 374
    as driver of landownership changes, 10, 90–2
    increased social role of, 92
    landownership, 10, 18, 98–9, 109, 370,
        371–2
    relationship with crofting community, 352
    relationship with private landowners, 79, 82,
        90–2
    see also public authorities; Scottish
        Parliament
Statutes of Iona, 25
statutory nuisance, 167
statutory tenancies, 272, 275, 278, 284
steam-powered reaper, 36
stewardship, 252, 373
Stewart, Elizabeth, countess of Moray, 128
Stewart, James, earl of Moray, 128
Stewart, James, of Appin, 32
Stewart-Murray, John, marquis of Tullibardine,
    100
stocks and shares, 30, 36–7
Stornoway, 109, 177, 358
subdivision of holdings, 296, 370, 379; see also
    fragmentation of ownership
subsidies, 8, 19, 208, 307, 361, 372, 378–80,
    389, 390, 395–6, 399; see also government
    funding
subsistence agriculture, 7, 313
subtenants, 53, 275
succession law, 372, 391
succession rights, 272, 275, 287, 295, 297,
    314, 315–16, 322, 408
sugar, 31, 37
supermarket contracts, 395, 396

supervisory jurisdiction, 126, 134
Supreme Court, 220–1, 224–5, 319
surveying, 36
sustainable development
    assessment criteria, 239, 247–9, 254–5, 256,
        259, 261
    Brundtland definition, 236, 238, 240, 242,
        252, 255
    of communities, 373, 375–87
    and community right to buy, 15, 163, 165,
        166, 168–70, 179, 181, 201–2, 236–40,
        243–62, 374
    and economic development, 375, 379–82
    and the economy, 241, 242, 247, 249, 251,
        262
    and environmental development, 375, 384
    and housing, 343–4, 382–3, 385
    and human rights, 239, 256–61
    interpretation tailored to specific regimes,
        239, 240, 248–9, 250–1, 255, 262
    and land management, 236, 251–2, 253,
        259, 373
    and land use, 236, 251–2, 253, 255, 258–62,
        373
    measurement of outcomes, 374–5
    in Norway, 389, 390, 404
    and planning, 337, 343–4
    policies on, 10, 15, 236–42, 247–52, 255,
        259–62, 373
    prioritisation of factors, 238–9, 252, 373
    and private landowners, 18–19, 368–87
    and public interest, 237, 239, 243, 246–7,
        249, 254–62
    and scales of landholding, 18–19, 368–87
    and social development, 375, 382–4
    state definitions of, 238, 239, 243, 254–5,
        374
    sustainable development equations, 238–40,
        245–6, 249–50, 251, 253, 255, 258, 261
    and urban development, 337, 343–4
Sutherland, Angus, 62, 64, 66, 69
Sutherland, dukes of, 66–7, 84, 89
Sutherland-Leveson-Gower, Cromartie, Lord
    Stafford and 4th duke of Sutherland, 66,
    84
Sutherland-Leveson-Gower, George, 3rd duke
    of Sutherland, 67
Sweden, 26, 30, 32

tacit relocation, 271, 272, 275, 288
tacksmen, 28
tariffs, 28
taxation, 27, 62, 91, 95, 109, 191, 208, 372,
    375, 384
Taylor Commission on Crofting Reform, 98,
    296, 297, 304, 310
technology, 35, 36, 375, 389
tenancies see agricultural tenancies; crofting;
    landlords; leases; rents; residential
    tenancies
tenancy agreements, 284–5
tenancy deposit schemes, 281, 291
tenancy information packs, 281
Tenant Farming Commissioner, 321–2

Tenant League, 61
tenants-at-will, 42, 51
Tenants' Rights, etc. (Scotland) Act (1980),
    273–5
tenure *see* customary tenure; feudal tenure
    systems; military tenure; security of
    tenure
Tenures Abolition Act (1746), 47
textiles, 26, 28, 31, 33, 34, 35, 46
Thatcher, Margaret, 274, 348
thin markets, 182–3, 201, 202
third-party purchasers, 170, 181, 208–9
third-party right of appeal (TPRA), 332,
    336–41, 349
Third Reform Act (1884), 90
Thompson, F. M. L., 80
threshing machine, 36
tied housing, 381, 383
Times, 64
Title Conditions (Scotland) Act (2003), 156
Titles to Land Consolidation (Scotland) Act
    (1858), 147
tobacco, 31
tourism, 381, 383, 385
Town and Country Planning Act (1947),
    329–30, 337
Town and Country Planning (Scotland) Act
    (1947), 329–30, 337
Town and Country Planning (Scotland), Act
    (1997), 340, 346
town planning, 17–18, 91, 329–30, 332, 334,
    337, 346
trade, 23, 24, 27, 29, 30–2, 46
trade unions, 60
tramp-trading, 24, 30, 31–2
Transfer of Crofting Estates (Scotland) Act
    (1997), 154, 157, 159–60, 165, 170–1,
    178
transport, 191, 241, 334, 383, 403, 407
Treaty of Union, 23, 28, 30–2, 36
trespassing, 54
Tribunals (Scotland) Act (2014), 282
Tullibardine, marquis of *see* Stewart-Murray,
    John, marquis of Tullibardine
Tully, James, 353–4, 365

udal law, 26
*UK shared framework for sustainable
    development*, 241, 242
Ulster, 25, 30, 78; *see also* Ireland
Underkuffler, Laura, 187, 188, 196
undersea mining, 25
United Irish League (UIL), 70–1
United Nations, 216–17, 219–20, 221, 337,
    349, 355–6, 359
United States, 186–7, 188–93, 197, 199,
    209–11, 229–30, 313
Universal Declaration of Human Rights
    (UDHR), 217
universities, 24–5, 48, 49; *see also* academic
    research; knowledge production

urban areas
    community landownership, 3, 19, 162, 178,
        196, 210, 244
    economic development, 381
    importance of inclusion in land debates, 3,
        19
    residential tenancies *see* residential tenancies
    and sustainable development, 337, 333–4
    town planning, 17–18, 91, 329–30, 332,
        334, 337, 346
Urban Partnership Zones, 199, 205
urbanisation, 13–14, 24, 35, 77–8, 337
US Steel, 189
Uthwatt Report, 330

Venice Commission, 353
venture capital, 26, 29–30
Voluntary Guidelines on the Responsible
    Governance of Tenure (VGGTs), 355–6,
    358–9

wages, 28–9, 53
Wales, 68, 79, 83, 105, 164
Walker, John, 48
Wallace, Alfred Russel, 95–6
Walpole, Robert, 31
Walter, son of Sibbald, 120–3
War of the Spanish Succession, 31
warrandice, 128–30
wastelands, 54
Watchman, Paul, 273
Wednesbury unreasonableness, 207
wellbeing *see* environmental wellbeing; health;
    social wellbeing
West Harris, 160
West Highland Free Press, 103
West Indies *see* Caribbean
Whitbread v. Macdonald, 298, 299
Who Owns Scotland? (McEwen), 106–7
Wightman, Andy, 5, 107–8
Wild Harbour (MacPherson), 102
William I, 122, 125
William of Lindsay, 114–15
William of Orange, 29
Williamite Wars, 29
Wilson, Brian, 104
Wilson, Harold, 273
Wishart, Sir John, of Pittarow, 128–30
wool, 31, 35; *see also* textiles
World Commission on Environment and
    Development, 236
written leases, 51, 275, 284
Wyndham Land Act, 71–2

yeoman class, 26
York Buildings Company, 32
Young, Coleman, 190
Young v. Leith, 147
Youngstown, OH, 188–9

Zasinaite, Agne, 245